Lecture Notes in Computer Science   8255

Commenced Publication in 1973
Founding and Former Series Editors:
Gerhard Goos, Juris Hartmanis, and Jan van Leeuwen

T0212724

Teruo Higashino   Yoshiaki Katayama
Toshimitsu Masuzawa   Maria Potop-Butucaru
Masafumi Yamashita (Eds.)

Stabilization, Safety, and Security of Distributed Systems

15th International Symposium, SSS 2013
Osaka, Japan, November 13-16, 2013
Proceedings

 Springer

Volume Editors

Teruo Higashino
Osaka University, Suita, Japan
E-mail: higashino@ist.osaka-u.ac.jp

Yoshiaki Katayama
Nagoya Institute of Technology, Japan
E-mail: katayama@nitech.ac.jp

Toshimitsu Masuzawa
Osaka University, Suita, Japan
E-mail: masuzawa@ist.osaka-u.ac.jp

Maria Potop-Butucaru
University Paris 6, France
E-mail: maria.gradinariu@lip6.fr

Masafumi Yamashita
Kyushu University, Fukuoka, Japan
E-mail: mak@csce.kyushu-u.ac.jp

ISSN 0302-9743   e-ISSN 1611-3349
ISBN 978-3-319-03088-3   e-ISBN 978-3-319-03089-0
DOI 10.1007/978-3-319-03089-0
Springer Cham Heidelberg New York Dordrecht London

Library of Congress Control Number: Applied for

CR Subject Classification (1998): D.4.5, D.4.7, F.3.1, F.1, C.2.4, K.6.5

LNCS Sublibrary: SL 1 – Theoretical Computer Science and General Issues

Typesetting: Camera-ready by author, data conversion by Scientific Publishing Services, Chennai, India

Printed on acid-free paper

Springer is part of Springer Science+Business Media (www.springer.com)

Preface

The papers in this volume were presented at the 15th International Symposium on Stabilization, Safety, and Security of Distributed Systems (SSS), held during November 13–16, 2013, in Osaka, Japan.

SSS is an international forum for researchers and practitioners working on the design and development of distributed systems with self-* properties: (classical) self-stabilizing, self-configuring, self-organizing, self-managing, self-repairing, self-healing, self-optimizing, self-adaptive, and self-protecting. Research in distributed systems is now at a crucial point in its evolution, marked by the importance of dynamic systems such as peer-to-peer networks, large-scale wireless sensor networks, mobile ad hoc networks, cloud computing, robotic networks, etc. Moreover, new applications such as grid and Web services, banking and e-commerce, e-health and robotics, aerospace and avionics, automotive, industrial process control, etc. have joined the traditional applications of distributed systems.

The theory of self-stabilization has been enriched in the last 30 years by high-quality research contributions in the areas of algorithmic techniques, formal methodologies, model theoretic issues, and composition techniques. All these areas are essential to the understanding and maintenance of self-* properties in fault-tolerant distributed systems.

This year the program was organized into several tracks reflecting most topics related to self-* systems. The tracks were: (1) Self-Stabilization, (2) Fault-Tolerance and Dependability, (3) Formal Methods and Distributed Systems, (4) Ad Hoc, Sensors, Mobile Agents and Robot Networks, and (5) P2P, Social, Self-Organizing, Autonomic and Opportunisitic Networks.

We received 68 submissions from 20 countries. Each submission was reviewed by at least three Program Committee members with the help of external reviewers. Out of the 68 submissions, 23 papers were selected as regular papers, and 12 papers were accepted as brief announcements. Among the 23 regular papers, we considered two papers for special awards. The best paper award was given to Heger Arfaoui, Pierre Fraigniaud, and Andrzej Pelc for "Local Decision and Verification with Bounded-Size Outputs," and the best student paper award was given to Fabienne Carrier, Ajoy K. Datta, Stéphane Devismes, Lawrence L. Larmore, and Yvan Rivierre for "Self-Stabilizing (f,g)-Alliances with Safe Convergence." This year, we were very fortunate to have two distinguished tutorial speakers, Onur Altintas (Toyota InfoTechnology Center) and Shlomi Dolev (Ben-Gurion University of the Negev), and two distinguished keynote speakers, Kazuo Iwano (Mitsubishi Corporation) and Michel Raynal (Institut Universitaire de France and IRISA, Université de Rennes 1).

On behalf of the Program Committee, we would like to thank all the authors who submitted their work to SSS. We sincerely acknowledge the tremendous time and effort the program track chairs and the Program Committee members invested in the symposium. We are also grateful to the external reviewers for their valuable and insightful comments and to EasyChair for tremendously simplifying the review process and the generation of the proceedings. We also thank the Steering Committee members for their valuable advice and the Organizing Committee members for their time and effort to ensure a successful meeting. Finally, we greatly appreciate the support from the Graduate School of Information Science and Technology at Osaka University, and the Support Center for Advanced Telecommunications Technology Research (SCAT).

November 2013   Maria Gradinariu Potop-Butucaru
                                                  Teruo Higashino
                                           Toshimitsu Masuzawa
                                           Masafumi Yamashita

Organization

General Chair

Toshimitsu Masuzawa   Osaka University, Japan

Program Chairs

Maria Gradinariu Potop-Butucaru   University Pierre et Marie Curie (Paris 6), France
Masafumi Yamashita   Kyushu University, Japan
Teruo Higashino   Osaka University, Japan

Program Co-chairs

Taisuke Izumi   Nagoya Institute of Technology, Japan
Ralf Klasing   CNRS and University of Bordeaux, France
Sandeep Kulkarni   Michigan State University, USA
Zvi Lotker   Ben-Gurion University of the Negev, Israel
Achour Mostéfaoui   University of Nantes, France
Christian Scheideler   University of Paderborn, Germany
Oliver Theel   Carl von Ossietzky University of Oldenburg, Germany
Sébastien Tixeuil   UPMC Sorbonne Universites and IUF, France
Tatsuhiro Tsuchiya   Osaka University, Japan
Koichi Wada   Hosei University, Japan

Local Arrangements Chairs

Hirotsugu Kakugawa   Osaka University, Japan
Fukuhito Ooshita   Osaka University, Japan

Publication Chair

Yoshiaki Katayama   Nagoya Institute of Technology, Japan

Publicity Chairs

Doina Bein   Pennsylvania State University, USA
Francois Bonnet   JAIST, Japan

Sylvie Delaët   LRI, University of Paris-Sud 11, France
Taisuke Izumi   Nagoya Institute of Technology, Japan
Tomoko Izumi   Ritsumeikan University, Japan

Program Committee

Self-Stabilization

Chairs: Sébastien Tixeuil and Koichi Wada

Sylvie Delaët   LRI, University of Paris-Sud 11, France
Stéphane Devismes   University of Grenoble, France
Emmanuel Godard   Aix-Marseille University, France
Ted Herman   University of Iowa, USA
Taisuke Izumi   Nagoya Institute of Technology, Japan
Colette Johnen   University of Bordeaux, France
Sayaka Kamei   Hiroshima University, Japan
Jun Kiniwa   University of Hyogo, Japan
Mikhail Nesterenko   Kent State University, USA
Fukuhito Ooshita   Osaka University, Japan
Riko Jacob   ETH Zurich, Switzerland
Stefan Schmid   TU Berlin and Telekom Innovation
                              Laboratories, Germany
Mordo Shalom   Tel-Hai College, Israel
Josef Widder   Technische Universität Wien, Austria
Yukiko Yamauchi   Kyushu University, Japan
Shmuel Zaks   Technion, Israel

Fault-Tolerance and Dependability

Chairs: Achour Mostéfaoui and Tatsuhiro Tsuchiya

Bernadette Charron-Bost   Ecole Polytechnique, France
Xavier Defago   JAIST and LIP6, UPMC, CNRS
Martin Hutle   Fraunhofer AISEC, Germany
Michiko Inoue   Nara Institute of Science and Technology,
                              Japan
Kenichi Kourai   Kyushu Institute of Technology, Japan
Mikel Larrea   University of the Basque Country UPV/EHU,
                              Spain
Fernando Pedone   University of Lugano, Switzerland
Lucia Penso   Universität Ulm, Germany
Luis Rodrigues   Universidade Técnica de Lisboa, INESC-ID,
                              Portugal
Oliver Theel   Carl von Ossietzky University of Oldenburg,
                              Germany
Roman Vitenberg   University of Oslo, Norway

Formal Methods and Distributed Systems

Chairs: Sandeep Kulkarni and Oliver Theel

Borzoo Bonakdarpour	University of Waterloo, Canada
Stéphane Devismes	University of Grenoble, France
Ali Ebnenasir	Michigan Technological University, USA
Vijay Garg	University of Texas at Austin, USA
Bernd Hauck	C1 WPS
Oday Jubran	Carl von Ossietzky University of Oldenburg, Germany
Sven Koehler	Tel Aviv University, Israel
Sayan Mitra	University of Illinois at Urbana Champain, USA
Achour Mostéfaoui	University of Nantes, France
Scott A. Smolka	Stony Brook University, USA
Volker Turau	Humburg University of Technology, Germany

Ad Hoc, Sensors, Mobile Agents, and Robot Networks

Chairs: Ralf Klasing and Zvi Lotker

Ittai Abraham	Microsoft Research Silicon Valley, USA
Keren Censor-Hillel	Technion, Israel
Colin Cooper	King's College London, UK
Jurek Czyzowicz	Université du Québec en Outaouais, Canada
Robert Elsässer	University of Salzburg, Austria
Thomas Erlebach	University of Leicester, UK
Pierre Fraigniaud	CNRS and University of Paris Diderot, France
Satoshi Fujita	Hiroshima University, Japan
Leszek Gąsieniec	University of Liverpool, UK
Sun-Yuan Hsieh	National Cheng Kung University, Taiwan, ROC
Adrian Kosowski	INRIA Bordeaux, France
Fabian Kuhn	University of Freiburg, Germany
Shay Kutten	Technion, Israel
Gopal Pandurangan	Nanyang Technological University and Brown University, Singapore/USA
Rajmohan Rajaraman	Northeastern University, USA

P2P, Social, Self-Organizing, Autonomic and Opportunistic Networks

Chairs: Taisuke Izumi and Christian Scheideler

Gregory Chockler	University of London, UK
Anwitaman Datta	Nanyang Technological University, Singapore

John Douceur	Microsoft Research
Pascal Felber	University of Neuchatel, Switzerland
Kalman Graffi	University of Düsseldorf, Germany
Qiang-Sheng Hua	Tsinghua University, China
Valerie King	University of Victoria, Canada
Lukasz Krzywieki	Wroclaw University of Technology, Poland
Laura Ricci	University of Pisa, Italy
Nicolas Schiper	Cornell University, USA
Siddhartha Sen	Princeton University, USA
Thorsten Strufe	TU Darmstadt, Germany
Hirozumi Yamaguchi	Osaka University, Japan

Steering Committee

Anish Arora	Ohio State University, USA
Ajoy K. Datta	University of Nevada, USA
Shlomi Dolev (Chair)	Ben-Gurion University of the Negev, Israel
Sukumar Ghosh	University of Iowa, USA
Mohamed Gouda	University of Texas at Austin, USA
Ted Herman	University of Iowa, USA
Toshimitsu Masuzawa	Osaka University, Japan
Vincent Villain	Université de Picardie Jules Verne (UPJV), France

Additional Reviewers

Altisen, Karine	Bridgman, John
Burman, Janna	Chauhan, Himanshu
Chen, Lin	Cournier, Alain
Datta, Ajoy K.	Daum, Sebastian
Duggirala, Parasara Sridhar	Faghih, Fathiyeh
Falcone, Ylies	Foreback, Dianne
Függer, Matthias	Gouda, Mohamed
Gu, Zhaoquan	Huang, Zhenqi
Hung, Wei-Lun	Izumi, Tomoko
Jubran, Oday	Konnov, Igor
Lafourcade, Pascal	Matsumae, Susumu
Niebert, Peter	Paes Leme, Renato
Petit, Franck	Rahaman Molla, Anisur
Robinson, Peter	Singh, Abhishek
Weiss, Stephane	Zemmari, Akka

Invited Papers

Tutorial on Vehicular Networking

Onur Altintas

Toyota InfoTechnology Center
6-6-20 Akasaka, Minato-ku, Tokyo Japan 107-0052

Abstract. Vehicular networking serves as one of the most important enabling technologies required to implement a myriad of applications related to vehicles, vehicle traffic, drivers, passengers and pedestrians. In this tutorial we will look into applications and use cases of vehicular networking with select examples from US, Europe and Japan. We will follow by looking into the requirements of applications ranging from safety to infotainment. Next we will cover some of the deployment plans and field tests around the world. System level approaches and a brief comparison of V2V, V2R, V2I communications will be given, followed by an overview of the standardization activities. We will provide a comparison of IEEE 802.11p/WAVE, ETSI (Europe) and Japan (ARIB) standards. Before concluding, we will take a glimpse at the recently emerging reality of electric vehicles and issues surrounding them. Finally we will conclude with open issues that require further research.

Practically Stabilizing and Secure Replicated State Machines
(Tutorial Abstract)

Shlomi Dolev

Department of Computer Science,
Ben-Gurion University of the Negev, Beer-Sheva, Israel
`dolev@cs.bgu.ac.il`

The tutorial focuses in two paradigms for reliable and secure distributed computation using multi-party computation. Replicated state machine and secure multi-party commutation. Recent results in self-stabilizing replicated state machine and in communicationless multi-party computation will be described.

Practically Stabilizing Replicated State Machine. Replicated state machines are used in practice to overcome faults in distributed systems. The Chubby, ZooKeeper (see e.g., [2]) that are used by Google and Yahoo are based on distributed implementation of replicated state machine. Other data centers also use the repeated consensus abstraction achieved by distributed algorithms such as Paxos [23]. Paxos ensures safety, namely, when a step is distributively selected (from a set of proposed steps) to be executed by a machine, all the other active machines will (eventually) execute this step too. Liveness is conditional (as [22] proved that asynchronous consensus does not exist) to the synchrony level encapsulated by the definition of an unreliable failure detection distributed algorithm [5]. The unreliable failure detector tries to exploit heuristics on the relative speed of responsiveness of machines to give (unreliable) hints on the machine that are suspected to be failed. The hints are used by a quorum of active machines to safely decide and proceed in implementing the common abstract state machine. The abstract state machine is distributively implemented by the machines using their replicas.

Chubby, ZooKeeper and in fact Paxos start in a consistent initial configuration and preserve consistency (in particular safety properties) by arguing that machines take actions according to the program (algorithm) and proving that these actions preserve consistency. Unfortunately, such a time-lined proof is very fragile in distributed systems, as unpredictable faults can temporarily cause the system configuration to be in inconsistent state, possibly caused by: accepting messages that are corrupted (while the error correcting code attached to them did not identify them as such), electricity spikes, single event upsets and crosstalks that flip the value of bits, and in fact any temporal violation of the assumptions made by the system designer [24, 7, 15, 6]. Self-stabilization is a property of systems, a property that ensures convergence to the desired behavior from any arbitrary configuration, where a configuration is described by a cartesian product of values, an arbitrary value to each variable in the system. The system is proven to have an attractor, which is the desired behavior. Thus, the fragility of the proof thread of claims becomes robust, even when unexpected (illegal) set of actions are taken, the system converges to the desired behavior following the undesired actions. Note that there exist systems that tolerate Byzantine faults [4], where even malicious actions of a subset of the machines is tolerated, and in particular errors in their programs. Here too the system consistency is still preserved by the correctly acting machines, and the correctness proof is inductive, starting from a consistent state and preserving consistency when taking steps, rather than being, attracted from any configuration to converge (here in the presence of the Byzantine participants) to behave as desired [21]. Such systems are (still) too expensive to be widely used as the communication and complexity overhead is costly.

One important ingredient of the replicated state machine is the use of a sequence number for the steps. The sequence number is *practically unbounded* which encapsulate the fact that when the system starts with sequence number 0 it will take more than the life time of the system to exhaust the sequence number. Recently a line of works in the scope of self-stabilization, argue that it is sufficient to ensure that a self-stabilizing system converges to exhibit the desired behavior for such a practically unbounded executions as well. As compared with the original non-stabilizing specifications the system acts correctly "only" for practically infinite period (say "only" for one million years). In some sense the practically stabilizing notion can be viewed as an extension of the pseudo-stabilizing notion where the number of divergences from the desired behavior in an infinite execution is bounded, whereas in practically stabilizing systems the scope is almost or practically infinite execution rather than strictly infinite. In the pseudo stabilizing case the pigeon hole principle ensures an infinite execution with no divergence from the desired behavior, while in the case of practically stabilization, the pigeon hole principle ensures the existence of practically infinite execution in which the system does not diverge from the desired behavior [16, 1, 3]. In addition we have to recall that the assumption of fault-free infinite suffix in which the system stabilizes is only an abstraction, as the system should converge in every long enough fault-free period. Finally, self-stabilizing replicated state machines have been considered in different scopes using different techniques in [14, 10, 18, 20, 9, 8].

Communicationless Practically Unbounded Secure Multi Party Computation. Decomposing automaton into several automata such that the original automaton operations are encoded in the operations of the new automata is the approach that will be described. Now the settings is different as every machine receives (secret shares of) the same (streaming) inputs, and a secure computation should be carried by the machines, optimally without revealing any information to the participating machines. The motivation comes from cloud computing where a user would not like to reveal neither the data nor the processing to the cloud machines, while still using their storage and computation power.

Consider an input sequences that is (at least, practically) infinite. One challenge we have is to cope with a split of inputs, such that no information is revealed from the input received by a subset of the automaton portions. Another related challenge is to allow the adversary to record the state and inputs of a subset of the automaton portions for a finite or preferably infinite sequences. Additional challenge is to overcome corruptions in several automaton portions. At last proactive security issues are inherent consideration for systems with unbounded computation length.

The tutorial summarizes several recent works in which a dealer wants to delegate a computation to processes in the cloud by sending them a stream of inputs. The dealer is able to harvest the result by collecting the states of the processes at any given time, while processes have limited or no information concerning the current state of the computation. In particular the following solutions will be described:

- Reactive secret sharing, that changes the secret according to unbounded sequence of common inputs, where no communication among the (dynamic set of) participants is allowed, a fully secure solution for simple functions but somewhat non perfectly secure solution for any function [19].
- Dynamic online multiparty computation, in which a dynamic group of participants that should not know the sequence of inputs they process nor the program computed. The solution is based on a secret share based implementation of oblivious Turing machine [11].
- Infinite execution with no communication among the participants where the input is revealed to all participants. We prove that any automaton can be executed without revealing any information concerning the current state of the automaton. The construction is based on Krohn-Rhodes decomposition technique. Using pseudo random sequence, we present a simpler efficient technique for securing the current state of the automaton [12, 13].
- Computation of a class of automata and in particular automata for general string matching, in which both the inputs and the state are information theoretically secure [17].

References

1. Noga Alon, Hagit Attiya, Shlomi Dolev, Swan Dubois, Maria Potop-Butucaru, Sebastien Tixeuil, "Pragmatic Self-stabilization of Atomic Memory in Message-Passing Systems", SSS, pp. 19-31, 2011.
2. Flavio Paiva Junqueira and Benjamin Reed, "The life and times of a zookeeper", PODC, 2009.
3. Peva Blanchard, Shlomi Dolev, Joffroy Beauquier, Sylvie Delaet, "Self-Stabilizing Paxos", CoRR abs/1305.4263, 2013.
4. Miguel Castro, Barbara Liskov, "Practical byzantine fault tolerance and proactive recovery", ACM Trans. Comput. Syst. 20(4), 2002.
5. Tushar Deepak Chandra, Sam Toueg, "Unreliable Failure Detectors for Reliable Distributed Systems", J. ACM, 43(2), 1996.

6. Sylvie Delaet, Shlomi Dolev, Olivier Peres, "Safe and Eventually Safe: Comparing Self-stabilizing and Non-stabilizing Algorithms on a Common Ground", *OPODIS*, pp. 315-329, 2009. Also, "Safer Than Safe: On the Initial State of Self-stabilizing Systems", *SSS* 2009: 775-776.
7. Shlomi Dolev, *Self-Stabilization*, MIT Press 2000.
8. Shlomi Dolev, "Dynamic Multi-party Computation Forever for Swarm and Cloud Computing and Code Obfuscation", *ALGOSENSORS*, 2011.
9. Shlomi Dolev, Ori Gersten, "A framework for robust active super tier systems". *STTT* 12(1): 53-67, 2010.
10. Shlomi Dolev, Seth Gilbert, Limor Lahiani, Nancy Lynch, Tina Nolte, "Timed Virtual Stationary Automata for Mobile Networks", *9th International Conference on Principles of Distributed Systems* (OPODIS), December, 2005. Also Technical Report MIT-LCS-TR-979a, MIT CSAIL, Cambridge, MA 02139, 2005.
11. Shlomi Dolev, Juan Garay, Niv Gilboa, Vladimir Kolesnikov, "Swarming Secrets", *47th Annual Allerton Conference on Communication, Control, and Computing*, 2009. Also brief Announcement PODC pp. 231-232, 2010.
12. Shlomi Dolev, Juan A. Garay, Niv Gilboa, Vladimir Kolesnikov, "Secret Sharing Krohn-Rhodes: Private and Perennial Distributed Computation", *ICS* 2011.
13. Shlomi Dolev, Juan A. Garay, Niv Gilboa, Vladimir Kolesnikov, Yelena Yuditsky, "Towards Efficient Private Distributed Computation on Unbounded Input Streams,", pp. 69-83, ACNS 2013.
14. Shlomi Dolev, Seth Gilbert, Nancy A. Lynch, Alexander A. Shvartsman, Jennifer L. Welch, "GeoQuorums: implementing atomic memory in mobile ad hoc networks", *Distributed Computing*, 18(2), 2005.
15. Shlomi Dolev, Yinnon A. Haviv "Self-Stabilizing Microprocessor: Analyzing and Overcoming Soft Errors", *IEEE Trans. Computers* 55(4): 385-399, 2006.
16. Shlomi Dolev, Ronen I. Kat, Elad Michael Schiller, "When consensus meets self-stabilization", *J. Comput. Syst. Sci.* 76(8), 2010.
17. Shlomi Dolev, Niv Gilboa and Ximing Li, "Accumulating Automata and Cascaded Equations Automata, for Communicationless Information Theoretically Secure Multi-Party Computation Over (Practically) Unbounded Input Streams", submitted for publication, 2013.
18. Shlomi Dolev, Limor Lahiani, Nancy Lynch, and Tina Nolte, "Self-Stabilizing Mobile Location Management and Message Routing", *Proc. of the 7th International Symposium on Self-Stabilizing Systems*, (SSS 2005), LNCS 3764, pp. 96-112, 2005. Also Technical Report MIT-LCS-TR-999, Massachusetts Institute of Technology, 2005.
19. Shlomi Dolev, Limor Lahiani, Moti Yung, "Secret swarm unit: Reactive k-secret sharing", *Ad Hoc Networks* 10(7), 2012.
20. Shlomi Dolev, Elad Schiller, Jennifer L. Welch, "Random Walk for Self-Stabilizing Group Communication in Ad Hoc Networks", *IEEE TMC* 5(7), 2006.
21. Shlomi Dolev, Jennifer L. Welch, "Self-stabilizing clock synchronization in the presence of Byzantine faults", *JACM* 51(5), 2004.
22. Michael J. Fischer, Nancy Lynch and Mike Paterson, "Impossibility of Distributed Consensus with One Faulty Process", *J. ACM*, 32:2, pp. 374-382, 1985.
23. Leslie Lamport, "The Part-Time Parliament", *ACM TOCS*, 16 (2), 1998.
24. Eric C. Rosen. "Vulnerabilities of network control protocols: an example", *SIGCOMM Comput. Commun. Rev.*, 11(3):10 16, July 1981.
25. Rodrigo Rodrigues, Barbara Liskov, Kathryn Chen, Moses Liskov, David A. Schultz, "Automatic Reconfiguration for Large-Scale Reliable Storage Systems", *IEEE TDSC* 9(2): 145-158, 2012.

Concurrency-Related Distributed Recursion

Michel Raynal

*Institut Universitaire de France & †IRISA, Université de Rennes 1 (France)
raynal@irisa.fr

Recursion. Recursion is a powerful algorithmic technique that consists in solving a problem of some size (where the size of the problem is measured by the number of its input data) by reducing it to problems of smaller size, and proceeding the same way until we arrive at basic problems that can be solved directly. This algorithmic strategy is often capture by the Latin terms *"divide ut imperes"*.

Recursive algorithms are often simple and elegant. Moreover, they favor invariant-based reasoning, and their time complexity can be naturally captured by recurrence equations. In a few words, recursion is a fundamental concept addressed in all textbooks devoted to sequential programming (e.g., [5, 7, 10] to cite a few). It is also important to say that, among the strong associations linking data structures and control structures, recursion is particularly well suited to trees and more generally to graph traversal [5].

Recursive algorithms are also used since a long time in parallel programming. In this case, parallel recursive algorithms are mainly extensions of sequential recursive algorithms, which exploit data independence. Simple examples of such algorithms are the parallel versions of the quicksort and mergesort sequential algorithms.

Recursion and distributed computing. In the domain of distributed computing, the first (to our knowledge) recursive algorithm that has been proposed is the algorithm solving the Byzantine general problem [9]. This algorithm is a message-passing synchronous algorithm. Its formulation is relatively simple and elegant, but it took time to understand its deep nature.

Similarly to parallelism, recursion has been used in distributed algorithms to exploit data independence or provide time-efficient implementations of data structures. As an example, the distributed implementation of a store-collect object described in [2] uses a recursive algorithm to obtain an efficient tree traversal, which provides an efficient adaptive distributed implementation.

Capture the essence of distributed computing. The aim of real-time computing is to ensure that no deadline is missed, while the aim of parallelism is to allow applications to be efficient (crucial issues in parallel computing are related to job partitioning –flow graphs– and scheduling). Differently, when considering distributed computing, the main issue lies in mastering the uncertainty created by the multiplicity and the geographical dispersion of computing entities, their asynchrony and the possibility of failures.

At some abstract level and from a "fundamentalist" point of view, such a distributed context is captured by the notion of a task, namely, the definition of a distributed computing unit which capture the essence of distributed computing [8]. Tasks are the distributed counterpart of mathematical functions encountered in sequential computing (where some of them are computable while others are not).

The talk: recursive algorithms for computable tasks. This invited talk is on the design of recursive algorithms that compute tasks. A seminal related work can be found in [6]. It appears that, for each process participating to a task, the recursion parameter x is not related to the size of a data structure but to the number of processes that the invoking process perceives as participating to the task computation. In a very interesting way, it follows from this feature that it is possible to design a general recursion pattern, which can be appropriately instantiated for particular tasks.

When designing such a pattern, the main technical difficulty come from the fact that processes may run concurrently, and, at any time, distinct processes can be executing at the same recursion level or at different recursion levels. To cope with such an issue, recursion relies on an underlying data structure (basically, an array of atomic read/write registers) which keeps the current state of each recursion level.

After having introduced the general recursion pattern, the talk will instantiate it to solve two tasks, namely, the write-snapshot task [3] and the renaming task [1, 4]. Interestingly, the first instantiation of the pattern is based on a notion of linear time (there is single sequence of recursive calls, and each participating process executes a prefix of it), while the second instantiation is based on a notion of branching time (when considering the recursion tree, a process executes a prefix of a single branch, while the whole set of branches captures all the possible process execution paths).

In addition to its methodological dimension related to the new use of recursion in a distributed setting, the talk has a pedagogical flavor in the sense that it focuses on and explains fundamental notions of distributed computing. Hence, an aim of this talk is to provide the reader with a better view of the nature of fault-tolerant distributed recursion when the processes are concurrent, asynchronous, prone to crash failures, and communicate through read/write registers.

Where to find the technical content. The technical content of this invited talk can be found in [12], and in Chapters 8 and 9 of [13]. A topological perspective of distributed recursion can be found in [11].

References

1. Attiya H., Bar-Noy A., Dolev D., Peleg D. and Reischuk R., Renaming in an asynchronous environment. *Journal of the ACM*, 37(3):524-548, 1990.
2. Attiya H., Fouren A., and Gafni E., An adaptive collect algorithm with applications. *Distributed Computing*, 15(2): 87-96, 2002.

3. Borowsky E. and Gafni E., Immediate atomic snapshots and fast renaming. *Proc. 12th ACM Symposium on Principles of Distributed Computing (PODC'93)*, pp. 41-51, 1993.

4. Castañeda, Rajsbaum S., and Raynal M., The renaming problem in shared memory systems: An introduction. *Computer Science Review*, 5(3):229-251, 2011.

5. Dahl O.J., Dijkstra E.W., and Hoare C.A.R., *Structured programming*. Academic Press, 220 pages, 1972 (ISBN 0-12-200550-3).

6. Gafni E. and Rajsbaum S., Recursion in distributed computing. *Proc. 12th Int'l l Symposium on Stabilization, Safety, and Security of Distributed Systems (SSS '10)*, Springer LNCS 6366, pp. 362-376, 2010.

7. Harel D. and Feldman Y., *Algorithmics: the spirit of computing* (third edition). Springer, 572 pages, 2012 (ISBN 978-3-642-27265-3).

8. Herlihy M.P., Rajsbaum S., and Raynal M., Power and limits of distributed computing shared memory models. To appear *Theoretical Computer Science*, 2013/2014.
(http://dx.doi.org/10.1016/j.tcs.2013.03.002),

9. Lamport L., Shostak E., and Pease M.C., The Byzantine general problem. *ACM Transactions on Programming Languages and Systems*, 4(3):382-401, 1982.

10. Mehlhorn K. and Sanders P., *Algorithms and data structures*. Springer, 300 pages, 2008 (ISBN 978-3-540-77977-3).

11. Onofre J.-C., Rajsbaum S., and Raynal M., A topological perspective of recursion in distributed computing. *Mexican Conference on Discrete Mathematics and Computational Geometry*, Oaxaca (Mexico), November 2013.

12. Rajsbaum S. and Raynal M., An introductory tutorial to concurrency-related distributed recursion. *Research report #2006*, IRISA, Université de Rennes (France), to appear in *Electronic Bulletin of EATCS*, 20 pages (October 2013/February 2014).

13. Raynal M., *Concurrent programming: algorithms, principles and foundations*. Springer, 515 pages, 2013 (ISBN 978-3-642-32026-2).

Table of Contents

Dependability and Fault-tolerance

Self-Stabilization I

Formal Methods and Distributed Systems

P2P, Social, Self-Organizing, Autonomic and Opportunistic Network

Self-Stabilization II

Ad-hoc, Sensors, Mobile Agents and Robot Networks

Brief Announcement I and II

Transactional Encoding for Tolerating Transient Hardware Errors

Jons-Tobias Wamhoff[1], Mario Schwalbe[1], Rasha Faqeh[1], Christof Fetzer[1], and Pascal Felber[2]

[1] Dresden University of Technology, Germany
[2] University of Neuchâtel, Switzerland

Abstract. The decreasing feature size of integrated circuits leads to less reliable hardware with higher likelihood for errors. Without adding additional failure detection and masking mechanisms, the next generations of CPUs would at least be unfit for executing mission- and safety-critical applications. One common approach is the replicated execution of programs on redundant cores, which is increasingly difficult considering that most programs are non-deterministic. To be able to detect and mask execution errors, one typically need to execute three copies of each thread.

In this paper, we propose and evaluate *transactional encoding*, a novel approach to detect and mask transient hardware errors such that one can build safe applications on top of unreliable components. Transactional encoding relies on a combination of arithmetic codes for detecting transient hardware errors and transactional memory for recovery and tolerance of transient errors. We present a prototype software implementation that encodes applications using an LLVM-based compiler and executes them with a customized software transactional memory algorithm. Our evaluation shows that our system can successfully survive between 90-96% of transient hardware errors.

1 Introduction

The dependability of hardware components in a computing systems is influenced by several factors. Some are related to the environment (e.g., system operating in tough conditions such as in space or at extreme temperatures) while others are driven by the evolution of technology. Notably, the increase in transistor density of integrated circuits leads to less reliable hardware and higher likelihood for transient errors [4]. Recent research has also shown that significant energy savings can be achieved by operating at lower, almost unsafe voltage levels, albeit at the price of increased error rates (e.g., [21]). Such *transient hardware errors* are particularly difficult to handle as they cannot be detected easily.

Traditionally, wrong executions of programs are detected by means of redundant executions and comparison of the results. Redundant execution is effective under the assumption that the program is deterministic, i.e., the result of a computation only depends on its input. However, most non-trivial applications nowadays are non-deterministic, e.g., because of concurrency or errors returned

T. Higashino et al. (Eds.): SSS 2013, LNCS 8255, pp. 1–16, 2013.

by some replicated system calls. This non-determinism makes replicated execution challenging because one must rely not only on synchronization of the input but also of thread scheduling and system calls. Moreover, to be able to not only detect but also to mask transient errors, one needs triple executions and voting.

In this paper, we tackle the problem of building possibly non-deterministic software systems that can tolerate a large fraction of transient execution errors. Indeed, safety critical systems require that, depending on the safety integrity level, a specified fraction of failures do not result in a safety violation. By tolerating a large fraction of failures, hardware consisting of unreliable components can be used in mission and safety-critical applications.

The underlying idea of our approach is to combine two techniques: (1) encoded processing [8], which provides means to detect incorrect execution of code and guarantees data integrity, and (2) transactional memory (TM) [10], which supports speculative execution of code and provides checkpoint/rollback mechanisms to restart erroneous operations. This novel combination of techniques allows us to detect and tolerate a significant fraction of transient errors such as data corruptions or execution errors. We show a proof-of-concept implementation that can detect and recover from a wide range of errors, albeit a with some runtime overhead resulting from the software-only nature of our prototype. Note that our focus in this study is not on performance as there are ongoing efforts to put these mechanisms in hardware.

The paper makes the following contributions: (1) We introduce a novel approach to *detect* and *tolerate* transient errors when executing applications on unreliable hardware (Section 3). Error detection is achieved using encoded processing and symptom-based error detection. Fault tolerance is supported by TM, providing means to recover to a correct state. (2) We automatically transform and instrument applications written in C using an encoding compiler (Section 4). This allows to apply our approach to existing applications without manual adaption of memory accesses. (3) We base the checkpointing mechanism on TM that we streamlined for high performance failure atomicity (Section 5). The TM selectively replicates memory so that the runtime system can tolerate errors that are not recoverable by a rollback. The replica is used to check and correct the consistency of the memory without aborting the transaction. (4) We present a prototype implemented in software and study the design of our self-healing approach. We evaluate the effectiveness of the aspirated error tolerance and its resource overhead (Section 6).

2   Related Work

Dependable mainframe systems typically add fault tolerance by introducing redundancy at different levels in hardware [11,26]. Faults are mitigated by combining information redundancy (e.g., checksums) and redundant execution, either using replicated hardware components or sequential re-execution over time.

Error detection and correction (ECC) uses information redundancy in form of parity data. Current ECC hardware implementations correct single event upsets that result in a single bit flip and detect double bit flips. However, ECC is applied to register files or ALU circuits only in custom processors and causes a high space and computing overhead.

Combinational logic within processors can be protected by either hardware-based [31] or software-based [16,17] duplication. A common hardware approach uses multiple identical lock-stepped processors to run copies of the same program in parallel [1, 12] and check for identical results. However, this requires high synchronization and comparison overhead.

Custom hardware solutions are often too costly for general use. Instead, software-only techniques achieve reliability using unreliable commodity hardware and redundancy on the application level. For example, SWIFT [19] is an instrumentation technique that computes in software duplicate versions of all register values and inserts validation instructions before control flow and memory operations. With the lack of duplicated memory operations, no end-to-end detection of hardware faults is provided. ReStore [29] detects failures by its symptoms (e.g., exceptions) but sacrifices error coverage if no symptom gets activated. DieHard [2] uses probabilistic memory safety based on randomization and process replication to overcome memory errors.

Error recovery techniques are generally based on checkpoint/rollback mechanisms [14,27] and can be triggered by error detection [20]. Checkpointing alone has the drawback that it can get corrupted by hardware errors and does not allow a selective repair but only a rollback. Samurai [18] is a robust runtime system that protects critical memory without rollback but forward recovery, i.e., fixing the memory using the replica, but requires an explicit programming model.

TM [10] provides an automated form of checkpoint/rollback. It supports speculative execution of code and is originally used as a synchronization mechanism to provide a simpler alternative for locks. It has been argued [5,7], however, that in the context of embedded systems TM should be limited to achieve failure control rather than concurrency control, and thus to provide a lightweight recovery control mechanism. SymptomTM provides a recovery strategy based on the abort operation of hardware TM, triggered by symptom-based error detection [32]. FaulTM uses TM for error detection and recovery [9]. The detection is based on a redundant execution of the application at thread-level and checks that the update logs of replicated transactions match upon commit. It requires twice the number of processors plus additional memory for the replicated logs.

3 System Design

Our goal is to allow applications to execute in a fault tolerant manner in an environment that is prone to transient errors. Traditionally, such dependability is achieved by replicating the entire execution of the application, either in time or space. Compared to existing approaches (see Section 2), we want to minimize the replication overhead. Our approach is to replicate the application's state in memory only, and to add parity information for operations. The latter is used for error detection and the former for error recovery.

3.1 System Model

The system model captures the properties of commodity hardware, the application, and the errors that can occur. *Commodity hardware* is composed of unreliable off-the-shelf components. It does not provide hardware support for error detection or correction in any of its components.

The hardware executes operations using the *CPU*. It consists of processor cores with *registers* and attached *memory*. The registers and memory hold the *state* of the application and are connected by *bus* or *interconnect networks*. The *operations* access and modify the state. Each operation consists of an instruction with *operands* as parameters, to which it applies an *operator*.

The hardware can suffer from *transient faults* that are bound in time, i.e., if the operation is repeated the resulting transient error will not re-occur, but may result in incorrect operation execution by altering state, operands or operators. Typical examples are bit flips due to radiation or noise from the power supply.

Following the error model of Forin [8], the system can suffer on the software-level from the following symptoms caused by hardware errors: (1) a *modified operand* with a transient error read from the state; (2) a *faulty operation* uses correct operands but a corrupted operator produces incorrect state; (3) an *exchanged operand* is executed by the operation, e.g., after a fault on an address line; (4) an *exchanged operator* is executed with correct operands, e.g., addition instead of subtraction; or (5) a *lost update* does not manifest the operation's result in the state, i.e., the state is not up-to-date The symptoms can be combined with one another to represent other symptoms using the error model.

Error detection allows us to identify activated hardware errors before they propagate to a failure. The correction of an error requires *recovery* in order to revert the system to a correct state. The *tolerance* of transient errors is based on a combination of detection and recovery. It can selectively correct and decide on a re-execution of operations. If tolerance fails, the error is considered permanent.

3.2 Design Overview

The design is based on a combination of arithmetic codes for error detection and transactional memory for error recovery. We extend the system by a runtime that allows us to tolerate unrecoverable errors by selectively correcting the state. Figure 1 depicts an overview of the transactional encoding process.

Arithmetic codes provide end-to-end error detection and are implemented in software, so all unreliable components are covered. This is achieved by adding redundancy to the data, so that one can detect errors that affect data during storage, transport, or operation, according to the error model (see Section 4).

Transactional memory (TM) continuously captures in a log all state changes performed by the operations of a transaction. Thus, TM provides a straightforward check-pointing technique that we use for error recovery. If an error is detected during the execution of an operation, the transaction will be aborted and all changes will be rolled back using the log, thus returning to the state prior to the start of the transaction. This property is called *failure atomicity*.

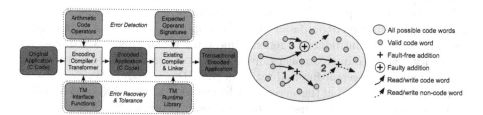

Fig. 1. The encoding enables the application to detect transient errors while the TM provides error recovery and tolerance mechanisms

Fig. 2. Code word domain of arithmetic codes and possible computation [22]

No guarantee is given that the application returns to a valid state after an abort. Therefore, TM additionally maintains replicas of all memory update operations in the log. The replicas allow us to detect corruptions not discoverable by arithmetic codes and to tolerate and repair corrupted state during the re-execution of the transaction (see Section 5).

4 Error Detection

Our error detection is based upon encoded processing, which applies arithmetic codes automatically to C code using an encoding compiler. It validates the correctness of the operand's state output and activates the error tolerance mechanisms if an inconsistency is detected.

4.1 Encoded Processing

Encoded processing adds redundancy to any value that is part of an application's state. This redundancy transforms the original domain of values into a larger domain where only a small subset of values are valid code words (see Figure 2). Correctly-executed arithmetic operations on code words preserve the code (case 1). However, a hardware error affecting the computation, e.g., a bit-flipped operand (case 2) or a erroneous arithmetic operation (case 3), results with a high probability in an invalid code word. Additionally, encoded processing allows us to detect errors during transport or storage of values, as they most likely also destroy the code word property.

For adding the redundancy, the encoding compiler uses arithmetic error detection codes. Well known codes comprise: (1) *AN:* For AN codes, the set of valid code words comprises the integral multiples of a compile-time constant A. Consequently, the code only allows for detection of value errors such as modified operands and faulty operations according to the error symptom model (see Section 3). (2) *ANB:* If the control flow gets modified, the processor might (a) use a different operand than the intended one (exchanged operand), or (b) perform a different computation (exchanged operator). Therefore, Forin [8] introduced value-independent static signatures, such that the resulting signature depends on both the correct operand signatures and operator. (3) *ANBDmem:* In order to detect the utilization of outdated values (lost update), e.g., due to address bus errors, Forin [8] also introduced a generic timestamp for all values (ANBD code). In contrast, the encoding compiler only applies timestamps to values stored in memory but not processor-internal registers (ANBDmem code) [23].

Measurements show that the increased detection capability of ANB and ANBD-mem codes comes at the expense of more processing overhead [25]. In our proto-type, we use AN codes because it is the only encoding currently supported by the compiler and combine it with symptom-based error detection that identifies anomalous application behavior (e.g., crashes) [15, 29]. We extend the transac-tional memory with masking of values to protect from an exchanged operand, and we validate the transaction at commit to discover lost updates (see Section 5). This allows us to cover symptoms not detectable by AN codes.

4.2 Application Encoding

The encoding compiler is a C source-to-source compiler [28]. Doing so has the advantage of being able to be used in existing tool chains in front of a target C compiler and support a whole range of target platforms. It consists of two major components as part of Figure 1: (1) A library of *encoded operations* provides encoded variants of all operations present in the original application and floating point arithmetics [30]. (2) The *transformer* operates on LLVM intermediate bitcode [13] replacing each original operation (e.g., arithmetic, logical, address computations) with an appropriate encoded one.

As some parts of applications are usually more safety-critical that others, the encoding compiler can adapt the scope of protection at a fine granularity by only encoding selected modules. Algorithm 1 shows the transformer output for an example application originally comprising two modules. The main module (lines 1–3) initializes the application and is not encoded. The encoded module (lines 11–16) contains the safety-critical algorithm, i.e., a counter using a global variable as its state.

Since the interfaces of unencoded and encoded functions have different seman-tics, the encoding compiler additionally generates wrappers for public functions (lines 4–10). Those *public wrappers* (1) encode their parameters, (2) call their encoded counterpart, and (3) optionally decode the return value (lines 6–8). Similarly, if encoded code attempts to call external functions (e.g., library or system calls), the transformer generates *external wrappers* working in the op-posite direction. For combining encoded processing and TM, the wrappers also contain transaction demarcations (lines 5 and 9).

Thus, any state being externalized is decoded and checked, allowing the run-time to take recovery actions if necessary (see Section 5). Note, to avoid ex-pensive checks of intermediate values, our approach defers code word checks to the latest possible point by relying on the error propagation of the employed arithmetic code. Hence, the system does not fail fast, but optimistically exe-cutes until the end of the transaction based on the assumption that errors occur

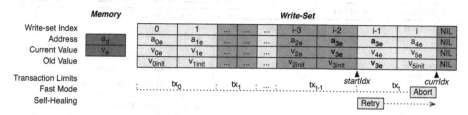

Fig. 3. The write-set keeps the history of all transactions and replicates the values currently written to memory. Addresses (a_e) and values (v_e) are stored encoded. The address must be decoded (a_d) before the memory can be updated. The initial value (v_{init}) is from before the application started. The current transaction executes within the boundaries *startIdx* and *currIdx*.

rarely. Consequently, it requires means to recover even if the fault leading to an error corrupted the application state in a previous transaction.

5   Error Recovery and Tolerance

The detection of an error is a violation of the application's integrity and triggers the recovery. Error recovery and tolerance are implemented by TM, which is traditionally used for concurrency control. However, here the focus is on dependability and we use a streamlined TM variant that does not suffer from overheads introduced by synchronization capabilities. The TM supports two modes: The *fast mode* is optimized for high throughput in the good case when no errors occur. Error detection is lazy, i.e., only at commit, and TM is used for failure atomicity. The TM performs backward recovery and the transaction is restarted from its beginning. The *self-healing mode* implies more checks and can fix the state selectively during execution instead of aborting the transaction. It is enabled upon retry of the transaction and performs eager error detection, i.e., on each state access. Upon error detection, the replica is used for forward recovery.

The TM is integrated with AN encoding such that an abort will be requested in case a non-valid code word was detected in an operand. In order to support a rollback, a valid checkpoint is required, which is built incrementally by recording all write operations that update the state. If a recovery based on rollback is not successful, the TM will identify the location of the state inconsistency and replace it with the most recent correct version from the state in the checkpoint.

5.1   Failure Atomicity

The TM runtime library is called from the encoded operations (see Algorithm 1). Transactions are started in the generated wrapper of an encoded function invocation and committed when it returns (lines 5 and 9). Within the transaction's boundaries, other functions can be called, but no state can be made externally visible. Native functions (not encoded) are not executed within transactions, thus, no recovery is provided. This also resolves irrevocability constraints known

---

Algorithm 1. Counter application.

```
1  function MAIN      // Main function module
2  |  c ← INCCOUNTER(42)
3  |_ PRINT(c)

4  function INCCOUNTER(inc)      // Wrapper
   function
5  |  START
6  |  inc_e ← ENCODE(inc)
7  |  c_e ← INCCOUNTER_e(inc_e)
8  |  c ← DECODE (c_e)
9  |  COMMIT
10 |_ return c

11 counter_e ← 0_e
12 function INCCOUNTER_e(inc_e)      // Encoded
   module
13 |  c_e ← READ(counter_e)
14 |  c_e ← c_e +_e inc_e
15 |  WRITE(counter_e, c_e)
16 |_ return c_e
```

Algorithm 2. TM for dependability.

```
1  currIdx ← startIdx ← 0      // Initialize
   write-set indices
2  function DECODE(val_e)      // Check and
   decode word
3  |  if VALID(val_e) then
4  |  |  return GET(val_e)      // Return
   |  |_   decoded value
5  |  else
6  |  |_ ABORT      // Abort transaction

7  function START      // Begin or restart a
   transaction
8  |  fastMode ← true
9  |_ setjmp (ctxt)      // Store the register
   state

10 function COMMIT      // Commit a
   transaction
11 |_ startIdx ← currIdx      // Advance
   write-set index
```

```
12 function READ(addr_e)      // Read encoded
   value
13 |  addr_d ← DECODE(addr_e)
14 |  if fastMode or VALID(*addr_d) then
15 |  |  return *addr_d      // Return
   |  |_   encoded mem value
16 |  val_e ← MRU(addr_e, 0, currIdx)
   |  // Find replica in log
17 |  if VALID(val_e) then
18 |  |  *addr_d ← val_e      // Fix memory
   |  |   with encoded value
19 |  |  return val_e      // Return encoded
   |  |_   value
20 |_ ABORT      // Abort because no valid
      state

21 function WRITE(addr_e, val_e)      // Write
   encoded value
22 |  if ¬VALID(val_e) then
23 |  |_ ABORT      // Abort because invalid
   |     operand
24 |  addr_d ← DECODE(addr_e)
25 |  writeSet [currIdx] ← (addr_e, *addr_d,
   |   val_e)
26 |  currIdx ← currIdx + 1 // Append to
   |   write-set
27 |_ *addr_d ← val_e      // Update memory
      with encoded value

28 function ABORT      // Abort a transaction
29 |  if ¬fastMode then
30 |  |_ KILL      // Kill upon abort during
   |      self-healing
31 |  fastMode ← false      // Enable
   |   self-healing
32 |  UNDO(writeSet (currIdx, startIdx))
   |   // Roll back state
33 |  currIdx ← startIdx      // Reset
   |   write-set index
34 |_ longjmp (ctxt)      // Reset register
      state & jump to start
```

---

for TM from concurrency control [3] because system calls and calls to external code will be executed outside the transaction (line 3 causes an irrevocable system call). All accesses to the state are redirected to the TM by invoking read and write functions from the encoded operations (lines 13 and 15).

Update operations of the state will not only be reflected by the current state in memory but also by a history at a different memory location. The history is maintained by the TM and is called *write-set* (see Figure 3). One entry is attached per update operation. A memory location of the state is identified using a decoded address and has an encoded value. Each write-set entry consists of the encoded address, the current encoded value of the memory at the time the entry was created, and the memory's previous encoded value. Note that we replicate (1) the value in memory as current value in the entry, and (2) the historic value as old value (e.g., v_{3e} is overwritten for a_{3e}).

The write-set maintains a history of all executed transactions and their entries. The current transaction's subset is identified using indices: *startIdx* points to the first entry and *currIdx* points to the next free entry after the subset. We assume for our prototype that sufficient memory is available for an infinite history. All entries other than the current transaction and the most recently used for each encoded address can be garbage collected.

We now explain the implementation of failure atomicity using the TM in Algorithm 2. With each switch from an unencoded to an encoded module, a new transaction is started. At the START of a transaction, we enable the fast mode and store the current register state (lines 8–9).

The WRITE function is called when an operation updates the memory state. It takes as parameters the encoded address and the encoded operand's value. We check if the value is a VALID operand (lines 22–23) to protect the write-set replica of the memory. An invalid currenty value in the write-set would prevent our self-healing after the transaction committed. We must DECODE the address (line 24) in order to find the actual location in the state. If the address is a valid code word, its decoded value is returned, otherwise the transaction is aborted (line 3–6). The encoded address, its dereferenced current value, and the new encoded value are appended to the write-set and the index that points to the current write-set entry is advanced (lines 25–26). Finally, the memory state is updated with the new encoded value at the decoded address (line 27).

The READ function must also DECODE the address (line 13), but in fast mode it simply returns the encoded value from the memory address without checking if it is a valid code word (lines 14–15).

Transactions reach their COMMIT if no errors were detected during their execution. Only the return value of the encoded function is exposed from the state, so only this value is validated during the DECODE before the COMMIT (see Algorithm 1, line 8 and Algorithm 2, line 3). The TM prepares for the next transaction by advancing the write-set index *startIdx* to *currIdx* (line 11).

The error detection mechanisms can trigger an ABORT of a transaction. All changes to the state made by the current transaction must be rolled back. This is done by applying the old encoded values of the write set (see Figure 3) in reverse order to the state (line 32). We enable the self-healing mode and reset *currIdx* back to the *startIdx* of the write-set (lines 31, 33). Finally, the transaction is restarted by resetting the register state.

5.2   Self-healing

The error tolerance of transactional encoding is based on the assumption that transient errors will not occur again when the operation is repeated. Abort and retry will re-execute the operation, but there is no guarantee that the aborted transaction in fast mode has rolled back to a valid state. ABORT (see Algorithm 2, line 32) does not validate the old values from the write-set written back to the state because the initial values of the state might not be valid code words. Any invalid values restored by ABORT will not be externally visible. Upon next access of the invalid state, we use the replicated state information from the write-set to heal the state during transaction re-execution.

Table 1. Overview of state and write-set corruptions how the error can be tolerated (m.*: memory state and w.*: current (most recently used) write-set entry)

Corruption	Self-Healing Mechanism
$\neg\text{VALID}(\text{m.addr}_e)$	READ will ABORT because no read or MRU lookup is possible
	WRITE will ABORT because storing and logging is impossible
$\neg\text{VALID}(\text{m.val}_e)$	READ uses MRU lookup to find last w.val_e at m.addr_e
$\neg\text{VALID}(\text{w.addr}_e)$	READ will ABORT because no MRU lookup is possible
	ABORT will KILL because no UNDO is possible without location
$\neg\text{VALID}(\text{w.val}_e)$	WRITE will ABORT because the write-set would get corrupted
	READ will KILL because MRU lookup failed (also $\neg\text{VALID}(\text{m.val}_e)$)
$\neg\text{VALID}(\text{w.old}_e)$	ABORT writes back invalid value, gets fixed upon next READ
$\text{VALID}(\text{m.val}_e) \wedge \text{VALID}(\text{w.val}_e) \wedge$ $\text{m.val}_e \neq \text{w.val}_e$	READ will KILL because indistinguishable which is latest version
Leads to crash	Catch signal and ABORT

The self-healing mode is enabled after an ABORT in the fast mode. We add three extensions: (1) validation can identify inconsistencies between the state and the write-set; (2) additional masking of values enhances the encoding semantically and can detect if a value belongs to a given address; and (3) signal handling enables the recovery from errors that were not immediately identified.

Table 1 summarizes which self-healing mechanism will be activated on different kinds of state corruptions. Three outcomes are possible: (1) the ABORT fixed the state based on failure atomicity, (2) the state is corrected during a READ, or (3) KILL application if the state cannot be corrected or an invalid address was encountered during a re-execution.

The READ is extended by a validation that checks if the value in memory is a valid code word before it is returned (see Algorithm 2, line 14). The validation protects from modified memory operands and faulty operations that produce invalid results and manifest in the state. If an invalid code word is detected, we access the most recently used value from the replica (MRU, line 16). Note that the most recent entry might not be in the boundaries of the current transaction but in the history of all transactions (see Figure 3). If the replicated value is valid, we correct the state by copying the value to memory and return it (lines 17–19). Otherwise, no valid state could be found and we must ABORT (line 20).

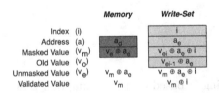

Fig. 4. Values in memory and write-set are masked using XOR to protect against exchanged operands and operators

We additionally extend the encoding with an XOR mask for the detection of incorrect state and write-set accesses when an operation suffers from an exchanged operand or exchanged operator. If the address could be decoded successfully, it can still point to an incorrect memory location, e.g., caused by a bus error. Therefore, we XOR the current value with the encoded address and the index $currIdx$, as illustrated in Figure 4. The encoded address is also added to the values of the state in memory. It can detect if the encoded value belongs to the requested address ($v_m = v_e \oplus a_e$). The $currIdx$ allows to check during DECODE if the correct entry is accessed by comparing the masked values in memory and at *currIdx* in the write-set ($v_m = v_{ei} \oplus a_e \oplus i$). The index i is determined by searching for the encoded address a_e in the write-set. We then compare the masked value in memory at address a_d with the partially unmasked value of the write-set entry ($v_m \oplus i$) for a match. This guarantees that memory values that are not stored at the correct memory address will be detected upon access. In any of the above cases, the XOR mask breaks the encoding of the value and can be detected during DECODE.

AN codes cannot detect if a valid but incorrect value is accessed, e.g., upon exchanged operands or lost updates. Accesses to incorrect values may lead to an inconsistent state. For our prototype, we rely upon signal handling to avoid crashes and recover when such an inconsistent state triggers exceptions and segmentation faults. This mechanism is used both in fast and self-healing mode. Recent work [6] has shown that transactions can be sand-boxed transparently for POSIX C code. It additionally requires timeouts to break endless loops and recursion caused by errors.

6   Evaluation

In this section, we evaluate and analyze the error tolerance and performance of our transactional encoding prototype (TE) that is implemented entirely in software. We are specifically interested in showing that (1) the majority of transient errors will indeed not result in a safety violation, (2) a fraction of errors not detected by encoded processing will be tolerated on a higher level using transactional memory (TM), and (3) the tolerance of errors introduces only a reasonable performance overhead compared to the error-free case.

Table 2. Incremental extensions

Variant	AN	TM	Valid	XOR	Signal
Native					
Encoded	✓				
TE $_{basic}$	✓	✓			
TE $_{val}$	✓	✓	✓		
TE $_{mask}$	✓	✓	✓	✓	
TE $_{exc}$	✓	✓	✓	✓	✓

We used the following test applications: bubble-sort (2500 numbers) and quicksort (10^4 numbers) sort integers, crc32 computes a CRC-32 checksum (10^7 bytes), md5 computes the MD5 hash of a string (10^7 bytes), sha256 computes a SHA-256 checksum (10^7 bytes), and aes256 encrypts a buffer with AES in ECB mode (10^7 bytes). Table 2 lists the different TE extensions we compared and executed on a machine with an Intel Core i7-3720QM CPU running Mac OS X 10.8. The applications were compiled using GCC 4.8 with inlining enabled.

6.1   Tolerance of Injected Errors

To evaluate the error tolerance capabilities, we used the injection tool EIS described in [24]. EIS consists of a static and dynamic injector. The static injector instruments the application with trigger points capable of injecting one or multiple errors into each instruction at the level of LLVM bitcode according to the selected error symptom model. In our experiments we used the symptoms modified operands (MO), faulty operations (FO), exchanged operands (EOD),

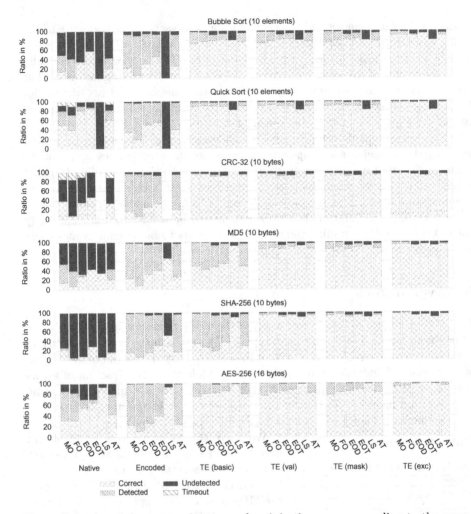

Fig. 5. Behavior of the test applications when injecting errors according to the error symptom models

exchanged operators (EOT), lost stores (LS), as well as the aggregation of all types of transient faults (AT) instrumenting both the application code and the transactional runtime. For the error injection experiments we use small input parameters for the tested applications (bubble-sort: 10 numbers, quick-sort: 10 numbers, crc32: 10 bytes, md5: 10 bytes, sha256: 10 bytes, and aes256: 16 bytes), because they already result in a large number of trigger points. Note that this does not reduce the variety of instructions being covered. The dynamic injector runs the target application under supervision monitoring its behavior and checking its output against an error-free golden run. Each error symptom gets injected once at each possible trigger point in a single run. The applied modification is selected randomly for each trigger point, e.g., which bits get flipped. Depending on its outcome the runs are categorized as follows: (1) *Correct:* The

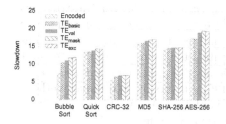
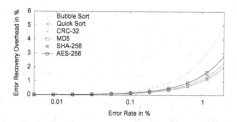

Fig. 6. Slowdown compared to the native execution of applications in the error-free case

Fig. 7. Cost of error tolerance for different error rates relative to the execution in fast mode

application terminated successfully and produced the same output as the golden run. (2) *Detected:* The application aborted because (a) the operating system delivered a signal, or (b) the encoding detected an uncorrectable error. (3) *Undetected:* The application terminated successfully but its output differs from the golden run, i.e., it silently corrupted data (SDC). (4) *Timeout:* The application exceeded its time limit (5 seconds) and was killed.

The outcome of our error injection experiments are presented in Figure 5. Note that the native and encoded versions of `crc32` contain no stores to inject faults (LS). Overall, the figure shows that TE is able to tolerate a high degree of transient errors. A large fraction (up to 79%) of detected or undetected *native* executions are converted into correct executions (TE $_{exc}$). Encoded processing already detects many injected error symptoms. A basic abort and retry of the erroneous transaction (TE $_{basic}$) already fixes many of those errors for `bubble-sort`, `quick-sort`, `crc32`, and `aes256`. The masking of TE $_{mask}$ seems to be ineffective. Its purpose is to protect against accesses of wrong or erroneously overwritten memory locations. However, this symptom is unlikely because invalid addresses are already detected while decoding by TE $_{val}$, or signaled by the operating system where only the exception handling of TE $_{exc}$ can recover.

The encoded functions of `md5` and `sha256` do not return a result and, thus, no code word is validated at the end of the transaction. This manifests in a low tolerance rate for TE $_{basic}$ because transactions are not aborted. Instead, the written incorrect state remains and is detected upon access in a following transaction, which will abort without returning to a correct state and enter self-healing mode. The self-healing mode uses the write-set to fix invalid loaded values, but cannot recover if the initial erroneous transaction already stored an invalid code word causing both the write-set entry and the memory to be invalid. The validation of each store of TE $_{val}$ is then capable of correcting the state by rolling-back the initial transaction containing the erroneous computation.

6.2 Performance Overhead

We now want to evaluate the performance overhead introduced by TE in terms of time and space, executing in fast and self-healing mode. The overhead in time compared to the *native* execution is presented in Figure 6. Most of the slowdown is caused by encoded processing because it replaces all instructions to support arithmetic codes. In the error-free case TE operates in fast mode (TE $_{basic}$) and does not incur much additional overhead for most applications because it only appends new entries to the write-set. The inefficient `bubble-sort` algorithm represents the worst-case scenario as it swaps numbers unnecessarily often, hence yielding very large write-sets. TE $_{val}$ incurs the additional overhead to first validate the values to be stored. Enabling XOR masking results in a slightly higher overhead due to the computation of the mask.

The detection of an error aborts the transaction and enables the self-healing mode. The execution time gets extended by the roll back and re-execution with extensive validation. Figure 7 shows the ratio by which the execution is extended depending on the rate of detected errors. The overhead is the slowdown when comparing the error-free case in fast mode with the fault-tolerant execution in self-healing mode, modeled as: $Overhead_{avg} := Rate_{error} * \frac{(Time_{abort} + Time_{heal})}{Time_{fast}}$. For our applications, the overhead in execution time stays below 2.5% for an error rate up to 1%. Typically, the error rate of unreliable hardware is much lower.

7   Conclusion

Depending on their safety integrity level, mission and safety critical systems typically require that a specified fraction of errors is masked, i.e., will not result in a safety violation. In this paper, we have addressed the problem of how to ensure that a large fraction of execution errors will indeed be masked. Our solution combines encoded processing for detecting incorrect execution of code and guaranteeing data integrity, and transactional memory for recovering from errors using a checkpoint/rollback approach. Moreover, we investigated mechanisms that support repair of the state beyond what is possible by a simple checkpoint/rollback approach.

We have implemented a software prototype composed of an LLVM-based compiler for encoded processing and a lightweight transactional memory library optimized for dependability—rather than for concurrent synchronization. Experimental results show that a high degree of error tolerance can be achieved on unreliable hardware. The presence of errors has only a small impact on the overall performance, i.e., this mechanism could for example be used to lower the voltage of CPU cores to reduce their energy consumption.

Acknowledgments. This work is partly supported by the German Research Foundation (DFG) within the Cluster of Excellence Center for Advancing Electronics Dresden and by the European Communitys Seventh Framework Programme under the ParaDIME Project, grant agreement 318693.

References

[1] Andrew Frame, C.T.: Introducing new armæ cortextm-r technology for safe and reliable systems. Technical report, ARM Ltd. (2011)
[2] Berger, E.D., Zorn, B.G.: Diehard: probabilistic memory safety for unsafe languages. In: ACM SIGPLAN (2006)

[3] Blundell, C., Lewis, E., Martin, M.: Deconstructing transactional semantics: The subtleties of atomicity. In: WDDD (2005)

[4] Borkar, S.: Designing reliable systems from unreliable components: the challenges of transistor variability and degradation. IEEE Micro, 25 (2005)

[5] Cristal, A., Felber, P., Fetzer, C., Harmanci, D., Sobe, A., Unsal, O., Wamhoff, J.-T., Yalcin, G.: Leveraging transactional memory for energy-efficient computing below safe operation margins. In: TRANSACT 2013 (2013)

[6] Dalessandro, L., Scott, M.L.: Sandboxing transactional memory. In: PACT (2012)

[7] Fetzer, C., Felber, P.: Transactional memory for dependable embedded systems. In: HotDep (2011)

[8] Forin, P.: Vital Coded Microprocessor Principles and Application for Various Transit Systems. In: FAC-GCCT (1989)

[9] Yalcin, G., Unsal, O., Cristal, A., Valero, M.: FaulTM-multi: Fault tolerance for multithreaded applications running on transactional memory hardware. In: WANDS (2011)

[10] Harris, T., Larus, J., Rajwar, R.: Transactional Memory, 2nd edn. Morgan & Claypool (2010)

[11] Horst, R.W., Harris, R.L., Jardine, R.L.: Multiple instruction issue in the nonstop cyclone processor. In: SIGARCH (1990)

[12] IBM. Powerpc 750gx lockstep facility- application note. Technical report, International Business Machines Corporation (2008)

[13] Lattner, C., Adve, V.: LLVM: A Compilation Framework for Lifelong Program Analysis & Transformation. In: CGO 2004 (2004)

[14] Lenharth, A., Adve, V.S., King, S.T.: Recovery domains: an organizing principle for recoverable operating systems. In: ASPLOS (2009)

[15] Li, M.-L., Ramachandran, P., Sahoo, S.K., Adve, S.V., Adve, V.S., Zhou, Y.: Understanding the propagation of hard errors to software and implications for resilient system design. In: ASPLOS (2008)

[16] Oh, N., Mitra, S., McCluskey, E.J.: Ed4i: Error detection by diverse data and duplicated instructions. IEEE Trans. Comput. (2002)

[17] Oh, N., Shirvani, P.P., McCluskey, E.J.: Control-flow checking by software signatures. IEEE Transactions on Reliability (2002)

[18] Pattabiraman, K., Grover, V., Zorn, B.G.: Samurai: protecting critical data in unsafe languages. In: ACM SIGOPS/EuroSys. (2008)

[19] Reis, G.A., Chang, J., Vachharajani, N., Rangan, R., August, D.I.: Swift: Software implemented fault tolerance. In: CGO (2005)

[20] Rinard, M., Cadar, C., Dumitran, D., Roy, D., Leu, T.: A dynamic technique for eliminating buffer overflow vulnerabilities (and other memory errors). In: ACSAC (2004)

[21] Roberts, D., Austin, T., Blauww, D., Mudge, T., Flautner, K.: Error analysis for the support of robust voltage scaling. In: ISQED (2005)

[22] Schiffel, U.: Hardware Error Detection Using AN-Codes. PhD thesis, Technische Universität Dresden (2011)

[23] Schiffel, U., Schmitt, A., Süßkraut, M., Fetzer, C.: ANB- and ANBDmem-Encoding: Detecting Hardware Errors in Software. In: Schoitsch, E. (ed.) SAFE-COMP 2010. LNCS, vol. 6351, pp. 169–182. Springer, Heidelberg (2010)

[24] Schiffel, U., Schmitt, A., Süßkraut, M., Fetzer, C.: Slice Your Bug: Debugging Error Detection Mechanisms using Error Injection Slicing. In: IEEE TC (2010)

[25] Schiffel, U., Schmitt, A., Süßkraut, M., Fetzer, C.: Software-Implemented Hardware Error Detection: Costs and Gains. In: DEPEND (2010)

[26] Slegel, T.J., Averill III, R.M., Check, M.A., Giamei, B.C., Krumm, B.W., Krygowski, C.A., Li, W.H., Liptay, J.S., MacDougall, J.D., McPherson, T.J., Navarro, J.A., Schwarz, E.M., Shum, K., Webb, C.F.: Ibm's s/390 g5 microprocessor design. In: IEEE Micro (1999)
[27] Sorin, D.J., Martin, M.M.K., Hill, M.D., Wood, D.A.: Safetynet: improving the availability of shared memory multiprocessors with global checkpoint/recovery. In: SIGARCH (2002)
[28] Süßkraut, M., Schmitt, A., Schiffel, U., Brünink, M., Fetzer, C.: Silistra compiler: Building reliable systems with unreliable hardware. In: DSN (2011)
[29] Wang, N., Patel, S.: Restore: Symptom-based soft error detection in microprocessors. In: TDSC (2006)
[30] Wappler, U., Fetzer, C.: Hardware Failure Virtualization Via Software Encoded Processing. In: INDIN (2007)
[31] Webber, S., Beirne, J.: The stratus architecture. In: FTCS (1991)
[32] Yalcin, G., Unsal, O., Cristal, A., Hur, I., Valero, M.: SymptomTM: Symptom-based error detection and recovery using hardware transactional memory. In: PACT (2011)

Universal Model Simulation:
BG and Extended BG as Examples

Petr Kuznetsov

Télécom ParisTech
petr.kuznetsov@telecom-paristech.fr

Abstract. This paper focuses on simulations as a means of deriving the relative power of distributed computing models. We describe an abstract simulation algorithm that enables reducing the question of solvability of a generic distributed task in one model to an equivalent question in another model. The technique implies simple equivalents to the fundamental reduction by Borowsky and Gafni, known as BG simulation, as well as to Extended BG, a more recent extension of it to colored tasks. We also sketch how the parameters of our technique can be tuned to derive recent equivalence results for models that use, in addition to basic read-write memory, k-set agreement or k-process consensus objects, or make assumptions on active resilience.

1 Introduction

When do we say that a given problem is hard or even impossible to solve? In computing, this typically means that, in a given model of computation, the problem cannot be solved by any algorithm with desired properties. But if we found the answer to the question in one model, can we derive it for another? This is where *simulations* may be handy.

This paper focuses on simulations of distributed computing models. Here a model specifies a collection of computing units, called *processes*, that communicate via invoking operations on shared-memory variables or sending messages. We restrict our attention to a class of decision problems called *tasks*, where every process starts with its private *input* value and is expected, after some information exchange with other processes, to produce an *output* value, so that the inputs and the outputs are consistent with the task specification. For example, in the *consensus* task, the processes are expected to agree on one of the inputs.

In this setting, informally, to simulate a model A in a model B means to guarantee that in every execution of B, the processes in B reach a form of *agreement* on the behaviour of the processes in A that is (1) consistent with some execution of A, and (2) somehow reflects the *inputs* provided to the processes in B. The first condition means that the simulation is *correct*, i.e., it indeed produces something that could have happened in A. The second condition means that the simulation is *useful*, i.e., the simulated run allows the simulators to compute some outputs based on their inputs. These outputs depend on the goal

T. Higashino et al. (Eds.): SSS 2013, LNCS 8255, pp. 17–31, 2013.
© Springer International Publishing Switzerland 2013

of the simulation, which in turn depends on the kind of relations between the models we intend to capture.

The main concern of this paper is *distributed computability*: what can and what cannot be computed in a given model. We aim at reductions of the question of whether a task T is solvable in model A to an equivalent question in model B.

We focus first on read-write shared-memory simulations. We assume that processes run the *full-information protocol* using the atomic snapshot memory [1] where every process first writes its input in the memory and then alternates snapshots with updates, where every next update writes the result of the preceding snapshot.

We define an abstract simulation technique in which a set of *simulators* use agreement protocols to reconcile on the evolution of the *simulated* processes. The input of the simulated processes is agreed upon too based on a specific *initialization* rule, which is a parameter of our simulation. A simulator may decide to join the simulation using an *activation* rule based on the inputs of other simulators, which is the second parameter of our simulation. At any point in the simulation, a simulator may decide to terminate, using a specific *termination* rule, which is the third parameter. By varying these three parameters, we can obtain a wide spectrum of computability results.

One application of our abstract techinque is the celebrated result that the question of t-resilient solvability of a colorless task T is equivalent to the question of wait-free solvability of T in a system of $t+1$ processes [5,7]. We derive the result by simply allowing each simulator to consider itself active, to use its input value in initializing any simulated process, and terminate as soon as one simulated process outputs.

We then go further and apply our simulation framework to the generic (not necessarily colorless) tasks and show that t-resilient solvability can be reduced to the wait-free solvability (obtained in [13] via *Extended* BG-simulation). We speculate that our technique can be extended to other classes of simulation algorithms, such as adversarial models [10,16,21] or models equipped with k-set agreement primitives [15,14]. In particular, we sketch how a simple modification of parameters in our simulation framework may establish the recently shown equivalence between a system in which any number of processes communicate via read-write memory and k-set agreement objects and a system in which no more than $k - 1$ *active* processes fail (*k-active resilience*).

The rest of the paper is organized as follows. In Section 2, we overview existing model simulations and hint how they can be unified in a common framework. In Section 3, we briefly discuss our basic system model and introduce agreement protocols as principal building blocks of our simulation. In Section 4, we present our simulation framework and in Section 5, we use the framework to derive equivalence results analogous to BG [5,7] and Extended BG [13]. Section 6 sketches applications of our framework to models beyond read-write t-resilience.

2   Related Work

Simulations improve our understanding of distributed computing by establishing equivalence between seemingly different phenomena: synchrony and asynchrony [12], message-passing and read-write shared memory [3], read-write shared memory and atomic snapshot [1], atomic snapshot and immediate snapshot [6], wait-freedom and t-resilience for distributed tasks [7,13], k-set agreement and k-concurrency [14], wait-freedom and superset-closed adversarial models [18], etc. The motivation behind this paper is to establish a unifying simulation framework that would encompass all existing and emerging equivalence results: by tuning a small set of well-defined parameters of our framework, we should be able produce the desired simulation protocol.

Our abstract simulation builds upon a weak simulation algorithm that always ensures *safety* [2], i. e., it guarantees that the simulated execution indeed could have taken place in the simulated model. A basic building block of the simulation is an agreement protocol, e.g., the safe agreement protocol of [7] or obstruction-free consensus [19,4]. Since no asynchronous fault-tolerant protocol can achieve agreement providing both safety and liveness [11], the liveness properties of the simulation depend on the liveness properties exported by the agreement protocols it employs. Interestingly, different simulated steps can use different agreement protocols which enables a variety of simulation protocols suitable for different models. The variants of BG and Extended BG proposed in this paper employ obstruction-free consensus [19,4] as an agreement protocol. Intuitively, to make progress with this kind of agreement protocols, we must ensure that eventually at least some of concurrently simulated processes is driven forward by exactly one correct simulator, which was inspired by the simulations proposed earlier in [17,9].

Gafni and Guerraoui [15] have recently established that providing the processes with k-set agreement objects is, in a precise sense, equivalent to having access to k state machines, where at least one is guaranteed to progress. In particular, as is informally shown in [14], providing k-set agreement is equivalent, with respect to task solvability, to assuming k-concurrency or active $(k-1)$-resilience. In this paper, we sketch how the latter equivalence result can be seen as a straightforward application of our simulation framework.

3   Model

Processes. We consider a system Π of n processes, $p_1, \ldots, p_n$, that communicate via reading and writing in the shared memory. We assume that the system is *asynchronous*, i.e., relative speeds of the processes are unbounded. Without loss of generality, we assume that processes communicate via an *atomic snapshot* memory [1], where every process may update its dedicated position and take atomic snapshot of the whole memory. More precisely, atomic snapshot memory exports two atomic operations: $update(i, v)$ $(i \in \{1, \ldots, n\})$ that writes value v to position i, and $scan()$ that returns the vector of the most recently written values to positions $1, \ldots, n$.

Simulators. An execution of the processes $p_1, \ldots p_n$ can be *simulated* by a set of *simulators* $s_1, \ldots, s_\ell$ that mimic the steps of the full-information protocol in a *consistent* way: for every execution E_s, there exists an execution E of the full-information protocol on $p_1, \ldots, p_n$ such that the sequence of simulated snapshots for every process p_i in E_s have also been observed by p_i in E.

A process or a simulator may only fail by crashing, and otherwise it must respect the algorithm it is given. A *correct* process or simulator never crashes.

Tasks. In this paper, we focus on a specific class of distributed computing problems, called *tasks* [20]. In a distributed task [20], every participating process starts with a unique input value and, after the computation, is expected to return a unique output value, so that the inputs and the outputs across the processes satisfy certain properties. More precisely, a *task* is defined through a set $\mathcal{I}$ of input vectors (one input value for each process), a set $\mathcal{O}$ of output vectors (one output value for each process), and a total relation $\Delta : \mathcal{I} \mapsto 2^{\mathcal{O}}$ that associates each input vector with a set of possible output vectors. An input $\bot$ denotes a *not participating* process and an output value $\bot$ denotes an *undecided* process.

For example, in the task of *k-set consensus*, input values are in $\{\bot, 0, \ldots, k\}$, output values are in $\{\bot, 0, \ldots, k\}$, and for each input vector I and output vector O, $(I, O) \in \Delta$ if the set of non-$\bot$ values in O is a subset of values in I of size at most k. The special case of 1-set consensus is called *consensus* [11].

We assume that every process runs a *full-information* protocol: initially it writes its input value and then alternates between taking snapshots of the memory and writing back the result of its latest snapshots. After a certain number of such asynchronous rounds, a process may gather enough state to *decide*, i.e., i.e., to produce an irrevocable non-$\bot$ output value. There is no loss of generality in this assumption since the full-information protocol provides at least as much information about the execution as any other protocol.

In *colorless* tasks (also called *convergence* tasks [7]), processes are free to use each others' input and output values, so the task can be defined in terms of input and output *sets* instead of vectors. Formally, let $val(U)$ denote the set of non-$\bot$ values in a vector U. In a colorless task, for all input vectors I and I' and all output vectors O and O', such that $(I, O) \in \Delta$, $val(I) \subseteq val(I')$, $val(O') \subseteq val(O)$, we have $(I', O') \in \Delta$. The k-set consensus task is colorless.

Note that to solve a colorless task, it is sufficient to find a protocol (a decision function) that allows just one process to decide. Indeed, if such a protocol exists, we can simply convert it into a protocol that allows every correct process to decide: every process simply applies the decision function to the observed state of any other process and adopts the decision.

The task of (m, k)-*renaming* involves m participating processes (out of n) that are expected to select *names* in the range $\{1, \ldots, k\}$ so that no two processes choose the same name. Renaming is a *colored* (not colorless) task.

Agreement. A basic building block of our simulations is an *agreement* abstraction that can be seen as a safe part of consensus. It exports one operation *propose*() taking $v \in V$ as a parameter and returning $w \in V$, where V is a (possibly infinite) *value set*. When a process p_i invokes *propose*(v) we say that

p_i *proposes* v, and when the invocation returns v' we say that p_i *decides on* v. Agreement ensures three properties:

(i) every decided value has been previously proposed,
(ii) no two processes decide on different values, and
(iii) if a process decides, then, eventually, every process that takes sufficiently many steps decides.

There are many protocols that satisfy the three properties above, additionally offering some liveness guarantees.

The consensus protocol using the Ω failure detector [8] guarantees that every correct process eventually decides, where Ω, at every correct process, eventually outputs the same identifier of a correct process.

The *BG agreement* protocol [5,7], guarantees that if every participating process takes enough steps, then eventually every correct participant decides.

The *obstruction-free* consensus protocol (*OF consensus*) [19,4], which is of special interest for us here, guarantees that a process decides if it eventually runs *solo*, i.e., it eventually encounters no step contention.

4 Abstract Simulation

We present our simulation algorithm in a modular way. First, we describe the procedure by which simulators advance one more step of a given simulated process p_i (Section 4.1). The procedure is using an agreement protocol that is, as stated above, safe but not necessarily live. Thus, a correct simulator may block forever in the middle of simulating a step.

Assuming that this procedure is used correctly, i.e., while a simulator is in the middle of simulating a step of p_i, it does not start simulating a new step of p_i, we show that the resulting simulated execution is *consistent* with some execution of the full-information protocol on the simulated processes, where inputs come from the simulators. simulation (Section 4.2).

4.1 Simulating One Step

To simulate a step of a given process p_i, every simulator follows the algorithm in Figure 1. First, the simulator takes a snapshot of the current states of the simulated processes (line 1). The states of the simulated systems is stored in an atomic snapshot object St. Each simulator s_j stores its view of the states of all simulated processes in position j of St. The $getState()$ call returns the vector of most recent simulated states, and the $updateState(i, [s, k + 1])$ performed by s_j updates the state of process p_i in jth position of St. Both operations can be easily implemented using atomic snapshot memory shared by the simulators.

If p_i has not yet performed a single simulated step, then p_i's evaluated state is just its input value (line 4). Note that the procedure by which a simulator chooses the input for p_i is a parameter of the simulation, and we give concrete

---

Shared variables:
   $A_1^i, A_2^i, \ldots$, agreement protocols   { *used to simulate steps* $1, 2, \ldots$ *of* p_i }
   St, atomic snapshot object, initially $[\bot, 0], \ldots, [\bot, 0]$

To simulate the next step of p_i:
1    $[S, K] := St.getState()$ { *get the most recent simulated states* }
2    $k := K[i]$ { *get the number of simulated steps of* p_i }
3   **if** $k = 0$ **then**
4      $s := p_i$ *'s input value (using the provided initialization procedure)*
5   **else**
6      $s := S$ { *the current simulated state* }
7    $s := A_{k+1}^i.propose(s)$ { *agree on the next state of* p_i }
8    $St.updateState(i, [s, k + 1])$

Fig. 1. Safety: simulating one step of process p_i

examples in Sections 5.1 and 5.2. Otherwise, the state of p_i is evaluated as the result of the last snapshot of the simulated state (line 1).

Then the simulated process p_i is driven forward using a new instance of agreement A_{k+1}^i. When A_{k+1}^i returns s, the simulator *publishes* $[s, k + 1]$ as the simulated state of p_i resulted after its $(k + 1)$th snapshot (line 8) .

We assume that every simulator is *well-formed*: it never starts simulating a new step of p_i (using the algorithm in Figure 1) if it has not yet computed an input value for p_i and it is not yet done with simulating p_i's previous step. Respectively, an execution is *well-formed* if every simulator is well-formed in it. We say that a process p_i takes r simulated steps in a well-formed execution if at least one simulator returned from an invocation of $A_r^i.propose(s)$ (line 7).

Correctness. Now we show that any well-formed execution of the simulation using the agreement protocol in Figure 1 indeed produces an execution of the full-information protocol on $p_1, \ldots, p_n$. More precisely, the sequence of simulated snapshots obtained by every process p_i settled by the agreement protocols $A_1^i, A_2^i, \ldots$ in the well-formed execution could have been indeed observed in some execution of the full-information protocol.

Any well-formed execution of the algorithm exports, for each process p_i, a sequence of *states* $v_1^i, v_2^i, \ldots$ of the full-information protocol returned by the agreement instances $A_1^i, A_2^i, \ldots$, each next state "extending" the previous one. This sequence is well defined, since each of these agreement instances returns at most one value and the instances are used one-by-one.

Intuitively, if the sequence of states $v_1^i, v_2^i, \ldots$ is finite (only finitely many invocations of $A_1^i, A_2^i, \ldots$ return), p_i takes only finitely many steps in the simulation. Otherwise, if the sequence of p_i's states is infinite, then p_i appears correct (takes infinitely many steps) in the simulated execution.

Now we say an execution E_s of the algorithm in Figure 1 is *consistent with* an execution E of the full-information protocol for processes $p_1, \ldots, p_n$ if, for each p_i, the sequence of states $v_1^i, v_2^i, \ldots$ exported to p_i by E_s is the sequence of states of p_i observed in E.

Lemma 1. *Let E_s be any well-formed execution on $s_1, \ldots, s_\ell$ using the algorithm in Figure 1. There exists an execution E of the full-information protocol on $p_1, \ldots, p_n$, such that E_s is consistent with E and the input of every process participating in E is proposed in E_s by some simulator in line 4.*

Proof. Given a well-formed execution E_s, we construct the corresponding execution E of the full-information protocol as follows.

First of all, we observe that, thanks to the use of agreement protocols, the evolution of the state of every simulated process is observed consistently by all simulators: the outcome of the kth snapshot of each process p_i is witnessed in the same way by all simulators in E_s.

The inputs of each simulated process is agreed using the agreement protocol in line 7, where each decided value is chosen by some simulator in line 4.

Further, since all snapshots of St are totally ordered, we can also totally order all snapshots of the simulated states that were agreed in line 7 for some simulated processes, so that every next snapshot contains the preceding one. Thus, all snapshots obtained by the simulated processes in E_s are related by *containment*.

Also, a simulator only accesses agreement protocol A^i_{k+1} if it observes (in line 1) that p_i performed k simulated snapshots so far. Since the full-information state proposed by a simulator to the agreement protocol in line 7 contains p_i's most recent snapshot, we also have *self-inclusion*: every simulated snapshot of a process p_i contains the most recent update of p_i.

Now we construct E as follows: we place simulated snapshot operations in E_s respecting the containment order, and then place each kth update of a process p_i before the first snapshot operation that returns a vector containing the $(k-1)$th snapshot of p_i. Here the first update operation of p_i simply writes the input of p_i. □

4.2   Simulating a Run Using OF Consensus

Our simulation algorithm using obstruction-free (OF) consensus as an agreement protocol is presented in Figure 2. The simulation is parameterized by:

- The *initialization* condition: how a simulator computes an input of any process it is simulating (line 9).
- The *activation* condition: how a simulator decides when to participate in the simulation (line 10).
- The *termination* condition: how a simulator decides when to depart from the simulation (line 28).

Concrete examples of how these parameters can be defined are given in Sections 5.1 and 5.2. For now we only assume that the activation and termination conditions are publicly known: each simulator can look at the simulated state St and decide which simulators are active and which are able to terminate. We assume that the conditions are *monotone*: if a condition holds given the current snapshot of the simulated state, it holds given any subsequent snapshot in the simulation.

In our simulation, each simulator s_i first *registers* its input (line 9) and then waits until it is *activated*. Once s_i becomes active, it writes 1 as its round number in register R_i (line 14). Therefore, we say that a simulator s_i is *active* in a given state of the simulations if $R_i \neq \perp$.

Every active simulator s_i proceeds in rounds. In each round, s_i picks one simulated process p_ℓ and tries to move it forward using the algorithm in Figure 1 with OF consensus objects [19,4] as the agreement abstractions. The simulated process p_ℓ is chosen based on the following rule:

- s_i computes the set U of currently active (but not yet terminated) simulators. Let $m = |U|$.
- s_i computes its *rank* k in U, i.e., the number of simulators in U with ids $j \leq i$.
- If $m \leq n$, i.e., the number of simulators in U does not exceed the number of processes to simulate, s_i chooses p_ℓ as the k-th smallest process in $S^m_{r \mod \binom{n}{m}}$, the "next" set of m simulated processes. Here, for all m, the set of process subsets of size m is ordered as $S^m_0, ..., S^m_{\binom{n}{m}-1}$. (Note that the simulation may block if the number of active simulators exceeds the number of simulated processes, which is not extremely surprising.)

The simulation of p_ℓ in round r is performed until p_ℓ moves forward (takes one more simulated snapshot according to the algorithm in Figure 1) or another simulator reaches a round higher than r. Note that in the special case when the input value for p_ℓ is not yet known, the simulation simply moves round $r + 1$.

I_i is an n-vector that contains inputs for processes in Π proposed by simulator s_i. If the jth position in the vector is $\perp$, it means that s_i does not have an input for p_i. The inputs given to different simulators do not have to be mutually consistent: different simulators can be given different input values for the same simulated process. We say that a process p_j is *initialized* if in a given execution of our simulation, at least one simulator s_i has written a non-$\perp$ value in the jth position of I_i (line 9).

Note that the simulation is well-formed: no simulator starts simulating a step of a process p_i before it finishes simulating p_i's previous step. Thus, by Lemma 1, it produces a correct execution of the full-information protocol where every participating simulated process starts with an input proposed by one of the active simulators.

Moreover, our abstract simulation ensures the following property that will be instrumental (in our concrete examples in Section 5.1 and 5.2).

Theorem 1. *If, eventually, there are exactly m active and not terminated simulators, at least one of which is correct, and at least $\ell \geq m$ processes are initialized, then at least $\ell - m + 1$ processes take infinitely many steps in the simulated execution.*

Shared variables:
    I_i, for each simulator s_i, initially $\perp$
    R_i, for each simulator s_i, initially $\perp$

Code for each simulator s_i with input V:

```
9    I_i := initialize(V)      { the initialization rule }
10   wait until active()       { the activation rule }
11   r := 0
12   repeat
13       r := r + 1
14       R_i := r
15       repeat
16           U := active and not yet terminated simulators
17           m := |U|
18           k := rank of s_i in U
19           if m ≤ n then
20               p_ℓ := the k-th process in S^m_{r mod (n choose m)}   { pick a process in S^m_{r mod (n choose m)} }
21               if p_ℓ is initialized in one of I_1,...,I_n then
22                   run one step of the algorithm in Figure 1 for p_ℓ using OF consensus
                     (start a new snapshot simulation if done with the previous one)
23               else
24                   break
25           else
26               break
27       until ∃s_j : R_j > r or p_ℓ moves forward
28   until decided in St    { the termination rule }
29   return the output
```

Fig. 2. Abstract simulation: the code of each simulator s_i

Proof. We show first that every correct simulator proceeds through infinitely many rounds of the algorithm in Figure 2. Suppose, without loss of generality, that r is the smallest round that is never completed by some correct simulator s_i. Since a simulator completes round r as soon as it observes that another simulator reaches a higher round (line 28), we derive that every correct process is blocked forever in round r.

Consider the moment after which the set W of active and not yet terminated simulators is of size m. Recall that the termination condition for each simulator is publicly known. Therefore, there is a time after which every correct simulator evaluates the set of such simulators as W in line 16.

Every simulator with rank k in W chooses kth process in the set $S^m_{r \bmod \binom{n}{m}}$ to simulate. Since no simulator reaches a round higher than r by breaking in line 24, we observe that every correct active simulator is blocked in simulating a step of an initialized process. But there are exactly m processes in $S^m_{r \bmod \binom{n}{m}}$, thus, eventually, at most one simulator is promoting every initialized process in $S^m_{r \bmod \binom{n}{m}}$.

Since we use OF consensus as the agreement protocol in Figure 1 and s_i is the only process to take steps of the protocol, eventually, the agreement protocol in line 7 returns. Thus, s_i eventually simulates one more step of its process in $S^m_{r \bmod \binom{n}{m}}$ and moves to round $r + 1$—a contradiction.

Thus, a correct simulator s_i goes through infinitely many rounds of the algorithm in Figure 2. Suppose, by contradiction, that there is a set W of m initialized simulated processes that take only finitely many steps in the resulting simulated execution. Note that since all sets of size m are continuously explored in the round-robin fashion, eventually, s_i infinitely often reaches round r such that $S^m_{r \bmod \binom{n}{m}} = W$. Since all processes in W are initialized, at least one of them is takes at least one simulated step. By repeating this argument, we derive that at least one process in W takes infinitely many simulated steps—a contradiction.

Thus, at most $m - 1$ initialized processes can take only finitely many steps in the simulated execution, i.e., at least $\ell - m + 1$ processes take infinitely many steps. $\qquad\square$

5   Applications

Now we apply our abstract simulation to establish the equivalence of t-resilient systems and wait-free $(t + 1)$-process systems, first for colorless tasks [5,7] and then for generic (colored) tasks [13].

5.1   BG Simulation: Characterizing t-Resilient Solvability of Colorless Tasks

BG simulation [5,7] is a technique by which $k+1$ simulators $s_1, \ldots, s_{k+1}$ $(k < n)$ can wait-free simulate a *t-resilient* execution on processes $p_1, \ldots, p_n$ $(n > t)$ of a protocol solving a colorless task. The technique is applied to derive the following result which we now obtain using our abstract simulation:

Theorem 2. *A colorless task T is t-resiliently solvable if and only if it is wait-free solvable by $t + 1$ processes.*

Proof. The "if" part of this result is straightforward. Suppose that T is solvable wait-free by $t + 1$ processes. We just let processes $p_1, \ldots, p_{t+1}$ run the wait-free algorithm, where each p_i $(i = 1, \ldots, t + 1)$ runs the algorithm of s_i. As soon as a process in $\{p_1, \ldots, p_{t+1}\}$ decides, it posts its decision value in the shared memory. Every process periodically checks the memory, and returns the first decision value it finds. In any t-resilient execution, every correct process returns.

To obtain the "only if" part, suppose that there is a t-resilient solution of T on processes $p_1, \ldots, p_n$. We want to show that T can thus be solved wait-free by $s_1, \ldots, s_{t+1}$. To use our abstract simulation, we need to specify the initialization, activation, and termination parameters for the algorithm in Figures 1 and 2.

To initialize simulated processes, s_i puts its input value v_i in all positions of the vector I_i: $I_i = [v_i, ..., v_n]$. Every simulator s_i that reached line 10 is considered active.

The termination condition is also straightforward. A simulator terminates as soon it observes (in line 28) a simulated state St in which some simulated process decides. The simulator then simply returns the value decided by the simulated process.

By Theorem 1, the resulting simulated execution is going to be t-resilient and, thus, eventually, some simulated process must decide. Therefore, every correct simulator eventually decides and, since the task is colorless and the inputs of the simulated processes come from the simulators, the decisions of the simulators are consistent with the inputs in regard to the task specification.   □

5.2 Extended BG Simulation: Characterizing Generic Tasks

In EBG [13], any task $T = (\mathcal{I}, \mathcal{O}, \Delta)$ defined for n processes $p_1, \ldots, p_n$, is associated with a task $T' = (\mathcal{I}', \mathcal{O}', \Delta')$ defined for $t + 1$ simulators $s_1, \ldots, s_{t+1}$ as follows:

- In every input vector $I' \in \mathcal{I}'$, each simulator s_i is given a set of input values for p_i and $n - t - 1$ processes with ids higher than i. No two simulators are given different input values for the same process.
- In every output vector $O' \in \mathcal{O}'$, each simulator s_i obtains a set of output values for p_i and $n - t - 1$ processes with ids higher than i. No two simulators obtain different output values for the same process.
- For every $(I', O') \in \Delta'$, the corresponding input vector I and output vector O for processes in Π satisfy $(I, O) \in \Delta$.

We apply our abstract simulation to derive the following result originally presented in [13]:

Theorem 3. *T can be solved t-resiliently if and only if T' can be solved wait-free.*

Proof. In both directions we use the simulation described in Figures 1 and 2 where the agreement protocols are instances of OF consensus. Recall that, in addition to the three properties of agreement, OF consensus guarantees that every process that, from some point on, runs solo eventually decides.

The "only if" Part. Suppose we are given an algorithm that t-resiliently solves T. In a wait-free solution of T' for $t + 1$ simulators $s_1, \ldots, s_{t+1}$, every simulator that reached line 10 is considered active. As in Section 5.1, every simulator s_i simply uses its input in T' to initialize its vector I_i. Then every active s_i runs the algorithm in Figures 1 and 2 until it observes outputs for p_i and $n - t - 1$ processes with ids higher than i (the termination condition in line 28).

Again, we show first that every correct simulator eventually terminates. Suppose, by contradiction, that there is a set W of exactly $m \geq 1$ active simulators

---

Initialization (line 9):

$I_i := V$ { V is s_i's input of T', a vector of at least $n - t$ input values of T }

Activation (line 10):

   true

Termination (line 28):

   p_i and $n - t - 1$ processes with ids higher than i decided in St

---

Fig. 3. The parameters of $T \Rightarrow T'$ (lines 9, 10 and 28 in Figure 2)

that never terminate, and at least one of them is correct. Since there are m active simulators, exactly $\ell \geq n - t + m - 1$ simulated processes are initialized.

By Theorem 1, in the resulting execution, at most $m - 1 \leq t$ initialized processes take only finitely many steps in the resulting simulated execution. Since the simulated algorithm is t-resilient, we derive that at most $m - 1$ initialized processes never decide.

Let $\{s_{i_1}, \ldots, s_{i_m}\}$ be the simulators in W sorted in the order of increasing ids. Note that there are at least $n - t + m - 1$ initialized processes with ids i_1 and higher, and at most $m - 1$ of them never decide. Hence, s_{i_1} eventually observes at least $n - t$ decided processes with ids i_1 or higher. We derive that p_{i_1} never decides, otherwise s_{i_1} would observe that p_{i-1} and $n - t - 1$ processes with ids higher than i_1 are decided and terminate. Inductively, s_j observes at least $n - t + m - j$ initialized decided processes with ids i_j and higher and at most $m - j$ of them never decide. But for $j = m$ this gives at least $n - t$ decided processes with ids i_m and higher, and, thus, s_{i_m} terminates—a contradiction.

Thus, eventually, every correct simulator outputs.

The "if" Part. Now suppose we are given a wait-free solution of T' for processes $p_1, \ldots, p_{t+1}$. We derive a t-resilient solution for T on n simulators $s_1, \ldots, s_n$ as follows.

Every simulator registers its participation by writing its input of T in the shared memory. As soon as a simulator $s_i \in \{s_1, \ldots, s_{t+1}\}$ witnesses the participation of at least $n - t - 1$ processes with ids higher than its own, it joins the simulation of the wait-free algorithm solving T'. Respectively, in the simulation, a process p_i is considered initialized if s_i and $n - t - 1$ simulators with ids higher than i have posted their inputs of T.

Note that, initially, every active simulator $s_i \in \{s_1, \ldots, s_{t+1}\}$ corresponds to a distinct initialized simulated process p_i. Thus, the number of active not yet terminated simulators does not exceed the number of simulated processes, and, by Theorem 1, at least one simulated process takes sufficiently many steps to decide (the simulated protocol is wait-free).

Once at least one simulated process decides (i.e., at least $n - t$ participating simulators terminate), every simulator s_i without output (whether it is in $\{s_1, \ldots, s_{t+1}\}$ or not) joins the simulation and runs it until some simulated process produces an output for it (see the activation procedure in Figure 4).

Initialization (line 9):
  $I_i := V$ { V is s_i's input in T }
Activation (line 10):
  if $s_i \notin \{s_1, \ldots, s_{t+1}\}$ **then**
    wait until at least one simulated process in $\{p_1, \ldots, p_{t+1}\}$ decides
Termination (line 28):
  some p_j decides with an output containing the value of s_i

Fig. 4. The parameters of $T' \Rightarrow T$ (lines 9, 10 and 28 in Figure 2)

A simulator terminates as soon as its output is produced by some decided simulated process (the termination condition in 28).

Again, suppose, by contradiction that there are $\ell > 0$ participating simulators that never decide, at least one of which is correct. We observe first that there are at least ℓ initialized processes in $\{p_1, \ldots, p_{t+1}\}$ that never terminate. Indeed, since $n - t$ simulators decided in the first phase of our simulation, the total number of participating simulators is $n - t + k \geq n - t + \ell$, where k is the exact number of participating simulators in $\{s_1, \ldots, s_{t+1}\}$.

Note that, since exactly ℓ out of m simulators are undecided in the current simulation, exactly ℓ out of k initialized simulated processes never terminate. Indeed if we imagine that $k - \ell + 1$ out of k initialized simulators terminate, the total number of decided simulators must be $n - t + k - \ell + 1$ which, together with the ℓ participating simulators that never decide gives $n - t + k + 1$ participating simulators in total.

By Theorem 1, at most $\ell - 1$ simulated process takes only finitely many steps in the simulated execution. Thus, at least one of the ℓ never terminated simulators take infinitely many steps, and, since the simulated protocol is wait-free, eventually decides—a contradiction.

Thus, our construction indeed ensures that every live simulator eventually decides. Since the decision come from an execution of a protocol solving T' with the same inputs, the solution is correct with respect to T.   □

6   Concluding Remarks and Speculations

This paper proposes a simple and intuitive simulation technique that is general enough to derive a wide variety of models equivalence results. At a high level, the technique maintains the invariant that the number of simulators conincides with the number of currently simulated processes. Therefore, as long as there is a live simulator, at least one of the simulated processes makes progress. To maintain the invariant, a terminated process may bring the number of simulators by one. As our algorithms in Section 5 suggest, multiple existing and new equivalence results can be established by simply parameterizing initialization, activation, and termination rules in our simulation framework.

Below we briefly sketch how the equivalence between the "generalized k-state machine"' [15] and active $(k - 1)$-resilience. Sorting out details of the sketched algorithms and proving their correctness is left for (immediate) future work. We also show how to extend the technique to models equipped with k-process consensus objects.

Bounded Active Resilience. Suppose that we have a protocol solving task T assuming that at most $k - 1$ active processes may fail. Recall that a process is considered active if it has started the protocol and have not yet output. Without loss of generality, we assume that in the first step of the protocol, each process registers its input value in the shared memory. Thus, at any point of the execution, active processes are not yet terminated processes whose input values are registered.

In a $(k - 1)$-active resilient model, we can easily solve k-set agreement as follows. Assuming active $(k - 1)$-resilience, the active processes simulate the first steps of at most k processes $q_1, \ldots, q_k$. As soon as the first step of at least one simulated process q_i is completed, every process can decide on the posted value. A process participates in the simulation as long as it is among the first k active processes. In that case, the process with rank $\ell \in \{1, \ldots, k\}$ is assigned to simulate process q_ℓ. If there are k or more active processes with smaller ids, then the process simply waits until a decision value is posted. Since at most $k - 1$ active processes may fail, at least one simulated process will eventually complete its first step, and every correct process will eventually decide.

In the other direction, we employ the simulation algorithm of Section 4.2 run on $\min(k, \ell)$ state machines, where ℓ is the number of active processes. The construction of [15] guarantees that at most $\min(k, \ell) - 1$ state machines may stall. Moreover, as long as there is at least one correct active process, at least one machine makes progress by simulating an active k-resilient execution. Therefore, every correct active process eventually terminates.

Beyond Read-Write. It is straightforward to extend our colorless simulations to the models where simulators can use k-process consensus objects so that, e.g., ℓ simulators can simulate a system of $\lceil \ell/k \rceil$ processes in the wait-free manner.

Indeed, consider the one-step simulation in Figure 1, where the agreement protocol A^i_{k+1} is augmented with k-processes consensus. "Augmented" means here that the protocol additionally guarantees that if at least one process among the first k to access it is correct, then every correct simulator returns. We can easily implement such an abstraction using k-process consensus object and read-write registers.

Now we apply our abstract simulation in Figure 2 and observe that a simulated process can only block forever if some k faulty simulators died in the middle of its simulation. As long as there is one correct simulator, at most $\lceil k/\ell \rceil - 1$ simulated processes can fail.

Acknowledgements. The author is grateful to Eli Gafni for multiple discussions on model simulations and to Armando Castañeda for sharing his confusions about the original EBG algorithm [13], which inspired deriving the technique proposed in this paper.

References

1. Afek, Y., Attiya, H., Dolev, D., Gafni, E., Merritt, M., Shavit, N.: Atomic snapshots of shared memory. J. ACM 40(4), 873–890 (1993)
2. Alpern, B., Schneider, F.B.: Defining liveness. Inf. Process. Lett. 21(4), 181–185 (1985)
3. Attiya, H., Bar-Noy, A., Dolev, D.: Sharing memory robustly in message passing systems. J. ACM 42(2), 124–142 (1995)
4. Attiya, H., Guerraoui, R., Hendler, D., Kuznetsov, P.: The complexity of obstruction-free implementations. J. ACM 56(4) (2009)
5. Borowsky, E., Gafni, E.: Generalized FLP impossibility result for t-resilient asynchronous computations. In: STOC, pp. 91–100. ACM Press (May 1993)
6. Borowsky, E., Gafni, E.: Immediate atomic snapshots and fast renaming. In: PODC, pp. 41–51. ACM Press, New York (1993)
7. Borowsky, E., Gafni, E., Lynch, N.A., Rajsbaum, S.: The BG distributed simulation algorithm. Distributed Computing 14(3), 127–146 (2001)
8. Chandra, T.D., Toueg, S.: Unreliable failure detectors for reliable distributed systems. J. ACM 43(2), 225–267 (1996)
9. Delporte-Gallet, C., Fauconnier, H., Gafni, E., Kuznetsov, P.: Wait-freedom with advice. In: PODC, pp. 105–114 (2012)
10. Delporte-Gallet, C., Fauconnier, H., Guerraoui, R., Tielmann, A.: The disagreement power of an adversary. Distributed Computing 24(3-4), 137–147 (2011)
11. Fischer, M.J., Lynch, N.A., Paterson, M.S.: Impossibility of distributed consensus with one faulty process. J. ACM 32(2), 374–382 (1985)
12. Gafni, E.: Round-by-round fault detectors (extended abstract): Unifying synchrony and asynchrony. In: Proceedings of the 17th Symposium on Principles of Distributed Computing (1998)
13. Gafni, E.: The extended BG-simulation and the characterization of t-resiliency. In: STOC, pp. 85–92 (2009)
14. Gafni, E., Guerraoui, R.: Simulating few by many: Limited concurrency = set consensus. Technical report, UCLA (2009), http://www.cs.ucla.edu/~eli/eli/kconc.pdf
15. Gafni, E., Guerraoui, R.: Generalized universality. In: Katoen, J.-P., König, B. (eds.) CONCUR 2011. LNCS, vol. 6901, pp. 17–27. Springer, Heidelberg (2011)
16. Gafni, E., Kuznetsov, P.: On set consensus numbers. Distributed Computing 24(3-4), 149–163 (2011)
17. Gafni, E., Kuznetsov, P.: Relating $\mathcal{L}$-Resilience and Wait-Freedom via Hitting Sets. In: Aguilera, M.K., Yu, H., Vaidya, N.H., Srinivasan, V., Choudhury, R.R. (eds.) ICDCN 2011. LNCS, vol. 6522, pp. 191–202. Springer, Heidelberg (2011)
18. Gafni, E., Rajsbaum, S.: Distributed programming with tasks. In: Lu, C., Masuzawa, T., Mosbah, M. (eds.) OPODIS 2010. LNCS, vol. 6490, pp. 205–218. Springer, Heidelberg (2010)
19. Herlihy, M., Luchangco, V., Moir, M.: Obstruction-free synchronization: Double-ended queues as an example. In: ICDCS, pp. 522–529 (2003)
20. Herlihy, M., Shavit, N.: The topological structure of asynchronous computability. J. ACM 46(2), 858–923 (1999)
21. Kuznetsov, P.: Understanding non-uniform failure models. Bull. Eur. Assoc. Theor. Comput. Sci. EATCS 106, 54–77 (2012)

Helical Entanglement Codes: An Efficient Approach for Designing Robust Distributed Storage Systems*

Veronica Estrada Galinanes and Pascal Felber

University of Neuchâtel, Switzerland

Abstract. This paper presents a new approach for data entanglement in a distributed storage system. The introduction of dependencies between stored content was initially proposed as a deterrent factor in censorship resistant systems. The strategies found in the literature fail, however, to simultaneously provide a high level of robustness while being sufficiently efficient to be deployed in real-world systems. To address this limitation, we propose a novel design, called helical entanglement code (HEC), that entangles files with both previously-stored and forthcoming data and provides a sound compromise between strong robustness, pragmatism, and efficiency. HEC provides self-repair capabilities inside a cluster of entangled documents while only requiring cheap encoding mechanisms. We further describe the architecture of a storage system that leverages HEC's implicit redundancy properties and can be used in combination with conventional encoding methods to protect data against various types of faults.

1 Introduction

Cloud computing [1] offers a wide range of opportunities to the IT industry, but also represents a radical departure from traditional distributed computing architectures. One of the most important paradigm shifts is the move from self-hosted services towards "pay as you go" platforms deployed and managed by external cloud providers. While interesting from an economical perspective, this separation of roles makes the customers reliant on the cloud providers, notably regarding the dependability and security of hosted applications and data. The use of commodity servers in highly distributed scenarios where users and nodes are geographically distributed has already caused important incidents [2], with several leading storage service providers recently experiencing downtimes (e.g., [3]). In this work we specifically focus on the problem of persistently storing data in cloud environments prone to failures and attacks.

Availability and reliability are major concerns in large-scale distributed systems. They are traditionally addressed by the means of redundancy, which is applied in many different flavors. The Google and Hadoop file systems [4,5], for

---

* The work described in this paper was founded by SNF grant Sinergia Project No. CRSII2_1363181.

T. Higashino et al. (Eds.): SSS 2013, LNCS 8255, pp. 32–44, 2013.

instance, adopt a triple replication policy. But a storage overhead of 200% becomes a concern considering the growing rates of "Big Data". Erasure coding [6] is a popular approach to reduce storage overhead. Cloud storage solutions usually adopt *maximum distance separable* erasures codes, notably the *Reed-Solomon* error-correcting codes. Reed-Solomon is a mathematical technique that takes k data symbols of s bits to create n symbols based on the coefficients of a polynomial $p(x)$ over a finite field. Most storage systems that use erasure codes first split files into fixed size chunks before applying erasure codes and storing the resulting data blocks on geographically distributed servers [7,8,9,10]. A problem arises when a single server fails. Various sophisticated repair strategies exist in the literature [11], but de-facto solution is a naive method that involves high bandwidth overhead: all original data blocks are recreated even to reconstruct a single missing encoded block.

A question that remains poorly answered is how storage providers can guarantee data durability and recovery in untrusted settings. Durability requires that data is not permanently lost after failures, which typically involves the maintenance of high levels of data redundancy. Reed-Solomon codes are not yet a wide accepted industry standard because their expensive bandwidth cost. Researchers at Facebook revealed that in a 3000 node production cluster only 8% of the data is currently RS encoded [12]. Higher degrees of replication will also increase the bandwidth and storage requirements of the system [13].

This work is an on-going research that primarily focus on effective ways to offer technical guarantees for data durability. Our source of inspiration are censorship resistant systems, in which dependencies between stored content was proposed as a deterrent to censor attacks. For instance, in Tangler [14], an entanglement process establishes a one-to-many relationship between blocks and files. Moreover, the process of uploading a new document contributes to the replication of blocks from other documents as dependencies generate implicit redundancy. Our goal is to achieve high levels of data dependencies while designing an entanglement function with minimal requirements in terms of bandwidth, computation, and storage. In particular, durability mechanisms should be practical and efficient enough to be deployed in real-world systems.

At a high level, our approach works as follows. To upload a piece of data to the system, a client must first download some existing blocks (three by default, chosen deterministically as will be explained in Section 3) and combine them with the new data using a simple exclusive-or (XOR) operation. The combined blocks are then uploaded to different servers, whereas the original data is not stored at all. The newly uploaded blocks will be subsequently used in combination with future blocks, hence creating intricate dependencies that provide strong durability properties. The original piece of data can be reconstructed in several ways by combining different pairs of blocks stored in the system. These blocks can themselves be repaired by recursively following dependency chains.

In this work we make the following contributions:

- We propose a novel method to entangle files with both previously-stored and forthcoming data, called *helical entanglement codes* (HEC). These codes are named after the helical lattice structure that supports our entanglement process, which is defined by $2 * p + 2$ independent chains of entanglements. HEC ensures all-or-nothing integrity, i.e., maximum achievable dependency, inside a cluster of entangled documents while requiring only cheap encoding mechanisms based on XOR computations.
- We sketch the architecture of an entangled data storage system that leverages HEC to provide a sound compromise between strong robustness, pragmatism, and efficiency.
- We analyze the properties of HEC and the trade-off between system robustness and lattice topology. The way the entanglement is done plays an important role in the durability of the file: dependency limitations are related to the factor p that describes the number of distinct helical strands that follow the same direction (left-handed or right-handed helix). In its default configuration, HEC's space overhead is similar to other solutions with 3 blocks generated per uploaded block.

2   Related Work

The general problem of anonymity in distributed systems has been largely studied in the literature, refer to [15] from an extensive bibliography. Several approaches have been proposed to address the particular aspect of censorship resistance. They can be loosely classified according to data replication, anonymous communication server deniability, and data entanglement [16]. Our main focus is on the latter.

Two existing systems, Tangler [14] and Dagster [17], use entanglement as an anti-censorship mechanism in document storage systems. Another entanglement model, called all-or-nothing integrity [18], has been proposed for protecting data from an untrusted storage provider that might be tempted to damage or destroy it.

Tangler consists of three main components: a publisher program that breaks the file in fixed-size (16K) blocks, a reconstruction program that reconstruct the file from fetched blocks, and a server daemon that distributes and retrieves blocks. The system assumes that all participating servers know each other and interact in a peer-to-peer fashion. Tangler uses consistent hashing to route queries among servers and relies on cryptographic hashes (SHA-1 and hash trees) to certified data published by the servers. Participants can inject blocks in a public pool that will feed the entanglement algorithm. The publisher program performs the entanglement using polynomial interpolation. It takes two random blocks from the public pool and one data block of the file, and produces two new server blocks that are injected to the pool. A data block can be reconstructed with any three of the four associated server blocks.

Dagster also has three architectural components: an anonymous channel between clients and servers, an out-of-band channel for document announcing, and the publishing server. Dagster's XOR-based entanglement model proposes that files are intertwined with a number of pre-existing documents (c factor) while constructing a direct acyclic graph of dependencies. The user announces the document when she believes that legitimate blocks are linked with her blocks. When retrieving a document, the user has the additional cost of reading all the c documents that were used in the entanglement process.

Aspnes *et al.* [18] observed that both aforementioned systems achieve a weak share-block notion of entanglement that has several drawbacks. In particular, deleting a document will affect only a small number of entangled files in Dagster and almost none in Tangler. Therefore, they introduced a theoretical framework for entanglement in which two interesting notions are defined: (1) *document dependency:* if document d_i depends on document d_j, then whenever d_j cannot be recovered, neither can d_i; (2) *all-or-nothing integrity:* a storage system is all-or-nothing when document dependency exists between every d_i and d_j, i.e., the system provides maximum achievable dependency.

3   Entanglement Model

In this section, we briefly discuss our design goals, before presenting in depth the components and operation of our entanglement approach.

3.1   Design Goal

Data entanglement in censorship-resistant systems is used to break the one-to-one relationship between a block an a document, and turn it into a one-to-many relationship, i.e., one block becomes part of many documents. In such systems, entanglement is used to discourage censorship attacks: a side-effect of removing a document is the destruction of other documents. The technique should be applied in combination with other methods to act as an effective deterrent to censorship. Anonymity as well as other typical requirements of censorship-resistant systems are provided by different layers of the storage system.

Entanglement introduces extra redundancy to the system and, hence, also contributes to its robustness. The way entanglement is performed plays an important role in the durability of the file. In this paper, we focus on the problem of *durability*: how can we persistently store a file and guarantee recovery properties in untrusted scenarios? Durability requires that the data is not permanently lost after failures. This typically involves repair actions to recover data stored in failed nodes (servers).

Our objective is to achieve high levels of document dependency and use the created redundancy to increase file durability. A further objective is to design an entanglement function that can be implemented efficiently. Indeed, high performance is a priority for the success of a practical system. Further, the disentanglement process should require as few data as possible, and we aim for low bandwidth, computation time, and storage requirements. The ultimate goal of our design is to provide strong file durability, relying on documents in the system to repair missing files and avoid data lost.

3.2   HEC Components

We introduce below the main components of our model. An extra layer is placed on top of the data store to coordinate the entanglement operation. This layer is modeled by an unbalanced (6,2)-biregular graph $G = (F, S, E)$, where F is the set of file blocks (*F-block* nodes), S the set of server blocks (*S-block* nodes), and E the set of edges that represents the entanglement relations. The graph topology corresponds to a helical lattice as described later in this section.

Blocks. All block types have the same fixed-size. File blocks, denoted by *F-blocks*, hold the data of user files. We assume for simplicity that files have the size of one block. In practice, larger files will be split and smaller ones will be padded. File blocks are not actually stored in the system, they are instead indirectly kept in the data store through their *entanglement tuples*. As F-blocks arrive to the system they are placed in an available lattice's compartment called *bucket*. Blocks are sequentially labeled with consecutive identifiers.

A new server block, or *S-block*, is generated each time an F-block is entangled with a previously stored S-block. The new S-block is stored in the system and will be entangled with a forthcoming F-block. Once that S-block is entangled again, it is said to be *actively entangled* with its left adjacent F-block and *passively entangled* with its right adjacent F-block. The S-block identification is based on both adjacent F-blocks, e.g., $S\text{-}block_{A\_B}$ is right adjacent to $F\text{-}block_A$ and left adjacent to $F\text{-}block_B$.

Anchor blocks, or *A-blocks*, are used to initialize the system (when there are not enough S-blocks). The number of A-blocks depends on the number of *helix'* starts.

Entanglement Function. The entanglement function takes one stored S-block and one F-block to produce a new S-block. When bootstrapping the system, the input S-block may be replaced by an A-block. We use a simple bitwise XOR to achieve high performance entanglement.

Helical Lattice. The stored blocks used in the entanglement function are selected according to rules that describe a repeated pattern forming a double-helix that uniformly grows when users upload files. The complete lattice is described by $2p+s$ chains of entanglements, where p strands are twisted into a right-handed helix, another p strands are twisted into a left-handed helix, and the remaining s chains constitute the parallel strands that follow the outline of the cylinder enclosing the double-p-helix shape. In the standard configuration presented in this paper, $s = 2$. A helical lattice with p independent threads in the same direction is denoted by *p-start helical lattice*. Figure 1 shows a 2D representation of a *5-start* helical entanglement structure. During one helix turn, a left-hand helix strand connects two consecutive F-blocks, e.g., $F\text{-}block_{26}$ and $F\text{-}block_{27}$, then it turns and the next F-block id is calculated using the *LH_Spring* value (+9). In the right-hand helix, the next connected block is founded by adding 3 to the id of the first block, e.g., $F\text{-}block_{25}$ and $F\text{-}block_{28}$. After rotation, the next block is obtained using the *RH_Spring* value (+7).

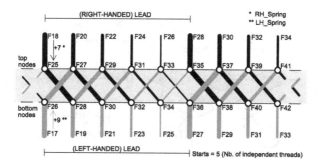

(a)View of F-blocks only (circles).

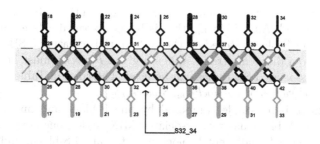

(b)View of F-blocks and associated S-blocks (diamonds).

Fig. 1. 2D representation of the helical lattice

Lead Window. In a cylindrical helix, the axial displacement of a point that moves on a thread in a circumferential direction during one complete revolution of the cylinder is called *lead*. We measure the lead in terms of the increment of the F-block number. Since F-block nodes are labeled consecutively, the lead size is $2p$. The *lead window* is composed by a set of *lead* $- 2$ files enclosed by the same helix strand.

Especially noteworthy is the maximum achievable dependency that exist between files stored inside a lead window. For every F-block$_i$, F-block$_j$ stored inside the same lead, whenever F-block$_i$ cannot be recovered, neither can F-block$_j$. To be more precise, given an odd value of p, the maximum number of files that can be deleted[1] without affecting the repair capabilities of the lattice is $2(p-1)$. The deleted files will be available again after a repair process. But, when $2p$ consecutive files, i.e., a complete lead, are deleted, the entanglement chains that allow repairs in backward and forward directions are broken. As a direct consequence, the deleted files are permanently lost.

Entanglement Tuples. An entanglement tuple is a two-element set that can be used to regenerate F-blocks and S-blocks. There are two types of entanglement tuples, *SB-tuples* and *MIX-tuples*, illustrated in Figure 2.

---

[1] F-blocks are deleted when all its 6 entangled S-blocks are deleted.

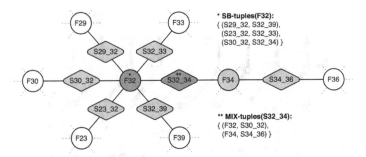

Fig. 2. Example of entanglement tuples

1. An *SB-tuple* is a 2-tuple composed by two consecutive S-blocks located on the same strand. Any F-block$_{id}$ that is being uploaded gets entangled with three distinct S-blocks stored on the system, thus creating 3 SB-tuple, each belonging to a different strand. When a given *F-block$_{id}$* must be recovered, any of its associated SB-tuples can be used. The rules in Table 1 determine the L and R values of $\{$*S-block$_{L\_id}$, S-block$_{id\_R}$*$\}$.
2. A *MIX-tuple* is a 2-tuple composed by one F-block and one adjacent S-block. Every S-block has two associated MIX-tuples, one corresponding to the preceding (left) adjacent F-block and its paired S-block, and the other corresponding to the following (right) adjacent F-block and its paired S-block. A missing S-block can be recovered directly using any of its two MIX-tuples.

3.3 Storing and Retrieving Data

To store an F-block, the algorithm identifies for each strand the left adjacent S-block (or A-block when bootstrapping the system) and generates a new S-block using the XOR entanglement function:

$$S\text{-}block_{id\_R} \leftarrow S\text{-}block_{L\_id} \oplus F\text{-}block_{id} \tag{1}$$

The new S-blocks (one per strand) are then stored in the system and the F-block is discarded.[2]

To retrieve an F-block, the rebuilding process takes any of the block's three SB-tuples and performs an XOR operation between the pair of elements. Thus, to regenerate *F-block$_{id}$*, a user must download one SB-tuple with L and R values obtained from the entanglement rules:

$$F\text{-}block_{id} \leftarrow S\text{-}block_{L\_id} \oplus S\text{-}block_{id\_R} \tag{2}$$

---

[2] This avoids individual servers to be able to read and tamper with locally-stored F-blocks.

3.4   Repairing Data

Under certain failures scenarios, none of the three SB-tuples may be available. The recovery process needs to regenerate the elements of one tuple to recover the F-block node. These S-blocks can be recovered via their associated MIX-tuples using any of the two equations:

$$S\text{-}block_{L\_R} \leftarrow F\text{-}block_L \oplus S\text{-}block_{X\_L} \tag{3}$$

$$S\text{-}block_{L\_R} \leftarrow F\text{-}block_R \oplus S\text{-}block_{R\_Y} \tag{4}$$

where the corresponding X and Y are obtained from the entanglement rules. In severe failure scenarios, multiple elements may be missing but the lattice topology can still allow repairing missing blocks by recursively applying Equations 3 and 4. In fact, the entanglement tuples define a binary *recovery tree* where at level 0, the root is the target F-block. Any of the three possible SB-tuples are at level 1 and each subsequent level is formed by a combination of MIX- and SB-tuples. A breadth-first search algorithm visits nodes until the root is restored. Each missing node in the tree can be recovered by using its two children nodes.

Table 1. HEC rules with $s = 2$, $LH\_Spring = sp - (s-1)^2$, $RH\_Spring = sp - (s^2 - 1)$

| | F-block$_{id}$ is top node | | F-block$_{id}$ is bottom node | |
	S-block$_{L\_id}$|L =	S-block$_{id\_R}$|R =	S-block$_{L\_id}$|L =	S-block$_{id\_R}$|R =
RH strand	$id - RH\_Spring$	$id + s + 1$	$id - (s+1)$	$id + RH\_Spring$
LH strand	$id - 1$	$id + LH\_Spring$	$id - LH\_Spring$	$id + (s-1)$
Horiz. strand	$id - s$	$id + s$	$id - s$	$id + s$

4   Entangled Data Storage

In this section, we describe how HEC may be used in a distributed storage system. We present the architectural components of such a system and the interactions between the different parties involved in the storage and retrieval operations.

4.1   Architecture

For clarity, we describe the main abstractions layers at the client and servers side. The client application has three main modules: an application layer (user interface), a security layer, and an entanglement client layer. The main components at the backend servers are: an entanglement coordination layer, an integrity layer, a distributed hash table (DHT) layer, and a storage layer.

On the user side, files are pre-processed upon upload (compressed, encrypted, and split in blocks). For performance reasons, block entanglement is performed at the backend but the client application is also able to reproduce the process independently and verify the content published on servers. A thin client reduces the bandwidth requirements on the user side, since uploading a file only requires to upload all its component F-blocks while S-blocks used for entanglements remain on the server side, where communication channels typically have higher bandwidth. Upon download, the client simply retrieves the blocks and reverses the process by applying combination, decryption, and decompression.

On the server side, an entanglement coordination agent handles the upload and download requests and applies the entanglement functions. The integrity layer has two functions: generate and publish Merkle trees [19], and manage available positions in the lattices. Merkle trees are data structures used in one-time signature schemes to authenticate an arbitrary number of messages. Only one single public key is required for validation: the root of the hash tree.

The DHT layer is in charged of locating values stored at the storage layer and identified by keys, i.e., it provides a key-value API to the data store. Our entanglement protocol does not put any special restrictions on the organization of the storage network. It may, for instance, be based on a multi-hop DHT deployed in a peer-to-peer overlay network. The selected DHT should support storage and retrieval operations of {*key,value*} pairs. More specifically, given a *key*, it should be possible to invoke a store operation in the form of *(put(key,value))* and a retrieval operation *(value=get(key))* as illustrated in Figure 2 of [20]. Thus, it should be possible to use any DHT.

4.2 Interactions

We now present the interactions and the messages exchanged by the main actors in response to an upload request made by a client application. Figure 3 depicts the sequence diagram of messages exchanged between the client, the coordination layer, the integrity layer, and the DHT layer.

The algorithm to upload a document works in stages. The *pre-processing stage* takes place at the client side. The file is compressed, encrypted, and split in blocks following a similar approach to [8]. When the client makes a request for uploading one block, the entanglement coordination layer initiates a *bucket allocation stage*. A bucket is a container for a F-block in the helical lattice. It consist of compartments to store the data produced by the entanglement operation. The integrity layer confirms that a bucket is available if the 3 S-blocks needed for entanglement are already stored in the system. The reservation is valid for a given duration of time. Thus, if the bucket not filled with 3 new S-blocks after a time-out, it will be released. When the confirmation arrives, the coordination layer continues with the *entanglement stage*. The input to the entanglement function are the F-block and a previously stored S-block determined by the bucket identifier included in the allocation confirmation. The coordination agent launches three processes in parallel to get the necessary 3 S-blocks from the DHT. As soon as the entanglement completes, the new S-block is stored in the DHT (*storage*

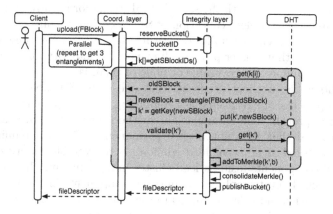

Fig. 3. Sequence diagram for the file upload process

stage) and the key is transmitted to the integrity layer that initiates a *server-side verification stage*. To that end, it verifies that the new blocks are stored in the DHT and closes the bucket reservation. It also maintains Merkle trees that can be made public to allow tracking modifications and detect inconsistencies. At the final step, during a *publication stage*, the client receives confirmation of the upload together with the file descriptor, which essentially consists of the keys of S-blocks and the root of the Merkle tree.

The coordination role can be performed by any of the servers, which may be chosen using a leader election algorithm. The bucket allocation service can be provided by an implementation based on a distributed lock manager (DLM) such as Chubby [21] or Zookeeper [22]. Both layers can be deployed on the same nodes, while the DHT logically represents an independent tier.

The proposed multi-tier architecture provides a separation between services; thus, it enables the coexistence of different vendors. Although the participation of multiple parties makes the system more complex, it allows for better security control and favors fault tolerance and scalability. In addition, considering untrusted scenarios, the chances of colluding servers among services managed by different parties are reduced.

5 Discussion

File Durability. Studies on the the reliability of storage system components are scarce in the literature [23]. Some services claim to provide a certain level of durability (e.g., Amazon S3 guarantees "eleven nines" durability[3]) but it is difficult to verify these numbers as the way they are computed is usually not publicly disclosed. In this paper, we use a simple, tractable model based on the number of missing blocks that the system can tolerate.

---

[3] https://aws.amazon.com/s3/faqs/

All files that are bound with the same helical strand form a strong dependable data structure. The complete collection of S-blocks that belong to any of the 3 SB-tuples associated with such files constitute the lead window. The dependencies created inside that cluster provide all-or-nothing integrity; in a sense, every file inside that window is recoverable or none of them is.

To rebuild a file, a client needs at least one of its SB-tuples. Recall that missing components are recovered by combining recovery equations following a top-down approach. The entanglement method allow to recover all files on a chain provided that it is not broken permanently. Then, a requirement is that all data stored at adjacent lead windows is recoverable. In critical failure scenarios, all components inside a lead cluster may be missing. In such a worst case, the system tolerates only a few missing components in the two neighbor lead windows (when no other failures are seen in the next adjacent windows). To be more conservative, we use a strict requirement: none of the immediately adjacent window's components must be missing. Therefore, the lattice admits in any 3 consecutive lead windows $2(p-1)$ missing F-blocks or its equivalent $7p$ S-blocks. In other words, the whole lattice tolerates $p-1$ missing files every $2p$ files. Using the S-blocks we calculate:

$$Block\ Error\ Rate = \frac{Nb.\ of\ missing\ blocks}{Nb.\ of\ stored\ blocks} = \frac{7p}{(2p)6} > 58\% \qquad (5)$$

Note that, although systems that use random triple replication can theoretically tolerate 2/3 error rate in the best case, a file is irrecoverable as soon as all 3 of its replicas are lost. Our solution is designed to cope with random failures since files can be recovered using the entangled data remaining on the system.

File Repair. The lattice can be built with a self-healing mechanism that regularly checks for missing blocks and eagerly repair them. In the presence of temporarily failures, however, a delayed repair policy can reduce overheads [24]. Therefore, our system can advantageously be configured to use a lazy repair strategy, i.e., only repair blocks once a file cannot be reconstructed directly from its adjacent S-blocks. The rationale is that the helical entanglements produce an implicit redundancy that extends deeply to both extremes of the lattice structure. In addition, the process of repairing file lazily will trigger recursive repair of other files as part of the same operation.

The problem of developing a strategy for guaranteeing file availability is not trivial. We have put our effort on creating a structure that generates high levels of redundancy without increasing storage overhead prohibitively, and investigation of repair policies is part of our on-going work. One approach is to run several agents on the servers to monitor different sectors of the lattice. A repair threshold can indicate when to launch repair operations before lost blocks diminish redundancy to a level that might jeopardize the file's durability.

Overheads. Each time a block of data is uploaded to the system, some existing blocks are used for the entanglement. By default, the client needs to download three deterministically chosen blocks. The client communication costs can be transferred to the servers if entanglements are performed in the coordination layer, as explained in Section 4. The storage servers contains only derived data. To download a file, two blocks are required in the general case.

The storage overhead is equivalent to systems that use triple replication policies: for each uploaded block the system stores three new blocks. Given that the price per unit of storage becomes cheaper every year, these costs are negligible when the added redundancy is taken in consideration. The HEC based structure has a remarkable property not found in the classical approaches to applying erasure codes or replication: the entanglements create intricate dependencies extending the durability of the file and providing multiple ways of recovering it using other files stored previously and subsequently.

6 Conclusion

We presented an efficient approach for designing robust distributed storage systems based on a novel entanglement method called helical entanglement code (HEC). HEC leverages dependencies between stored content, creating implicit redundancy to increase system robustness. The lattice tolerates a block error rate bigger than 58%. Repairs are based on cost-effective XOR operations. The system can be implemented on an untrusted infrastructure, relying on a multi-tier architecture run by different parties while providing the client with an API that allows integrity controls on the system to detect data corruptions. Further research might investigate different repair mechanisms.

References

1. Armbrust, M., Fox, A., Griffith, R., Joseph, A.D., Katz, R., Konwinski, A., Lee, G., Patterson, D., Rabkin, A., Stoica, I., Zaharia, M.: A view of cloud computing. Commun. ACM 53(4), 50–58 (2010)
2. Cachin, C., Keidar, I., Shraer, A.: Trusting the cloud. SIGACT News 40(2), 81–86 (2009)
3. Craig, C.: Google, linkedin, and microsoft prove no cloud is too big to fail (March 2013), http://www.infoworld.com/t/cloud-computing/google-linkedin-and-microsoft-prove-no-cloud-too-big-fail-215006?source=fssr
4. Ghemawat, S., Gobioff, H., Leung, S.T.: The google file system. In: Proceedings of the Nineteenth ACM Symposium on Operating Systems Principles, SOSP 2003, pp. 29–43. ACM, New York (2003)
5. Shvachko, K., Kuang, H., Radia, S., Chansler, R.: The hadoop distributed file system. In: Proceedings of the 2010 IEEE 26th Symposium on Mass Storage Systems and Technologies, MSST 2010, pp. 1–10. IEEE Computer Society, Washington, DC (2010)
6. Plank, J.S.: Erasure codes for storage applications. Tutorial Slides, Presented at 4th Usenix Conference on File and Storage Technologies, FAST 2005 (2005)
7. Dabek, F., Kaashoek, M.F., Karger, D., Morris, R., Stoica, I.: Wide-area cooperative storage with cfs. In: Proceedings of the Eighteenth ACM Symposium on Operating Systems Principles, SOSP 2001, pp. 202–215. ACM, New York (2001)

8. Wilcox-O'Hearn, Z., Warner, B.: Tahoe: the least-authority filesystem. In: Proceedings of the 4th ACM International workshop on Storage Security and Survivability, pp. 21–26. ACM, New York (2008)
9. LaCie, A.: The wuala project (2007), http://www.wuala.com
10. Kubiatowicz, J., Bindel, D., Chen, Y., Czerwinski, S., Eaton, P., Geels, D., Gummadi, R., Rhea, S., Weatherspoon, H., Weimer, W., Wells, C., Zhao, B.: Oceanstore: an architecture for global-scale persistent storage. SIGPLAN Not 35(11), 190–201 (2000)
11. Dimakis, A.G., Ramchandran, K., Wu, Y., Suh, C.: A survey on network codes for distributed storage. Proceedings of the IEEE 99(3), 476–489 (2011)
12. Sathiamoorthy, M., Asteris, M., Papailiopoulos, D., Dimakis, A.G., Vadali, R., Chen, S., Borthakur, D.: Xoring elephants: novel erasure codes for big data. In: Proceedings of the 39th International Conference on Very Large Data Bases, PVLDB 2013. VLDB Endowment, pp. 325–336 (2013)
13. Venkatesan, V., Iliadis, I., Hu, X.Y., Haas, R., Fragouli, C.: Effect of replica placement on the reliability of large-scale data storage systems. In: MASCOTS, pp. 79–88. IEEE (2010)
14. Waldman, M.: Tangler: A censorship-resistant publishing system based on document entanglements. In: Proceedings of the 8th ACM Conference on Computer and Communications Security, pp. 126–135 (2001)
15. Dingledine, R., Freedman, M., Molnar, D.: Free haven's anonymity bibliography (March 2013), https://git.torproject.org/anonbib.git
16. Perng, G., Reiter, M.K., Wang, C.-X.: Censorship resistance revisited. In: Barni, M., Herrera-Joancomartí, J., Katzenbeisser, S., Pérez-González, F. (eds.) IH 2005. LNCS, vol. 3727, pp. 62–76. Springer, Heidelberg (2005)
17. Stubblefield, A., Wallach, D.S.: Dagster: Censorship resistant publishing without replication. Technical Report TR01-380, Rice University, Houston, Texas (July 2001)
18. Aspnes, J., Feigenbaum, J., Yampolskiy, A., Zhong, S.: Towards a theory of data entanglement. Theoretical Computer Science 389(1-2) (December 2007)
19. Merkle, R.C.: A digital signature based on a conventional encryption function. In: Pomerance, C. (ed.) CRYPTO 1987. LNCS, vol. 293, pp. 369–378. Springer, Heidelberg (1988)
20. Lua, E.K., Crowcroft, J., Pias, M., Sharma, R., Lim, S.: A survey and comparison of peer-to-peer overlay network schemes. IEEE Communications Surveys and Tutorials 7, 72–93 (2005)
21. Burrows, M.: The chubby lock service for loosely-coupled distributed systems. In: Proceedings of the 7th Symposium on Operating Systems Design and Implementation, OSDI 2006, pp. 335–350. USENIX Association, Berkeley (2006)
22. Hunt, P., Konar, M., Junqueira, F.P., Reed, B.: Zookeeper: wait-free coordination for internet-scale systems. In: Proceedings of the 2010 USENIX Conference on USENIX Annual Technical Conference, USENIXATC 2010, pp. 11–11. USENIX Association, Berkeley (2010)
23. Vishwanath, K.V., Nagappan, N.: Characterizing cloud computing hardware reliability. In: Proceedings of the 1st ACM Symposium on Cloud Computing, SoCC 2010, pp. 193–204. ACM, New York (2010)
24. Bhagwan, R., Tati, K., Cheng, Y.C., Savage, S., Voelker, G.M.: Total recall: system support for automated availability management. In: Proceedings of the 1st Conference on Symposium on Networked Systems Design and Implementation, NSDI 2004, vol. 1, p. 25. USENIX Association, Berkeley (2004)

Concurrent Wait-Free Red Black Trees*,**

Aravind Natarajan, Lee H. Savoie, and Neeraj Mittal

Erik Jonsson School of Engineering and Computer Science
The University of Texas at Dallas
Richardson, TX 75080, USA

Abstract. We present a new *wait-free* algorithm for concurrent manipulation of a red-black tree in an asynchronous shared memory system that supports search, insert, update and delete operations using single-word compare-and-swap instructions. Search operations in our algorithm are fast and execute only read and write instructions (and no atomic instructions) on the shared memory. The algorithm is obtained through a progressive sequence of modifications to an existing general framework for deriving a concurrent wait-free tree-based data structure from its sequential counterpart. Our experiments indicate that our algorithm significantly outperforms other concurrent algorithms for a red-black tree for most workloads.

1 Introduction

With the growing prevalence of multi-core, multi-processor systems, concurrent data structures are becoming increasingly important. In such a data structure, multiple processes may need to operate on overlapping regions of the data structure at the same time. Contention between different processes must be managed in such a way that all operations complete correctly and leave the data structure in a valid state.

Concurrency is most often managed through locks. However, locks are blocking; while a process is holding a lock, no other process can access the portion of the data structure protected by the lock. If a process stalls while it is holding a lock, then it will cause other processes to wait on the stalled process for extended periods of time. As a result, lock-based implementations of concurrent data structures are vulnerable to problems such as deadlock, priority inversion and convoying [1].

Non-blocking algorithms avoid the pitfalls of locks by using special (hardware-supported) *read-modify-write* instructions such as *load-link/store-conditional (LL/SC)* [1] [2] and *compare-and-swap (CAS)* [2] [1]. Non-blocking implementations of

---

* This work was supported, in part, by the National Science Foundation (NSF) under grant number CNS-1115733.
** This work has appeared as a brief announcement in the Proceedings of the 26th International Symposium for Distributed Computing (DISC), pages 421–422, 2012.
[1] A load-link instruction returns the current value of a memory location; a subsequent store-conditional instruction to the same location will store a new value only if no updates have occurred to that location since the load-link was performed.
[2] A compare-and-swap instruction compares the contents of a memory location to a given value and, only if they are the same, modifies the contents of that location to a given new value.

T. Higashino et al. (Eds.): SSS 2013, LNCS 8255, pp. 45–60, 2013.
© Springer International Publishing Switzerland 2013

common data structures such as queues, stacks, linked lists, hash tables, and search trees have been proposed [1, 3–8].

Non-blocking algorithms may provide varying degrees of progress guarantees [1]. Three widely accepted progress guarantees are: obstruction-freedom, lock-freedom, and wait-freedom. An algorithm is said to be *obstruction-free* if any process that executes in isolation will finish its operation in a finite number of steps. It is said to be *lock-free* if some process will complete its operation in a finite number of steps. Finally, it is said to be *wait-free* if every process will complete its every operation in a finite number of steps.

Binary search tree is one of the fundamental data structures for organizing *ordered* data that supports search, insert, update and delete operations [9]. Red-black tree is a type of self-balancing binary search tree that provides good worst-case time complexity for all tree operations. As a result, they are used in symbol table implementations within systems like C++, Java, Python and BSD Unix [10]. They are also used to implement completely fair schedulers in Linux kernel [11]. However, red-black trees have been remarkably resistant to parallelization using both lock-based and lock-free techniques. The tree structure causes the root and high level nodes to become the subject of high contention and thus become a bottleneck. This problem is only exacerbated by the introduction of balance requirements.

Related Work: Designing an efficient concurrent non-blocking data structure that guarantees wait-freedom is hard. Several universal constructions exist that can be used to derive a concurrent wait-free data structure from its sequential version [1, 12, 13]. Due to the general nature of the constructions, when applied to a binary search tree, the resultant data structure is quite inefficient. This is because universal constructions involve either: (a) applying operations to the data structure in a serial manner, or (b) copying the entire data structure (or parts of it that will change and any parts that directly or indirectly point to them), applying the operation to the copy and then updating the relevant part of the data structure to point to the copy. The first approach precludes any concurrency. The second approach, when applied to a tree, also precludes any concurrency since the root node of the tree indirectly points to every node in the tree.

Several customized non-blocking implementations of concurrent unbalanced search trees [4–7], and balanced search trees such as B-tree [3] and B^+-tree [8] have been proposed, that are more efficient than those obtained using universal constructions.

In [14], Ma presented a "lock-free" algorithm for a concurrent red-black tree that supports search and insert operations using CAS, DCAS (double-word[3] CAS) and TCAS (triple-word[3] CAS) instructions [14]. Kim *et al.* extended Ma's algorithm to support delete operations as well as eliminate the use of multi-word CAS instructions [15]. However, a closer inspection of the algorithm reveals that it is actually a blocking algorithm. It is only lock-free in the sense that CAS instructions are used for synchronization (setting and unset-ting flags at nodes) and no "locks" are used. But, if a process blocks while holding the flag on the root of the tree, *all other processes* will be prevented from making progress. Concurrent algorithms for a red-black tree based on the transactional memory framework have also been proposed (*e.g.*, [16, 17]). The algorithm in [17] maintains a relaxed red-black tree in which the balance requirements of a red-

---

[3] Words need not be adjacent.

black tree may be violated temporarily. In contrast to the aforementioned algorithms, our algorithm has the following desirable properties: (a) it uses only single word CAS instruction, which is commonly available in many hardware architectures including Intel 64 and AMD64, (b) it does not require any additional underlying system support such as transactional memory, and (c) it never allows the tree to go out of balance.

For a tree-based data structure that supports operations executing in top-down manner using small-sized windows, Tsay and Li's framework [18] can be used to derive a concurrent wait-free data structure from its sequential version. Operations are injected into the tree at the root node, and work their way toward a leaf node by operating on small portions of the tree at a time. Wait-freedom is achieved using helping; as an operation traverses the tree, it helps any operation that it encounters on its way "move out" of its way. The framework requires that an operation (including a search operation) makes a copy of every node that it encounters as it traverses the tree. Our wait-free algorithm is based on Tsay and Li's framework, but significantly modified to (a) overcome some of its practical limitations, and (b) reduce the overhead for search and modify operations.

Contributions: In this paper, we present a new *wait-free* algorithm for concurrent manipulation of a red-black tree in an asynchronous shared memory system that supports search, insert, update and delete operations using single-word CAS instructions. Search operations in our algorithm are fast and perform only read and write instructions (and no atomic instructions) on the shared memory. The algorithm is obtained through a progressive sequence of modifications to the Tsay and Li's framework for deriving a concurrent wait-free tree-based data structure from its sequential counterpart. Our experiments indicate that our algorithm *significantly outperforms* all other concurrent algorithms for maintaining a (non-relaxed) red-black tree that can be implemented directly without any additional system support.

2 Preliminaries

2.1 Tsay and Li's Wait-Free Framework for Tree-Based Data Structures

Tsay and Li described a framework in [18] (or TL-framework for short) that can be used to develop wait-free operations for a tree-based data structure provided operations work on the tree in top-down manner. The framework is based on the concept of a *window*, which is simply a *rooted subtree* of the tree structure, that is, a small, contiguous piece of the tree. We say that a window is *located* at its root node. The execution of a top-down operation can be modeled using a sequence of windows starting from the root and ending at a leaf of the tree. For example, Fig. 1(a) shows a sequence of three windows W_1, W_2 and W_3; the shaded nodes denote the root node of the respective windows. Note that different windows of an operation may be of different shapes and sizes. We refer to actions performed by an operation as part of its window as *transaction*.

In the TL-framework, when an operation starts, it first needs to be "injected" into the tree. This involves obtaining the ownership of the root of the tree. This step "initializes" the first window of the operation. Thereafter the operation performs a sequence of window transactions until it reaches the bottom of the tree at which point the it terminates. Consecutive windows of an operation always *overlap*. The root of the next window is

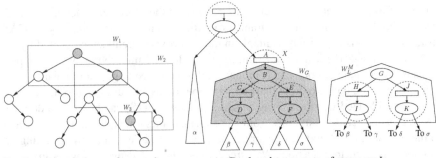

Overlapping windows of a top-down operation.

Dual node structure of a tree node.

Fig. 1. Windows in Tsay and Li's framework

part of the current window. For an example, see Fig. 1(a). A process table is used to store the current state of the most recent operation of each process. We now explain how a window transaction is performed in the TL-framework. To execute a window transaction of an operation α with current window W_G in the tree, a process p needs to perform the following four steps:

1. *Explore-Help-And-Copy:* In this step, p traverses nodes in W_G starting from the root node of the window. On visiting a node X (in W_G), if p finds that X is owned by another operation β, then p helps β "move out" of α's way by performing a window transaction on β's behalf. As p traverses W_G, it also makes its copy, denoted by say W_L. Note that, at this point, only p can access nodes in W_L.

2. *Transform-And-Lock:* In this step, p modifies W_L as needed (*e.g.*, performing rotations). Let W_L^M denote the window obtained after applying all transformations to W_L. Let Y denote the node in W_L^M that corresponds to the root node of the next window of α (recall that consecutive windows of an operation overlap). Process p then obtains the ownership of node Y. Note that actions in this step do not require any synchronization because, at this point, only p can access nodes in W_L^M.

3. *Install:* In this step, p replaces the window W_G in the tree with the window W_L^M in its local memory using a synchronization instruction. If this step succeeds, then nodes in W_L^M become accessible from the root of the tree and are thus visible to all processes in the system. Further, nodes in W_G are no longer accessible from the root of the tree (but some processes may still hold references to them). We refer to nodes that are reachable from the root of the tree as *active nodes*, and nodes that were once active but not any more as *passive nodes*. Note that, on performing this step, α's ownership of the root node of the current window in the tree is released and that of the next window in the tree gained *atomically*.

4. *Announce:* Let α belong to process q, where q may be p. In this step, p announces the location of α's new window to other processes in the system by updating q's (process) table entry using a synchronization instruction. It is possible for this step to be performed by another process, say r, where r may be different from both p and q, since α's new window is now visible to all processes in the system. Sufficient information is stored in the root node of the window to enable this to happen.

Consider a window rooted at some tree node, say X. A window transaction may involved changing multiple attributes of X (*e.g.*, color, key and/or children pointers). This, in general, cannot be performed using a single synchronization instruction. To address this problem, a tree node in the TL-framework has *dual* structure; it consists of a *pointer* node and a *data* node. The pointer node contains a reference to the data node, and information about whether the tree node (it represents) is owned by some operation. The data node stores all other attributes of the tree node (color, key, *etc.*). This dual structure allows a window in the tree to be replaced by replacing the data node of its root node. For example, in Fig. 1(b), window W_G is rooted at tree node X with pointer and data nodes as A and B, respectively, and W_L^M denotes a transformed copy of W_G. Now, W_G can be replaced with W_L^M by changing the reference stored in A from B to G.

The TL-framework has several limitations. First, the pointer node, which is a single word, needs to store two distinct addresses. Second, it assumes the availability of a special hardware instruction *check_valid* that checks if the contents of a word have changed since they were last read using an LL instruction; to our knowledge, no hardware currently implements such an instruction. We have modified the framework to remove both the above limitations. A pointer node in our algorithm needs to only store a single address (and a small number of bits). Further, our algorithm uses only a single-word CAS instruction, which is widely available in hardware. Hereafter, we refer to the TL-framework, modified to make it more practical, as MTL-framework; our wait-free algorithm is built on top of this modified framework.

2.2 Red-Black Trees and Top-Down Operations

We assume that a red-black tree implements a dictionary of *key-value pairs* and supports the following four operations: A *search* operation explores the tree for a given key and, if the key is present in the tree, returns the value associated with the key. An *insert* operation adds a given key-value pair to the tree if the key is not already present in the tree. Otherwise, it becomes an *update* operation and changes the value associated with the key to the given value. A *delete* operation removes a key from the tree if the key is present in the tree. A *modify* operation is an insert, update or delete operation.

Traditional insert and delete operations for maintaining a red-black tree do not work in a top-down manner (a top-down phase may be followed by a bottom-up phase for re-balancing the tree). In [19], Tarjan proposed algorithms for insert and delete operations that work in a top-down manner on an *external* red-black tree in which all the data are stored in the leaf nodes. Basically, all operations begin at the root of the tree and traverse the tree towards the leaf nodes along a path called the *access path* using a constant-size window, while maintaining specific invariants. For more details of insert and delete operations, including invariants they maintain and various transformations they use to keep the tree balanced, please refer to [19].

3 A Wait-Free Algorithm for Red-Black Tree

We now describe how to reduce the overhead of search and modify operations in the MTL-framework to obtain a more efficient wait-free algorithm for a red-black tree.

3.1 Reducing the Overhead of Search Operation

Note that MTL-framework, when used with red-black tree operations that work in top-down manner [19], yields a wait-free red-black tree. But the resulting data structure has a serious limitation. In the MTL-framework, every operation including search operation: (i) only "acts" on active nodes, (ii) needs to make a copy of every node that it encounters, and (iii) needs to help every stalled operation on its path before it can advance further. This copying and helping makes an operation *expensive* to execute. Besides, every operation that is currently executing on the tree, including a search operation, owns a node in the tree and each node can only be owned by at most one operation at a time. This means that concurrently invoked search operations may conflict with each other, which is an unusual behavior for a concurrent algorithm.

To reduce the overhead of a search operation, we make the following observations. First, in the MTL-framework, a window transaction is *atomic* with respect to an operation; either the operation sees *all* modifications made by the transaction or *none* of them. This is because a process makes change to its *local* window first and then installs it in the tree using a *single* CAS instruction at which time it becomes accessible to all processes. Second, every window transaction applied to the tree maintains the *legality* of the red-black tree, that is, the set of active nodes in the tree always form a valid red-black tree. So, in our algorithm, a search operation simply traverses the tree, unaware of other operations and without helping other operations on their path complete. Clearly, a search operation can now proceed concurrently with other search and modify operations without interfering with them. Note that, as a modify operation traverses the tree from from top to bottom, it replaces all nodes in the current window with new copies before moving down. Thus, as a search operation proceeds, it may encounter nodes that are no longer part of the tree. Nevertheless, we show that the result of a search operation is still meaningful, that is, our algorithm only generates *linearizable* histories [20].

3.2 Reducing the Overhead of Modify Operation

We reduce the overhead of a modify operation in two ways, which are described one-by-one as follows.

Minimizing the Use of the MTL-Framework: By reducing the overhead of a search operation, we can also reduce the overhead of a modify operation by first using a search operation to determine whether the tree contains the key and, depending on the result, execute the modify operation using the MTL-framework [1]. For example, for an insert/update operation, if the search operation finds the key, then it returns the address of the leaf node containing the key and the insert/update operation can change the value associated with the key outside the MTL-framework. Note that, in the MTL-framework, a node is replaced with a new copy whenever it happens to be in the window of a modify operation. Hence, to be able to change the value associated with a key outside the MTL-framework, the value can no longer be stored inside a node. Rather, it has to be stored *outside* a node as a separate *record* with the node containing the *address* of the record. Also, a search operation is then changed to return the address of the record (containing the value) if it finds the given key in the tree.

An insert/update operation consists of three phases: (a) *Phase 1:* The tree is searched for the given key using the fast search operation. (b) *Phase 2:* If the key does not exist in the tree, then the key along with its associated value are added to the tree using the expensive MTL-framework, (c) *Phase 3:* If the key already exists in the tree, then the value stored in the record associated with the key is updated outside the MTL-framework. Note that an operation in phase 2 may find that the key already exists in the tree due to concurrent modifications to the tree. In that case, the insert operation becomes an update operation after completing its phase 2 and then executes phase 3 as well. To accomplish this, we modify the MTL-framework to return the address of the record in case the key is already present in the tree.

A delete operation consists of two phases: (a) *Phase 1:* The tree is searched for matching key using the fast search operation. If the key does not exist in the tree, no further action is required and the delete operation terminates. (b) *Phase 2:* If the key exists in the tree, the key and its associated value are removed from the tree using the expensive MTL-framework.

Updating the Value in a Record: To modify the value associated with a key in phase 3 of an update operation, we adopt the wait-free algorithm proposed by Chuong *et al.* in [12]. The algorithm uses two data structures that are shared by all processes: (i) an array *announce* that is used by processes to *announce* their operations to other processes, and (ii) a variable *gate* that is used by processes to *agree* on the next operation to execute. To maximize concurrency, we use a separate instance of Chuong *et al.*'s algorithm for each record. However, to reduce the space-complexity, all records share the same *announce* array, but each record has its own copy of the *gate* variable. We modify Chuong *et al.*'s algorithm so that a process helps an update operation only if the operation *conflicts* with its own update operation (wants to update the value stored in the same record). This would require storing the address of the record that an update operation wants to modify in the *announce* array. Processes whose update operations conflict use the *gate* variable stored in the (target) record to decide on the next update operation to be applied to the value.

Minimizing Copying of Nodes in the MTL-Framework: There may be situations when a transaction does not need to modify the window of the tree in any way because the required invariant already holds [19]. We refer to such transactions as *trivial* transactions. Clearly, it is wasteful for a trivial transaction to copy the entire window of the tree in local memory and then replace that window with an identical copy. It is instead desirable for the window to simply *slide down* to its next root. To avoid copying a window, acquiring ownership of the next root of the window and releasing ownership of the current root of the window is no longer an atomic step as in the MTL-framework. Rather, a process first needs to acquire ownership of the next root of the window and then release the ownership of the current root of the window in two separate steps.

The consequence of not copying the entire window is that a modify operation can now *overtake* a search operation that started before it. As a result, it is possible for a search operation to never complete if it is repeatedly overtaken by a constant stream of modify operations that continually cause the bottom of the tree to move down. To ensure that a search operation eventually terminates, a modify operation may now have

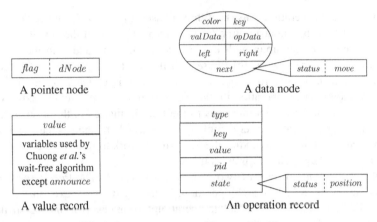

Fig. 2. Data structures used by our algorithm

to help a search operation complete. To that end, whenever a process executes a modify operation, at the beginning of phase 2, it selects a process to help in a round-robin manner. If the search operation of the process it selected at the beginning of phase 2 is still pending at the end of phase 2, then it helps that search operation complete.

3.3   Data Structures Used

Our algorithm uses four major data structures as shown in Fig. 2: (1) *pointer node* that stores reference to the data node, (2) *data node* that stores tree node attributes, (3) *value record* that stores the value associated with the key, and (4) *operation record* that stores information about the operation such as its type, arguments and current state.

A pointer node, which is a single word, contains the following fields: (a) *flag*: a bit that indicates whether the node is owned by an operation, and (b) *dNode*: the address of the data node. The *flag* field has two possible values: **FREE** or **OWNED**.

A data node contains the following fields: (a) node specific attributes such as color, key, pointers to left and right children nodes, denoted by *color*, *key*, *left* and *right*, respectively, (b) *valData*: the address of the record that contains the value associated with the key, (c) *opData*: the address of an operation record (only relevant if the node was/is the root of some window), and (d) *next*: information about the operation after executing window transaction (only relevant if the node was the root of some window); it contains two sub-fields (packed into a single word): (i) *status*: the new status of the operation, and (ii) *move*: the address of the next location of the operation's window. The *status* field has three possible values: **WAITING** (waiting to be injected into the tree), **IN_PROGRESS** (executing window transactions) and **COMPLETED** (terminated).

A value record contains the following fields: (a) *value*: the value associated with the key, and (b) variables used by the Chuong *et al.*'s wait-free algorithm (*e.g.*, *gate*).

An operation record contains the following fields: (a) operation specific attributes such as its type, arguments and process identifier, denoted by *type*, *key*, *value* and *pid*, and (b) *state*: information about the current state of the operation; it contains two sub-fields (packed into a single word): (i) *status*: the current status of the operation, and (ii) *position*: the address of the current location of the operation's window. In case of

```
 1   Value search( key )
 2   begin
 3   │   opData := create( SEARCH, key, ⊥ ) ;                      // create a new operation record
 4   │   opData → state := {IN_PROGRESS, null} ;                   // initialize the operation state
 5   │   ST[myid] := opData ;                                      // initialize the search table entry
 6   │   traverse( opData ) ;                                      // traverse the tree
 7   │   if (opData → state) ⤳ position ≠ null then
 8   │   │   read the value stored in the record using Chuong et al.'s algorithm and return it;
 9   └   else return ⊥

10   insertOrUpdate( key, value )
11   begin
12   │   valData := null;
     │   // phase 1: determine if the key already exists in the tree
13   │   search( key );
14   │   valData := (ST[myid] → state) ⤳ position;
15   │   if valData = null then
     │   │   // phase 2: try to add the key-value pair to the tree using the MTL-framework
     │   │   // select a search operation to help at the end of phase 2
16   │   │   pid := the process selected to help in round-robin manner;    pidOpData := ST[pid];
17   │   │   opData := create( INSERT, key, value ) ;              // create a new operation record
18   │   │   executeOperation( opData ) ;                          // add the key-value pair to the tree
19   │   │   valData := (opData → state) ⤳ position;
20   │   │   if pidOpData ≠ null then
21   │   │   └   traverse( pidOpData ) ;                           // help the selected search operation complete
22   │   if valData ≠ null then
     │   └   // phase 3: update the value in the record using Chuong et al.'s algorithm

23   delete( key )
24   begin
     │   // phase 1: determine if the key already exists in the tree
25   │   if search( key ) then
     │   │   // phase 2: try to delete the key from the tree using the MTL-framework
     │   │   // select a search operation to help at the end of phase 2
26   │   │   pid := the process selected to help in round-robin manner;    pidOpData := ST[pid];
27   │   │   opData := create( DELETE, key, ⊥ ) ;                  // create a new operation record
28   │   │   executeOperation( opData ) ;                          // remove the key from the tree
29   │   │   if pidOpData ≠ null then
30   │   │   └   traverse( pidOpData ) ;                           // help the selected search operation complete

31   traverse( opData )
32   begin
33   │   dCurrent := pRoot ⤳ dNode ;                               // start from the root of the tree
34   │   while dCurrent is not a leaf node do
     │   │   // abort the traversal if no longer needed
35   │   │   if (opData → state) ⤳ status = COMPLETED then return;
     │   │   // find the next node to visit
36   │   │   if opData → key < dCurrent → key then dCurrent := (dCurrent → left) ⤳ dNode;
37   │   └   else dCurrent := (dCurrent → right) ⤳ dNode;
     │   // check if the two keys match
38   │   if dCurrent → key = opData → key then valData := dCurrent → valData;
39   │   else valData := null;
40   └   opData → state := {COMPLETED, valData} ;                  // update the operation state
```

Fig. 3. Pseudo-code for MINIMALCOPY

search or update operation, the *position* field of its operation record is used to store the address of the record containing the value (if found).

Besides the above data structures, our algorithm also uses two tables, namely modify table, denoted by MT, and search table, denoted by ST. They are used to enable

```
41  executeOperation( opData )
42  begin
43  │   opData → state := {WAITING , root} ;                                    // initialize the operation state
44  │   MT[myid] := opData ;                                                     // initialize the modify table entry

        // select a modify operation to help later at the end
45  │   pid := the process selected to help in round-robin manner;    pidOpData := MT[pid];

        // inject the operation into the tree
46  │   injectOperation( opData );
        // repeatedly execute transactions until the operation completes
47  │   {status, pCurrent} := read( opData → state );
48  │   while status ≠ COMPLETED do
49  │   │   dCurrent := pCurrent ⤳ dNode;
50  │   │   if dCurrent → opData = opData then
51  │   │   └   executeWindowTransaction( pCurrent, dCurrent );
52  │   └   {status, pCurrent} := opData → state;

53  │   if pidOpData ≠ null then
54  │   └   injectOperation( pidOpData ) ;                                       // help inject the selected operation


55  injectOperation( opData )
56  begin
        // repeatedly try until the operation is injected into the tree
57  │   while (opData → state) ⤳ status = WAITING do
58  │   │   dRoot := pRoot ⤳ dNode;
        │   // execute a window transaction, if needed
59  │   │   if dRoot → opData ≠ null then  executeWindowTransaction( pRoot, dRoot )
60  │   │   dNow := pRoot ⤳ dNode ;                                      // read the address of the data node again
        │   // if they match, try to inject the operation into the tree; otherwise restart
61  │   │   if dRoot = dNow then
62  │   │   │   dCopy := clone( dRoot );       dCopy → opData := opData;
        │   │   // try to obtain the ownership of the root of the tree
63  │   │   │   result := CAS( pRoot, {FREE, dRoot}, {OWNED, dCopy} );
64  │   │   │   if result then
        │   │   │   // the operation has been successfully injected; update the operation state
65  │   │   └   └   CAS( opData → state, {WAITING, pRoot}, {IN_PROGRESS, pRoot} );
```

Fig. 4. Pseudo-code for MINIMALCOPY (continued)

helping so as to ensure the wait-freedom property. Each table contains one entry for every process; the entry stores the address of the operation record of the most recent operation generated by the process.

3.4   Formal Description

A detailed pseudo-code of the algorithm is given in Figs. 3-6. The pseudo-code contains extensive comments and is self-explanatory. It uses the following functions: (i) read to dereference a pointer node and extract both its fields, (ii) clone to make a copy of a data node (copies all fields except $opData$ and $next$), and (iii) create to allocate and initialize an operation record. Note that a data node in our algorithm is an *immutable* object. Once it becomes part of the tree, the contents of its fields never change. Thus, it can be safely copied without any issues. In the pseudo-code, we use $pRoot$ to refer to the pointer node of the root of the tree, which never changes. Further, we use the convention that a variable with prefix 'p' represents a pointer node and that with prefix 'd' represents a data node. For convenience, we assume that the tree is never empty and always contains at least one node. This can be ensured by using a sentinel key that is

```
66  executeWindowTransaction( pNode, dNode )
67  begin
        // execute a window transaction for the operation stored in dNode
68      opData := dNode → opData;
69      {flag, dCurrent} := read( pNode ) ;                        // read the contents of pNode again
70      if dCurrent → opData = opData then
71          if flag = OWNED then
72              if pNode = pRoot then
                    // the operation may have just been injected into the tree, but the operation state
                    // may not have been updated yet; update the state
73                  CAS( opData → state, {WAITING, pRoot}, {IN_PROGRESS, pRoot} );

74              if not (executeCheapWindowTransaction( pNode, dCurrent )) then
                    // traverse the window and make copies as required
75                  windowSoFar := {clone( dCurrent )};
76                  while more nodes need to be added to windowSoFar do
77                      pNextToAdd := the address of the pointer node of the next tree node to be copied;
78                      dNextToAdd := pNextToAdd ↝ dNode;
                        // help the operation located at this node, if any, move aside
79                      if dNextToAdd → opData ≠ null then
80                          executeWindowTransaction( pNextToAdd, dNextToAdd );
                        // read the address of the data node again as it may have changed
82                      dNextToAdd := pNextToAdd ↝ dNode;
83                      copy pNextToAdd and dNextToAdd, and add them to windowSoFar;

84                  window has been copied; now apply transformations dictated by Tarjan' algorithm to
                    windowSoFar;
85                  dWindowRoot := the address of the data node now acting as window root in
                                    windowSoFar;
86                  if last/terminal window transaction then
87                      status := COMPLETED;
88                      pMoveTo :=
                            ⎧ the address of the record containing the value   : if update operation;
89                  else    ⎨ null                                    ,         : otherwise;
90                      status := IN_PROGRESS;
91                      pMoveTo := the address of the pointer node of the node in windowSoFar to
                                    which the operation will now move;
92                      pMoveTo ↝ flag := OWNED;
93                      dMoveTo := pMoveTo ↝ dNode;
                        dMoveTo → opData := opData;

94                  dWindowRoot → opData := opData;
                    dWindowRoot → next := {status, pMoveTo};
                    // replace the tree window with the local copy and release the ownership
95                  CAS( pNode, {OWNED, dCurrent}, {FREE, dWindowRoot} );

        // at this point, no operation should own pNode; may still need to update the operation state
        // with the new position of the operation window
96      dNow := pNode ↝ dNode;
97      if dNow → opData = opData then
98          CAS( opData → state, {IN_PROGRESS, pNode}, dNow → next );
```

Fig. 5. Pseudo-code for MINIMALCOPY (continued)

larger than any other key value. For ease of exposition, we also assume that there is no reclamation of the memory allocated to nodes that have become garbage and are not "accessible" by any process. Thus all objects will have unique addresses. However, a *wait-free garbage collection operation* can be easily developed for our algorithm using the well-known notion of *hazard pointers* [21]. More details of the garbage collection operation can be found in [22].

To prove the correctness of our algorithm, we show that all its execution histories are linearizable and all its operations are wait-free. For the linearizability proof, we define

```
 99  Boolean executeCheapWindowTransaction( pNode, dNode )
100  begin
101      opData := dNode → opDate;      pid := opData → pid;

         // traverse the tree window using Tarjan's algorithm
102      while traversal not complete do
103          pNextToVisit := the address of the pointer node of the next node to be visited;
104          dNextToVisit := pNextToVisit ↝ dNode;

             // abort if transaction already executed
105          if (opData → state) ↝ position ≠ pNode then return true

             // if there is an operation residing at the node, help it move out of the way
106          if dNextToVisit → opData ≠ null then
                 // there are several cases to consider
107              if (dNextToVisit → opData) → pid ≠ pid then
                     // the operation residing at the node belongs to a different process
108                  executeWindowTransaction( pNextToVisit, dNextToVisit );

                     // read the address of the data node again as it may have changed
109                  dNextToVisit := pNextToVisit ↝ dNode;

                     // abort if transaction already executed
110                  if (opData → state) ↝ position ≠ pNode then return true
111              else if dNextToVisit → opData = dNode → opData then
                     // partial window transaction has already been executed; complete it if needed
112                  if (opData → state) ↝ position = pNode then
113                      slideWindowDown( pNode, dNode, pNextToVisit, dNextToVisit );

114                  return true;
115              else if MT[pid] ≠ opData then
116                  return true;                              // abort; transaction already executed

117          visit dNextToVisit;

118      if no transformation needs to be applied to the tree window then
119          if last/terminal window transaction then
120              pMoveTo := { the address of the record containing the value   : if an update operation;
                             null                                              : otherwise;
121              dMoveTo := null;
122          else
123              pMoveTo := the address of the pointer node of the node in the tree to which the operation
                           will now move;
124              dMoveTo := pMoveTo ↝ dNode;
125          if (opData → state) ↝ position = pNode then
126              slideWindowDown( pNode, dNode, pMoveTo, dMoveTo );
127          return true;
128      else return false;

129  slideWindowDown( pMoveFrom, dMoveFrom, pMoveTo, dMoveTo )
130  begin
131      opData = dMoveFrom → opData;

         // copy the data node of the current window location
132      dCopyMoveFrom := clone( dMoveFrom );
         dCopyMoveFrom → opData := opData;
133      if dMoveTo ≠ null then dCopyMoveFrom → next := {IN_PROGRESS, pMoveTo};
134      else dCopyMoveFrom → next := {COMPLETED, pMoveTo};

         // copy the data node of the next window location, if needed
135      if dMoveTo ≠ null then
136          if dMoveTo → opData ≠ opData then
137              dCopyMoveTo := clone( dMoveTo );      dCopyMoveTo → opData := opData;
                 // acquire the ownership of the next window location
138              CAS( pMoveTo, {FREE, dMoveTo}, {OWNED, dCopyMoveTo} );

         // release the ownership of the current window root and update the operation state
139      CAS( pMoveFrom, {OWNED, dMoveFrom}, {FREE, dCopyMoveFrom} );
140      CAS( opData → state, {IN_PROGRESS, pMoveFrom}, dCopyMoveFrom → next );
```

Fig. 6. Pseudo-code for MINIMALCOPY (continued)

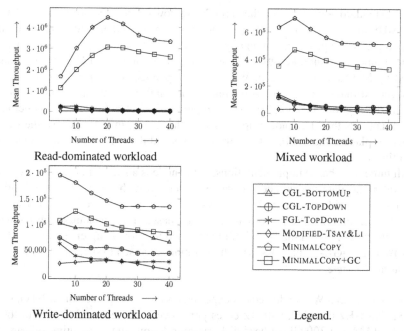

Fig. 7. Comparison of throughput of different implementations of red-black tree

the linearization point of a "completed" operation as follows. For an insert or delete operation, the linearization point is taken to be the time when the operation performed its last window transaction. All update and search operations that act on the *same* record are linearized in the order given by Chuong *et al.*'s wait-free algorithm, and are ordered immediately after the insert operation that created that record. For a search operation that does not find the key, the linearization point is taken to be the time when the *last* terminal window transaction that is visible to the search operation is performed by some modify operation working on the same key. If no such modify operation exists, then the linearization point is taken to be the time when the operation began its traversal. We use these linearization points to construct an equivalent sequential history that respects the relative order of non-overlapping operation and in which all operations are legal. The wait-freedom of an operation follows from the helping performed by modify operations during searching, injection and execution of window transaction. More details of the correctness proof can be found in [22].

We refer to our wait-free algorithm for concurrent red-black tree as MINIMALCOPY and the version that supports garbage collection as MINIMALCOPY+GC.

4   Experimental Evaluation

Other Concurrent Red-Black Tree Implementations: For our experiments, we considered four other implementations of concurrent red-black tree besides the two based on MINIMALCOPY and MINIMALCOPY+GC: (i) two based on coarse-grained-locking (using the standard bottom-up and the Tarjan's top-down approaches), denoted by CGL-BOTTOMUP and CGL-TOPDOWN, (ii) one based on fine-grained-locking (using the Tarjan's top-down approach), denoted by FGL-TOPDOWN and (iii) one based on Tsay and Li's framework (modified to use one-word pointer nodes and CAS instructions), denoted by MODIFIED-TSAY&LI. We did not implement Kim *et al.*'s algorithm for concurrent red-black tree because some important details about the algorithm are missing in the description given in [15]. For example, it is not clear how a search operation works. It appears that it cannot simply traverse the tree as in [14] because the tree is modified in-place using multiple CAS instructions and thus may be in an inconsistent state at times.

In all three lock-based implementations, a tree node is a singular entity and not split into pointer and data nodes, and the value associated with a key is stored inside a node and not outside in a record. Windows are modified in-place. Note that all the above changes improve the performance of lock-based implementations by reducing indirection and copying. Finally, in both lock-based top-down implementations CGL-TOPDOWN and FGL-TOPDOWN, search operations are used to speedup modify operations as appropriate.

Experimental Setup: We conducted our experiments on a dual-processor AMD Opteron 6180 SE 2.5 GHz machine, with 12 cores per processor (yielding 24 cores in total), 64 GB of RAM and 300 GB of hard disk, running 64-bit Linux operating system. All implementations were written in C. To compare the performance of different implementations, we considered the following parameters:

1. **Maximum Tree Size:** This depends on the size of the key space. We considered three different key space sizes of 10,000 (10K), 100,000 (100K) and 1 million (1M) keys. To ensure consistent results, as in [7], rather than starting with an empty tree, we populated the tree to a certain size prior to starting the simulation run.

2. **Relative Distribution of Various Operations:** We considered three different workload distributions: (a) *Read-dominated workload:* 90% search, 9% insert/update and 1% delete (b) *Mixed workload:* 70% search, 20% insert/update and 10% delete (c) *Write-dominated workload:* 0% search, 50% insert/update and 50% delete

3. **Maximum Degree of Contention:** This depends on the number of threads. We varied the number of threads from 5 to 40 in steps of 5.

We compared the performance of different implementations with respect to *system throughput*, which is given by the number of operations executed per unit time.

Evaluation Results: The results of our experiments are shown in Fig. 7. Each test was carried out for 60 seconds and the results were averaged over several runs to obtain values within 99% confidence interval. For MINIMALCOPY+GC, the garbage collection threshold was set to 25,000 nodes per thread. The results for the three key space sizes are very similar to each other; due to space limitations, we only show the results for the 100K key space size.

As the graphs show, for all the three categories of workloads, MINIMALCOPY and MINIMALCOPY+GC are the top two performers among all the implementations. Between the two, MINIMALCOPY+GC has 20%-45% lower throughput than MINIMAL-COPY indicating that garbage collection has relatively significant overhead. The third best performer for read-dominated workloads is FGL-TopDown, whereas for mixed and write-dominated workloads is CGL-BottomUp. For read-dominated workloads, MinimalCopy+GC has 350%-4,300% better throughput than FGL-TopDown. For mixed workloads, MinimalCopy+GC has 150%-660% better throughput than CGL-BottomUp. For write-dominated workloads, the gap between MinimalCopy+GC and CGL-BottomUp is much smaller; MinimalCopy+GC has only 3.4%-34% better throughput than CGL-BottomUp. More details about the experiments (*e.g.*, comparison of various implementations with respect to execution times of search and modify operations) can found in [22].

5   Conclusion

In this paper, we have presented an new wait-free algorithm for a concurrent red-black tree. Our experiments indicate that our algorithm has significantly better performance than other concurrent algorithms for a red-black tree including those based on locks.

References

1. Herlihy, M., Shavit, N.: The Art of Multiprocessor Programming, Revised Reprint. Morgan Kaufmann (2012)
2. Herlihy, M.: Wait-Free Synchronization. ACM Transactions on Programming Languages and Systems (TOPLAS) 13(1), 124–149 (1991)
3. Bender, M.A., Fineman, J.T., Gilbert, S., Kuszmaul, B.C.: Concurrent Cache-Oblivious B-Trees. In: Proceedings of the 17th ACM Symposium on Parallelism in Algorithms and Architectures (SPAA), pp. 228–237 (2005)
4. Ellen, F., Fataourou, P., Ruppert, E., van Breugel, F.: Non-Blocking Binary Search Trees. In: Proceedings of the 29th ACM Symposium on Principles of Distributed Computing (PODC), pp. 131–140 (2010)
5. Brown, T., Helga, J.: Non-Blocking *k*-ary Search Trees. In: Fernàndez Anta, A., Lipari, G., Roy, M. (eds.) OPODIS 2011. LNCS, vol. 7109, pp. 207–221. Springer, Heidelberg (2011)
6. Prokopec, A., Bronson, N.G., Bagwell, P., Odersky, M.: Concurrent Tries with Efficient Non-Blocking Snapshots. In: Proceedings of the 17th ACM Symposium on Principles and Practice of Parallel Programming (PPOPP), pp. 151–160 (2012)
7. Howley, S.V., Jones, J.: A Non-Blocking Internal Binary Search Tree. In: Proceedings of the 24th ACM Symposium on Parallelism in Algorithms and Architectures (SPAA), pp. 161–171 (June 2012)
8. Braginsky, A., Petrank, E.: A Lock-Free B+tree. In: Proceedings of the 24th ACM Symposium on Parallelism in Algorithms and Architectures (SPAA), pp. 58–67 (2012)
9. Cormen, T.H., Leiserson, C.E., Rivest, R.L.: Introduction to Algorithms. The MIT Press (1991)
10. Sedgewick, R.: Left-leaning Red-Black Trees
11. Jones, M.T.: Inside the Linux 2.6 Completely Fair Scheduler (December 2009)
12. Chuong, P., Ellen, F., Ramachandran, V.: A universal construction for wait-free transaction friendly data structures. In: Proceedings of the 22nd ACM Symposium on Parallelism in Algorithms and Architectures (SPAA), pp. 335–344 (2010)

13. Fatourou, P., Kallimanis, N.D.: A Highly-Efficient Wait-Free Universal Construction. In: Proceedings of the 23rd ACM Symposium on Parallelism in Algorithms and Architectures (SPAA), pp. 325–334 (2011)
14. Ma, J.: Lock-Free Insertions on Red-Black Trees. Master's thesis. The University of Manitoba, Canada (October 2003)
15. Kim, J.H., Cameron, H., Graham, P.: Lock-Free Red-Black Trees Using CAS. Concurrency and Computation: Practice and Experience, 1–40 (2006)
16. Fraser, K.: Practical Lock-Freedom. PhD thesis, University of Cambridge (February 2004)
17. Crain, T., Gramoli, V., Raynal, M.: A Speculation-Friendly Binary Search Tree. In: Proceedings of the 17th ACM Symposium on Principles and Practice of Parallel Programming (PPOPP), pp. 161–170 (2012)
18. Tsay, J.J., Li, H.C.: Lock-Free Concurrent Tree Structures for Multiprocessor Systems. In: Proceedings of the International Conference on Parallel and Distributed Systems (ICPADS), pp. 544–549 (December 1994)
19. Tarjan, R.E.: Efficient Top-Down Updating of Red-Black Trees. Technical Report TR-006-85, Department of Computer Science, Princeton University (1985)
20. Herlihy, M., Wing, J.M.: Linearizability: A Correctness Condition for Concurrent Objects. ACM Transactions on Programming Languages and Systems (TOPLAS) 12(3), 463–492 (1990)
21. Michael, M.M.: Hazard Pointers: Safe Memory Reclamation for Lock-Free Objects. IEEE Transactions on Parallel and Distributed Systems (TPDS) 15(6), 491–504 (2004)
22. Natarajan, A., Savoie, L., Mittal, N.: Concurrent Wait-Free Red Black Trees. Technical Report UTDCS-16-12, Department of Computer Science, The University of Texas at Dallas (October 2012)

Self-stabilizing *(f,g)*-Alliances with Safe Convergence

Fabienne Carrier[1], Ajoy K. Datta[2], Stéphane Devismes[1], Lawrence L. Larmore[2], and Yvan Rivierre[1]

[1] VERIMAG UMR 5104, Université Joseph Fourier, France
firstname.lastname@imag.fr
[2] School of Computer Science, University of Nevada Las Vegas, USA
firstname.lastname@unlv.edu

Abstract. Given two functions f and g mapping nodes to non-negative integers, we give a silent self-stabilizing algorithm that computes a minimal (f, g)-alliance in an asynchronous network with unique node IDs, assuming that every node p has a degree at least $g(p)$ and satisfies $f(p) \geq g(p)$. Our algorithm is *safely converging* in the sense that starting from any configuration, it first converges to a (not necessarily minimal) (f, g)-alliance in at most four rounds, and then continues to converge to a minimal one in at most $5n+4$ additional rounds, where n is the size of the network. Our algorithm is written in the shared memory model. It is proven assuming an unfair (distributed) daemon. Its memory requirement is $O(\log n)$ bits per process, and it takes $O(\Delta^3 n)$ steps to stabilize, where Δ is the degree of the network.

Keywords: Self-Stabilization, Safe Convergence, (f, g)-Alliance.

1 Introduction

Self-stabilization [2] is a versatile technique to withstand *any* transient fault in a distributed system. Informally, a distributed algorithm is self-stabilizing if, after transient faults hit the system and place it in some arbitrary configuration, the system recovers without external (*e.g.*, human) intervention in finite time. Thus, self-stabilization makes no hypothesis on the nature or extent of transient faults that could hit the system, and recovers from the effects of those faults in a unified manner. However, self-stabilization has some drawbacks; perhaps the main one is *temporary loss of safety*, *i.e.*, after the occurrence of transient faults, there is a finite period of time — called the *stabilization phase* — before the system returns to a legitimate configuration. During this phase, there is no guarantee of safety. Several approaches have been introduced to offer more stringent guarantees during the stabilization phase, *e.g.*, *fault-containment* [7], *super-stabilization* [4], *time-adaptivity* [12], and *safe convergence* [9].

We consider here the notion of *safe convergence*. The main idea behind this concept is the following: For a large class of problems, it is often hard to design self-stabilizing algorithms that guarantee small stabilization time, even after few transient faults [6]. Large stabilization time is usually due to strong specifications that a legitimate configuration must satisfy. The goal of a *safely converging self-stabilizing algorithm* is to first quickly converge ($O(1)$ rounds is usually expected) to a *feasible* legitimate configuration, where a minimum quality of service is guaranteed. Once such a feasible legitimate

T. Higashino et al. (Eds.): SSS 2013, LNCS 8255, pp. 61–73, 2013.

configuration is reached, the system continues to converge to an *optimal* legitimate configuration, where more stringent conditions are required. Safe convergence is especially interesting for self-stabilizing algorithms that compute optimized data structures, *e.g.*, minimal dominating sets [9], approximation of the minimum weakly connected dominating set [10], and approximately minimum connected dominating set [11].

We consider the (f, g)-*alliance problem*. Let $G = (V, E)$ be an undirected graph and f, g two functions mapping nodes to non-negative integers. For every node $p \in V$, $\mathcal{N}_p$ (resp. δ_p) denotes the set of neighbors (resp. the degree) of p in G. A subset of nodes $A \subseteq V$ is an (f, g)-*alliance* of G if and only if

$$(\forall p \in V \setminus A, |\mathcal{N}_p \cap A| \geq f(p)) \wedge (\forall p \in A, |\mathcal{N}_p \cap A| \geq g(p))$$

Moreover, A is *minimal* if and only if no proper subset of A is an (f, g)-alliance of G. The (f, g)-alliance problem is a generalization of several problems that are of interest in distributed computing. Consider any subset S of nodes:

1. S is a (minimal) dominating set if and only if S is a (minimal) $(1, 0)$-alliance;
2. more generally, S is a (minimal) k-domination set if and only if S is a (minimal) $(k, 0)$-alliance;
3. S is a (minimal) k-tuple domination set if and only if S is a (minimal) $(k, k - 1)$-alliance;
4. S is a (minimal) global defensive alliance if and only if S is a (minimal) $(f, 0)$-alliance, such that $\forall p \in V, f(p) = \lceil \delta_p/2 \rceil$;
5. S is a (minimal) global offensive alliance if and only if S is a (minimal) $(1, g)$-alliance, such that $\forall p \in V, g(p) = \lceil \delta_p/2 \rceil$.

Note that (f, g)-alliances also have applications in the field of population protocols [1], or server allocation in computer networks [8].

Our Contribution. We give a silent self-stabilizing algorithm, $\mathcal{MA}(f, g)$, that computes a minimal (f, g)-alliance in an asynchronous network with unique node IDs, where f and g are integer-valued functions on nodes, such that $f(p) \geq g(p)$ and $\delta_p \geq g(p)$ for all p.[1]

Given two functions f, g mapping nodes to non-negative integers, we say $f \geq g$ if and only if $\forall p \in V, f(p) \geq g(p)$. We remark that the class of minimal (f, g)-alliances with $f \geq g$ generalizes the classes of minimal dominating sets, k-domination sets, k-tuple domination sets, and global defensive alliance problems. However, minimal global offensive alliances do not belong to this class.

Our algorithm $\mathcal{MA}(f, g)$ is *safely converging* in the sense that starting from any configuration, it first converges to a (not necessarily minimal) (f, g)-alliance in at most four rounds, and then continues to converge to a minimal one in at most $5n + 4$ additional rounds, where n is the size of the network. Our algorithm is written in the shared memory model, and is proven assuming an unfair (distributed) daemon, the weakest daemon of this model. $\mathcal{MA}(f, g)$ uses $O(\log n)$ bits per process, and stabilizes to a terminal (legitimate) configuration in $O(\Delta^3 n)$ steps, where Δ is the degree of the network.

---

[1] We assume that $\delta_p \geq g(p)$ to ensure that an (f, g)-alliance always exists.

Finally, $\mathcal{MA}(f, g)$ does not need any knowledge of any bound on global parameters of the network (such as its size or its diameter).

Related Work. The (f, g)-alliance problem is introduced in [5]. In the same paper, the authors give several distributed algorithms for that problem and its variants, but none of them is self-stabilizing. To the best of our knowledge, this has been the only publication on (f, g)-alliances up to now. However, there have been results on particular instances of (minimal) (f, g)-alliances, *e.g.*, [9,13,14,15]. All of these consider arbitrary identified networks; however a safely converging solution is given only in [9]. Srimani and Xu [13] give a self-stabilizing algorithm to compute a minimal global defensive alliance in $O(n^3)$ steps; however, they assume a central daemon. Turau [14] gives a self-stabilizing algorithm to compute a minimal dominating set in $9n$ steps, assuming an unfair (distributed) daemon. Wang *et al* [15] give a self-stabilizing algorithm to compute a minimal k-domination set in $O(n^2)$ steps, assuming a central daemon. A safely converging self-stabilizing algorithm is given in [9] for computing a minimal dominating set. The algorithm first computes a (not necessarily minimal) dominating set in $O(1)$ rounds and then safely stabilizes to a *minimal* dominating set in $O(\mathcal{D})$ rounds, where $\mathcal{D}$ is the diameter of the network. However, they assume a synchronous daemon.

Roadmap. In the next section we describe our model of computation and give some basic definitions. We define our algorithm $\mathcal{MA}(f, g)$ in Section 3. In Section 4, we sketch the correctness of $\mathcal{MA}(f, g)$ and highlight its complexity analysis.[2] We write concluding remarks and perspectives in Section 5.

2 Preliminaries

Distributed Systems. We consider distributed systems of n processes equipped of *unique* IDs. By an abuse of notation, we identify a process with its ID whenever convenient. Each process p can directly communicate with a subset $\mathcal{N}_p$ of other processes, called its *neighbors*. We assume that if $q \in \mathcal{N}_p$, then $p \in \mathcal{N}_q$. For every process p, $\delta_p = |\mathcal{N}_p|$ is the *degree of p*. We assume that $\delta_p \geq g(p)$ for every process p. Let $\Delta = \max_{p \in V} \delta_p$ be the degree of the network. The topology of the system is a simple undirected graph $G = (V, E)$, where V is the set of processes and E is a set of edges representing (direct) communication relations.

Computational Model. We assume the *shared memory model* of computation introduced by Dijkstra [2], where each process communicates with its neighbors using a finite set of *locally shared variables*, henceforth called simply *variables*. Each process can read its own variables and those of its neighbors, but can write only to its own variables. Each process operates according to its (local) *program*. We define a *(distributed) algorithm* to be a collection of n *programs*, each operating on a single process. The program of each process is a finite ordered set of actions, where the ordering defines *priority*. This priority is the order of appearance of actions in the text of the program. A process p is not enabled to execute any (lower priority) action if it is enabled to execute an action of higher priority. Let $\mathcal{A}$ be a distributed algorithm, consisting of a

---

[2] All detailed proofs are given in a technical report available online at http://www-verimag.imag.fr/TR/TR-2012-19.pdf

local program $\mathcal{A}(p)$ for each process p. Each action in $\mathcal{A}(p)$ is of the following form: ⟨*label*⟩ :: ⟨*guard*⟩ → ⟨*statement*⟩. *Labels* are only used to identify actions. The *guard* of an action in $\mathcal{A}(p)$ is a Boolean expression involving the variables of p and its neighbors. The *statement* of an action in $\mathcal{A}(p)$ updates some variables of p. The *state* of a process in $\mathcal{A}$ is defined by the values of its variables in $\mathcal{A}$. A *configuration* of $\mathcal{A}$ is an instance of the states of processes in $\mathcal{A}$. $\mathcal{C}_{\mathcal{A}}$ is the set of all possible configurations of $\mathcal{A}$. (When there is no ambiguity, we omit the subscript $\mathcal{A}$.) An action can be executed only if its guard evaluates to *true*; in this case, the action is said to be *enabled*. A process is said to be enabled if at least one of its actions is enabled. We denote by *Enabled*(γ) the subset of processes that are enabled in configuration γ. When the configuration is γ and *Enabled*(γ) $\neq \emptyset$, a *daemon*[3] (scheduler) selects a non-empty set $\mathcal{X} \subseteq$ *Enabled*(γ); then every process of $\mathcal{X}$ *atomically* executes its highest priority enabled action, leading to a new configuration γ', and so on. The transition from γ to γ' is called a *step* (of $\mathcal{A}$). The possible steps induce a binary relation over configurations of $\mathcal{A}$, denoted by $\mapsto$. An *execution* of $\mathcal{A}$ is a maximal sequence of its configurations $e = \gamma_0 \gamma_1 \ldots \gamma_i \ldots$ such that $\gamma_{i-1} \mapsto \gamma_i$ for all $i > 0$. The term "maximal" means that the execution is either infinite, or ends at a *terminal* configuration in which no action of $\mathcal{A}$ is enabled at any process. As we saw previously, each step from a configuration to another is driven by a daemon. In this paper we assume the daemon is *unfair*; *i.e.*, the daemon might never permit an enabled process to execute unless it is the only enabled process.

We say that a process p is *neutralized* in the step $\gamma_i \mapsto \gamma_{i+1}$ if p is enabled in γ_i and not enabled in γ_{i+1}, but does not execute any action between these two configurations. Neutralization of a process can be caused by the following situation: at least one neighbor of p changes its state between γ_i and γ_{i+1}, and this change makes the guards of all actions of p false. To evaluate time complexity, we use the notion of *round*. The first round of an execution e, noted e', is the minimal prefix of e in which every process that is enabled in the initial configuration either executes an action or becomes neutralized. Let e'' be the suffix of e starting from the last configuration of e'. The second round of e is the first round of e'', and so forth.

Self-stabilization, Silence, and Safe Convergence. Let $\mathcal{A}$ be a distributed algorithm. Let P be a predicate over $\mathcal{C}$. $\mathcal{A}$ is *self-stabilizing w.r.t.* P if and only if there exists a non-empty subset $\mathcal{S}_P$ of $\mathcal{C}$ such that:

1. $\forall \gamma \in \mathcal{S}_P, P(\gamma)$ (*Correction*);
2. for each possible step $\gamma \mapsto \gamma'$ of $\mathcal{A}$, $\gamma \in \mathcal{S}_P \Rightarrow \gamma' \in \mathcal{S}_P$ (*Closure*);
3. each execution of $\mathcal{A}$ (starting from an arbitrary configuration) contains a configuration of $\mathcal{S}_P$ (*Convergence*).

The configurations of $\mathcal{S}_P$ are said to be *legitimate*, and other configurations are called *illegitimate*.

$\mathcal{A}$ is *silent* if all its executions are finite [3]. To show that $\mathcal{A}$ is silent and self-stabilizing *w.r.t.* P, it is sufficient to show that (1) all executions of $\mathcal{A}$ are finite and (2) all terminal configurations of $\mathcal{A}$ satisfy P.

Let P_1 and P_2 be two predicates over $\mathcal{C}$ such that $\forall \gamma \in \mathcal{C}, P_2(\gamma) \Rightarrow P_1(\gamma)$. $\mathcal{A}$ is *safely converging self-stabilizing w.r.t.* (P_1, P_2) if and only if the following three properties hold:

---

[3] The daemon realizes the asynchrony of the system.

1. $\mathcal{A}$ is *self-stabilizing w.r.t.* P_1;
2. $\mathcal{A}$ is *self-stabilizing w.r.t.* P_2; and
3. every execution of $\mathcal{A}$ starting from a configuration of $\mathcal{S}_{P_1}$ eventually reaches a configuration of $\mathcal{S}_{P_2}$, where $\mathcal{S}_{P_1}$ and $\mathcal{S}_{P_2}$ are respectively the sets of legitimate configurations for P_1 and P_2 (*Safe Convergence*).

The configurations of $\mathcal{S}_{P_1}$ are said to be *feasible legitimate*. The configurations of $\mathcal{S}_{P_2}$ are said to be *optimal legitimate*.

Assume that $\mathcal{A}$ is *safely converging self-stabilizing w.r.t.* (P_1, P_2). The *first convergence time* is the maximum time to reach a feasible legitimate configuration, starting from any configuration. The *second convergence time* is the maximum time to reach an optimal legitimate configuration, starting from any feasible legitimate configuration. The *stabilization time* is the sum of the first and second convergence times.

Minimality and 1-Minimality of (f, g)**-Alliances.** We recall that an (f, g)-alliance A of a graph G is *minimal* if and only if no proper subset of A is an (f, g)-alliance. Then, A is 1-*minimal* if and only if $\forall p \in A$, $A \setminus \{p\}$ is not an (f, g)-alliance. Surprisingly, a 1-*minimal* (f, g)-alliance is not necessarily a *minimal* (f, g)-alliance, [5]. However, we have the following property:

Property 1. [5] Given two functions f and g mapping nodes to non-negative integers, we have:
1. Every minimal (f, g)-alliance is a 1-minimal (f, g)-alliance, and
2. if $f \geq g$, every 1-minimal (f, g)-alliance is a minimal (f, g)-alliance.

3   The Algorithm

The formal code of $\mathcal{MA}(f, g)$ is given as Algorithm 1. Given input functions f and g, $\mathcal{MA}(f, g)$ computes a single Boolean variable $p.inA$ for each process p. For any configuration γ, let $A_\gamma = \{p \in V : p.inA\}$. (We omit the subscript γ when it is clear from the context.) If γ is terminal, then A_γ is a 1-*minimal* (f, g)-*alliance*, and consequently, if $f \geq g$, A_γ is a *minimal* (f, g)-*alliance*.

During an execution, a process may need to leave or join A. The basic idea of safe convergence is that it should be more difficult for a process to leave A than to join it. This permits quick recovery to a configuration in which A is an (f, g)-alliance, but not necessarily a minimal one.

3.1   Leaving A

Action Leave allows a process to leave A. To obtain 1-minimality, we allow a process p to leave A if
Requirement 1: p will have enough neighbors in A (*i.e.*, at least $f(p)$) once it has left, and
Requirement 2: each $q \in \mathcal{N}_p$ will still have enough neighbors in A (*i.e.*, at least $g(q)$ or $f(q)$, depending on whether q is in A) once p has been deleted from A.

Ensuring Requirement 1. To maintain Requirement 1, we implement our algorithm in such a way that deletion from A is *locally sequential*, *i.e.*, during a step, at most one process can leave A in the neighborhood of each process p (including p itself). Using this locally sequential mechanism, if a process p wants to leave A, it must first verify that $\text{NbA}(p) = |\{q \in \mathcal{N}_p : q.inA\}|$ is greater or equal to $f(p)$ before leaving A. Hence, if p actually leaves A, it is the only one in its neighborhood allowed to do so; consequently, Requirement 1 still holds once p has left A.

The locally sequential mechanism is implemented using a neighbor pointer $p.choice$ at each process p, which takes value in $\mathcal{N}_p \cup \{\bot\}$; $p.choice = q \in \mathcal{N}_p$ means that p authorizes q to leave A, while $p.choice = \bot$ means that p does not authorize any neighbor to leave A. The value of $p.choice$ is maintained using Action Vote, which will be defined later.

To leave A, a process p should not authorize any neighbor to leave A ($p.choice = \bot$) and should be authorized to leave by all of its neighbors ($\forall q \in \mathcal{N}_p$, $q.choice = p$). For example, consider the $(1,0)$-alliance in Figure 1. Only Process 2 is able to leave A. Process 2 can leave A because it has enough neighbors in A (i.e., 2 neighbors, while $f(2) = 1$); if Process 2 leaves A, it will still have two neighbors in A, and Requirement 1 will not be violated.

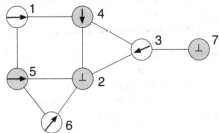

Fig. 1. Neighbor pointers when computing a minimal $(1,0)$-alliance. Numbers indicate IDs. A is the set of gray nodes. The value of *choice* is represented by an arrow or a tag "$\bot$" inside the node.

Ensuring Requirement 2. Requirement is also maintained by the fact that a process p must have authorization from each of its neighbors to leave A. A neighbor q can give such an authorization to p only if q still has enough neighbors in A without p. For a process q to authorize a neighbor p to leave A, p must currently be in A, i.e., $p.inA = true$, and q must have more neighbors than necessary in A, i.e., the predicate $\text{HasExtra}(q)$ should be true, meaning that $\mathcal{N}_q \cap A$ has more than $g(q)$, respectively $f(q)$, members if q is in A, respectively not in A. For example, consider the $(1,0)$-alliance in Figure 1. Processes 4 and 5 can designate Process 2 because they belong to A and $g(4) = g(5) = 0$. Moreover, Processes 3 and 6 can designate Process 2 because they do not belong to A and $f(3) = f(6) = 1$: if Process 2 leaves A, Process 3 (resp. Process 6) still has one neighbor in A, which is Process 7 (resp. Process 5).

Busy Processes. It is possible that a neighbor p of q cannot leave A — in this case p is said to be *busy* — because one of these two conditions is *true*:
(i) $\text{NbA}(p) < f(p)$: in this case, p does not have enough neighbors in A to be allowed to leave A.
(ii) $\neg\text{IsExtra}(p)$: in this case, at least one neighbor of p needs p to stay in A.
If q chooses such a neighbor p, this may lead to a deadlock. We use the Boolean variable $p.busy$ to inform q that one of the two aforementioned conditions holds for p. Action Flag maintains $p.busy$. So, to prevent deadlock, q must not choose any neighbor p for which $p.busy = true$.

A process p evaluates Condition (i) by reading the variables inA of all its neighbors. On the other hand, evaluation of Condition (ii) requires that p knows, for each of its neighbors, both its status (*inA*) and the number of its own neighbors that are in A. This latter information is obtained using an additional variable, *nbA*, where each process maintains, using Action `Count`, the number of its neighbors that are in A.

In Figure 2, consider the $(2,0)$-alliance. Process 5 is busy because of Condition (i): it has only one neighbor in A, while $f(5) = 2$. Process 2 is busy because of Condition (ii): its neighbor 1 is not in A, $f(1) = 2$, and has only two neighbors in A, so it cannot authorize any of its neighbors to leave. Consequently, Process 1

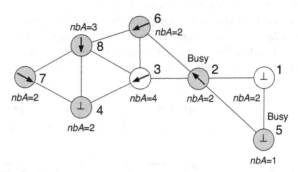

Fig. 2. Busy processes when computing a minimal $(2,0)$- alliance. Values of *nbA* are also given.

cannot designate any neighbor (all its neighbors in A are busy); while Process 3 should not designate Process 2.

Action Vote. Hence, the value of *p.choice* is chosen, using Action `Vote`, as follows:

1. *p.choice* is set to $\perp$ if the condition $\text{Cand}(p){\neq}\emptyset{\wedge}\text{HasExtra}(p){\wedge}(\text{IamCand}(p) \Rightarrow \text{MinCand}(p) < p)$ in Macro `ChosenCand`(p) is *false*, *i.e.*, if one of the following conditions holds:
   - $\text{Cand}(p) = \emptyset$, which means that no neighbor of p can leave A.
   - $\text{HasExtra}(p) = \textit{false}$, which means that p cannot authorize any neighbor to leave A.
   - $\text{IamCand}(p) \wedge p < \text{MinCand}(p)$, which means that p is also candidate to leave A and has higher priority to leave A than any other candidate in its neighborhood. (Remember that to be allowed to leave A, p should, in particular, satisfy *p.choice* $= \perp$.)

   The aforementioned priorities are based on process IDs, *i.e.*, for every two process u and v, u has higher priority than v if and only if the ID of u is smaller than the ID of v.
2. Otherwise, p uses *p.choice* to designate a neighbor that is in A, and not busy, in order to authorize it to leave A. If p has several possible candidates among its neighbors, it selects the one of highest priority (*i.e.*, of smallest ID). For example, if we consider the $(2,0)$-alliance in Figure 2, then we can see that Process 3 designates Process 4 because it is its smallest neighbor that is both in A and not busy.

There is one last problem: A process q may change its pointer while simultaneously one of its neighbors p leaves A, and consequently Requirement 2 may be violated. Indeed, q chooses new candidate assuming that p remains in A. This may happen only if the previous value of *q.choice* was p. To avoid this situation, we do not allow q to directly change *q.choice* from one neighbor to another. Each time q wants to change its pointer, if *q.choice* $\in \mathcal{N}_q$, q first resets *q.choice* to $\perp$; see `Choice`(q).

Figures 3 and 4 illustrate this last issue in the case of a $(1, 0)$-alliance. In the step from Configuration (a) to Configuration (b) of Figure 3, Process 2 directly changes its pointer from 3 to 1. Simultaneously, 3 leaves A. So, Process 2 authorizes Process 1 to leave A, while it should not do so. After that, Process 1 is authorized to leave A and does so at the step from Configuration (b) to Configuration (c), and thus Requirement 2 is violated. Figure 4 illustrates how we solve the problem. In Configuration (b), Process 3 has left, but the pointer of Process 2 is equal to $\bot$. So, Process 1 cannot leave yet, and Process 2 will not authorize it to leave.

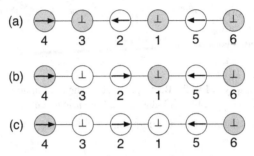

Fig. 3. Requirement 2 violation when computing a minimal $(1, 0)$-alliance. (We only show the values that are needed in the discussion.)

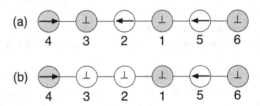

Fig. 4. The reset of the neighbor pointer is applied to the example of Figure 3

3.2 Joining A

Action $\mathtt{Join}$ allows a process to join A. A process p not in A must join A if:
(1) p does not have enough neighbors in A ($\mathtt{NbA}(p) < f(p)$), or
(2) a neighbor of p needs p to join A ($\mathtt{IsMissing}(p)$).

Moreover, to prevent p from cycling in and out of A, we require that every neighbor of p stop designating it (with their *choice* pointer) before p can join A (again). Note that all neighbors of p stop designating p immediately after it leaves A; see Action $\mathtt{Vote}$. (Actually, this introduces a delay of only one round.)

A process evaluates condition (1) by reading the variables *inA* of all its neighbors. To evaluate condition (2), it needs to know, for each neighbor q, both its status *w.r.t.* A ($q.inA$) and the number of its neighbors that are in A ($q.nbA$).

Algorithm 1. $\mathcal{MA}(f,g)$, code for each process p

Variables: $p.inA$, $p.busy$: Booleans; $p.choice \in \mathcal{N}_p \cup \{\perp\}$; $p.nbA \in [0..\delta_p]$

Macros:

$\text{NbA}(p) \qquad = |\{q \in \mathcal{N}_p, q.inA\}|$

$\text{Cand}(p) \qquad = \{q \in \mathcal{N}_p, q.inA \wedge \neg q.busy\}$

$\text{MinCand}(p) \quad = \min(\text{Cand}(p) \cup \{\infty\})$

$\text{ChosenCand}(p) = \textbf{if } \text{Cand}(p) \neq \emptyset \wedge \text{HasExtra}(p) \wedge (\text{IamCand}(p) \Rightarrow \text{MinCand}(p) < p)$
$\qquad\qquad\qquad \textbf{then } \text{MinCand}(p)$
$\qquad\qquad\qquad \textbf{else } \perp$

$\text{Choice}(p) \qquad = \textbf{if } p.choice = \perp \textbf{ then } \text{ChosenCand}(p) \textbf{ else } \perp$

Predicates:

$\text{IsMissing}(p) \equiv \exists q \in \mathcal{N}_p, (\neg q.inA \wedge q.nbA < f(q)) \vee (q.inA \wedge q.nbA < g(q))$

$\text{IsExtra}(p) \quad \equiv \forall q \in \mathcal{N}_p, (\neg q.inA \Rightarrow q.nbA > f(q)) \wedge (q.inA \Rightarrow q.nbA > g(q))$

$\text{HasExtra}(p) \equiv (\neg p.inA \Rightarrow \text{NbA}(p) > f(p)) \wedge (p.inA \Rightarrow \text{NbA}(p) > g(p))$

$\text{IsBusy}(p) \quad \equiv \text{NbA}(p) < f(p) \vee \neg \text{IsExtra}(p)$

$\text{IamCand}(p) \equiv p.inA \wedge \neg \text{IsBusy}(p)$

$\text{MustJoin}(p) \equiv \neg p.inA \wedge (\text{NbA}(p) < f(p) \vee \text{IsMissing}(p)) \wedge (\forall q \in \mathcal{N}_p, q.choice \neq p)$

$\text{CanLeave}(p) \equiv p.inA \wedge \text{NbA}(p) \geq f(p) \wedge (\forall q \in \mathcal{N}_p, q.choice = p) \wedge p.choice = \perp$

Actions:

$\text{Join} \;\; :: \text{MustJoin}(p) \qquad\qquad \rightarrow p.inA \leftarrow true$
$\qquad\qquad\qquad\qquad\qquad\qquad\quad\; p.choice \leftarrow \perp$
$\qquad\qquad\qquad\qquad\qquad\qquad\quad\; p.nbA \leftarrow \text{NbA}(p)$

$\text{Vote} \;\; :: p.choice \neq \text{ChosenCand}(p) \rightarrow p.choice \leftarrow \text{Choice}(p)$
$\qquad\qquad\qquad\qquad\qquad\qquad\quad\; p.nbA \leftarrow \text{NbA}(p)$
$\qquad\qquad\qquad\qquad\qquad\qquad\quad\; p.busy \leftarrow \text{IsBusy}(p)$

$\text{Count} :: p.nbA \neq \text{NbA}(p) \qquad\quad \rightarrow p.nbA \leftarrow \text{NbA}(p)$

$\text{Flag} \;\; :: p.busy \neq \text{IsBusy}(p) \qquad \rightarrow p.busy \leftarrow \text{IsBusy}(p)$

$\text{Leave} :: \text{CanLeave}(p) \qquad\qquad \rightarrow p.inA \leftarrow false$

---

4 Correctness

Recall that, for any configuration γ, we define the set $A = A_\gamma = \{p \in V : p.inA\}$. Moreover, throughout this section, we assume that $f \geq g$.

Termination. We first show that the unfair daemon cannot prevent $\mathcal{MA}(f,g)$ from reaching a terminal configuration, regardless the initial configuration. The proof consists of proving that the number of steps to reach a terminal configuration, starting from an arbitrary configuration, is bounded, regardless of the choices of the daemon.

The core of the proof consists of showing that each process can execute Join at most once. To join A, a process p should be not be pointed to by any neighbor. If later p leaves A, (1) it should satisfy $p.choice = \perp$ and (2) all its neighbors should have executed Vote so as to point to p with their variable *choice*, meaning that none of them needs p to stay in A. Hence, after leaving A, p will always have enough neighbors in A since by (1), Requirement 1 cannot be violated. Moreover, all its neighbors will always have enough neighbors in A since by (2), Requirement 2 is never violated. Hence, from that time forward, no process in the neighborhood of p (including p itself) will ever need p to rejoin A.

We can directly deduce that each process can execute Leave at most twice. Using similar reasoning, the number of times a process executes Count is bounded by one plus the number of times each of its neighbors joins or leaves A. We use the same approach for all other actions. Overall, we find that the maximum number of actions executed by all processes — and consequently the maximum number of steps to reach a terminal configuration — is bounded as follows:

Lemma 1. *Starting from any configuration, $\mathcal{MA}(f, g)$ reaches a terminal configuration in $O(n \times \Delta^3)$ steps.*

Partial Correctness. Let γ be any terminal configuration. To complete the proof, we have to show that the specification $\mathcal{MA}(f, g)$ is achieved at γ, *i.e.*, γ satisfies the following predicate:

$$SP_{Minimal} \overset{\text{def}}{=} A \text{ is a minimal } (f, g)\text{-alliance}$$

To prove this, we first show that A is an (f, g)-alliance in γ (Lemma 3); then we show that A is also minimal in γ (Lemma 4). To show these two results, we use two intermediate claims: Lemma 2 and Corollary 1. The former states that every process of A is busy in γ, meaning that either p does not have enough neighbors in A to leave A, or that at least one neighbor of p requires that p stay in A, *i.e.*, A is 1-minimal. The latter is a simple corollary of Lemma 2 and states that no process authorizes a neighbor to leave A at γ.

At γ, Action Count is disabled at every process, thus:

Remark 1. At γ, for every process p, $p.nbA = \text{NbA}(p) = |\{q \in \mathcal{N}_p : q.inA\}|$.

Lemma 2. *At γ, for every process p, p.inA $\Rightarrow p$.busy.*

Proof Outline. By contradiction. Assume that there is at least one process p such that $p.inA = true$ and $p.busy = false$ at γ. Then, for each such process p, we have $\text{IsBusy}(p) = false$ at γ, because Action Flag is disabled at every process. The remainder of the proof consists of showing that the process p_{min} having the smallest ID among all p satisfies $\text{CanLeave}(p_{min})$ at γ, and consequently is enabled to leave A, contradiction. Informally, if we made such an assumption, then p_{min} would be the smallest candidate to leave A, and consequently it would be designated by the pointer *choice* of all its neighbors and $p_{min}.choice = \bot$. □

By Lemma 2, for every process p, $\text{Cand}(p) = \emptyset$ at γ. Thus $\text{ChosenCand}(p) = \bot$ at γ, and from the negation of the guard of Action Vote, we have:

Corollary 1. *At γ, for every process p, p.choice $= \bot$.*

For every process p, let

$$\text{Fga}(p) \overset{\text{def}}{=} (\neg p.inA \Rightarrow \text{NbA}(p) \geq f(p)) \wedge (p.inA \Rightarrow \text{NbA}(p) \geq g(p))$$

When a process p satisfies $\text{Fga}(p)$, it is locally correct, *i.e.*, it has enough neighbors in A, according to its status. So, by definition we have:

Remark 2. A is an (f, g)-alliance if and only if $\texttt{Fga}(p)$ holds for all $p \in V$.

Lemma 3. *At γ, A is an (f, g)-alliance.*

Proof Outline. By Remark 2, we merely need show that every process p satisfies $\texttt{Fga}(p)$ in γ. Consider the following two cases:

$p \notin A$ **in** γ: First, $p.inA = false$ at γ. Then, γ being terminal, $\neg\texttt{MustJoin}(p)$ holds in γ. Now, by Corollary 1, since $p.inA = false$, $\texttt{NbA}(p) \geq f(p)$ holds at γ. Consequently $\texttt{Fga}(p)$ holds at γ.

$p \in A$ **at** γ: First, $p.inA = true$ at γ. Assume that $\texttt{Fga}(p) = false$ at γ. Since $\delta_p \geq g(p)$, we can show that $\exists q \in \mathcal{N}_p$ such that $\neg q.inA \wedge \texttt{IsMissing}(q) = true$ at γ. Then, by Corollary 1, we can conclude that q is enabled to join A at γ, contradiction. $\square$

Lemma 4. *At γ, A is a minimal (f, g)-alliance.*

Proof Outline. We already know that at γ, A defines an (f, g)-alliance. Moreover, by Property 1, if A is 1-minimal and $f \geq g$, then A is a minimal (f, g)-alliance. Thus, we only need to show the 1-minimality of A. Assume that A is not 1-minimal. Then, $\exists p \in A$ such that $A - \{p\}$ is an (f, g)-alliance. So:
1. $|A \cap \mathcal{N}_p| \geq f(p)$,
2. $\forall q \in \mathcal{N}_p, q \in A \Rightarrow |A \cap \mathcal{N}_q - \{p\}| \geq g(q)$, and
3. $\forall q \in \mathcal{N}_p, q \notin A \Rightarrow |A \cap \mathcal{N}_q - \{p\}| \geq f(q)$.

From the negation of the guard in the local program of p, we can show that 1, 2, and 3 imply that $p.busy = false$ at γ. As we assume that $p.inA = true$ at γ ($p \in A$), this contradicts Lemma 2. $\square$

By Lemmas 1-4, we can conclude:

Theorem 1. $\mathcal{MA}(f, g)$ *is silent and self-stabilizing w.r.t.* $SP_{Minimal}$, *and its stabilization time is* $O(\Delta^3 n)$ *steps.*

Complexity Analysis and Safe Convergence in Rounds. First, we recall the notion of a *closed predicate*: let P be a predicate over configuration of $\mathcal{MA}(f, g)$; P is *closed* if and only if $\forall \gamma, \gamma' \in \mathcal{C}$, $P(\gamma) \wedge \gamma \mapsto \gamma' \Rightarrow P(\gamma')$.

To establish safe convergence of $\mathcal{MA}(f, g)$, we have showed that it gradually converges to more and more specific closed predicates until reaching a terminal configuration. The gradual convergence to those specific closed predicates is given in Figure 5.

We have first showed that, regardless the initial configuration, in at most one round the system reaches a configuration from which the predicate $\forall p \in V$, $\texttt{ChoiceOk}(p)$ is forever *true*, where for every process p:

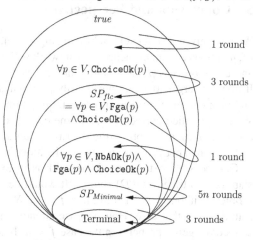

Fig. 5. Safe Convergence of $\mathcal{MA}(f, g)$

$$\text{ChoiceOk}(p) \overset{\text{def}}{=} (p.choice \neq \bot \wedge p.choice.inA) \Rightarrow \text{HasExtra}(p)$$

Once $\text{ChoiceOk}(p)$ holds at p, no neighbor of p can make p locally incorrect by leaving A.

Then, we have showed that, at most three rounds later, the system is forever in a *feasible legitimate configuration*, which is defined as any configuration that satisfies

$$SP_{flc} \overset{\text{def}}{=} \forall p \in V, \text{ChoiceOk}(p) \wedge \text{Fga}(p)$$

Note that, as expected, A defines an (f, g)-alliance in any feasible legitimate configuration (Remark 2).

Then, we have showed that after one more round, the system is in a configuration from which the predicate $\forall p \in V, \text{ChoiceOk}(p) \wedge \text{Fga}(p) \wedge \text{NbAOk}(p)$ is forever *true*, where for every process p,

$$\text{NbAOk}(p) \overset{\text{def}}{=} (\neg p.inA \Rightarrow p.nbA \geq f(p)) \wedge (p.inA \Rightarrow p.nbA \geq g(p))$$

When $\text{Fga}(p) \wedge \text{NbAOk}(p)$ is *true* at p, this means that p is locally correct and the variable $p.nbA$ gives this information to the neighbors of p.

From that point, we have showed that while A is not a minimal (f, g)-Alliance, at least one process definitely leaves A within the next five rounds. Hence, in most $5n$ additional rounds, the predicate $SP_{Minimal}$ is forever true, meaning that A is a minimal (f, g)-Alliance.

Finally, we have showed that three additional rounds are necessary to reach a terminal configuration. Hence, we can conclude:

Theorem 2. $\mathcal{MA}(f, g)$ *is silent and safely converging self-stabilizing w.r.t.* $(SP_{flc}, SP_{Minimal})$, *its first convergence time is at most four rounds, its second convergence time is at most $5n + 4$ rounds, and its stabilization time is at most $5n + 8$ rounds.*

5 Conclusion and Perspectives

We have given a silent self-stabilizing algorithm, $\mathcal{MA}(f, g)$, that computes a minimal (f, g)-alliance in an asynchronous network with unique node IDs, assuming that $f \geq g$ and every process p has a degree at least $g(p)$. $\mathcal{MA}(f, g)$ is also *safely converging*: It first converges to a (not necessarily minimal) (f, g)-alliance in at most four rounds and then continues to converge to a minimal one in at most $5n + 4$ additional rounds. We have verified correctness and time complexity of $\mathcal{MA}(f, g)$, assuming the weakest scheduling assumption: the distributed unfair daemon. Its memory requirement is $O(\log n)$ bits per process and its stabilization time in steps is $O(\Delta^3 n)$.

One possible extension of our work is to explore the possibility of reducing the stabilization time to $O(\mathcal{D})$ rounds. It would be interesting to study the (f, g)-alliance problem without the constraint that $f \geq g$. We conjecture that $\mathcal{MA}(f, g)$ is still self-stabilizing in that case. However, we already know that it does not guarantee a good safe convergence property in the case $f < g$: Indeed, in that case, any process can join A several times, giving us a round complexity of $\Omega(n)$ for convergence to a feasible legitimate configuration. We believe that when $f < g$, it is impossible to guarantee $O(1)$ round convergence to a feasible legitimate configuration, where a (not necessarily minimal) (f, g)-alliance is defined.

References

1. Angluin, D., Aspnes, J., Eisenstat, D., Ruppert, E.: The computational power of population protocols. Distributed Computing 20(4), 279–304 (2007)
2. Dijkstra, E.W.: Self-Stabilizing Systems in Spite of Distributed Control. Commun. ACM 17, 643–644 (1974)
3. Dolev, S., Gouda, M.G., Schneider, M.: Memory Requirements for Silent Stabilization. In: PODC, pp. 27–34 (1996)
4. Dolev, S., Herman, T.: Superstabilizing protocols for dynamic distributed systems. Chicago J. Theor. Comput. Sci. (1997)
5. Dourado, M.C., Penso, L.D., Rautenbach, D., Szwarcfiter, J.L.: The south zone: Distributed algorithms for alliances. In: Défago, X., Petit, F., Villain, V. (eds.) SSS 2011. LNCS, vol. 6976, pp. 178–192. Springer, Heidelberg (2011)
6. Genolini, C., Tixeuil, S.: A lower bound on dynamic k-stabilization in asynchronous systems. In: 21st Symposium on Reliable Distributed Systems (SRDS 2002), October 13-16. IEEE Computer Society, Osaka (2002)
7. Ghosh, S., Gupta, A., Herman, T., Pemmaraju, S.V.: Fault-containing self-stabilizing algorithms. In: Proceedings of the Fifteenth Annual ACM Symposium on Principles of Distributed Computing, May 23-26, pp. 45–54. ACM, Philadelphia (1996)
8. Gupta, A., Maggs, B.M., Oprea, F., Reiter, M.K.: Quorum placement in networks to minimize access delays. In: Aguilera, M.K., Aspnes, J. (eds.) Proceedings of the Twenty-Fourth Annual ACM Symposium on Principles of Distributed Computing, PODC 2005, July 17-20, pp. 87–96. ACM, Las Vegas (2005)
9. Kakugawa, H., Masuzawa, T.: A self-stabilizing minimal dominating set algorithm with safe convergence. In: IPDPS (2006)
10. Kamei, S., Kakugawa, H.: A self-stabilizing approximation for the minimum connected dominating set with safe convergence. In: Baker, T.P., Bui, A., Tixeuil, S. (eds.) OPODIS 2008. LNCS, vol. 5401, pp. 496–511. Springer, Heidelberg (2008)
11. Kamei, S., Kakugawa, H.: A self-stabilizing 6-approximation for the minimum connected dominating set with safe convergence in unit disk graphs. Theoretical Computer Science 428, 80–90 (2012)
12. Kutten, S., Patt-Shamir, B.: Time-adaptive self stabilization. In: Burns, J.E., Attiya, H. (eds.) Proceedings of the Sixteenth Annual ACM Symposium on Principles of Distributed Computing, August 21-24, pp. 149–158. ACM, Santa Barbara (1997)
13. Srimani, P.K., Xu, Z.: Distributed protocols for defensive and offensive alliances in network graphs using self-stabilization. In: ICCTA, pp. 27–31 (2007)
14. Turau, V.: Linear self-stabilizing algorithms for the independent and dominating set problems using an unfair distributed scheduler. Inf. Process. Lett. 103(3), 88–93 (2007)
15. Wang, G., Wang, H., Tao, X., Zhang, J.: A self-stabilizing algorithm for finding a minimal K-dominating set in general networks. In: Xiang, Y., Pathan, M., Tao, X., Wang, H. (eds.) ICDKE 2012. LNCS, vol. 7696, pp. 74–85. Springer, Heidelberg (2012)

A Self-stabilizing Algorithm for Maximal p-Star Decomposition of General Graphs

Brahim Neggazi[1], Volker Turau[2], Mohammed Haddad[1],
and Hamamache Kheddouci[1]

[1] University of Lyon, LIRIS UMR5205 CNRS, Claude Bernard Lyon 1 University
43 Bd du 11 Novembre 1918, F-69622, Villeurbanne, France
[2] Hamburg University of Technology, Institute of Telematics,
Schwarzenbergstraße 95, 21073 Hamburg, Germany

Abstract. A p-star is a complete bipartite graph $K_{1,p}$ with one center node and p leaf nodes. In this paper we propose the first distributed self-stabilizing algorithm for graph decomposition into p-stars. For a graph G and an integer $p \geq 1$, this decomposition provides disjoint components of G where each component forms a p-star. We prove convergence and correctness of the algorithm under an unfair distributed daemon. The stabilization time is $2\lfloor \frac{n}{p+1} \rfloor + 2$ rounds.

Keywords: Graph decomposition, stars, generalized matching, master-slave model, self-stabilizing algorithm.

1 Introduction

In the two past decades, computer networks began to expand and became larger, making control and management of these networks much harder. A new line of research on network decomposition is launched and motivated by the simplification and improvement of network management. The decomposition problem is a way for partitioning a network into small components that satisfy some specific properties (topology, number of nodes, density, etc.). On the other hand, fault-tolerance is among the most important requirements for distributed systems. *Self-stabilization* – introduced by Dijkstra – is one original approach for dealing with transient faults disturbing a distributed system [9].

It is natural to model a distributed system by a graph, where processes and links are represented respectively by nodes and edges. This way, several classic algorithms for graph parameters have been used in distributed systems. For example, self-stabilizing algorithms for finding minimal dominating sets, maximal independent sets, maximal matchings [14] , spanning trees [5] have been proposed. However, only few algorithms were proposed for graph decomposition problems within the self-stabilization paradigm.

F. Belkouch et al. in [3] considered a particular graph decomposition problem that consists in partitioning a graph of k^2 nodes into k partitions of order k. The proposed algorithm relies on a self-stabilizing spanning tree construction and converges within $3(h + 1)$ steps where h is the height of the spanning tree.

T. Higashino et al. (Eds.): SSS 2013, LNCS 8255, pp. 74–85, 2013.

E. Caron et al. in [8], *C. Johnen et al.* in [15] and *D. Bein et al.* [2] focused on decomposing graphs into clusters. *B. Neggazi et al.* in [24] considered decomposition of graphs into triangles.

A well studied graph decomposition problem is star decomposition [7,21,6,18,12]. This type of decomposition describes a graph as the union of disjoint stars [6]. An uniform decomposition into stars is one in which all stars have equal size. A p-star is a complete bipartite graph $K_{1,p}$ with one center node and p leaves where $p \geq 1$. A p-star decomposition subdivides a graph into p-stars [7,18]. This variant belongs to the class of generalized matchings and general graph factor problems that were proved to be NP-complete [16,17]. Note that a 1-star decomposition is equivalent to a maximum matching of a graph. Figure 1 presents an example of 3-star decomposition. The sets $\{i, s, j, l\}$, $\{m, k, n, t\}$, $\{p, o, q, r\}$ form a 3-star decomposition.

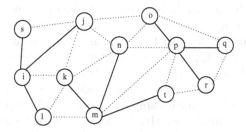

Fig. 1. An example of a 3-star decomposition

Star decompositions have several applications in areas such as scientific computing, scheduling, load balancing and parallel computing [1,25]. Furthermore, they have been used for studying the robustness of social networks [19,20]. In addition to applications in distributed systems, the decomposition into p-stars is also used in the field of parallel computing and programming. This decomposition offers similar paradigm as the Master-Slaves paradigm used in grid [23] and P2P infrastructures [4]. The Master-Slaves paradigm distinguishes between two entities: masters and slaves. A master is responsible for decomposing the problem into different tasks and distributes the tasks on its slaves and collects results in order to produce the final result of the computation.

The purpose of this paper is to develop a self-stabilizing algorithm for decomposing a graph into p-stars, where each node has only a local knowledge (distance-1 knowledge). To the best of our knowledge, this is the first work that considers such problem. The rest of this paper is organized as follows. The next section introduces the used model and further definitions. In Section 3, we give a self-stabilizing algorithm SMSD for decomposing a graph into $p$stars. The correctness is proved in Section 4 and the convergence proof under the unfair distributed daemon is contained in Section 5. Finally, Section 6 concludes the paper.

2   System Model and Definitions

A distributed system is self-stabilizing if it can start from any possible configuration and converges to a desired configuration in finite time by itself without using any external intervention. Convergence is also guaranteed when the system is affected by transient faults. This makes self-stabilization an elegant approach for non-masking fault-tolerance [10]. The concept of self-stabilization was first introduced by Dijkstra [9]. Each node has only a partial view - the *local state* - of the system. The node's local state includes the node's state itself and the states of all its neighbors. The union of the local states of all nodes defines the system's *global state*. Based on its local state, a node can decide to make *a move*. Therefore, self-stabilizing algorithms are given as a set of rules of the form

$$[\textbf{If } p(v) \textbf{ then } M]$$

where $p(v)$ is a predicate and M is a move. The predicate $p(v)$ is true when v's state is locally illegitimate. In this case, v is called an *enabled*.

Self-stabilizing algorithms can be designed according to different *daemons* (a.k.a. schedulers). Two types of daemons are often assumed in the literature on self-stabilizing algorithms: *central* and *distributed* daemon. At each step, the central daemon selects exactly one enabled node to make a move. Whereas the distributed daemon selects in each step a non-empty subset of all enabled nodes to make their moves simultaneously. A special kind of distributed daemon is the *synchronous* daemon; in each step all enabled nodes make their move. A taxonomy of existing daemons is proposed in [11].

Daemons are also associated with the notion of fairness. A daemon can be fair, or unfair (adversarial). A daemon is fair if every node that is continuously enabled will eventually be selected. The unfair daemon on the other hand may delay the move of a node as long as there are other enabled nodes. Self-stabilizing algorithms are designed for a specific daemon and cannot trivially operate under a more general daemon. Obviously, an algorithm designed for an unfair distributed daemon will work with all other daemons. This paper assumes the most general daemon, the unfair distributed daemon. As a communication model the shared variable model is used.

The *configuration* of a system is the n-tuple of the local states of all nodes of the distributed system. Let Σ denote the set of all configurations. An *execution* $\langle c_0, c_1, c_2, \ldots, c_k \rangle$ is a sequence of configurations c_i $(0 \leqslant i \leqslant k)$ where c_0 is the *initial configuration* and c_i is the configuration of the system after the i-th step. In other words, if the current configuration is c_i and all nodes selected in step $i + 1$ make a move, then this yields configuration c_{i+1}.

The time complexity of a self-stabilizing algorithm can be measured in moves and in rounds. The definition of a round is as follows. Let x be an execution and $x = x_0$. Then x is partitioned into rounds by induction. Round r_i is defined to be the minimal prefix of x_i, such that each node in the system has either made a move or has been disabled at least once within r_i. Execution x_{i+1} is obtained by removing prefix r_i from x_i. The intuition is that within a round, each node that is enabled at the beginning of the round, gets the chance to make a move if it has not become disabled by a move of its neighbors.

All graphs in this paper are undirected connected graphs. So, the system is represented by a graph $G = (V, E)$, such that V is a set of nodes and E is a set of edges. We assume that each node has a unique identifier and that these are locally distinct. We denote by $N(u)$ and $d(u)$ the open neighborhood and the degree of a node u, respectively.

Let $p > 0$. The problem of graph decomposition into p-star is defined as follows.

Definition 1. *A p-star is a complete bipartite graph $K_{1,p}$. We denote $S = (V, E)$ a p-star if $V = \{v_i \mid 0 \leq i \leq p\}$ and $E = \{(v_0, v_i) \mid 1 \leq i \leq p\}$. v_0 is called the center node and v_i for $1 \leq i \leq p$ the leaf nodes.*

Definition 2. *A p-star Decomposition of a graph $G = (V, E)$ is a set of subgraphs of the form $S_i = (V_i, E_i)$ such that the sets $V_i \subseteq V$ are disjoint and each S_i is a p-star. An p-star decomposition D of G is maximal p-star decomposition if the subgraph induced by the nodes of G not contained in a p-star of D does not contain a p-star as a subgraph.*

For notational convenience, the center node of a p-star will be called *master* and its leaves *slaves*.

3   Self-stabilizing Algorithm SMSD

This section presents the self-stabilizing algorithm SMSD for computing a maximal p-star decomposition of an arbitrary graph. Since the impossibility of finding a deterministic self-stabilizing algorithm for maximal matching in anonymous graph under a distributed daemon has been already proved in [22], and since the p-star decomposition is a generalization of the matching problem for which $p = 1$, the impossibility result remains valid for p-star decomposition for all $p \geq 1$. Hence, any distributed algorithm requires a mechanism for symmetry breaking. Thus, we suppose nodes to have unique identifiers. We say that a node v_1 is smaller as a node v_2 (denoted by $v_1 < v_2$) if v_1's identifier is smaller than that of v_2. For notational convenience we let $v < null$ for each node v.

The general idea of the proposed algorithm is as follows: A node becomes a slave by selecting the smallest possible node as a master. A node v becomes master only if all nodes smaller than v are either master or have decided not to become master. In other words, the node v with the smallest identifier having at least p neighbors becomes master. The p neighbors $v_1, \ldots, v_p$ of v with the smallest identifiers become the slaves of v. This procedure is recursively repeated for the subgraph of G consisting of all nodes except $v, v_1, \ldots v_p$. The challenge is to design an efficient distributed version of this algorithm.

Let X be a set and p is a positive integer. Algorithm SMSD uses two operators X^p and $\min X$ that are defined as follows:

$$X^p = \begin{cases} \emptyset & \text{if } |X| < p \\ \text{the } p \text{ smallest elements of } X & \text{otherwise.} \end{cases}$$

$$\min X = \begin{cases} null & \text{if } |X| = \emptyset \\ \text{the smallest element of } X & \text{otherwise.} \end{cases}$$

Each node v of G maintains two variables m and s. Variable s of v contains the list of pointers to its p slaves and the variable m contains the pointer to the selected master. If a node has not selected a master then $m = null$ and if it has not selected any slaves then $s = \emptyset$.

Note that during the execution of the algorithm, a node v can be a member of the set of slaves of many neighbors. For a node v, the set of such neighbors is denote by $M(v)$. Formally, $M(v) = \{w \in N(v) \mid v \in w.s\}$.

Moreover, the set of potential slaves of a node v is denoted by $S(v)$. This set contains all neighbors w of v such that w is either a master (*i.e.* $w.s \neq \emptyset$) and its identifier is bigger than v (*i.e.* $w > v$) or w is not a master (*i.e.* $w.s = \emptyset$) and w points to $null$ or to a master bigger or equal to v (*i.e.* $w.m \geqslant v$). Formally,

$$S(v) = \{w \in N(v) \mid (w.s = \emptyset \wedge w.m \geqslant v) \vee (w.s \neq \emptyset \wedge w > v)\}.$$

For each node v two cases have to be distinguished. Case (1): v can not be a master (*i.e.* $S(v)^p = \emptyset$) or v is pointed by a master having a smaller identifier than v (*i.e.* $minM(v) < v$). In this case the correct values for $v.s$ and $v.m$ are $\emptyset$ and $\min M(v)$ respectively. This means that v becomes a slave and v selects the smallest possible master of v. These values are denoted by $v.s_{new}$ and $v.m_{new}$ respectively.

Case (2): v can be master (*i.e.* $S(v)^p \neq \emptyset$) and v is pointed by master with larger identifier than v or v is not pointed to by any master (*i.e.* $\min M(v) > v$). In this case the correct values for $v.s$ and $v.m$ are $S(v)^p$ and $null$ respectively. This means that v becomes a master and v selects the nodes in $S(v)^p$ as slaves. These values are also denoted by $v.s_{new}$ and $v.m_{new}$ respectively.

Formally, Algorithm SMSD uses the following code permitting a node v to compute its new values of s_{new} and m_{new}.

> **if** $(\min M(v) < v \vee S(v)^p = \emptyset)$ **then**
> $v.s_{new} := \emptyset;\ v.m_{new} := \min M(v);$
> **else**
> $v.s_{new} := S(v)^p;\ v.m_{new} := null;$

The proposed Algorithm SMSD (Algorithm 1) consists of Rule R only. A node v is enabled if and only if $v.m \neq v.m_{new}$ or $v.s \neq v.s_{new}$. When v executes the rule R, v updates the values of s and m.

Algorithm 1. Star Decomposition (SMSD)

Nodes: v is the current node

$v.m \neq v.m_{new} \lor v.s \neq v.s_{new} \longrightarrow v.m := v.m_{new}; \; v.s := v.s_{new};$ [R]

It can be observed that Algorithm SMSD always finds a unique solution independent of the starting configuration. As an example for the execution of Algorithm SMSD consider $p = 3$ and a complete graph with a starting configuration, where each node v has $v.m = null$ and $v.s = \emptyset$. Figure 2 shows an example of the execution of Algorithm SMSD for such a graph with eight nodes. Using the synchronous daemon Algorithm SMSD finds two 3-stars after three rounds.

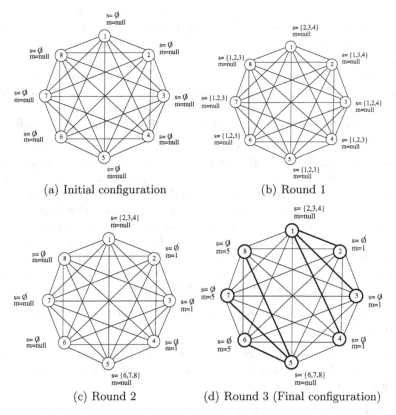

(a) Initial configuration   (b) Round 1

(c) Round 2   (d) Round 3 (Final configuration)

Fig. 2. Example of executing Algorithm SMSD under the synchronous daemon. The edges of the resulting two 3-stars are depicted in bold.

4 Correctness

Lemma 1. *In a configuration with no node is enabled, the following properties hold for each $v \in V$.*

(a) If $v.s \neq \emptyset$ then $v.s \subseteq N(v)$ and $|v.s| = p$ and $v.m = null$.
(b) If $v.m \neq null$ then $v.m \in N(v)$.
(c) If $v \in w.s$ then $v.m = w$ and $v.s = \emptyset$.

Proof. Let $v.s \neq \emptyset$. Then $v.s = v.s_{new} = S(v)^p$ since rule R is disabled. Thus, $v.s \neq \emptyset$ implies $v.s \subseteq N(v)$ and $|v.s| = p$. Moreover, if $v.s_{new} = S(v)^p$ then $v.m = v.m_{new} = null$. This proves property (a). Let $v.m \neq null$ then $v.m = v.m_{new} = \min M(v)$ since rule R is disabled. Thus, $\min M(v) \in N(v)$ implies $v.m \in N(v)$. This proves property (b).

Property (c) is proven by contradiction. Suppose there exists $v, w \in V$ such that $v \in w.s$ and $v.s \neq \emptyset$ or $v.m \neq w$. First assume $v.s \neq \emptyset$. Since $v \in w.s$, $w.s \neq \emptyset$. Then $v.s = v.s_{new} = S(v)^p$ since rule R is disabled for v. They are two cases to consider.

Case $v < w$. $v.s \neq \emptyset$ and $v \in S(w)^p$ implies $v > w$. Contradiction.

Case $v > w$. Then $v \in w.s$ implies $w \in M(v)$. Furthermore, $\min M(v) < v$ since $w < v$ and $w \in M(v)$. Thus, $v.s = v.s_{new} = \emptyset$. Contradiction.

This yields that $v \in w.s$ implies $v.s = \emptyset$.

Next consider the remaining case $v.m \neq w$. Using the previous result, if $v \in w.s$ then $v.s = \emptyset$. Hence, $v.m \neq w$ implies $v.m = null$ or $v.m = u$ such that $u \neq w$. By assumption, $v \in w.s$, *i.e.* $w \in M(v)$. This implies $\min M(v) \neq null$. To obtain a final contradiction the remaining proof is split into two cases for v:

1. If $\min M(v) < v$ or $S(v)^p = \emptyset$ then $v.s_{new} = \emptyset$ and $v.m_{new} = \min M(v)$. Further analysis depends on the value of $v.m$. If $v.m = null$ then we have $\min M(v) \neq null$ and $v.m = null$, this implies that $v.m \neq v.m_{new}$. Contradiction. On the other hand if $v.m = u$ and $u \neq w$ then $v \in u.s$. Assume that $u < v$ (resp. $u > v$) and by assumption $v \in S(w)$, this implies that $w.s \neq S(w)^p$. So, rule R is enabled for w (resp. for u). Contradiction.
2. If $\min M(v) \geq v$ and $S(v)^p \neq \emptyset$ then $v.s_{new} = S(v)^p$ and $v.m_{new} = null$. Node v is disabled by rule R, *i.e.* $v.m = v.m_{new} = null$. So, based on the previous result, if $v \in w.s$ then $v.s = \emptyset$. Hence, $v.s = \emptyset$ and we have $S(v)^p \neq \emptyset$. This implies $v.s \neq v.s_{new}$ and rule R is enabled for v. Contradiction.

We conclude that if $v \in w.s$ then $v.m = w$ and $v.s = \emptyset$. This completes the proof of property (c). □

Consider a configuration with no enabled node. Let S be the set of all nodes $v \in V$ with $v.s \neq \emptyset$. By Lemma 1, each node v of S together with the p nodes in $v.s$ forms a star in G. These stars do not overlap.

Lemma 2. *In a configuration with no enabled node the stars induced by all nodes v with $v.s \neq \emptyset$ form a maximal p-star decomposition of G.*

Proof. It is sufficient to prove that the decomposition is maximal. Let $v \in V$ such that $v.s = \emptyset$ and $v.m = null$. Assume that v is the center of a star with p slaves that are not contained in S nor are slaves of a master contained in S. Then $w.m = null$ and $w.s = \emptyset$ for every slave w of v. This implies that all p slaves of v are contained in $S(v)$. This is impossible because otherwise node v would be enabled.

5   Convergence under Unfair Distributed Daemon

In this section, the convergence of Algorithm SMSD under the unfair distributed daemon is proved. The time complexity of the algorithm is measured in rounds. Note that in general a round under an unfair distributed daemon may consist of an infinite number of moves. Thus, it is not sufficient to prove that the algorithm stabilizes after a finite number of rounds. For this reason, we first prove in Theorem 1 that Algorithm SMSD requires only a finite number of moves. This implies convergence. In the following the usage of the unfair distributed daemon is assumed.

A move of a node v is called m-move (resp. s-move) if v executes rule R and assigns a new value to $v.m$ (resp. $v.s$). Thus, a move can be a m-move and a s-move at the same time.

Lemma 3. *Let $v \in V$ and e an execution of Algorithm SMSD such that no node u with $u < v$ makes an s-move in e. Then v makes at most $d(v) + 2$ s-moves in e.*

Proof. We prove that each node $u \in N(v)$ may enter or leave the set $S(v)$ at most once during e. Since between two s-moves of v the set $S(v)$ must change the result follows. Let $w \in N(v)$ and c be the first configuration in e where w makes a move. Denote by e_c the remaining execution, *i.e.*, the suffix of e beginning in c. So, there are two possible cases for w:

Case $\min M(w) < v$. Let $u = \min M(w)$. Since $u < v$, by assumption $u.s$ will never change, thus $u \in M(w)$ holds forever and hence $\min M(w) < v$ holds forever. If $w > v$ then $\min M(w) < w$ holds forever, this implies that $w.s = \emptyset$ will be satisfied from now on. Hence, w will never be part of $S(v)$ in the future. If $w < v$ then because $\min M(w) < v$ holds forever, w will also never be part of $S(v)$ in the future. In summary, if $\min M(w) < v$, node w will at most once drop out of $S(v)$.

Case $\min M(w) \geq v$. Again by assumption $\min M(w) \geq v$ holds for the rest of the execution. Consider the case $w > v$. If there exists $u < v$ with $w \in u.s$ then w will never be part of $S(v)$ in the future. If $w \notin u.s$ for all $u < v$, then w will be forever in $S(v)$. Next let $w < v$. Then $w.s$ will never change by assumption. Then as in the previous case, node w will never be part of $S(v)$ in the future or will be forever contained in $S(v)$. In summary, if $\min M(w) \geq v$, node w will at most once drop out of $S(v)$ or will be inserted at most once into $S(v)$.

Hence, each neighbor of w induces at most one change of $S(v)$. Furthermore, all nodes u with $u < v$ cause together at most one change of $S(v)$. In total we have at most $d(v) + 2$ s-moves of v.   □

Lemma 4. *The total number of s-moves in any execution of Algorithm SMSD is finite.*

Proof. The proof is by induction on the identifier of the nodes. The node v with the smallest identifier makes at most $d(v) + 2$ s-moves by Lemma 3. Let $w \in V$, with $w \neq v$. By induction there exists a number C such that all nodes with identifiers less than w make together at most C s-moves. Then Lemma 3 implies that w makes at most $(C + 1)(d(w) + 2)$ s-moves. This completes the proof. □

Lemma 5. *Let Δ be the maximum node degree in the graph G. The total number of m-moves in any execution of Algorithm SMSD is at most $\Delta C + n$, here C denotes the total number of s-moves during the execution*

Proof. If a node v makes a m-move then the set $M(v)$ has changed since the last m-move of v or it is v's first m-move. The set $M(v)$ changes if the membership of v in $w.s$ for a node $w \in N(v)$ changes. This is caused by a s-move of w. In the worst case a s-move of a node u changes the sets $w.s$ of all neighbors w of u. This completes the proof. □

Theorem 1. *Algorithm SMSD is a self-stabilizing algorithm for computing a maximal p-star decomposition.*

Proof. The convergence property of Algorithm SMSD follows from Lemma 4 and 5. The correctness property was shown in Lemma 2. □

In the following, we analyze the round complexity of Algorithm SMSD under the unfair distributed daemon.

Lemma 6. *After round r_0 and in all following rounds, each node $v \in V$ satisfies the following properties.*

(a) $v.m = null$ or $v.m \in N(v)$.
(b) if $v.s \neq \emptyset$ then $|v.s| = p \wedge v.s \subseteq N(v) \wedge d(v) \geq p \wedge v.m = null$.

Proof. It is obvious that any node $v \in V$ that does not satisfy properties (a) and (b) is enabled and when v executes rule R during r_0, v will satisfy both of these properties because $v.m_{new} = null$ or $v.m_{new} \in N(v)$ and $v.s_{new} = \emptyset$ or $|v.s_{new}| = p$. Note that $v.s_{new} \subseteq N(v)$. □

Lemma 7. *After round r_1 and in all following rounds, each node $v \in V$ with $v.m = u$ satisfies $d(u) \geq p$ and $v.s = \emptyset$.*

Proof. After the first round r_0, if a node u has $d(u) < p$ then $u.s = \emptyset$ (Lemma 6). Moreover, u will never have $u.s \neq \emptyset$ because $S(u)^p = \emptyset$ independently of $\min M(u)$ and $S(u)^p$. Hence, u keeps its value $u.s = \emptyset$. So, after round r_1 and for all following rounds, we have $u \notin M(v)$ for all $v \in V$. This completes the proof. □

Lemma 8. *Let v^* be the smallest node in G such that $d(v^*) \geq p$. Then,*

(a) after round r_2 and in all following rounds, $v^*.m = null$ and $v^*.s = N(v^*)^p$.
(b) Let be $S^* = (v^* \cup v^*.s)$. After round r_3 and in all following rounds, $v.m \notin S^*$ and $v.s \cap S^* = \emptyset$ for all $v \in V(G) \setminus S^*$.

Proof. For proving property (a), it is sufficient to prove that during round r_2 and in all following rounds, we have $v^*.m_{new} = null$ and $v^*.s_{new} = S(v^*)^p$. This implies that $\min M(v^*) \geq v^* \wedge S(v^*)^p \neq \emptyset$.

By assumption and Lemmas 6 and 7, v^* is the smallest node such that $v^*.s \neq \emptyset$. Hence, after r_1, we have $\min M(v^*) > v^*$. Now, we prove that during round r_2, we always have $S(v^*)^p \neq \emptyset$.

By definition, $S(v^*) = \{w \in N(v^*) \mid (w.s = \emptyset \wedge w.m \geq v^*) \vee (w.s \neq \emptyset \wedge w > v^*)\}$. Now, we show that after round r_1, any neighbor w of v^* belongs to $S(v^*)$. For a node w two cases have to be considered.

Case $w.s \neq \emptyset$. Then using Lemma 6, $w > v^*$. This implies that $w \in S(v^*)$.

Case $w.s = \emptyset$. Then node w can have $w.m = null$ or $w.m \neq null$. If $w.m \neq null$ then by Lemma 6, $w.s = \emptyset$. By assumption and using Lemma 7, we have $w.m > v^*$ and $w.s = \emptyset$, this implies that $w \in S(v^*)$. If on the other hand $w.m = null$ then this yields $w.s = \emptyset$ and $w.m = null > v^*$. This implies that $w \in S(v^*)$.

We deduce that any neighbor w of the node v^* belongs of $S(v^*)$ independent of the values of $w.m$ or $w.s$. Hence, $S(v^*) = N(v^*) \neq \emptyset$. So, during round r_2 and in all following rounds, we have $S(v^*) = N(v^*) \neq \emptyset$. This implies $v^*.m_{new} = null$ and $v^*.s_{new} = N(v^*)^p$. Thus, if $v^*.m \neq v^*.m_{new}$ or $v^*.s \neq v^*.s_{new}$ then v^* executes rule R and updates its variables such that $v^*.m = null$ and $v^*.s = N(v^*)^p$ after round r_2 and v^* will never make a move again.

Property (b) means that after round r_3, there is no node $v \in V \setminus S^*$ depending on the star S^* formed by $v^* \cup v^*.s$. As previously shown, after round r_2 and in all following rounds, node v^* satisfies $v^*.m = null$ and $v^*.s = N(v^*)^p$. Hence, after round r_2, each node w not belonging to star S^* that satisfies $w.m \in S^*$ or $w.s \cap S^* \neq \emptyset$ will be enabled by rule R and must execute this rule before the end of round r_3. Thus, after round r_3, any node w not belonging to S^* will have $w.m \notin S^*$ and $w.s \cap S^* = \emptyset$.   □

Lemma 9. *Algorithm SMSD stabilizes after at most $2\lfloor \frac{n}{p+1} \rfloor + 2$ rounds.*

Proof. The proof is by induction. Consider the first two rounds r_0 and r_1. Each node satisfies the properties stated in Lemmas 6 and 7. Let be v^* the node with the smallest identifier in G with degree at least p (*i.e.* $d(v^*) \geq p$). Using Lemma 8, the star S^*, which contains the node v^* as a master and $v^*.s$ as slave nodes, will emerge after at most two successive rounds and any node belonging to this star (*i.e.* nodes in $\{v^*\} \cup v^*.s$) will never make a move again. Let G' be the graph obtained by removing the nodes of S^* from G. The argument given above can be repeated. Hence, by induction, each star stabilizes after at most two more rounds. Since G contains at most $\lfloor \frac{n}{p+1} \rfloor$ stars, Algorithm SMSD will stabilize after at most $2\lfloor \frac{n}{p+1} \rfloor + 2$ rounds.   □

The following theorem summarizes the main result of the paper.

Theorem 2. *Algorithm SMSD is self-stabilizing algorithm for maximal p-star decomposition and converges after at most $2\lfloor \frac{n}{p+1} \rfloor + 2$ rounds under the unfair distributed daemon using $O(p \log n)$ memory.*

Proof. The result follows from Theorem 1 and Lemma 9.   □

6   Conclusion

In this paper, we proposed the first self-stabilizing algorithm for graph decomposition into disjoint p-stars. The algorithm operates under the unfair distributed daemon and stabilizes after at most $2\lfloor\frac{n}{p+1}\rfloor + 2$ rounds using $O(p\log n)$ memory where n is the number of nodes in the graph G and p is a positive integer. The proposed algorithm generalizes maximal matching algorithms where $p = 1$. The time complexity in rounds of SMSD has the same order as the best known self-stabilizing algorithm for maximal matching under the synchronous daemon [13] or the distributed daemon [22].

Using the synchronous daemon, algorithm SMSD requires at most $O(n^2/p)$ moves. The exact move complexity of the algorithm under the unfair distributed daemon is unknown. We are not aware of an example where the algorithm requires an exponential number of moves. On the other hand we were unable to show the existence of a polynomial bound for the number of moves. We leave the move analysis and a generalization to weighted graphs as future work.

Acknowledgments. This work is partially supported by P2GE Rhone-Alpes Region project. The second author was funded by the Deutsche Forschungsgemeinschaft (DFG), contract number TU 221/6-1.

References

1. Andreev, K., Räcke, H.: Balanced graph partitioning. In: Proceedings 16th Annual ACM Symposium on Parallelism in Algorithms and Architectures, SPAA 2004, pp. 120–124 (2004)
2. Bein, D., Datta, A.K., Jagganagari, C.H., Villain, V.: A self-stabilizing link-cluster algorithm in mobile ad hoc networks. In: ISPAN, pp. 436–441 (2005)
3. Belkouch, F., Bui, M., Chen, L., Datta, A.: Self-stabilizing deterministic network decomposition. J. Parallel Distrib. Comput. 62(4), 696–714 (2002)
4. Bendjoudi, A., Melab, N., Talbi, E.-G.: P2p design and implementation of a parallel branch and bound algorithm for grids. Int. J. Grid Util. Comput. 1(2), 159–168 (2009)
5. Blin, L., Potop-Butucaru, M.G., Rovedakis, S., Tixeuil, S.: Loop-free super-stabilizing spanning tree construction. In: Dolev, S., Cobb, J., Fischer, M., Yung, M. (eds.) SSS 2010. LNCS, vol. 6366, pp. 50–64. Springer, Heidelberg (2010)
6. Bryant, D., El-Zanati, S., Eynden, C.H.: Star factorizations of graph products. J. Graph. Theory 36(2), 59–66 (2001)
7. Cain, P.: Decomposition of complete graphs into stars. Bull. Austral. Math. Soc. 10, 23–30 (1974)
8. Caron, E., Datta, A.K., Depardon, B., Larmore, L.L.: A self-stabilizing K-clustering algorithm using an arbitrary metric. In: Sips, H., Epema, D., Lin, H.-X. (eds.) Euro-Par 2009. LNCS, vol. 5704, pp. 602–614. Springer, Heidelberg (2009)
9. Dijkstra, E.W.: Self-stabilizing systems in spite of distributed control. Commun. ACM 17(11), 643–644 (1974)
10. Dolev, S.: Self-stabilization. MIT Press (2000)
11. Dubois, S., Tixeuil, S.: A taxonomy of daemons in self-stabilization. CoRR, abs/1110.0334 (2011)

12. Gnanadhas, N., Ebin Raja Merly, E.: Linear star decomposition of lobster. Int. J. of Contemp. Math. Sciences 7(6), 251–261 (2012)
13. Goddard, W., Hedetniemi, S., Jacobs, D., Srimani, K.: Self-stabilizing protocols for maximal matching and maximal independent sets for ad hoc networks. In: Proceedings of the 17th International Symposium on Parallel and Distributed Processing, IPDPS, p. 162.2 (2003)
14. Guellati, N., Kheddouci, H.: A survey on self-stabilizing algorithms for independence, domination, coloring, and matching in graphs. J. Parallel Distrib. Comput. (4), 406–415 (2010)
15. Johnen, C., Nguyen, L.H.: Robust self-stabilizing clustering algorithm. In: Shvartsman, A. (ed.) OPODIS 2006. LNCS, vol. 4305, pp. 410–424. Springer, Heidelberg (2006)
16. Kirkpatrick, D., Hell, P.: On the completeness of a generalized matching problem. In: STOC, pp. 240–245. ACM, New York (1978)
17. Kirkpatrick, D., Hell, P.: On the complexity of general graph factor problems. SIAM Journal on Computing 12(3), 601–609 (1983)
18. Lee, H., Lin, C.H.: Balanced star decompositions of regular multigraphs and λ-fold complete bipartite graphs. Discrete Mathematics 301(2-3), 195–206 (2005)
19. Lemmouchi, S., Haddad, M., Kheddouci, H.: Study of robustness of community emerged from exchanges in networks communication. In: Proceedings 11th International ACM Conference on Management of Emergent Digital EcoSystems, MEDES, pp. 189–196 (2011)
20. Lemmouchi, S., Haddad, M., Kheddouci, H.: Robustness study of emerged communities from exchanges in peer-to-peer networks. Computer Communications 36(1011), 1145–1158 (2013)
21. Lin, C., Shyu, T.: A necessary and sufficient condition for the star decomposition of complete graphs. J. Graph Theory 23(4), 361–364 (1996)
22. Manne, F., Mjelde, M., Pilard, L., Tixeuil, S.: A new self-stabilizing maximal matching algorithm. Theor. Comput. Sci. 410(14), 1336–1345 (2009)
23. Mezmaz, M., Melab, N., Talbi, E.-G.: A Grid-based Parallel Approach of the Multi-Objective Branch and Bound. In: Proceedings 15th Euromicro International Conference on Parallel, Distributed and Network-Based Processing, PDP, pp. 23–30 (2007)
24. Neggazi, B., Haddad, M., Kheddouci, H.: Self-stabilizing algorithm for maximal graph partitioning into triangles. In: Richa, A.W., Scheideler, C. (eds.) SSS 2012. LNCS, vol. 7596, pp. 31–42. Springer, Heidelberg (2012)
25. Pothen, A.: Graph partitioning algorithms with applications to scientific computing. Technical report, Norfolk, VA, USA (1997)

Space Complexity of Self-Stabilizing Leader Election in Population Protocol Based on k-Interaction

Xiaoguang Xu, Yukiko Yamauchi, Shuji Kijima, and Masafumi Yamashita

Graduate School of Information Science and Electrical Engineering,
Kyushu University, Fukuoka, Japan
{xiaoguang.xu,yamauchi,kijima,mak}@inf.kyushu-u.ac.jp

Abstract. Population protocol (PP) is a distributed computing model for passively mobile systems, in which a computation is executed by interactions between two agents. This paper is concerned with an extended model, *population protocol based on interactions of at most k agents* (PP_k). Beauquier et al. (2012) recently introduced the model, and showed a hierarchy of computational powers of PP_k with respect to k; a PP_{k+1} is strictly more powerful than a PP_k. Motivated by a further understanding of the model, this paper investigates the space complexity of PP_k for *self-stabilizing leader election* (SS-LE), which is a fundamental problem for a distributed system. Cai et al. (2012) showed that the space complexity of SS-LE for n agents by a PP (i.e., PP_2) is exactly n. This paper shows that the space complexity of SS-LE for n agents by a PP_k is exactly $\lceil (n-1)/(k-1) \rceil + 1$.

1 Introduction

Angluin et al. [2] proposed *Population Protocol* (PP), motivated by modeling networks such as networks of smart sensors attached to cars or animals, synthesis of chemical materials, complex biosystems, and so on (see also e.g., [5,11]). PP is a model of distributed systems consisting of mobile agents with limited computational resources, in which agent-to-agent communication (called interaction) is carried out only when two agents approach by accident. Every agent is an identical finite state machine, and two interacting finite state machines (i.e., two agents under communication) can update their states by using the transition function. Once an initial configuration is given, an execution of the system is determined by the order of interactions among the agents, which however is unpredictable and is assumed to be given by an adversarial scheduler satisfying a *fairness condition*.

Since PP was designed from a minimalist point of view, it can compute only a small set of semilinear predicates. We thus face the need of an enhancement of PP, when a larger class of predicates has turned out to be important in some killer applications. Angluin et al. [2] also suggested briefly an extension of PP to a model based on interactions by more than two agents. Recently, Beauquier et

T. Higashino et al. (Eds.): SSS 2013, LNCS 8255, pp. 86–97, 2013.
© Springer International Publishing Switzerland 2013

al. [6] investigated the *Population Protocol by interactions of at most k agents* (PP_k). They presented a computational hierarchy of PP_k with respect to k, i.e., PP_{k+1} is strictly more powerful than PP_k for any $k \in \{2, \ldots, n-1\}$, introducing the *non-deterministic population protocol* by interactions of at most k agents. We also remark *Mediated Population Protocol* (MPP) proposed by Chatzigiannakis, Michail and Spirakis [10], as another enhancement of PP. It extends PP by introducing "memories on communication links" (i.e., regarding agent-to-agent interaction as an analogue of conventional point-to-point communication through a bidirectional communication link implemented by shared memories).

A sensor network is typically characterized as a network consisting of huge inexpensive (and hence not highly reliable) sensor nodes. Such a system frequently encounters transient node failures, and its initialization is sometimes very difficult or even impossible. A system is said to be *Self-Stabilizing* (SS), if it eventually reaches a legitimate configuration regardless of its initial configuration [13]. A notable property of an SS system is that it autonomously reaches a legitimate computation, tolerating a finite number of transient failures. This motivates a series of works on SS protocols in PP.

The *Leader Election* (LE) problem is the problem of electing a unique leader agent, which frequently plays a key role in coordinating agents. Fischer et al. [14] thus discussed the problem of *Self-Stabilizing Leader Election* (SS-LE). A PP for SS-LE with an arbitrary initial configuration eventually reaches a legitimate configuration[1] such that all of its successive configurations contain exactly one leader agent.

Anglluin et al. [4] showed that there is no PP for SS-LE that works for any system of n agents, if n is not available to the agents. Fischer and Jiang [14] showed that there is a PP for SS-LE, if the scheduler is globally fair and the system can make use of the eventual leader detector $\Omega?$, that eventually detects the presence or absence of a leader. Canepa and Potop-Butucaru [9] proposed deterministic and probabilistic protocols when communication topologies (i.e., interaction graphs) are rooted trees and arbitrary graphs, under the same assumption as [14]. Cai, Izumi, Wada [8] returned to the original setting in [4] and asked a natural question: how many agent-states are necessary and sufficient in a PP for SS-LE? They then showed that n agent-states are necessary and sufficient. Thus we cannot solve this typical and important problem in PP, unless we enhance the amount of agent memory until this large size seems to contradict to the original design policy of PP. Note that [4,8,14] all assumed that the interaction graph is complete. For the enhanced model MPP, Mizoguchi et al. [17] showed that $(2/3)n$ agent-states are sufficient for SS-LE by a MPP, presenting a protocol. They also showed that any MPP requires $(1/2)\lg n$ agent-states, as a lower bound.

This paper investigates the space complexity of PP_k which solves SS-LE. We present a PP_k with $\lceil (n-1)/(k-1) \rceil + 1$ agent-states to solves SS-LE for n agents. We then show that there is no PP_k for SS-LE with $\lceil (n-1)/(k-1) \rceil$ agent-states, meaning that our PP_k is optimum in the sense of space complexity. Thus, our

---

[1] See Section 2 for details.

results may support the result by Beauquier et al. [6]. We also give an upper bound of the convergence time in terms of the number of "active" interactions, where active means at least one agent changes its state in the interaction. Precisely, our PP_k for SS-LE for n agents gets into a legitimate configuration in at most $(1/2)mn$ active interactions where m denotes the number of agent-states, i.e., $m = \lceil (n-1)/(k-1) \rceil + 1$.

Our analysis techniques are based on Cai et al. [8] and Mizoguchi et al. [17], while interactions of many agents must be carefully considered, particularly in the analysis of the lower bound. In fact, our upper bound holds even for a weaker model, in which a scheduler is allowed to choose exactly k agents instead of the condition that a scheduler can choose any of at most k agents. The lower bound clearly holds for the weaker model, and which implies that *interactions of strictly less than k agents do not help in improvement of the space complexity of SS-LE in PP_k*. See Section 5.1 for details. Our results may imply that investigating the role of interactions is an important task for further understanding of population protocols.

This paper is organized as follows. In Section 2, we describe the details of our model. In Section 3, we present a SS-LE PP_k with $\lceil (n-1)/(k-1) \rceil + 1$ agent-states for n agents. In Section 4, we show that any PP_k for SS-LE for n agents requires $\lceil (n-1)/(k-1) \rceil + 1$ agent-states. In Section 5, we give two remarks on our results.

2   Model Description

A population consists of n agents $(u_1, u_2, \ldots, u_n)$. A population protocol based on k-interaction (PP_k: $k \geq 2$) is defined by (Q, δ), where $Q = \{q_0, q_1, \ldots, q_{m-1}\}$ denotes a finite set of states and δ is a set of transition rules taken among k agents or less.

A configuration is a n-tuple $(s_1, s_2, \ldots, s_n)$ of states with s_i corresponding to the state of agent u_i. A configuration may contain multiple agents with the same state q. A transition from a configuration C to the next configuration C' in an PP_k is defined as follows. In the beginning, the scheduler chooses a k'-tuple ($2 \leq k' \leq k$) of agents $(u_1, u_2, \ldots, u_{k'})$. We assume that the scheduler can choose any k'-tuple. Suppose the states of the k'-tuple agents are $(s_1, s_2, \ldots, s_{k'})$ respectively, and let $R: (s_1, s_2, \ldots, s_{k'}) \rightarrow (s'_1, s'_2, \ldots, s'_{k'})$ be a transition rule of δ. Then, the k'-tuple agents $(u_1, u_2, \ldots, u_{k'})$ interact, writing as $C \xrightarrow{R} C'$, and the states of agents $(u_1, u_2, \ldots, u_{k'})$ in C' are $(s'_1, s'_2, \ldots, s'_{k'})$ respectively, while all other agents keep their states in the transition. We say that a transition $C \xrightarrow{R} C'$ is *active* if at least one agent changes its state or *silent* otherwise.

An execution E is defined as an infinite sequence of configurations and transitions in alternation $C_0, R_0, C_1, R_1, \ldots$ such that $C_i \xrightarrow{R_i} C_{i+1}$ for each i. Like most of the literature on PP, we assume that the scheduler in an PP_k is adversarial, but satisfying some *fairness* conditions [12].

A scheduler is said to be *globally fair* if C is a configuration that appears infinitely often in an execution, and $C \xrightarrow{R} C'$, then C' must also appear infinitely often in the execution. We sometimes abbreviate $C \xrightarrow{R} C'$ to $C \to C'$, unless it is confusing. The reflexive and transitive closure of $\to$ is denoted by $\xrightarrow{*}$. That is, $C \xrightarrow{*} C'$ means that a configuration C' is reachable from a configuration C by a sequence of transitions of length greater than or equal to 0.

We say that an element $q \in Q$ can be generated from a configuration $C \in Q^n$ if there exists a configuration C' such that $C \xrightarrow{*} C'$, containing an (multiple) agent(s) in state q. We say that a set of states G $(G \subseteq Q)$ cannot be generated from a configuration C unless at least one element in G can be generated from C. We say that $G \subseteq Q$ is closed if for any transition R: $(s_1, s_2, \ldots, s_k) \to (s_1', s_2', \ldots, s_k')$ of δ, $s_1, s_2, \ldots, s_k \in G$ indicates that $s_1', s_2', \ldots, s_k' \in G$. Let $\perp$ denotes an invalid state in which an agent is unable to be included in an interaction. We define the size of a configuration C (denoted as $|C|$) by the number of agents in states other than $\perp$. When C' is obtained by masking with $\perp$ some agents in C, we say that C' is a subconfiguration of C. For example, a configuration $C = (s_1, s_2, s_3, s_4)$ has size 4, and $C' = (s_1, \perp, s_3, \perp)$, which is a subconfiguration of C, has size 2.

The *Leader Election* (*LE*) in PP_k is a problem to assign a special state of Q, representing the "leader", to exactly one agent. A configuration $C \in Q^n$ is *legitimate* if C contains exactly one agent in the leader state, and so does in any configuration C' satisfying $C \xrightarrow{*} C'$. Let $\mathcal{L}$ $(\subseteq Q^n)$ denotes the set of all legitimate configurations. A protocol for LE is *Self-Stabilizing* (SS) (with respect to $\mathcal{L}$) if the following condition holds: For any configuration $C_0 \in Q^n$ and any execution $E = C_0 \xrightarrow{R_0} C_1 \xrightarrow{R_1} \ldots$ starting from C_0, there is an $i \geq 0$ such that $C_i \in \mathcal{L}$.[2] We use the term PP_k for SS-LE to indicate a self-stabilizing population protocol by k interactions for leader election.

3 Upper Bound of the Space Complexity

This section establishes the following theorem, which presents an upper bound of the space complexity of PP_k for SS-LE.

Theorem 3.1. *For any integer k ($k \geq 2$), and for any integer n ($n \geq k$), there exists a PP_k using $\lceil (n-1)/(k-1) \rceil + 1$ agent-states which solves the SS-LE for n agents.*

To begin with, we present Protocol 1, which is a PP_k for SS-LE in case of $n \equiv 1$ (mod $k - 1$). Let $m \stackrel{\mathrm{def}}{=} (n-1)/(k-1) + 1$ for convenience, in fact m denotes the size of agent-states. We later modify Protocol 1 for other cases of n.

Protocol 1 $Q = \{q_0, q_1, \ldots, q_{m-1}\}$, where q_0 denotes the leader state.
$\quad \delta = \{$
$\qquad R_1$: $(q_0, \ldots, q_0, q, \ldots, q') \to (q_0, q_{m-1}, \ldots, q_{m-1}, q, \ldots, q')$, for any $q, \ldots,$
$q' \in Q \setminus \{q_0\}$,

---

[2] All successive configurations in an execution after reached legitimate configuration contains exactly one leader agent, but allows leader state to change from one agent to another.

R_2: $(q_i, q_i, \ldots, q_i) \to (q_{i-1}, q_i, \ldots, q_i)$, *for any* $i \in \{1, 2, \ldots, m-1\}$,
R_3: $(q, \ldots, q') \to (q, \ldots, q')$, *in cases other than* R_1 *and* R_2.
}
R_1 *and* R_3 *are* k'-*tuple interactions where* $2 \leq k' \leq k$, *while* R_2 *is exactly* k-*tuple interaction.*

In Protocol 1, rule R_1 means that if two or more agents of a selected k'-tuple agents are in state q_0, then those agents except for exactly one change to q_{m-1}, and other agents remain their states. Rule R_2 means that if a selected k-tuple of agents are in the same state $q_i \in Q \setminus \{q_0\}$, then the first agent changes its state from q_i to q_{i-1} and other agents keep their states. In case that the selected k-tuple of agents does not satisfy the hypothesis of R_1 nor R_2, rule R_3 is applied, meaning that every agent keeps its state, i.e., R_1 and R_2 are active, but R_3 is *not*.

Now, we define a set of configurations $\mathcal{L} \subseteq Q^n$, such that $C \in \mathcal{L}$ if $\gamma_0(C) = 1$ and $\gamma_i(C) = k-1$ for $i \in \{1, 2, \ldots, m-1\}$ where $\gamma_i(C)$ denotes the number of agents in state q_i in C for each $i \in \{0, 1, \ldots, m-1\}$. Thus, $C \in \mathcal{L}$ contains exactly one leader.

Lemma 3.2. $\mathcal{L}$ *is the set of legitimate configurations, i.e., if* $C \in \mathcal{L}$ *and* $C \to C'$, *then* $C' \in \mathcal{L}$.

Proof. In an arbitrary legitimate configuration C, there is exactly one leader agent, meaning that R_1, which requires two leader agents, is not applicable to C. In a similar argument, there are $k-1$ agents in each state other than leader, meaning that R_2, which requires k agents in state q_i ($i \in \{1, \ldots, m-1\}$), is not applicable to C. Since rule R_3 is non-active, $C' = C$ holds, and we obtain the claim.

Lemma 3.3. *For any configuration* $C \in Q^n$, *there exists an execution that satisfies* $C \xrightarrow{*} C'$ *such that* $C' \in \mathcal{L}$.

Proof. To begin with, we remark the following facts. Suppose that a configuration $D \in Q^n$ satisfies $\gamma_0(D) \geq 1$, and suppose that $D \to D'$, then $\gamma_0(D') \geq 1$ holds by the definition of δ. By an induction, if a configuration $D \in Q^n$ satisfies $\gamma_0(D) \geq 1$ and $D \xrightarrow{*} D''$, then $\gamma_0(D'') \geq 1$ holds. In a similar way, for each $i \in \{1, \ldots, m-1\}$, if a configuration $D \in Q^n$ satisfies $\gamma_i(D) \geq k-1$ and $D \xrightarrow{*} D''$, then $\gamma_i(D'') \geq k-1$ holds.

If a configuration $D \in Q^n$ satisfies $\gamma_0(D) = 0$, then we claim that q_0 is generated by a sequence of transitions. In the case, there exists an index $i \in \{1, \ldots, m-1\}$ such that $\gamma_i(D) \geq k$ by the pigeon hole principle, otherwise the total number of agents $\sum_{j=0}^{m-1} \gamma_j(D) = (k-1)(m-1)$ is less than n since $m = (n-1)/(k-1) + 1$, which is a contradiction. Then, any active transition $D \to D'$ is due to R_2, and $\sum_{j'=0}^{j} \gamma_{j'}(D') > \sum_{j'=0}^{j} \gamma_{j'}(D)$ holds for an index $j \in \{0, \ldots, m-1\}$, by the definition of δ. Note that $\sum_{j=0}^{i} \gamma_j(D') \geq \sum_{j=0}^{i} \gamma_j(D)$ holds for any index $i \in \{0, \ldots, m-1\}$ by rule R_2. This implies that for any $D \in Q^n$ satisfying $\gamma_0(D) = 0$, $D \xrightarrow{*} D''$ such that $\gamma_0(D'') \geq 1$.

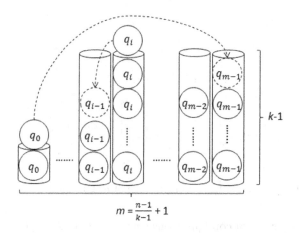

$$m = \frac{n-1}{k-1} + 1$$

Fig. 1. Active transitions in case of $n \equiv 1 \pmod{k-1}$

In a similar way, if a configuration $D \in Q^n$ satisfies $\gamma_i(D) < k - 1$, then q_i is generated by a sequence of transitions. Combining the above remark, we obtain the claim.

By combining Lemmas 3.2 and Lemmas 3.3, we obtain that Protocol 1 solves SS-LE for n agents in case of $n \equiv 1 \pmod{k-1}$. See Figure 1. The figure indicates that if the size of agents in any state is over the corresponding container, an active transition is available. And legitimate configuration is that agents in all states exactly fill the corresponding containers.

In case that $n \not\equiv 1 \pmod{k-1}$, let $m \stackrel{\text{def}}{=} \lceil (n-1)/(k-1) \rceil + 1$ and we simply modify δ of Protocol 1, inserting rule R_4, as follows:

Protocol 2 $Q = \{q_0, q_1, \ldots, q_{m-1}\}$, *where* q_0 *denotes the leader state.*
    $\delta = \{$
       $R_1 : (q_0, \ldots, q_0, q, \ldots, q') \rightarrow (q_0, q_{m-1}, \ldots, q_{m-1}, q, \ldots, q')$, *for any* $q, \ldots,$
$q' \in Q \setminus \{q_0\}$,
       $R_2 : (q_i, q_i, \ldots, q_i) \rightarrow (q_{i-1}, q_i, \ldots, q_i)$, *for any* $i \in \{1, \ldots, m-2\}$
       $R_4 : (q_{m-1}, q_{m-1}, \ldots, q_{m-1}, q, \ldots, q') \rightarrow (q_{m-2}, \ldots, q_{m-2}, q_{m-1}, \ldots, q_{m-1},$
$q, \ldots, q')$ *for any* $q, \ldots, q' \in Q$, *in cases other than* R_1
       $R_3 : (q, \ldots, q') \rightarrow (q, \ldots, q')$, *in cases other than* R_1, R_2 *and* R_4.
    $\}$
    R_4 *is* l-*tuple interaction where* $((n-1) \bmod (k-1) + 1) \leq l \leq k$

Rule R_4 means that if more than l' agents of a selected l-tuple agents are in state q_{m-1}, then the l' agents remain their states while others change to q_{m-2} and agents in other states keep, where $l' \stackrel{\text{def}}{=} n - (1 + (m-2)(k-1)) = (n - 1) \bmod (k-1)$.

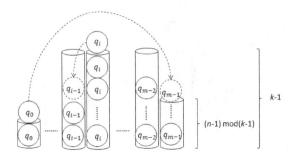

Fig. 2. Active transitions in case of $n \not\equiv 1 \pmod{k-1}$

Let $\mathcal{L} \subseteq Q^n$ be a set of configurations such that $C \in \mathcal{L}$ if $\gamma_0(C) = 1$, $\gamma_i(C) = k-1$ for $i \in \{1, 2, \ldots, m-2\}$, and $\gamma_{m-1}(C) = l'$. Then, we can show Lemmas 3.2 and 3.3, and hence we obtain Theorem 3.1. Proofs are similar to the case of $n \equiv 1 \pmod{k-1}$, and we omit them here (see Figure 2).

4 Lower Bound of the Space Complexity

Theorem 4.1. *Any PP_k requires agent states with size at least $\lceil (n-1)/(k-1) \rceil + 1$ to solve an SS-LE for n agents.*

To prove Theorem 4.1, we show the following Lemmas 4.2 and 4.3.

Lemma 4.2. *Let G be a finite subset of agent-states Q. Suppose that C is a (sub)configuration of a PP_k, and that G cannot be generated from C. Then, the following condition holds:*

Condition: If the complement of G (denoted by $\overline{G}$) is not closed, there exists a subconfiguration C' of C and a set $G' \supset G$ such that $|C| - (k-1) \leq |C'|$, $|G| + 1 \leq |G'|$, and the configuration C' cannot generate G'.

Proof. The assumption that $\overline{G}$ is not closed implies that there exists a transition $(s_1, s_2, \ldots, s_{k'}) \to (s'_1, s'_2, \ldots, s'_{k'})$ $(2 \leq k' \leq k)$ such that $s_1, s_2, \ldots, s_{k'} \in \overline{G}$, and at least one of $s'_1, s'_2, \ldots, s'_{k'} \notin \overline{G}$. We consider the condition in the following two cases:

Case 1: at least one state of $\{s_1, s_2, \ldots, s_{k'}\}$ cannot be generated from C. Without loss of generality, we may assume that s_1 cannot be generated from C. Then, we obtain the condition by setting $C' = C$ and $G' = G \cup \{s_1\}$.

Case 2: each of $\{s_1, s_2, \ldots, s_{k'}\}$ can be generated from C. Note that $(s_1, s_2, \ldots, s_{k'})$ cannot coexist in configuration C, otherwise, $(s'_1, s'_2, \ldots, s'_{k'})$ can be generated from C, which contradicts to the hypothesis of the lemma that G cannot be generated from C.

Then, suppose that at most l $(0 < l < k' \leq k)$ states of $(s_1, \ldots, s_{k'})$ can be generated at the same time. Without loss of generality, we may assume that $s_1, \ldots, s_l$ can be generated from C at the same time. We set a subconfiguration

C' of C by masking with $\perp$ the l agents each of which is respectively in states of $s_1, \ldots, s_l$, i.e., $|C'| = |C| - l \geq |C| - (k-1)$. Then $s_{l+1}, \ldots, s'_k$ cannot be generated from C', otherwise, contradicts to the assumption that l is maximum. Set $G' = G \cup \{s_{l+1}, \ldots, s'_k\}$, and we obtain the condition.

Lemma 4.3. *In an SS-LE protocol, the set of states excluding leader state would never be closed.*

Proof. If such kind of set exists, a configuration initialized by elements only in the set would be unable to generate the leader state which results in a contradiction.

Now we prove Theorem 4.1.

Proof (Proof of Theorem 4.1). Suppose for a contradiction that there exists a PP_k with $m := \lceil (n-1)/(k-1) \rceil$ agent-states to solve an SS-LE for n agents. Let $Q = \{q_0, q_1, \ldots, q_{m-1}\}$ denotes the set of agent-states of the protocol where q_0 is the leader state. Let C be a legitimate configuration of the protocol, thus C contains exactly one leader. We set C_0 by masking the agent with q_0 in C with $\perp$, thus $|C_0| = n - 1$. Then, set $G_0 = \{q_0\}$. Since C is a legitimate configuration, G_0 cannot be generated from C_0. Lemma 4.3 implies that $\overline{G_0}$ is not closed. By Lemma 4.2, we can obtain a configuration C_1 and a set G_1 such that $|C_1| \geq |C_0| - (k-1)$, $|G_1| \geq |G'| + 1$, and G_1 cannot be generated from C_1.

In a similar way, by recursively applying Lemma 4.3 $m-1$ times, we obtain a configuration C_{m-1} and $G_{m-1} \subseteq Q$ such that such that G_{m-1} cannot be generated from C_{m-1}. Note that

$$|C_{m-1}| \geq |C_0| - (k-1)(m-1) \geq n - 1 - (k-1)(m-1) > 0$$

where the last inequality follows from $m := \lceil (n-1)/(k-1) \rceil$, and also note that $|G_{m-1}| \geq |G_0| + m - 1 = m$, meaning that $G_{m-1} = Q$. Contradiction.

5 Two Remarks

5.1 Interactions of Strictly Less Than k Agents Are Helpless for SS-LE

In this section, we remark a "weaker" model, $PP_{=k}$. Instead a scheduler can choose any of at most k agents for an interaction in PP_k described in Section 2, a scheduler in $PP_{=k}$ is allowed only to choose exactly k of agents arbitrarily in an interaction.

It is easy to see that any protocol of $PP_{=k}$ is immediately emulated by a protocol of PP_k, by setting any interaction of strictly less than k agents to be silent. On the other hand, $PP_{=k}$ cannot emulate PP_k in general, by a counting argument; the size[3] of δ of $PP_{=k}$ is at most $\Delta(k, m)$, where $\Delta(k, m)$ denote the number of integers

---

[3] Here, we assume "symmetric" interactions, meaning that an interaction depends only on the multiset of states of chosen agents but independent of an order of them, however here we omit the detailed argument because of the page limitation.

in a k dimensional simplex with side length m, that is $\Delta(k, m) = \binom{m+k}{k} \simeq m^k$ in fact, while the size of δ of PP_k can be as large as $\sum_{k'=2}^{k} \Delta(k', m) \simeq \sum_{k'=2}^{k} m^{k'}$. This implies $PP_{=k}$ is a model "strictly weaker" than PP_k. For an intuitive example, we can design a PP_3 with δ containing rules such as

$r_1 \colon (q_1, q_1, *) \rightarrow (q_1, q_1, q_1)$ where $*$ represents an arbitrary state, and
$r_2 \colon (q_1, q_1) \rightarrow (q_1, q_0)$,

then r_1 and r_2 are not naturally designed in $PP_{=3}$.

Nevertheless, our results in Sections 3 and 4 imply that the space complexity of SS-LE of PP_k and $PP_{=k}$ are the same. In fact, we obtain Theorem 3.1 for $PP_{=k}$ by modifying Protocols 1 and 2 to ones for $PP_{=k}$: R_1 and R_4 in Protocol 2 are applied only when k agents are interacted. Theorem 4.1 is immediate for $PP_{=k}$ by the above argument that PP_k emulates $PP_{=k}$. This implies that interactions of strictly less than k agents does not contribute an improvement of the space complexity of SS-LE in PP_k.

5.2   Time Complexity of the Protocol

Though this paper is concerned with the space complexity of the SS-LE in PP_k, this section briefly discusses the convergence time of our PP_k, Protocols 1 and 2, from an arbitrary initial configuration to a legitimate configuration, in terms of the number of active interactions. This section assumes a scheduler defined in Section 2. Let T_C denote the number of active interactions which takes from a configuration C to a legitimate configuration.

We claim in Theorem 5.1 that the value of T_C is represented by a minimum cost integral flow (or a directed version of the minimum weight b-matching) problem (see e.g., [18]). Let $d_{ij} \stackrel{\text{def}}{=} i - j \pmod{m}$ for any $i, j \in \{0, \ldots, m-1\}$, i.e.,

$$d_{ij} = \begin{cases} i - j & \text{(if } i \geq j\text{)}, \\ m + i - j & \text{(otherwise)}. \end{cases}$$

For a configuration C, we define b_i for each $i \in \{0, \ldots, m-1\}$ by

$$b_i(C) = \begin{cases} \gamma_i(C) - 1 & (i = 0), \\ \gamma_i(C) - (k-1) & (i \in \{1, \ldots, m-2\}), \\ \gamma_i(C) - (n - 1 - (k-1)(m-2)) & (i = m-1), \end{cases}$$

where we note that $b_{m-1}(C) = \gamma_i(C) - (k-1)$ if $n \equiv 1 \pmod{k-1}$, otherwise, $b_{m-1}(C) = \gamma_i(C) - ((n-1) \bmod (k-1))$, i.e., b_i represents the surplus number of agents in state i. Then, we formulate the following integer programming problem for the configuration C,

(IP)

minimize $g_C(x) \stackrel{\text{def}}{=} \sum_{i=0}^{m-1} \sum_{j=0}^{m-1} d_{ij} x_{ij}$, subject to $\quad \displaystyle\sum_{j=0}^{m-1} x_{ij} = b_i(C) \quad$ for $i \in \{i' \in \{0, \ldots, m-1\} \mid b_{i'}(C) > 0\}$,

$\displaystyle\sum_{i=0}^{m-1} x_{ij} = -b_j(C) \quad$ for $i \in \{i' \in \{0, \ldots, m-1\} \mid b_{i'}(C) < 0\}$,

$x_{ij} \in \mathbb{Z}_{\geq 0} \qquad\qquad$ for $i, j \in \{0, \ldots, m-1\}$.

Theorem 5.1. *For any configuration C, T_C is equal to the optimum value of* (IP).

Proof. Let $f(C)$ denote the optimum value of (IP) for a configuration C. Suppose x_C^* is an optimum solution, i.e., $f(C) = g_C(x^*)$. Then, it is not difficult to see that x^* provides an execution of our PP_k by a "friendly" scheduler from a configuration C to a legitimate configuration, with $f(C)$ active interactions.

Thus, what we need to show is that the number of active iterations from C to a legitimate configuration is equal to $f(C)$, by any "proper"[4] scheduler. We show it by an induction on the size of $f(C) \in \mathbb{Z}_{\geq 0}$. In case of $f(C) = 0$, C is a legitimate configuration, meaning that $T_C = 0$.

Now, we assume that $T_{C'} = f(C')$ holds for any configuration C' satisfying $f(C') = k$, and show that $T_C = f(C)$ for any configuration C satisfying $f(C) = k + 1$. For the purpose, we show that if $C \xrightarrow{R} C'$ is an active transition then $f(C') = f(C) - 1$ holds, which implies that *an arbitrary active transition decreases the optimum value of* (IP) *by exactly one*, and hence we obtain $T_C = T_{C'} + 1$ by the inductive hypothesis. By the definition of Protocols 1 or 2, it is not difficult to see that there exists an index $i \in \{0, \ldots, m-1\}$, and $b_{i-1}(C') = b_{i-1}(C) + 1$, $b_i(C') = b_i(C) - 1$, and $b_j(C') = b_j(C)$ $(j \neq i-1, i)$ hold. Let x' be a solution obtained from x^* modifying that $x'_{i-1,j} = x^*_{i-1,j} + 1$ and $x'_{ij} = x^*_{ij} - 1$. It is not difficult that x' is a feasible solution of (IP) for C', as well as that $g_{C'}(x') = g_C(x^*) - 1$ holds, which implies $f(C') \leq f(C) - 1$. In a similar way, let y^* be a optimal solution of (IP) for C', and set y' modifying y^* such that $y'_{i-1,j} = y^*_{i-1,j} + 1$ and $y'_{ij} = y^*_{ij} - 1$. then $g_C(y') = g_{C'}(y) + 1$ which implies $f(C) \leq f(C') + 1$. We obtain the claim.

Note that it is well-known that (IP) is solved in $O(m^3)$ time. Theorem 5.1 implies the following.

Corollary 5.2. *For any $k \geq 2$ and $n \geq k$,*

$$\max_C T_C = \sum_{d=2}^{m-1} (d-1)(k-1) + n - 1 \leq \frac{1}{2} mn.$$

6 Concluding Remarks

This paper has been concerned with the space complexity of PP_k for the SS-LE with n agents, and showed that the space complexity is exactly

---

[4] Which is the weakest fairness assumption[12].

$\lceil (n-1)/(k-1) \rceil + 1$. As we stated in Section 5.1, interactions of less than k agents do not help an improvement of the space complexity of SS-LE in PP_k. Investigating the role of interactions is an important task for further understanding of population protocols, and a generalized model of population protocol based on interactions of many agents is an interesting and challenging subject. For instance, analysis of PP_k with an incomplete interaction hypergraph is an interesting future work.

Acknowledgment. This work is partly supported by JSPS KAKENHI Grant Number 23700019, Grant-in-Aid for Scientific Research on Innovative Areas "Exploring the Limits of Computation (ELC)" (No. 24106005), and Grant-in-Aid for Scientific Research on Innovative Areas "Molecular Robotics" (No. 24104003).

References

1. Angluin, D., Aspnes, J., Chan, M., Fischer, M.J., Jiang, H., Peralta, R.: Stably computable properties of network graphs. In: Prasanna, V.K., Iyengar, S.S., Spirakis, P.G., Welsh, M. (eds.) DCOSS 2005. LNCS, vol. 3560, pp. 63–74. Springer, Heidelberg (2005)
2. Angluin, D., Aspnes, J., Diamadi, Z., Fischer, M.J., Peralta, R.: Computation in networks of passively mobile finite-state sensors. Distributed Computing 18, 235–253 (2006)
3. Angluin, D., Aspnes, J., Eisenstat, D.: Fast computation by population protocols with a leader. Distributed Computing 21, 183–199 (2008)
4. Angluin, D., Aspnes, J., Fischer, M.J., Jiang, H.: Self-stabilizing population protocols. ACM Transactions on Autonomous and Adaptive Systems 3, Article 13 (2008)
5. Aspnes, J., Ruppert, E.: An introduction to population protocols. Bulletin of the EATCS 93, 98–117 (2007)
6. Beauquier, J., Burman, J., Rosaz, L., Rozoy, B.: Non-deterministic population protocols. In: Baldoni, R., Flocchini, P., Binoy, R. (eds.) OPODIS 2012. LNCS, vol. 7702, pp. 61–75. Springer, Heidelberg (2012)
7. Beauquier, J., Clement, J., Messika, S., Rosaz, L., Rozoy, B.: Self-stabilizing counting in mobile sensor networks. In: Proc. of PODC 2007, pp. 396–397 (2007)
8. Cai, S., Izumi, T., Wada, K.: How to prove impossibility under global fairness: on space complexity of self-stabilizing leader election on a population protocol model. Theory of Computing Systems 50, 433–445 (2012)
9. Canepa, D., Potop-Butucaru, M.G.: Stabilizing leader election in population protocols. INRIA Rocquencourt, RR-6269 (2007), http://hal.inria.fr/inria-00166632/en/
10. Chatzigiannakis, I., Michail, O., Spirakis, P.G.: Mediated population protocols. Theoretical Computer Science 412, 2434–2450 (2011)
11. Chatzigiannakis, I., Michail, O., Spirakis, P.G.: Recent advances in population protocols. In: Královič, R., Niwiński, D. (eds.) MFCS 2009. LNCS, vol. 5734, pp. 56–76. Springer, Heidelberg (2009)
12. Devismes, S., Tixeuil, S., Yamashita, M.: Weak vs. self vs. probabilistic stabilization. In: Proc. of ICDCS 2008, pp. 681–688 (2008)
13. Dijkstra, E.W.: Self stabilizing systems in spite of distributed control. Communications of the Association of the Computing Machinery 17, 643–644 (1974)

14. Fischer, M., Jiang, H.: Self-stabilizing leader election in networks of finite-state anonymous agents. In: Shvartsman, A. (ed.) OPODIS 2006. LNCS, vol. 4305, pp. 395–409. Springer, Heidelberg (2006)
15. Guerraoui, R., Ruppert, E.: Names trump malice: Tiny mobile agents can tolerate byzantine failures. In: Albers, S., Marchetti-Spaccamela, A., Matias, Y., Nikolet-seas, S., Thomas, W. (eds.) ICALP 2009, Part II. LNCS, vol. 5556, pp. 484–495. Springer, Heidelberg (2009)
16. Michail, O., Chatzigiannakis, I., Spirakis, P.G.: Mediated population protocols. Theoretical Computer Science 412, 2434–2450 (2011)
17. Mizoguchi, R., Ono, H., Kijima, S., Yamashita, M.: On space complexity of self-stabilizing leader election in mediated population protocol. Distributed Computing 25, 451–460 (2012)
18. Schrijver, A.: Combinatorial Optimization. Springer (2003)

Self-Healing of Byzantine Faults*

Jeffrey Knockel, George Saad, and Jared Saia

Department of Computer Science, University of New Mexico
{jeffk,george.saad,saia}@cs.unm.edu

Abstract. Recent years have seen significant interest in designing networks that
are *self-healing* in the sense that they can automatically recover from adversarial
attacks. Previous work shows that it is possible for a network to automatically
recover, even when an adversary repeatedly deletes nodes in the network. However, there have not yet been any algorithms that self-heal in the case where an
adversary takes over nodes in the network. In this paper, we address this gap.

In particular, we describe a communication network over n nodes that ensures
the following properties, even when an adversary controls up to $t \leq (1/8 - \epsilon)n$
nodes, for any non-negative ϵ. First, the network provides a point-to-point communication with bandwidth and latency costs that are asymptotically optimal.
Second, the expected total number of message corruptions is $O(t(\log^* n)^2)$ before the adversarially controlled nodes are effectively quarantined so that they
cause no more corruptions. Empirical results show that our algorithm can reduce
bandwidth cost by up to a factor of 70.

Keywords: Byzantine Faults, Threshold Cryptography, Self-Healing Algorithms.

"Fool me once, shame on you. Fool me twice, shame on me." - English proverb

1 Introduction

Self-healing algorithms protect critical properties of a network, even when that network
is under repeated attack. Such algorithms only expend resources when it is necessary
to repair damage done by an attacker. Thus, they provide significant resource savings
when compared to traditional robust algorithms, which expend significant resources
even when the network is not under attack.

The last several years have seen exciting results in the design of self-healing algorithms [1–6]. Unfortunately, none of these previous results handle *Byzantine faults*,
where an adversary takes over nodes in the network and can cause them to deviate arbitrarily from the protocol. This is a significant gap, since traditional Byzantine-resilient
algorithms are notoriously inefficient, and the self-healing approach could significantly
improve efficiency.

In this paper, we take a step towards addressing this gap. For a network of n nodes,
we design self-healing algorithms for communication that tolerate up to $1/8$ fraction of
Byzantine faults. Our algorithms enable any node to send a message to any other node
in the network with bandwidth and latency costs that are asymptotically optimal.

---

* This research is partially supported by NSF grants: CISE-1117985 and CNS-1017509.

T. Higashino et al. (Eds.): SSS 2013, LNCS 8255, pp. 98–112, 2013.

Moreover, our algorithms limit the expected total number of message corruptions. Ideally, each Byzantine node would cause $O(1)$ corruptions; our result is that each Byzantine node causes an expected $O((\log^* n)^2)$ corruptions. [1] Now we must amend our initial proverb to: *"Fool me once, shame on you. Fool me $\omega((\log^* n)^2)$ times, shame on me."*.

1.1 Our Model

We assume an adversary that is *static* in the sense that it takes over nodes before the algorithm begins. The nodes that are compromised by the adversary are *bad*, and the other nodes are *good*. The bad nodes may arbitrarily deviate from the protocol, by sending no messages, excessive numbers of messages, incorrect messages, or any combination of these. The good nodes follow the protocol. We assume that the adversary knows our protocol, but is unaware of the random bits of the good nodes.

We further assume that each node has a unique ID. We say that node p has a link to node q if p knows q's ID and can thus directly communicate with node q. Also, we assume the existence of a public key digital signature scheme, and thus a computationally bounded adversary. Finally, we assume a partially synchronous communication model: any message sent from one good node to another good node requires at most h time steps to be sent and received, and the value h is known to all nodes. Also, we allow for the adversary to be *rushing*, where the bad nodes receive all messages from good nodes in a round before sending out their own messages.

Our algorithms make critical use of quorums and a quorum graph. We define a *quorum* to be a set of $\Theta(\log n)$ nodes, of which at most $1/8$-fraction are bad. Many results show how to create and maintain a network of quorums [7–13]. All of these results maintain what we will call a *quorum graph* in which each vertex represents a quorum. The properties of the quorum graph are: 1) each node is in $O(\log n)$ quorums; 2) for any quorum Q, any node in Q can communicate directly to any other node in Q; and 3) for any quorums Q_i and Q_j that are connected in the quorum graph, any node in Q_i can communicate directly with any node in Q_j and vice versa. Moreover, we assume that for any two nodes x and y in a quorum, node x knows all quorums that node y is in.

The communication in the quorum graph typically occurs as follows. When a node s sends another node r some message m, there is a canonical *quorum path*, $Q_1, Q_2, \ldots, Q_\ell$, through the quorum graph. This path is determined by the ID's of both s and r. A naive way to route the message is for s to send m to all nodes in Q_1. Then for $i = 1$ to $\ell - 1$, for all nodes in Q_i to send m to all nodes in Q_{i+1}, and for each node in Q_{i+1} to do majority filtering on the messages received in order to determine the true value of m. Then all nodes in Q_ℓ send m to node r that does a majority filter on the received messages. Unfortunately, this algorithm requires $O(\ell \log^2 n)$ messages and a latency of $O(\ell)$. This paper shows how to reduce the message cost to $O(\ell + \log n)$, in an amortized sense.

---

[1] Recall that $\log^* n$ or the iterated logarithm function is the number of times logarithm must be applied iteratively before the result is less than or equal to 1. It is an extremely slowly growing function: e.g. $\log^* 10^{10} = 5$.

As we show in Section 4, this reduction can be large in practice. In particular, we reduce the bandwidth cost by a factor of 58 for $n = 14{,}116$, and by a factor of 70 for $n = 30{,}509$.

1.2   Our Results

This paper provides a self-healing algorithm, *SEND*, that sends a message from a source node to a target node in the network. Our main result is summarized in the following theorem.

Theorem 1. *Assume we have a network with n nodes and $t \leq (1/8 - \epsilon)n$ bad nodes, for any non-negative ϵ, and a quorum graph as described above. Then our algorithm ensures the following.*

- *For any call to SEND, the expected number of messages is $O(\ell + \log n)$ and the expected latency is $O(\ell)$, in an amortized sense.[2]*
- *The expected total number of times that SEND fails to deliver a message reliably is at most $3t(\log^* n)^2$.*

Due to the space constraints, the proof of this theorem is not given here [3].

1.3   Related Work

Several papers [14–18] have discussed different restoration mechanisms to preserve network performance by adding capacity and rerouting traffic streams in the presence of node or link failures. They present mathematical models to determine global optimal restoration paths, and provide methods for capacity optimization of path-restorable networks.

Our results are inspired by recent work on self-healing algorithms [1–6]. A common model for these results is that the following process repeats indefinitely: an adversary deletes some nodes in the network, and the algorithm adds edges. The algorithm is constrained to never increase the degree of any node by more than a logarithmic factor from its original degree. In this model, researchers have presented algorithms that ensure the following properties: the network stays connected and the diameter does not increase by much [1–3]; the shortest path between any pair of nodes does not increase by much [4]; and expansion properties of the network are approximately preserved [5].

Our results are also similar in spirit to those of Saia and Young [19] and Young et al. [20], which both show how to reduce message complexity when transmitting a message across a quorum path of length ℓ. The first result, [19], achieves expected message complexity of $O(\ell \log n)$ by use of bipartite expanders. However, this result is impractical due to high hidden constants and high setup costs. The second result, [20],

---

[2] In particular, if we perform any number of message sends through quorum paths, where ℓ_M is the longest such path, and $\mathcal{L}$ is the sum of the quorums traversed in all such paths, then the expected total number of messages sent will be $O(\mathcal{L} + t \cdot (\ell_M \log^2 n + \log^5 n))$. Note that, since t is fixed, for large $\mathcal{L}$, the expected total number of messages is $O(\mathcal{L})$.

[3] A full version with all the proofs is available at the authors' homepages.

achieves expected message complexity of $O(\ell)$. However, this second result requires the sender to iteratively contact a member of each quorum in the quorum path.

As mentioned earlier, several peer-to-peer networks have been described that provably enable reliable communication, even in the face of adversarial attack [7–10, 12, 21]. To the best of our knowledge, our approach applies to each of these networks, with the exception of [21]. In particular, we can apply our algorithms to asymptotically improve the efficiency of the peer-to-peer networks from [7–10, 12].

Similarly to Young et al. [22], we use threshold cryptography as an alternative to Byzantine Agreement.

1.4 Organization of Paper

The rest of this paper is organized as follows. In Section 2, we describe our algorithms. The analysis of our algorithms is shown in Section 3. Section 4 gives empirical results showing how our algorithms can improve the efficiency of the butterfly networks of [7]. Finally, we conclude and describe problems for future work in Section 5.

2 Our Algorithms

In this section, we describe our algorithms: *BROADCAST, SEND, SEND-PATH, CHECK* and *UPDATE*.

2.1 Overview

Recall that when node s wants to send a message to a node r, there is a canonical *quorum path* $Q_1, Q_2, \ldots, Q_\ell$, determined by the IDs of s and r. We assume that Q_1 is the leftmost quorum and Q_ℓ is the rightmost quorum; and we let $|Q_j|$ be the number of nodes in quorum Q_j, for $1 \leq j \leq \ell$.

The objective of our algorithms is marking all bad nodes in the network, where no more message corruption occurred. In order to do that, we mark nodes after they are *in conflict*, where a pair of nodes is *in conflict* if at least one of these nodes accuses the other node in this pair. If the half of nodes in any quorum are marked, we unmark these nodes. Note that when we mark (or unmark) a node, it is marked (or unmarked) in its quorums and in their neighboring quorums. Note that all nodes in the network are initially unmarked.

In our algorithms, we assume that when any node x in a quorum Q broadcasts a message m to a set of nodes S, it executes $BROADCAST(m, Q, S)$. Before discussing our main algorithm, *SEND*, we describe *BROADCAST* procedure (Algorithm 1).

In *BROADCAST*, we make use of the threshold cryptography as an alternative to Byzantine Agreement. We briefly describe the threshold cryptography, (η, d)-threshold scheme.

Threshold Cryptography. In (η, d)-threshold scheme, the secret key is distributed among η parties, and any subset of more than d parties can jointly reassemble the key. The secret key can be distributed by a completely distributed approach, *Distributed Key*

Algorithm 1. $BROADCAST(m, Q, S)$

Declarations: *BROADCAST* is being called by a node x in a quorum Q in order to send a message m to a set of nodes S.

1. Node x sends message m to all nodes in Q.
2. Each node in Q signs m by its private key share to obtain a signed-message share, and sends this signed-message share back to node x.
3. Node x interpolates at least $\frac{7|Q|}{8}$ of the received signed-message shares to obtain the signed-message of Q.
4. Node x sends the signed-message of Q to all nodes in S.

Algorithm 2. SEND$(m, \mathbf{r})$

Declaration: node s wants to send message m to node $\mathbf{r}$.

1. Node s calls *SEND-PATH* $(m, \mathbf{r})$.
2. With probability p_{call}, node s calls *CHECK* $(m, \mathbf{r})$.

Generation (DKG) [23]. The *Distributed Key Generation* (DKG) generates the public/private key shares of all nodes in every quorum and the public/private key pair of each quorum. The public key share of any node is known only to the nodes that are in the same quorum. Moreover, the public key of each quorum is known to all nodes of this quorum and its neighboring quorums, but the private key of any quorum is unknown to all nodes.

BROADCAST Algorithm. In $BROADCAST(m, Q, S)$, we use in particular a $(|Q|, \frac{7}{8}|Q| - 1)$-threshold scheme, where $|Q|$ is the quorum size. Throughout the paper, when any node x in a quorum Q broadcasts a message m to a set of nodes S, it calls $BROADCAST(m, Q, S)^4$. In $BROADCAST(m, Q, S)$, node x sends m to all nodes in Q. Then each node in the quorum signs m by its private key share, and sends the signed message share to node x. Node x interpolates at least $\frac{7|Q|}{8}$ of the received signed-message shares to construct a signed-message of the quorum. We know that at least $7/8$-fraction of the nodes in any quorum are good. So if this signed-message is constructed, it ensures that at least $7/8$-fraction of the nodes in this quorum has received the same message m, agrees upon the content of the message and gives the permission to node x of broadcasting this message. Then node x sends this constructed signed-message to all nodes in S.

Now we describe our main algorithm, *SEND*, that is stated formally in Algorithm 2. *SEND* calls *SEND-PATH*, which is formally described in Algorithm 3. In *SEND-PATH*, node s sends message m to node $\mathbf{r}$ through a path of unmarked nodes selected uniformly at random. However, *SEND-PATH* algorithm is vulnerable to corruption. Thus, with probability p_{call}, *SEND* calls *CHECK*, which detects if a message was corrupted in the previous call to *SEND-PATH*, with probability p_{detect}.

---

[4] When node s broadcasts m to a set of nodes S, it calls $BROADCAST(m, Q_1, S)$.

Algorithm 3. SEND-PATH$(m, \mathbf{r})$

Declarations: m is the message to be sent, and $\mathbf{r}$ is the destination.

1. Node $\mathbf{s}$ selects an unmarked node, q_1, in Q_1 uniformly at random.
2. Node $\mathbf{s}$ broadcasts to all nodes in Q_1 the message m and q_1's ID.
3. All nodes in Q_1 forward the message to node q_1.
4. For $i = 1, \ldots, \ell - 1$ do
    (a) Node q_i selects an unmarked node, q_{i+1}, in Q_{i+1} uniformly at random.
    (b) Node q_i sends m to node q_{i+1}.
5. Node q_ℓ in Q_ℓ broadcasts m to all nodes in Q_ℓ.
6. All nodes in Q_ℓ send m to node $\mathbf{r}$.

In *CHECK*, the message is propagated from the leftmost quorum to the rightmost quorum in the quorum path through a path of subquorums, where a subquorum is a subset of unmarked nodes selected uniformly at random in a quorum.

CHECK is implemented as either *CHECK1* (Algorithm 4) or *CHECK2* (Algorithm 5). For *CHECK1*, $p_{call} = 1/(\log \log n)^2$ and $p_{detect} = 1 - o(1)$, and it requires $O(\ell(\log \log n)^2 + \log n \cdot \log \log n)$ messages and has latency $O(\ell)$. For *CHECK2*, $p_{call} = 1/(\log^* n)^2$ and $p_{detect} \geq 1/2$, and it has message cost $O((\ell + \log n)(\log^* n)^2)$ and latency $O(\ell \log^* n)$.

Unfortunately, while *CHECK* can determine if a corruption occurred, it does not specify the location where the corruption occurred. Thus, if *CHECK* detects a corruption, *UPDATE* (Algorithm 6) is called. When *UPDATE* is called, it identifies two neighboring quorums Q_i and Q_{i+1} in the path, for some $1 \leq i < \ell$, such that at least one pair of nodes in these quorums is in conflict and at least one node in such pair is bad. Then quorums Q_i and Q_{i+1} mark these nodes and notify all other quorums that these nodes are in. All quorums in which these nodes are notify their neighboring quorums. Recall that if the half of nodes in any quorum have been marked, these nodes are set unmarked in all quorums they are in, and their neighboring quorums are notified.

Moreover, we use *BROADCAST* in *SEND-PATH* and *CHECK* to handle any accusation in *UPDATE* against node $\mathbf{s}$ or node $\mathbf{r}$. In *SEND-PATH* (or *CHECK*), we make node $\mathbf{s}$ broadcast the message to all nodes in Q_1 that forward the message to the selected unmarked node (or subquorum) in Q_1; and when the message is propagated to the selected unmarked node (or subquorum) in Q_ℓ, the message is broadcasted to all nodes in Q_ℓ.

Our model does not directly consider concurrency. In a real system, concurrent calls to UPDATE that overlap at a single quorum may allow the adversary to achieve multiple corruptions at the cost of a single marked bad node. However, this does not effect correctness, and, in practice, this issue can be avoided by serializing concurrent calls to SEND. For simplicity of presentation, we leave the concurrency aspect out of this paper.

Throughout this paper, we let U_i be the set of unmarked nodes in Q_i, and we let $|U_i|$ be the number of nodes in U_i, for $1 \leq i \leq \ell$.

2.2   CHECK1

Algorithm 4. CHECK1$(m, \mathbf{r})$

Initialization: let the subquorums $S_1, S_2, ..., S_\ell$ be initially empty.

1. Node s constructs R to be an ℓ by $|Q_{max}|$ by $\log \log n$ array of random numbers, where $|Q_{max}|$ is the maximum size of any quorum and $\log \log n$ is the size of any subquorum. Note that $R[j, k]$ is a multiset of $\log \log n$ numbers selected uniformly at random with replacement between 1 and k.
2. Node s sets m' to be a message consisting of m, $\mathbf{r}$, and R.
3. Node s broadcasts m' to all nodes in Q_1.
4. The nodes in Q_1 calculate the nodes of S_1 using the numbers in $R[1, |U_1|]$ to index U_1's nodes sorted by their IDs.
5. The nodes in Q_1 send m' to the nodes of S_1.
6. For $j \leftarrow 1, \ldots, \ell - 1$ do
    (a) The nodes of S_j calculate the nodes of S_{j+1} using the numbers in $R[j + 1, |U_{j+1}|]$ to index U_{j+1}'s nodes sorted by their IDs.
    (b) The nodes of S_j send m' to all nodes of S_{j+1}.
7. The nodes of S_ℓ broadcast m' to all nodes in Q_ℓ.

Note that: throughout *CHECK1*, if a node receives inconsistent messages or fails to receive an expected message, then it initiates a call to *UPDATE*.

Now we describe *CHECK1* that is stated formally as Algorithm 4. *CHECK1* is a simpler *CHECK* procedure compared to *CHECK2*, and, although it has a worse asymptotic message cost, it performs well in practice.

In *CHECK1*, each subquorum S_i has $\log \log n$ nodes that are chosen uniformly at random with replacement from the nodes in U_i in the quorum path, for $1 \leq i \leq \ell$.

First, node s broadcasts the message to all nodes in Q_1, which send the message to the nodes of S_1. Then the nodes of S_1 forward this message to the nodes of S_ℓ through a path of subquorums in the quorum path via all-to-all communication. Once the nodes in S_ℓ receive the message, they broadcast this message to all nodes in Q_ℓ. Further, if any node receives inconsistent messages or fails to receive an expected message, it initiates a call to *UPDATE*.

Now we show that if the message was corrupted during the last call to *SEND-PATH*, the probability that *CHECK1* fails to detect a corruption is $o(1)$ when $\ell = O(\log n)$.

Lemma 1. *If $\ell = O(\log n)$, then CHECK1 fails to detect any message corruption with probability $o(1)$.*

Proof. *CHECK1* succeeds in detecting the message corruption if every subquorum has at least one good node. We know that at least $1/2$-fraction of the nodes in any quorum are unmarked, then the probability that an unmarked bad node is selected uniformly at random is at most $1/4$. Thus the probability of any subquorum having only bad nodes is at most $(1/4)^{\log \log n} = 1/\log^2 n$. Union-bounding over all ℓ subquorums, the probability of *CHECK1* failing is at most $\ell/\log^2 n$. For $\ell = O(\log n)$, the probability that *CHECK1* fails is $o(1)$.   □

2.3 CHECK2

Algorithm 5. CHECK2$(m, \mathbf{r})$

Initializations: node s generates public/private key pair k_p, k_s to be used in this procedure; also let the subquorums $S_1, S_2, ..., S_\ell$ be initially empty.

for $i \leftarrow 1, ..., 4\log^* n$ do

1. Node s constructs R to be an ℓ by $|Q_{max}|$ array of random numbers, where $|Q_{max}|$ is the maximum size of any quorum. Note that $R[j, k]$ is a uniformly random number between 1 and k.

2. Node s sets m' to be m, k_p, $\mathbf{r}$, and R signed by k_s.

3. Node s broadcasts m' to all nodes in Q_1.

4. The nodes in Q_1 calculate the node, $x_1 \in U_1$, to be added to S_1 using the number $R[1, |U_1|]$ to index U_1's nodes sorted by their IDs.

5. The nodes in Q_1 send m' to the nodes of S_1.

6. For $j \leftarrow 1, ..., \ell - 1$ do
   (a) All i nodes in S_j calculate the node, $x_{j+1} \in U_{j+1}$, to be added to S_{j+1} using the number $R[j + 1, |U_{j+1}|]$ to index U_{j+1}'s nodes sorted by their IDs.
   (b) The nodes in S_j send m' to node x_{j+1}.
   (c) Node x_{j+1} sends m' to all the nodes in S_{j+1}.

7. The nodes in S_ℓ broadcast m' to all nodes in Q_ℓ.

end for

Note that: throughout this procedure, if a node has previously received k_p, then it verifies each subsequent message with it; also if a node receives inconsistent messages or fails to receive and verify an expected message, then it initiates a call to *UPDATE*.

In this section, we describe *CHECK2* algorithm, which is stated formally as Algorithm 5. Firstly, node s generates a public/private key pair k_p, k_s to let the nodes verify any message received. Then *CHECK2* runs for $4\log^* n$ rounds, and has a subset $S_j \subset U_j$ for each quorum Q_j in the quorum path, for $1 \leq j \leq \ell$. Every S_j is an incremental subquorum, where each S_j is initially empty; and in each round, an unmarked node, x_j, is selected uniformly at random from all nodes in U_j and is added to S_j, for all $1 \leq j \leq \ell$.

In each round, node s broadcasts the message to all nodes in Q_1, which forward such message to the nodes of S_1. Then for all $1 \leq j < \ell$, all nodes in S_j send the message to node x_{j+1}, which forwards the message to all nodes in S_{j+1}. Finally, all nodes in S_ℓ broadcast the message to all nodes in Q_ℓ.

Note that if any node receives inconsistent messages or fails to receive and verify any expected message in any round, it initiates a call to *UPDATE*.

An example run of *CHECK2* is illustrated in Figure 1. In this figure, there is a column for each quorum in the quorum path and a row for each round of *CHECK2*. For a given row and column, there is a G or B in that position depending on whether the node selected in that particular round and that particular quorum is good (G) or bad (B).

Recall that the adversary knows *CHECK2* algorithm, but in any round, the adversary does not know which nodes will be selected to participate for any subsequent round. The adversary's strategy is to maintain an interval of bad nodes in each row to corrupt (or drop) the message so that *CHECK2* will not be able to detect the corruption.

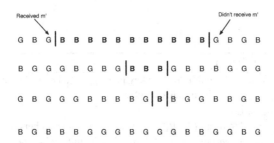

Fig. 1. Example run of *CHECK2*

In Figure 1, the intervals maintained by the adversary are outlined by a left and a right bar in each row; where the best interest of the adversary is to maintain the longest interval of bad nodes in the first row. The left bar in each row specifies the rightmost subquorum in which there is some good node that receives m'. The right bar in each row specifies the leftmost subquorum in which there is some good node that does not receive m'.

Note that, as rounds progress, the left bar can never move leftwards, because a node that has already received k_p will call *UPDATE* unless it receives messages signed with k_p for all subsequent rounds. Note further that the right bar can never move rightwards, since the nodes of each subset S_j send m' to the node x_{j+1}, which forwards such message to all nodes that are currently in S_{j+1}, for $1 \leq j < \ell$. Finally, when these two bars meet, a corruption is detected.

Intuitively, the reason *CHECK2* requires only $4 \log^* n$ rounds is because of a probabilistic result on the maximum length run in a sequence of coin tosses. In particular, if we have a coin that takes on value "B" with probability at most $1/4$, and value "G" with probability at least $3/4$, and we toss it x times, then the expected length of the longest run of B's is $\log x$. Thus, if in some round, the distance between the left bar and the right bar is x, we expect in the next round this distance will shrink to $\log x$. Intuitively, we might expect that, if the quorum path is of length ℓ, then $O(\log^* \ell)$ rounds will suffice before the distance shrinks to 0. This intuition is formalized in Lemmas 2 and 3 of Section 3.

In contrast to *CHECK1*, even though all nodes in column 9 are bad in Figure 1, *CHECK2* algorithm handles this case since the good node in row 3 and column 10 receives the message m'.

2.4   UPDATE

When a message corruption occurs and *CHECK* detects this corruption, *UPDATE* is called. Now the task of *UPDATE* is to 1) determine the location in which the corruption occurred; 2) mark the nodes that are in conflict. The *UPDATE* algorithm is described formally as Algorithm 6. When *UPDATE* starts, all nodes in each quorum in the quorum path are notified.

To determine the location in which the corruption occurred, each node previously involved in *SEND-PATH* or *CHECK* broadcasts to all nodes in its quorum and the

---

Algorithm 6. *UPDATE*

---

1. The node x in a quorum Q' making the call to *UPDATE* broadcasts this fact to all nodes in Q' along with all the messages that x has received during this call to *SEND*. The nodes in Q' verify that x received inconsistent messages before proceeding.
2. The quorum Q' propagates the fact that a call to *UPDATE* is occurring, via all-to-all communication, to all quorums $Q_1, Q_2, \ldots, Q_\ell$.
3. Each node involved in the last call to *SEND-PATH* or *CHECK*, except node s and node r, compiles all messages they have received (and from whom) in that last call, and broadcasts all these messages to all nodes in its quorum and the neighboring quorums.
4. Each node involved in the last call to *SEND-PATH*, except node s and node r, broadcasts all messages they have sent (and to whom) in that last call, to all nodes in its quorum and the neighboring quorums.
5. A node v is *in conflict* with a node u if:
   (a) node u was scheduled to send a message to node v at some point in the last call to *SEND-PATH* or *CHECK*; and
   (b) node v does not receive an expected message from node u in step 3 or step 4, or node v receives a message in step 3 or step 4 that is different than the message that it has received from node u in the last call to *SEND-PATH* or *CHECK*.
6. For each pair of nodes, (u, v), that are in conflict in (Q_k, Q_{k+1}), for $1 \leq k < \ell$:
   (a) node v sends a *conflict* message "(u,v)" to all nodes in Q_v,
   (b) each node in Q_v forwards this conflict message to all nodes in Q_v and all nodes in Q_u,
   (c) quorum Q_u (or Q_v) sends the conflict message to all other quorums that node u (or v) is in, and
   (d) each quorum that node u or node v is in sends such conflict message to its neighboring quorums.
7. Each node that receives this conflict message mark the nodes u and v.
8. If the half of nodes in any quorum have been marked, they are set unmarked in all quorums these nodes are in, and their neighboring quorums are notified.

---

neighboring quorums all messages they have received in the previous call to *SEND-PATH* or *CHECK*. Moreover, to announce the unmarked nodes that are selected uniformly at random in the last call to *SEND-PATH*, every node involved in the last call to *SEND-PATH*, broadcasts all messages they have sent (and to whom) in such call, to all nodes in its quorum and the neighboring quorums.

We say that a node v is *in conflict* with a node u if 1) node u was scheduled to send a message to node v at some point in the previous call to *SEND-PATH* or *CHECK*; and 2) node v does not receive an expected message from node u in this call to *UPDATE*, or node v receives a message in this *UPDATE* that is different than the message that it has received from node u in the previous call to *SEND-PATH* or *CHECK*.

For each pair of nodes, (u, v), that are in conflict in quorums (Q_k, Q_{k+1}) for $1 \leq k < \ell$, these two quorums send a *conflict* message "(u,v)" to all quorums in which node u or node v is and to all neighboring quorums to mark these nodes. Recall that if the half of nodes in any quorum are marked, this quorum notifies all other quorums in which these nodes are via all-to-all communication to unmark such nodes, and their neighboring quorums are notified as well.

3   Analysis

In this section, we prove the lemmas required for Theorem 1. Throughout this section, *SEND-PATH* calls *CHECK2*. Also we let all logarithms be base 2.

Lemma 2. *When a coin is tossed x times independently given that each coin has a tail with probability at most $1/4$, then the probability of having any substring of length $\max(1, \log x)$ being all tails is at most $1/2$.*

Proof. The probability of a specific substring of length $\log x$ being all tails is

$$\left(\frac{1}{4}\right)^{\log x} = \frac{1}{x^2}.$$

Union bounding over all possible substrings of length $\log x$, then the probability of any all-tailed substring existing is at most $x\frac{1}{x^2}$; or equivalently, for $x \geq 2$, $\frac{1}{x} \leq \frac{1}{2}$; and for $x = 1$, the probability of having a substring of $\max(1, \log x)$ tail is trivially $1/4$.   □

The next lemma shows that the algorithm *CHECK2* catches corruptions with probability at least $1/2$.

Lemma 3. *Assume some node selected uniformly at random in the last call to SEND-PATH has corrupted a message. Then when the algorithm CHECK2 is called, with probability at least $1/2$, some node will call UPDATE.*

Lemma 4. *If some node selected uniformly at random in the last call to SEND-PATH has corrupted a message, then the algorithm UPDATE will identify a pair of neighboring quorums Q_j and Q_{j+1}, for some $1 \leq j < \ell$, such that at least one pair of nodes in these quorums is in conflict and at least one node in such pair is bad.*

Proof. First we show that if a pair of nodes x and y is in conflict, then at least one of them is bad. Assume not. Then both x and y are good. Then node x would have truthfully reported what it received; any message that x received would have been sent directly to y; and y would have truthfully reported what it received from x. But this is a contradiction, since for x and y to be in conflict, y must have reported that it received from x something different than what x reported receiving.

Now consider the case where a selected unmarked bad node corrupted a message in the last call to *SEND-PATH*. By the definition of corruption, there must be two good nodes q_j and q_k such that $j < k$ and q_j received the message m' sent by node **s**, and q_k did not. We now show that some pair of nodes between q_j and q_k will be in conflict. Assume this is not the case. Then for all x, where $j \leq x < k$, nodes q_x and q_{x+1} are not in conflict. But then, since node q_j received the message m', and there are no pairs of nodes in conflict, it must be the case that the node q_k received the message m'. This is a contradiction. Thus, *UPDATE* will find two nodes that are in conflict, and at least one of them will be bad.

Now we prove that at least one pair of nodes is found to be in conflict as a result of calling *UPDATE*. Assume that no pair of nodes is in conflict. Then for every pair of nodes x and y, such that x was scheduled to send a message to y during any round i of

CHECK2, x and y must have reported that they received the same message in round i. In particular, this implies via induction, that for every round i, for all j, where $1 \leq j \leq \ell$, all nodes in the sets S_j must have broadcasted that they received the message m' that was initially sent by node s in round i. But if this is the case, the node x that initially called *UPDATE* would have received no inconsistent messages. This is a contradiction since in such a case, node x would have been unsuccessful in trying to initiate a call to *UPDATE*. Thus, some pair of nodes must be found to be in conflict, and at least one of them is bad.   □

The next lemma bounds the number of times that *UPDATE* must be called before all bad nodes are marked.

Lemma 5. *UPDATE is called at most $3t/2$ times before all bad nodes are marked.*

Proof. By Lemma 4, if a message corruption occurred in the last call to *SEND-PATH*, and is caught by *CHECK2*, then *UPDATE* is called. *UPDATE* identifies at least one pair of nodes that are in conflict.

Now let g be the number of good nodes that are marked, and let b be the number of bad nodes that are marked. Also let $f(g,b) = b - g/3$.

For each corruption caught, at least one bad node is marked, and so $f(g,b)$ increases by at least $2/3$ since b increases by at least 1 and g increases by at most 1. When a $1/2$-fraction of nodes in any quorum Q of size $|Q|$ are unmarked, $f(g,b)$ further increases by at least 0 since g decreases by at least $\frac{3|Q|}{8}$ and b decreases by at most $\frac{|Q|}{8}$.

Hence, $f(g,b)$ is monotonically increasing by at least $2/3$ for each corruption caught. When all bad nodes are marked, $f(g,b) \leq t$. Therefore, after at most $3t/2$ calls to *UPDATE*, all bad nodes are marked.   □

4 Empirical Results

4.1 Setup

In this section, we empirically compare the message cost and the fraction of messages corrupted of two algorithms via simulation. The first algorithm we simulate is *no-self-healing* algorithm from [24]. This algorithm has no self-healing properties, and simply uses all-to-all communication between quorums that are connected in a butterfly network. The second algorithm is *self-healing*, wherein we apply our self-healing algorithm in the butterfly networks using *CHECK1*.

In our experiments, we consider two butterfly network sizes: $n = 14{,}116$ and $n = 30{,}509$, where $\ell = \lfloor \log n \rfloor - 2$, the quorum size is $\lfloor 4 \log n \rfloor$ and the subquorum size is $\lfloor \log \log n \rfloor$. Moreover, we do our experiments for several fractions of bad nodes such as f equal to $1/8, 1/16, 1/32$ and $1/64$, where $f = t/n$.

Our simulations consist of a sequence of calls to *SEND* over the network, given a pair of nodes s, r, chosen uniformly at random, such that node s sends a message to node r. We simulate an adversary who chooses at the beginning of each simulation a fixed number of nodes to control uniformly at random without replacement. Our adversary attempts to corrupt messages between nodes whenever possible. Aside from attempting to corrupt messages, the adversary performs no other attacks.

4.2   Results

The results of our experiments are shown in Figures 2 and 3. Our results highlight two strengths of our self-healing algorithms (*self-healing*) when compared to algorithms without self-healing (*no-self-healing*). First, the message cost per *SEND* decreases as the total number of calls to *SEND* increases, as illustrated in Figure 2. Second, for a fixed number of calls to *SEND*, the message cost per *SEND* decreases as the total number of bad nodes decreases, as shown in Figure 2 as well. In particular, when there are no bad nodes, *self-healing* has dramatically less message cost than *no-self-healing*.

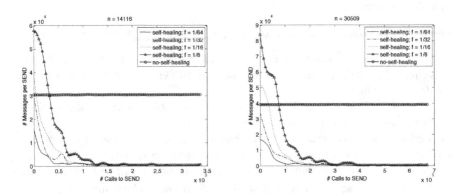

Fig. 2. # Messages per *SEND* versus # calls to *SEND*, for $n = 14,116$ and $n = 30,509$

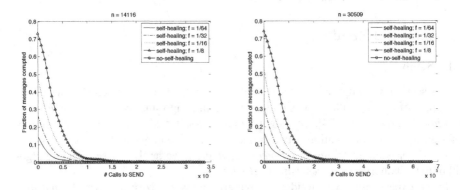

Fig. 3. Fraction of messages corrupted versus # calls to *SEND*, for $n = 14,116$ and $n = 30,509$

Figure 2 shows that for $n = 14,116$, the number of messages per SEND for *no-self-healing* is 30,516; and for *self-healing*, it is 525. Hence, the message cost is reduced by a factor of 58. Also for $n = 30,509$, the number of messages per SEND for *no-self-healing* is 39,170; and for *self-healing*, it is 562; which implies that the message cost is reduced by a factor of 70.

In Figure 3, *no-self-healing* has 0 corruptions; however, for *self-healing*, the fraction of messages corrupted per *SEND* decreases as the total number of calls to *SEND* increases. Also for a fixed number of calls to *SEND*, the fraction of messages corrupted per *SEND* decreases as the total number of bad nodes decreases.

Furthermore, in Figure 3, for each network, given the size and the fraction of bad nodes, if we integrate the corresponding curve, we get the total number of times that a message can be corrupted in calls to *SEND* in this network. These experiments show that the total number of message corruptions is at most $3t(\log \log n)^2$.

5   Conclusion and Future Work

We have presented algorithms that can significantly reduce communication cost in attack-resistant peer-to-peer networks. The price we pay for this improvement is the possibility of message corruption. In particular, if there are $t \leq n/8$ bad nodes in the network, our algorithm allows $O(t(\log^* n)^2)$ message transmissions to be corrupted in expectation.

Many problems remain. First, it seems unlikely that the smallest number of corruptions allowable by an attack-resistant algorithm with optimal message complexity is $O(t(\log^* n)^2)$. Can we improve this to $O(t)$ or else prove a non-trivial lower bound? Second, can we apply techniques in this paper to problems more general that enabling secure communication? For example, can we create self-healing algorithms for distributed *computation* with Byzantine faults? Finally, can we optimize constants and make use of heuristic techniques in order to significantly improve our algorithms' empirical performance?

References

1. Boman, I., Saia, J., Abdallah, C.T., Schamiloglu, E.: Brief announcement: Self-healing algorithms for reconfigurable networks. In: Datta, A.K., Gradinariu, M. (eds.) SSS 2006. LNCS, vol. 4280, pp. 563–565. Springer, Heidelberg (2006)
2. Saia, J., Trehan, A.: Picking up the pieces: Self-healing in reconfigurable networks. In: IEEE International Symposium on Parallel and Distributed Processing, IPDPS 2008, pp. 1–12 (2008)
3. Hayes, T., Rustagi, N., Saia, J., Trehan, A.: The forgiving tree: a self-healing distributed data structure. In: PODC 2008, pp. 203–212 (2008)
4. Hayes, T.P., Saia, J., Trehan, A.: The forgiving graph: a distributed data structure for low stretch under adversarial attack. In: PODC 2009, pp. 121–130 (2009)
5. Pandurangan, G., Trehan, A.: Xheal: localized self-healing using expanders. In: PODC 2011, pp. 301–310 (2011)
6. Das Sarma, A., Trehan, A.: Edge-preserving self-healing: keeping network backbones densely connected. In: 2012 IEEE Conference on Computer Communications Workshops (INFOCOM WKSHPS), pp. 226–231 (2012)
7. Fiat, A., Saia, J.: Censorship resistant peer-to-peer networks. Theory of Computing 3(1), 1–23 (2007)
8. Hildrum, K., Kubiatowicz, J.D.: Asymptotically efficient approaches to fault-tolerance in peer-to-peer networks. In: Fich, F.E. (ed.) DISC 2003. LNCS, vol. 2848, pp. 321–336. Springer, Heidelberg (2003)

9. Naor, M., Wieder, U.: A simple fault tolerant distributed hash table. In: Kaashoek, M.F., Stoica, I. (eds.) IPTPS 2003. LNCS, vol. 2735, pp. 88–97. Springer, Heidelberg (2003)

10. Scheideler, C.: How to spread adversarial nodes? rotate! In: STOC 2005 (2005) 704–713

11. Fiat, A., Saia, J., Young, M.: Making chord robust to byzantine attacks. In: Brodal, G.S., Leonardi, S. (eds.) ESA 2005. LNCS, vol. 3669, pp. 803–814. Springer, Heidelberg (2005)

12. Awerbuch, B., Scheideler, C.: Towards a scalable and robust dht. Theory of Computing Systems 45(2), 234–260 (2009)

13. King, V., Lonargan, S., Saia, J., Trehan, A.: Load balanced scalable byzantine agreement through quorum building, with full information. In: Aguilera, M.K., Yu, H., Vaidya, N.H., Srinivasan, V., Choudhury, R.R. (eds.) ICDCN 2011. LNCS, vol. 6522, pp. 203–214. Springer, Heidelberg (2011)

14. Frisanco, T.: Optimal spare capacity design for various protection switching methods in atm networks. In: ICC 1997 Montreal, vol. 1, pp. 293–298 (1997)

15. Iraschko, R., MacGregor, M., Grover, W.: Optimal capacity placement for path restoration in stm or atm mesh-survivable networks. IEEE/ACM Transactions on Networking 6(3), 325–336 (1998)

16. Murakami, K., Kim, H.: Comparative study on restoration schemes of survivable atm networks. In: INFOCOM 1997, vol. 1, pp. 345–352 (1997)

17. Van Caenegem, B., Wauters, N., Demeester, P.: Spare capacity assignment for different restoration strategies in mesh survivable networks. In: Communications, ICC 1997 Montreal, vol. 1, pp. 288–292 (1997)

18. Xiong, Y., Mason, L.: Restoration strategies and spare capacity requirements in self-healing atm networks. IEEE/ACM Transactions on Networking 7(1), 98–110 (1999)

19. Saia, J., Young, M.: Reducing communication costs in robust peer-to-peer networks. Information Processing Letters 106(4), 152–158 (2008)

20. Young, M., Kate, A., Goldberg, I., Karsten, M.: Practical robust communication in dhts tolerating a byzantine adversary. In: ICDCS 2010, pp. 263–272 (2010)

21. Datar, M.: Butterflies and peer-to-peer networks. In: Möhring, R.H., Raman, R. (eds.) ESA 2002. LNCS, vol. 2461, pp. 310–322. Springer, Heidelberg (2002)

22. Young, M., Kate, A., Goldberg, I., Karsten, M.: Towards practical communication in byzantine-resistant dhts. IEEE/ACM Transactions on Networking 21(1), 190–203 (2013)

23. Kate, A., Goldberg, I.: Distributed key generation for the internet. In: ICDCS 2009, pp. 119–128 (2009)

24. Fiat, A., Saia, J.: Censorship resistant peer-to-peer content addressable networks. In: SODA 2002, pp. 94–103 (2002)

Leader Election and Centers and Medians in Tree Networks

Ajoy K. Datta and Lawrence L. Larmore

Department of Computer Science, University of Nevada Las Vegas, USA

Abstract. We give a *weak leader election* algorithm, which elects a leader or two neighboring co-leaders of an anonymous tree network, as well as give distributed algorithms for finding centers and medians of anonymous tree networks. All algorithms are in the comparison model, are self-stabilizing and silent under the unfair daemon. Each of the three problems is solved in $O(Diam)$ rounds with step complexity $O(n \cdot Diam)$. The per process space complexity is $O(1)$ for weak leader election, $O(\log Diam)$ for finding centers, and $O(\log n)$ for finding medians. These are the minimum possible space complexities for self-stabilizing silent algorithms. The main innovation is the introduction of the constant space implementation of parent pointers using the finite Abelian group $\mathbb{Z}_5$.

Keywords: Self-stabilization, anonymous network, tree network, leader election, center, median.

1 Introduction

In this paper, we consider three problems on distributed networks with a tree topology; leader election, center finding, and median finding. We give silent self-stabilizing [10] algorithms for all three problems. Since leader election is impossible in an anonymous tree with the unfair daemon, we solve the weak version, where we elect either a leader or two neighboring processes as *co-leaders*.

Centers and Medians. In any connected graph G, the *eccentricity* of a node x is defined to be the maximum distance from x to any other node, while the *weight* of x can be defined to be the sum of the distances from x to all other nodes. A node x is a *center* of G if it has minimum eccentricity, and is a *median* of G if it has minimum weight. A tree graph has either one or two centers and either one or two medians. If there are two centers (or two medians) in a tree, those two nodes are neighbors.

1.1 Related Work

Antonoiu and Srimani have published three papers on these problems. In [1], they give a distributed leader election algorithm for trees. In [2], they give a distributed algorithm for finding the centers of a tree network, while in [3], they

T. Higashino et al. (Eds.): SSS 2013, LNCS 8255, pp. 113–132, 2013.

give a distributed algorithm for finding the medians of a tree network. All three algorithms are self-stabilizing and silent, use the composite model of atomicity, and do not assume that the processes have unique IDs. They do not use the unfair daemon; they assume that no two neighboring processes can be simultaneously selected. Their daemon is thus equivalent to the *central* daemon, which selects one enabled process at each step. This daemon allows an algorithm to break symmetry. For example, the algorithm of [1] computes a unique leader. All three of their algorithms assume existence of known upper bound C on the size of the network, and use space complexity $\Theta(\log C)$ per process.

In [4], Xu and Srimani give a distributed algorithm for leader election in an anonymous tree network, which takes $O(n^4)$ steps and uses $O(\log n)$ space per process, using the composite model. Again, the daemon is not allowed to select adjacent processes simultaneously. In [5], Blair and Manne give algorithms for leader election, and center and median finding for a tree network with unique IDs. They use the composite model, assume the unfair daemon, and use $O(\delta_x \log n)$ bits for each process x, where δ_x is the degree of x. Their algorithm for leader election requires $O(n^2)$ steps.

In [6], Bruell *et al.* give silent self-stabilizing algorithms for center and median finding in an anonymous tree network, in the composite model using the central daemon. Their space complexity is $O(\log Diam)$ bits per process for finding centers and $O(\log n)$ for finding medians. Both algorithms take $O(Diam)$ rounds. Their step complexity is $O(n^3 + n^2 c_h)$ for finding centers, and $O(n^3 c_s)$ for finding medians, where c_h, c_s are the maximum initial values of certain variables in the algorithm.

In [9], Chepoi *et al.* explore the problems of center and median finding in more general classes of graphs.

1.2   Contributions

We give four self-stabilizing silent distributed algorithms on an anonymous tree network T of size n and diameter $Diam$. The first, ATWLE, solves the weak leader election problem, and takes $O(Diam)$ rounds. ATWLE is used as a module of the other three algorithms, ATWLEU, ATC, and ATM, each of which takes $O(Diam)$ rounds, $O(n \cdot Diam)$ steps, and uses a $\mathbb{Z}_3$ *unison* similar to that of Boulinier [8]. The space complexity of ATWLEU is $O(1)$ per process, of ATC is $O(\log Diam)$ per process, and of ATM is $O(\log n)$ per process. These space complexities are asymptotically minimal for silent self-stabilizing algorithms for these problems on a tree.

During execution of ATWLE, each process, other than the leader or the co-leaders, chooses one of its neighbors to be its *parent*, so that the network becomes a rooted tree rooted at the leader or two rooted trees rooted at the co-leaders. In most published algorithms, the parent of a process x is encoded as a pointer which takes $\lceil \log_2 \delta_x \rceil$ bits to encode, where δ_x is the degree of x. We introduce a different technique, making use of a *tag* variable, which takes its value in the cyclic Abelian group $\mathbb{Z}_5$, utilizing only finite space in each process. If x, y are neighboring processes, x is a parent of y if $y.tag = x.tag + 1$ or $y.tag = x.tag + 2$.

We call this the $\mathbb{Z}_5$ *implementation* of the parent pointers. This innovation allows space complexity to be independent of degree.

We use $\mathbb{Z}_5$ instead of the simpler $\mathbb{Z}_3$, so that the tag values of neighboring processes, say x and y, can be changed arbitrarily many times while maintaining a parent child relation, as illustrated in Figure 2.

It is in step complexity that our algorithms are substantially better than prior published algorithms. The $\mathbb{Z}_3$ unison (synchronizer) forces each process to execute approximately the same number of times, yielding our upper bound on the number of steps. We suggest that if the unison were added to the algorithms of [6], the step complexity of each of those algorithms would also be $O(n \cdot Diam)$.

1.3   Outline of the Paper

In Section 2, we describe our model of computation. In Section 3, we give ATWLE, an algorithm for weak leader election in a tree network which takes $O(Diam)$ rounds. In Section 4, we give ATWLEU, a modification of ATWLE obtained by adding a $\mathbb{Z}_3$ unison. In Section 5, we give ATC, which finds the centers of a tree network, and which uses ATWLE as a module. In Section 6, we give ATC, which finds the medians of a tree network, and which also uses ATWLE as a module. Correctness of ATC and ATM is unaffected by the failure of ATWLE to guarantee a unique leader.

In Section 7, we give a proof supporting our claim that the space complexities of ATC and ATM are optimal for self-stabilizing silent algorithms. Section 8 concludes.

2   Preliminaries

We use the *composite* model of computation, and we assume an anonymous network of processes. Each process can read its own and its neighbors' registers, and can write only its own registers. A process x is *enabled* to execute a given action if the *guard* of that action, a Boolean function of the states of x and those of its neighbors, evaluates to true. At each step of a computation, if there is at least one enabled process, the scheduler (daemon) selects a set of enabled processes, and those processes each execute an action. We assume the *unfair* daemon; there is no requirement that it select any specific enabled process unless it is the only enabled process. We measure time both by steps and by *rounds*. A round is a minimal sequence of one or more steps during which every process that is enabled prior to the first of those steps executes or becomes neutralized at some step during the round. A distributed algorithm $\mathcal{A}$ is called *self-stabilizing* if there is a closed predicate, called *legitimacy*, such that every computation of $\mathcal{A}$ eventually satisfies that predicate. In addition, we say that $\mathcal{A}$ is *silent* if no computation of $\mathcal{A}$ has infinitely many steps.

2.1   Problem Definition

The *weak leader election problem* on T is defined by one output condition, namely that there will be some Boolean variable, which we call *is_leader*, which will eventually be true for either exactly one process, which we call the *leader*, or for exactly two neighboring processes, which we call the *co-leaders*. Any process, or pair of adjacent processes, could be elected. In this paper, we address the weak leader election problem for anonymous tree networks, as well as the center finding and median finding problems for those networks.

3   ATWLE

ATWLE (Anonymous Tree Weak Leader Election) is based on what we call *simple leader election*, or Simp_LE, a non-self-stabilizing composite model version of the leader election algorithm ST_to_Leader on a tree networks given by Lynch [7, p. 501]. ST_to_Leader assumes that processes have unique IDs, but Simp_LE assumes that processes are anonymous, and elects either a leader or two co-leaders.

Simp_LE. Starting with a tree where all nodes are unmarked, any unmarked node which has at most one unmarked neighbor marks itself, simultaneously choosing its unmarked neighbor, if any, to be its *parent*. Eventually, all nodes are marked. Those one node or two nodes without parents are the leaders.

ATWLE is a self-stabilizing version of Simp_LE, which works on an anonymous (*i.e.*, no UID) tree network. ATWLE uses constant space per process and is silent. ATWLE uses two innovations: the implementation of parent pointers using $\mathbb{Z}_5$ tags, and the top-down waves which increment these tags to permit additional processes to be marked. The round complexity of ATWLE is $O(Diam)$.

3.1   Overview of ATWLE

ATWLE uses an error-correction method to return a computation to what is essentially a clean start, if necessary, using an *error status* variable that has three possible values. ATWLE also uses a *tag* variable, which has five possible values, in each process to implement the parent pointers. Two additional bits are used to indicate whether a process is a leader and and whether the computation is finished. Thus, ATWLE needs $O(1)$ space per process.

Starting from an arbitrary configuration, the first phase of ATWLE is error correction, in which any process in an *erroneous* state initiates a contagious error-correction cycle. All processes execute this cycle, and eventually every process returns to a *clear* state, where it is free to execute the other phases of ATWLE.

The second phase of ATWLE consists of a convergecast *marking wave*, analogous to the marking wave of ST_to_Leader or Simp_LE. Each step of the marking wave causes two *adjustment* waves to be generated, as explained below. Because of asynchrony, the marking wave terminates at an arbitrary position in the tree, causing one or two processes to elect themselves leaders. Finally, a broadcast *finishing wave* informs all processes that a leader, or leaders, have been elected.

Figure 1 shows two possible executions of the marking phase of Simp_LE (or ATWLE) for the same tree. In the first step, all leaves mark themselves and choose their parents. In the first computation, A and C mark themselves in the second step, as shown in (c), and in the third step, B marks itself and becomes the leader, as shown in (d). An alternative computation is shown as the sequence (a), (b), (e), (f). In the second step, A is enabled but not selected. In the third step, both A and B mark themselves, and both become leaders.

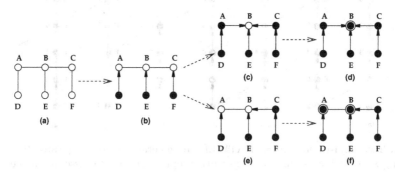

Fig. 1. Two possible computations of ST_to_Leader, or ATWLE, for the same tree. Only the marking wave is shown. Arrows indicate virtual pointers. Processes are named only for discussion purposes. Marked processes are solid dots, unmarked open dots. The two computations consist of (a), (b), (c), (d), in which B is elected leader, and (a), (b), (e), (f), in which A and B are elected leaders.

Adjustment Waves. The tag of a process is in $\mathbb{Z}_5$, and the difference of the tags of neighboring processes determines their relationship. A process x is a child of a neighbor y if the tag of x is equal to the tag of y plus 1 or 2. If x and y have equal tags, neither is a child of the other. It is this indeterminacy, *i.e.,* the fact that differences of 1 and 2 have the same meaning, that permits implementation of the top-down *adjustment waves* in the marked processes, which in turn permit additional processes to be marked.

Each time the bottom-up marking wave advances one level, two adjustment waves are generated. These waves are necessary in order to maintain the rule that all unmarked processes have tag zero. When a process x marks itself, x changes its tag from 0 to 1, initiating a *primary adjustment wave* during which the tag of every descendant of x is incremented. Either x then elects itself leader, or waits until the primary wave passes its children and then changes its tag to 2, initiating a *secondary adjustment wave* during which the tag of every descendant of x is incremented again. When ATWLE is finished, the tag of each leader is 1, and the tag of each child is the same as its parent's tag, plus 2.

Figure 2 illustrates the interaction between the single bottom-up *marking wave* and the adjustment waves. Each process increments its tag once each time it participates in a wave At the step from (a) to (b), C marks itself as part of the marking wave, incrementing its tag, and thus choosing B as its parent. This initiates a top-down primary adjustment wave, indicated by solid diagonal arrows in the figure. After the primary wave is out of the way, C initiates a *secondary adjustment wave*, in the step from (c) to (d), as indicated by the dashed diagonal arrows. Primary and secondary adjustment waves initiated by D and B are also shown.

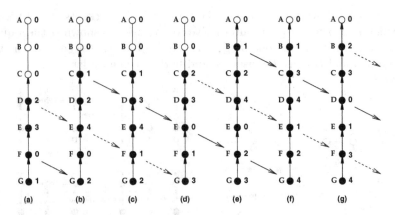

Fig. 2. Two adjustment waves of ATWLE are generated at each upward step of the marking wave. Columns illustrate consecutive configurations. Processes are named only for discussion purposes. Solid headed arrows are virtual pointers. Marked processes are solid dots, unmarked open dots. Tag values in $\mathbb{Z}_5$ are shown.

3.2   Variables of ATWLE

1. $x.es \in \mathbb{Z}_3$, the *error status* of x; a value of 0 means that there is no error.
2. $x.marked$, Boolean, meaning that x is *marked*. If $\neg\, x.marked$, we say x is *unmarked*.
3. $x.tag \in \mathbb{Z}_5$, the *tag value* of x.
4. $x.is\_leader$, Boolean.
5. $x.finished$, Boolean.

$\mathbb{Z}_3 = \{0,1,2\}$ and $\mathbb{Z}_5 = \{0,1,2,3,4\}$ are the cyclic Abelian groups of orders 3 and 5, respectively.

3.3   Functions of ATWLE

These functions can be computed by any process x.

1. $N(x)$ is the set of *neighbors* of x, and $U(x) = N(x) \cup \{x\}$, the *neighborhood* of x.
2. $\Delta\_tag(x,y) = x.tag - y.tag \in \mathbb{Z}_5$, where subtraction is computed modulo 5.
3. $Chldrn(x) = \{y \in N(x) : \Delta\_tag(y,x) \in \{1,2\}\}$.
4. $Parents(x) = \{y \in N(x) : \Delta\_tag(y,x) \in \{3,4\}\} = \{y \in N(x) : x \in Chldrn(y)\}$.
5. $Parent(x) \in N(x) \cup \{\bot\}$, the *parent* of x. If $Parents(x)$ consists of exactly one process, that process is $Parent(x)$. Otherwise, $Parent(x) = \bot$, *i.e.*, undefined.
6. $Is\_Child(x) \equiv Parent(x) \neq \bot$, Boolean.
7. $Finished(x) \equiv x.is\_leader \vee (Parent(x).finished \wedge (x.tag = 2 + Parent(x).tag))$, Boolean.

8. $Clean(x) \equiv (x.es = 0) \wedge (x.tag = 0) \wedge \neg x.marked \wedge \neg x.is\_leader \wedge \neg x.finished$, Boolean.

9. $Valid(x)$, Boolean, which is the conjunction of the following list of conditions.

   (a) $\neg x.marked \implies x.tag = 0$. The tag value of an unmarked process must be zero.

   (b) $|Parents(x)| \leq 1$. A process can have at most one parent.

   (c) $x.marked \implies 1 + |Chldrn(x)| \geq |N(x)|$. All neighbors but at most one of a marked process must be its children.

   (d) $x.marked \wedge \neg y.marked \wedge (y \in N(x)) \implies y = Parent(x)$. An unmarked neighbor of a marked process must be its parent.

   (e) $x.is\_leader \implies x.marked$. A leader must be marked.

   (f) $x.is\_leader \implies Parents(x) = \emptyset$. A leader cannot be the child of another process.

   (g) $x.finished \implies Finished(x)$. No "false positive" is permitted for this Boolean variable.

10. $Error(x) \equiv (\neg Valid(x) \wedge (\forall y \in U(x) y.es = 0)) \vee (\neg Clean(x) \wedge ((x.es = 1) \vee (\exists y \in U(x) y.es = 2)))$, Boolean, x is *erroneous*.

11. $Can\_Reset(x) \equiv Error(x) \vee (\exists y \in N(x)(y.es = 1))$, Boolean, x can initiate its error-correction cycle.

12. $Can\_Inc\_Err\_St(x) \equiv (x.es \in \{1, 2\}) \wedge (\forall (y \in N(x)) (y.es - x.es \in \{0, 1\}))$, Boolean, x can continue its error-correction cycle. Subtraction is in $\mathbb{Z}_5$.

13. $Clear(x) \equiv Valid(x) \wedge (\forall y \in U(x) \; y.es = 0)$, Boolean.

The following functions are not used during execution of ATWLE, but are needed when ATWLE is used as a black box for ATC or ATM.

14. $Is\_Sole\_Leader(x) \equiv x.is\_leader \wedge (\forall y \in N(x) \; \neg y.is\_leader)$

15. $Is\_Co\text{-}Leader(x) \equiv x.is\_leader \wedge (\exists y \in N(x) \; y.is\_leader)$

16. $Co\text{-}Leader(x) = \begin{cases} y \text{ if } x.is\_leader \wedge y.is\_leader \wedge y \in N(x) \\ \bot \text{ otherwise.} \end{cases}$

   That is, $Co\text{-}Leader(x) = y$ if x and y are both leaders.

17. $Level(x)$, integer, the distance from x to the nearest leader.

3.4   Detailed Overview of ATWLE

Error Correction. The *error status* of a process x, written $x.es$, is 0 during any error-free computation. If any process has error status 0 and detects that the computation is faulty, it *resets* by executing Action A1, setting its error status to 1. In a flooding wave, all processes change their error status to 1, then to 2, then back to 0, by executing Action A1 once and then Action A2 twice, bringing every process to a clean state, effectively restarting the computation. The computation will subsequently be error-free.

At the top level, an error-free computation of ATWLE consists of a bottom-up wave which marks all processes. During execution of this wave, every process executes Action A3 exactly once. Election of the leader, or leaders, occurs when either one or two processes, noting that they are marked but have no parents, execute Action A5. A final, top-down, wave informs all processes that the computation is finished, as each process executes Action A6.

During the bottom-up wave, there are $O(Diam)$ top-down waves which adjust tag values of the marked processes. Each time a process x executes Action A3, it generates a *primary adjustment wave* during which all descendants of x increment their tags by executing Action A4. After that wave is "out of the way," x executes Action A4, initiating a *secondary adjustment wave*, during which all processes in T_x execute Action A4, once again incrementing their tag values. Thus, the marking of one process x gives rise to incrementation of all tags of processes in T_x by 2, unless x is a leader, in which case all tags are incremented by only 1.

Finishing. In order to facilitate the use of ATWLE as a "black box" in ATC and ATM, we introduce one additional flag which informs x that ATWLE is done, namely *x.finished*. The flag is set for each process in a top-down wave starting at the elected leader, or leaders. If *x.finished* = TRUE, it indicates not only that the leaders have been elected, but also that x will never again execute an action of ATWLE.

The following loop invariant holds at every step of a clean computation of ATWLE.

1. $\neg x.marked \implies x.tag = 0$, *i.e.*, the tag value of an unmarked process is 0.
2. The set of marked processes is the disjoint union of trees $T_1 \cup \ldots \cup T_k$, which we call the *marked trees*. Each marked tree is a rooted tree using virtual parent pointers. Let r_i be the root of T_i.
3. One of the following three conditions holds:
   (a) There is one marked tree which includes all processes.
   (b) There are two marked trees which together include all processes. The roots of these trees are neighbors.
   (c) There is at least one unmarked process. Each r_i has one unmarked neighbor, which is $Parent(r_i)$. No other member of T_i has a neighbor outside T_i. Thus, the unmarked processes form a connected subgraph of the network. Figure 3 shows an example of such a configuration.
4. If *x.finished* = TRUE, either *x.is_leader*, or $Parent(x).finished$ = TRUE and $\Delta\_tag(x, Parent(x)) = 2$.

When ATWLE halts, the following additional conditions hold for each x.

5. *x.finished* = TRUE.
6. $x.tag = 1 + 2 \cdot Level(x)$. Computation is in $\mathbb{Z}_5$.

Table 1 gives the actions of ATWLE. In this table, as in Tables 2, 3, and 4, the clauses of the guard of each action are written in the third column. The actual guard is the conjunction of those clauses.

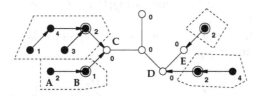

Fig. 3. Configuration satisfying the loop invariant. Marked processes are solid. Unmarked processes are open. Each marked tree is enclosed in a dashed polygon. Roots of the marked trees are doubly circled. Tag values are shown. Virtual parent pointers are indicated by arrows. Names of processes are for discussion purposes only. One or two of the unmarked processes will eventually be elected leaders.

Table 1. Actions of ATWLE for Process x

A1 priority 1	Reset	$Can\_Reset(x)$	$\longrightarrow$	$x.es \leftarrow 1$ $x.marked \leftarrow$ FALSE $x.tag \leftarrow 0$ $x.is\_leader \leftarrow$ FALSE $x.finished \leftarrow$ FALSE
A2 priority 1	Increment Error Status	$Can\_Inc\_Err\_St(x)$	$\longrightarrow$	$x.es \leftarrow x.es + 1$
A3 priority 2	Mark	$Clear(x)$ $\neg x.marked$ $\forall y \in Chldrn(x)(y.tag = 2)$ $\neg Is\_Child(x)$ $1 + |Chldrn(x)| \geq |N(x)|$	$\longrightarrow$	$x.marked \leftarrow$ TRUE $x.tag \leftarrow 1$
A4 priority 2	Increment Tag	$Clear(x)$ $x.marked$ $\forall y \in Chldrn(x)(y.tag = 2 + x.tag)$ $Is\_Child(x)$ $x.tag = 1 + Parent(x).tag$	$\longrightarrow$	$x.tag \leftarrow x.tag + 1$
A5 priority 2	Elect Myself Leader	$Clear(x)$ $x.marked$ $\forall y \in N(x)\ y.marked$ $\neg Is\_Child(x)$ $\neg x.is\_leader$	$\longrightarrow$	$x.is\_leader \leftarrow$ TRUE
A6 priority 2	Announce Election	$Clear(x)$ $Finished(x)$ $\neg x.finished$	$\longrightarrow$	$x.finished \leftarrow$ TRUE

Figure 3 shows an error-free configuration. Process C cannot execute Action A3 because $\Delta\_tag(B, C) \neq 2$, while B is unable to execute Action A4 because $\Delta\_tag(A, B) \neq 2$. A must execute first, then B can execute, then C. Process D is unable to execute Action A3 because $\Delta\_tag(E, D) \neq 2$. After E executes Action A3, D will be able to execute.

Figure 4 below shows the steps involved for one unmarked process, namely C in the figure, to be marked.

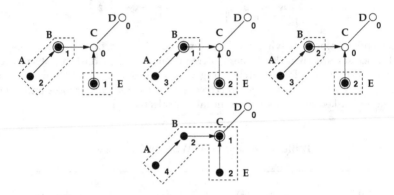

Fig. 4. A sequence of configurations illustrating growth of the marked forest. Names of processes are for discussion purposes only. Marked processes are solid dots, unmarked open dots. Marked subtrees are enclosed in dashed polygons, and the roots of those subtrees are doubly circled. The tag values of the processes are indicated, and virtual pointers are indicated by arrows. In the first step, A and E execute Action A4. In the second step, B executes A4. In the third step, A executes A4, and C executes Action A3, becoming marked and becoming the root of the new marked subtree.

Theorem 1. ATWLE *is silent and self-stabilizing on an anonymous tree network of diameter Diam, uses $O(1)$ space for each process, and halts within $O(Diam)$ rounds.*

Proof Sketch. Within $O(Diam)$ rounds, all errors have been eliminated; thereafter, Action A1 is not executed. The marking wave must move up $O(Diam)$ times, and each time it generates two $O(Diam)$-round adjustment waves. However, the adjustment waves are pipelined, and thus all adjustment waves take only $O(Diam)$ rounds.

To achieve the desired step complexity of $O(n \cdot Diam)$, we need each process to execute approximately the same number of times. To accomplish this goal, we modify ATWLE by introducing a *union* to obtain the algorithm ATWLEU in the next section.

4   ATWLEU

ATWLEU (Anonymous Weak Leader Election with a Unison) is essentially ATWLE together with a *synchronizer* to prevent processes from executing repeatedly while other processes languish.

ATWLEU uses a $\mathbb{Z}_3$-synchronizer, a unison in the spirit of [8]. In any computation of ATWLEU, regardless of length, all processes execute approximately equally often; more specifically, if processes x and y execute $t(x)$ and $t(y)$ times, respectively, during a computation, then $|t(x) - t(y)| \leq 2 \cdot dist(x, y)$. Consequently, the number of steps of any computation of ATWLEU cannot exceed n times the number of rounds plus $O(n \cdot Diam)$.

The variable $x.clck \in \mathbb{Z}_3$ increments at every action of x. We say that x is "ahead of" its neighbor y if $x.clck = 1 + y.clck$, and "behind" y if $y.clck = 1 + x.clck$. Otherwise, it is "even with" y. No process can execute any action of ATWLEU if it is ahead of any of its neighbors. The predicate $Can\_Tick(x)$ is true if x is not ahead of any neighbor, and the predicate $Must\_Tick(x)$ is true if $Can\_Tick(x)$ and x is behind some neighbor. A process x cannot execute any action of ATWLEU if $Can_Tick(x) = $ FALSE, and it is always enabled if $Must_Tick(x) = $ TRUE. In any computation of ATWLEU, the guards of Actions A1 through A6 are eventually all FALSE, and hence ATWLEU cannot further execute Action B1. After that, processes will continue to execute Action B2 until all processes are even with their neighbors, i.e., all values of $clck$ are the same. At that configuration, no process will be enabled.

The fundamental reason that the unison gives us a bound on the step complexity is that, during a computation of ATWLEU of $\Theta(Diam)$ rounds, each process executes $O(1)$ times, on the average, during each round. The actual detailed proof of this fact will be in the full paper.

4.1   Definition of ATWLEU

ATWLEU has the following variables and functions.

1. All the variables and functions of ATWLE.
2. The variable $x.clck \in \mathbb{Z}_3$.
3. $Enabled^{\mathrm{ATWLE}}(x)$, Boolean, meaning that x is enabled to execute some action of ATWLE.
4. $Can\_Tick(x) \equiv \forall y \in N(x)(y.clck - x.clck \in \{0, 1\})$, indicating that the unison can advance.
5. $Must\_Tick(x) \equiv Can\_Tick(x) \wedge (\exists y \in N(x)(y.clck - x.clck = 1))$, indicating that the unison can advance and that x has a neighbor whose clock is ahead of the clock of x.

Table 2. Actions of ATWLEU for Process x

B1	Emulate	$Enabled^{\mathrm{ATWLE}}(x)$	$\longrightarrow$	Action of ATWLE
priority 1	ATWLE	$Can\_Tick(x)$		$x.clck \leftarrow x.clck + 1$
B2	Must	$Must\_Tick(x)$	$\longrightarrow$	$x.clck \leftarrow x.clck + 1$
priority 2	Tick			

Theorem 2. ATWLEU *is silent and self-stabilizing on an anonymous tree network of size n and diameter Diam, takes $O(Diam)$ rounds and $O(n \cdot Diam)$ steps, and uses $O(1)$ space for each process.*

Proof Sketch: The proof that the round complexity is $O(Diam)$ is similar to the proof of Theorem 1. By the use of the $\mathbb{Z}_3$ unison, we can show that the difference between the numbers of executions of any two processes is $O(Diam)$. From that, it is possible to prove the upper bound on the number of steps.

5 ATC

The first phase of ATC (Anonymous Tree Center) consists of electing one or two leaders, using the algorithm ATWLE. No process can execute any other action of ATC until its *finished* flag is TRUE, indicating that there will be no further actions of ATWLE. Because of arbitrary initialization, *x.finished* could be true even if ATWLE has not converged. In this case, T will reset and ATWLE will start over and eventually converge. At that point, the other variables of ATC can have arbitrary values. The leaders elected by ATWLE are taken to be roots, making T a rooted tree or a *bi-rooted* tree, as defined in Section 5.1 below.

The second phase of ATC consists of three pipelined bottom-up waves. The first computes the *height* $H(x)$ of each process x, the length of the longest path from x to a leaf of T_x, while the second, which follows immediately, computes the secondary height, $H_2(x)$, which is the length of the second-longest path from x to a leaf of T_x which does not meet the longest path except at x. The third of those waves, which follows immediately after the second, computes the diameter of T_x for each process x, using Remarks 1 and 2. The third phase of ATC consists of a top-down wave, starting at the leaders, which tells every process the correct value of the diameter of T. The fourth and final phase is not a wave; each process determines whether it is a center by comparing its height to $Diam$ using the Remark 3.

All these phases, together, take only $O(Diam)$ rounds. Just as in ATWLEU, a $\mathbb{Z}_3$ synchronizer is used to ensure fairness, thus keeping the number of steps of ATC to $O(n \cdot Diam)$. The implementation of the synchronizer is identical to that of ATWLEU.

5.1 Heights and Secondary Heights

If S is any multiset of non-negative numbers, we define max $\_2(S)$ to be the *second largest* element of S, that is, max $\_2(S) = \max\{S \backslash \{\max(S)\}\}$. If $|S| < 2$, let max $\_2(S) = 0$.

In the following definitions, we let T be a rooted tree with root R.

- Let $Diam(T)$ be the diameter of T.
- Let $Level(x) = dist(x, \mathrm{R})$, for any $x \in T$, the *level* of x.
- If x is any node of T, let T_x be the subtree of T rooted at x.
- Let $H(x)$, the *height* of x, be the height of T_x, defined to be the length of the longest path from x to a leaf of T_x.

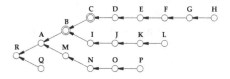

x	R	A	B	C	D	E	F	G	H	I	J	K	L	M	N	O	P	Q
H	8	7	6	5	4	3	2	1	0	3	2	1	0	3	2	1	0	0
H_2	1	4	4	0	0	0	0	0	0	0	0	0	0	0	0	0	0	0

Fig. 5. Table shows $H(x)$ and $H_2(x)$ for each node x in T, where R is the root. $Diam(T) = 11$, the maximum value of $H(x) + H_2(x)$, which is achieved for $x = $ A. Since $Diam(T)$ is odd, there are two co-centers, B and C, since $H(B) = \frac{Diam}{2} + \frac{1}{2}$ and $H(C) = \frac{Diam}{2} - \frac{1}{2}$. The co-centers are doubly circled.

- Let $H_2(x)$ be the *secondary height* of x, defined as follows. If x has fewer than two children, the secondary height is zero. Otherwise, pick a child y of x such that the height of x is one more than the height of y. The secondary height of x is one plus the maximum height of any child of x other than y.

ATC is driven by Remarks 1, 2, and 3.

Remark 1. If T is a rooted tree, then $Diam(T) = \max\{H(x) + H_2(x) : x \in T\}$.

We say that a tree graph T is a *bi-rooted tree* if there are two distinguished *root nodes*, R_1 and R_2, which are neighbors. In this case, we can write $T = T_1 \cup T_2$, where T_1 consists of all nodes closer to R_1 than to R_2, and T_2 is defined similarly. If $x \in T_i$, we define $Level(x)$, $H(x)$, $H_2(x)$, T_x, and $Chldrn(x)$ by considering T_i to be a rooted tree.

Remark 2. If T is a bi-rooted tree with roots R_1 and R_2, then

$$Diam(T) = \max\{1 + H(R_1) + H(R_2), \max\{H(x) + H_2(x) : x \in T\}\}$$

Remark 3. Let x be a process of a rooted or bi-rooted tree T of diameter d.
(a) If d is even, then T has one center, and x is the center of T if and only if $H(x) = \frac{d}{2}$.
(b) If d is odd, T has two centers; x is a center if and only if $H(x)$ equals either $\frac{d-1}{2}$ or $\frac{d+1}{2}$.

An example which illustrates Remark 1 and Remark 3(b) is illustrated in Figure 5.

5.2   Variables of ATC

1. All the variables of ATWLE.
2. $x.clck \in \mathbb{Z}_3$, the current value of the unison.
3. $x.height$, integer, whose correct value is $H(x)$.
4. $x.height\_2$, integer, whose correct value is $H_2(x)$.

5. $x.subtree\_diam$, integer, whose correct value is the diameter of T_x.
6. $x.diameter$, integer, whose correct value is $Diam(T)$.
7. $x.is\_center$, integer, whose correct value is TRUE if and only if x is a center of T.

5.3 Functions of ATC

1. All the functions of ATWLE.
2. $Enabled^{\text{ATWLE}}(x)$, $Can\_Tick(x)$, $Must\_Tick(x)$, Boolean, identical to the functions of the same names in the definition of ATWLEU.
3. $Height(x) = \begin{cases} 0 \text{ if } Chldrn(x) = \emptyset \\ \max\{1 + y.height : y \in Chldrn(x)\} \text{ otherwise} \end{cases}$
   The correct value of $Height(x)$ is the height of x.
4. $Height\_2(x) = \max\_2\{1 + y.height : y \in Chldrn(x)\}$. The correct value of $Height\_2(x)$ is the secondary height of x.
5. $Subtree\_Diam(x) = \max \begin{cases} \max\{y.subtree\_diam : y \in Chldrn(x)\} \\ x.height + x.height\_2 \end{cases}$
6. $Diameter(x) = \begin{cases} x.subtree\_diam \text{ if } Is\_Sole\_Leader(x) \\ \max\left\{ \begin{array}{l} x.subtree\_diam \\ x.height + Co\text{-}Leader(x).height \end{array} \right\} \text{ if } Is\_Co\text{-}Leader(x) \\ Parent(x).Diameter \text{ if } Is\_Child(x) \\ 0 \text{ otherwise. This option never occurs in an error-free computation.} \end{cases}$
   The value of this function, at each process, eventually equals the diameter of T.
7. $Is\_Center(x) \equiv |2 \cdot x.height - x.diameter| \leq 1$, Boolean, x is a center of T.

5.4 Detailed Overview of ATC

ATC consists of a sequence of *phases*. The first phase consists of electing one two leaders, using the algorithm ATWLE. The leaders elected by ATWLE then become the roots, making T a rooted tree, or a *bi-rooted* tree as defined in Section 5.1.

ATWLE is used as a "black box," which is implemented as Action C1. If x is enabled to execute any action of ATWLE, or if a $x.finished$ = FALSE, then x is not enabled to execute any other action of ATC. This first phase of ATC takes $O(Diam)$ rounds, during which each process of T executes Action C1 or C7 in $O(Diam)$ rounds. The second phase of ATC is implemented by Actions C2, C3, and C4. The third phase is implemented by Action C5, and the fourth by Action C6.

Actions C1 through C7 are prioritized; no action is enabled if any action of higher priority is enabled. This rule is justified by the fact that correctness of the value calculated by each of those actions depends on correctness of the values calculated by higher priority actions.

Table 3. Actions of ATC for Process x

C1 priority 1	Emulate ATWLE	$Enabled^{\text{ATWLE}}(x)$ $Can\_Tick(x)$	$\longrightarrow$	Action of ATWLE $x.clck \leftarrow x.clck + 1$
C2 priority 2	Update Height	$x.height \neq Height(x)$ $x.finished$ $Can\_Tick(x)$	$\longrightarrow$	$x.height \leftarrow Height(x)$ $x.clck \leftarrow x.clck + 1$
C3 priority 3	Update Secondary Height	$height\_2 \neq Height\_2(x)$ $x.finished$ $Can\_Tick(x)$	$\longrightarrow$	$x.height\_2 \leftarrow Height\_2(x)$ $x.clck \leftarrow x.clck + 1$
C4 priority 4	Update Subtree Diameter	$x.subtree\_diam \neq Subtree\_Diam(x)$ $x.finished$ $Can\_Tick(x)$	$\longrightarrow$	$x.subtree\_diam \leftarrow Subtree\_Diam(x)$ $x.clck \leftarrow x.clck + 1$
C5 priority 5	Update Diameter	$x.diameter \neq Diameter(x)$ $x.finished$ $Can\_Tick(x)$	$\longrightarrow$	$x.diameter \leftarrow Diameter(x)$ $x.clck \leftarrow x.clck + 1$
C6 priority 6	Declare Myself Center	$x.is\_center \neq Is\_Center(x)$ $x.finished$ $Can\_Tick(x)$	$\longrightarrow$	$x.is\_center \leftarrow Is\_Center(x)$ $x.clck \leftarrow x.clck + 1$
C7 priority 7	Must Tick	$Must\_Tick(x)$	$\longrightarrow$	$x.clck \leftarrow x.clck + 1$

Calculating Height, Secondary Height, and Subtree Diameter. During the second phase of ATC, heights and secondary heights of all processes and the diameters of all subtrees are computed. This phase consists of each process executing Action C2 once, followed by Action C3 once, followed by Action C4 once. These actions take place in three pipelined bottom-up waves. It is possible that some of those processes "out of turn," *i.e.,* before they are ready to compute the correct values. The synchronizer will put a bound on how many times this can happen, thus forcing all three waves to be completed in $O(n \cdot Diam)$ steps. The third wave uses Remarks 1 and 2.

In the full paper, we will formally prove that the step complexity of ATC is $O(n \cdot Diam)$. Intuitively, the argument is as follows. It takes $O(Diam)$ rounds for ATWLE to reach a final configuration. Thereafter, each of the three bottom-up waves takes one round to move up one level, thus every x knows its height and secondary height, as well as the diameter T_x, within $O(Diam)$ rounds. Thereafter, it takes one round per level for the top-town wave, after which every process knows the diameter of T. Within one more round, every process knows whether it is a center.

As we stated above, it is then possible to prove that the worst case step complexity exceeds the worst case round complexity only by a factor of $O(n)$. Our main theorem for ATC is as follows.

Theorem 3. ATC *is silent and self-stabilizing on an anonymous tree network of size n and diameter $Diam$, uses $O(\log Diam)$ space for each process, and halts within $O(Diam)$ rounds and $O(n \cdot Diam)$ steps.*

Proof Sketch: It takes $O(Diam)$ rounds for the emulated ATWLE to reach a final configuration. After ATWLE converges, the bottom-up wave of ATC takes one round to move up each level, and hence within $O(Diam)$ rounds all values of *subtree_diam* will be computed. Thereafter, it takes one round per level for the top-town wave, after which $x.diameter = Diam$ for all x. Within one more round, every process knows whether it is a center. The upper bound on steps is maintained by the action of the unison.

6   ATM

ATM (Anonymous Tree Median) also consists of a sequence of phases. The first phase is identical to the first phase of ATC, namely the execution of ATWLE, which we treat as a black box in our code. The leaders elected by ATWLE become the roots, making T a rooted tree, or a bi-rooted tree.

The second phase of ATM is a bottom-up wave which computes $|T_x|$, the size of the subtree T_x, for each x. The third phase is a top-down wave which tells each process the value of n, the size of T. The fourth and final phase is not a wave; using Remark 4, each process determines whether it is a median.

All these phases, together, take $O(Diam)$ rounds. Just as in ATWLEU and ATC, we use a $\mathbb{Z}_3$ synchronizer to ensure fairness, thus keeping the number of steps of ATM to $O(n \cdot Diam)$. The implementation of the synchronizer is identical to that of ATWLEU and ATC.

Remark 4. Let T be a rooted or bi-rooted tree consisting of n nodes, and x a node of T.

(a) x is the sole median of T if and only if $|T_x| > \frac{n}{2}$ and $|T_y| < \frac{n}{2}$ for all $y \in Chldrn(x)$.

(b) x is a one of two medians of T if and only if either $|T_x| = \frac{n}{2}$, or there is some $y \in Chldrn(x)$ such that $|T_y| = \frac{n}{2}$.

Example. In Figure 5, $n = 18$ and B is the sole median, since $|T_B| = 13 > \frac{n}{2}$ while $|T_C| = 6$ and $|T_I| = 4$, both less than $\frac{n}{2}$.

Just as in ATC, a $\mathbb{Z}_3$ synchronizer is used to ensure fairness, thus keeping the number of steps of ATM to $O(n \cdot Diam)$. The implementation of the synchronizer is identical to that in ATC and ATWLEU.

6.1   Variables of ATM

1. All the variables of ATWLE.
2. $x.size$, integer, which will be computed to be the number of processes in the subtree rooted at x.
3. $x.total$, integer, which will be computed to be n, the number of processes in the network.
4. $x.is\_median$, Boolean, whose correct value if TRUE if and only if x is a median of T.

6.2   Functions of ATM

1. All the functions of ATWLE.
2. $Enabled^{\text{ATWLE}}(x)$, $Can\_Tick(x)$, $Must\_Tick(x)$, Boolean, identical to the functions of the same names in the definitions of ATWLEU and ATC.
3. $Size(x) = 1 + \sum_{y \in Chldrn(x)} y.size$, whose correct value is $|T_x|$.
4. $Total(x) = \begin{cases} x.size & \text{if } Is\_Sole\_Leader(x) \\ x.size + Co\text{-}Leader(x).size & \text{if } Is\_Co\text{-}Leader(x) \\ Parent(x).total & \text{if } Is\_Child(x) \\ 0 & \text{otherwise. This value never occurs if } x \text{ is not erroneous} \end{cases}$
   whose correct value is n.
5. $Is\_Sole\_Median(x) \equiv (x.size > x.total/2) \wedge (\forall y \in Chldrn(x)\ y.size < x.total/2)$
6. $Is\_Co\_Median(x) \equiv (x.size = x.total/2) \vee (\exists y \in Chldrn(x)\ y.size = x.total/2)$
7. $Is\_Median(x) \equiv Is\_Sole\_Median(x) \vee Is\_Co\_Median(x)$, whose correct value is TRUE if and only if x is a median of T.

Table 4. Actions of ATM for Process x

D1 priority 1	Emulate ATWLE	$Enabled^{\text{ATWLE}}(x)$ $Can\_Tick(x)$	$\longrightarrow$	Action of ATWLE $x.clck \leftarrow x.clck + 1$
D2 priority 2	Update Size	$x.size \neq Size(x)$ $x.finished$ $Can\_Tick(x)$	$\longrightarrow$	$x.size \leftarrow Size(x)$ $x.clck \leftarrow x.clck + 1$
D3 priority 3	Update Total	$x.total \neq Total(x)$ $x.finished$ $Can\_Tick(x)$	$\longrightarrow$	$x.total \leftarrow Total(x)$ $x.clck \leftarrow x.clck + 1$
D4 priority 4	Declare Myself Median	$x.is\_median \neq Is\_Median(x)$ $x.finished$ $Can\_Tick(x)$	$\longrightarrow$	$x.is\_median \leftarrow Is\_Median(x)$ $x.clck \leftarrow x.clck + 1$
D5 priority 5	Must Tick	$Must\_Tick(x)$	$\longrightarrow$	$x.clck \leftarrow x.clck + 1$

ATM consists of a sequence of *phases*. The first phase is identical to the first phase of ATC, and uses ATWLE to compute the leaders, making T into either a rooted or a bi-rooted tree. This phase is implemented as a "black box," using Actions D1 and D5. The second phase of ATM is implemented by Action D2, the third phase by Action D3, and the fourth by Action D4.

Priorities are used in the same manner as in ATM, since the correctness of each value calculated by Action D2, D3, or D4, depends on correctness of the values calculated by higher priority actions. ATM uses a $\mathbb{Z}_3$-synchronizer in the same manner as ATC.

Theorem 4. ATM *is silent and self-stabilizing on an anonymous tree network of size n and diameter $Diam$, uses $O(\log n)$ space for each process, and halts within $O(Diam)$ rounds and $O(n \cdot Diam)$ steps.*

Proof Sketch: It takes $O(Diam)$ rounds for the emulated ATWLE to reach a final configuration. After ATWLE converges, the bottom-up wave of ATM takes one round to move up each level, and hence within $O(Diam)$ rounds all values of *size* will be computed. Thereafter, it takes one round per level for the top-town wave, after which $x.total = n$ for all x. Within one more round, every process knows whether it is a median. The upper bound on steps is maintained by the action of the unison.

7   Lower Bound on Space Complexity

We now prove that, among silent self-stabilizing center and median finding algorithms on tree networks, our algorithms ATC and ATM have asymptotically optimal space complexity. For given N and D, we define $\mathcal{T}_{N,D}$ to be the class of all networks with a tree topology of size at most N and diameter at most D.

Theorem 5. *For any integers N and D, such that $5 \leq D < N$:*

(a) *If $\mathcal{A}$ is a silent self-stabilizing distributed algorithm which computes the center of any network in the class $\mathcal{T}_{N,D}$, the per node space complexity of $\mathcal{A}$ is at least $\frac{1}{2} \log \left\lfloor \frac{D-3}{2} \right\rfloor$.*

(b) *If $\mathcal{A}$ is a silent self-stabilizing distributed algorithm which computes the median of any network in the class $\mathcal{T}_{N,D}$, the per node space complexity of $\mathcal{A}$ is at least $\frac{1}{2} \log \left\lfloor \frac{N-2}{2} \right\rfloor$.*

Proof. The proofs of both parts are the same, except for a few details.

If T_L and T_R are rooted trees, let $\mathbb{T}[T_L, T_R]$ be the network consisting of two processes P_L and P_R, which are neighbors, which we call the *middle* processes, together with T_L, whose root is a neighbor of P_L, and T_R, whose root is a neighbor of P_R. (Figure 6 illustrates $\mathbb{T}[T_L, T_R]$.)

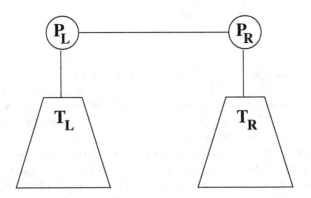

Fig. 6. $\mathbb{T}[T_L, T_R]$

We first prove (a). For any integer $1 \leq i \leq D - 5$, let T_i be a rooted tree of height i consisting of a single chain where the root is at one end, and let

$\mathbb{T}_{i,j} = \mathbb{T}[T_i, T_j]$, a tree (actually, a chain) with diameter $i + j + 3$ and size $i + j + 4$.

When the algorithm $\mathcal{A}$ is executed on $\mathbb{T}_{i,i}$ For any $1 \leq i \leq \lfloor \frac{D-3}{2} \rfloor$, a final configuration $\gamma^{i,i}$ is reached. Both P_L and P_R will be selected as centers.

There is a fixed number m such that P_L and P_R each have m possible states in $\mathcal{A}$, and hence at least $\log_2 m$ bits of memory. There are m^2 possible combinations of states of P_L and P_R.

Suppose $m^2 < \lfloor \frac{D-3}{2} \rfloor$. By the pigeon-hole principle, there must exist distinct i and j, where $1 \leq i < jm^2 + 1 \leq \lfloor \frac{D-3}{2} \rfloor$, such that P_L and P_R each have the same state in both $\gamma^{i,i}$ and $\gamma^{j,j}$.

Now, consider the tree $\mathbb{T}[i, j]$. Let $\gamma^{i,j}$ be the configuration which agrees with $\gamma^{i,i}$ on $T_L \cup \{P_L, P_R\}$ and which agrees with $\gamma^{j,j}$ on $T_R \cup \{P_L, P_R\}$. Since both $\gamma^{i,i}$ and $\gamma^{j,j}$ are final, $\gamma^{i,j}$ is also final, since any process in $T_L \cup P_L$ cannot distinguish between $\gamma^{i,j}$ and $\gamma^{i,i}$, and thus cannot be enabled, and any process in $T_R \cup P_R$ cannot distinguish between $\gamma^{i,j}$ and $\gamma^{j,j}$, and thus cannot be enabled.

In this final configuration, P_L must be designated a co-center, since it has the same state it would have if the network were $\mathbb{T}[i, i]$. But P_L is not a co-center of $\mathbb{T}[i, j]$, contradicting the hypothesis that $\mathcal{A}$ is correct for the class $\mathcal{T}_{N,D}$.

We conclude that $m^2 \geq \lfloor \frac{D-3}{2} \rfloor$. Thus, the per process space complexity of $\mathcal{A}$ is at least $\frac{1}{2} \log_2 \lfloor \frac{D-3}{2} \rfloor$.

The proof of (b) is similar. The only change is that we choose T_i to be a rooted tree of size i and diameter at most 1. P_L and P_R are co-medians of $\mathbb{T}[T_i, T_i]$, and $\mathcal{A}$ must find the median or medians on $\mathbb{T}[T_i, T_j]$ for all i, j such that $i + j \leq N - 2$. Let m be the number of states of a process of degree 2. If $m^2 < \lfloor \frac{N-2}{2} \rfloor$, then, by the pigeonhole principle, there must be some $1 \leq i < j \leq \lfloor \frac{N-2}{2} \rfloor$ such that both P_L and P_R have the same states for final configurations of $\mathcal{A}$ on both $\mathbb{T}[T_i, T_i]$ and $\mathbb{T}[T_i, T_i]$. and hence on $\mathbb{T}[T_i, T_j]$ as well, if we pick a final configuration of $\mathcal{A}$ on $\mathbb{T}[T_i, T_j]$ by combining final configurations of $\mathbb{T}[T_i, T_i]$ and $\mathbb{T}[T_i, T_i]$ in the same manner as in the proof of (a). However, P_L is a co-median of $\mathbb{T}[T_i, T_i]$, but not of $\mathbb{T}[T_i, T_j]$, contradiction.

We conclude that $m^2 \geq \lfloor \frac{N-2}{2} \rfloor$. Thus, the per process space complexity of $\mathcal{A}$ is at least $\frac{1}{2} \log_2 \lfloor \frac{N-2}{2} \rfloor$.

8 Conclusion

Algorithms ATWLEU, ATC, and ATM each have round complexity $O(Diam)$, which is asymptotically optimal since it must take at least $Diam$ rounds for a processes to have a chance to react to the states of all other processes. Trivially, the constant space complexity of ATWLEU is asymptotically optimal. By Theorem 5, the space complexities of ATC and ATM are asymptotically optimal as well for silent self-stabilizing distributed algorithms. The worst case step complexity of all three algorithms is $O(n \cdot Diam)$, a substantial improvement over previous work. We conjecture that this complexity is asymptotically optimal for all three problems.

The main contribution of this paper is the introduction of the constant space implementation of parent pointers using $\mathbb{Z}_5$. By using $\mathbb{Z}_5$, instead of the obvious and simpler $\mathbb{Z}_3$, we enable the implementation to be adjusted without changing the pointers, permitting a process to become the parent of two or more other processes. Our method uses top-down *adjustment waves* to make this possible.

References

1. Antonoiu, G., Srimani, P.K.: A self-stabilizing leader election algorithm for tree graphs. J. Parallel Distrib. Comput. 34(2), 227–232 (1996)
2. Antonoiu, G., Srimani, P.K.: A self-stabilizing distributed algorithm to find the center of a tree graph. Parallel Algorithms Appl. 10(3-4), 237–248 (2007)
3. Antonoiu, G., Srimani, P.K.: A self-stabilizing distributed algorithm to find the median of a tree graph. Journal of Computer and System Sciences 58(1), 215–221 (1999)
4. Xu, Z., Srimani, P.K.: Self-stabilizing anonymous leader election in a tree. Int. J. Found. Comput. Sci. 17(2), 323–336 (2006)
5. Blair, J.R., Manne, F.: Efficient self-stabilizing algorithms for tree networks. In: Proceedings of the 23rd International Conference on Distributed Computing Systems, pp. 20–26. IEEE (2003)
6. Bruell, S.C., Ghosh, S., Karaata, M.H., Pemmaraju, S.V.: Self-stabilizing algorithms for finding centers and medians of trees. SIAM J. Comput. 29(2), 600–614 (1999)
7. Lynch, N.: Distributed Algorithms. Morgan Kaufmann (1996)
8. Boulinier, C., Petit, F., Villain, V.: When graph theory helps self-stabilization. In: Proceedings of the Twenty-third Annual ACM Symposium on Principles of Distributed Computing, PODC 2004, pp. 150–159 (2004)
9. Chepoi, V., Fevat, T., Godard, E., Vaxès, Y.: A Self-stabilizing algorithm for the median problem in partial rectangular grids and Their relatives. Algorithmica 62(1-2), 146–168 (2012)
10. Dijkstra, E.: Self stabilizing systems in spite of distributed control. Communications of the Association of Computing Machinery 17, 643–644 (1974)

Local Decision and Verification
with Bounded-Size Outputs

Heger Arfaoui[1], Pierre Fraigniaud[1,*], and Andrzej Pelc[2,**]

[1] CNRS and University Paris Diderot, France
[2] Université du Québec en Outaouais, Canada

Abstract. We are dealing with the design of algorithms using few resources, enabling to decide whether or not any given n-node graph G belongs to some given graph class $\mathcal{C}$. Our model borrows from property testing the way the decision is taken, by an *unconstrained interpretation function* applied to the set of outputs produced by individual queries (instead of an interpretation function limited to the conjunction operator as in local distributed decision). It borrows from local distributed decision the fact that *all nodes are involved* in the decision (instead of $o(n)$ nodes as in property testing). The unique, but severe restriction we impose to the nodes is a limitation on the amount of information they are enabled to output: every node is bounded to output a *constant* number of bits. In this paper, we provide separation results between distributed decision and verification classes, and we analyze the size of the certificates enabling to verify distributed languages.

1 Introduction

Objective. The ability to computationally *decide* a language using few resources is at the core of computer science, where, e.g., P can be interpreted as the class of languages *decidable* using little computation time, L can be interpreted as the class of languages decidable using little memory space, and NP and NL, the non deterministic versions of P and L, can be interpreted as the classes of languages *verifiable* using little computation time and little memory space, respectively, with small certificates. Still in the spirit of minimizing resources, *property testing* [17] is aiming at identifying languages that can be decided without accessing the whole instance. In particular, for any fixed graph class $\mathcal{C}$, property testing on graphs [18] aims at designing algorithms able to decide whether or not any given n-node graph G belongs to $\mathcal{C}$, by querying only $o(n)$ (random) nodes of the graph. In essence, the result of querying a node u is a value $out(u)$ such as, e.g., the degree of u. The decision algorithm acts and

---

* The first and second authors receive support from the ANR project DISPLEXITY, and from the INRIA project GANG.
** Partially supported by NSERC discovery grant and by the Research Chair in Distributed Computing at the Université du Québec en Outaouais. Additional support from the Foundation Sciences Mathématiques de Paris.

T. Higashino et al. (Eds.): SSS 2013, LNCS 8255, pp. 133–147, 2013.

decides depending on the set of values collected so far. There are no restrictions imposed to this algorithm, except that one aims at designing algorithms deciding in polynomial time. In the distributed setting, the theory of *local distributed decision* [12,26] also aims at understanding the ability to decide graph properties, with or without inputs at nodes, using few resources. In this framework, all nodes are involved, each node u computes and outputs a single bit value b_u by inspecting its local neighborhood, and the result of the distributed decision is obtained by applying the conjunctive operator $\bigwedge_u b_u$ on these 1-bit-per-node outputs. (That is, the input configuration is accepted if and only if all nodes locally accept).

The restriction to the conjunctive operator in the framework of local distributed decision is conceptually elegant, and is well motivated by practical applications. For instance, the output $b_u = 0$ at node u can be interpreted as node u "raising an alarm". This alarm can be used by a central entity collecting data, like in, e.g., sensor networks. It can also be used in a distributed manner. For instance, in the framework of *self-stabilzation*, the alarm at node u may correspond to the detection of an invalid state of the system, and yields the launch of a recovery procedure [4,20]. Also, since the conjunctive operator is idempotent, commutative, and associative, it is easy to conceive a gossip procedure enabling all nodes to become aware of the global decision, by flooding in diameter rounds, where each round involves exchanging a single bit on each link (see, e.g., [5] for decision and verification in the $\mathcal{CONGEST}$ model).

Nevertheless, restricting ourselves to the conjunctive operator in the framework of local distributed decision is not a law carved in stone. In fact, there are several arguments against restricting the distributed decision setting to this specific operator. For instance, this restriction does not fit with elementary algebraic operations on sets. Typically, one may be able to distributedly decide locally two distributed properties $\mathcal{P}$ and $\mathcal{P}'$, and yet be unable to distributedly decide $\mathcal{P} \vee \mathcal{P}'$. For instance, using the conjunctive operator, one cannot decide locally whether nodes are properly k-colored if the set of k colors is not specified (this holds even if this set of colors is specified as being either {green, orange, red} or {green, orange, blue}). Last but not least, recent results in the framework of distributed local decision [11] reveal that restricting ourselves to the conjunction operator prevents us from "boosting" probabilistic decisions. That is, using the conjunction operator, and as opposed to, say, languages in BPP, there are classes of distributed languages that can be decided distributedly with a fixed probabilistic guarantee, but which cannot be decided distributedly with better guarantees. In fact, there are computational models (e.g., distributed quantum computing) in which the exclusive-disjunction operator is known to be far more practical and efficient than the conjunctive operator (see [2], and the references therein).

To sum up the above discussion, while using the conjunctive operator in the framework of local distributed decision is well grounded for some settings, there are no reasons to stick to this specific operator in general. The objective of this paper is thus to revisit local distributed decision, without restricting ourselves to the conjunctive operator.

Framework. We consider the $\mathcal{LOCAL}$ model [27], which is a standard network computing model capturing the essence of locality. In this model, processors have individual inputs, and arbitrary pairwise distinct identities. The algorithms should work properly for every possible identity assignment. They are woken up simultaneously, and computation proceeds in fault-free synchronous rounds during which every processor exchanges messages of unlimited size with its neighbors, and performs arbitrary computations on its data. Our aim is to decide distributed languages, locally, i.e., in a constant number of rounds. A distributed language is a (TM-decidable) collection $\mathcal{L}$ of pairs $(G, \mathbf{x})$, where G is a (connected) graph, and $\mathbf{x} = \{\mathbf{x}_u, u \in V(G)\}$ denotes the set of inputs given to the nodes (node u receives the binary string $\mathbf{x}_u$ as input). Typical examples of distributed languages are

$$\texttt{IsColored} = \{(G, \mathbf{x}) \text{ s.t. } \forall u \in V(G), \forall v \in N(u), \mathbf{x}_u \neq \mathbf{x}_v\}$$

where $N(u)$ denotes the (open) neighborhood of u, that is, all nodes at distance exactly 1 from u, and

$$\texttt{Tree} = \{(G, \mathbf{x}) \text{ s.t. } G \text{ is a tree}\}.$$

Deciding a distributed language $\mathcal{L}$ relies on two ingredients. One ingredient is a distributed algorithm $\mathcal{A}$ enabling each node u to output some value $out(u)$ in a constant number of rounds t, that is, after inspecting all nodes in the ball of radius t. This includes the structure of that ball, and the input values given to the nodes in this ball. The second ingredient is an interpretation operator $\mathcal{I}$, which applies to the collection $\{out(u), u \in V(G)\}$ of all values output by the nodes. As in classical local distributed decision, the interpretation is taken over all outputs. However, as in property testing, we allow any form of interpretation. Obviously, all distributed languages would be decidable in a single round in this setting if one did not impose restrictions on the values output by the nodes. We restrict every node to output a *constant* number k of bits. Hence, our framework is the extension of the model in [11,12,19,26] where:

1. every node outputs a number of bits bounded by a language-specific constant (rather than only one bit), and
2. the interpretation of these outputs is allowed to be any binary valued function $\mathcal{I}$ whose arguments are the unordered multi-sets of outputs of all nodes (rather than only the conjunction operator applied to these outputs).

Note that, using the interpretation function $\mathcal{I}$, an instance is accepted or rejected on the basis of the number of outputs of each type, regardless by which node a given output is produced.

For a non-negative integer t, we define the class ULD(t) (for *Unrestricted Local Decision*) as the class of distributed languages that can be decided in t

communication rounds in the $\mathcal{LOCAL}$ model, where decision is taken according to the rules specified above. We then define one of two classes of main interest for the purpose of this paper: ULD = $\cup_{t\geq 0}$ULD(t).

We are also concerned with distributed *verification*, which can be seen as the nondeterministic version of decision, in the same way as NP is the nondeterministic version of P. In distributed verification, every node $u \in V(G)$ is given a *certificate* $\mathbf{y}_u$, in addition to the input $\mathbf{x}_u$. Each certificate is an arbitrary binary string. A distributed language $\mathcal{L}$ is locally verifiable if there exists a pair $(\mathcal{A}, \mathcal{I})$, where $\mathcal{A}$ is a distributed algorithm performing in a constant number of rounds, and $\mathcal{I}$ is an interpretation of the outputs produced by $\mathcal{A}$ at all nodes, such that the following holds:

- if $(G, \mathbf{x}) \in \mathcal{L}$ then there exists a collection of certificates $\mathbf{y} = \{\mathbf{y}_u, u \in V(G)\}$ satisfying that $\mathcal{A}$ running in G, with the pair $(\mathbf{x}_u, \mathbf{y}_u)$ given to each node u, returns $out(u)$ at every node u such that $\mathcal{I}$ accepts the multi-set $\{out(u), u \in V(G)\}$;
- if $(G, \mathbf{x}) \notin \mathcal{L}$ then for any collection of certificates $\mathbf{y} = \{\mathbf{y}_u, u \in V(G)\}$, $\mathcal{A}$ running in G, with the pair $(\mathbf{x}_u, \mathbf{y}_u)$ given to each node u, returns $out(u)$ at every node u such that $\mathcal{I}$ rejects the multi-set $\{out(u), u \in V(G)\}$.

For a non-negative integer t, we define the class UNLD(t) (for *Unrestricted Nondeterministic Local Decision*) as the class of distributed languages that can be verified in t communication rounds in the $\mathcal{LOCAL}$ model, where the verification is performed according to the rules specified above. We then define our second class of interest: UNLD = $\cup_{t\geq 0}$UNLD(t).

Observe that, for both decision and verification, the global outcome should not depend on the identities assigned to the nodes. In particular, the certificate $\mathbf{y}$ for a legal instance $(G, \mathbf{x})$, i.e., for an instance $(G, \mathbf{x}) \in \mathcal{L}$, enabling the interpretation to accept $(G, \mathbf{x})$ should not depend on the identity assignment to the nodes. This is in accordance to distributed verification, as studied in [11,12], but should not be mixed up with *proof-labeling schemes* [19,25] in which the certificates can possibly depend on the identity assignment.

Our Results. We first establish a set of classification and separation results, by placing various languages in their appropriate decision and verification classes. These results are summarized in Figure 1, where the classes LD and NLD are the classes of locally decidable languages, and of non-deterministic locally decidable languages, respectively, defined in [12]. These classes can alternatively be defined as the restriction of ULD and UNLD to the setting in which each node can output a single bit, and the interpretation is the result of the conjunction operator on these outputs.

We then prove that, in our "universal" decision and verification model, as opposed to classical distributed decision, *all* distributed languages can be *verified*. More specifically, all distributed languages on n-node networks with k-bit input per node can be verified using certificates of $O(n^2 + kn)$ bits, by having each node inspecting its neighborhood at distance 1 only, with just 1-bit-per-node outputs.

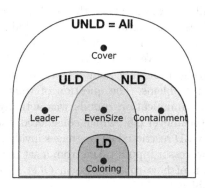

Fig. 1. *Four distributed decision and verification classes, with representatives*

Hence, in other words, UNLD = All. This result is essentially obtained by proving that the problem Cover, known to be a "hardest" local decision problem up to local reduction [12], is in UNLD. (Formally, Cover is BPNLD-complete[1] [12]).

The above upper bound on the certificate size enabling to put any language in UNLD is tight. Indeed, we prove that there are languages which require $\Omega(n^2 + kn)$ bits to be verified, even if the nodes are allowed to perform an arbitrarily large number of communication rounds, and even if each node can output an arbitrarily large number of bits.

From the fact that all distributed languages can be *verified*, it results that, as for *proof-labeling scheme*, one major issue in our setting is minimizing the size of the certificates. We prove that just enabling two output bits per node instead of just one, and just enabling a slightly more complex interpretation that the conjunction operator, has a tremendous impact on the size of the certificates. For instance, it is known that verifying trees using the logical conjunction operator, on 1-bit-per-node outputs, requires certificates of $\Omega(\log n)$ bits. (This holds even in the proof-labeling setting, i.e., when the certificates can possibly depend on the identity assignment). One of our perhaps most surprising results is a proof that, by simply using the conjunction and the disjunction operators together, on only 2-bit-per-node outputs, one can verify trees using certificates of only $O(1)$ bits.

Importantly, several of our positive results use interpretations of the outputs that have desirable properties. In particular, they are idempotent, commutative and associative. As a consequence, all nodes can become aware of the decision result by a simple gossip protocol performing in $O(\log n)$ time whenever such a mechanism can be implemented on top of the network. Alternatively, the global decision can be computed by all nodes in $O(D)$ time in the $\mathcal{CONGEST}(1)$ model [27], where D denotes the diameter of the network. Our universal verifier, used to establish UNLD = All, does not satisfy the idempotence property. Nevertheless, the global decision can still be computed by all nodes in $O(D)$ time in the $\mathcal{CONGEST}(\log n)$ model.

---

[1] BPNLD stands for Bounded-error Probabilistic Non-deterministic Local Decision.

Related Work. Locality issues have been thoroughly studied in the literature, via the analysis of various *construction* problems, including coloring and maximal independent set (MIS), minimum-weight spanning tree (MST), matching, dominating set, spanners, etc. We refer to the book [27] for an excellent introduction to local computing, providing pointers to the most relevant techniques for solving construction problems. The question of what can be computed in a constant number of communication rounds was actually posed in the seminal work of Naor and Stockmeyer [26], which considered a subclass of LD, called LCL, which is essentially LD restricted to languages involving graphs of constant maximum degree and processor inputs taken from a set of constant size. In fact, [26] studies the question of how to compute in $O(1)$ rounds the constructive versions of decision problems in LCL.

Recently, several results were established concerning *decision* problems in distributed computing. For example, [5] and [21] study specific decision problems in the $\mathcal{CONGEST}$ model. Specifically, tight bounds are established in [21] for the time and message complexities of the problem of deciding whether a given subgraph is an MST of the network, and time lower bounds for many other subgraph-decision problems (e.g., spanning tree, connectivity) are established in [5]. Decision problems have recently received attention in the asynchronous setting too, in the framework of wait-free computing [15]. In particular, [16] extends the results in [15] by allowing interpretations beyond the simple conjunction operator. Similarly, decision problem have also received attention in the context of computing with mobile agents [14].

The theory of proof labeling schemes [19,23,25] was designed to tackle the issue of locally verifying (with the aid of a "proof", i.e., a certificate, at each node) solutions to problems that cannot be decided locally. Investigations in this framework mostly focus on the minimum size of the certificate necessary so that verification can be performed in a single round [19,23,25], or in t rounds [24]. Hence, the model of proof labeling schemes has some resemblance to our definition of the class UNLD. The notion of proof labeling schemes also has interesting similarities with the notions of local detection [1], local checking [3], or silent stabilization [6], which were introduced in the context of self-stabilization.

The use of oracles that provide information to nodes was studied intensively in the context of distributed construction tasks. In particular, it was studied in the framework of *local computation with advice*. In this framework, MST construction was studied in [10], 3-coloring of cycles in [7], and broadcast and wake up in [8]. Finally, in [22] it is shown that, in the context of local computation, access to the oracle providing the number of nodes is not required for solving efficiently several central problems (e.g., $O(\Delta)$-coloring, MIS, etc.), while previous algorithms in the literature explicitly or implicitly assumed the use of this oracle.

2   Classification and Separation

Recall that the classes LD and NLD, defined in [12], are the respective restrictions of ULD and UNLD to the setting in which each node can output a single bit, and the interpretation is the result of the conjunction operator on these outputs. Hence, by definition, LD $\subseteq$ ULD, and NLD $\subseteq$ UNLD. Also, by definition, ULD $\subseteq$ UNLD. The purpose of this section is to show that these inclusions are strict (the strict inclusion LD $\subset$ NLD is established in [12]), and to study the relationship between ULD and NLD. The following result is illustrated in Figure 1.

Theorem 1. ULD $\setminus$ NLD $\neq \emptyset$, NLD $\setminus$ ULD $\neq \emptyset$, *and* LD $\subset$ (ULD $\cap$ NLD) $\subset$ (ULD $\cup$ NLD) $\subset$ UNLD = All.

The proof of the above theorem is direct by combining the following four lemmas, including Lemma 2 which, in addition, provides an upper bound on the size of the certificates enabling to place every language in UNLD.

Lemma 1. ULD $\setminus$ NLD $\neq \emptyset$ *and* LD $\subset$ ULD $\cap$ NLD.

Proof. Let $\mathtt{Leader} = \{(G, \mathbf{x})$ s.t. $\forall u \in V(G), \mathbf{x}_u \in \{0,1\}$, and $\sum_{u \in V(G)} \mathbf{x}_u = 1\}$. We have $\mathtt{Leader} \notin$ NLD because this language is not closed under lift (see [9] for the characterization of NLD in term of lifts). To establish that $\mathtt{Leader} \in$ ULD, we describe a local distributed algorithm enabling each node to output a constant number of bits, with the associated interpretation. The algorithm performs in zero rounds: every node u simply returns the single bit $b_u = \mathbf{x}_u$. The decision is then made according to the collection $\{b_i \in \{0,1\}, i \in [n]\}$ of outputs[2], by applying the logical operator $\mathcal{I} = \bigvee_{i=1}^n \left(b_i \wedge \bigwedge_{j \neq i} \overline{b_j}\right)$ which is true if and only if there is a unique b_i equal to 1. Hence, the input configuration is accepted if and only if there is a unique node u with $x_u = 1$, as desired. This proves that ULD $\setminus$ NLD $\neq \emptyset$.

Let $\mathtt{EvenSize} = \{(G, \mathbf{x})$ s.t. G has an even number of nodes$\}$. This language is in NLD because it is closed under lift (see [9]). To establish that $\mathtt{EvenSize} \in$ ULD, consider the algorithm performing in zero rounds consisting, for each node u, in outputting the single bit $b_u = 1$. The decision is then made by applying the operator $\mathcal{I} = 1 - \bigoplus_{i=1}^n b_i$ to the collection $\{b_i \in \{0,1\}, i \in [n]\}$ of output bits, where $\oplus$ denotes the exclusive-disjunctive operator. The value of $\mathcal{I}$ is equal to 1 if and only if the graph has an even number of nodes. Now, we also have $\mathtt{EvenSize} \notin$ LD. This is because if some node u outputs 0 in an odd cycle C with some identity assignment (there must be such a node for C being rejected by the conjunction operator), then it also outputs 0 in some even cycle, causing this latter legal instance to be wrongly rejected. (Take the same cycle C with the same identity assignment, and insert one node between the two nodes at distance $\lfloor n/2 \rfloor$ from u, with some arbitrary identity distinct from the existing ones: node u still outputs 0 in this cycle). This proves LD $\subset$ ULD $\cap$ NLD, which completes the proof. $\square$

Let us consider the language

$$\mathtt{Cover} = \{(G, (\mathbf{e}, \mathbf{S})) \mid \exists v \in V(G), \exists S \in \mathbf{S}_v \text{ s.t. } S = \{\mathbf{e}_u : u \in V(G)\}\}$$

---

[2] The indexes $i = 1, \dots, n$ are only for the purpose of notation. The decision is made based on an unordered multiset of outputs.

introduced in [12]. This language is formed by all configurations $(G, \mathbf{x})$ with $\mathbf{x}_u = (\mathbf{e}_u, \mathbf{S}_u)$, where $\mathbf{e}_u$ is an element of some universe U, and $\mathbf{S}_u = \{S_1, \ldots, S_{k_u}\}$ is a collection of sets with elements in U, such that there exists a node v whose collection $\mathbf{S}_v$ contains a set S that is equal to the set formed of all the elements $\mathbf{e}_u$ for all $u \in V(G)$. We have Cover $\in$ UNLD as a consequence of the combined observations that (1) by providing every node with an oracle deciding Leader, all distributed languages are in NLD, and (2) Leader $\in$ ULD. The first claim is implicit in [12], and the second has been established in the proof of Lemma 1. In other words, Cover $\in$ UNLD simply because UNLD $=$ NLD$^{\text{Leader}} =$ All. We provide a complete proof of UNLD $=$ All below, for the purpose of completeness and further references in the text, and refer to [12] for more details on the impact of using oracles on the theory of local decision.

Lemma 2. *Every TM-decidable distributed language is in UNLD. Moreover, the verification of languages on n-node networks with k-bit input per node can be achieved using certificates of $O(n^2 + kn)$ bits, by having each node inspecting its neighborhood at distance 1, and with 1-bit-per-node outputs.*

Proof. Let $\mathcal{L}$ be a language. We describe a 1-round nondeterministic verification scheme $(\mathcal{A}, \mathcal{I})$ for $\mathcal{L}$. The certificate $\mathbf{y}$ of an instance $(G, \mathbf{x}) \in \mathcal{L}$ is a $n \times n$ adjacency matrix M of G, with vertices indexed arbitrarily by distinct integers in $[1, n]$, plus a n-dimensional vector I where I_i is the input of vertex $i \in [1, n]$. In addition, every node v receives the index $\lambda(v) \in [1, n]$ corresponding to v in M and I. More formally, the certificate at node v is $\mathbf{y}_v = ((G', \mathbf{x}'), i)$, where G' is an isomorphic copy of G with nodes labeled by λ from 1 to n, $\mathbf{x}'$ is an n-dimensional vector such that $\mathbf{x}'_{\lambda(u)} = \mathbf{x}_u$ for every node u, and $i = \lambda(v)$. In n-node networks with k-bit input per node, such a certificate is on $O(n^2 + kn)$ bits.

The local algorithm $\mathcal{A}$ executed on an instance $(G, \mathbf{x})$ with certificate $\mathbf{y}$ outputs one bit c_u at every node u. Let us first describe an algorithm with two bits a_u and b_u at every node u, and then we will show how to reduce these two bits into just one. Every node u with index $\lambda(u) = 1$ sets $a_u = 1$. The others set $a_u = 0$. For computing b_u, every node performs a single round of communication. First, every node u checks that it has received the input as specified by $\mathbf{x}'$, i.e., u checks whether $\mathbf{x}'_{\lambda(u)} = \mathbf{x}_v$, and set $b_u = 0$ if this does not hold. Second, each node u communicates with its neighbors to check that (1) they all got the same graph G' and the same input vector $\mathbf{x}'$, and (2) they are indexed the way they should be according to the map G'. If some inconsistency is detected by a node, then this node sets $b_u = 0$. At this point, each node u that has not yet set the variable b_u sets it to 1 if $(G', \mathbf{x}') \in \mathcal{L}$, and to 0 otherwise. All nodes u output the pair (a_u, b_u). The decision is then made according to the collection $\{(a_i, b_i) \in \{0,1\}^2, i \in [n]\}$ of outputs, by applying the operator

$$\mathcal{I} = \left(\bigvee_{i=1}^{n} \left(a_i \wedge \bigwedge_{j \neq i} \overline{a_j} \right) \right) \wedge \left(\bigwedge_{i=1}^{n} b_i \right)$$

which is 1 if and only if $(G, \mathbf{x}) \in \mathcal{L}$. To see why, observe that if every node u passes the tests regarding the certificates without setting b_u to 0, then all nodes agree on the graph G' and on the input vector $\mathbf{x}'$. Moreover, they know that their respective neighborhood in G fits with the corresponding one in G'. Therefore, if every node u passes the tests regarding the certificates without setting b_u to 0, then $(G', \mathbf{x}')$ is either identical to $(G, \mathbf{x})$ or to a lift of it[3]. It follows that, if all bits b_u are 1, then $(G', \mathbf{x}') = (G, \mathbf{x})$ if and only if there exists exactly one node $v \in G$, whose index $\lambda(v) = 1$. This is precisely the Leader problem, which is decided using the a_us.

Now, we reduce the two bits a_u and b_u into just one bit c_u. This reduction is based on the observation that if any node u detects some inconsistencies, then at least one of it neighbors also detects the same inconsistencies. As a consequence, if some node "raises an alarm" (i.e., set $b_u = 0$), then at least another node does the same. Thus, every node u sets $c_u = a_u \vee \overline{b_u}$ and output c_u. The decision is then made according to the collection $\{c_i \in \{0, 1\}, i \in [n]\}$ of outputs, by applying the operator

$$\mathcal{I}' = \bigvee_{i=1}^{n} \left(c_i \wedge \bigwedge_{j \neq i} \overline{c_j} \right)$$

which is 1 if and only if $(G, \mathbf{x}) \in \mathcal{L}$. Indeed, $c_u = 1$ if and only if u detects some inconsistencies (i.e., $b_u = 0$) or $\lambda(u) = 1$ (i.e., $a_u = 1$). However, if u has detected some inconsistencies, then one of its neighbors u' has also detected the same inconsistencies, which guarantees $c_{u'} = 1$ for u' as well. Thus $\mathcal{I}' = 0$ if $(G, \mathbf{x}) \notin \mathcal{L}$. (The case where G is reduced to a single node is an exception: in this case, the unique node u sets $c_u = a_u \wedge b_u$). This completes the proof that UNLD = All.   □

Lemma 3. ULD $\cup$ NLD $\subset$ UNLD.

Proof. It is known that Cover $\notin$ NLD [12]. We prove that Cover $\notin$ ULD by contradiction, using arguments from communication complexity. Assume that there exists a local algorithm $\mathcal{A}$ and an interpretation $\mathcal{I}$ of the individual outputs produced by $\mathcal{A}$ enabling to decide Cover. In particular, $(\mathcal{A}, \mathcal{I})$ must decide the restricted version of Cover, defined on paths $P = (v_1, \dots, v_n)$ with $U = \{0, 1\}^k$, defined as follows. Let $\bar{0}$ denote the k-bit string formed by k consecutive 0s. We set

$$\mathbf{e}_1 = x, \mathbf{e}_n = y, \text{ and } \mathbf{e}_i = \bar{0} \text{ for } 1 < i < n,$$

and $\mathbf{S}_i = \{S_i\}$ for $i = 1, \dots, n$ with

$$S_1 = \{\bar{0}, x\}, S_n = \{\bar{0}, y\} \text{ and } S_i = \emptyset \text{ for } 1 < i < n.$$

Such a configuration is in Cover if and only if $x = y$. We show that, using $(\mathcal{A}, \mathcal{I})$, one could solve the communication complexity problem "Equality" between Alice and Bob, by exchanging less than k bits. Assume $\mathcal{A}$ performs in t

---

[3] A graph H is a lift of a graph G if there exists a homomorphism from H to G preserving the neighborhood of each node.

rounds. Then, given x as input, Alice simulates the algorithm $\mathcal{A}$ applied at the $n - t - 1$ nodes $v_1, \ldots, v_{n-t-1}$, while, given y as input, Bob simulates $\mathcal{A}$ applied to the $t+1$ nodes $v_{n-t}, \ldots, v_n$. Assume that $\mathcal{A}$ produces B bits of output at each node. The simulation of $\mathcal{A}$ allows Alice to compute $(n - t + 1)B$ bits, i.e., the $n - t - 1$ outputs of the nodes $v_1, \ldots, v_{n-t-1}$. Similarly, Bob computes $(t + 1)B$ bits. It is thus sufficient for Bob to send these $(t + 1)B = O(1)$ bits to Alice so that she can apply $\mathcal{I}$ on these bits together with her own $(n - t + 1)B$ bits to determine whether $x = y$ or not. This holds for any $x, y \in \{0, 1\}^k$. This is a contradiction, whenever $k > (t + 1)B$ because "Equality" requires k bits to be exchanged between Alice and Bob for being solved. Hence Cover $\notin$ ULD $\cup$ NLD, which completes the proof. □

Lemma 4. NLD $\setminus$ ULD $\neq \emptyset$.

Proof. Let us consider the following language, similar to Cover:

Containment $= \{(G, (\mathbf{e}, \mathbf{S})) \mid \exists v \in V(G), \exists S \in \mathbf{S}_v \text{ s.t. } S \supseteq \{\mathbf{e}_u : u \in V(G)\}\}$

The two languages Cover and Containment differ only in the fact that Cover asks for $S = \{\mathbf{e}_u : u \in V(G)\}$ while Containment simply asks for $S \supseteq \{\mathbf{e}_u : u \in V(G)\}$. It is known [12] that Containment $\in$ NLD. Now, by the same arguments as for proving Cover $\notin$ ULD, one can show Containment $\notin$ ULD as well. □

Remark. Lemma 2 states that all distributed languages are verifiable using certificates of $O(n^2 + kn)$ bits, which is the same upper bound as for proof-labeling schemes [25]. However, while proof-labeling schemes allows certificates to depend on the identity assignment, our verification algorithm uses certificates that are independent of the identity assignment.

3   Minimum Certificate Size for Universal Verification

By Lemma 2, we know that every TM-decidable distributed language with k-bit inputs is locally verifiable by providing nodes with certificates of $O(n^2 + kn)$ bits in n-node networks. Moreover, the verification is performed in one round, with 1-bit outputs. The following theorem proves that this bound is tight, in the sense that, for every k, there exist languages with k-bit inputs which require certificates of size $\Omega(n^2 + nk)$ bits to be verified in t rounds for b-bit outputs, for all t and b.

Theorem 2. *There exist languages with k-bit inputs that require certificates of size $\Omega(n^2 + nk)$ bits in n-node networks to be verified locally (i.e., to be placed in UNLD).*

Proof. We define the language Symmetry as follows. Given a graph G with k-bit input $\mathbf{x}_u$ per node u, an *input-preserving* automorphism ϕ of G is an automorphism satisfying $\mathbf{x}_u = \mathbf{x}_{\phi(u)}$ for every node u. Let

Symmetry $= \{(G, \mathbf{x}) : \text{there is a non-trivial input-preserving automorphism for } G\}$.

The proof that Symmetry requires $\Omega(n^2 + nk)$ bits to be verified in n-node networks with k-bit inputs is based on a construction used in [19] to prove a lower bound on the size of the certificates when using the conjunction operator. We extend the arguments from [19] so that they apply to languages with inputs (and not only to graph properties), and apply to all possible operators for interpreting b-bit outputs (and not only the conjunction operator for 1-bit outputs).

Let $\mathcal{F}_{n,k}$ be the family of configurations $(G, \mathbf{x})$ where G is a non-symmetric graph with n-nodes, and $|\mathbf{x}_u| = k$ for every node u of G. More precisely, by labeling the nodes of G from 1 to n in arbitrary manner, we select a unique (labeled) instance of each non-symmetric graph with n nodes, to be placed in $\mathcal{F}_{n,k}$. It results from the same analysis as in [19] that

$$|\mathcal{F}_{n,k}| = 2^{kn} \frac{(1 - o(1))2^{\binom{n}{2}}}{n!}$$

and thus $\log |\mathcal{F}_{n,k}| = \Theta(n^2 + nk)$. Now, for every two configurations $(F_1, \mathbf{x}_1)$ and $(F_2, \mathbf{x}_2)$ in $\mathcal{F}_{n,k}$, let $(G, \mathbf{x}) = (F_1, \mathbf{x}_1) + (F_2, \mathbf{x}_2)$ be the configuration formed by a copy of F_1 together with its inputs $\mathbf{x}_1$, a copy of F_2 together with its inputs $\mathbf{x}_2$, and a path P of $4t + 1$ nodes (without inputs), connecting the node with label 1 in F_1 to the node with label 1 in F_2. The number of nodes in G is $2n + 4t + 1 = \Theta(n)$. Let

$$\mathcal{C} = \{(G, \mathbf{x}) = (F_1, \mathbf{x}_1) + (F_2, \mathbf{x}_2) \ : \ (F_1, \mathbf{x}_1) \in \mathcal{F}_{n,k} \text{ and } (F_2, \mathbf{x}_2) \in \mathcal{F}_{n,k}\}.$$

We show that even verifying Symmetry-membership for configurations in $\mathcal{C}$ requires $\Omega(n^2 + nk)$-bit certificates. Since all graphs in $\mathcal{F}_{n,k}$ are non-symmetric, we get that, for any $(G, \mathbf{x}) \in \mathcal{C}$, we have $(G, \mathbf{x}) \in$ Symmetry if and only if $(F_1, \mathbf{x}_1) = (F_2, \mathbf{x}_2)$. (Recall that the graphs in $\mathcal{F}_{n,k}$ are labeled, and thus equality here means the existence of a label-preserving input-preserving isomorphism between F_1 and F_2). Let $\mathcal{C}_{\text{sym}}$ be the subset of $\mathcal{C}$ consisting of symmetric graphs in $\mathcal{C}$, i.e., $\mathcal{C}_{\text{sym}} = \mathcal{C} \cap$ Symmetry. We have:

$$\mathcal{C}_{\text{sym}} = \{(G, \mathbf{x}) = (F, \mathbf{x}') + (F, \mathbf{x}') \ : \ (F, \mathbf{x}') \in \mathcal{F}_{n,k}\}.$$

Note that $|\mathcal{C}_{\text{sym}}| = |\mathcal{F}_{n,k}| \geq 2^{c(n^2 + nk)}$ for some constant $c > 0$ and for big enough values of n. Assume now, for the sake of contradiction, that one can verify Symmetry in t rounds with certificates of size $s = o(n^2 + nk)$ bits per node, using algorithm $\mathcal{A}$ with interpretation $\mathcal{I}$. Then, for every configuration in $\mathcal{C}$, the path P includes $4t + 1$ certificates, for a total of $(4t + 1)s$ bits, that is still $o(n^2 + nk)$ bits since t is constant. Therefore, there are at least

$$R = 2^{c'(n^2 + nk)}$$

graphs in $\mathcal{C}_{\text{sym}}$, that have the same collection of certificates on their respective paths P, for some c', $0 < c' < c$. On the other hand, for an $(n+t)$-node graph with b bits of output per node, the total number of possible multi-sets the verification algorithm $\mathcal{A}$ can produce on this graph is upper bounded. If $\left(\binom{x}{y}\right)$ denotes the multinomial coefficient "x multichoose y", then this number is:

$$N = \left(\binom{2^b}{n+t}\right) = \binom{2^b + n + t - 1}{n + t}.$$

Therefore

$$N = \frac{(n + t + 1)(n + t + 2)...(n + t + 2^b - 1)}{(2^b - 1)!} = O(n^{2^b}).$$

So, let us assign identities to every graphs $(G, \mathbf{x}) = (F, \mathbf{x}') + (F, \mathbf{x}')$ in $\mathcal{C}_{\text{sym}}$ as follows. One copy of $(F, \mathbf{x}')$ is given identities from 1 to n, while the other copy of $(F, \mathbf{x}')$ is given identities from $n + 1$ to $2n$. In both copies, the identity assignment is set with respect to the labeling of F, i.e., node labeled i receive identity i in one copy, and $n + i$ in the other copy. Nodes in the path P are given identities from $2n + 1$ to $2n + 4t + 1$.

Since R is very large compared to N^2, there exist two configurations $(G_1, \mathbf{x}_1) = (F_1, \mathbf{x}'_1) + (F_1, \mathbf{x}'_1)$ and $(G_2, \mathbf{x}_2) = (F_2, \mathbf{x}'_2) + (F_2, \mathbf{x}'_2)$ in $\mathcal{C}_{\text{sym}}$ that receive the same collection of certificates on their respective path P, and for which $\mathcal{A}$ produces the same multi-set M_1 of outputs in the copies of $(F_1, \mathbf{x}'_1)$ and $(F_2, \mathbf{x}'_2)$ connected to the nodes with identities $2n + 1, \ldots, 2n + t$ on P, and the same multi-set M_2 of outputs in the copies of $(F_1, \mathbf{x}'_1)$ and $(F_2, \mathbf{x}'_2)$ connected to the nodes with identities $2n + 3t + 1, \ldots, 4t + 1$ on P. Let us denote by M_0 the multi-set of produced produced by $\mathcal{A}$ on the $2t + 1$ nodes at the middle of P in both configuration $(G_1, \mathbf{x}_1)$ and $(G_2, \mathbf{x}_2)$.

Now, consider the following configuration $(G, \mathbf{x})$ formed by "cutting and gluing" $(G_1, \mathbf{x}_1)$ and $(G_2, \mathbf{x}_2)$. More precisely, $(G, \mathbf{x})$ is formed by connecting $(F_1, \mathbf{x}_1)$, $(P, \varnothing)$, and $(F_2, \mathbf{x}_2)$, with identities in $[1, n]$ for F_1, in $[n + 1, 2n]$ for F_2, and, as usual, in $[2n + 1, 2n + 4t + 1]$ for P. Let us provide these nodes with the certificates inherited from these respective copies of $(F_1, \mathbf{x}_1)$, and $(F_2, \mathbf{x}_2)$. Each node with identities $\{1, ..., n\} \cup \{2n+1, \ldots, 2n+t\}$ (resp., with identities in $\{n+1, \ldots, 2n\} \cup \{2n+3t+1, \ldots, 2n+4t+1\}$) has the same local view of radius t in $(G, \mathbf{x})$ as in $(F_1, \mathbf{x}_1)$ (resp., $(F_2, \mathbf{x}_2)$). Moreover, nodes in the middle part of the path, with identities in $[2n+t+1, 2n+3t]$ have the same view in $(G, \mathbf{x})$ as in $(G_1, \mathbf{x}_1)$ and $(G_2, \mathbf{x}_2)$. Therefore, the verification algorithm $\mathcal{A}$ outputs the same multi-set $M_0 \cup M_1 \cup M_2$ for the illegal configuration $(G, \mathbf{x})$, as it does for the legal configurations $(G_1, \mathbf{x}_1)$ and $(G_2, \mathbf{x}_2)$, yielding the desired contradiction. $\square$

Remark. By inspecting R and N in the proof of Theorem 2, we can notice that the theorem holds even if the number of output bits per node is up to $c \log(n^2 + nk)$, for $c < 1$, and, by the construction of the accepted illegal configuration, even for verification algorithms performing in time up to $o(n)$ rounds.

4   Verifying Trees with Constant-Size Certificates

In this section, we show that, for languages in NLD, restricting the interpretation to the use of the conjunctive operator may have a significant cost in terms of certificate size. For instance, it is known [25] that verifying Tree using the conjunction operator requires $\Omega(\log n)$-bit certificates for n-node trees. This holds even if the certificates can depend on the identity assignment, and even if the verification can take an arbitrarily large (but constant) number of rounds. In contrast, we show that using conjointly the conjunction and disjunction operators, on 2-bit outputs, enables to verify Tree in one round, using certificates of only $O(1)$ bits. Moreover, as we can see in the proof of this result, the decision is made according to the application of a 2-bit logical operator $\mathcal{I}$ that is idempotent, commutative, and associative, and thus with all the desirable properties to be used in environments supporting gossip protocols, as well as in the $\mathcal{CONGEST}(1)$ model.

Theorem 3. Tree *can be verified in one round, with certificates of constant size, and two output bits per node.*

Proof. To establish the theorem, we first describe the collection of $O(1)$-bit certificates assigned to the nodes in the case of a valid instance of Tree, i.e., for a tree T. The certificate assigned to node v is a pair $\mathbf{y}_v = (r(v), d(v))$, where $r(v)$ is on one bit, and $d(v)$ is on two bits. Every certificate is thus encoded using three bits. To define the assignment of these bits at node v, let us pick an arbitrary node u_0 of T, and set u_0 as the root of T. Set $r(u_0) = 1$, and $r(v) = 0$ for every node $v \neq u_0$. For every $v \in V(T)$, let $d(v) = dist_T(v, u_0) \bmod 3$, where $dist_T(x, y)$ denotes the distance in T between nodes x and y, i.e., the minimum number of edges of a path from x to y in T.

We now describe the verification algorithm. It performs in just one round, during which every node v sends its certificate $\mathbf{y}_v$ to all its neighbors, and receives all the certificates of its neighbors. Given its own certificate and the certificates of its neighbors, every node v then computes a pair of bits (a_v, b_v) as follows. First, every node v checks whether it has at most one neighbor w with $d(w) = d(v) - 1$ (mod 3). Node w is called the parent of v. More precisely, if $r(v) = 1$ then there must be no parent for v, and, if $r(v) = 0$ then there must be exactly one parent for v. Similarly, v checks whether all its neighbors w different from its parent satisfy $d(w) = d(v) + 1$ (mod 3). All such nodes are called the children of v. If any of these tests is not passed, then v aborts, and outputs $(0, 0)$. If node v has not aborted, then it has identified its parent and its children (apart the root which has no parent), and it outputs $(1, r(v))$. This completes the description of the verification algorithm.

We now describe the interpretation of the collection of 2-bit outputs $\{(a_i, b_i), i = 1, \ldots, n\}$. It is the result of the following operator:

$$\mathcal{I} = \left(\bigwedge_{i=1}^{n} a_i \right) \wedge \left(\bigvee_{i=1}^{n} b_i \right).$$

By construction, if T is a tree, then $\mathcal{I} = 1$. Indeed, all tests are passed successfully, and thus the (unique) node v with $r(v) = 1$ returns $(1, 1)$ while all the other nodes return $(1, 0)$.

Establishing that $\mathcal{I} = 0$ whenever T is not a tree, independently from the certificates given to the nodes, is based on the fact that, if all tests are passed (i.e., if $\bigwedge_{i=1}^{n} a_i = 1$) then there cannot be a node v with $r(v) = 1$, and therefore $\bigvee_{i=1}^{n} b_i = 0$, yielding $\mathcal{I} = 0$. To see why this is indeed the case, assume that the current input (connected) graph G is not a tree. Assume moreover that the verification algorithm returns a set $\{(a_i, b_i), i = 1, \ldots, n\}$ such that $\bigwedge_{i=1}^{n} a_i = 1$. (Note that if this is not the case, then $\mathcal{I} = 0$, and we are done).

Since $\bigwedge_{i=1}^{n} a_i = 1$, every edge of G is given an orientation, from child to parent, and this orientation in locally consistent. That is, every node has exactly one outgoing edge, and a (potentially empty) set of incoming edges, apart from nodes marked $r(v) = 1$, if any, which may have no outgoing edges. Since G is not a tree, there is a cycle C in G. Since $a_i = 1$ for all i, it must be the case that all edges of the cycle are consistently oriented along C. That is, each node in C has exactly one outgoing edge in C and one incoming edge in C. In particular, all edges incident to C are entering C. As a consequence, there is a unique cycle in G. Indeed, if there were two node-disjoint cycles, then one could not guarantee consistency of the edge orientation along a path connecting these two cycles. The same holds if the two cycles would share one or more nodes. So, G is an "octopus". That is, it consists of a cycle C to which are attached a collection of trees, whose edges are all consistently oriented toward the cycle. Therefore, every node has an outgoing edge, and thus there cannot be a root node in G, i.e., a node v with $r(v) = 1$. Thus, $b_i = 0$ for all i, yielding $\mathcal{I} = 0$, which completes the proof of the theorem. $\qquad\Box$

Acknowledgements. the authors are thankful to Amos Korman for fruitful discussions regarding the subject of this paper.

References

1. Afek, Y., Kutten, S., Yung, M.: The local detection paradigm and its applications to self stabilization. Theoretical Computer Science 186(1-2), 199–230 (1997)
2. Arfaoui, H., Fraigniaud, P.: What Can Be Computed without Communications? In: Even, G., Halldórsson, M.M. (eds.) SIROCCO 2012. LNCS, vol. 7355, pp. 135–146. Springer, Heidelberg (2012)
3. Awerbuch, B., Patt-Shamir, B., Varghese, G.: Self-Stabilization By Local Checking and Correction. In: Proc. IEEE Symp. on the Foundations of Computer Science (FOCS), pp. 268–277 (1991)
4. Awerbuch, B., Patt-Shamir, B., Varghese, G., Dolev, S.: Self-Stabilization by Local Checking and Global Reset. In: Tel, G., Vitányi, P. (eds.) WDAG 1994. LNCS, vol. 857, pp. 326–339. Springer, Heidelberg (1994)
5. Das Sarma, A., Holzer, S., Kor, L., Korman, A., Nanongkai, D., Pandurangan, G., Peleg, D., Wattenhofer, R.: Distributed Verification and Hardness of Distributed Approximation. In: Proc. 43rd ACM Symp. on Theory of Computing, STOC (2011)
6. Dolev, S., Gouda, M., Schneider, M.: Requirements for silent stabilization. Acta Informatica 36(6), 447–462 (1999)
7. Fraigniaud, P., Gavoille, C., Ilcinkas, D., Pelc, A.: Distributed Computing with Advice: Information Sensitivity of Graph Coloring. In: Arge, L., Cachin, C., Jurdziński, T., Tarlecki, A. (eds.) ICALP 2007. LNCS, vol. 4596, pp. 231–242. Springer, Heidelberg (2007)

8. Fraigniaud, P., Ilcinkas, D., Pelc, A.: Communication algorithms with advice. J. Comput. Syst. Sci. 76(3-4), 222–232 (2008)
9. Fraigniaud, P., Halldórsson, M.M., Korman, A.: On the Impact of Identifiers on Local Decision. In: Baldoni, R., Flocchini, P., Binoy, R. (eds.) OPODIS 2012. LNCS, vol. 7702, pp. 224–238. Springer, Heidelberg (2012)
10. Fraigniaud, P., Korman, A., Lebhar, E.: Local MST computation with short advice. In: Proc. 19th ACM Symp. on Parallelism in Algorithms and Architectures (SPAA), pp. 154–160 (2007)
11. Fraigniaud, P., Korman, A., Parter, M., Peleg, D.: Randomized Distributed Decision. In: Aguilera, M.K. (ed.) DISC 2012. LNCS, vol. 7611, pp. 371–385. Springer, Heidelberg (2012)
12. Fraigniaud, P., Korman, A., Peleg, D.: Local Distributed Decision. In: Proc. 52nd Annual IEEE Symp. on Foundations of Computer Science (FOCS), pp. 708–717 (2011)
13. Fraigniaud, P., Göös, M., Korman, A., Suomela, J.: What can be decided locally without identifiers? In: 32nd ACM Symp. on Principles of Distributed Computing, PODC (2013)
14. Fraigniaud, P., Pelc, A.: Decidability Classes for Mobile Agents Computing. In: Fernández-Baca, D. (ed.) LATIN 2012. LNCS, vol. 7256, pp. 362–374. Springer, Heidelberg (2012)
15. Fraigniaud, P., Rajsbaum, S., Travers, C.: Locality and Checkability in Wait-Free Computing. In: Peleg, D. (ed.) DISC 2011. LNCS, vol. 6950, pp. 333–347. Springer, Heidelberg (2011)
16. Fraigniaud, P., Rajsbaum, S., Travers, C.: An Impossibility Result for Run-Time Monitoring (submitted, 2013)
17. Goldreich, O. (ed.): Property Testing. LNCS, vol. 6390. Springer, Heidelberg (2010)
18. Goldreich, O., Ron, D.: Property Testing in Bounded Degree Graphs. Algorithmica 32(2), 302–343 (2002)
19. Göös, M., Suomela, J.: Locally checkable proofs. In: Proc. 30th ACM Symp. on Principles of Distributed Computing, PODC (2011)
20. Katz, S., Perry, K.: Self-stabilizing extensions to for message-passing systems. Distributed Computing 7, 17–26 (1993)
21. Kor, L., Korman, A., Peleg, D.: Tight Bounds For Distributed MST Verification. In: Proc. 28th Int. Symp. on Theoretical Aspects of Computer Science, STACS (2011)
22. Korman, A., Sereni, J.S., Viennot, L.: Toward More Localized Local Algorithms: Removing Assumptions Concerning Global Knowledge. In: Proc. 30th ACM Symp. on Principles of Distributed Computing, PODC, pp. 49–58 (2011)
23. Korman, A., Kutten, S.: Distributed verification of minimum spanning trees. Distributed Computing 20, 253–266 (2007)
24. Korman, A., Kutten, S., Masuzawa, T.: Fast and Compact Self-Stabilizing Verification, Computation, and Fault Detection of an MST. In: Proc. 30th ACM Symp. on Principles of Distributed Computing, PODC (2011)
25. Korman, A., Kutten, S., Peleg, D.: Proof labeling schemes. Distributed Computing 22, 215–233 (2010)
26. Naor, M., Stockmeyer, L.: What can be computed locally? SIAM J. Comput. 24(6), 1259–1277 (1995)
27. Peleg, D.: Distributed Computing: A Locality-Sensitive Approach. SIAM (2000)

How Good is Weak-Stabilization?

Narges Fallahi and Borzoo Bonakdarpour

School of Computer Science
University of Waterloo
200 University Avenue West, Waterloo, Ontario, Canada, N2L 3G1
{nfallahi,borzoo}@cs.uwaterloo.ca

Abstract. A *weak-stabilizing* system is one that guarantees only the
possibility of convergence to a correct behavior; *i.e.*, a recovery path may
visit an execution cycle before reaching a good behavior. To our knowledge, there has been no work on analyzing the power and performance
of weak-stabilizing algorithms. In this paper, we investigate a metric
for characterizing the recovery time of weak-stabilizing algorithms. This
metric is based on expected mean value of recovery steps for resum-
ing a correct behavior. Our method to evaluate this metric is based on
probabilistic state exploration. We show that different weak-stabilizing
algorithms perform differently during recovery, because of their structure
(e.g., the length and reachability of cycles). We also introduce an automated technique that can improve the performance of implementation
of weak-stabilizing algorithms through state encoding.

Keywords: Weak stabilization, Performance evaluation, Recovery time.

1 Introduction

A *self-stabilizing* [4, 5, 13] (SS) system is one that always recovers a correct behavior when the system is hit by transient faults and consequently reaches some
arbitrary state [15]. Such recovery is guaranteed to reach a set of *legitimate states*
within a *finite* number of execution steps. Self-stabilization is a strong property
and there have been several results on impossibility of designing SS algorithms for
token circulation and leader election in anonymous networks. To tackle this problem, several relaxations have been introduced. Examples include *probabilistic*
SS [11], where recovery is guaranteed with probability 1, and *k*-stabilization [1],
which assumes some arbitrary states cannot be reached and recovery takes place
within k local state changes for each process. *Weak-stabilization* [9] requires that
starting from any arbitrary state, there *exists* an execution path that eventually
reaches a legitimate state. Thus, in a weak-stabilizing (WS) system, a recovery
path may reach a cycle on its way to legitimate states (see Figure 1(b)).

There has been little attention to weak-stabilization in the literature due to
relaxation of finiteness of stabilization. It is also unclear how one would evaluate
the performance of a WS algorithm. In fact, conventional metrics for evaluating
the performance of self-stabilization (e.g., asymptotic computation complexity)

T. Higashino et al. (Eds.): SSS 2013, LNCS 8255, pp. 148–162, 2013.
© Springer International Publishing Switzerland 2013

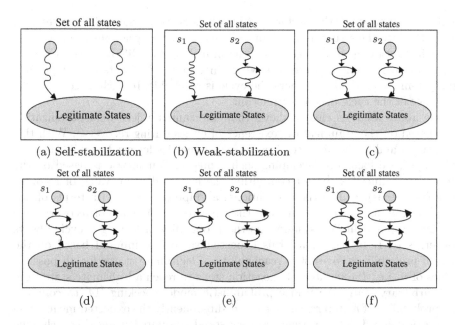

Fig. 1. Self-stabilization and different algorithm structure for weak-stabilization

become irrelevant in the context of WS algorithms. We argue that the relaxation of convergence finiteness by itself is not a plausible reason to reject weak-stabilization as a practical solution to deal with fault recovery in distributed systems for the following reasons:

- A WS algorithm in the presence of a fair scheduler is guaranteed to reach a correct behavior within a finite number of execution steps.
- In many commonly considered systems, actions happen with some probability. For example, in data networks, a packet reaches its destination with some probability. This implies that a cycle of actions that involves data re-transmission eventually ends.
- Recovery in a WS algorithm heavily depends on the structure of the algorithm and, in particular, reachability and length of cycles outside the legitimate states. In other words, existence of cycle(s) in an algorithm by itself is not a good measure to judge the performance of a WS algorithm.

To explain the latter reason in more detail, consider the structures in Figure 1. In Figure 1(b), the recovery path that starts from state s_2 reaches a cycle, but the one that starts from state s_1 does not. Such an algorithm is expected to perform better than the one shown in Figure 1(c), since in the latter both recovery paths reach a cycle. Likewise, the algorithm in Figure 1(c) is expected to perform better than the one shown in Figure 1(d), as in the latter, the path that starts from state s_2 reaches two cycles during recovery. Also, the algorithm in Figure 1(d) is expected to perform better than the one shown in Figure 1(e), since the latter reaches a cycle whose length is longer. On the other hand, it is difficult to compare the performance of the structures shown in Figures 1(d) and 1(f), since the structure in Figure 1(f) has a longer cycle, but the path that starts from state s_1 may avoid a cycle by branching to a different recovery sub-path. Another example is the case where in Figure 1(b) faults do not perturb the system to a state from where the cycle is reachable. In such a scenario, the existence of the cycle becomes irrelevant.

The above analysis clearly shows that one cannot reject weak-stabilization only based on the argument of "existence of cycles during recovery". With this motivation and in the absence of performance metrics for weak-stabilization, in this paper, we focus on developing such a metric. Our metric is based on the method introduced in [8] for computing the expected mean value of recovery time (i.e., steps). Unlike the conventional asymptotic metrics (in terms of, for instance, the number of rounds [6]), the expected mean value of recovery time can be computed in WS systems, as the probability of leaving a cycle always converges to 1. In particular, this expected value is computed based on the sum of probabilities for n-step reachability of legitimate states for all possible values of n; *i.e.*, the number of execution steps to reach a legitimate state from each arbitrary state. We utilize probabilistic model checking [14] to compute the probability of n-step reachability and subsequently the expected mean value of recovery speed. The average recovery speed computed using this technique represents the overall performance of a WS algorithm.

Since the absolute value of recovery time does not reveal much about the structure of a WS algorithm, we also propose a graph-theoretic metric that characterizes the performance of a WS algorithm by identifying its strongly connected components and incorporating their size, density, centrality, and reachability. Our analysis and experiments on a WS leader election algorithm [3] clearly show that the performance of a WS algorithm heavily depends on its structure as well as the location and length of cycles. We also introduce an algorithm that automatically generates a *state encoding* scheme for a given WS algorithm that can reduce the recovery time of the algorithm without changing its functional behavior.

Organization. In Section 2, we recap the preliminary concepts. Our performance evaluation method is described in Section 3. We introduce our graph-theoretic metric in Section 4. The algorithm for state encoding are discussed in Section 5. Finally, we make concluding remarks in Section 6.

2 Preliminaries

2.1 Distributed Systems

We model a *distributed system* as a simple self-loopless *static* undirected graph $\mathcal{G} = (V, E)$, where V is a finite set of vertices representing *processes* and E is a finite set of *edges* representing bidirectional communication, such that for all $(p, q) \in E$, we have $p, q \in V$. In this case, p and q are called *neighbors*. We

$$
\begin{array}{rcl}
x = 0 & \longrightarrow & \textbf{print} \, (\text{``safe''}) \\
x = 1 & \longrightarrow & x := 0 \\
x = 1 & \longrightarrow & x := 3 \\
x = 2 & \longrightarrow & x := 1 \\
x = 3 & \longrightarrow & x := 2 \\
x = 3 & \longrightarrow & x := 1 \\
x = 3 & \longrightarrow & x := 0
\end{array}
$$

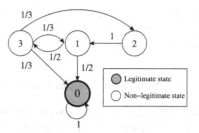

Fig. 3. Markov chain of guarded commands in Figure 2

Fig. 2. A set of guarded commands

assume that each process can distinguish all its neighbors using local indices. These indices are stored in $Neig_p = \{0, \ldots, \Delta_p - 1\}$.

The communication between processes are carried out using *locally shared variables*. Each process owns a finite set of locally shared variables, henceforth, referred to as *variables*. Each variable ranges over a fixed domain and the process can read and write them. Moreover, a process can also read variables of its neighbors in one atomic step. The *state* of a process is defined by a mapping from each variable to a value in its finite domain[1]. A process can change its state by executing its *local algorithm*. The local algorithm of a process is described using a finite set of Dijkstra's *guarded commands* (also called *actions*) of the form:

$$\langle label \rangle \; :: \; \langle guard \rangle \longrightarrow \langle statement \rangle$$

The *guard* of an action at process p is a Boolean expression involving a subset of variables of p and its neighbors. The *statement* of an action of p updates a subset of variables of p.

Example. We utilize the following running example to describe the concepts. Consider a system that consists of only one process. This process has a variable x that ranges over domain $\{0, 1, 2, 3\}$. The process actions are shown in Figure 2.

A *global state* s of a distributed system is an instance of the local state of its processes. We denote the set of all states of a distributed system G by S (called its *state space*). The concurrent execution of the set of all local algorithms defines a *distributed algorithm*. We say that an action of a process p is *enabled* in a state s if and only if its guard is true in s. By extension, process p is said enabled in s if and only if at least one of its actions is enabled in s. An action can be executed only if its guard is enabled. If *atomic* execution of an action in state s results in state s', we call (s, s') a *transition*.

Definition 1 (Computation). *A computation of a distributed algorithm is a maximal sequence of states $\overline{\sigma} = s_0 s_1 \ldots$, such that for all $i \geq 0$, each pair*

---

[1] We note that finiteness of processes, variables, and domains is due to the fact that our approach in this paper is based on model checking.

(s_i, s_{i+1}) *is a transition. Maximality of a computation means that the computation is either infinite or eventually reaches a terminal state; i.e., a state where no action is enabled.*   □

2.2 Probabilistic Model Checking

In order to reason about distributed systems, we focus on their state space and set of transitions. Let AP be a set of atomic propositions.

Definition 2 (Markov Chains). *A discrete-time Markov chain is a tuple $D = (S, S^0, \mathbb{P}, L)$, where*

- *S is the finite state space*
- *$S^0 \subseteq S$ is the set of initial states*
- *$\mathbb{P} : S \times S \to [0, 1]$ is a function such that for all $s \in S$, we have*

$$\sum_{s' \in S} \mathbb{P}(s, s') = 1$$

- *$L : S \to 2^{AP}$ is a labeling function assigning to each state a set of atomic propositions.*   □

It is straightforward to see that one can represent a distributed algorithm as a Markov chain. In a Markov chain, the fact that $\mathbb{P}(s, s') \neq 0$ for two states $s, s' \in S$ stipulates there is a transition from s to s' that can be executed with some probability. We emphasize that representing a distributed algorithm in our framework based on a Markov chain does not make our approach in this paper suitable for only probabilistic distributed algorithms (e.g., [11]). In particular, if a distributed algorithm is not probabilistic, then it can be modeled as a Markov chain, where the probability of all outgoing transitions from each state are equal, unless the system scheduler imposes certain probability constraints. Also, as argued in [8], for a distributed system, its corresponding Markov chain can be constructed in such a way that it is augmented with a certain type of scheduler (i.e., central, distributed, fair, etc).

Example. The Markov chain of the guarded commands in Figure 2 is shown in Figure 3. Each state is labeled by the value of variable x. Each transition is annotated by the probability of its occurrence.

Probabilistic model checking is based on the definition of a probability measure over the set of paths that satisfy a given property specification. Our specification language in this paper is the Probabilistic Computation Tree Logic (PCTL).

Definition 3 (PCTL Syntax). *Formulas in PCTL [10] are inductively defined as follows:*

$$\varphi ::= p \mid \neg\varphi \mid \varphi_1 \vee \varphi_2 \mid \mathbb{P}_{\sim\lambda}(\varphi_1 \, \mathcal{U}^h \, \varphi_2)$$

where $p \in AP$, $\sim \in \{<, \leq, \geq, >, =\}$ is a comparison operator, and λ is probability threshold. The sub-formula $\varphi_1 \mathcal{U}^h \varphi_2$ is the classic (bounded/unbounded) "until" operator.   □

Definition 4 (PCTL Semantics). *Let $\overline{\sigma} = s_0 s_1 \ldots$ be an infinite computation, i be a non-negative integer, and $\models$ denote the satisfaction relation. Semantics of* PCTL *is defined inductively as follows:*

$$\overline{\sigma}, i \models true$$

$$
\begin{array}{llll}
\overline{\sigma}, i \models p & \text{iff} & p \in L(s_i) \\
\overline{\sigma}, i \models \neg\varphi & \text{iff} & \overline{\sigma}, i \not\models \varphi \\
\overline{\sigma}, i \models \varphi_1 \vee \varphi_2 & \text{iff} & (\overline{\sigma}, i \models \varphi_1) \vee (\overline{\sigma}, i \models \varphi_2) \\
\overline{\sigma}, i \models \varphi_1 \mathcal{U}^h \varphi_2 & \text{iff} & \exists k \geq i : (k - i = h) \wedge (\overline{\sigma}, k \models \varphi_2) \wedge \\
& & \qquad \forall j : i \leq j < k : \overline{\sigma}, j \models \varphi_1.
\end{array}
$$

In addition, $\overline{\sigma} \models \varphi$ holds   iff $\overline{\sigma}, 0 \models \varphi$ holds. Finally, for a state s, we have $s \models \mathbb{P}_{\sim\lambda}\varphi$ iff   the probability of taking a path from s that satisfies φ is $\sim \lambda$.   □

Following Definition 4, we use the usual abbreviation $\Diamond\varphi \equiv (true\,\mathcal{U}\,\varphi)$ for "eventually" formulas. Moreover, $\Box\varphi \equiv \neg\Diamond\neg\varphi$ is the classical "globally" path formula.

Example. It is straightforward to see that the Markov chain in Figure 3 satisfies the following PCTL properties:

- $\mathbb{P}_{=\frac{1}{3}}(x = 3) \Rightarrow \Diamond^1(x = 0)$.
- $\mathbb{P}_{=\frac{2}{9}}(x = 3) \Rightarrow \Diamond^3(x = 0)$.
- $\mathbb{P}_{=1}\Diamond(x = 0)$, which is logically equal to $\mathbb{P}_{=1}(1 \leq x \leq 3)\,\mathcal{U}\,(x = 0)$

Definition 5. *Let $D = (S, S^0, \mathbb{P}, L)$ be a Markov chain. A* state predicate *of D is a subset of S.*   □

Observe that a state predicate is a PCTL formula constructed by only atomic propositions and Boolean operators $\neg$ and $\vee$.

2.3   Weak-Stabilization

Intuitively, a weak-stabilizing (WS) system is one that if its execution starts from any *arbitrary* state, then from that state there *exists* an execution path that reaches a good behavior (called the *convergence* property) and after convergence, it behaves normally unless its state is perturbed by transient faults (called *closure* property). The so-called "good behavior" is normally modeled by a state predicate called *legitimate states*. Since a WS system can start executing from any arbitrary state, in the context of Markov chains, we assume that $S = S^0$; *i.e.*, an initial state can be any state in the state space. Following the result in [3] that a non-probabilistic finite-state weak-stabilizing protocol in the presence of a probabilistic scheduler can be turned into a probabilistic self-stabilizing protocol, we formally define the notion of weak-stabilization as follows.

Definition 6 (Weak-stabilization). *Let* $D = (S, S^0, \mathbb{P}, L)$ *be a Markov chain, representing a distributed algorithm, and LS be a non-empty state predicate. We say that* D *is* weak-stabilizing *for legitimates states LS* iff *the following two conditions hold:*

- (Closure) *For each state* $s \in LS$, *if there exists a state* s', *such that* $\mathbb{P}(s, s') \neq 0$, *then* $s' \in LS$; *i.e., execution of a transition in LS results in a state in LS.*
- (Convergence) *We have* $\mathbb{P}_{=1} \square \lozenge LS$; *i.e., starting from any arbitrary state, the probability of reaching the legitimate states is always 1.* $\square$

In Definition 6, the convergence property is also called *recovery* and a computation that starts from a state in $\neg LS$ and reaches a state in LS is called a *recovery path*.

Example. It is straightforward to see that the Markov chain in Figure 3 is weak-stabilizing for $LS \equiv (x = 0)$.

3   Rigorous Computation of Recovery Time in Weak-Stabilization

Let $D = (S, S^0, \mathbb{P}, L)$ be a Markov chain with legitimate states LS and $\mathfrak{s}$ be a state in $\neg LS$. Following Definition 4, the PCTL property

$$\mathbb{P}_{\geq p}(\mathfrak{s} \Rightarrow \lozenge^h LS)$$

holds in D, if starting from $\mathfrak{s}$ the probability of reaching LS in h steps is greater than or equal to p. In order to analyze the speed of recovery of a self-stabilizing algorithm, we consider the other side of the coin by computing the probability of truthfulness of the following expression

$$(\mathfrak{s} \Rightarrow \lozenge^h LS)$$

for each state $\mathfrak{s} \in \neg LS$. Let μ be the probability distribution on recovery paths and $R(\mathfrak{s})$ denote the length of a recovery path that starts from $\mathfrak{s}$. One can compute the probability of existence of recovery paths of length at most N from state $\mathfrak{s}$ as follows:

$$\mathbb{P}\{R(\mathfrak{s}) \leq N\} = \sum \{\mu(\bar{\sigma} = s_0 s_1 \ldots) \,|\, (s_0 = \mathfrak{s}) \wedge (\bar{\sigma} \models \lozenge^h LS) \wedge (h \leq N)\} \quad (1)$$

Example. For the Markov chain in Figure 3, the probability of recovery of length at most 2 from state 3 to state 0 is: $\frac{1}{3} \times \frac{1}{2} + \frac{1}{3} = \frac{1}{2}$.

One can also compute the expected mean value of $R(\mathfrak{s})$, that is, the average length of all recovery paths that start from state $\mathfrak{s}$. Again, this value can be computed by direct summation as follows:

$$\mathbb{E}\{R(\mathfrak{s})\} = \sum \{\mu(\bar{\sigma} = s_0 s_1 \ldots) \times h \,|\, (s_0 = \mathfrak{s}) \wedge (\bar{\sigma} \models \lozenge^h LS)\} \quad (2)$$

Example. For the Markov chain in Figure 3, the expected mean value of recovery steps for the three states in $\neg LS$ are $\mathbb{E}\{R(1)\} \approx 2.5$, $\mathbb{E}\{R(2)\} \approx 3.5$, and $\mathbb{E}\{R(3)\} \approx 3$. These values can be obtained by computing infinite Taylor series that handle convergence of cycles in Figure 3.

In order to compute the expected value of recovery time, one can also incorporate the likelihood of execution from an arbitrary initial states. Thus, we associate a probability $p(\mathfrak{s})$ to each state $\mathfrak{s} \in \neg LS$, such that

$$\sum_{\mathfrak{s} \in \neg LS} p(\mathfrak{s}) = 1$$

Subsequently, the mean expected value of recovery steps for a weak-stabilizing algorithm represented by a Markov chain D is the following:

$$\mathbb{E}\{R(D)\} = \sum \left\{ \mathbb{E}\{R(\mathfrak{s})\} \times p(\mathfrak{s}) \mid \mathfrak{s} \in \neg LS \right\} \qquad (3)$$

Example. For the Markov chain in Figure 3, assuming uniform probability distribution for all non-legitimate state, the expected mean value of recovery is

$$2.5 \times \frac{1}{3} + 3.5 \times \frac{1}{3} + 3 \times \frac{1}{3} = 3$$

Another observation is that removing the transition from state 3 to 2 will break one of the cycles and results in expected recovery time 2.3 and removing the transition from state 3 to 1 will break all cycles and reduces the recovery time to 1.5.

Given $D_1 = (S_0, S_1^0, \mathbb{P}_1, L_1)$ and $D_2 = (S_2, S_2^0, \mathbb{P}_2, L_2)$, we say that D_1 outperforms D_2 iff

$$\mathbb{E}\{R(D_1)\} < \mathbb{E}\{R(D_2)\}$$

---

4   Structural Analysis of Weak-Stabilization

Although our approach in Section 3 can be applied to any WS algorithm, we choose the WS leader election algorithm for anonymous trees introduced in [3] for our study (see Algorithm 1). The state space of this algorithm includes cycles due to computations in which a process keeps changing its parent to its neighboring processes (*i.e.*, in Line 2). Thus, the length of cycles in $\neg LS$ directly depends on the number of neighbors of processes.

Consider the network topologies shown in Figure 4 and their expected recovery times obtained from Equation 3 through implementing the algorithms in the probabilistic model checker PRISM [12]. Although the recovery times clearly show which topology converges faster when running Algorithm 1, one needs more insightful information in order to analyze the behavior of the algorithm. To this end, we analyze the structure of the Markov chain of Algorithm 1 running on each topology in Figure 4. Before analyzing Algorithm 1, we introduce our structural analysis technique for performance evaluation of WS algorithms.

Algorithm 1. WS Leader Election [3] for any Process p

Variable: $Par_p \in Neig_p \cup \{\bot\}$
Macro: $Children_p = \{q \mid q \in Neig_p \wedge Par_q = p\}$
Predicate: $isLeader(p) \equiv (Par_p = \bot)$

Actions:
1: $(Par_p \neq \bot) \wedge (|Children_p| = |Neig_p|)$ $\longrightarrow$ $Par_p := \bot$
2: $(Par_p \neq \bot) \wedge [Neig_p \backslash (Children_p \cup \{Par_p\}) \neq \emptyset]$ $\longrightarrow$ $Par_p := (Par_p + 1) \mod \Delta_p$
3: $(Par_p = \bot) \wedge (|Children_p| < |Neig_p|)$ $\longrightarrow$ $Par_p := \min_{\prec_p}(Neig_p \backslash Children_p)$

4.1   A Graph-Theoretic Metric for Performance Evaluation of WS Algorithms

As mentioned earlier, measuring the performance of WS algorithms boils down to analyzing the structure of its cycles outside legitimate states. Since enumerating all cycles and computing their reachability from each other incurs an exponential time complexity in the size of Markov chain, we focus on two graph-theoretic abstractions that represent the existence and connectivity of cycles:

- *Strongly connected components (SCC).* An SCC is a subgraph in which each pair of vertices are reachable from each other. An SCC contains at least one cycle. In order to analyze nested cycles in an SCC, we also consider the number of states and transitions in the SCC. That is, the higher the number of transitions, the more likely it is for the SCC to have nested cycles.
- *Betweenness centrality (BC) [2].* Betweenness centrality quantifies the number of times a vertex acts as a bridge along the shortest path between two other vertices. We, in particular, employ vertex betweenness to compute the centrality of states in Markov chains. Formally, for a Markov chain with set of states S, BC of a state $s \in S$ is defined as follows:

$$C_B(s) = \sum_{s \neq s' \neq s''} \frac{SP_{s's''}(s)}{SP_{s's''}}$$

where $SP_{s's''}$ is the total number of shortest paths from state s' to state s'' and $SP_{s's''}(s)$ is the number of those paths that pass through s. In the context of our problem, we compute betweenness of states in SCCs in order to identify the number of paths that pass through cycles.

Thus, in general, we characterize the performance of a WS algorithm modeled by Markov chain D using the above factors as follows:

$$\mathcal{R} = |D_{scc}| \cdot \sum_{scc \in D} \left(C_B(scc) \cdot \frac{E_{scc}}{V_{scc}} \right) \tag{4}$$

where D_{scc} denotes the set of SCCs in D whose states are in $\neg LS$, $C_B(scc)$ is the average BC of the states in scc, and V_{scc} and E_{scc} denote the number of states (respectively, transitions) in scc. The last fraction in Equation 4 incorporates the *graph density* of an SCC. We note that since Equation 4 is an abstraction

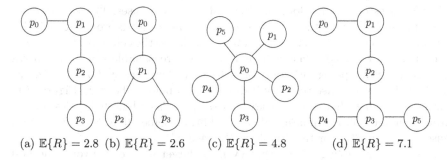

(a) $\mathbb{E}\{R\} = 2.8$ (b) $\mathbb{E}\{R\} = 2.6$ (c) $\mathbb{E}\{R\} = 4.8$ (d) $\mathbb{E}\{R\} = 7.1$

Fig. 4. Different topologies for Algorithm 1

to explain to the performance of a WS algorithm, it may fail by outliers. For instance, Equation 4 fails in Markov chains whose SCCs are small (*i.e.*, less than 4 states).

4.2 Analysis of WS Leader Election Algorithm

Figures 4(a) and 4(b) show the two possible topologies for a network of size 4 for Algorithm 1. The Markov chain of the topology in Figure 4(a) includes three SCCs: one SCC of size 3 states and 6 SCCs of size 2. SCCs of size two are due to the fact that processes p_1 and p_2 can keep changing their parents. For example, in global state $(p_1, \perp, p_3, \perp)$ (*i.e.*, $Par_{p_0} = p_1$, $Par_{p_1} = \perp$, $Par_{p_2} = p_3$, and $Par_{p_3} = \perp$), process p_2 has process p_1 as its neighbor which is neither its parent nor its child. Hence, p_2 can execute Line 2 of Algorithm 1 and choose p_1 as its parent, where the new global state is $(p_1, \perp, p_1, \perp)$. From this state, p_2 can again choose p_3 as its parent by executing the same action, hence, the cycle. There are $3 * 2 = 6$ combinations of such cycles. The SCC of size 3 is due to the following scenario. In state $s_0 = (\perp, p_0, p_3, \perp)$, the system can reach either state $s_1 = (\perp, p_0, p_1, \perp)$ or state $s_2 = (\perp, p_2, p_3, \perp)$. Thus, there is a cycle of length 2 between s_0 and s_1 and another cycle of length 2 between s_0 and s_2, hence, an SCC of size 3.

On the contrary, the Markov chain of the topology in Figure 4(b) includes only one SCC (due to process p_1 and its three neighbors) of size 18 states and 36 transitions. This implies that although this SCC has at least one (not necessarily simple) cycle of length 18, it is quite sparse. In other words, the SCC does not contain a high number of nested cycles and, hence, does not incur a high recovery time. Nested cycles and chain of cycles tend to increase expected recovery time exponentially. While the topology in Figure 4(b) has a long cycle, it does not have a high number of nested cycles and it does not have chain of individual cycles. Unlike this case, in the topology in Figure 4(a), the SCCs form a relatively long chain of cycles, which causes higher recovery time. We note that due to the size of SCCs for 4 processes, Equation 4 does not reflect the structure of its Markov chains properly.

For 6 processes, we only focus on the best and worst cases. The star topology in Figure 4(c) exhibits the best performance among all 6-process topologies. Intuitively, this is because the network tends to choose the center of the star (*i.e.*, process p_0) as the leader faster. This intuition is reasonable since the Markov chain of the star topology has only one SCC with low density 3.3, BC 272, and $\mathcal{R} = 899$. The worst case recovery is due to the topology shown in Figure 4(d). Our analysis shows that this topology creates 27 SCCs with nested cycles chained throughout the non-legitimate states. In addition, some larger SCCs are highly dense with high BC. For this topology $\mathcal{R} = 438,152$.

Likewise, our analysis shows that even for larger sizes of network, the best and worst case performance belongs to similar topologies. In particular, for 7 processes, the best performance is due to the star topology ($\mathbb{E}\{R\} = 5.8$ and $\mathcal{R} = 10,664$) and the worst performance is due to the line topology with ending branching ($\mathbb{E}\{R\} = 8.2$ and $\mathcal{R} = 1,474,708$).

To summarize, the importance of the above discussion is threefold:

- Equation 3 provides us with a rigorous fine-grained approach to evaluate the performance of WS algorithms.
- Equation 4 characterizes a coarse-grained approach to obtain the performance of a WS algorithm, but provides us the means to analyze and reason about the performance and structure of WS algorithms.
- These equations together are valuable tools for developers of distributed and network protocols to design more efficient WS algorithms.

5   Automated State Encoding for Weak-stabilizing Algorithms

State encoding consists in assigning bit patterns to abstract algorithm states [8]. For example, two states s and s' can be associated to bits 0 and 1, respectively. Another possibility is to have bit patterns of size two and mapping s to $\{00\}$ and s' to $\{01, 10, 11\}$. In the first case, there is a bijection between bit pattern and abstract states. In the second case, the mapping is injective, but not surjective.

In the context of WS algorithms, the purpose of such state encoding is twofold:

1. increase the proportion of LS as compared to $\neg LS$ states by making states appearing in $\neg LS$ less likely to appear (compared to the default choice of a bijective mapping) if bits can, for instance, randomly get flipped.
2. decrease the average expected recovery time by making states that are engaged in cycles outside legitimate states and incur long recovery time executions less likely to appear than those belong to short recovery time executions.

Example. As shown for the Markov chain in Figure 3, $\mathbb{E}\{R(1)\} = 2.5$, $\mathbb{E}\{R(2)\} = 3.5$, $\mathbb{E}\{R(3)\} = 3.0$, and $\mathbb{E}\{R\} = 3$. The set of states before encoding is $\{0, \ldots, 3\}$. Let the new domain of states be $\{0, \ldots, 6\}$. Since state 1 has the smallest expected value for recovery, we map it to values $\{1, 4, 5\}$. Likewise, we map state 3

Algorithm 2. State Encoding for WS Algorithms (based on feedback arc set)

Input: Processes $\{p_0 \ldots p_{n-1}\}$ and corresponding Markov chain $D = (S, S^0, \mathbb{P}, L)$
Output: Bit pattern state encoding

1: Let $G = (V, A)$ be the digraph, where $V = S$ and $(v_s, v_{s'}) \in A$ if $\mathbb{P}(s, s') \neq 0$ for all $s, s' \in S$.
2: Let $rank(v_s)$ be the length of the shortest path from vertex v_s, where $s \notin LS$, to a vertex $v_{s'}$, where $s' \in LS$
3: $A' := FAS(G)$
4: $V' := \{v \mid \exists u : (v, u) \in A'\}$
5: Let U_1 (respectively, U_2) be the sorted list of $rank(v)$ for each $v \in V'$ (respectively, $rank(u)$ for each $u \notin V'$)
6: $U := U_1 \cdot U_2$
7: Divide U into n sub-lists $\{u_0 \ldots u_{n-1}\}$
8: **for** $(i = 0$ to $n - 1)$ **do**
9:     Encode(u_i)
10: **end for**

---

to $\{3, 6\}$ and state 2 to $\{2\}$. By applying this encoding, the new expected mean value of recovery will reduce to $\mathbb{E}\{R\} = 2.83$.

We now introduce a state encoding algorithm based on the insights gained through our performance analysis techniques presented in Sections 3 and 4. We emphasize that state encoding is only an *implementation* technique and does not change the functional behavior of the original algorithm. Intuitively, the algorithm attempts to map more state bits to states that do not appear on a cycle. To this end, the algorithm utilizes the concept of *feedback arc set* (FAS); *i.e.*, a set of arcs whose removal makes a digraph acyclic. The algorithm uses the source vertices of these arcs to generate a state bit mapping.

The input to Algorithm 2 are n processes and a Markov chain D. First, it transforms D into a directed graph (Line 1). Then it ranks all states in $\neg LS$ based on the length of their shortest path to some state in LS (Line 2). Next, it attempts to find the minimum FAS (Line 3). Since finding minimum FAS is NP-complete, we utilize an approximation algorithm [7] to find a near-optimal solution. Next, we sort the vertices that originate from an arc in the FAS in the list U_1 and the rest of the vertices in the list U_2 (Line 6) based on their ranks. The actual encoding (Line 9) occurs on n equal-size slices of concatenation of U_1 and U_2.

The function Encode works as follows. For each variable in process p_i, we define two domains for before and after encoding, denoted D_i and D_i'. Initially, D_i' is empty. For each u_i and value $j \in D_i$, we calculate the probability that process p_i takes value j. Then, we map the most probable value onto i values in D_i' and subsequently remove the original value from D_i. Since the states in $u_0 \cdots u_{n-1}$ are sorted, we are guaranteed that for every process i, each value in D_i will be mapped to at least 1 value in D_i'. Also, the most probable values in u_{n-1} are mapped to n values in D_i'. If D_i has only one element left and there are still some u_j's left to analyze, we compare the probability of that value in different

u_i's, and decide on the mapping with the most probable one. In case of a tie, we skip the slice.

Example. Consider Algorithm 1 with 4 processes with the topology shown in Figure 4(a), where range $\{-1, 0, \ldots, 3\}$ represents $\{\perp, p_0, p_1, p_2, p_3\}$. Thus, considering the neighborig processes in the topology, we have $D_0 = \{-1, 1\}$, $D_1 = \{-1, 0, 2\}$, $D_2 = \{-1, 1, 3\}$, and $D_3 = \{-1, 2\}$. By applying Algorithm 2, we obtain the following slices:

$$u_0 = \{(-1, 0, -1, -1), (-1, 0, 1, -1), (-1, 0, 3, -1),$$
$$(-1, 2, -1, -1), (-1, 2, 3, -1), (1, -1, 3, -1), (1, 0, 3, -1)\}$$
$$u_1 = \{(-1, -1, 1, -1), (-1, -1, 3, -1), (-1, 0, -1, 2),$$
$$(-1, 0, 3, 2), (-1, 2, -1, 2), (1, 2, 3, 2)\}$$
$$u_2 = \{(-1, 2, 1, -1), (1, 2, -1, -1), (1, 2, 1, -1), (1, 0, 1, 2), (1, 2, 1, 2)\}$$
$$u_3 = \{(-1, -1, -1, -1), (-1, -1, -1, 2), (-1, -1, 1, 2), (-1, -1, 3, 2), (-1, 2, 1, 2),$$
$$(1, -1, -1, -1), (1, -1, -1, 2), (1, -1, 3, 2), (1, 0, -1, -1), (1, 0, -1, 2), (1, 0, 3, 2)\}$$

Now, for u_0, we have the following (initially $D'_0 = D'_1 = D'_2 = D'_3 = \emptyset$):

$$\mathbb{P}(Par_{p_0} = -1) = \frac{5}{7} \qquad \mathbb{P}(Par_{p_0} = 1) = \frac{2}{7}$$

$$\mathbb{P}(Par_{p_1} = -1) = \frac{1}{7} \qquad \mathbb{P}(Par_{p_1} = 0) = \frac{4}{7} \qquad \mathbb{P}(p_1 = 2) = \frac{2}{7}$$

$$\mathbb{P}(Par_{p_2} = -1) = \frac{2}{7} \qquad \mathbb{P}(Par_{p_2} = 1) = \frac{1}{7} \qquad \mathbb{P}(Par_{p_2} = 3) = \frac{4}{7}$$

$$\mathbb{P}(Par_{p_3} = -1) = \frac{7}{7} \qquad \mathbb{P}(Par_{p_3} = 2) = \frac{0}{7}$$

Thus, we map $-1 \in D_0$ to only 1 value in D'_0 and update D_0 by removing -1 and D'_0 by adding -1. The application of this mapping to domains $D_1 \cdots D_3$ and $D'_1 \cdots D'_3$ are illustrated in Table 1.

For u_1, the probabilities are the following,

$$\mathbb{P}(Par_{p_0} = 0) = \frac{0}{6} \qquad \mathbb{P}(Par_{p_1} = -1) = \frac{2}{6} \qquad \mathbb{P}(Par_{p_1} = 2) = \frac{2}{6}$$

$$\mathbb{P}(Par_{p_2} = 1) = \frac{1}{6} \qquad \mathbb{P}(Par_{p_2} = 3) = \frac{3}{6} \qquad \mathbb{P}(Par_{p_3} = 2) = \frac{4}{6}$$

For process p_0 and p_3 there is also only one value remaining. Thus, we will decide on their mapping when processing u_2. For process p_2, we map 3 in D_2 to two values $\{3, 4\}$ in D'_2 and update D_2 by removing 3 from it. The remainder of this iteration is summarized in Table 1.

For u_2, we have:

$$\mathbb{P}(Par_{p_0} = 1) = \frac{4}{5} \qquad \mathbb{P}(Par_{p_1} = -1) = \frac{0}{5} \qquad \mathbb{P}(Par_{p_1} = 2) = \frac{4}{5}$$

$$\mathbb{P}(Par_{p_2} = 1) = \frac{4}{5} \qquad \mathbb{P}(p_3 = 2) = \frac{2}{5}$$

Table 1. Iterations of state encoding for $i = 0$ to 3 (Line 9 of Algorithm 2 for WS leader election and 4 processes for the topology shown in Figure 4(a))

	$i = 0$			$i = 1$			$i = 2$			$i = 3$		
	max $\mathbb{P}$	D	D'	max $\mathbb{P}$	D	D'	max $\mathbb{P}$	D	D'	max $\mathbb{P}$	D	D'
p_0	-1	$\{1\}$	$\{-1\}$		$\{1\}$	$\{-1\}$		$\{1\}$	$\{-1\}$	1	$\emptyset$	$\{-1,0,1,2\}$
p_1	0	$\{-1,2\}$	$\{0\}$		$\{-1,2\}$	$\{0\}$	2	$\{-1\}$	$\{0,2,5,6\}$	-1	$\emptyset$	$\{-1,0,1,2,3,4,5,6\}$
p_2	3	$\{-1,1\}$	$\{3\}$	-1	$\{1\}$	$\{-1,0,3\}$		$\{1\}$	$\{-1,0,3\}$	1	$\emptyset$	$\{-1,0,1,2,3,4\}$
p_3	-1	$\{2\}$	$\{-1\}$		$\{2\}$	$\{-1\}$		$\{2\}$	$\{-1\}$	2	$\emptyset$	$\{-1,0,1,2,3\}$

Finally, for u_3, we have:

$$\mathbb{P}(Par_{p_0} = 1) = \frac{6}{11} \qquad \mathbb{P}(Par_{p_1} = -1) = \frac{7}{11} \qquad \mathbb{P}(p_3 = 2) = \frac{8}{11}$$

The result of the iterations for u_2 and u_3 are in summarized in Table 1. Using the above state encoding technique, the expected recovery time of WS leader election for the topology shown is Figure 4(a) (respectively, Figure 4(b)) reduces to 1.6 (respectively, 1.7) from 2.8 (respectively, 2.6). We note that the encoded models use 26 times more space than the original model.

6 Conclusion

Evaluating the performance of weak-stabilizing (WS) algorithms has not been studied in the literature, since such algorithms may exhibit behaviors that never stabilize. In this paper, we proposed an automated method for evaluating the performance of distributed WS algorithms using probabilistic verification. Our method computes the expected recovery time of each state of a WS algorithm using rigorous state exploration from which the overall expected mean value of recovery time of the algorithm can be obtained. To our knowledge, this is the first attempt in studying the performance of WS systems.

Since the expected recovery time as an absolute value is not particularly insightful, we also proposed a graph-theoretic method to analyze the structure of WS algorithms. This method is based on identifying strongly connected components and their betweenness centrality in the reachability graph of a WS algorithm. We showed that the corresponding metric is in strong correlation with expected recovery time in WS algorithms. All our claims are backed by experiments on a WS leader election algorithm [3]. Using our insights, we also introduced an algorithm that generate state bit maps (called *state encoding*) that improve the recovery time in an implementation of a WS system.

As for future work, we are planning to design algorithms that synthesize WS systems that satisfy given recovery time objectives. Another interesting direction is to design parametric model checking techniques to analyze the performance of WS algorithms when the exact number of processes is not given.

Acknowledgements. This research was supported in part by Canada NSERC Discovery Grant 418396-2012 and NSERC Strategic Grant 430575-2012.

References

1. Beauquier, J., Genolini, C., Kutten, S.: k-stabilization of reactive tasks. In: Proceedings of the 17th ACM Symposium on Principles of Distributed Computing (PODC), pp. 318–327 (1998)
2. Brandes, U.: On variants of shortest-path betweenness centrality and their generic computation. Social Nnetworks 30(2) (2008)
3. Devismes, S., Tixeuil, S., Yamashita, M.: Weak vs. self vs. probabilistic stabilization. In: Proceedings of the 28th IEEE International Conference on Distributed Computing Systems (ICDCS), pp. 681–688 (2008)
4. Dijkstra, E.W.: Self-stabilizing systems in spite of distributed control. Communications of the ACM 17(11), 643–644 (1974)
5. Dolev, S.: Self-stabilization. MIT Press (March 2000)
6. Dolev, S., Israeli, A., Moran, S.: Uniform dynamic self-stabilizing leader election. IEEE Transactions on Parallel Distributed Systems 8(4), 424–440 (1997)
7. Eades, P., Lin, X., Smyth, W.F.: A fast effective heuristic for the feedback arc set problem. Information Processing Letters (IPL) 47, 319–323 (1993)
8. Fallahi, N., Bonakdarpour, B., Tixeuil, S.: Rigorous performance evaluation of self-stabilization using probabilistic model checking. In: Proceedings of the 32nd IEEE International Conference on Reliable Distributed Systems, SRDS (to appear 2013)
9. Gouda, M.G.: The theory of weak stabilization. In: Datta, A.K., Herman, T. (eds.) WSS 2001. LNCS, vol. 2194, p. 114. Springer, Heidelberg (2001)
10. Hansson, H., Jonsson, B.: A logic for reasoning about time and reliability. Formal Aspect of Computing (FAOC) 6(5), 512–535 (1994)
11. Herman, T.: Probabilistic self-stabilization. Information Processing Letters 35(2), 63–67 (1990)
12. Kwiatkowska, M., Norman, G., Parker, D.: PRISM 4.0: Verification of probabilistic real-time systems. In: Gopalakrishnan, G., Qadeer, S. (eds.) CAV 2011. LNCS, vol. 6806, pp. 585–591. Springer, Heidelberg (2011)
13. Tixeuil, S.: Self-stabilizing Algorithms. In: Algorithms and Theory of Computation Handbook, Chapman & Hall/CRC Applied Algorithms and Data Structures, 2nd edn., pp. 26.1–26.45. CRC Press, Taylor & Francis Group (November 2009)
14. Vardi, M.Y.: Automatic verification of probabilistic concurrent finite-state programs. In: Proceedings of the 26th Annual Symposium on Foundations of Computer Science (FOCS), pp. 327–338 (1985)
15. Varghese, G., Jayaram, M.: The fault span of crash failures. J. ACM 47(2), 244–293 (2000)

Verifying Livelock Freedom on Parameterized Rings and Chains*

Alex P. Klinkhamer and Ali Ebnenasir

Department of Computer Science,
Michigan Technological University, Houghton MI 49931, U.S.A.
{apklinkh,aebnenas}@mtu.edu

Abstract. This paper investigates the complexity of verifying livelock freedom, self-stabilization, and weak stabilization in parameterized unidirectional ring and bidirectional chain topologies. Specifically, we illustrate that verifying livelock freedom of parameterized rings consisting of self-disabling and deterministic processes is undecidable (specifically, Π_1^0-complete). This result implies that verifying self-stabilization and weak stabilization for parameterized rings of self-disabling processes is also undecidable. The results of this paper strengthen previous work on the undecidability of verifying temporal logic properties in symmetric ring protocols. The proof of undecidability is based on a reduction from the periodic domino problem.

1 Introduction

Verifying *strong convergence* is known to be a difficult task [17], where from any state, *every* execution of a distributed system recovers to a set of legitimate states. From any state, a *weakly* converging system has at least one execution that recovers to legitimate states. Designing and verifying convergence are important problems as they have applications in several fields such as network protocols [7,19], multi-agent systems [16], cloud computing [23], and equilibrium in socioeconomic systems [18]. A common feature of such systems is that they comprise a finite but unbounded number of components/processes that communicate based on a specific network topology; i.e., *parameterized systems*. Deadlock freedom and livelock freedom outside legitimate states are necessary and sufficient conditions for strong convergence, whereas a system is weakly converging if and only if the system can reach the legitimate states from each illegitimate state via some execution. There are numerous methods [6,11,14,15] for the verification of safety properties of parameterized systems, where safety requires that nothing bad happens in system executions (e.g., no deadlock state is reached). Apt and Kozen [3] illustrate that, in general, verifying Linear Temporal Logic (LTL) [8] properties for parameterized systems is Π_1^0-complete. Suzuki [25] shows that the verification problem remains Π_1^0-complete even for unidirectional rings where all processes have a similar code that is parameterized in the number of nodes.

Contributions. In this paper, we extend this result for the special case where the property of interest is livelock freedom and every system state is under

---

* This work was sponsored by the NSF grant CCF-1116546.

T. Higashino et al. (Eds.): SSS 2013, LNCS 8255, pp. 163–177, 2013.
© Springer International Publishing Switzerland 2013

consideration. We make restrictive assumptions about processes, that they are deterministic, have constant state spaces, and are *self-disabling*, i.e., no action of a process is enabled immediately after it acts. Specifically, we illustrate that, even when processes are symmetric, deterministic, self-disabling, and have a constant state space, livelock detection is undecidable (Σ_1^0-complete) on unidirectional ring and bidirectional chain topologies. Further, we conclude that verifying strong or weak convergence on these topologies is Π_1^0-complete. The proof of undecidability in our work is based on a reduction from the periodic domino problem.

Organization. Section 2 presents some basic concepts. Section 3 provides a formal characterization of livelocks in unidirectional rings. Then, Section 4 represents a well-known undecidable problem, which we will use to show the undecidability of verifying livelock freedom in rings. Section 5 illustrates that verifying livelock freedom of unidirectional ring and bidirectional chain protocols is undecidable. Section 6 discusses related work, and Section 7 summarizes our contributions and outlines some future work.

2   Basic Concepts

This section presents the definition of protocols and action graphs. A protocol p defines the behavior for a network of $N > 1$ processes (finite-state machines), where each process P_i owns a set of variables whose valuation determines its *state*. The state of the network/system is defined by the current states of all processes. A process *acts* when it atomically changes its state based on its current state and the states of its neighboring processes, where neighbors are defined by the network topology. For example, in a unidirectional ring topology consisting of N processes, each process P_i has a neighbor P_{i-1}, where $i \in \mathbb{Z}_N$ (i.e., $0 \le i \le N - 1$) and subtraction is in modulo N. A *global transition* is a change in the system state. We assume that one process acts at a time (i.e., interleaving semantics), therefore each global transition corresponds to the action of a single process from some global state. An *execution* of a protocol is a sequence of states $C_0, C_1, \ldots, C_k$ where there is a transition from C_i to C_{i+1} for every $i \in \mathbb{Z}_k$.

We consider *symmetric* protocols, where each process has identical rules for changing its state. Furthermore, we assume that the state space Σ and rules for each process are independent of the topology (e.g., number of processes).

Definition 1 (Transition Function). *Let P_i be any process in a unidirectional ring protocol p which owns one variable x_i. We define its transition function $\xi : \Sigma \times \Sigma \to \Sigma$ as a partial function such that $\xi(a, b) = c$ if and only if P_i has an action $(x_{i-1} = a \land x_i = b \longrightarrow x_i := c;)$. In other words, ξ can be used to define all actions of P_i in the form of a single parametric action:*

$$((x_{i-1}, x_i) \in \text{PRE}(\xi)) \longrightarrow x_i := \xi(x_{i-1}, x_i);$$

where $(x_{i-1}, x_i) \in \text{PRE}(\xi)$ checks to see if the current x_{i-1} and x_i values are in the preimage of ξ.

We use triples of the form (a, b, c) to denote actions $(x_{i-1} = a \wedge x_i = b \longrightarrow x_i := c;)$ of any process P_i in a unidirectional ring protocol. To visually represent actions, we depict a protocol by a labeled directed multigraph where each action (a, b, c) in the protocol appears as an arc from node a to node c labeled b in the graph. For example, consider the self-stabilizing sum-not-2 protocol given in [12]. Each process P_i has a variable $x_i \in \mathbb{Z}_3$ and actions $(x_{i-1} = 0 \wedge x_i = 2 \longrightarrow x_i := 1)$, $(x_{i-1} = 1 \wedge x_i = 1 \longrightarrow x_i := 2)$, and $(x_{i-1} = 2 \wedge x_i = 0 \longrightarrow x_i := 1)$. This protocol converges to a state where the sum of each two consecutive x values does not equal 2 (i.e., the state predicate $\forall i : (x_{i-1} + x_i \neq 2)$). We represent this protocol with a graph containing arcs $(0, 2, 1)$, $(1, 1, 2)$, and $(2, 0, 1)$ as shown in Figure 1.

Since protocols consist of *self-disabling* processes, an action (a, b, c) cannot coexist with action (a, c, d) for any d. Moreover, when the protocol is deterministic, a process cannot have two actions enabled at the same time; i.e., an action (a, b, c) cannot coexist with an action (a, b, d) where $d \neq c$.

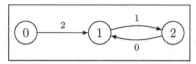

Fig. 1. Graph representing sum-not-2 protocol.

Livelock, deadlock, and closure. A *legitimate* state is a state which we want the system to be in. Let I be a predicate representing the legitimate states for some protocol p. A *livelock* of p is an infinite execution which never reaches I. When legitimate states are not specified, we assume a livelock is any infinite execution. A *deadlock* of p is a state in $\neg I$ which has no outgoing transition; i.e., no process is enabled to act. The state predicate I is *closed* under p when no transition exists which brings the system from a state in I to a state in $\neg I$. These concepts allow us to define self-stabilization and weak stabilization (from [17]).

Definition 2 (Self-Stabilization). *A protocol p is self-stabilizing with respect to its legitimate state predicate I if and only if from each illegitimate state, all executions reach and remain in the set of legitimate states. That is, p is livelock-free and deadlock-free, and I is closed under p.*

Definition 3 (Strong Fairness). *An execution is strongly fair if and only if for any state C_0 and transition (C_0, C_1), if C_0 is reached infinitely often, then (C_0, C_1) is executed infinitely often [17].*

Definition 4 (Weak Stabilization). *A protocol p is weakly stabilizing with respect to its legitimate state predicate I if and only if from each illegitimate state, an execution exists to a legitimate state, and I is closed under p.*

Notice that deploying a weakly stabilizing protocol under a strongly fair scheduler guarantees convergence to I, even if there are livelocks under no fairness.

3   Livelock Characterization

This section presents a formal characterization of livelocks in parameterized rings, which is an extension of [12,14]. This characterization is based on a notion of sequences of actions that are propagated in a ring, called *propagations* and a *leads* relation between the propagations. We shall use propagations and the leads relation to specify necessary and sufficient conditions for the existence of livelocks in symmetric unidirectional ring protocols of self-disabling processes.

Propagations. When a process acts and enables its successor, it propagates its ability to act. The successor may enable its own successor by acting, and the pattern may continue indefinitely. This behavior is called a *propagation* and is represented by a sequence of parameterized actions. Consider a propagation $\langle(a,b,c),(d,e,f)\rangle$ of length 2 which says a state exists which allows some P_i to perform action (a,b,c) which enables P_{i+1} to perform (d,e,f). Since P_i assigns its variable x_i to c and P_{i+1} is then enabled to perform (d,e,f) which relies on $x_i = d$ and $x_{i+1} = e$, we know $c = d$. We therefore write the jth action of a propagation as (a_{j-1},b_j,a_j). It follows that a propagation is a walk through the protocol's graph. For example, the sum-not-2 protocol has a propagation $\langle(0,2,1),(1,1,2),(2,0,1),(1,1,2)\rangle$ whose actions can be executed in order by processes P_i, P_{i+1}, P_{i+2}, and P_{i+3} from a state $(x_{i-1},x_i,x_{i+1},x_{i+2},x_{i+3}) = (0, 2,1,0,1)$. A propagation is *periodic* with period m if its jth action and $(j+m)$th action are the same for every index j. A periodic propagation corresponds to a closed walk of length m in the graph. The sum-not-2 protocol has such a propagation of period 2: $\langle(1,1,2),(2,0,1)\rangle$.

"Leads" Relation. Consider two actions A_1 and A_2 in a process P_i. We say the action A_1 *leads* A_2 if and only if the value of the variable x_i after executing A_1 is the same as the value required for P_i to execute A_2. Formally, this means an action (a,b,c) leads (d,e,f) if and only if $e = c$. Similarly, a propagation leads another if and only if, for every index j, its jth action leads the jth action of the other propagation. Therefore if we have a propagation whose jth action is (a_{j-1},b_j,a_j) which leads another propagation whose jth action is (d_{j-1},e_j,d_j), then we know $e_j = a_j$ and write the led action as (d_{j-1},a_j,d_j). In the context of the protocol graph, this corresponds to two walks (representing propagations) where the jth destination node label of the first walk matches the jth arc label of the second walk for each index j. After some first propagation executes through a ring segment $P_q,\ldots,P_{q+m-1}$, a second propagation can execute through the same segment only if the first propagation leads the second. This is true since each process P_{q+j} performs the jth action of the first propagation, assigning its variable x_{q+j} to some value a_j. If the second propagation executes through the segment, each P_{q+j} must perform the jth action of the second propagation from a state where $x_{q+j} = a_j$. As such, each jth action of the first propagation must lead the jth action of the second propagation. Thus, the first propagation itself must lead the second.

We focus on scenarios where for some positive integers m and n, there are m periodic propagations with period n where the ith propagation leads the $(i+1)$th propagation for each i (and the last propagation leads the first). This case can be represented succinctly. Using X as a wildcard value (i.e., any value, do not assume X = X), recall that an action is defined to lead another action $(\mathtt{X},a,\mathtt{X})$ when it has the form $(\mathtt{X},\mathtt{X},a)$. Also recall that a propagation of period n has the form

$\langle(a_{n-1}, X, a_0), (a_0, X, a_1), \ldots, (a_{n-2}, X, a_{n-1})\rangle$. Thus, if we write each ith propagation as $\langle(a^i_{n-1}, X, a^i_0), (a^i_0, X, a^i_1), \ldots, (a^i_{n-2}, X, a^i_{n-1})\rangle$, then we can determine the X values as $\langle(a^i_{n-1}, a^{i-1}_0, a^i_0), (a^i_0, a^{i-1}_1, a^i_1), \ldots, (a^i_{n-2}, a^{i-1}_{n-1}, a^i_{n-1})\rangle$. This case is succinctly visualized by an $m \times n$ matrix as shown in Remark 1 where for each row i and column j, the triple $(a^i_{j-1}, a^{i-1}_j, a^i_j)$ is an action in the protocol.

Remark 1. Consider the following $m \times n$ matrix M whose element at row i and column j is denoted as $M[i, j] = a^i_j$.

$$M = \begin{bmatrix} a^0_0 & a^0_1 & \cdots & a^0_{n-1} \\ a^1_0 & a^1_1 & \cdots & a^1_{n-1} \\ \vdots & \vdots & \vdots & \vdots \\ a^{m-1}_0 & a^{m-1}_1 & \cdots & a^{m-1}_{n-1} \end{bmatrix}$$

Assuming a unidirectional ring protocol of self-disabling, symmetric processes, the following statements are equivalent:

- The triple $(a^i_{j-1}, a^{i-1}_j, a^i_j)$ is an action in the protocol for every row $i \in \mathbb{Z}_m$ and column $j \in \mathbb{Z}_n$.
- The protocol contains m propagations of period n where each ith propagation leads the $(i+1)$th propagation for each $i \in \mathbb{Z}_m$. For each $i \in \mathbb{Z}_m$ and $j \in \mathbb{Z}_n$, the jth action of the ith propagation is $(a^i_{j-1}, a^{i-1}_j, a^i_j)$.

Example 1. Livelock freedom of the sum-not-2 protocol.

Recall from Figure 1 that the sum-not-2 protocol consists of three parameterized actions $(0, 2, 1)$, $(1, 1, 2)$, and $(2, 0, 1)$. Every periodic propagation in this protocol alternates between actions $(2, 0, 1)$ and $(1, 1, 2)$. These propagations require x_i values to alternate between 0 and 1 for each subsequent i. However, these propagations assign x_i values alternating between 1 and 2 for each subsequent i. Clearly no periodic propagation can execute through a ring segment of alternating 1 and 2 values, therefore no periodic propagation leads another in this protocol. For any ring size, an infinite execution requires that actions propagate around the ring. This is not possible since no periodic propagation leads another, therefore the protocol is livelock-free.

We form the same argument in terms of walks in the protocol's graph. Every closed walk in the graph alternates between visiting node 1 and node 2 indefinitely. No closed walk exists which alternates between visiting arcs labeled 1 and 2, therefore no periodic propagation leads another in the this protocol. As such, no livelock exists. We have also investigated livelocks in a 3-coloring unidirectional ring protocol (which is omitted due to space constraints) [22].

Lemma 1. *Assume a ring protocol where processes are symmetric. Let $C = (c_0, \ldots, c_{N-1})$ and $C' = (c'_0, \ldots, c'_{N-1})$ be states of a ring of size N such that $\exists k : \forall i : c'_i = c_{i+k}$. In other words, if C is rotated clockwise by k positions, then it equals C'. If an execution exists from C to C', then an infinite execution exists.*

Proof. Since processes are symmetric, we know a second execution exists from C' to a state $C'' = (c_0'', \ldots, c_{N-1}'')$ where $c_i'' = c_{i+k}' = c_{i+2k}$ for each i. States C' and C'' meet the same respective conditions as C and C', therefore an infinite execution exists. Emerson and Namjoshi [10] similarly use this notion of rotational symmetry to reason about rings of symmetric processes.   □

Lemma 2. *Assume a unidirectional ring protocol of symmetric, self-disabling processes. Given m propagations with period n, where the $(i-1)$th propagation leads the ith propagation for each index i (note: $(n-1)$th leads 0th when $i = 0$), the protocol contains a livelock for some ring size.*

Proof. Write the ith propagation as

$$\langle (a_{n-1}^i, a_0^{i-1}, a_0^i), (a_0^i, a_1^{i-1}, a_1^i), \ldots, (a_{n-2}^i, a_{n-1}^{i-1}, a_{n-1}^i) \rangle$$

Construct a ring of mn processes with an initial state

$$\left(a_0^{m-1}, a_1^{m-1}, \ldots, a_{n-1}^{m-1}, \ldots, a_0^1, a_1^1, \ldots, a_{n-1}^1, a_0^0, a_1^0, \ldots, a_{n-1}^0 \right)$$

In this state, every process whose index is a multiple of n is enabled. If each process executes its enabled action, we obtain the following state.

$$\left(a_0^0, a_1^{m-1}, \ldots, a_{n-1}^{m-1}, \ldots, a_0^2, a_1^1, \ldots, a_{n-1}^1, a_0^0, a_1^0, \ldots, a_{n-1}^0 \right)$$

If each propagation executes $n-1$ more times, we reach the following state.

$$\left(a_0^0, a_1^0, \ldots, a_{n-1}^0, \ldots, a_0^2, a_1^2, \ldots, a_{n-1}^2, a_0^1, a_1^1, \ldots, a_{n-1}^1 \right)$$

Every x_i now holds the initial value of x_{i-n}, therefore a livelock exists by Lemma 1.   □

Lemma 3. *Assume a unidirectional ring protocol of symmetric, self-disabling processes. The protocol has a livelock if and only if there exist some m propagations with some period n, where the $(i-1)$th propagation leads the ith propagation for each index i.*

Proof. Consider a fixed state C in the livelock where m processes are enabled at indices $i_0, \ldots, i_{m-1}$. Between two visitations of C, the propagation which started at index i_j has shifted to index i_{j+k} for some $k \in \mathbb{Z}_m$. Regardless of the value of k, we know that if C is visited m times after the initial visitation, the propagation which started at index i_j will be at $i_{j+mk} = i_j$. Thus, each of the m propagations will repeat at least every mth time the system reaches C. Such a list of propagations is necessary to form a livelock, and Lemma 2 shows it is sufficient, thus completing the proof.   □

4   Tiling

With our new characterization of livelocks in a unidirectional ring protocol from Lemma 3, we can explore the difficulty of livelock detection. We use the protocol graph as an intuitive bridge between problems. To complete the bridge, we introduce a well-studied undecidable problem, the domino problem, and reduce a variant of the problem to the problem of livelock detection.

4.1   Variants of the Domino Problem

Problem 1 (The Domino Problem).
- **Input:** A set of square tiles with a color (label) on each edge. All tiles are the same size.
- **Question:** Can copies of these tiles cover an infinite plane by placing them side-by-side, without changing tile orientations, such that edge colors match where tiles meet? In other words, can the following be satisfied for each tile $T[i, j]$ at row i and column j on the plane?

$$(T[i,j].N = T[i-1,j].S) \wedge (T[i,j].W = T[i,j-1].E)$$

where $T[i,j].N$ is the color on the north edge of tile $T[i,j]$. Similarly, the $.S$, $.W$, and $.E$ suffixes refer to south, west, and east edge colors of their respective tiles.

The domino problem was introduced by Wang [27], and the square tiles are commonly referred to as Wang tiles. Berger showed the problem to be undecidable [4]. Specifically, the problem is co-semi-decidable, also written as Π_1^0-complete using the arithmetical hierarchy notation of Rogers [24].

A tile set is *NW-deterministic* when each tile in the set can be identified uniquely by its north and west edge colors. In this case, if a tile meets another at its southwest (resp. northeast) corner, then the tile to its south (resp east) side is uniquely determined. Kari proved that the domino problem remains undecidable for NW-deterministic tile sets [21].

Problem 2 (The Periodic Domino Problem). This domino problem asks whether an infinite plane can be covered by placing copies of a fixed rectangular arrangement of tiles side-by-side such that a *repeating pattern* forms. In other words, can Problem 1 be solved such that there exist m and n such that the following is satisfied for each tile $T[i, j]$ at row i and column j on the plane?

$$(T[i,j] = T[i+m,j]) \wedge (T[i,j] = T[i,j+n])$$

Problem 2 is equivalent to asking whether a torus can be completely covered using the same tiling rules. Gurevich and Koriakov [20] give a semi-algorithm which terminates if the given tile set can periodically tile the plane or cannot tile the plane, otherwise it does not halt and the plane can be tiled, but not periodically. It follows that this problem is semi-decidable, also written as Σ_1^0-complete using notation of Rogers [24].

Action Tiles. A tile is *SE-identical* when it has identical south and east edge colors. For such sets, we refer to the south and east edge colors of a tile $T[i, j]$ as $T[i,j].SE$. We write (a, b, c) to denote such a tile with colors a, b, c, and c on its west, north, east, and south edges respectively. A set of SE-identical tiles is *W-disabling* when no two tiles which have the same west color have matching north and south colors respectively. In other words, a SE-identical tile set is W-disabling if and only if for every tile (a, b, c) in the set, no color d exists such that (a, c, d) is also in the set. Due to the following lemma (Lemma 4), we use the term *action tile* strictly to denote tiles in a SE-identical W-disabling tile set and *action tile set* to denote the set itself.

The triples that we use to represent tiles in an action tile set are subject to the same constraints as actions in a unidirectional ring protocol of symmetric, self-disabling processes. That is, the W-disabling constraint for tiles is equivalent to the self-disabling constraint for actions. As such, we have a bijection between these kinds of tile sets and protocols.

4.2   Equivalence to Livelock Detection

Lemma 4. *There is a bijective function which maps an action tile set to a unidirectional ring protocol of self-disabling processes such that the tile set admits a periodic tiling if and only if the protocol contains a livelock. The mapping preserves determinism (resp. NW-determinism) in the protocol (resp. tile set).*

Proof. Recall that a livelock can be characterized by a list of m periodic propagations of period n where each propagation leads the next one in the list (and the last leads the first). From Remark 1, we know that this is equivalent to an $m \times n$ matrix where for each row i and column j, the element a_j^i forms an action $(a_{j-1}^i, a_j^{i-1}, a_j^i)$ in the protocol with the help of its west and north neighbors a_{j-1}^i and a_j^{i-1} (with indices computed modulo the matrix bounds). It is straightforward to see that satisfying these constraints is equivalent to solving the periodic domino problem, where each action $(a_{j-1}^i, a_j^{i-1}, a_j^i)$ must exist as a tile in the action tile set as shown in Figure 2.

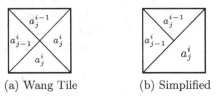

(a) Wang Tile   (b) Simplified

Fig. 2. Tile for action $(a_{j-1}^i, a_j^{i-1}, a_j^i)$

We already know that there is a bijection between action tile sets and unidirectional ring protocols of symmetric, self-disabling processes since the tiles and actions respectively are triples conforming to the same conditions. Therefore, the periodic tiling problem for action tile sets is equivalent to the livelock detection problem for unidirectional ring protocols of symmetric, self-disabling processes.

Similarly, an action tile set is NW-deterministic if and only if its corresponding protocol is deterministic. That is, for each triple (a, b, c) in the set, no triple (a, b, d) exists in the set where $c \neq d$. Thus, our bijective function (the identity) preserves determinism.   □

Example 2. Fictional "A-b-C" protocol with a livelock.

Figure 3 shows the graph of our example unidirectional ring protocol where each arc corresponds to an action. Note that the labels $a_0, \ldots, c_4$ are constants which could equivalently be changed to numbers $0, \ldots, 13$. The protocol does not attempt to function in any meaningful way, but it does provide an interesting livelock. First, propagations which characterize the livelock do not correspond to simple cycles in the protocol's graph. Secondly, 3 of these 6 propagations correspond to walks which are unique regardless of the starting node.

A livelock can be found by taking a walk through the graph. We start by choosing a closed walk starting with node a_2 and visiting nodes a_0, a_1, a_2, a_0, a_3, and a_2 without considering which arcs were taken.

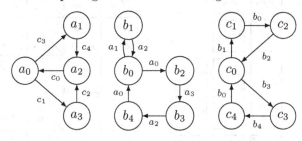

Fig. 3. "A-b-C" protocol graph

1. Using the previous nodes as arc labels a_0, a_1, a_2, a_0, a_3, and a_2, start from node b_4 to form a closed walk visiting nodes b_0, b_1, b_0, b_2, b_3, and b_4. This corresponds to the periodic propagation:
   $$\langle (b_4, a_0, b_0), (b_0, a_1, b_1), (b_1, a_2, b_0), (b_0, a_0, b_2), (b_2, a_3, b_3), (b_3, a_2, b_4) \rangle$$
2. Using the previous nodes as arc labels b_0, b_1, b_0, b_2, b_3, and b_4, start from node c_4 to form a closed walk visiting nodes c_0, c_1, c_2, c_0, c_3, and c_4. This corresponds to the periodic propagation:
   $$\langle (c_4, b_0, c_0), (c_0, b_1, c_1), (c_1, b_0, c_2), (c_2, b_2, c_0), (c_0, b_3, c_3), (c_3, b_4, c_4) \rangle$$
3. Using the previous nodes as arc labels, start at node a_2, etc.
4. Using the previous nodes as arc labels, start at node b_0, etc.
5. Using the previous nodes as arc labels, start at node c_2, etc.
6. Using the previous nodes as arc labels c_0, c_3, c_4, c_0, c_1, and c_2, start from node a_2 to form a closed walk visiting nodes a_0, a_1, a_2, a_0, a_3, and a_2. We started with this same sequence of nodes, therefore we are done and have found the first periodic propagation to be:
   $$\langle (a_2, c_0, a_0), (a_0, c_3, a_1), (a_1, c_4, a_2), (a_2, c_0, a_0), (a_0, c_1, a_3), (a_3, c_2, a_2) \rangle$$

To compactly illustrate all 6 propagations, we follow the method of Remark 1 and construct a matrix M where, for each row i and column j, the elements $(M[i, j-1], M[i-1, j], M[i, j])$ form the jth action of the ith propagation of our livelock.

$$
M = \begin{bmatrix}
a_0 & a_1 & a_2 & a_0 & a_3 & a_2 \\
b_0 & b_1 & b_0 & b_2 & b_3 & b_4 \\
c_0 & c_1 & c_2 & c_0 & c_3 & c_4 \\
a_0 & a_3 & a_2 & a_0 & a_1 & a_2 \\
b_2 & b_3 & b_4 & b_0 & b_1 & b_0 \\
c_0 & c_3 & c_4 & c_0 & c_1 & c_2
\end{bmatrix}
$$

The equivalent periodic tiling problem has an input tile set and solution shown in Figure 4. Recall that the solution is a block of tiles which can have a copy of itself placed on any side without breaking the tiling rules, therefore it can be used to periodically tile the infinite plane.

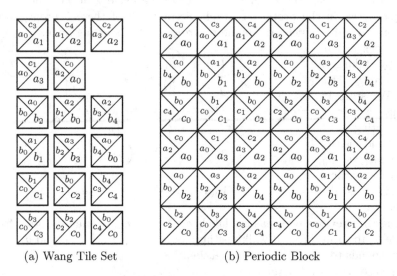

(a) Wang Tile Set   (b) Periodic Block

Fig. 4. Instance and solution for the periodic domino problem which corresponds to finding a livelock in the "A-b-C" protocol

4.3   Equivalent Tile Sets

The remainder of this section shows how to transform a NW-deterministic Wang tile set into a NW-deterministic action tile set which is equivalent with respect to the domino problems. This gives us the tools to reduce the periodic domino problem to livelock detection in the next section which proves that livelock detection is undecidable for unidirectional ring protocols of symmetric, deterministic, self-disabling processes.

Lemma 5. *For any set of SE-identical tiles which is not W-disabling, a W-disabling set of SE-identical tiles (i.e., an action tile set) exists which gives the same result to Problem 1 and Problem 2 and preserves NW-determinism.*

Proof. Recall that if a SE-identical tile set is W-disabling, then for every tile (a, b, c), there exists no tile (a, c, d) in the set for any d. If a tile set does contain such tiles, we can create a new tile set which is W-disabling. The new tile set has colors: $a_\rightarrow$ and $a_\uparrow$ for every color a in the original tile set, abc for every tile (a, b, c) in the original set, and a new color \$. The new set has tiles $(a_\rightarrow, b_\uparrow, abc)$, $(abc, \$, c_\rightarrow)$, $(\$, abc, c_\uparrow)$, and $(c_\uparrow, c_\rightarrow, \$)$ for each tile (a, b, c) in the original set. This reduction is shown clearly in Figure 5.

Tiling Correspondence. Observe that if a tile with a color of the form abc is placed on the plane, we can determine three other tiles which must be placed

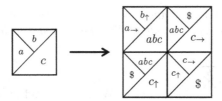

Fig. 5. Transform (a, b, c) tile to 4 W-disabling tiles

near it to form the 2×2 arrangement shown in Figure 5. Two of these are determined since the color abc appears on exactly three tiles in the set (for the W, N, and SE edges). The third tile $(c_\uparrow, c_\rightarrow, \$)$ is determined since no other tile has a color $c_\uparrow$ on its west edge (or $c_\rightarrow$ on its north edge).

Conversely, if a tile of the form $(c_\uparrow, c_\rightarrow, \$)$ is placed on the plane, then its west neighbor must have the form $(\$, abc, c_\uparrow)$ for some a and b corresponding to the original set of colors. After knowing these a and b, the two tiles to the north are determined due to the reasoning in the previous paragraph. Thus, any valid tiling T' using the new tile set consists of 2×2 blocks corresponding to the tiles in the original set. Further, since the $\$$ colors must match across these 2×2 blocks, the blocks must be aligned.

For correspondence, it remains to show that a valid tiling T exists using the original tile set if and only if a valid tiling T' exists using the new set. This is easy to see since two tiles (a, b, c) and (x, y, z) in the original set can border each other if and only if their corresponding 2×2 blocks in the new set can border each other.

The New Tile Set is W-Disabling. We want to show that for every tile (a, b, c) in the new set, there does not exist another tile (a, c, d) in the set for any d.

Partition the new tile set into four classes whose west edge colors have the form $X_\rightarrow$, XXX, $X_\uparrow$, and $\$$ respectively. Note that the forms of the north and southeast edge colors are also the same across tiles of the same class. Within each of these classes, the form of the north color differs from the form of the southeast color. Thus, no tile has a north color which matches the southeast color of a tile in the same class. Since tiles of different classes have different west colors, this implies that the new tile set is W-disabling.

The New Tile Set Preserves NW-Determinism. Recall that a tile set is NW-deterministic when for every tile (a, b, c), there does not exist another tile (a, b, d) in the set for any $d \neq c$. If this is the case in the original set, then any tile in the new set with a west color of $a_\rightarrow$ and a north color of $b_\uparrow$ for any a and b has a uniquely determined southeast color.

Each other tile in the new set (those with $\$$ on some edge) can be uniquely identified by its west or north color. For any abc, a tile whose west color is abc uniquely has the form $(abc, \$, c_\rightarrow)$. Similarly, a tile whose north color is abc uniquely has the form $(\$, abc, c_\uparrow)$. Lastly, for any c, a tile whose west color is $c_\uparrow$ uniquely has the form $(c_\uparrow, c_\rightarrow, \$)$. This covers all forms of tiles in the new set, therefore the new set preserves NW-determinism. $\square$

Lemma 6. *For any set of Wang tiles, an equivalent set of SE-identical tiles exists which gives the same result to Problem 1 and Problem 2 and preserves NW-determinism.*

Proof. For each tile 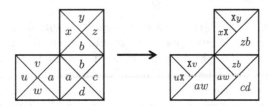 in the set of Wang tiles, and for every two colors w and z in the Wang tile set, construct a SE-identical tile (aw, zb, cd).

Fig. 6. Transform Wang tiles to SE-identical tiles

Recall from Problem 1 that a tiling is valid if and only if the following formula is satisfied for every tile $T[i, j]$ at row i and column j on the plane.

$$(T[i, j].N = T[i - 1, j].S) \land (T[i, j].W = T[i, j - 1].E)$$

Consider a tiling T' using the new set of SE-identical tiles. For any $T'[i, j] = (aw, zb, cd)$, we know that $T'[i, j - 1].E = aw$ and $T'[i - 1, j].S = zb$ must hold. By the construction of the new set, this is possible if and only if there are three Wang tiles from the original set whose edge colors correspond with aw, zb, and cd which can be placed on a plane at $T[i, j-1]$, $T[i-1, j]$, and $T[i, j]$ respectively (as illustrated on the left side of Figure 6). As such, a valid tiling T' exists using the new set if and only if a valid tiling T exists using the original set.

This transformation also preserves NW-determinism. Assume the input tile set is NW-deterministic. For any tile in the set, its east and south colors c and d are uniquely determined by its west and north colors a and b. This tile results in an SE-identical tile (aw, zb, cd) for each unique pair of w and z values. Still, the southeast color cd of these tiles is uniquely determined by a and b, therefore each SE-identical tile is uniquely determined by its west and north colors aw and zb. As such, the transformation preserves NW-determinism.   □

5   Undecidability Results

This section presents the undecidability of verifying livelock freedom in symmetric unidirectional ring and bidirectional chain protocols. The proofs of the theorems in this section heavily rely on the results of previous sections. Moreover, the results of this section apply even in the case of a *locally-conjunctive invariant*, which means that the predicate defining legitimate states has the form $I \equiv (\forall i : L(x_{i-1}, x_i))$, where $L(x_{i-1}, x_i)$ is a predicate checkable by process P_i.

Theorem 1. *Livelock detection on a unidirectional ring of symmetric, deterministic, finite-state, self-disabling processes is undecidable (Σ_1^0-complete). (Proof in [22])*

Corollary 1. *Detection of a livelock where exactly one process is enabled at all times on a unidirectional ring of symmetric, deterministic, finite-state, self-disabling processes is undecidable (Σ_1^0-complete). (Proof in [22])*

Corollary 2. *Verifying self-stabilization or weak stabilization on a unidirectional ring is undecidable (Π_1^0-complete). (Proof in [22])*

Corollary 3. *Verifying self-stabilization or weak stabilization on a segment of a bidirectional chain of symmetric, deterministic, self-disabling processes is undecidable (Π_1^0-complete). (Proof in [22])*

6   Related Work

This section discusses related work regarding necessary and/or sufficient conditions for livelock freedom and decidability of livelock freedom in parameterized systems. Specifically, Farahat and Ebnenasir investigate sufficient conditions for livelock freedom in symmetric unidirectional ring protocols of self-disabling processes [14]. They also present necessary and sufficient conditions for deadlock detection in symmetric unidirectional and bidirectional ring protocols. This paper complements their work by showing that, even when assuming deterministic and self-disabling properties, livelock freedom on ring and chain topologies is undecidable in general.

Decidability. In [3], Apt and Kozen prove that verifying an LTL formula holds for a parameterized system is Π_1^0-complete. Suzuki [25] builds on this result, showing that the problem remains Π_1^0-complete on symmetric unidirectional ring protocols where only the number of processes is parameterized. Emerson and Namjoshi [11] show that the result holds even when a token which can take two different values is passed around such a ring. Abello and Dolev [2] present a reduction from any Turing machine to a self-stabilizing bidirectional chain protocol. While one could use their reduction to build a proof for Corollary 3, such a proof would be complex since they rely on the existence of a distinguished processes.

Regular Model Checking. In regular model checking [1,5], system states are represented by strings of arbitrary length, and a protocol is represented by a transducer. Let R be the relation of this transducer and let R^+ be its transitive closure. A sufficient condition for the existence of a livelock would then be if some state is related to itself under the relation R^+. Touili [26] presents widening techniques which help compute R^+, which is uncomputable in general.

Our reasoning strongly resembles that of regular model checking. We can interpret the graph of a protocol p as a transducer, where arc and node labels denote input and output symbols respectively (i.e., a Moore machine). A periodic propagation would then be represented by some strings s and w such that the transducer accepts w^k and outputs s^k for all k. The protocol p therefore has a livelock if and only if some string w exists such that $(\forall k : (w^k, w^k) \in R^+)$, where R is the transducer's relation and R^+ is its transitive closure. While this technique can be applied to find livelocks in symmetric unidirectional ring protocols, regular model checking can be used with other topologies and LTL properties.

Cutoff Theorems. Emerson *et al.* [9, 10] present cutoff theorems for the verification of temporal logic properties in parameterized systems, where a property $\mathcal{P}$ holds for a parameterized protocol p if and only if $\mathcal{P}$ holds for an instantiation of p with a fixed number of processes k, called the *cutoff*. This method is mainly applicable for properties that are specified in terms of the locality of each process.

7   Conclusion and Future Work

We illustrated that verifying livelock freedom is undecidable for parameterized unidirectional ring and bidirectional chain protocols, where every process has similar code up to variable renaming. While Suzuki [25] shows that the verification of general case temporal logic properties is undecidable for symmetric unidirectional ring protocols, this paper illustrates that the verification problem remains undecidable even if processes are *self-disabling*; i.e., a process is disabled after acting. The proof of undecidability presented in this paper is based on a reduction from the periodic domino problem [27]. We also showed that verifying self-stabilization or weak stabilization is undecidable for these parameterized unidirectional ring and bidirectional chain protocols. As an extension of this work, we will investigate the design of a framework that will be an integration of our automated synthesis tools [13] and theorem proving. In this framework, we will first synthesize small instances of parameterized systems that are self-stabilizing for a specific number of processes. Then, we will use theorem proving techniques to generalize the synthesized systems for an arbitrary number of processes.

References

1. Abdulla, P.A., Jonsson, B., Nilsson, M., Saksena, M.: A survey of regular model checking. In: Gardner, P., Yoshida, N. (eds.) CONCUR 2004. LNCS, vol. 3170, pp. 35–48. Springer, Heidelberg (2004)
2. Abello, J., Dolev, S.: On the computational power of self-stabilizing systems. Theoretical Computer Science 182(1-2), 159–170 (1997)
3. Apt, K.R., Kozen, D.C.: Limits for automatic verification of finite-state concurrent systems. Information Processing Letters 22(6), 307–309 (1986)
4. Berger, R.: The Undecidability of the Domino Problem. Memoirs; No 1/66. American Mathematical Society (1966)
5. Bouajjani, A., Jonsson, B., Nilsson, M., Touili, T.: Regular model checking. In: Emerson, E.A., Sistla, A.P. (eds.) CAV 2000. LNCS, vol. 1855, Springer, Heidelberg (2000)

6. Cachera, D., Morin-Allory, K.: Verification of safety properties for parameterized regular systems. ACM Transactions on Embedded Computing Systems 4(2), 228–266 (2005)
7. Dijkstra, E.W.: Self-stabilizing systems in spite of distributed control. Communications of the ACM 17(11), 643–644 (1974)
8. Emerson, E.A.: Temporal and modal logic. In: Handbook of Theoretical Computer Science, Volume B: Formal Models and Sematics (B), pp. 995–1072. Elsevier (1990)
9. Emerson, E.A., Kahlon, V.: Reducing model checking of the many to the few. In: McAllester, D. (ed.) CADE 2000. LNCS, vol. 1831, pp. 236–254. Springer, Heidelberg (2000)
10. Emerson, E.A., Namjoshi, K.S.: Reasoning about rings. In: Cytron, R.K., Lee, P. (eds.) POPL, pp. 85–94. ACM Press (1995)
11. Emerson, E.A., Namjoshi, K.S.: On reasoning about rings. International Journal of Foundations of Computer Science 14(4), 527–550 (2003)
12. Farahat, A.: Automated Design of Self-Stabilization. PhD thesis, Michigan Technological University (2012)
13. Farahat, A., Ebnenasir, A.: A lightweight method for automated design of convergence in network protocols. TAAS 7(4), 38 (2012)
14. Farahat, A., Ebnenasir, A.: Local reasoning for global convergence of parameterized rings. In: ICDCS, pp. 496–505. IEEE (2012)
15. Fribourg, L., Olsén, H.: Reachability sets of parameterized rings as regular languages. Electronic Notes in Theoretical Computer Science 9, 40 (1997)
16. Funk, P., Zinnikus, I.: Self-stabilization as multiagent systems property. In: AAMAS, pp. 1413–1414. ACM (2002)
17. Gouda, M.G.: The theory of weak stabilization. In: Datta, A.K., Herman, T. (eds.) WSS 2001. LNCS, vol. 2194, pp. 114–123. Springer, Heidelberg (2001)
18. Gouda, M.G., Acharya, H.B.: Nash equilibria in stabilizing systems. In: Guerraoui, R., Petit, F. (eds.) SSS 2009. LNCS, vol. 5873, pp. 311–324. Springer, Heidelberg (2009)
19. Gouda, M.G., Multari, N.J.: Stabilizing communication protocols. IEEE Trans. Computers 40(4), 448–458 (1991)
20. Gurevich, Y., Koriakov, I.O.: A remark on Berger's paper on the domino problem. Siberian Mathematical Journal 13(2), 319–321 (1972)
21. Kari, J.: The nilpotency problem of one-dimensional cellular automata. SIAM Journal on Computing 21(3), 571–586 (1992)
22. Klinkhamer, A.P., Ebnenasir, A.: Verifying livelock freedom on parameterized rings. Technical Report CS-TR-13-01, Michigan Technological University (July 2013), http://www.cs.mtu.edu/html/tr/13/13-01.pdf
23. La, H.J., Kim, S.D.: A self-stabilizing process for mobile cloud computing. In: SOSE, pp. 454–462. Computer Society (2013)
24. Rogers, H.: Theory of recursive functions and effective computability. MIT Press (1987) (reprint from 1967)
25. Suzuki, I.: Proving properties of a ring of finite-state machines. Information Processing Letters 28(4), 213–214 (1988)
26. Touili, T.: Regular model checking using widening techniques. Electronic Notes in Theoretical Computer Science 50(4), 342–356 (2001)
27. Wang, H., Telephone, A., Company, T.: Proving Theorems by Pattern Recognition -II. American Telephone and Telegraph Company (1961)

Certified Impossibility Results
for Byzantine-Tolerant Mobile Robots[*]

Cédric Auger, Zohir Bouzid[4], Pierre Courtieu[2],
Sébastien Tixeuil[4,5], and Xavier Urbain[1,3]

[1] École Nat. Sup. d'Informatique pour l'Industrie et l'Entreprise (ENSIIE), Évry, F-91025
[2] CÉDRIC – Conservatoire national des arts et métiers, Paris, F-75141
[3] LRI, CNRS UMR 8623, Université Paris-Sud, Orsay, F-91405
[4] UPMC Sorbonne Universités
[5] Institut Universitaire de France

Abstract. We propose a framework to build formal developments for robot networks using the COQ proof assistant, to state and prove formally various properties. We focus in this paper on *impossibility* proofs, as it is natural to take advantage of the COQ higher order calculus to reason about algorithms as abstract objects. We present in particular formal proofs of two impossibility results for convergence of oblivious mobile robots if respectively more than one half and more than one third of the robots exhibit Byzantine failures, starting from the original theorems by Bouzid *et al.*. Thanks to our formalisation, the corresponding COQ developments are quite compact. To our knowledge, these are the first certified (in the sense of formally proved) impossibility results for robot networks.

1 Introduction

Networks of static and/or mobile sensors (that is, robots) [19] received increasing attention in the past few years from the Distributed Computing community. On the one hand, the use of cooperative swarms of inexpensive robots to achieve various complex tasks in potentially hazardous environments is a promising option to reduce human and material costs and assess the relevance of Distributed Computing in a practical setting. On the other hand, execution model differences warrant extreme care when revisiting "classical results" from Distributed Computing, as very small changes in assumed hypotheses may completely change the feasibility of a particular problem. Negative results such as impossibility results are fundamental in Distributed Computing to establish what can and cannot be computed in a given setting, or permitting to assess optimality results through lower bounds for given problems. Two notorious examples are the impossibility of reaching consensus in an asynchronous setting when a single process may fail by stopping unexpectedly [18], and the impossibility of reliably exchanging information when more than one third of the processes can exhibit arbitrary behaviour [29]. As noted by Lamport, Shostak and Pease [25], correctly proving results in the context of Byzantine (*a.k.a.* arbitrary behaviour capable) processes is a major challenge, as [they

---

[*] This work was supported in part by the Digiteo Île-de-France project PACTOLE 2009-38HD. A preliminary version of this work appears as a 2-pages Brief Announcement in DISC 2013.

T. Higashino et al. (Eds.): SSS 2013, LNCS 8255, pp. 178–190, 2013.
© Springer International Publishing Switzerland 2013

knew] *of no area in computer science or mathematics in which informal reasoning is more likely to lead to errors than in the study of this type of algorithm.*

An attractive way to assess the validity of distributed algorithm is to use *tool assisted* verification, be it based on process algebra [4,20], local computations [27], Event-B [8], CoQ [9], HOL [10], Isabelle/HOL [23], or TLA [25,24] that can enjoy an Isabelle backend for its provers [13]. Surprisingly, only few works consider using mechanised assistance for networks of mobile entities, be it population protocols [14,11] or mobile robots [15,5]. In this paper, our goal is to propose a formal provable framework in order to prove positive or negative results for localised distributed protocols in mobile robotic networks, based on recent advances in mechanical proving and related areas, and in particular on *proof assistants*. Proof assistants are environments in which a user can express programs, state theorems and develop interactively proofs that will be mechanically checked (that is machine-checked). They have been successfully employed for various tasks such as the formalisation of programming language semantics [26,28], verification of cryptographic protocols [2], certification of RSA keys [31], mathematical developments as involved as the 4-colours [21] or Feit-Thompson [22] theorems.

Our Contribution. We developed a general framework relying on the CoQ proof assistant to prove possibility and impossibility results about mobile robotic networks. The key property of our approach is that its underlying calculus is of higher order: instead of providing the code of the distributed protocols executed by the robots, we may quantify universally on those programs/algorithms, or just characterise them with an abstract property. This genericity makes this approach complementary to the use of model-checking methods for verifying distributed algorithms [7,11,15,17] that are highly automatic, but address mainly particular instances of algorithms. In particular, quantifying over algorithms allows us to express in a natural way *impossibility results*.

We illustrate how our framework allows for such certification by providing CoQ proofs of two earlier impossibility and lower bound theorems by Bouzid *et al.* [6], guaranteeing soundness of the first one, and of the SSYNC fair version of the second one. More precisely, in the context[1] of oblivious robots that are endowed with strong global multiplicity detection and whose movements are constrained along a rational line, and assuming that the demon (that is, the way robots are scheduled for execution) is fair, the convergence problem cannot be solved if respectively at least one half (Theorem 1) and at least one third (Theorem 2) of robots are Byzantine.

The interestingly short size of the CoQ proofs we obtained using our framework not only makes it easily human-readable, but is also very encouraging for future applications and extensions of our framework.

Related Work. With reference to proof assistants, Küfner *et al.* [23] develop a methodology to develop ISABELLE-checked proofs of properties of fault-tolerant distributed algorithms in an asynchronous message passing style setting. This work's motivations are similar to ours, however the setting (message passing distributed algorithms) is different, moreover it focuses on positive results only whereas we provide negative results, *i.e.* proofs of impossibility.

---

[1] Distributed Robot model assumptions are presented in Section 2.

Chou [10] develops a methodology based on the HOL proof assistant to prove properties of concrete distributed algorithms via proving simulation with abstract ones. The
methodology does not allow to prove impossibility results. Casteran *et al.* [9] propose
proofs of negative results in CoQ for some kinds of distributed algorithms. Though
very interesting, their approach is based on labeled graph rewriting and does not address robot networks. Another interesting approach is that of Deng and Monin [14] that
uses CoQ to prove the correctness of distributed self-stabilizing protocols in the population protocol model. This model permits to describe interactions of an arbitrary large
size of mobile entities, but the considered entities lack movement control and geometric awareness that are characteristic of robot networks such as those we envision, and is
thus not suitable for our purpose. This approach also only considers positive results.

Preliminary attempts for automatically proving impossibility results in robot networks properties are due to Devismes *et al.* [15], Bonnet *et al.* [5], and Bérard *et al.*[3].
The first paper [15] uses the LUSTRE formalism and model-checking to search exhaustively all possible 3-robots protocols that explore every node of a 3×3 grid (and
conclude that no such algorithm exists). The second paper [5] uses an ad hoc tool to
generate all possible unambiguous protocols of k robots operating in an n-sized ring (k
and n are given as parameters) and check exhaustively the properties of the generated
protocols (and in the paper conclude that no protocol of 5 robots on a 10 sized ring
can explore all nodes infinitely often with every robot). The third proposal [3] uses the
DiVinE model-checker to verify the correctness of two existing algorithms for exploration with stop and exclusive perpetual exploration in uniform anonymous rings of size
n. Those three proposals differ from our goal in several ways. Firstly, they are limited
to a so called *discrete space*, where the robots may only occupy a *finite* number of positions, while we focus on the more realistic setting where an infinite number of positions
are possible for the robots. Also, contrary to all three, we do not want to restrict our
tools to a particular setting (*e.g.* 3 robots on a 3×3 grid), but rather have results that
are general with respect to all considered parameters. Then, unlike the second proposal,
we want universal impossibility results (*i.e.* consider not only unambiguous protocols
– that permit to limit combinatorial explosion to some extent – but also ambiguous
ones – resulting from symmetrical situations that are likely to occur in practice). Finally, we want to integrate the possibility of misbehaving robots (*e.g.* robots crashing or
exhibiting arbitrary and potentially malicious behaviour), rather than assuming that all
considered robots are correct. This enables to state formally and assess the amount of
faults and attack resilience a given robot protocol may guarantee, which is crucial when
robots are deployed in dangerous areas as it is often the case.

Roadmap. The sequel of the paper is organised as follows. First, we recall the context
of robot networks in Section 2. Then, in Section 3 we give a brief description of CoQ
and its main principles. Section 4 contains the basis of our formal model for robot
networks, and some useful theorems. We show in Section 5 how convenient it is to
carry out formal proofs of various properties, as we study previous results by Bouzid *et
al.* [6]. We provide some concluding remarks in Section 6.

Note that for the sake of readability we slightly simplified CoQ notations (mostly to
avoid syntactic sugar). The actual development for CoQ 8.4pl3 is available at
http://pactole.lri.fr/pub/framework.tgz

2   Robot Networks

We borrow most of the notions in this section from [30,1,19]. The network consists in a set of n mobile entities, called robots, arbitrarily located in the space. Robots cannot communicate directly by sending messages to each others. Instead, their communication is based on vision: they observe the positions of other robots, and based on their observations, they compute destination points to which they move.

Robots are *homogeneous* and *anonymous*: they run the same algorithm (called *robogram*), they are completely indistinguishable by their appearance, and no identifier can be used in their computations. They are also *oblivious*, i.e. they cannot remember any previous observation, computation or movement performed in any previous step.

For simplicity, we assume that robots are *without volume, i.e.* they are modeled as points that cannot obstruct the movement or vision of other robots. Visibility is *global*: the entire set of robots can always be seen by any robot at any time. Robots that are able to determine the exact number of robots occupying the same position enjoy *strong* multiplicity detection ; if they can only know if a given position is inhabited or not, their multiplicity detection is said to be *weak*. Each robot has its own local coordinate system and its own unit measure. They do not share any origin, orientation, and more generally any frame of reference.

The multiset of positions of robots at a given time is called a *configuration*. We assume that the actions of robots are controlled by a fictitious entity called the *demon* (or adversary). Each time a robot is activated by the demon, it executes a complete three-phases cycle: Look, Compute and Move. During the Look phase, using its visual sensors, the robot gets a snapshot of the current configuration. Then, based only on this observed configuration, it computes a destination in the Compute phase using its robogram and moves towards it during the subsequent Move phase. Movements of robots are *atomic, i.e.* the demon cannot stop them before they reach the destination.

A *run* (or execution) is an infinite sequence of rounds. During each round, the demon chooses a subset of robots and activates them to execute a cycle. We assume the scheduling to be *fair, i.e.* each robot is activated infinitely often in any infinite execution, and *atomic* in the sense that robots that are activated at the same round execute their actions synchronously and atomically. An atomic demon is called fully-synchronous (FSYNC) if all robots are activated at each round, otherwise it is said to be semi-synchronous (SSYNC). The impossibility results we focus on are given in the FSYNC and SSYNC models, and hence remain valid in less constrained ones (*e.g.* non-atomic, unfair scheduling, etc.).

A robot is *Byzantine* (or faulty) if it does not comply with the robogram and behaves in an arbitrary and unpredictable way. We assume that the movements of Byzantine robots are controlled by the adversary that uses them in order to make the algorithm fail. Let $f \in [0, n]$ be a parameter that denotes the number of faulty robots. Robots that are not Byzantine are called *correct*. Correct robots are supposed to know an upper bound on the number of Byzantine robots.

3 The COQ Proof Assistant

COQ is based on *type theory*. Its *formal language* can express objects, properties and proofs in a unified way; all these are represented as terms of an expressive λ-calculus: the *Calculus of Inductive Constructions* (CIC) [12]. λ-abstraction is denoted **fun** x:T $\Rightarrow$ t, and application is denoted t u. A proof development with COQ consists in trying to build, interactively and using tactics, a λ-term the type of which corresponds to the proven theorem (Curry-Howard style).

The kernel of COQ is a *proof checker* that checks the validity of proofs written as CIC-terms. Indeed, in this framework, a term is a *proof* of its type, and checking a proof consists in typing a term. Roughly speaking, the small kernel of COQ simply type-checks λ-terms to ensure soundness.

A very powerful feature of COQ is the ability to define *inductive types* to express inductive data types and inductive properties. For example the following inductive types define the data type nat of natural numbers, O and S (successor) being the two constructors, and the property even of being an even natural number. In this setting the term even_S(S(S O))(even_S O (even_O)) is of type even(S(S(S(S O)))) so it is a proof that 4 is even.

```
Inductive nat : Set := O : nat | S : nat → nat.
Inductive even : nat → Prop :=
  | even_O : even O
  | even_S : ∀ n : nat, even n → even (S(S n)).
```

We also make use of *coinductive* types to express infinite data types and properties on them. For example in the robot networks setting a set of robots has an infinite behaviour. For example one can define infinite streams of natural numbers and the property all_even of being an infinite stream of even natural number as follows:

```
CoInductive stm : Set :=
  | scons : nat → stm → stm.
CoInductive all_even : stm → Prop :=
  | Ceven_all: ∀ n s, even n → all_even s → all_even (scons n s).
```

4 The Formal Model

We present our formal model and the relevant notations. Robots are anonymous, however we need to identify some of them in the proofs. Thus, we consider the union of two given disjoint finite sets of *identifiers*: G referring to robots that behave correctly, and B referring to the set of Byzantine ones. We will omit Sets G and B most of the time, except in Section 5 where they characterise the number of robots. Note that those sets are isomorphic to segments of $\mathbb{N}$ but we keep our formalisation as abstract as possible. If needed in the model, we can make sure that names are not used by the embedded algorithm, as shown below.

```
Variable G B : finite.
Inductive ident := Good : G → ident | Byz : B → ident.
```

Locations, Positions, Similarities. Robots are distributed in space, at places called *locations*. We define a *position* as a *function* from a set of identifiers to the space of locations. As the space of locations in the paper of Bouzid *et al.* [6] is an infinite line, we use $\mathbb{Q}$ for locations. Note that going from one to many dimensions is not a problem with respect to our formalisation. Throughout this article, and unless specified otherwise gp denotes a position for correct robots, and bp a position for Byzantine ones. The position of all robots is then given by the combination gp $\uplus$ bp.

```
Record position:= { gp: G → location ; bp: B → location }.
(* Getting the location of a robot *)
Definition locate p (id: ident): location :=
    match id with Good g ⇒ p.(gp) g | Byz b ⇒ p.(bp) b end.
```

Robots compute their target position from the observed configuration of their siblings in the considered space. We also define permutations of robots, that is bijective applications from $G \cup B$ to itself, usually denoted hereafter by Greek letters. Moreover, any correct robot is supposed to act as any other correct robot in the same context, that is, with a *similar* perception of the environment. For two rational numbers $k \neq 0$ and t, a *similarity* is a function mapping a location x to $k \times (x - t)$, denoted $[\![k,t]\!]$. Rational number k is called the homothetic factor, and $-k \times t$ is called the translation factor. For simplicity we restrict this definition to the uni-dimensional case; otherwise rotational factors may have to be provided too. Similarities are invertible; they form a group for the law of composition $([\![k,t]\!]^{-1} = [\![k^{-1}, -k^{-1} \times t]\!])$. Similarities can be extended to positions, by applying the similarity transform to the extracted location.

```
Definition similarity (k t : Q) (p:position) : position := {
    gp := fun n ⇒ k * (p.(gp) n - t) ;
    bp := fun n ⇒ k * (p.(bp) n - t) }.
```

This operation will be (abusively) written $[\![k,t]\!](\text{gp} \uplus \text{bp})$. Similarities will be used as transformations of frames of reference.

Robograms. We now model what an algorithm r embedded in a correct robot is. For a robot $r\text{-}id_i$, a computation takes as an input an entire position gp $\uplus$ bp as seen by $r\text{-}id_i$, in its own frame of reference (scale, origin, etc.),[2] and returns a rational number l_i corresponding to a location (the *destination point*) in the same frame.

Remark 1. Recall that robots in G cannot decide whether another robot is Byzantine, and have no access to a symmetry breaking mechanism such as an identifier. In such a case: the result of r must be invariant by permutations of robots. This is a fundamental property that *any* embedded algorithm must fulfil.

Embedded computation algorithms verifying Remark 1 are called *robograms*. They are naturally defined in our CoQ model as follows.

---

[2] Note that the scale factor is taken anew at each cycle for *oblivious* robots; in the context of Byzantine failures, it is convenient to consider it as chosen by some adversary.

```
Record robogram := {
  algo : position → location ;
  AlgoMorph : ∀ p q σ, (q ≡ p ∘ σ⁻¹) → algo p = algo q }.
```

It is worth noticing that this definition is completely abstract and makes no use of concrete code whatsoever.

Computation. So as to provide to r the locations of robots in terms of the considered robot's local frame of reference, and to obtain an absolute location in the *global* coordinate system from the result of r (thus local) we use the notion of similarity. Let us consider a robot $r\text{-}id_i$ the location of which is at t, and the scale of which is k times the global one, defining a similarity $[\![k, t]\!]$. To obtain the resulting location in terms of the global coordinate system:

1. We center the origin of the position in t, and we zoom according to the homothetic factor k to express the position in the local frame of $r\text{-}id_i$.
2. The algorithm r computes a local destination point.
3. We apply the inverse of the similarity to obtain the global destination point, that is: according to the global coordinate system.

We denote this operation $r_{[\![k,t]\!]}(\mathtt{gp} \uplus \mathtt{bp}) = [\![k, t]\!]^{-1}(r([\![k, t]\!](\mathtt{gp} \uplus \mathtt{bp})))$. This way we ensure that the global destination point does not depend on the individual frame of reference of robots.[3]

Demons and Properties. A demon provides the position for Byzantine robots, and selects the correct robots to be activated at the current round. As noticed in Footnote 2, we may consider that the demon, acting as an adversary, selects also the scale of the frame of reference for each activated correct robot at each round. A demonic action is thus a record

```
Record demonic_action:= {locate_byz: B → location; frame: G → ℚ}.
```

consisting of a position for Byzantine robots (`locate_byz`), and a function associating to each correct robot a rational number k such that $k = 0$ and the robot is not activated, or $k \neq 0$ and the robot is activated with a scale factor. The actual *demon* is simply an infinite sequence (stream) of demonic actions.

```
CoInductive demon :=  NextDemon: demonic_action → demon → demon.
```

Characteristic properties of demons include *fairness* and synchronous aspects. A demon (seen as a sequence) is locally fair for a robot (inductive property `LocallyFairForOne`) if either this robot is activated during the first demonic action, or if the robot is not activated during the first round but the sequel of the demon is locally fair for that robot. This is related to the classical notion of accessibility. The demon will be fair if it is locally fair for all robots and if its *infinite* sequel is fair.

---

[3] Note that in this presentation, any considered robot perceives itself as the origin of its local frame of reference.

```
Inductive LocallyFairForOne g (d : demon) : Prop :=
  | ImmediatelyFair : ((demon_head d).frame g) ≠ 0
      → LocallyFairForOne g d
  | LaterFair : ((demon_head d).frame g) = 0
      → LocallyFairForOne g (demon_tail d)
      → LocallyFairForOne g d.
```

```
CoInductive Fair (d : demon) : Prop :=
  AlwaysFair : Fair (demon_tail d) → (∀ g, LocallyFairForOne g d)
      → Fair d.
```

To be fully synchronous for a demon can be defined similarly. Recall that a fully synchronous demon is a particular case of fair demon such that all correct robots are activated at each round. This is done easily in our setting where we only have to state that the demonic action's frame never returns 0. An inductive property FullySynchronousForOne states that the first demonic action activates a given robot. A demon is then fully synchronous if FullySynchronousForOne holds for all robots and this demon, and if its *infinite* sequel is fully synchronous.

```
CoInductive FullySynchronous d :=
  NextfullySynch: FullySynchronous (demon_tail d)
      → (∀ g, FullySynchronousForOne g d) → FullySynchronous d.
```

Execution. Finally, given an initial position for correct robots gp_0, and a demon

$$D = (\text{locate\_byz}_i, \text{frame}_i)_{i \in \mathbb{N}},$$

we may define an infinite sequence $(gp_i)_{i \in \mathbb{N}}$ called the *execution* (from gp_0 according to D) as

$$gp_{i+1}(x) = \begin{cases} r_{[\![\text{frame}_i(x), gp_i(x)]\!]}(gp_i \uplus bp_i) & \text{if } \text{frame}_i(x) \neq 0 \\ gp_i(x) & \text{otherwise} \end{cases}$$

Its type is thus:

```
CoInductive execution := NextExecution : (G → location) → execution → execution.
```

and its computation is reflected by the following corecursive function execute:

```
Definition round (r : robogram) (da : demonic_action) (gp: G → location)
  : G → location := fun g ⇒
  let k := da.(frame) g in let t := g.(gp) in
    if k = 0 then t
    else t + 1/k * (algo r ([k,t]{gp := gp; bp := locate_byz da})).
```

```
Definition execute (r : robogram): demon → (G → location) → execution :=
  cofix execute d gp :=
    NextExecution gp (execute (demon_tail d) (round r (demon_head d) gp)).
```

5   Case Study: Impossibility Proofs with Byzantine Behaviours

Let us illustrate how well-suited our formalisation is to prove impossibility results, with two theorems by Bouzid *et al.* [6]. Those results address the problem known as *convergence*. Given any initial configuration of robots, the convergence problem requires *correct* robots to approach asymptotically the same, but unknown beforehand, location. That is, for every initial configuration, convergence requires the existence of a point c in space such that for every $\varepsilon > 0$, there exists a time τ_ε such that $\forall \tau > \tau_\varepsilon$, all correct robots are within a distance of at most ε of c at τ. The impossibility results in [6] are as follows:

Theorem 1 ([6], Thm 4.3). *It is impossible to achieve convergence if $n \leq 2f$ in the FSYNC uni-dimensional model, where n denotes the number of robots and f denotes the number of Byzantine robots.*

Theorem 2 ([6], Thm 4.4). *Byzantine-resilient convergence is impossible for $n \leq 3f$ in the SSYNC uni-dimensional model and a 2-bounded demon.*

Proofs of Impossibility. Providing a solution to a problem in robot networks usually implies giving a robogram such that the expected property holds at some point in the execution, whatever the demon (seen as an adversary, thus including the Byzantine robots) might do. More precisely, it amounts to showing that there exists a robogram such that for all demons, the property is eventually satisfied. An immediate way of proving such a fact is to provide the actual code for the robogram.

When it comes to impossibility proofs, one has to show instead that for all robogram pretending to be a solution, there exists a demon such that the considered robogram will fail. In fact, the usual attempts to achieve this involve looking for a stronger result: exhibiting a demon that will make any candidate robogram for solution to fail. In both cases the statement of such a result is quantified universally on robograms. Giving any concrete code will not help. However, working with higher-order mechanical theorem proving allows us to consider programs as abstract objects and to quantify over them. Robograms will be just characterised by some invariants and the fact that they are supposed to be a solution of a considered problem.

The Theorems in our Formal Model. First of all we need to define formally the convergence problem. In the atomic FSYNC and SSYNC models, an execution $(\mathsf{gp}_i)_{i \in \mathbb{N}}$ is said to be convergent when for any $\varepsilon > 0$ there exists a number of rounds $N_\varepsilon \in \mathbb{N}$ and a location l_ε (in the particular context of [6], $l_\varepsilon \in \mathbb{Q}$) such that for all $n > N_\varepsilon$, all correct robots at round n are no further than ε from l_ε.

$$\forall \varepsilon > 0, \exists N_\varepsilon \in \mathbb{N}, l_\varepsilon \in \mathbb{Q}, \forall n > N_\varepsilon, \forall x \in G, |\mathsf{gp}_n(x) - l_\varepsilon| < \varepsilon$$

Convergence expresses that all correct robots will be gathered forever (thus involving a coinductive construct) in a disc of radius ε...

```
CoInductive imprisoned (prison_center : location) (radius : Q)
                       (e : execution) : Prop :=
  InDisk : (∀ g, [(prison_center - execution_head e g)] <= radius)
           → imprisoned prison_center radius (execution_tail e)
           → imprisoned prison_center radius e.
```

...that they reach eventually (thus involving an inductive part).

```
Inductive attracted (pc: location) (radius: Q) (e: execution): Prop :=
 | Captured : imprisonned pc radius e → attracted pc radius e
 | WillBeCaptured : attracted pc radius (execution_tail e)
                   → attracted pc radius e.
```

A *solution* to the Convergence problem is a robogram such that for any initial position and assuming a fair demon, the execution eventually imprisons all correct robots.

```
Definition solution (r: robogram) : Prop :=
 ∀ (gp: G → location), ∀ d: demon, Fair d
 → ∀ ε: Q, 0 < ε → ∃ lim: location, attracted lim ε (execute r d gp).
```

Remark 2. Our current model considers locations in $\mathbb{Q}$, however the final destination (limit) for convergence is allowed to be in $\mathbb{R} \setminus \mathbb{Q}$, in which case the sequence of l_{ε_i} is a sequence in $\mathbb{Q}$, which has a limit in $\mathbb{R}$.

In this section, we shall make explicit the given two sets (i.e. objects of type finite) that were provided as variables G and B in the formal model on page 182, so as to characterise the numbers of corrects and byzantine robots in the COQ statement of theorems.

A formal version of Theorem 1. Let us focus on Theorem 1. As the premises require the demon to be fully-synchronous (FSYNC model) we may as well define what a fully-synchronous demon is, as mentioned on page 185, and specialise with it a version of solution. It is worth noticing that our development contains a proof that a fully-synchronous demon is fair and that therefore a solution for any fair scheduler is also a solution for a FSYNC one.

```
Definition solution_FSYNC (r : robogram) : Prop :=
 ∀ (gp : G → location), ∀ (d : demon), FullySynchronous d
 → ∀ ε: Q, 0 < ε → ∃ lim: location, attracted lim ε (execute r d gp).
Lemma solution_FAIR_FSYNC : ∀ r, solution r → solution_FSYNC r.
Theorem th1:
 ∀ (g b:finite) (g ≠ ∅) → (r: robogram ({·} ⊎ g) (b ⊎ (g ⊎ {·}))),
   ¬ solution_FSYNC r.
```

It may seem surprising that we use g both for correct and Byzantine robots. As a matter of fact, since unions are disjoint by construction, this notation just ensures that the sets of names share the same cardinal. Adding another arbitrary set b to the Byzantine part is thus a way of saying that there are at least as many Byzantine robots as correct ones.

Further note that this expression of the theorem clearly states that *there are at least 2 correct robots*; this is not implicit (as no assumption can be in COQ): the considered set of correct robots is indeed a singleton {·} added to a non-empty set.

This theorem and its complete formal proof can be found in our development, as Theorem no_solution in File NoSolutionFSYNC_2f.v. The file itself is a hundred lines long and relies on various lemmas provided by our framework.

A formal SSYNC fair version of Theorem 2. Akin to the previous theorem the addition of an arbitrary set b denotes that the total number of robots is not more than three times the number of Byzantine ones.

We prove in fact a sligthly different result, instead of assuming the demon 2-bounded (that is, the demon may execute a particular robot at most two times between any two executions of *any* other robot [16]), we show that the impossibility result holds for a demon that is fair in SSYNC, and for a number f of Byzantine robots such that $2f < n \leq 3f$ where n is the total number of robots. The bound about f and n by Bouzid *et al.* can be obtained by combining this theorem with the previous one and using lemma `solution_FAIR_FSYNC` above.

Theorem th2′:
$\forall$ (g b: finite) (g ≠ ∅) → (r : robogram ((b ⊎ g) ⊎ g) (b ⊎ g)),
  ¬ solution r.

As before, the theorem and its complete formal proof can be found in our development, as Theorem `no_solution` in File `NoSolutionFAIR_3f.v`. The file itself is 125 lines long and relies on various lemmas provided by our framework.

6   Remarks and Perspectives

The choice of the usual topology of $\mathbb{Q}$ as the basic one is driven by three main reasons. First, it allows arbitrary homotheties (which is not the case for $\mathbb{N}$). Then, it preserves arbitrary precision (thus excluding IEEE754 floating point numbers). Finally, it is axiom-free, while $\mathbb{R}$ is not. As noticed in Remark 2, considering rational numbers is not a handicap for convergence properties.

The total size of our development, including the framework and the proofs of the aforementioned theorems is quite small, as it is approximately 450 lines of specifications and 950 lines of proofs. This is encouraging with reference to how adequate our framework is, as it indicates that proofs are not too intricate and remain human readable.

It is worth noticing that our formalism is robust enough to take into account several alternative models with few modifications. For instance, and thanks to the high abstraction level of our framework, considering a multi-dimensional space (instead of just a line) only amounts to considering tuples for locations (and not simply rational numbers) and adding a rotation for some similarities. The effort is thus put on the actual proof and not on the modeling tasks. Hence, a first short-term perspective is to tackle impossibility proofs for convergence on the rational plane or three dimensional space. Similarly, going from strong multiplicity to weak multiplicity is only a redefinition of the equality relation between positions... The same remark applies to demons' characteristics. Adding constraints such as being fully-synchronous is just *(i)* Defining this constraint, and *(ii)* Adding this constraint as an assumption in the statement of a theorem. Of course proofs may be very demanding in all those models, but we want to emphasise that relevant adaptations of our framework are rather non-expensive.

A noteworthy added benefit of our abstract formalisations is that keeping them as general as possible may lead to relaxing premises of theorems, thus potentially discovering new results (*e.g.* formalising weaker daemons [16] and weaker forms of Byzantine behaviours could lead to stronger impossibility results).

Finally, we plan to use our development for positive results also, that is, to prove properties of concrete algorithms. The language of CoQ can handle data-types, programs, and properties about them. Our general framework should allow for certification of embedded algorithms, as both concrete code for robots and global properties of the network fit in. Notice that such proofs would guarantee the expected properties in infinite spaces, *i.e.* without limits on locations.

References

1. Agmon, N., Peleg, D.: Fault-tolerant gathering algorithms for autonomous mobile robots. SIAM Journal on Computing 36(1), 56–82 (2006)
2. Almeida, J.B., Barbosa, M., Bangerter, E., Barthe, G., Krenn, S., Béguelin, S.Z.: Full Proof Cryptography: Verifiable Compilation of Efficient Zero-Knowledge Protocols. In: Yu, T., Danezis, G., Gligor, V.D. (eds.) ACM Conference on Computer and Communications Security, pp. 488–500. ACM (2012)
3. Berard, B., Millet, L., Potop-Butucaru, M., Thierry-Mieg, Y., Tixeuil, S.: Formal verification of Mobile Robot Protocols. Technical report (May 2013)
4. Bezem, M., Bol, R., Groote, J.F.: Formalizing Process Algebraic Verifications in the Calculus of Constructions. Formal Aspects of Computing 9, 1–48 (1997)
5. Bonnet, F., Défago, X., Petit, F., Potop-Butucaru, M.G., Tixeuil, S.: *Brief Announcement:* Discovering and Assessing Fine-Grained Metrics in Robot Networks Protocols. In: Richa, A.W., Scheideler, C. (eds.) SSS 2012. LNCS, vol. 7596, pp. 282–284. Springer, Heidelberg (2012)
6. Bouzid, Z., Potop-Butucaru, M.G., Tixeuil, S.: Optimal Byzantine-Resilient Convergence in Uni-Dimensional Robot Networks. Theoretical Computer Science 411(34-36), 3154–3168 (2010)
7. Cadilhac, M., Hérault, T., Lassaigne, R., Peyronnet, S., Tixeuil, S.: Evaluating complex MAC protocols for sensor networks with APMC. Electronic Notes in Theoretical Computer Science 185, 33–46 (2007)
8. Cansell, D., Méry, D.: The Event-B Modelling Method: Concepts and Case Studies. In: Logics of Specification Languages, pp. 47–152. Springer (2007)
9. Castéran, P., Filou, V., Mosbah, M.: Certifying Distributed Algorithms by Embedding Local Computation Systems in the Coq Proof Assistant. In: Bouhoula, A., Ida, T. (eds.) Symbolic Computation in Software Science, SCSS 2009 (2009)
10. Chou, C.-T.: Mechanical Verification of Distributed Algorithms in Higher-Order Logic. The Computer Journal 38, 158–176 (1995)
11. Clément, J., Delporte-Gallet, C., Fauconnier, H., Sighireanu, M.: Guidelines for the verification of population protocols. In: ICDCS, Minneapolis, Minnesota, USA, pp. 215–224. IEEE Computer Society (June 2011)
12. Coquand, T., Paulin-Mohring, C.: Inductively Defined Types. In: Martin-Löf, P., Mints, G. (eds.) COLOG 1988. LNCS, vol. 417, pp. 50–66. Springer, Heidelberg (1990)
13. Cousineau, D., Doligez, D., Lamport, L., Merz, S., Ricketts, D., Vanzetto, H.: TLA + Proofs. In: Giannakopoulou, D., Méry, D. (eds.) FM 2012. LNCS, vol. 7436, pp. 147–154. Springer, Heidelberg (2012)
14. Deng, Y., Monin, J.-F.: Verifying Self-stabilizing Population Protocols with Coq. In: Chin, W.-N., Qin, S. (eds.) Third IEEE International Symposium on Theoretical Aspects of Software Engineering (TASE 2009), Tianjin, China, pp. 201–208. IEEE Computer Society (July 2009)
15. Devismes, S., Lamani, A., Petit, F., Raymond, P., Tixeuil, S.: Optimal Grid Exploration by Asynchronous Oblivious Robots. In: Richa, A.W., Scheideler, C. (eds.) SSS 2012. LNCS, vol. 7596, pp. 64–76. Springer, Heidelberg (2012)

16. Dubois, S., Tixeuil, S.: A Taxonomy of Daemons in Self-stabilization. Technical Report 1110.0334, ArXiv eprint (October 2011)
17. Fellahi, N., Bonakdarpour, B., Tixeuil, S.: Rigorous performance evaluation of self-stabilization using probabilistic model checking. In: Proceedings of the International Conference on Reliable Distributed Systems (SRDS 2013), Braga, Portugal. IEEE Computer Society (September 2013)
18. Fischer, M.J., Lynch, N.A., Paterson, M.: Impossibility of Distributed Consensus with One Faulty Process. J. ACM 32(2), 374–382 (1985)
19. Flocchini, P., Prencipe, G., Santoro, N.: Distributed Computing by Oblivious Mobile Robots. Synthesis Lectures on Distributed Computing Theory. Morgan & Claypool Publishers (2012)
20. Fokkink, W.: Modelling Distributed Systems. EATCS Texts in Theoretical Computer Science. Springer (2007)
21. Gonthier, G.: Formal–Proof The Four-Color Theorem. Notices of the AMS 55, 1370 (2008)
22. Gonthier, G.: Engineering Mathematics: the Odd Order Theorem Proof. In: Giacobazzi, R., Cousot, R. (eds.) POPL, pp. 1–2. ACM (2013)
23. Küfner, P., Nestmann, U., Rickmann, C.: Formal Verification of Distributed Algorithms. In: Baeten, J.C.M., Ball, T., de Boer, F.S. (eds.) TCS 2012. LNCS, vol. 7604, pp. 209–224. Springer, Heidelberg (2012)
24. Lamport, L.: Byzantizing Paxos by Refinement. In: Peleg, D. (ed.) DISC 2001. LNCS, vol. 6950, pp. 211–224. Springer, Heidelberg (2011)
25. Lamport, L., Shostak, R., Pease, M.: The Byzantine Generals Problem. ACM Transactions on Programming Languages and Systems 4(3), 382–401 (1982)
26. Leroy, X.: A Formally Verified Compiler Back-End. Journal of Automated Reasoning 43(4), 363–446 (2009)
27. Litovsky, I., Métivier, Y., Sopena, É.: Graph Relabelling Systems and Distributed Algorithms. In: Ehrig, H., Kreowski, H.-J., Montanari, U., Rozenberg, G. (eds.) Handbook of Graph Grammars and Computing by Graph Transformation, vol. 3, pp. 1–56. World Scientific (1999)
28. Mccarthy, J., Painter, J.: Correctness of a Compiler for Arithmetic Expressions. In: Proceedings of Applied Mathematica. Mathematical Aspects of Computer Science, vol. 19, pp. 33–41. American Mathematical Society (1967)
29. Pease, M.C., Shostak, R.E., Lamport, L.: Reaching Agreement in the Presence of Faults. J. ACM 27(2), 228–234 (1980)
30. Suzuki, I., Yamashita, M.: Distributed Anonymous Mobile Robots: Formation of Geometric Patterns. SIAM Journal of Computing 28(4), 1347–1363 (1999)
31. Théry, L., Hanrot, G.: Primality Proving with Elliptic Curves. In: Schneider, K., Brandt, J. (eds.) TPHOLs 2007. LNCS, vol. 4732, pp. 319–333. Springer, Heidelberg (2007)

Self-stabilizing Balancing Algorithm
for Containment-Based Trees[*]

Evangelos Bampas[1], Anissa Lamani[2], Franck Petit[3], and Mathieu Valero[4]

[1] School of Elec. & Comp. Eng., National Technical University of Athens, Greece
[2] Graduate School of Information Science and Electrical Engineering, Kyushu
University, Japan
[3] LIP6, 4 place Jussieu, F-75005 Paris, France
[4] Orange Labs, 92130 Issy-les-Moulineaux, France
ebamp@cs.ntua.gr, first.last@lip6.fr

Abstract. Containment-based trees are widely used to build data indexes, range-queryable overlays, publish/subscribe systems both in centralized and distributed contexts. In addition to their versatility, their
balanced shape ensures an overall satisfactory performance. Recently,
it has been shown that their distributed implementations can be fault-
resilient. However, this robustness is achieved at the cost of unbalancing
the structure. While the structure remains correct in terms of searcha-
bility, its performance can be significantly decreased. In this paper, we
propose a distributed self-stabilizing algorithm to balance containment-
based trees.

Keywords: self-stabilization, balancing algorithms, containment-based
trees.

1 Introduction

These last few years have seen the development of very large scale systems like
Peer-to-Peer systems and computational grids. One key feature of such large
distributed systems is that they maintain large-scale distributed data structures
allowing access to resources. This led to the development of various distributed
tree-based overlays used to maintain the most correct view of available resources
and to answer the requests efficiently. Furthermore, overlays must be able to
handle the high dynamism of such systems and tolerate numerous types of faults.

Self-stabilization [11] is a general technique to cope with transient faults and
dynamism. A self-stabilizing system is guaranteed to converge to the intended
behavior in finite time, regardless of the initial state of the processes and initial messages in the links. Its "self-*" feature—"self-healing", "self-repair", "self-
configuration", etc.—also provides to self-stabilization the ability to tolerate high
dynamism of the system.

---

[*] This research was initiated while Evangelos Bampas and Anissa Lamani was with
MIS Lab., University of Picardie Jules Verne, France. It was partially funded by
french National Research Agency (08-ANR-SEGI-025). Details of the project on
http://graal.ens-lyon.fr/SPADES.

T. Higashino et al. (Eds.): SSS 2013, LNCS 8255, pp. 191–205, 2013.

Tree construction has been widely addressed in the area of self-stabilization—refer to [12] for such algorithms. Work took also interest in preserving the *tree nature* in a self-stabilizing manner, *e.g.*, [16,15,3,8,7,4,17]. This means that, starting from any arbitrary configuration in which the essential feature of the tree is corrupted, the goal is to reconfigure the tree so that the feature is eventually satisfied. One of the main difficulties in solving this problem is that the distributed algorithm must be responsible for restoring a global property whereas the nodes of the tree (most likely, processes) have a partial vision of the tree.

One very desirable property of tree-based overlays is logarithmic height. This ensures a fast access time to resources. In this work, we consider a slightly stronger property: For every node, the heights of every pair of its children differ by at most a positive constant α. Trees having this property are said to be *balanced*.

Containment-based trees belong to this category with two extra constraints: **Containment**, every non-root node n satisfies $label(n) \sqsubseteq label(father(n))$, and **Siblings**, which means that every non-leaf node possesses at least two children. *B+-trees* [2] are somehow the most popular containment-based trees. However, they have two extra strong requirements: First, their implementation is very restrictive compared to the containment-based trees. Indeed, for a fixed integer constant $m > 1$, each non-root node maintains between $m+1$ and $2m+1$ children, except the root that have either 0 or between 2 and $2m$ children. Second, they obey a considerably stronger balancing constraint: the length of the paths going from the root to any pair of leaves must be exactly the same. R-trees [14] and M-trees [9] are also containment-based trees. They have the same requirements as B+-trees, except that instead of handling one-dimensional intervals, they have been designed to handle multi-dimensional intervals, respectively rectangles and balls.

The self-stabilizing algorithms proposed in [16,15,3] focus on 2-3 trees, heap trees, and binary search trees, respectively. 2-3 trees belong to the category of balanced trees, but the data structure proposed in [16] is not distributed. Basically, the algorithm in [16] has been designed for a single central memory prone to transient faults. The algorithm proposed in [15] assumes the same setting. In [3], the authors present a distributed solution for the Binary Search Tree (BST) problem. Their solution has the nice property of being *snap-stabilizing* [5], i.e., it guarantees that it always behaves according to its specification. (By contrast, a self-stabilizing implementation only guarantees that the system *eventually* behaves according to its specification.) It requires $O(n)$ rounds to rebuild the BST (n is the number of nodes), which is proved to be asymptotically optimal for this problem in the same paper. However, their solution assumes a fixed underlying binary topology, meaning that their algorithm rearranges the keys embedded within the tree so that the tree eventually satisfies the BST requirements. In other words, their solution has no impact on the tree topology, that can be quite unbalanced.

The solutions in [8,7] arrange both node labels (or keys) and the tree topology. Both maintain Proper Greatest Common Prefix trees. The former is snap-stabilizing and works in the semi-synchronous model introduced in [11]. The latter is only self-stabilizing but it works in the asynchronous message-passing model. However, the shape of the resulting tree depends on the stored keys and is not balanced.

Self-stabilizing Containment-Based Trees are considered in [4,17]. In [4], the authors propose a self-stabilizing distributed version of R-trees (DR-trees, for short), developed to maintain a dependable Peer-to-Peer publish/subscribe system. Their algorithm can be roughly sketched as follows: When a peer detects an inconsistency between a node u and its father, all the keys within the subtree of u are removed from the tree and reinserted at some point between the root and the father of u. By doing so, the resulting tree satisfies the desirable property of all paths from the root to the leaves eventually having the same length, i.e., it eventually satisfies the strong requirement of being an R-tree. However, the stabilization time is $O(n^2)$, where n is the number of nodes. Thus, their solution is not scalable. The solution proposed in [17] deals with this problem. It assumes that every non-leaf node has no more than two children. It proceeds by restoring the connectivity and the containment relation. However, the tree may not be balanced.

In this paper, we propose a distributed self-stabilizing algorithm for balancing containment-based trees. Our solution is based on an edge swapping technique. It guarantees that the heights of any pair of children of any node differ by at most α, which in turn guarantees that the height of the tree is logarithmic. Our algorithm is devoted to be combined with self-stabilizing containment-based tree algorithms requiring to be balanced, e.g., [17]. We prove the correctness of the algorithm and investigate its practical convergence performance through simulations.

In Section 2, we argue that edge swapping is practically better suited than rotations to balance containment-based trees. In Section 3, we present the model we use to describe our algorithm. In Section 4, we propose a distributed self-stabilizing algorithm that relies on edge swapping to balance any containment-based tree. In Section 5, we prove the termination and correctness of the algorithm. In Section 6, we investigate the practical termination time of our algorithm through simulations. Section 7 contains some concluding remarks and possible directions for future work. All missing proofs are omitted due to lack of space and will appear in the full version of the paper.

2   Balancing Primitive

Let $\alpha \in \mathbb{N}$. A tree is balanced iff all its nodes are balanced. A node is balanced iff the heights of any pair of its children differ at most by α. In the remainder of this paper, we make two assumptions: **(a)** $\alpha \geq 1$ and **(b)** each non-leaf node has at least two children. The assumption on α is weaker than those of [13,17,18] and still ensures logarithmic height of the tree [19]. The degree assumption is also weaker than those of [13,17,18] and allows more practical tree configurations.

Basically, a balancing primitive is an operation that eventually reduces the difference between the heights of some subtrees by modifying several links of

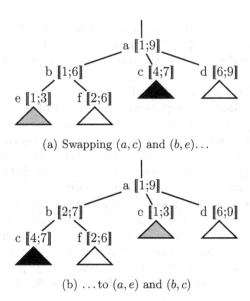

(a) Swapping (a, c) and (b, e). . .

(b) . . . to (a, e) and (b, c)

Fig. 1. An example of edge swapping. Node labels are intervals. The fathers of c and e are modified. The label of b is updated.

the tree. Those link modifications may have some semantic impact if they break node labeling invariants.

2.1   Rotation

In BST [10] and AVL [1], the well known rotation primitive is used to ensure the balanced shape of the tree. However, when dealing with structures relying on partially ordered data, rotations do have a semantic impact. Moreover, in a distributed context, if a node n and its father or grandfather concurrently execute rotations, they may both "write" $father(n)$. It follows that the use of distributed rotations requires synchronization to preserve *tree structure*.

2.2   Edge Swapping

Given two edges (a, b) and (c, d), swapping them involves exchanging their tails (or, equivalently, their heads). Formally, $swap((a, b), (c, d))$ modifies the edges of the graph as follows: $E(G) := E(G) - \{(a, b), (c, d)\} + \{(a, d), (c, b)\}$. Figure 1 contains an illustration similar to our use of edge swapping; between a node and one of his nephews (c and e). Note that as a consequence each edge swapping leads to recompute the label of at most one node. Indeed by transitivity of containment relation the label of each node contains the label of all nodes in its subtree. When edge swapping is applied between a node and one of its nephews, only one subtree is modified; the one rooted by the brother of the node (i.e., the father of the nephew). It follows that on Figure 1 the label of a remains correct as its subtree contains the same nodes after edge swapping. Only the label of b is updated. With the algorithm that we present in Section 4, concurrent swaps cannot conflict. The use of this balancing primitive is thus more suitable in a distributed context.

3   Model

In this paper, we consider the classical local shared memory model, known as the state model, that was introduced by Dijkstra [11]. In this model, communications between neighbours are modeled by direct reading of variables instead of exchange of messages. The program of every node consists of a set of shared variables (henceforth referred to as "variables") and a finite number of actions. Each node can write in its own variables and read its own variables and those of its neighbors. Each action is constituted as follows:

$$< Label >::< Guard > < Statement >$$

The guard of an action is a boolean expression involving the variables of a node u and its neighbours. The statement is an action which updates one or more variables of u. Note that an action can be executed only if its guard is true. Each execution is decomposed into steps.

The state of a node u is defined by the value of its variables. It consists of the following pieces of information: (a) an integer value which we call the *height value* or *height information* of node u and (b) two arrays that contain the IDs of the children of u and their height values. For the sake of generality, we do not make any assumptions about the number of bits available for storing height information, thus the height value of a node can be an arbitrarily large (positive or negative) integer.

The *configuration* of the system at any given time t is the aggregate of the states of the individual nodes. We will sometimes use the term "configuration" to refer to the rooted tree formed by the nodes.

Definition 1. *We denote by $\mathcal{C}(t)$ the configuration of the system at time $t \geq 0$. For a node u, we denote by $h_u(t)$ the value of its height variable in $\mathcal{C}(t)$, by $h_u^\star(t)$ its actual height in the tree in $\mathcal{C}(t)$, by $\mathcal{S}_u(t)$ the set of children of u in $\mathcal{C}(t)$, and by $\mathcal{S}_u^\star(t)$ the set of nodes in the subtree rooted at u in $\mathcal{C}(t)$.*

Let $\mathcal{C}(t)$ be a configuration at instant t and let I be an action of a node u. I is *enabled* for u in $\mathcal{C}(t)$ if and only if the guard of I is satisfied by u in $\mathcal{C}(t)$. Node u is enabled in $\mathcal{C}(t)$ if and only if at least one action is enabled for u in $\mathcal{C}(t)$. Each step consists of two sequential phases executed atomically: (i) Every node evaluates its guard; (ii) One or more enabled nodes execute their enabled actions. When the two phases are done, the next step begins. This execution model is known as the *distributed daemon* [6]. To capture asynchrony, we assume a semi-synchronous scheduler which picks any non-empty subset of the enabled nodes in the current configuration and executes their actions simultaneously. We do not make any fairness assumptions, thus the scheduler is free to effectively ignore any particular node or set of nodes as long as there exists at least one other node that can be activated.

Definition 2. *We refer to the activation of a non-empty subset A of the enabled nodes in a given configuration as an* execution step. *If C is the configuration of the system before the activation of A and C' is the resulting configuration, we denote this particular step by $C \longrightarrow_A C'$. An execution starting from an initial configuration C_0 is a sequence $C_0 \longrightarrow_{A_1} C_1 \longrightarrow_{A_2} C_2 \longrightarrow \dots$ of execution steps. Time is measured by the number of steps that have been executed. An execution is completed when it reaches a configuration in which no node is enabled. After that point, no node is ever activated.*

If a node was enabled before a particular execution step, was not activated in that step, and is not enabled after that step, then we say that it was *neutralized* in that step.

Definition 3. *Given a particular execution, an* execution round *(or simply* round*) starting from a configuration C consists of the minimum-length sequence of steps in which every enabled node in C is activated or neutralized at least once.*

Remark 1. To simplify the presentation, we will assume throughout the rest of the paper that the arrays containing the IDs of the children of each node and copies of their height values are consistent with the height values stored by the children themselves in the current configuration of the system. It should be clear that maintaining these copies up to date can be achieved with a constant overhead per execution step.

4   Self-stabilizing Balancing Solution

In this section, we present our self-stabilizing algorithm for balancing containment-based trees, we provide some termination properties, and we prove that any execution converges to a balanced tree.

Assuming that each node knows the correct heights of its subtrees, a very simple distributed self-stabilizing algorithm balances the tree: each node uses the *swap* operation whenever two of its children heights are "too different". However, in a distributed context, height information may be inaccurate. This inaccuracy could lead the aforementioned naive balancing algorithm to make some "wrong moves." For example, in Figure 1, assume that c "thinks" that its own height is 4 and e "thinks" that its own height is 9 while their actual heights are respectively 10 and 8; the illustrated *swap* would actually unbalance the tree. On one hand, maintaining heights in a self-stabilizing fashion is easy and ensures that height information will eventually be correct. On the other hand, no node can know when height information is correct; as a consequence, height maintenance and balancing have to run concurrently. But their concurrent execution raises an obvious risk: the *swap* operation modifies the tree structure and could thus compromise the convergence of the height maintenance subprotocol.

Guard	Statement
G1 $\neg$stable(u)	**S1** $h_u := 1 + \max_{w \in \mathcal{S}_u} h_w$ (or $h_u := 0$ if u is a leaf)
G2 stable(u) $\wedge$ stable(max(u))$\wedge$ $\neg$balanced(u)	**S2** swap the two edges $(u, \min(u))$ and $(\max(u), \max(\max(u)))$

Fig. 2. Distributed self-stabilizing balancing algorithm

Basically, the algorithm that we propose in this section consists of two concurrent actions: one maintaining heights, the other one balancing the tree. We formalize both actions and prove that their concurrent execution converges to a balanced tree.

4.1 Algorithm

At any time t, each node u is able to evaluate the following functions and predicates for itself and its children:

- max(x): returns a node in $\arg\max_{w \in \mathcal{S}_x(t)} h_w(t)$. If x is a leaf, returns $\bot$ (undefined).
- min(x): returns a node in $\arg\min_{w \in \mathcal{S}_x(t)} h_w(t)$. If x is a leaf, returns $\bot$.
- stable(x): returns true if and only if $h_x(t) = 1 + \max_{w \in \mathcal{S}_x(t)} h_w(t)$. If x is a leaf, returns true if and only if $h_x(t) = 0$.
- balanced(x): returns true if and only if for all $z, z' \in \mathcal{S}_x(t)$, $|h_z(t) - h_{z'}(t)| \leq \alpha$.

When there are more than one possible return values for max(x) and min(x), an arbitrary choice is made. For simplicity, we can consider that the candidate node with the smallest ID is returned, although this will not be crucial for our results. Each node u executes the algorithm in Figure 2 (the value of stable($\bot$) is assumed to be false). Note that the guards **G1** and **G2** are mutually exclusive and, by definition, the height update action effectively has priority over the edge swapping action. We say that a node is *enabled for a height update* if **G1** is true, or *enabled for a swap* if **G2** is true.

When a node u performs a swap, four nodes are involved: u itself, max(u), min(u), and max(max(u)). We refer to these nodes as the *source*, the *target*, the *swap-out*, and the *swap-in* nodes of the swap, respectively.

The following proposition can be proved directly from the definitions.

Proposition 1. *If $\mathcal{C}$ is a rooted tree with root r, then after any execution step $\mathcal{C} \longrightarrow_A \mathcal{C}'$, $\mathcal{C}'$ is still a directed tree with root r.*

4.2 Termination Properties

In the following section, we will prove that for any initial configuration, every possible execution is completed in a finite number of steps. For the moment, we give two properties of the resulting tree, assuming of course that the execution consists of a finite number of steps.

Proposition 2. *If the execution is completed at time t^*, then in the final configuration $\mathcal{C}(t^*)$ all nodes are balanced and have correct height information.*

The next proposition, regarding the height of the resulting tree, follows directly from the analysis in [19, Sections II and III]. In our case, the initial conditions of the recurrence studied in [19] are slightly different, but this does not affect the asymptotic behavior of the height.

Proposition 3. *If the execution is completed at time t^*, then in the final configuration $h_r^*(t^*) = \mathcal{O}(\log n)$, where r is the root and n is the number of nodes in the system.*

5   Proof of Convergence

The concept of a "bad node" will be useful in the analysis of the algorithm. Intuitively, a bad node is a node that "wants" to increase its height value.

Definition 4 (Bad nodes). *In a given configuration $\mathcal{C}(t)$, an internal node u is a bad node if $h_u(t) \leq \max_{v \in \mathcal{S}_u(t)} h_v(t)$. A leaf is a bad node if $h_u(t) < 0$.*

Let $P = \mathcal{C} \longrightarrow_A \mathcal{C}'$ be a step of the execution. The set A is partitioned into subsets A_h, A_b, and A_s, where A_h is the set of non-bad nodes which perform a height update, A_b is the set of bad nodes which perform a height update, and A_s is the set of nodes which are sources of a swap. Let A_t be the set of nodes which are targets of a swap and let B and B' denote the set of bad nodes in configuration $\mathcal{C}$ and $\mathcal{C}'$, respectively. For each node u, let $\mathcal{S}_u$ be the set of children of u in $\mathcal{C}$ and $\mathcal{S}_u^*$ be the set of nodes of the subtree rooted at u in $\mathcal{C}$, and let $\mathcal{S}_u'$ and $\mathcal{S}_u^{*'}$ be the corresponding sets in $\mathcal{C}'$. Finally, let $\mathcal{G}(A_b)$ be the subgraph induced by A_b in the configuration $\mathcal{C}$.

5.1   Preliminaries

Lemmas 1 to 6 below state some basic properties of an execution step, which are used throughout the proofs.

Lemma 1.   *1. $A_b \subseteq B$.*
2. $A_s \cap A_h = A_s \cap B = A_t \cap A_h = A_t \cap B = \emptyset$.
3. For all nodes u, $\mathcal{S}_u' = \mathcal{S}_u$ if and only if $u \notin A_s \cup A_t$.
4. The set of leaves in $\mathcal{C}'$ is equal to the set of leaves in $\mathcal{C}$.

Lemma 2. *If $u \notin A \cup B$ and $\mathcal{S}_u' \cap A_b = \emptyset$, then $u \notin B'$.*

Lemma 3. *If $u \in A_h$ and $\mathcal{S}_u' \cap A_b = \emptyset$, then $u \notin B'$.*

Lemma 4. *If $u \in A_s$ and $\mathcal{S}_u' \cap A_b = \emptyset$, then $u \notin B'$.*

Lemma 5. *$|B' \setminus B| \leq |A_b \setminus B'|$.*

Lemma 6. *If $\mathcal{C}(t)$ contains no bad nodes, then for all $t' \geq t$, $\mathcal{C}(t')$ contains no bad nodes.*

It will be convenient to view any execution of the algorithm as consisting of two phases: The first phase starts from the initial configuration and ends at the first configuration in which the system is free of bad nodes. The second phase starts at the end of the first phase and ends at the first configuration in which no node is enabled, i.e., at the end of the execution. In view of Lemma 6, the system does not contain any bad nodes during the second phase. We will prove that each phase is concluded in a finite number of steps, starting with the second phase.

5.2   Second Phase

We prove convergence for the second phase by bounding directly the number of height updates and the number of swaps that may occur during that phase. The fact that there are no bad nodes in the second phase is crucial for bounding the number of height updates. It follows that the number of swaps also has to be bounded, since a long enough sequence of steps in which only swaps are performed incurs more height updates.

Lemma 7. *For any node u, if $h_u(t) < h_u^\star(t)$, then there exists in $\mathcal{C}(t)$ at least one bad node in the subtree rooted at u.*

Lemma 8. *In the second phase, if a node becomes enabled for a height update, it will remain enabled for a height update at least until it is activated.*

Lemma 9. *Starting from a configuration with no bad nodes, no execution can perform an infinite number of height updates.*

Proof. Consider an execution of the algorithm in which an infinite number of height updates are executed. Since the number of nodes is finite, at least one node must execute a height update an infinite number of times. By the fact that the initial configuration contains no bad nodes and by Lemma 6, each time that node executes a height update, its height variable decreases. At some point, its height variable will become negative and at that point, by Lemma 7, some node in its subtree will become bad. This contradicts with Lemma 6.   □

Lemma 10. *Starting from a configuration with no bad nodes, no execution can perform an infinite number of swaps.*

Proof. By Lemma 9, there exists a finite time t_0 after which no height updates are performed. For each node u, let h_u denote the value of its height variable at time t_0 and, since it remains constant thereafter, at all subsequent times. Furthermore, for $t \geq t_0$, let $\hat{\mathcal{S}}_u(t)$ denote the set of children of u at time t whose height variable is equal to $h_u - 1$.

Note that u is enabled for a height update at time t if and only if $|\hat{\mathcal{S}}_u(t)| = 0$. We observe now that in every step, if u is the target of a swap then $|\hat{\mathcal{S}}_u(t)|$ is decreased by 1, otherwise it remains the same. By Lemma 8, if $|\hat{S}_u(t)|$ becomes 0 then it remains equal to 0 until u performs a height update.

Suppose, now, for the sake of contradiction, that an infinite number of swaps are performed after time t_0. For each swap, there exists a node that is the target of that swap. It follows, then, that after at most $\sum_u |\hat{S}_u(t_0)|$ swaps have been performed after time t_0, all nodes in the system will be either idle or enabled for a height update (idle nodes will include nodes that are so low in the tree that they cannot possibly be the source of a swap and the root of the tree which will not be able to perform a swap since all of its children will be enabled for a height update). At that point, either all nodes are idle and thus the execution is completed, which contradicts with the fact that an infinite number of swaps are performed after time t_0, or the only choice of the scheduler is to activate a node for a height update, which contradicts with the fact that no height updates are performed after time t_0.   □

Lemmas 9 and 10 directly imply the following:

Theorem 1. *In any execution, the second phase is completed in a finite number of steps.*

5.3   First Phase

For the sake of presentation, it will be helpful to sometimes consider that the root of the tree has an imaginary father $\mathfrak{r}$, which is never enabled and is always a bad node.

Definition 5 (Extended configuration). *We denote by $\tilde{C}(t)$ an auxiliary extended configuration at time t, which is identical to $C(t)$ except that the root node in $C(t)$ has a new father node $\mathfrak{r}$ with $h_{\mathfrak{r}}(t) = -\infty$, for all $t \geq 0$.*

The bad nodes induce a partition of the nodes of the extended configuration into components: each bad node belongs to a different component, and each non-bad node belongs to the component that contains its nearest bad ancestor.

Definition 6 (Partition into components). *For each bad node b in $\tilde{C}(t)$, the component $T_b(t)$ is the maximal weakly connected directed subgraph of $\tilde{C}(t)$ that has b at its root and contains no other bad nodes.*

If $P = C \longrightarrow_A C'$ is an execution step, let $\tilde{C}$ and $\tilde{C}'$ denote the extended configurations corresponding to C and C', and let $\tilde{B}$ and $\tilde{B}'$ denote the corresponding sets of bad nodes. Moreover, let $\{T_b\}_{b \in \tilde{B}}$ and $\{T_b'\}_{b \in \tilde{B}'}$ be the partition of nodes into components for the two configurations, and if T is any such component, let $V(T)$ denote its set of nodes.

A useful property of this partition into components is that it remains unchanged as long as the set of bad nodes remains the same:

Lemma 11. *If $\tilde{B}' = \tilde{B}$, then $V(T_b') = V(T_b)$, for all $b \in \tilde{B}$.*

Lemma 12. *There cannot be an infinite sequence of steps in which no bad node is activated or becomes non-bad.*

Proof. By Lemma 11, in a sequence of steps in which no bad node is activated or becomes non-bad, each of the connected components behaves in the same way as a tree that does not contain bad nodes.[1] Therefore, by Lemmas 9 and 10, each component will stabilize in finite time and the bad nodes will be the only candidates for activation. □

We associate a *badness vector* with each configuration. This vector reflects the distribution of bad nodes in the system and serves to quantify a certain notion of progress toward the extinction of bad nodes. In particular, we prove that the badness vector decreases lexicographically in every step in which at least one bad node is activated or becomes non-bad.

Definition 7 (Badness vector). *For $t \geq 0$, let $b_1, b_2, \ldots, b_{|\tilde{B}(t)|}$ be an ordering of the bad nodes in $\tilde{C}(t)$ by non-decreasing number of bad nodes contained in the path from $\mathfrak{r}$ to b_i, breaking ties arbitrarily. Note that $b_1 \equiv \mathfrak{r}$. We define the badness vector at time $t \geq 0$ to be the vector*

$$b(t) = (|\mathcal{T}_{b_1}(t)|, \ldots, |\mathcal{T}_{b_{|\tilde{B}(t)|}}(t)|) \ ,$$

where the size of a connected component is the number of nodes belonging to that component.

We refer the reader to Figure 3 for an example of an extended configuration, its partition into components, and the corresponding badness vector.

Lemma 13. *If at least one bad node becomes non-bad without being activated in step P, then $|B'| < |B|$.*

Proof. Let N be the set of bad nodes that become non-bad without being activated. We can partition the set B as follows: $B = N \cup (A_b \setminus B') \cup (B \cap B')$. Moreover, we can naturally partition the set B' as follows: $B' = (B' \setminus B) \cup (B \cap B')$. If $|N| > 0$, then from the first equation we get $|B| > |A_b \setminus B'| + |B \cap B'|$, and then from the second equation and Lemma 5 we have that $|B'| = |B' \setminus B| + |B \cap B'| \leq |A_b \setminus B'| + |B \cap B'| < |B|$. □

Definition 8 (Lexicographic ordering). *Consider two badness vectors $b = (x_1, \ldots, x_k)$ and $b' = (x'_1, \ldots, x'_{k'})$. We say that b' is lexicographically smaller than b if one of the following holds:*

1. *$k' < k$, or*
2. *$k' = k$ and for some i in the range $1 \leq i \leq k$, $x'_i < x_i$ and $x'_j = x_j$ for all $j < i$.*

---

[1] That is slightly inaccurate: Certain nodes of the component may contain in their children set some bad nodes, which are at the root of other components. From the point of view of the father's component, these bad nodes will behave as if they are leaves whose height value is fixed to some arbitrary value, smaller than the height value of their father. However, it should be clear that this does not change the fact that the component will stabilize after a finite number of steps.

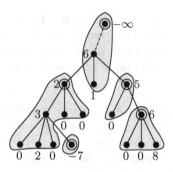

Fig. 3. An illustration of the notions introduced in Definitions 4, 5, 6, and 7. Node labels indicate their height values. Circled nodes represent bad nodes. The dashed edge exists only in the extended configuration and connects the real root of the tree to the artificial node r. Each group of nodes is one component of the partition. The badness vector corresponding to this configuration is $(3, 7, 2, 1, 4)$.

Let b and b' denote the badness vectors corresponding to C and C'.

Lemma 14. *If at least one bad node is activated or becomes non-bad in step* $C \longrightarrow C'$, *then* b' *is lexicographically smaller than* b.

Theorem 2. *In any execution, the first phase is completed in a finite number of steps.*

Proof. By Lemma 14, the badness vector decreases lexicographically whenever at least one bad node is activated or becomes non-bad. By Lemma 12, we cannot have an infinite sequence of steps in which no bad node is activated or becomes non-bad. Moreover, during such a sequence of steps, the set of bad nodes remains the same by Lemmas 2, 3, and 4, and thus the badness vector remains the same by Lemma 11. The theorem follows from these observations and the fact that no configuration can have a corresponding badness vector that is lexicographically smaller than the single-component badness vector $(n+1)$, where n is the number of nodes in the system.   □

6   Simulation

To investigate the dynamic behavior and properties of our algorithm, we implemented a round based simulator. Each simulation (i) builds a full binary tree, (ii) initializes heights, and (iii) runs the balancing protocol. We used a synchronous daemon to run simulations, i.e., all the enabled nodes of the system execute their enabled actions simultaneously. The impact of non-deterministic daemons and/or the weaker daemon that is required to run our algorithm will be tackled in future work.

In the following, for a given simulation we will denote by n the number nodes of the tree, by h_i its initial height (i.e. after generation), by h_f its final height (i.e. after balancing) and by t the execution time in rounds.

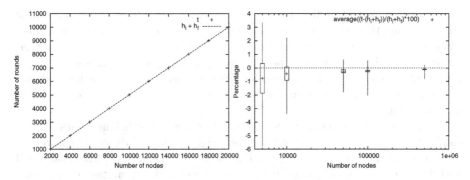

Fig. 4. t for almost linear trees   **Fig. 5.** t for random trees

6.1   Almost Linear Trees

Intuitively, almost linear trees are stressing for a balancing algorithm because they are "as unbalanced as possible". In the following, for a given n, the initial tree is the structurally unique full binary tree of height $\lceil n/2 \rceil$. The only unspecified part of the simulation is the initial height values. It turns out that this has practically a very small impact on termination time. For each n we ran thousands of simulations starting from the corresponding linear tree. For a given n they always converged in the same number of rounds. As a consequence, all runs starting from the same linear tree will have approximately the same results.

Figure 4 shows the termination time of simulations for different numbers of nodes. It contains two curves: the first one is plotted from our experiment and each point stands for an almost linear tree. The second curve is the sum of initial and final tree heights. This plot tends to show that the round complexity of our algorithm is $\mathcal{O}(n)$ in the worst case.

6.2   Random Trees

To showcase the applicability of our algorithm to an existing system, trees are generated using the join protocol of [17]. Figure 5 shows the distance between the sum of initial and final tree heights and experimental termination times. The vertical axis gives the average variation between $h_i + h_f$ and experimental termination times. For each n we ran thousands of simulations. Each candlestick sums up statistics on those runs; the whiskers indicates minimum and maximum variation, the cross indicates the average variation and the box height indicates the standard deviation. The greater n is, the closer $h_i + h_f$ and experimental results are. This result indicates that the average round complexity of our algorithm is $\mathcal{O}(h_i + h_f)$.

7   Concluding Remarks

In this work, we propose a new distributed self-stabilizing algorithm to balance containment-based trees using edge swapping. Simulation results indicate that the algorithm is quite efficient in terms of round complexity. As a matter of fact, it seems that we can reasonably expect $\mathcal{O}(n)$ to be a worst-case bound, whereas in the average case the running time is closer to $\mathcal{O}(h_i + h_f)$ rounds. Interestingly, this average-case bound also appears in a different setting in [8]. Note that the conjectured average-case bound is close to $\mathcal{O}(\log n)$ in a practically relevant scenario in which some faults appear (or new nodes are inserted) in an already balanced tree.

We have assumed that nodes keep correct copies of the height values of their children, so that each node can read the height values of its grandchildren by looking at the memory of its children. For the sake of simplicity, we have not dealt with the extra synchronization that would be required to maintain these copies up-to-date, but it should be possible to achieve this with a constant overhead per execution step. Furthermore, we have assumed that internal nodes have degree of at least two. Degenerate internal nodes with degree one could be accommodated by a bottom-up protocol that runs in parallel and essentially disconnects them from the tree, attaching their children to their parents. Finally, note that in Section 2 we remarked that edge swaps may have semantic impact if they rearrange nodes so as to violate the containment relation. This can also be fixed by another bottom-up protocol that restores each node label to the minimum that suffices to contain the labels of its children.

Possible directions for future work include establishing the conjectured upper bounds of $\mathcal{O}(n)$ and $\mathcal{O}(h_i + h_f)$ for the round complexity. We already have some preliminary results in this direction: the first phase of the algorithm (which lasts until no bad nodes remain in the system) is indeed concluded in at most n rounds. The proof of this claim will appear in the full version. An extension of the present work would be to adapt the proposed algorithm in the message passing model.

References

1. Adelson-Velskii, G., Landis, E.M.: An algorithm for the organization of information. Proceedings of the USSR Academy of Sciences 146, 263–266 (1962)
2. Bayer, R., McCreight, E.M.: Organization and maintenance of large ordered indices. Acta Inf. 1, 173–189 (1972)
3. Bein, D., Datta, A.K., Villain, V.: Snap-stabilizing optimal binary search tree. In: Tixeuil, S., Herman, T. (eds.) SSS 2005. LNCS, vol. 3764, pp. 1–17. Springer, Heidelberg (2005)
4. Bianchi, S., Datta, A.K., Felber, P., Gradinariu, M.: Stabilizing peer-to-peer spatial filters. In: ICDCS, p. 27. IEEE Computer Society (2007)
5. Bui, A., Datta, A.K., Petit, F., Villain, V.: Snap-stabilization and PIF in tree networks. Distributed Computing 20(1), 3–19 (2007)
6. Burns, J.E., Gouda, M.G., Miller, R.E.: On relaxing interleaving assumptions. In: Proceedings of the MCC Workshop on Self-Stabilizing Systems, MCC Technical Report No. STP-379-89 (1989)
7. Caron, E., Datta, A.K., Petit, F., Tedeschi, C.: Self-stabilization in tree-structured peer-to-peer service discovery systems. In: SRDS, pp. 207–216. IEEE (2008)

8. Caron, E., Desprez, F., Petit, F., Tedeschi, C.: Snap-stabilizing prefix tree for peer-to-peer systems. Parallel Processing Letters 20(1), 15–30 (2010)
9. Ciaccia, P., Patella, M., Zezula, P.: M-tree: An efficient access method for similarity search in metric spaces. In: Jarke, M., Carey, M.J., Dittrich, K.R., Lochovsky, F.H., Loucopoulos, P., Jeusfeld, M.A. (eds.) VLDB, pp. 426–435. Morgan Kaufmann (1997)
10. Cormen, T.H., Leiserson, C.E., Rivest, R.L., Stein, C.: Introduction to Algorithms, 2nd edn. The MIT Press (2001)
11. Dijkstra, E.W.: Self-stabilizing systems in spite of distributed control. Commun. ACM 17(11), 643–644 (1974)
12. Dolev, S.: Self-Stabilization. The MIT Press (2000)
13. du Mouza, C., Litwin, W., Rigaux, P.: SD-Rtree: A scalable distributed Rtree. In: Chirkova, R., Dogac, A., Özsu, M.T., Sellis, T.K. (eds.) ICDE, pp. 296–305. IEEE (2007)
14. Guttman, A.: R-trees: A dynamic index structure for spatial searching. In: Yormark, B. (ed.) SIGMOD Conference, pp. 47–57. ACM Press (1984)
15. Herman, T., Masuzawa, T.: Available stabilizing heaps. Inf. Process. Lett. 77(2-4), 115–121 (2001)
16. Herman, T., Masuzawa, T.: A stabilizing search tree with availability properties. In: ISADS, p. 398. IEEE Computer Society (2001)
17. Izumi, T., Gradinariu Potop-Butucaru, M., Valero, M.: Physical expander in virtual tree overlay. In: Peleg, D. (ed.) DISC 2011. LNCS, vol. 6950, pp. 82–96. Springer, Heidelberg (2011)
18. Jagadish, H.V., Ooi, B.C., Vu, Q.H., Zhang, R., Zhou, A.: VBI-Tree: A peer-to-peer framework for supporting multi-dimensional indexing schemes. In: Liu, L., Reuter, A., Whang, K.-Y., Zhang, J. (eds.) ICDE, p. 34. IEEE Computer Society (2006)
19. Luccio, F., Pagli, L.: On the height of height-balanced trees. IEEE Trans. Computers 25(1), 87–91 (1976)

On the Effectiveness of Punishments
in a Repeated Epidemic Dissemination Game

Xavier Vilaça and Luís Rodrigues

INESC-ID, Instituto Superior Técnico, Universidade de Lisboa
xvilaca@gsd.inesc-id.pt,
ler@ist.utl.pt

Abstract. This work uses Game Theory to study the effectiveness of punishments as an incentive for rational nodes to follow an epidemic dissemination protocol. The dissemination process is modeled as an infinite repetition of a stage game. At the end of each stage, a monitoring mechanism informs each player of the actions of other nodes. The effectiveness of a punishing strategy is measured as the range of values of the benefit-to-cost ratio that sustain cooperation. This paper studies both public and private monitoring. Under public monitoring, we show that direct reciprocity is not an effective incentive, whereas full indirect reciprocity provides a nearly optimal effectiveness. Under private monitoring, we identify necessary conditions regarding the topology of the graph in order for punishments to be effective. When punishments are coordinated, full indirect reciprocity is also effective under private monitoring.

Keywords: Epidemic Dissemination, Game Theory, Peer-to-Peer.

1 Introduction

Epidemic broadcast protocols are known to be extremely scalable and robust [1,3,10]. As a result, they are particularly well suited to support the dissemination of information in large-scale peer-to-peer systems, for instance, to support live streaming [12,11]. In such an environment, nodes do not belong to the same administrative domain. On the contrary, many of these systems rely on resources made available by self-interested nodes that are not necessarily obedient to the protocol. In particular, participants may be rational and aim at maximizing their utility, which is a function of the benefits obtained from receiving information and the cost of contributing to its dissemination.

Two main incentive mechanisms may be implemented to ensure that rational nodes are not interested in deviating from the protocol: one is to rely on balanced exchanges [12,11]; other is to monitor the degree of cooperation of every node and punish misbehavior [6]. When balanced exchanges are enforced, in every interaction, nodes must exchange an equivalent amount of messages of interest to each other. This approach has the main disadvantage of requiring symmetric interactions between nodes. In some cases, more efficient protocols may be achieved with asymmetric interactions [3,10,6], where balanced exchanges

T. Higashino et al. (Eds.): SSS 2013, LNCS 8255, pp. 206–220, 2013.

become infeasible. Instead, nodes are expected to forward messages without immediately receiving any benefit in return. Therefore, one must consider repeated interactions for nodes to able to collect information about the behavior of their neighbors, which may be used to detect misbehavior and trigger punishments.

Although monitoring has been used to detect and expel free-riders from epidemic dissemination protocols [6], no theoretical analysis studied the ability of punishments to sustain cooperation among rational nodes. Therefore, in this paper, we tackle this gap by using Game Theory [14]. The aim is to study the existence of equilibria in an infinitely repeated Epidemic Dissemination game. The stage game consists in a sequence of messages disseminated by the source, which are forwarded by every node i to each neighbor j with an independent probability $p_i[j]$. At the end of each stage, a monitoring mechanism provides information to each node regarding $p_i[j]$.

Following work in classical Game Theory that shows that cooperation in repeated games can be sustained using punishing strategies [5], we focus on this class of strategies. We assume that there is a pre-defined target for the reliability of the epidemic dissemination process. To achieve this reliability, each node should forward every message to each of its neighbors with a probability higher than some threshold probability p, known a priory by the two neighboring nodes. We consider that a player i defects from a neighbor j if it uses a probability lower than p when forwarding information to j. Each node i receives a benefit β_i per received message, but incurs a cost γ_i of forwarding a message to a neighbor. Given this, we are particularly interested in determining the range of values of the benefit-to-cost ratio (β_i/γ_i) that allows punishing strategies to be equilibria. The wider is this range, the more likely it is for all nodes to cooperate.

The main contribution of this paper is a quantification of the effectiveness of different punishing strategies under two types of monitors: public and private. Public monitors inform every node of the actions of every other node with no delays. On the other hand, private monitoring informs only a subset of nodes of the actions of each node, and possibly with some delays. In addition, we study two particular types of punishing strategies: direct and full indirect reciprocity. In the former type, each node is solely responsible for monitoring and punishing each neighbor, individually. The latter type specifies that each misbehaving node should eventually be punished by every neighbor.

More precisely, we make the following contributions. With public monitoring, we analyze the existence of Subgame Perfect Equilibrium with strategies that use direct and full indirect reciprocity. We first derive an upper bound for the effectiveness of the former type of strategies. We observe that this value decreases very quickly with an increasing reliability, in many scenarios. If full indirect reciprocity is used, then this problem can be avoided. We derive a lower bound for the effectiveness of these strategies, which is independent from the desired reliability and close to the theoretical optimum, under certain circumstances.

Under private monitoring with delays, information collected by each node may be imperfect. We thus consider the alternative solution concept of Sequential Equilibrium, which requires the specification of a belief system that captures the belief held by each player regarding past events of which it has not been informed. For a punishing strategy to be an equilibrium, this belief must be consistent. We provide a definition of consistency that is sufficient to derive the effectiveness of punishing strategies. Then, we show that certain topologies are ineffective when monitoring is fully distributed and, unless full indirect reciprocity is possible, the effectiveness decreases monotonically with the reliability. To avoid this problem, punishments should be coordinated, i.e., punishments applied to a misbehaving node i by every neighbor of i should overlap in time. We derive a lower bound for the effectiveness of full indirect reciprocity strategies with coordinated punishments. The results indicate that the number of stages during which punishments overlap should be at least of the order of the maximum delay of the monitoring mechanism. This suggests that, when implementing a distributed monitoring mechanism, delays should be minimized.

Due to space constraints, we only include the most important results and an intuition of their correctness. The complete proofs can be found in the technical report [16]. The remainder of the paper is structured as follows. Section 2 discusses some related work. The general model is provided in Section 3. The analysis of public and private monitoring are given in Sections 4 and 5, respectively. Section 6 concludes the paper and provides directions of future work.

2   Related Work

There are examples of work that use monitoring to persuade rational nodes to engage in a dissemination protocol. In Equicast [8], the authors perform a Game Theoretical analysis of a multicast protocol where nodes monitor the rate of messages sent by their neighbors and apply punishments whenever the rate drops below a certain threshold. The protocol is shown to be a dominating strategy. However, the authors consider deterministic delivery of messages and the actions available to each node are restricted to the adjustments of some parameters of the protocol. This contrasts with our analysis, where we consider non-deterministic delivery of messages and a more general set of strategies available to nodes.

Guerraoui et al. [6] propose a mechanism that monitors the degree of cooperation of each node in epidemic dissemination protocols. The goal is to detect and expel free-riders. This mechanism performs statistical inferences on the reports provided by every node regarding its neighbors, and estimates the cooperation level of each node. If this cooperation level is lower than a minimum value, then the node is expelled from the network. The authors perform a theoretical and experimental analysis to show that this mechanism guarantees that free-riders only benefit by deviating from the protocol if the degree of deviation is not significantly high. However, no Game Theoretical analysis is performed to determine in what conditions are free-riders willing to abide to the protocol.

In [12,11], the authors rely on balanced exchanges to provide incentives for nodes to cooperate in dissemination protocols for data streaming. In BAR Gossip [12], the proposed epidemic dissemination protocol enforces strictly balanced exchanges. This may force nodes to send garbage as a payment for any unbalance in the amount of information exchanged with a neighbor. A stepwise analysis shows that nodes cannot increase their utility by deviating in any step of the protocol. In FlightPath [11], the authors remove the need for sending garbage by allowing imbalanced exchanges. By limiting the maximum allowed imbalance between every pair of nodes, the authors show that it is possible for the protocol to be an 1/10-Nash equilibrium, while still ensuring a streaming service with high quality. Unfortunately, these results might not hold for other dissemination protocols that rely on more imbalanced exchanges. In these cases, a better alternative might be to rely on a monitoring approach.

Other game theoretical analysis have addressed a similar problem, but in different contexts. The most popular examples are the analysis of the tit-for-tat strategy used in BitTorrent, a P2P file sharing system (e.g., [4,15]). These works consider a set of n nodes deciding with which nodes to cooperate, given a limited number of available connections, with the intent to share content. Therefore, there is no non-determinism in content delivery.

3   Model

We now describe the System and Game Theoretical models, followed by the definition of effectiveness. The epidemics model is thoroughly described in [16].

3.1   System Model

There is a set of nodes $\mathcal{N}$ organized into a directed graph G. Each node has a set of in ($\mathcal{N}_i^{-1}$) and out-neighbors ($\mathcal{N}_i$). Communication channels are assumed to be reliable. We consider the existence of a single external source s that introduces messages into the network. Its behavior is described by a profile $\boldsymbol{p}_s$, which defines for each node $i \in \mathcal{N}_s$ the probability $p_s[i] \in [0,1)$ of i receiving a message directly from s, where $p_s[i] > 0$ for some i. We also consider the graph to be connected from the source s, i.e., there is a path from s to every node i. Conversely, every node i forwards messages to every neighbor $j \in \mathcal{N}_i$ with an independent probability $p_i[j]$. Given a vector $\boldsymbol{p}$, which includes $\boldsymbol{p}_s$ and $\boldsymbol{p}_i$ used by s and by every $i \in \mathcal{N}$, respectively, the reliability of the dissemination protocol is $1 - q_i[\boldsymbol{p}]$, where $q_i[\boldsymbol{p}]$ is the probability of a node i *not* receiving a message.

3.2   Monitoring Mechanism

The monitoring mechanism emits a signal $s \in \mathcal{S}$, where every player i may observe a different private signal $s_i \in s$. This signal can take two values for every pair of nodes $j \in \mathcal{N}$ and $k \in \mathcal{N}_j$: $s_i[j,k] = $ *cooperate* notifies i that j forwarded messages to k with a probability higher than a specified threshold, and $s_i[j,k] = $ *defect* signals the complementary action. This signal may be public, if all nodes read the same signal, or private, otherwise. Moreover, if the signal is perfectly correlated with the action taken by a node, then monitoring is perfect; otherwise, monitoring is said to be imperfect.

We consider that monitoring is performed locally by every node. A possible implementation of such monitoring mechanism in the context of P2P networks could be based on the work of [6]. A simpler mechanism would instead consist in every out-neighbor j of a given node i recording the fraction of messages sent by i to j during the dissemination of a fixed number M of messages. Then, j may use this information along with an estimate of the reliability of the dissemination of messages to i in order to assess the behavior of i. When a defection is detected, j disseminates an accusation against i towards other nodes. If i is expected to use $p_i[j] < 1$ towards j, then monitoring is imperfect. Furthermore, accusations may be blocked, disrupted, or wrongly emitted against one node due to both malicious and rational behavior. However, in this paper, we consider only perfect monitoring, faithful propagation of accusations, and that nodes are rational. Almost perfect monitoring can be achieved with a large M. Faithful propagation may be reasonable to assume if the impact of punishments on the reliability of each non-punished node is small and the cost of sending accusations is not significant. We intend to relax these assumptions in future work.

In our model, an accusation emitted by a node j against an in-neighbor i may only be received by the nodes that are reachable from j by following paths in the graph. In addition, if we consider the obvious possibility that i might block any accusation emitted by one of its neighbors, then these paths cannot cross i. Finally, the number of nodes informed of each defection may be further reduced to minimize the monitoring costs. This restricts the set of in-neighbors of i that may punish i for defecting j. In this paper, we consider two alternative models. First, we study public monitoring, where all nodes may be informed about any defection with no delays. Then, we study the private monitoring case, taking into consideration the possible delay of the dissemination of accusations.

3.3   Game Theoretical Model

Our model considers an infinite repetition of a stage game. Each stage consists in the dissemination of a sequence of messages and is interleaved with the execution of the monitoring mechanism, which provides every node with some information regarding the actions taken by other nodes during the stage game. This game is modeled as a strategic game, where $\mathcal{N}$ is the set of players. An action of a player i is a vector of probabilities $\boldsymbol{p}_i \in \mathcal{P}_i$, such that $p_i[j] > 0$ only if $j \in \mathcal{N}_i$. Thus, $\boldsymbol{p}_i$ represents the average probability used by i to forward messages during the stage. It is reasonable to consider that i adheres to $\boldsymbol{p}_i$ during the complete stage, since i expects to be monitored by other nodes with regard to a given $\boldsymbol{p}_i$. Hence, changing strategy is equivalent to following a different $\boldsymbol{p}_i$. The utility of a player i is a function of the benefit β_i obtained per received message and the cost γ_i of forwarding a message to each neighbor. More precisely, this utility is given by the product of the reliability by the difference between the benefit per message (β_i) and the expected cost of forwarding the message ($\gamma_i \sum_{j \in \mathcal{N}_i} p_i[j]$)):

$$u_i[\boldsymbol{p}] = (1 - q_i[\boldsymbol{p}])(\beta_i - \gamma_i \sum_{j \in \mathcal{N}_i} p_i[j]). \tag{1}$$

The repeated game consists in the infinite interleaving between the stage game and the execution of the monitoring mechanism, where future payoffs are discounted by a factor ω_i for every player i. The game is characterized by (possibly infinite) sequences of previously observed signals, named histories. The set of finite histories observed by player i is represented by $\mathcal{H}_i$ and $\mathcal{H} = (\mathcal{H}_i)_{i \in \mathcal{N}}$ is the set of all histories observed by any player. A pure strategy for the repeated game $\sigma_i \in \Sigma_i$ maps each history to an action p_i, where $\sigma \in \Sigma$ is a profile of strategies. The expected utility of player i after having observed h_i is given by $\pi_i[\sigma|h_i]$. The exact definitions of equilibrium and expected utility will be provided in each of the sections regarding public and private monitoring. Throughout the paper, we will conveniently simplify the notation as follows. Whenever referring to a profile of strategies σ, followed by all nodes except i, we will use the notation σ_{-i}. Also, (σ_i, σ_{-i}) denotes the composite of a strategy σ_i and a profile σ_{-i}. The same reasoning applies to profiles of strategies of the stage game. Finally, (h, s) is the history that follows h and the observation of signal s. Since the focus of this paper is on pure punishing strategies, we omitted the definition of non-deterministic strategies for both games, which are analyzed in [16].

3.4   Effectiveness

We know from the Game Theoretic literature that certain punishing strategies can sustain cooperation if the discount factor ω_i is sufficiently close to 1 [5]. This minimum value is a function of the parameters β_i and γ_i for every player i. More precisely, for larger values of the benefit-to-cost ratio β_i/γ_i, the minimum required value of ω_i is smaller. In addition, for certain values of the benefit-to-cost ratio, no value of ω_i can sustain cooperation. Notice that these parameters are specified by the environment and thus cannot be adjusted in the protocol. Thus, a strategy is more effective if it is an equilibrium for wider ranges of ω_i, β_i, and γ_i. In this paper, we only measure the effectiveness of a profile of strategies σ as the allowed range of values for the benefit-to-cost ratio.

Definition 1. *The effectiveness of a profile $\sigma \in \Sigma$ is given by $\psi[\sigma] \subseteq [0, \infty)$, such that, if, for every $i \in \mathcal{N}$, $\frac{\beta_i}{\gamma_i} \in \psi[\sigma]$, then there exists $\omega_i \in (0, 1)$ for every $i \in \mathcal{N}$ such that σ is an equilibrium.*

4   Public Monitoring

In this section, we assume that the graph allows public monitoring to be implemented. That is, every node is informed about each defection at the end of the stage when the defection occurred. We can thus simplify the notation by considering only public signals $s \in \mathcal{S}$ and histories $h \in \mathcal{H}$. With perfect monitoring, the public signal observed after players follow $p \in \mathcal{P}$ is deterministic. This type of monitoring requires accusations to be broadcast. However, since the dissemination of accusations is interleaved with the dissemination of a sequence of messages, monitoring costs may not be relevant if the size of each accusation is small, compared to the size of messages being disseminated.

4.1 Public Signal and Punishing Strategies

We study a wide variety of punishing strategies, by considering a parameter τ that specifies the duration of punishments. Of particular interest to this analysis is the case where the duration of punishments is infinite, commonly known as the Grim Trigger strategy. Furthermore, a punishing strategy specifies a Reaction Set $RS[i, j] \subseteq \mathcal{N}$ of nodes that are expected to react to every defection of i from j during τ stages. This set always contains i and j. In addition, a third node $k \in RS[i, j]$ that is an in-neighbor of i is expected to stop forwarding any messages to i, as a punishment. If k is not a neighbor of i, then k may also adapt the probabilities used towards its out-neighbors, for instance, to keep the reliability high for every unpunished node.

Formally, a punishing strategy σ_i^* defines for every history $h \in \mathcal{H}$ a threshold probability $p_i[j|h]$ with which i should forward messages to j. We will denote by $\boldsymbol{\sigma}^* \in \Sigma$ the profile of punishing strategies. The restrictions imposed on every $p_i[j|h]$ by σ_i^* can be defined as follows. Every node i evaluates the set of defections observed in a history h by i and every neighbor j to which both nodes should react. If a defection of j from some out-neighbor or of i from j is observed in one of the last τ stages, then $p_i[j|h] = 0$; otherwise, $p_i[j|h]$ is a deterministic function of the set of observed defections. Given this, the public signal is defined as a function of every $p_i[j|h]$.

Definition 2. *For every $h \in \mathcal{H}$ and $\boldsymbol{p}' \in \mathcal{P}$, let $s = sig[\boldsymbol{p}'|h]$ be the public signal observed when players follow $\boldsymbol{p}'$. For every $i \in \mathcal{N}$ and $j \in \mathcal{N}_i$, $s[i, j] =$ cooperate if and only if $p_i'[j] \geq p_i[j|h]$.*

4.2 Expected Utility and Solution Concept

For any history $h \in \mathcal{H}$, let $\boldsymbol{p} = \boldsymbol{\sigma}[h]$. The expected utility of any player i is

$$\pi_i[\boldsymbol{\sigma}|h] = u_i[\boldsymbol{p}] + \omega_i \pi_i[\boldsymbol{\sigma}|(h, sig[\boldsymbol{p}|h])]. \qquad (2)$$

The considered solution concept for this model is the notion of Subgame Perfect Equilibrium (SPE) [14], which refines the solution concept of Nash Equilibrium (NE) for repeated games. In particular, a profile of strategies is a NE if no player can increase its utility by deviating, given that other players follow the specified strategies. The solution concept of NE is adequate for instance for strategic games, where players choose their actions prior to the execution of the game. However, in repeated games, players have multiple decision points, when they may adapt their actions according to the observed history of signals. In this case, the notion of NE ignores the possibility of players being faced with histories that are not consistent with the defined strategy, e.g., when some defection is observed. In some cases, this results in a NE being sustained by non-credible threats. The notion of SPE was proposed to address this issue, which imposes the additional requirement that the defined strategy must be a NE after any history. This intuition is formalized as follows.

Definition 3. *A profile of strategies* σ^* *is a Subgame Perfect Equilibrium if and only if for every player* $i \in \mathcal{N}$, *history* $h \in \mathcal{H}$, *and strategy* $\sigma_i' \in \Sigma_i$,

$$\pi_i[\sigma_i^*, \sigma_{-i}^*|h] \geq \pi_i[\sigma_i', \sigma_{-i}^*|h]. \tag{3}$$

4.3 Optimal Effectiveness

Proposition 1 establishes a minimum necessary benefit-to-cost ratio for any profile of strategies to be a SPE of the repeated Epidemic Dissemination Game. Intuitively, the benefit-to-cost ratio must be greater than the expected number of forwarded messages $(\bar{p}_i)$, since otherwise a player has incentives to not forward any messages. Consequently, this establishes an upper bound for the effectiveness of any profile of strategies. It is important to notice that this result follows directly from the Folk Theorems [5], since the minmax utility of the considered game is 0. However, the Folk Theorems only allows us to derive a strictly necessary benefit-to-cost, which is not always sufficient for the generic family of punishing strategies considered in this paper.

Proposition 1. *For every profile of punishing strategies* σ^*, *if* σ^* *is a SPE, then, for every* $i \in \mathcal{N}$, $\frac{\beta_i}{\gamma_i} > \bar{p}_i = \sum_{j \in \mathcal{N}_i} p_i[j|\emptyset]$. *Consequently,*

$$\psi[\sigma^*] \subseteq (\max_{i \in \mathcal{N}} \bar{p}_i, \infty). \tag{4}$$

4.4 Direct Reciprocity is Not Effective

If G is undirected, then it is possible to use direct reciprocity, by defining $\mathrm{RS}[i, j] = \{i, j\}$ for every $i \in \mathcal{N}$ and $j \in \mathcal{N}_i$. That is, if i defects from j, then only j punishes i. Direct reciprocity is the ideal incentive mechanism in a fully distributed environment, since it does not require any accusations to be sent. Unfortunately, in some scenarios, this incentive is not effective, as shown in Lemma 1. Namely, by letting q_i^* to be the probability of delivery of messages in equilibrium, we find that, if $p_i[j|\emptyset] + q_i^* \ll 1$, then the effectiveness is of the order $(1/q_i^*, \infty)$, which decreases to $\emptyset$ very quickly with an increasing reliability. The conditions under which direct reciprocity is ineffective are easily met, e.g., when a node has more neighbors than what is necessary to ensure high reliability.

Lemma 1. *Suppose that for any* $i \in \mathcal{N}$ *and* $j \in \mathcal{N}_i$, $p_i[j|\emptyset] + q_i^* \ll 1$. *If* σ^* *is a SPE, then:*

$$\psi[\sigma^*] \subseteq (1/q_i^*, \infty). \tag{5}$$

Proof. The proof defines an alternative strategy σ_i' where i defects from j. In order for σ^* to be a SPE, Equation 3 must hold for the empty history and σ_i'. After some manipulations, we can derive Equation 5. This derivation uses Inequality 6, where q_i' results from j punishing i.

$$q_i' \leq q_i^*/(1 - p_i[j|\emptyset]). \tag{6}$$

4.5   Full Indirect Reciprocity Is Sufficient

Unlike direct reciprocity, if full indirect reciprocity is used, then the effectiveness may be independent of the reliability of the dissemination protocol. This consists in the case where for every $i \in \mathcal{N}$ and $j \in \mathcal{N}_i$ we have

$$\mathcal{N}_i^{-1} \subseteq \text{RS}[i, j]. \tag{7}$$

Theorem 1 derives a lower bound for the effectiveness of a profile of punishing strategies σ^* that uses full indirect reciprocity. The proof of this result relies on Assumption 4. Let $q_i[h, r | \sigma]$ denote the value of q_i in stage r following the observation of h, when players follow σ.

Definition 4. *(Assumption). There must exist a constant $c \geq 1$ such that for every history $h \in \mathcal{H}$:*

$$q_i[h, 0 | \sigma^*] \geq 1 - c(1 - q_i[h, 1 | \sigma^*]).$$

The intuition of this assumption is that the variation of q_i from one stage to the following is never too large, regardless of the punishments being applied in h. We can now derive a lower bound for the effectiveness of the considered strategy. Let $\bar{p}_i[h | \sigma^*]$ be the expected number of forwarded messages after h.

Theorem 1. *If there exists a constant $c \geq 1$ such that, for every $h \in \mathcal{H}$ and $i \in \mathcal{N}$, Assumption 4 holds, then $\psi[\sigma^*] \supseteq (v, \infty)$, where*

$$v = \max_{h \in \mathcal{H}} \max_{i \in \mathcal{N}} \bar{p}_i[h | \sigma^*](1 + c/\tau). \tag{8}$$

Proof. Using full indirect reciprocity, the best strategy is for i to either follow σ_i^* or σ_i' where i defects from all neighbors. Using this fact, we find that the history h that minimizes Equation 3 has the property that any punishment being applied in h is concluded exactly $\tau - 1$ stages after h is observed. With this and Assumption 4, it is possible to derive v as a sufficient benefit-to-cost ratio for i to not have incentives to defect from all neighbors.

We can then conclude that if c is small or τ is large, and the maximum of $\bar{p}_i[h | \sigma^*]$ is never much larger than $\bar{p}_i$ for every i and h, then the effectiveness of full indirect reciprocity is close to the optimum derived in Proposition 1. In particular, Grim Trigger achieves optimal effectiveness if $\bar{p}_i$ is maximal.

5   Private Monitoring

When using public monitoring, we make the implicit assumption that the monitoring mechanism is able to provide the same information instantly to every node, which requires the existence of a path from every out-neighbor j of any node i to every node of the graph, that does not cross i. In addition, public monitoring is only possible if accusations are broadcast to every node. We now consider private monitoring, where the dissemination of accusations may be restricted by the topology and scalability constraints and may be delayed.

5.1   Private Signals

In private monitoring, signals are also a function of a history $h \in \mathcal{H}$ and a profile $p \in \mathcal{P}$. However, every node i observes only its private signal $s_i \in s$. We denote by $h_i \in h$ the private history observed by i when all players observe $h \in \mathcal{H}$. The distinction between cooperation and defection is now determined by a threshold probability $p_i[j|h_i]$. If a node i defects an out-neighbor j in stage r, then k is informed of this defection with a delay $d_k[i,j]$ if the delay is finite, i.e., k is informed only at the end of stage $r + d_k[i,j]$. We consider that the delay is infinite iff accusations emitted by j against i may never reach k. These delays are assumed to be common knowledge among all players. With this, we no longer need the definition of reaction set RS.

5.2   Private Punishments

A punishing strategy σ_i^* specifies the threshold probabilities $p_i[j|h_i]$ for every player i, private history h_i, and out-neighbor j. The definition of private signals states that an accusation by j against i is emitted iff i uses $p_i[j] < p_i[j|h_i]$. In public monitoring, since we considered public histories, this was reasonable to assume. In private monitoring, if i observes $h_i \in h$ and j observes $h_j \in h$, then the set of defections observed by both nodes may vary, since h_i may differ from h_j. Thus, σ_i^* should also define $p_i[j|h_j]$. In order for monitoring to be accurate, $p_i[j|h_i]$ and $p_i[j|h_j]$ must be computed as a function of the same set of signals. The only issue with this requirement is that defection signals may arrive at different stages to i and j. For instance, if k_1 defects from k_2 in stage r and $d_i[k_1,k_2] < d_j[k_1,k_2]$, then i must wait for stage $r + d_j[k_1,k_2]$ before taking this defection into consideration in the computation of the threshold probability. Furthermore, as in public monitoring, i and j are expected to react to a given defection for a finite number of stages. However, as we will see later, this number should vary according to the delays in order for punishments to be effective. Thus, for every $k_1 \in \mathcal{N}$ and $k_2 \in \mathcal{N}_{k_1}$, we define $\tau[k_1, k_2|i,j]$ to be the number of stages during which i and j react to a given defection of k_1 from k_2.

5.3   Expected Utility and Solution Concept

We now model the interactions as a repeated game where players are imperfectly informed about the strategies of other players. In this context, the solution concept of Sequential Equilibrium is adequate [9]. Its definition requires the specification of a belief system μ. More precisely, after player i observes $h_i \in \mathcal{H}_i$, i must form some expectation regarding the history $h \in \mathcal{H}$ observed by every other player. This is captured by a probability distribution $\mu_i[.|h_i]$ over $\mathcal{H}$. By defining $\mu = (\mu_i)_{i \in \mathcal{N}}$, we call a pair (σ, μ) an assessment, which is assumed to be common knowledge among all players. Let $\pi_i[\sigma|h]$ be defined as in the public monitoring case. The expected utility of a profile of strategies σ for a player i and private history h_i is then defined as:

$$\pi_i[\sigma|\mu, h_i] = \sum_{h \in \mathcal{H}} \mu_i[h|h_i]\pi_i[\sigma|h]. \tag{9}$$

An assessment $(\boldsymbol{\sigma}^*, \boldsymbol{\mu}^*)$ is a Sequential Equilibrium if and only if $(\boldsymbol{\sigma}^*, \boldsymbol{\mu}^*)$ is Sequentially Rational and Consistent. The definition of sequential rationality is identical to that of subgame perfection:

Definition 5. *An assessment $(\boldsymbol{\sigma}^*, \boldsymbol{\mu}^*)$ is Sequentially Rational if and only if for every $i \in \mathcal{N}$, $h_i \in \mathcal{H}_i$, and $\sigma_i' \in \Sigma_i$,*

$$\pi_i[\boldsymbol{\sigma}^* | \boldsymbol{\mu}^*, h_i] \geq \pi_i[\sigma_i', \boldsymbol{\sigma}_{-i}^* | \boldsymbol{\mu}^*, h_i].$$

However, defining consistency for an assessment $(\boldsymbol{\sigma}, \boldsymbol{\mu})$ is more intricate. The idea of defining this concept was introduced in [9]. For any profile $\boldsymbol{\sigma}$, every private history h_i that may be reached with positive probability when players follow $\boldsymbol{\sigma}$ is said to be consistent with $\boldsymbol{\sigma}$; otherwise, h_i is inconsistent. For any consistent h_i, $\mu_i[h|h_i]$ must be defined using the Bayes rule. The definition of μ_i for inconsistent private histories varies with the specific definition of Consistent Assessment. It turns out that in our case the notion of Preconsistency introduced in [7] is sufficient. We opt not to include in this paper the formal definition of Preconsistency, which is rather technical. Instead, we provide only an intuition for our context. An assessment is Preconsistent if and only if the following condition is met. After having observed h_i, i never believes that any defection was performed other than what has been observed in h_i. More precisely, $\mu[h|h_i] = 1$ if and only if h is the history containing h_i and the set of defections observed by any node $j \in \mathcal{N}$ in $h_j \in h$ is a subset of the set of defections observed in h_i. One important consequence of this definition is that the *optimal effectiveness* for private monitoring is *identical* to what is stated in Proposition 1.

5.4   Ineffective Topologies

Our first result for this model shows that not every topology allows the existence of equilibria for punishing strategies. In fact, if there is some node i and a neighbor j such that every node k that is reachable from j without crossing i is never in between s and i, then no in-neighbor of i is ever informed about any defection of i from j. Therefore, i can decrease the incurred costs while maintaining the expected benefits by dropping j. This intuition is formalized in Lemma 2, where $PS[i, j]$ denotes the set of paths from i to j in G.

Lemma 2. *If the assessment $(\boldsymbol{\sigma}^*, \boldsymbol{\mu}^*)$ is Preconsistent and Sequentially Rational, then for every $i \in \mathcal{N}$ and $j \in \mathcal{N}_i$, there is $k \in \mathcal{N} \setminus \{i\}$, $x \in PS[s, i]$, and $x' \in PS[j, k]$, such that $k \in x$ and $i \notin x'$.*

The main implication of this result is that many non-redundant topologies, i.e., that do not contain multiple paths between s and every node, are ineffective at sustaining cooperation. This is not entirely surprising, since it was already known that cooperation cannot be sustained using punishments as incentives in non-redundant graphs such as trees [13]. But even slightly redundant structures, such as directed cycles, do not fulfill the necessary condition specified in Lemma 2. Although redundancy is desirable to fulfill the above condition, it might decrease the effectiveness of punishments unless full indirect reciprocity may be used, as shown in the following section.

5.5 Redundancy May Decrease Effectiveness

Besides the need to fulfill the necessary condition of Lemma 2, a higher redundancy increases tolerance to failures. We show in Theorem 2 that if the graph is redundant and it does not allow full indirect reciprocity to be implemented, then the effectiveness decreases monotonically with the increase of the reliability. More precisely, the reliability increases as the probabilities $p_i[j|\emptyset]$ approach 1 for every node i and out-neighbor j. This is denoted by $\lim_{\sigma^* \to 1}$. We find that the effectiveness of any punishment strategy that cannot implement full indirect reciprocity converges to $\emptyset$. Thus, no benefit-to-cost ratio sustains cooperation.

Theorem 2. *If G is redundant and there exist $i \in \mathcal{N}$, $j \in \mathcal{N}_i$, and $k \in \mathcal{N}_i^{-1}$ such that for every $x \in PS[j,k]$ we have $i \in x$, then Equality 10 holds:*

$$\lim_{\sigma^* \to 1} \psi[\sigma^*|\mu^*] = \cdot_{i \in \mathcal{N}, j \in \mathcal{N}_i} \lim_{p_i[j|\emptyset] \to 1} \psi[\sigma^*|\mu^*] = \emptyset. \tag{10}$$

Proof. If i defects from j, then k is not informed of this fact. Since G is redundant, there is a path x from s to i that crosses k. Thus, every node along x also does not react to the defection of i and the probability of any message being delivered to i along this path converges to 1. In the limit, i can avoid the costs of forwarding messages to j, without decreasing the benefits. Thus, no benefit-to-cost ratio ensures that σ^* is an equilibrium.

Notice that this result does not imply that only full indirect reciprocity is effective at incentivizing rational nodes to cooperate. In fact, it might suffice for a majority of the in-neighbors of a node i to punish i after any defection. A more sensible analysis would take into consideration the rate of converge to $\emptyset$ as the reliability increases. Nevertheless, full indirect reciprocity is necessary for the effectiveness to be independent of the reliability in any redundant graph.

5.6 Coordination is Desirable

We now show that for some definitions of punishing strategies and redundant graphs, full indirect reciprocity might not be sufficient if monitoring incurs large delays. We find that nodes also need to coordinate the punishments being applied to any node, such that these punishments overlap during at least one stage after the defection. This intuition is formalized as follows.

Definition 6. *An assessment (σ^*, μ^*) enforces coordination if and only if for every $i \in \mathcal{N}$ and $j \in \mathcal{N}_i$, there exists $r > 0$ such that, for every $k \in \mathcal{N}_i^{-1}$,*

$$r \in \{d_k[i,j] + 1 \ldots d_k[i,j] + \tau[i,j|k,i]\}.$$

Theorem 3 states, if coordination is not enforced, then the effectiveness decreases to $\emptyset$ with the reliability, as in Theorem 2.

Theorem 3. *If G is redundant and σ^* does not enforce coordination, then there is a definition of σ^* such that Equality 10 holds.*

Proof. One example of such definition is when nodes only react to defections performed by their out-neighbors. Given this, there is a node i and neighbor j such that if i defects j, then in every stage r following the defection there is some in-neighbor k of i that is not reacting to the defection of i during r. This always ensures the existence of a path from s to i composed only of nodes not reacting to the defection of i in r. The rest of the proof proceeds as in Theorem 2.

To avoid this problem, punishments should overlap in $\tau > 0$ stages. More precisely, for every node i, let $\bar{d}_i$ denote the maximum delay of accusations against i to reach every in-neighbor of i. It is sufficient to provide a definition of $\tau[i, j | k, i]$ for every $k \in \mathcal{N}_i^{-1}$ and $j \in \mathcal{N}_i$ such that every in-neighbor of i stops reacting to a given defection in the same stage. Formally:

$$\tau[i, j | k, i] = \bar{d}_i - d_k[i, j] + \tau. \tag{11}$$

5.7 Coordinated Full Indirect Reciprocity

We now study the set of punishing strategies that use full indirect reciprocity. Under some circumstances, the effectiveness of a Preconsistent assessment (σ^*, μ^*) that uses full indirect reciprocity does not increase with the reliability of the dissemination process. As seen in the previous section, this requires punishments to be coordinated, which we assume to be defined as in 11. The main result of this section is presented in Theorem 4, which derives a lower bound for the effectiveness of coordinated full indirect reciprocity. The proof of this theorem is very similar to that of Theorem 1, except that now we need two assumptions. Assumption 7 states that punishing strategies should be defined in a reasonable manner. More precisely, if in reaction to a defection of node i other nodes increase the probabilities used towards out-neighbors other than i, then i should never expect a large increase in its reliability during the initial stages, before every in-neighbor starts punishing i. For any $p'_i \in \mathcal{P}_i$, let $\sigma_i^*[h|p'_i]$ denote the strategy where i only deviates from σ_i^* by following p'_i in the first stage after h.

Definition 7. *(Assumption) There exists a constant $\epsilon \in [0, 1)$ such that, for every $h \in \mathcal{H}$, $i \in \mathcal{N}$, $p'_i \in \mathcal{P}_i$, and $r > 0$,*

$$q_i[h, r | \sigma^*] - q_i[h, r | \sigma_i^*[h|p'_i], \sigma_{-i}^*] < \epsilon.$$

Furthermore, Assumption 8 requires that, if a node i defects from some out-neighbor, then the reliability i would obtain during the initial stages when it is not being punished by all in-neighbors is not significantly greater than the reliability i would obtain in the subsequent stages, had i not defected.

Definition 8. *(Assumption). There exists a constant $c > 0$, such that, for every $i \in \mathcal{N}$, $r \in \{0 \ldots \bar{d}_i\}$, and $r' \in \{\bar{d}_i + 1 \ldots \bar{d}_i + \tau\}$,*

$$q_i[h, r | \sigma^*] \geq 1 - c(1 - q_i[h, r' | \sigma^*]).$$

A lower bound of the effectiveness of coordinated full indirect reciprocity is derived for values of τ and ϵ such that $\tau \geq \bar{d}+1$ and $\epsilon \ll 1$, where $\bar{d} = \max_{i \in \mathcal{N}} \bar{d}_i$ is the maximum delay between defections and corresponding punishments.

Theorem 4. *If (σ^*, μ^*) is Preconsistent, Assumptions 7 and 8 hold for $\epsilon \ll 1$, and $\tau \geq \bar{d}+1$, then there is a constant $c > 0$ such that $\psi[\sigma^*|\mu^*] \supseteq (v, \infty)$, where*

$$v = \max_{i \in \mathcal{N}} \max_{h \in \mathcal{H}} \bar{p}_i[h|\sigma^*](1 + c).$$

Proof. The proof follows similar guidelines to the proof of Theorem 1.

As in public monitoring, the effectiveness is close to optimal only if $\bar{p}_i$ is close to $\bar{p}_i[h|\sigma^*]$ for any history h. Provided this guarantee, if ϵ is small and τ is chosen to be at least of the order of $\bar{d}$, then the effectiveness differs from the optimal by a constant factor. Notice that, although we can adjust the value of τ to compensate for higher delays, it is desirable to have a low maximum delay. First, if monitoring is imperfect, then a node may be wrongly accused, in which case we want to avoid very harsh punishments. Second, a larger τ may decrease the range of values of ω_i that sustain cooperation for each benefit-to-cost ratio.

6   Discussion and Future Work

From our analysis, we can derive several desirable properties of a fully distributed monitoring mechanism for an epidemic dissemination protocol with asymmetric interactions, which uses punishments as the main incentive. This monitoring mechanism is expected to operate on top of an overlay network that provides a stable membership to each node. The results of this paper determine that the overlay should optimally explore the tradeoff between maximal randomization and higher clustering coefficient. The former is ideal for minimizing the latency of the dissemination process and fault tolerance, whereas the latter is necessary to minimize the distances between the neighbors of each node, while maximizing the number of in-neighbors of every node i informed about any defection of i. The topology of this overlay should also fulfill the necessary conditions identified in this paper. Furthermore, the analysis of private monitoring shows that each accusation may be disseminated to a subset of nodes close to the accused node, without hindering the effectiveness. As future work, we plan to extend this analysis by considering imperfect monitoring, unreliable dissemination of accusations, malicious behavior, and churn. One possible application of the considered monitoring mechanism would be to sustain cooperation in a P2P news recommendation system such as the one proposed in [2]. Due to the lower rate of arrival of news, a monitoring approach may be better suited for this context.

Acknowledgements. This work was partially supported by Fundação para a Ciência e Tecnologia (FCT) via the INESC-ID multi-annual funding through the PIDDAC Program fund grant, under project PEst-OE/ EEI/ LA0021/ 2013, and via the project PEPITA (PTDC/EEI-SCR/2776/2012).

References

1. Birman, K.P., Hayden, M., Ozkasap, O., Xiao, Z., Budiu, M., Minsky, Y.: Bimodal multicast. ACM Trans. Comput. Syst. 17(2), 41–88 (1999)
2. Boutet, A., Frey, D., Guerraoui, R., Jegou, A., Kermarrec, A.-M.: Whatsup: A decentralized instant news recommender. In: 27th IEEE International Symposium on Parallel Distributed Processing, IPDPS, pp. 741–752. IEE Press, New York (2013)
3. Deshpande, M., Xing, B., Lazardis, I., Hore, B., Venkatasubramanian, N., Mehrotra, S.: Crew: A gossip-based flash-dissemination system. In: Proceedings of the 26th IEEE International Conference on Distributed Computing Systems, ICDCS, p. 45. IEEE Computer Society, Washington, DC (2006)
4. Feldman, M., Lai, K., Stoica, I., Chuang, J.: Robust incentive techniques for peer-to-peer networks. In: Proceedings of the 5th ACM Conference on Electronic Commerce, EC, pp. 102–111. ACM, New York (2004)
5. Fudenberg, D., Maskin, E.: The folk theorem in repeated games with discounting or with incomplete information. Econometrica 54(3), 533–554 (1986)
6. Guerraoui, R., Huguenin, K., Kermarrec, A.-M., Monod, M., Prusty, S.: liFTinG: Lightweight freerider-tracking in gossip. In: Gupta, I., Mascolo, C. (eds.) Middleware 2010. LNCS, vol. 6452, pp. 313–333. Springer, Heidelberg (2010)
7. Hendon, E., Jacobsen, H., Sloth, B.: The one-shot-deviation principle for sequential rationality. Games and Economic Behavior 12(2), 274–282 (1996)
8. Keidar, I., Melamed, R., Orda, A.: Equicast: Scalable multicast with selfish users. Comput. Netw. 53(13), 2373–2386 (2009)
9. Kreps, D., Wilson, R.: Sequential equilibria. Econometrica 50(4), 863–894 (1982)
10. Li, B., Xie, S., Qu, Y., Keung, G.Y., Lin, C., Liu, J., Zhang, X.: Inside the new coolstreaming: Principles, measurements and performance implications. In: The 27th Conference on Computer Communications, INFOCOM, pp. 1031–1039. IEEE Press, New York (2008)
11. Li, H.C., Clement, A., Marchetti, M., Kapritsos, M., Robison, L., Alvisi, L., Dahlin, M.: Flightpath: obedience vs. choice in cooperative services. In: Proceedings of the 8th USENIX Symposium on Operating Systems Design and Implementation, OSDI, pp. 355–368. USENIX Association, Berkeley (2008)
12. Li, H.C., Clement, A., Wong, E.L., Napper, J., Roy, I., Alvisi, L., Dahlin, M.: BAR gossip. In: Proceedings of the 7th Symposium on Operating Systems Design and Implementation, OSDI, pp. 191–204. USENIX Association, Berkeley (2006)
13. Ngan, T., Druschel, P., Wallach, D.: Incentives-Compatible Peer-to-Peer Multicast. In: 2nd Workshop on Economics of Peer-to-Peer Systems (2004)
14. Osborne, M., Rubinstein, A.: A course in game theory. The MIT Press (1994)
15. Qiu, D., Srikant, R.: Modeling and performance analysis of bittorrent-like peer-to-peer networks. SIGCOMM Comput. Commun. Rev. 34(4), 367–378 (2004)
16. Vilaca, X., Rodrigues, L.: On the effectiveness of punishments in a repeated epidemic dissemination game. Arxiv preprint arXiv:1308.6526v2 (August 2013)

Linearizing Peer-to-Peer Systems with Oracles

Rizal Mohd Nor[1,*], Mikhail Nesterenko[2], and Sébastien Tixeuil[3,**]

[1] International Islamic University, Malaysia
[2] Kent State University, USA
[3] UPMC Sorbonne Universités & IUF, France

Abstract. We study distributed linearization or topological sorting in peer-to-peer networks. We define strict and eventual variants of the problem. We consider these problems restricted to existing peer identifiers or without this restriction. None of these variants are solvable in the asynchronous message-passing system model. We define a collection of oracles and prove which oracle combination is necessary to enable a solution for each variant of the linearization problem. We then present a linearization algorithm. We prove that this algorithm and a specific combination of the oracles solves each stated variant of the linearization problem.

1 Introduction

Oracles and Limits of Solvability in peer-to-peer Systems. Mohd Nor et al [17] showed that construction of structured peer-to-peer systems in asynchronous systems have fundamental limits such as inability to connect a disconnected network or discard peer identifiers that are not present in the system. These limits do not appear to be reducible to just the properties of asynchronous systems alone, such as lack of consensus [10]. That is, the limits are specific to peer-to-peer problems.

In this paper we endeavor to systematically study these limits. We intentionally pattern our work on the classic proof of impossibility of crash-robust consensus [10] and its resolution with failure detector oracles [4, 5]. That is, we identify peer-to-peer system specific oracles and isolate the source of impossibility in them, we then show the minimality of oracles by proving their necessity for solution existence and then solve the problem by providing an oracle-based algorithm.

We focus on the problem of linearization (topological sort). Let us motivate our choice of the problem. Linearization requires each process p to determine two peers whose identifiers are consequent, i.e. next to one another in topological order, with this p's identifier. This problem underlies most popular peer-to-peer systems [1, 2, 14–16, 19, 20] as more sophisticated constructions start by topologically sorting the peer-to-peer network. While being foundational for many

---

* This work is supported in part by a Research Acculturation Grant Scheme RAGS 12-042-0042, IIUM, MOHE Malaysia.
** This work was supported in part by LINCS.

T. Higashino et al. (Eds.): SSS 2013, LNCS 8255, pp. 221–236, 2013.

peer-to-peer systems, linearization is similar to consensus in the following sense. Linearization is simple enough so that one can observe how the results established for this problem pertain to all peer-to-peer systems.

Our Contribution. Similar to consensus, we define two variants of the problem: strict linearization, where each process has to output its consequent identifiers exactly once; and eventual linearization where a process may make a finite number of mistakes in its output. We introduce a restriction that is specific to peer-to-peer systems: the initial input may contain only process identifiers that exist in the system. We study the linearization problems with and without this restriction, i.e. we consider four different linearization problem variants.

In present work, we show that none of the four variants of the linearization problem are solvable in the asynchronous message-passing systems. We use the concept of oracles to encapsulate the impossible. We define the weak connectivity oracle that detects the system to be disconnected and restores its connectivity. We show that this oracle is necessary to solve all four variants of the problem. We define the participant detector oracle that removes non-existent identifiers from the system. We then show that this oracle is necessary to solve the linearization problem that allows non-existent identifier input. We define the oracle property of subset splittability. Intuitively, a subset splittable oracle does not provide information about the state of the outside system to a particular subset of processes. We then prove that a non-subset splittable oracle is necessary to solve strict linearization.

On the constructive side, we use a simple linearization algorithm [17] and show that it solves each variant of the linearization problem with a particular combination of oracles. Specifically, this algorithm solves eventual linearization problem with existent identifiers using only weak connectivity oracle; the addition of participant detector oracle enables solution to the problem with non-existent identifiers. Taken together with the necessary results, this demonstrates that the particular combinations of oracles are necessary and sufficient to solve the variants of the linearization problem with existing identifiers. We define the consequent detector oracle, a specific non-subset splittable oracle that can output consequent identifier once the process stores it in its memory. We then show that using the consequent detector oracle, our algorithm solves the strict linearization problem. These results are summarized in Figure 4.

Related Literature. Mohd Nor et al [17] provided impetus for this work. As a part of the work presented in their paper, they showed that there are limitations of achievable results in peer-to-peer systems. However, the applicability of their negative results is limited, as Mohd Nor et al considered only self-stabilizing algorithms [7, 21]. To prove impossibility of stabilization, it is sufficient to show that there exists a global state from which no program can possibly recover. However, such results may not be applicable to regular, non-stabilizing programs, as non-stabilizing programs are only required to solve the problem from a particular non-faulty initial state. Therefore, such programs may never reach the degenerate states that self-stabilizing programs have to address. Hence, proving the limits for regular programs is significantly more involved.

Onus et al [18] recognize the importance of linearization as a fundamental problem in peer-to-peer system construction and study it in the context of self-stabilization. Gall et al [11] consider linearization performance bounds. Emek et al [9] study various definitions of connectivity for overlay networks. There are several studies on participant detectors [3, 13] for consensus.

2   Notation and Execution Model

Peer-to-peer Systems. A peer-to-peer overlay system consists of a set of N processes with unique identifiers. When it is clear from the context, we refer to a process and its identifier interchangeably. A process stores other process identifiers in its local memory. Once the peer identifier is stored, the process is able to communicate with its peer by sending messages to it. Message routing is handled by the underlying network. We thus assume that the peers are connected by a communication channel. Processes may store identifiers of peers that do not exist in the system. If a message is sent to such non-existent identifier, the message is discarded. A process a *forwards* identifier b to process c, if a sends a message containing identifier b to process c and erases b from its memory.

The peer identifiers are assumed to be totally ordered, i.e. for any two distinct identifiers a and b, either $a < b$ or $a > b$. Two processes a and b of set N are *consequent*, denoted **cnsq**(a, b) if any other process that belongs to N is either less than a or greater than b. Negative infinity is consequent with the smallest process of N and positive infinity is consequent with the largest process. Note that the total order of identifiers implies that if two non-identical sets are merged, the consequent process changes for at least one process in each set.

Graph terminology helps in reasoning about peer-to-peer systems. A *link*, denoted (a, b), between a pair of identifiers a and b is defined as follows: either message $message(b)$ carrying identifier b is in the incoming channel of process a, or process a stores identifier b in its local memory. Thus defined, link is directed. When referring to link (a, b), we always state the predecessor process first and the successor process second.

A *channel connectivity* multigraph CC includes both locally stored and message-based links. Self-loop links are not considered. Links to non-existent identifiers are not considered either. Note that besides the processes, CC may contain two nodes $+\infty$ and $-\infty$ and the corresponding links to them. Graph CC reflects the connectivity data that is stored in the process memory and, implicitly, in communication channels messages.

Computation Model. Each process contains a set of variables and actions. A *channel* is a special variable type whose values are sets of messages. That is, we consider non-FIFO channels. The channels may contain an arbitrary number of messages, i.e. the channels are unbounded. We assume that the only information any message can carry is process identifiers. We further assume that each message carries only one identifier. Message loss is not considered. Since message order is unimportant, we consider all messages sent to a particular process as belonging to the single incoming channel of this process.

An action has the form ⟨*guard*⟩ ⟶ ⟨*command*⟩. *guard* is either a predicate over the process variables or the incoming channel or **true**. In the latter case, the predicate and its action are *timeout*. *command* is a sequence of statements assigning new values to the variables of the process or sending messages to other processes.

Program state is an assignment of a value to every variable of each process and messages to each channel. An action is *enabled* in some program state if its guard is **true** in this state. The action is *disabled* otherwise. A timeout action is always enabled.

A computation on a set N of processes is a fair sequence of states such that for each state s_i, the next state s_{i+1} is obtained by executing the command of an action of the processes of N that is enabled in s_i. This disallows the overlap in action execution. That is, the action execution is atomic. The computation is either infinite or it ends in a state where no actions are enabled. This execution semantics is called *interleaving semantics* or central daemon [8]. We assume two kinds of fairness: weak fairness of action execution and fairness of message receipt. *Weak fairness* of action execution means that if an action is enabled in all but finitely many states of the computation, then this action is executed infinitely often. *Fair message receipt* means that if the computation contains a state where there is a message in the channel, this computation contains a later state where this message is no longer in the channel, i.e. the message is received. Besides the fairness, our computation model places no bounds on message propagation delay or relative process execution speed, i.e. we consider fully asynchronous computations.

Computation suffix is the sequence of computation states past a particular state of this computation. In other words, the suffix of the computation is obtained by removing the initial state and finitely many subsequent states. Note that a computation suffix is also a computation.

We consider algorithms that do not manipulate the internals of process identifiers which we call copy-store-forward algorithms. An algorithm is *copy-store-forward* if the only operations that it does with process identifiers is comparing them, storing them in local process memory and sending them in a message. That is, operations on identifiers such as addition, radix computation, hashing, etc. are not used. In a copy-store-forward algorithm, if a process does not store an identifier in its local memory, the process may learn this identifier only by receiving it in a message. A copy-store-forward algorithm can not introduce new identifiers to the system, it can only operate on the ids that are already there. Hence, if a computation of a copy-store-forward algorithm starts from a state where every identifier is existing, each state of this computation contains only existing identifiers.

Oracles. An *oracle* is a specialized set of actions used to abstract a problem in distributed computing. The actions of a single oracle may be defined in multiple processes. An oracle action of a process may mention the state of variables of other processes and even the global state of the whole system.

An oracle is *subset splittable* for a linearization algorithm $\mathcal{A}$, if there exist two non-intersecting sets of processes S_1 and S_2 as well as a computation σ_1 on S_1 of $\mathcal{A}$ and state s_2 of processes in S_2 with the following property. For every state s_1 of σ_1 where this oracle is enabled, this oracle is also enabled in $s_1 \cup s_2$. In other words, if the processes of S_2 in state s_2 are added to any such state s_1, the oracle still remains enabled. An oracle is just subset splittable, if it is subset splittable for any linearization algorithm. Intuitively, subset splittability prevents a subset of processes from learning about the state of the rest of the system on the basis of an oracle. Subset splittable and not-subset splittable oracles are respectively denoted as $\mathcal{SS}$ and $\mathcal{NSS}$.

A linearization algorithm is *proper* if it satisfies the following requirements.

- If a process a has identifiers b and c, such that $a < b < c$ then process a forwards c to b. The requirement is similar in the opposite direction. That is, a process forwards each identifier closer to its destination.
- A process that does not contain identifiers to its right or left is *orphan*. A process does not orphan itself. That is, the process does not discard its only single left, or single right, identifier. Note that oracle actions may still orphan the process.

3   The Linearization Problem and Solution Oracles

Linearization Problem Statement. The linearization problem is stated as follows. Each process p of a given set N of processes, is input a left l and a right r neighbor such that $l < p$ and $r > p$. These values may be $-\infty$ and $+\infty$ respectively. The communication channels are empty. In the solution, each process should output two identifiers: cl and cr such that each identifier is consequent with p. The smallest process should output negative infinity as its left neighbor while the largest process should output positive infinity as it right neighbor.

Depending on the certainty of the output, the problem has two variants. The *strict linearization problem* $\mathcal{SL}$ requires each process to output its neighbors exactly once and allows only correct output. The *eventual linearization problem* $\mathcal{EL}$ states that each computation contains a suffix where the output of each process is correct. That is, each process is allowed to make a finite number of mistakes. The problem statement also depends on whether non-existent identifiers may be present in the initial state. *Non-existing identifier variant* $\mathcal{NID}$ allows such identifiers while *existing-only identifiers variant* $\mathcal{EID}$ prohibits them.

The combination of these conditions defines four different linearization problem statements. When we refer to the specific linearization problem, we state the particular conditions. For example, strict linearization problem with non-existing identifiers is referred to as $\mathcal{SL}+\mathcal{NID}$.

Oracles. The oracle actions are shown in Figure 1. An oracle may have one or two actions. The two actions operate on the right and left variable of the process and are respectively distinguished by letters r and l.

process p

constants and global variables
N, // set of processes in the system
CC // system channel connectivity graph

shortcuts
$\mathbf{cnsq}(a, b) \equiv (\forall c : c \in N : (c < a) \vee (b < c))$

local variables
r, l, // input, right ($> p$) and left ($< p$) neighbors
cl, cr // output, right and left consequent process,
initially $\bot$

oracle actions

$\mathcal{WC}$: CC contains disconnected components
$C1$ and $C2$ such that $(p \in C1) \wedge (q \in C2) \longrightarrow$
send $message(q)$ **to** p

$\mathcal{PD}$l: $l \notin N \longrightarrow l := -\infty$
$\mathcal{PD}$r: $r \notin N \longrightarrow r := +\infty$

$\mathcal{NO}$l: $cl \neq l \longrightarrow cl := l$
$\mathcal{NO}$r: $cr \neq r \longrightarrow cr := r$

$\mathcal{CD}$l: $(cl \neq l) \wedge \mathbf{cnsq}(l, p) \longrightarrow cl := l$
$\mathcal{CD}$r: $(cr \neq r) \wedge \mathbf{cnsq}(p, r) \longrightarrow cr := r$

Fig. 1. Linearization algorithm oracles

We define the following oracles to be used in solving the linearization problem. Weak connectivity oracle $\mathcal{WC}$ has a single action that selects a pair of processes p and q such that they are disconnected in the channel connectivity graph CC and adds q to the incoming channel of p creating a link (p, q) in CC thus connecting the graph. Participant detector $\mathcal{PD}$ oracle removes a non-existent identifier stored in p. The actions of neighbor output oracle $\mathcal{NO}$ just output identifiers stored in left and right variables of p. In fact, $\mathcal{NO}$ is not a true oracle. It is trivially built from scratch as it uses only local variables of p. However, for ease of exposition, $\mathcal{NO}$ actions are described among oracles. The actions of consequent process detector $\mathcal{CD}$ are similar to the actions of $\mathcal{NO}$ in effect. However, each action of $\mathcal{CD}$ outputs the stored identifier only if it is consequent with p. That is, unlike $\mathcal{NO}$, the guard of $\mathcal{CD}$ mentions all the identifiers of the system.

Lemma 1. Oracles $\mathcal{NO}$, $\mathcal{PD}$ and $\mathcal{WC}$ are subset splittable while $\mathcal{CD}$ is not.

Proof: To prove subset splittability of an oracle, by definition, we need to identify two non-intersecting sets of processes S_1 and S_2, a computation σ_1 on

S_1 of an arbitrary linearization algorithm $\mathcal{A}$ and a state s_2 of S_2, such that if this oracle is enabled in some state of s_1 of σ_1, it remains enabled in $s_1 \cup s_2$.

Indeed, $\mathcal{NO}$ is trivially subset splittable since its guards only mention local variables. To see why $\mathcal{PD}$ is subset splittable, consider a set of processes S_1 and a computation σ_1 of some algorithm $\mathcal{A}$ on this set. We form another set of processes S_2 such that it does not intersect with S_1 and does not contain any of the non-existing identifiers appearing in σ_1. Let s_2 be an arbitrary state of processes of S_2. If some identifier nid is non-existent in a state s_1 of σ_1, it remains non-existent in state $s_1 \cap s_2$. Hence, if an action of $\mathcal{PD}$ is enabled in s_1, it is enabled in $s_1 \cup s_2$ as well.

Let us now consider $\mathcal{WC}$. Again, let S_1 be a set of processes and σ_1 be a computation of some algorithm $\mathcal{A}$ on it. Let S_2 be a set of processes that does not intersect with S_1. Let state s_2 of processes of S_2 be such that none of these processes stores identifiers of S_1. Let us consider a state that is formed by merging some state s_1 of σ_1 and s_2. If channel connectivity graph CC is disconnected in s_1, it remains disconnected in $s_1 \cup s_2$. Hence, if an action of $\mathcal{WC}$ is enabled in s_1, it is also enabled in $s_1 \cup s_2$. That is, $\mathcal{WC}$ is subset splittable.

Let us discuss $\mathcal{CD}$. Consider an arbitrary set of processes S_1 and a computation σ_1 of some linearization algorithm $\mathcal{A}$ on it. Each process of a linearization algorithm has to output process identifiers consequent with itself. If a process stores consequent identifiers, its $\mathcal{CD}$ actions are enabled. However, since the identifier space is totally ordered, regardless of the composition of S_2, if S_2 is added to S_1, at least one process in S_1 changes its consequent process. This disables an action of $\mathcal{CD}$. Hence, $\mathcal{CD}$ is not subset splittable. □

4 Necessary Conditions

Lemma 2. If the channel connectivity graph CC is disconnected in the initial state of copy-store-forward algorithm computation, then either CC is disconnected in every state of the computation or this computation contains an execution of a weak connectivity oracle action.

Proof: Let us consider the computation σ of an arbitrary copy-store-forward algorithm such that σ contains states where CC is at least weakly connected yet CC is disconnected in the initial state of σ. Let s_2 be the first state of σ where CC is connected. Assume, without loss of generality, that in s_2 process a has a link to process b in CC while in all previous states, including the state s_1 that directly precedes s_2, the two processes are disconnected. The link may be due to the action of the algorithm or an oracle.

Let us consider the possibility of algorithm action first. Refer to Figure 2 for illustration. Since processes in the message passing system model do not share local memory, an algorithm action may create link (a, b) in CC only by adding process b to the incoming channel of a. That is, some process c sends a message carrying b to a. This message transmission moves the system from s_1 to s_2. Since the algorithm is copy-store-forward, to send a message to a, process c needs to store the identifier of a in its local memory in the preceding state s_1. That is,

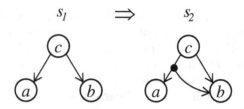

Fig. 2. Illustration to the proof of Lemma 2. Transition from state s_1 where processes a and b are disconnected to s_2 where they are connected via a link (a, b) in the incoming channel of process a, requires initial overall system connectivity, i.e. CC needs to be connected.

c has to be connected to a in CC of s_1. Also, c sends identifier b to a. That is, c is connected to b in s_1. This means that for this message transmission, a and b need to be weakly connected in s_1. However, we assumed that s_2 is the first state where a and b are connected.

Hence, the action that moves the system from s_1 to s_2 can only be an oracle action. This action connects two disconnected processes. That is, it has to be the action of the weak connectivity oracle. Therefore, if a computation of a copy-store-forward algorithm starts from a state where CC is disconnected, the only way this computation produces a state with connected CC is through the action of a weak connectivity oracle.   □

Theorem 1. Every solution to the linearization problem requires a weak connectivity oracle.

Proof: Let $\mathcal{A}$ be a linearization algorithm. Let us consider the set of processes to be linearized. Let us further consider a computation of $\mathcal{A}$ that starts in a state where this set is separated into two arbitrary subsets S_1 and S_2 such that if process $a \in S_1$ stores identifier b then $b \notin S_2$. Similarly if process $c \in S_2$ stores identifier d then $d \notin S_1$. Note that in thus formed initial state, the sets S_1 and S_2 are disconnected in the channel connectivity graph CC.

Since process identifiers are totally ordered, there has to be at least two consequent processes $p_1 \in S_1$ and $p_2 \in S_2$. Since $\mathcal{A}$ is a linearization algorithm, p_1 has to eventually output p_2. According to Lemma 2, this may only happen if the computation contains the actions of the weak connectivity oracle.   □

Theorem 2. A solution to the strict linearization problem requires a non-subset splittable oracle.

Proof: Assume the opposite. Let there be an algorithm $\mathcal{A}$ that solves the strict linearization problem with only subset splittable oracle $\mathcal{O}$. Since $\mathcal{O}$ is subset splittable, there are two non-intersecting sets of processes S_1 and S_2 as well as a computation σ_1 of $\mathcal{A}$ on S_1 and a state s_2 of S_2 such that the addition of s_2 to every state of σ_1 keeps the actions of $\mathcal{O}$ in processes of S_1 enabled.

We construct a computation σ_3 of $\mathcal{A}$ on $S_1 \cup S_2$ as follows. The computation starts with the initial state of σ_1 merged with s_2. We then consider the first action of σ_1. If the action is non-oracle, since processes of S_1 in σ_3 have the same initial state as in σ_1, the action is enabled and can be executed. If the first action is an oracle $\mathcal{O}$ action, since the oracle is subset splittable, this action is enabled and can be executed. We continue building σ_3 by sequentially executing the actions of σ_1. Computation σ_1 is produced by $\mathcal{A}$ which, by assumption, is a solution to the strict linearization problem. By the statement of the problem, during σ_1, every process has to output the identifier of its consequent process exactly once. We stop adding the actions of σ_1 to σ_3 once every process of S_1 does so. We conclude the construction of σ_3 by executing the actions of $\mathcal{A}$ and $\mathcal{O}$ in an arbitrary fair manner. Thus constructed, σ_3 is a computation of $\mathcal{A}$.

Let us examine σ_3. By construction, every process p_1 in S_1 outputs an identifier that p_1 is consequent with in S_1. Since the identifier state space is totally ordered, the consequent identifiers of at least one process of S_1 differ if S_2 is added to S_1. This means that this process outputs incorrect identifier in σ_3 that is executed on $S_1 \cup S_2$. However, this violates the requirements of the strict linearization problem. This means that, contrary to our initial assumption, $\mathcal{A}$ is not a solution to $\mathcal{SL}$ and the strict linearization problem indeed requires a non-subset splittable oracle. $\qquad\square$

Theorem 3. A proper solution to the linearization problem that allows non-existing identifiers requires a participant detector oracle.

Proof: Assume the opposite. Let $\mathcal{A}$ be a proper algorithm that solves a linearization problem with non-existing identifiers and does not use $\mathcal{PD}$. That is, oracles used by the algorithm do not remove non-existing identifiers.

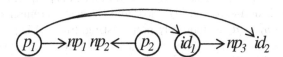

Fig. 3. Illustration to the proof of Theorem 3. In the initial state of constructed computation, two consequent processes p_1 and p_2 hold non-existent identifiers np_1 and np_2. An oracle action at p_1 adds identifiers id_1 and id_2 to process p_1. Process p_1 forwards id_2 to id_1.

Let us construct a computation σ on some set of processes. We select the initial state of σ as follows. Refer to Figure 3 for illustration. Processes do not have links to existing identifiers. That is, each process is disconnected from all other processes. Each process stores exactly two non-existing identifiers. For any two neighbor processes p_1 and p_2 such that $p_1 < p_2$, the non-existing identifier np_1 stored at p_1 is such that $p_1 < np_1 < p_2$, the non-existing identifier np_2 stored at p_2 is $p_1 < np_2 < p_2$. That is, the non-existing ids are between neighbors. If the process has the largest, or smallest identifier in the set, this process contains respectively lower and higher non-existing identifier.

Since $\mathcal{A}$ is proper, a process cannot orphan itself. Hence, the actions of the algorithm cannot remove the non-existent identifiers from this initial state either. Since $\mathcal{A}$ is copy-store-forward, its actions cannot add new identifiers to the system. That is, there are no enabled actions of $\mathcal{A}$ that change its topology in the initial state of σ.

Since $\mathcal{A}$ does not use the participant detector oracle, the oracles that it does use cannot remove the non-existing identifiers either. That is, the only oracle actions that are enabled in the initial state of σ add process identifiers.

We construct σ as follows. Let p_1 be the process that has an enabled oracle action. We execute this action and consider the identifiers that the oracle action adds to p_1. The identifiers may be greater or smaller than p_1. Moreover, they may be existent or non-existent.

We consider the added identifiers that are greater than p_1. The case of smaller identifiers is similar. Process p_1 already holds $np_1 > p_1$. Since $\mathcal{A}$ is proper, process p_1 has to select two identifiers id_1 and id_2 such that $p_1 < id_1 < id_2$ and forward id_2 to id_1. Thus, p_1 eliminates id_2 from its memory. We add this forwarding action to σ. We continue this process of identifier elimination until p_1 holds only a single identifier greater than its own.

If p_1 ever forwards non-existing np_1 to some process id_1, then $p_1 < id_1 < np_1$. That is, the remaining identifier id_1 is non-existing. Therefore, once p_1 is left with a single identifier, this identifier is non-existing and p_1 remains disconnected from the higher-id processes.

Let us now consider what happens with the identifiers that p_1 forwards. The recipient identifier id_1 may be existing or non-existing. If id_1 is non-existing, the forwarded identifier id_2 is lost. Let us address the situation when id_1 is existing. Note that id_2 is greater than than id_1. Once id_2 is received by id_1, its operation depends on the value of its right non-existent identifier np_3. There may be two cases. In the first case, id_2 is greater than np_3. Since $\mathcal{A}$ is proper, id_2 is forwarded to np_3. Since np_3 is non-existing, id_2 is lost and the system remains disconnected. If id_2 is less than np_3, id_2 is definitely non-existing. Since $\mathcal{A}$ is proper, id_1 keeps id_2 and forwards np_3 to id_2. That is, np_3 is discarded. The system, however, remains disconnected. We construct the computation σ by thus processing all identifiers forwarded by p_1.

The resultant state resembles the initial state of σ in the sense that all processes are disconnected and the only actions that may be enabled are the actions of an id-adding oracle. We continue constructing σ by executing an enabled oracle action in a fair manner and then letting the algorithm handle the added identifiers. We proceed with this construction either indefinitely or until there are no more enabled oracle actions.

Thus constructed σ is a computation of $\mathcal{A}$. However, no process outputs the identifiers of its consequent processes. That is, contrary to our assumption, $\mathcal{A}$ is not a solution to the linearization problem with non-existing identifiers.   □

The theorems of this section specify the oracles that are necessary to solve each variant of the linearization problem. These requirements are summarized in Figure 4(a).

	$\mathcal{EL}$	$\mathcal{SL}$
$\mathcal{EID}$	$\mathcal{WC}$	$\mathcal{WC}+\mathcal{NSS}$
$\mathcal{NID}$	$\mathcal{WC}+\mathcal{PD}$	$\mathcal{WC}+\mathcal{PD}+\mathcal{NSS}$

(a) Necessary oracles.

	$\mathcal{EL}$	$\mathcal{SL}$
$\mathcal{EID}$	$\mathcal{L}+\mathcal{WC}+\mathcal{NO}$	$\mathcal{L}+\mathcal{WC}+\mathcal{CD}$
$\mathcal{NID}$	$\mathcal{L}+\mathcal{WC}+\mathcal{NO}+\mathcal{PD}$	$\mathcal{L}+\mathcal{WC}+\mathcal{CD}+\mathcal{PD}$

(b) Solution algorithm and oracles sufficient for solution.

Fig. 4. Necessary and sufficient conditions for a linearization problem solution

5   Linearization Solutions

Algorithm Description. The linearization algorithm $\mathcal{L}$ is adapted from [17]. The algorithm contains two actions: $\mathcal{REC}$ and $\mathcal{TO}$. The actions are shown in Figure 5. The first is a message receipt action $\mathcal{REC}$. This action is enabled if the incoming channel of process p contains a message bearing some identifier id. If the received id is greater than the right neighbor r of p, p forwards this identifier to r to process. If id is between p and r, then p, selects id to be its new right neighbor and forwards the old neighbor for id to handle. Process p handles received id smaller than its own in a similar manner. If p receives its own identifier, p discards it. The second action is a timeout action $\mathcal{TO}$. It is always enabled. This means that the correctness of the algorithm does not depend on the timing of the action execution, which is left up to the implementer. The action sends identifier p to its right and left neighbor provided they exist. Note that the linearization algorithm $\mathcal{L}$ is proper.

Lemma 3. If channel connectivity graph contains only existing identifiers, the operation of the linearization algorithm $\mathcal{L}$ in combination with any of the oracles does not disconnect any pair of processes in the channel connectivity graph CC.

Proof: Let us consider the actions of the oracles first. The actions of $\mathcal{WC}$ may only add identifiers to CC. Hence it does not disconnect the processes in CC. Since there are no non-existent identifiers, the actions of $\mathcal{PD}$ are disabled. Oracles $\mathcal{NO}$ and $\mathcal{CD}$ only copy the identifiers in the same process. Hence, they do not affect CC either.

Let us now consider the actions of $\mathcal{L}$. The operation of receive action $\mathcal{REC}$ depends on the value of the received identifier id. If id is the same as p, it is discarded. However, since self-loops are not considered in CC, this discarding of the identifier does not change CC. Let us consider the case $p > id$. If $id > r$, then p forwards id to r to deal with. That is, the link (p, id) in CC is replaced by the path (p, r), (r, id). If $p > id \geq r$, process p replaced its right neighbor with p and forwards its old right neighbor to id. That is, the link (p, id) is preserved in CC while (p, r) is replaced by (p, id), (id, r). In either case no path in CC is disconnected. The case of $p < id$ is similar. The timeout action $\mathcal{TO}$ only adds links to CC so it does not disconnect it.   □

Lemma 4. Starting from an arbitrary state that contains only existing identifiers, the linearization algorithm $\mathcal{L}$ in combination with the weak connectivity

process p

local variables
r, l // input, right $(> p)$ and left $(< p)$ neighbors

algorithm action
$\mathcal{REC}$: $message(id)$ is in the coming channel of p $\longrightarrow$
    receive $message(id)$
    if $id > p$ **then**
        if $id < r$ **then**
            if $r < +\infty$ **then**
                send $message(r)$ **to** id
            $r := id$
        else
            send $message(id)$ **to** r
    if $id < p$ **then**
        if $id > l$ **then**
            if $l > -\infty$ **then**
                send $message(l)$ **to** id
            $l := id$
        else
            send $message(id)$ **to** l

$\mathcal{TO}$: **true** $\longrightarrow$
    if $l > -\infty$ **then**
        send $message(p)$ **to** l
    if $r < +\infty$ **then**
        send $message(p)$ **to** r

Fig. 5. Linearization algorithm actions

oracle $\mathcal{WC}$ and any other oracles, arrives at a state where the channel connectivity graph CC is connected.

Proof: Indeed, if CC is disconnected, actions of $\mathcal{WC}$ are enabled in the processes of the disconnected components. Once such action is executed, the two components are connected. According to Lemma 3, the components are not disconnected again regardless of used oracles. Hence, CC is eventually connected in every computation of the linearization algorithm where $\mathcal{WC}$ is used. $\qquad\square$

Lemma 5. Any computation of the linearization algorithm $\mathcal{L}$ in combination with participant detector oracle $\mathcal{PD}$ and any other oracles has a suffix with only existing identifiers.

Proof: Observe that none of the oracles introduce new non-existing identifiers. Since $\mathcal{L}$ is copy-store-send, it does not create new identifiers either. Hence, to prove the lemma we need to show that all non-existent identifiers present in the initial state are removed.

Note that each process of the linearization algorithm either keeps an identifier or forwards it to its neighbors. That is, processes of $\mathcal{L}$ do not duplicate non-existent identifiers. Moreover, the identifier is forwarded only in one direction: either to the left or to the right. This means that during the computation each identifier will be forwarded a finite number of times. Let us consider process p that holds non-existent identifier nid and does not forward it. Since nid is non-existent, an action of participant detector $\mathcal{PD}$ is enabled at p. Since nid is not forwarded, the action remains enabled until executed. Once executed, the action removes the non-existent identifier. That is, every non-existent identifier is eventually removed.   □

Lemma 6. Starting from an arbitrary state where CC is connected and only existing identifiers are present, the linearization algorithm combined with the timeout oracle and regardless of the operation of other oracles contains a suffix where the variables r and l of each process p hold identifiers consequent with p.

The proof of Lemma 6 is in [17].

Theorem 4. The linearization algorithm combined with neighbor output, and weak connectivity oracles solves eventual linearization with existing identifiers problem. The linearization algorithm combined with consequent process detector and weak connectivity oracles solves strict linearization with existing identifiers problem.

The addition of participant detector enables the solution to the non-existent identifier variants of these problems.

The specific oracles sufficient for each problem solution as stated in Theorem 4 are summarized in Figure 4(b).

Proof: Let us first address the case of existing identifiers only. According to Lemma 6, if a computation starts in an arbitrary state where CC is connected, this computation contains a suffix where each process p stores its consequent identifiers in r and l. The argument differs depending on whether $\mathcal{NO}$ or $\mathcal{CD}$ is being used.

In case $\mathcal{NO}$ is used, if p stores different identifiers in r and cr, then $\mathcal{NO}r$ is enabled. Once executed, the identifier stored in r is output. That is, if there is a suffix of a computation containing consequent right identifier in r of p, there is a suffix that contains this identifier cr. Similar argument applies to the left identifier of p. That is, every computation of $\mathcal{L}+\mathcal{NO}+\mathcal{WC}$ contains a suffix where consequent left and right neighbors are output. In other words, this combination of the linearization algorithm and oracles solves $\mathcal{EL}+\mathcal{EID}$.

Let us consider the case of $\mathcal{CD}$. Note that consequent process detector oracle outputs the identifier if and only if it is consequent. However, every computation of the algorithm contains a suffix where each process stores its consequent identifiers. If the process holds its consequent identifier, $\mathcal{CD}$ is enabled. Once $\mathcal{CD}$ is executed, the correct identifier is output. That is, every computation of $\mathcal{L}+\mathcal{CD}+\mathcal{WC}$ every process outputs its consequent identifiers exactly once.

In other words, this combination of the linearization algorithm and oracles solves $\mathcal{SL}+\mathcal{EID}$.

Let us address the case of non-existing identifiers. According to Lemma 5, participant process detector oracle $\mathcal{PD}$ eventually removes non-existent identifiers from the system. That is, every computation contains a suffix with only existing identifiers. In this case $\mathcal{NO}$ eventually outputs correct identifiers that satisfies the conditions of eventual linearization problem. By its specification, consequent process detector oracle $\mathcal{CD}$ never outputs non-existent identifiers. That is, the presence of non-existent identifiers does not compromise the solution to the strict linearization problem if $\mathcal{CD}$ is used. Hence, the addition of $\mathcal{PD}$ enables the solution of the non-existing identifier variants of the linearization problems.   □

6   Oracle Implementation and Optimality

Oracle Nature and Implementation. The three oracles required to solve the linearization problem variants described in this paper are weak connectivity, participant process detector and consequent process detector. None of them are implementable in the computation model we consider. Nonetheless, let us discuss possible approaches to their construction.

Oracle $\mathcal{WC}$, that repairs the network disconnections, is an encapsulation of bootstrap service [6] commonly found in peer-to-peer systems. One possible implementation of such oracle is as follows. One bootstrap process b is always present in the system. This identifier may be part of the oracle implementation and, as such, not visible to the application program using the oracle. The responsibility of this process is to maintain the greatest and smallest identifier of the system. All other processes are supplied with b's identifier. If a regular system process p does not have a left or right neighbor, it assumes that its own identifier is the greatest or, respectively, smallest. Process p then sends its identifier to b. Process b then either confirms this assumption or sends p, its current smallest or greatest identifier. This way, if the system is disconnected, the weak connectivity is restored.

Oracle $\mathcal{PD}$ encapsulates the limits between relative process speeds and maximum message propagation delay. This oracle may be implemented using a heartbeat protocol [12]. For example, if process p contains an identifier q, p sends q a heartbeat message requesting a reply. If p does not receive this reply after the time above the maximum network delay, p considers q non-existent and discards it.

Oracle $\mathcal{CD}$ may be the most difficult to implement. We believe that to implement $\mathcal{CD}$ one has to solve the strict linearization problem itself. That is, $\mathcal{CD}$ serves to illustrate the difficulty of the strict linearization problem rather than encode any particular oracle implementation.

Oracle Optimality. This paper states the necessary and sufficient conditions for both strict and eventual linearization problem. The conditions for the eventual linearization are sharp as we use the necessary oracles to provide the algorithmic solution for the problem. For the strict linearization, there is a gap between these conditions. Specifically, our algorithmic solution relies on $\mathcal{CD}$, which is a specific kind of the necessary non-subset splittable detector. Narrowing the gap between necessary and sufficient conditions for the solution to the strict linearizability problem remains to be addressed in future research.

References

1. Aspnes, J., Shah, G.: Skip graphs. ACM Transactions on Algorithms 3(4), 1–37 (2007)
2. Awerbuch, B., Scheideler, C.: The hyperring: a low-congestion deterministic data structure for distributed environments. In: SODA 2004: Proceedings of the Fifteenth Annual ACM-SIAM Symposium on Discrete Algorithms, pp. 318–327. Society for Industrial and Applied Mathematics, Philadelphia (2004)
3. Cavin, D., Sasson, Y., Schiper, A.: Consensus with unknown participants or fundamental self-organization. In: Nikolaidis, I., Barbeau, M., An, H.-C. (eds.) ADHOC-NOW 2004. LNCS, vol. 3158, pp. 135–148. Springer, Heidelberg (2004)
4. Chandra, T.D., Hadzilacos, V., Toueg, S.: The weakest failure detector for solving consensus. Journal of ACM 43(4), 685–722 (1996)
5. Chandra, T.D., Toueg, S.: Unreliable failure detectors for reliable distributed systems. Journal of the ACM 43(2), 225–267 (1996)
6. Cramer, C., Fuhrmann, T.: ISPRP: a message-efficient protocol for initializing structured P2P networks. In: International Performance Computing and Communications Conference (IPCCC), pp. 365–370 (2005)
7. Dijkstra, E.W.: Self-stabilization in spite of distributed control. Communications of the ACM 17(11), 643–644 (1974)
8. Dubois, S., Tixeuil, S.: A taxonomy of daemons in self-stabilization. Technical Report 1110.0334, ArXiv eprint (October 2011)
9. Emek, Y., Fraigniaud, P., Korman, A., Kutten, S., Peleg, D.: Notions of connectivity in overlay networks. In: Even, G., Halldórsson, M.M. (eds.) SIROCCO 2012. LNCS, vol. 7355, pp. 25–35. Springer, Heidelberg (2012)
10. Fischer, M.J., Lynch, N.A., Paterson, M.S.: Impossibility of distributed consensus with one faulty process. J. ACM 32(2), 374–382 (1985)
11. Gall, D., Jacob, R., Richa, A.W., Scheideler, C., Schmid, S., Täubig, H.: Time complexity of distributed topological self-stabilization: The case of graph linearization. In: López-Ortiz, A. (ed.) LATIN 2010. LNCS, vol. 6034, pp. 294–305. Springer, Heidelberg (2010)
12. Gouda, M.G., McGuire, T.M.: Accelerated heartbeat protocols. In: 18th International Conference on Distributed Computing Systems (ICDCS), pp. 202–209 (May 1998)
13. Greve, F., Tixeuil, S.: Knowledge connectivity vs. synchrony requirements for fault-tolerant agreement in unknown networks. In: Proceedings of IEEE International Conference on Dependable Systems and networks (DSN), pp. 82–91. IEEE (June 2007)
14. Harvey, N.J.A., Ian Munro, J.: Deterministic skipnet. Inf. Process. Lett. 90(4), 205–208 (2004)
15. Malkhi, D., Naor, M., Ratajczak, D.: Viceroy: a scalable and dynamic emulation of the butterfly. In: PODC 2002: Proceedings of the Twenty-first Annual Symposium on Principles of Distributed Computing, pp. 183–192. ACM, New York (2002)

16. Munro, J.I., Papadakis, T., Sedgewick, R.: Deterministic skip lists. In: SODA 1992: Proceedings of the Third Annual ACM-SIAM Symposium on Discrete Algogrithms, pp. 367–375. Society for Industrial and Applied Mathematics, Philadelphia (1992)
17. Nor, R.M., Nesterenko, M., Scheideler, C.: Corona: A stabilizing deterministic message-passing skip list. In: Défago, X., Petit, F., Villain, V. (eds.) SSS 2011. LNCS, vol. 6976, pp. 356–370. Springer, Heidelberg (2011)
18. Onus, M., Richa, A.W., Scheideler, C.: Linearization: Locally self-stabilizing sorting in graphs. In: ALENEX 2007: Proceedings of the Workshop on Algorithm Engineering and Experiments. SIAM (January 2007)
19. Rowstron, A., Druschel, P.: Pastry: Scalable, decentralized object location, and routing for large-scale peer-to-peer systems. In: Guerraoui, R. (ed.) Middleware 2001. LNCS, vol. 2218, pp. 329–350. Springer, Heidelberg (2001)
20. Stoica, I., Morris, R., Liben-Nowell, D., Karger, D.R., Kaashoek, M.F., Dabek, F., Balakrishnan, H.: Chord: a scalable peer-to-peer lookup protocol for Internet applications. IEEE/ACM Transactions on Networking 11(1), 17–32 (2003)
21. Tixeuil, S.: Self-stabilizing Algorithms. In: Algorithms and Theory of Computation Handbook, 2nd edn., pp. 26.1–26.45. CRC Press, Taylor & Francis Group (2009); Chapman & Hall/CRC Applied Algorithms and Data Structures

Synchronous Counting
and Computational Algorithm Design

Danny Dolev[1], Janne H. Korhonen[2], Christoph Lenzen[3],
Joel Rybicki[2], and Jukka Suomela[2]

[1] School of Engineering and Computer Science,
The Hebrew University of Jerusalem
[2] Helsinki Institute for Information Technology HIIT,
Department of Computer Science, University of Helsinki
[3] Computer Science and Artificial Intelligence Laboratory, MIT

Abstract. Consider a complete communication network on n nodes, each of which is a state machine with s states. In *synchronous 2-counting*, the nodes receive a common clock pulse and they have to agree on which pulses are "odd" and which are "even". We require that the solution is *self-stabilising* (reaching the correct operation from any initial state) and it tolerates f *Byzantine failures* (nodes that send arbitrary misinformation). Prior algorithms are expensive to implement in hardware: they require a source of random bits or a large number of states s. We use computational techniques to construct very compact deterministic algorithms for the first non-trivial case of $f = 1$. While no algorithm exists for $n < 4$, we show that as few as 3 states are sufficient for all values $n \geq 4$. We prove that the problem cannot be solved with only 2 states for $n = 4$, but there is a 2-state solution for all values $n \geq 6$.

1 Introduction

Synchronous Counting. In the *synchronous C-counting* problem, n nodes have to count clock pulses modulo C. Starting from any initial configuration, the system has to *stabilise* so that all nodes agree on the clock value.

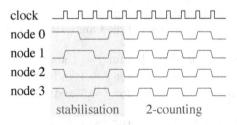

Each node is a finite state machine with s states, and after every state transition, each node *broadcasts* its current state to all other nodes—effectively, each node can see the current states of all other nodes. An algorithm specifies (1) the new state for each observed state, and (2) how to map the internal state of a node to its output.

T. Higashino et al. (Eds.): SSS 2013, LNCS 8255, pp. 237–250, 2013.

Byzantine Fault Tolerance. In a fault-free system, the C-counting problem is trivial to solve. For example, we can designate node 0 as a leader, and then all nodes (including the leader itself) can follow the leader: if the current state of the leader is c, the new state is $c + 1 \bmod C$. This algorithm will stabilise in time $t = 1$, and we only need $s = C$ different states.

However, we are interested in algorithms that tolerate *Byzantine failures*. Some number f of the nodes may be *faulty*. A faulty node may send arbitrary misinformation to non-faulty nodes, including *different* information to different nodes within the same round. For example, if we have nodes $0, 1, 2, 3$ and node 2 is faulty, node 0 might observe the state vector $(0, 1, 1, 1)$, while node 1 might observe the state vector $(0, 1, 0, 1)$.

Our goal is to design an algorithm with the following guarantee: even if we have up to f faulty nodes, no matter what the faulty nodes do, the system will stabilise so that after t rounds all non-faulty nodes start to count clock pulses consistently modulo C. We will give a formal problem definition in Section 4.

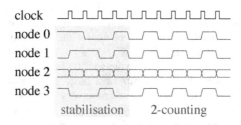

Contributions. Both randomised and deterministic algorithms for synchronous counting have been presented in the literature (see Section 2). However, prior algorithms tend to be expensive to implement in hardware: they require a source of random bits or complicated circuitry.

In this work, we use a single parameter s, the number of states per node, to capture the complexity of an algorithm. We employ *computational* techniques to design 2-counting algorithms that have the smallest possible number of states. Our focus is on the first non-trivial case of $f = 1$.

The case of $n = 1$ is trivial, and by prior work it is known that there is no algorithm for $1 < n < 4$. We give a detailed analysis of 2-counting for $n \geq 4$:

- there is no deterministic algorithm for $f = 1$ and $n = 4$ with $s = 2$ states,
- there is a deterministic algorithm for $f = 1$ and $n \geq 4$ with $s = 3$ states,
- there is a deterministic algorithm for $f = 1$ and $n \geq 6$ with $s = 2$ states.

With such a small state space, the algorithms are easy to implement in hardware. For example, a straightforward implementation of our algorithm for $f = 1$, $n = 4$, and $s = 3$ requires just 2 bits of storage per node, and a simple lookup table with 81 entries.

Our results are related to synchronous 2-counting, but we can compose b copies of a 2-counter to construct a 2^b-counter (see Section 3 for details).

Structure. Section 2 covers related work and Section 3 discusses applications of synchronous 2-counters. Section 4 gives a formal definition of the problem, and Section 5 gives a graph-theoretic interpretation that is helpful in the analysis of counting algorithms. In Section 6 we show that we can increase n for free, without affecting the parameters f, s, or t; this enables us to focus on small values of n. Section 7 demonstrates the use of computers in algorithm design, and Section 8 shows how we can use computers to construct compact proofs of the *non-existence* of algorithms for given values of n, f, and s.

2   Related Work

Randomised Algorithms. Randomised algorithms for synchronous 2-counting are known, with different time–space tradeoffs.

The algorithm by Dolev and Welch [9] requires only $s = 3$ states, but the stabilisation time is $t = 2^{O(f)}$. Here we are assuming that $n = O(f)$; for a large n, we can run the algorithm with $O(f)$ nodes only and let the remaining nodes follow the majority.

The algorithm by Ben-Or et al. [2] stabilises in expected constant time. However, it requires $\Omega(2^f)$ states and private channels (i.e., the adversary has limited information on the system's state).

Deterministic Algorithms. The fastest known deterministic algorithm is due to Dolev and Hoch [7], with a stabilisation time of $O(f)$. However, the algorithm is not well suited for a hardware implementation. It uses as a building block several instances of algorithms that solve the Byzantine consensus problem—a non-trivial task in itself. The number of states is also large, as some storage is needed for each Byzantine consensus instance.

Consensus Lower Bounds. *Binary consensus* is a classical problem that has been studied in the context of Byzantine fault tolerance; see, e.g., the textbook by Lynch [15] for more information. It is easy to show that synchronous 2-counting is at least as difficult to solve as binary consensus.

Lemma 1. *If we have a 2-counting algorithm $\mathcal{A}$ that stabilises in time t, we can design an algorithm that solves binary consensus in time t, for the same parameters n and f.*

Proof. We can find configurations $\boldsymbol{x}(0)$ and $\boldsymbol{x}(1)$ with the following properties:

– For any $a = 0, 1$ and $j = 0, 1, 2, \ldots$, if we initialise the system with configuration $\boldsymbol{x}(a)$ and run $\mathcal{A}$ for j rounds, all nodes output $(a + j) \bmod 2$.

In essence, $\boldsymbol{x}(0)$ and $\boldsymbol{x}(1)$ are some examples of configurations that may occur during 2-counting.

First assume that t is even. Each node i receives its input a for the binary consensus problem. We use the element i of $\boldsymbol{x}(a)$ to initialise the state of node

i. Then we run $\mathcal{A}$ for t rounds. Finally, the output of algorithm $\mathcal{A}$ forms the output of the binary consensus instance. To see that the algorithm is correct, we make the following observations: (1) All non-faulty nodes produce the same output at time t, regardless of the input. (2) If all inputs had the same value a, we used $\boldsymbol{x}(a)$ to initialise all nodes, and hence the final output is a.

For an odd t, we can use the same approach if we complement the inputs. In summary, $\mathcal{A}$ can be used to solve binary consensus in time t.   □

Now we can invoke the familiar lower bounds related to the consensus problem:

- no algorithm can tolerate $f \geq n/3$ failures [18],
- no deterministic algorithm can solve the problem in $t < f + 1$ rounds [10].

Pulse Synchronisation. Both 2-counting and *pulse synchronisation* [6,9] have a superficially similar goal: produce well-separated, (approximately) synchronised clock pulses in a distributed system in a fault-tolerant manner. However, there are also many differences: in pulse synchronisation the task is to construct a clock pulse without any external reference, while in 2-counting we are given a reference clock and we only need to construct a clock that ticks at a slower rate. Also the models of computation differ—for pulse synchronisation, a relevant model is an asynchronous network with some bounds on propagation delays and clock drifts.

A 2-counting algorithm does not solve the pulse synchronisation problem, and a pulse synchronisation algorithm does not solve the 2-counting problem. However, if one is designing a distributed system that needs to produce synchronised clock ticks in a fault-tolerant manner, either of the approaches may be applicable.

Computational Algorithm Design. The computational element of our work can be interpreted as a form of *algorithm synthesis*. In prior work, similar approaches have been proposed to synthesise protocols for both shared-memory and message-passing protocols [5,16] by solving the satisfiability of certain temporal logic formulas.

In our work, we construct distributed algorithms with the help of modern SAT solvers [4]. Recently, such tools have been used in related problems, e.g., for finding small logic circuits [11,12,14].

3   Applications

Counters as Frequency Dividers. We can visualise a C-counter as an electronic circuit that consists of n components (nodes); see Fig. 1. Each node i has a register x_i that stores its current state—one of the values $0, 1, \ldots, s-1$. There is a logical circuit g that maps the current state to the output, and another logical circuit A_i that maps the current states of all nodes to the new state of node i. At each rising edge of the clock pulse, register x_i is updated.

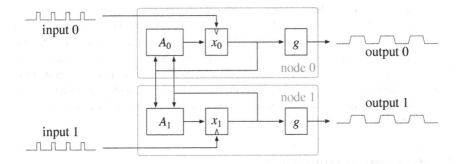

Fig. 1. A 2-counter for $n = 2$, viewed as an electronic circuit

If the clock pulses are synchronised, regardless of the initial states of the registers, after t clock pulses the system has stabilised so that the outputs are synchronised and they are incremented (modulo C) at each clock pulse.

In particular, if we have an algorithm for 2-counting, it can be used as a *frequency divider*: given synchronous clock pulses at rate 1, it produces synchronous clock pulses at rate $1/2$.

From 2-Counters to C-counters. We can compose b layers of 2-counters to build a clock that counts modulo 2^b; see Fig. 2. A composition of self-stabilising algorithms is self-stabilising [8]. For the purposes of the analysis, we can wait until layer $i - 1$ stabilises, use this as the initial state of layer i, and then argue that the nodes on layer i receive a synchronous clock pulse and hence they will eventually stabilise.

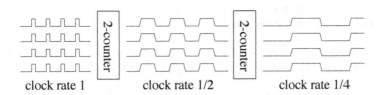

Fig. 2. Composition of 2-counters

Fault-Tolerant Counting. Assume that we have n nodes that are supposed to count events that can be observed by all nodes. However, some nodes might occasionally miss some events, and we may have transient failures. A synchronous C-counter provides an elegant solution to the problem: observations of the events are interpreted as clock pulses. A node that misses an event is merely one kind of faulty behaviour; if there are at most f such nodes, all other nodes will keep counting correctly. Moreover, if we have at most f nodes whose current counter values are incorrect, these nodes will eventually catch up with the others.

Counters in Mutual Exclusion. With a C-counter we can implement *mutual exclusion* and *time division multiple access* in a fairly straightforward manner. If we have $C = n$ nodes and one shared resource (e.g., a transmission medium), we can let node i to access the resource when its own counter has value i. Care is needed with the actions of faulty nodes, though—for further information on achieving *fault-tolerant* mutual exclusion, see, e.g., Moscibroda and Oshman [17]. Again 2-counting is of particular interest, as it may be leveraged by more complex mutual exclusion algorithms.

4   Problem Formulation

We will now formalise the C-counting problem and introduce the definitions that we will use in this work. Throughout this work, we will follow the convention that nodes, states, and time steps are indexed from 0. We use the notation $[k] = \{0, 1, \ldots, k - 1\}$.

Simplifications. As our focus is on 2-counters, we will now fix $C = 2$; the definitions are straightforward to generalise.

In prior work, algorithms have made use of a function that maps the internal state x_i of a node to its output $g(x_i)$. However, in this work we do not need any such mapping: for our positive results, an identity mapping is sufficient, and for the negative result, we study the case of $s = 2$ which never benefits from a mapping. Hence we will now give a formalisation that omits the output mapping.

Algorithms. Fix the following parameters:

- n = the number of nodes,
- f = the maximum number of faulty nodes,
- s = the number of internal states.

An algorithm $\boldsymbol{A}$ specifies a *state transition* function $A_i \colon [s]^n \to [s]$ for each node $i \in [n]$. Here $[s]^n$ is the set of *observed configurations* of the system.

Projections. Let $F \subseteq [n]$, $|F| \leq f$ be the set of *faulty* nodes. We define the projection π_F as follows: for any observed configuration $\boldsymbol{s}$, let $\pi_F(\boldsymbol{s})$ be a vector $\boldsymbol{x}$ such that $x_i = *$ if $i \in F$ and $x_i = s_i$ otherwise. For example,

$$\pi_{\{2,4\}}((0, 1, 0, 1, 1)) = (0, 1, *, 1, *).$$

This gives us the set $V_F = \pi_F([s]^n)$ of *actual configurations*. Two actual configurations are particularly important:

$$\boldsymbol{0}_F = \pi_F((0, 0, \ldots, 0)), \quad \boldsymbol{1}_F = \pi_F((1, 1, \ldots, 1)).$$

Executions. Let $x, y \in V_F$. We say that configuration y is *reachable* from x if for each non-faulty node $i \notin F$ there exists some observed configuration $u_i \in [s]^n$ satisfying $\pi_F(u_i) = x$ and $A_i(u_i) = y_i$. Intuitively, the faulty nodes can feed such misinformation to node i that it chooses to switch to state y_i. We emphasise that u_i may be different for each i; the misinformation need not be consistent.

An *execution* of an algorithm A for given set of faulty nodes F is an infinite sequence of actual configurations $X = (x^0, x^1, x^2, \dots)$ such that x^{r+1} is reachable from x^r for all r.

Stabilisation. For an execution $X = (x^0, x^1, x^2, \dots)$, define its t-tail $X[t] = (x^t, x^{t+1}, x^{t+2}, \dots)$. We say that X *stabilises in time* t if one of the following holds:

$$X[t] = (0_F, 1_F, 0_F, \dots) \quad \text{or} \quad X[t] = (1_F, 0_F, 1_F, \dots).$$

We say that an algorithm A *stabilises in time* t if for any set of faulty nodes F with $|F| \leq f$, all executions of A stabilise in time t.

5 Projection Graphs

Before discussing how to *find* an algorithm (or prove that an algorithm does not exist), let us first explain how we can *verify* that a given algorithm is correct. Here the concept of a *projection graph* is helpful.

Fix the parameters s, n, and f, and consider a candidate algorithm A that is supposed to solve the 2-counting problem. For each set $F \subseteq [n]$ of faulty nodes, construct the directed graph $G_F(A) = (V_F, R_F(A))$ as follows:

1. The set of nodes V_F is the set of actual configurations.
2. There is an edge $(u, v) \in R_F(A)$ if configuration $v \in V_F$ is reachable from configuration $u \in V_F$. In general, this may produce self-loops.

Note that the outdegree of each node in $G_F(A)$ is at least 1. Directed walks in $G_F(A)$ correspond to possible executions of algorithm A, for this set F of faulty nodes. To verify the correctness of algorithm A, it is sufficient to analyse the projection graphs G_F. The following lemmas are straightforward consequences of the definitions.

Lemma 2. *Algorithm A stabilises in some time t iff for every F, graph $G_F(A)$ contains exactly one directed cycle, $0_F \mapsto 1_F \mapsto 0_F$.*

Lemma 3. *Algorithm A stabilises in time t iff the following holds for all F:*

1. *In $G_F(A)$, the only successor of 0_F is 1_F and vice versa.*
2. *In $G_F(A)$, every directed walk of length t reaches node 0_F or 1_F.*

Lemma 4. *Let A be an algorithm. Consider any four configurations $x, u, v, w \in V_F$ with the following properties: $(x, u) \in R_F(A)$, $(x, v) \in R_F(A)$, and $w_i \in \{u_i, v_i\}$ for each $i \notin F$. Then $(x, w) \in R_F(A)$.*

6   Increasing the Number of Nodes

It is not obvious how to use computational techniques to design an algorithm that solves the 2-counting problem for a fixed $f = 1$ but arbitrary $n \geq 4$. However, as we will show next, we can generalise any algorithm so that it solves the same problem for a larger number of nodes, without any penalty in time or space complexity. Therefore it is sufficient to design an algorithm for the special case of $f = 1$ and $n = 4$.

Lemma 5. *Fix $n \geq 4$, $f < n/2$, $s \geq 2$, and $t \geq 1$. Assume that $\boldsymbol{A}$ is an algorithm that solves the 2-counting problem for n nodes, out of which at most f are faulty, with stabilisation time t and with s states per node. Then we can design an algorithm $\boldsymbol{B}$ that solves the 2-counting problem for $n+1$ nodes, out of which at most f are faulty, with stabilisation time t and with s states per node.*

Proof. The claim would be straightforward if we permitted the stabilisation time of $t + 1$. However, some care is needed to avoid the loss of one round.

We take the following approach. Let p be a projection that removes the last element from a vector, for example, $p((a, b, c)) = (a, b)$. In algorithm $\boldsymbol{B}$, nodes $i \in [n]$ simply follow algorithm $\boldsymbol{A}$, ignoring node n:

$$B_i(\boldsymbol{u}_i) = A_i(p(\boldsymbol{u}_i)).$$

Node n tries to predict the majority of nodes $0, 1, \ldots, n - 1$, i.e., what most of them are going to output after this round:

- Assume that node n observes a configuration $\boldsymbol{u}_n$. For each $i \in [n]$, define $h_i = A_i(p(\boldsymbol{u}_n))$. If a majority of the values h_i is 1, then the new state of node n is also 1; otherwise it is 0.

To prove that the algorithm is correct, fix a set $F \subseteq [n + 1]$ of faulty nodes, with $|F| \leq f$. Clearly, all nodes in $[n] \setminus F$ will start counting correctly at the latest in round t. Hence any execution of $\boldsymbol{B}$ with $n \in F$ trivially stabilises within t rounds; so we focus on the case of $F \subseteq [n]$, and merely need to show that also node n counts correctly.

Fix an execution $X = (\boldsymbol{x}^0, \boldsymbol{x}^1, \ldots)$ of $\boldsymbol{A}$, and a point of time $r \geq t$. Consider the state vector $\boldsymbol{x}^{r-1}$. By assumption, $\boldsymbol{A}$ stabilises in time t. Hence the successors of $\boldsymbol{x}^{r-1}$ in the projection graph must be in $\{\boldsymbol{0}_F, \boldsymbol{1}_F\}$.

The key observation is that only one of the configurations $\boldsymbol{0}_F$ and $\boldsymbol{1}_F$ can be the successor of $\boldsymbol{x}^{r-1}$. Otherwise Lemma 4 would allow us to construct another state that is a successor of $\boldsymbol{x}^{r-1}$, contradicting the assumption that $\boldsymbol{A}$ stabilises.

We conclude that for all rounds $r \geq t$ and all nodes $i \in [n] \setminus F$, the value h_i is independent of the states communicated by nodes in F. Since the values h_i are identical and $n - f > f$, node n attains the same state as other correct nodes in rounds $r \geq t$.   □

7 Computer-Designed Algorithms

In principle, we could now attempt to use a computer to tackle our original problem. By the discussion of Section 6, it suffices to discover an algorithm with the smallest possible s for the special case of $n = 4$ and $f = 1$. We could try increasing values of $s = 2, 3, \dots$. Once we have fixed n, f, and s, the problem becomes finite: an algorithm is a lookup table with $\ell = ns^n$ entries, and hence there are s^ℓ candidate algorithms to explore. For each candidate algorithm, we could use the projection graph approach of Section 5 to quickly reject any invalid algorithm.

Unfortunately, the search space is huge. As we will see, there is no algorithm with $n = 4$ and $s = 2$. For $n = 4$ and $s = 3$, we have approximately 10^{154} candidates. We use two complementary approaches to tackle the task:

1. Narrow down the search space by considering restricted classes of algorithms.
2. Encode the problem as a Boolean formula and apply SAT solvers.

While SAT solvers are not a panacea, it is not uncommon to see modern general-purpose SAT solvers outdo carefully engineered application-specific algorithms.

Cyclic Algorithms. We will consider two classes of algorithms—general algorithms (without any restrictions) and *cyclic* algorithms. We say that algorithm A is cyclic if

$$A_i((x_i, x_{i+1}, \dots x_{n-1}, x_0, x_1, \dots, x_{i-1})) = A_0((x_0, x_1, \dots, x_{n-1}))$$

for all i and all $\boldsymbol{x}$. That is, a cyclic algorithm is invariant under cyclic renaming of the nodes.

There is no a priori reason to expect that the most efficient algorithms are cyclic. However, cyclic algorithms have many attractive features: for example, in a hardware implementation of a cyclic algorithm we only need to take n copies of identical modules. Furthermore, the search space is considerably smaller: we only need to define transition function A_0. For $n = 4$ and $s = 3$, we have approximately 10^{38} candidate algorithms.

Cyclic algorithms are also much easier to verify. The projection graphs $G_F(\boldsymbol{A})$ are isomorphic for all $|F| = 1$ and hence it is sufficient to check one of them.

Encoding. At a high level, we take the following approach.

1. Fix the parameters s, n, f, t, and the algorithm family (cyclic or general).
2. Construct a Boolean circuit C that verifies whether a given algorithm A is correct. The circuit receives the transition table of A encoded as a binary string.
3. Translate circuit C to an equivalent Boolean formula $\mathcal{F}$.
4. Use SAT solvers to find a satisfying assignment $\boldsymbol{a}$ of $\mathcal{F}$.
5. Translate $\boldsymbol{a}$ to an algorithm A that passes the verification of circuit C.

Table 1. Positive results. The size of the search space is approximately 2^b.

Parameters					SAT instance		Solver running time (s)		
s n f t family				b	variables	clauses	picosat	lingeling	plingeling
2 6 1 8				384	78546	336098	—	—	140000
2 7 1 8	cyclic			128	37230	171626	—	47	48
2 8 1 4	cyclic			256	79423	436929	410	17	12
3 4 1 7	cyclic			129	10338	42030	4	3	3
3 5 1 4				1926	374871	1712779	—	—	140000
3 5 1 6	cyclic			386	66793	304091	—	3000	1200
3 6 1 3	cyclic			1156	319726	1753824	11000	450	530
4 4 1 5	cyclic			512	62272	269892	64000	320	77
4 5 1 5	cyclic			2048	760892	3691498	—	41000	25000

In essence, circuit $\mathcal{C}$ applies Lemma 3 to verify $\boldsymbol{A}$. More concretely, it is a hard-wired implementation of a computer program that performs the following steps (in parallel for all possible sets F):

1. Construct the projection graph $G_F(\boldsymbol{A})$.
2. Verify that there are no self-loops in G_F.
3. Verify that the only successor of $\boldsymbol{0}_F$ is $\boldsymbol{1}_F$ and vice versa.
4. For each $d = 1, 2, \ldots, t$, find the subset $B_F(d) \subseteq V_F$ of states with the following property: for each $\boldsymbol{u} \in B_F(d)$ there is a directed walk of length d in G_F that starts from $\boldsymbol{u}$ and does not traverse $\boldsymbol{0}_F$ or $\boldsymbol{1}_F$.
5. Verify that set $B_F(t)$ is empty.

For cyclic algorithms, we identify equivalent transitions in the input and simplify the circuit accordingly.

Results. The Boolean circuits were constructed with a program written in C++. We used Junttila's **bc2cnf** tool, version 0.35 [13] to convert the circuit to a SAT instance, and then we experimented with two SAT solvers: **lingeling**, version ala-b02aa1a [4], and **picosat**, version 954 [3]. We ran our experiments on a computing cluster in which each node had 2 processors (Intel Xeon E5540), 2×4 cores, and 32 GB RAM. In this environment **plingeling**, the parallel version of **lingeling**, automatically uses up to 8 threads and up to 16 GB memory.

The positive results are reported in Table 1, along with some statistics. The b column indicates how many bits are needed to encode an algorithm—equivalently, it is the base-2 logarithm of the size of the search space, rounded up.

The key findings are a cyclic algorithm for $s = 3$, $n = 4$, and $f = 1$, and a non-cyclic algorithm for $s = 2$, $n = 6$, and $f = 1$. The table also gives example of space-time tradeoffs: we can often obtain faster stabilisation if we use a larger number of states.

For the sake of comparison, we note that the *fastest* deterministic algorithm from prior work [7] stabilises in time $t = 13$ for $f = 1$ and it requires a large state space. Our algorithms achieve the stabilisation time of $t = 5$ for $s = 4$ and $t = 7$ for $s = 3$.

Machine-readable versions of all positive results, together with a Python script that can be used to verify the correctness of the algorithms, are freely available online [1]. Selected examples of the algorithms are also given in Appendix A.

8 Computer-Designed Lower Bounds

We can use the approach of Section 7 to discover not only positive but also negative results. If we use a SAT encoding that applies Lemma 2 instead of Lemma 3, we can use the same approach to prove, for example, that the case of $s = 2$, $n < 6$, and $f = 1$ is not solvable for any stabilisation time t.

However, such an approach would not admit easy independent verification. It is true that modern SAT solvers are able to produce, e.g., resolution proofs showing the unsatisfiability of the propositional formula. However, these proofs tend to be long, and more importantly, require us to prove that (1) the encoding exactly captures the problem at hand and (2) the computer program that outputs the formula is correct. Hence we apply different techniques.

Using C++, we implemented a backtracking algorithm that analyses the case of $s = 2$, $n = 4$, and $f = 1$. The algorithm produces a proof that shows that there is no solution.

The proof is a case analysis with 106 cases, each of them easy to verify. A machine-readable version of the proof is freely available online [1]. We have also provided a simple Python script that can be used to check that the proof is indeed correct: all possible cases are covered and the contradiction that we exhibit for each case is verified.

While it is straightforward to construct *some* proof (in principle, an exhaustive enumeration of all candidate algorithms would suffice), it is difficult to come up with a *small* proof that is short enough for a (very patient) human being to verify. Briefly, the key milestones are as follows.

1. An exhaustive enumeration: 2^{64} cases.
2. Trivial cases eliminated: 2^{32} cases.
3. A straightforward backtracking search: ≈ 10000 cases.
4. A heuristic rule that attempts to find the best possible branching order for the backtracking search: 243 cases.
5. Merging cases that can be covered with a single proof: 106 cases.

While a long proof is easy to construct, the short proofs required extensive computations in a cluster environment (in total several years of CPU time).

9 Conclusions

In this work, we have used computational techniques to study the synchronous counting problem. At first sight the problem is not well-suited for computational algorithm design—we need to reason about stabilisation from any given starting configuration, for any adversarial behaviour, in a system with arbitrarily many nodes. Nevertheless, we have demonstrated that computational techniques can be used in this context, both to discover novel algorithms and to prove lower-bound results.

Our computational results were constructed with a fairly complicated tool-chain. However, the end results are compact, machine readable, and easy to verify with a straightforward script.

Our algorithms outperform the best human-designed algorithms: they are deterministic, small ($2 \leq s \leq 3$), fast ($3 \leq t \leq 8$), and easy to implement in hardware or in software—a small lookup table suffices. In summary, our work leaves very little room for improvement in the case of $f = 1$. The general case of $f > 1$ is left for future work; we are optimistic that the algorithms designed in this work can be used as subroutines to construct algorithms that tolerate a larger number of failures.

Acknowledgments. Many thanks to Matti Järvisalo for discussions and advice related to SAT encoding and SAT solvers.

DD: Danny Dolev is Incumbent of the Berthold Badler Chair in Computer Science. This research project was supported in part by The Israeli Centers of Research Excellence (I-CORE) program, (Center No. 4/11), by grant 3/9778 of the Israeli Ministry of Science and Technology, and by the ISG (Israeli Smart Grid) Consortium, administered by the office of the Chief Scientist of the Israeli Ministry of Industry and Trade and Labor.

JHK, JR, JS: This work is supported in part by the Helsinki Doctoral Pro-gramme in Computer Science – Advanced Computing and Intelligent Systems, by the Academy of Finland (grants 132380 and 252018), and by the Research Funds of the University of Helsinki.

CL: This material is based upon work supported by the National Science Foundation under Grant Nos. CCF-AF-0937274, CNS-1035199, 0939370-CCF and CCF-1217506, the AFOSR under Award number FA9550-13-1-0042, and the German Research Foundation (DFG, reference number Le 3107/1-1).

References

1. Computer-generated proofs, https://github.com/suomela/counting (primary), https://bitbucket.org/suomela/counting (backup)
2. Ben-Or, M., Dolev, D., Hoch, E.N.: Fast self-stabilizing Byzantine tolerant digi-tal clock synchronization. In: Proc. 27th Symposium on Principles of Distributed Computing (PODC 2008), pp. 385–394. ACM Press, New York (2008)
3. Biere, A.: PicoSAT essentials. Journal on Satisfiability, Boolean Modeling and Computation 4, 75–97 (2008)
4. Biere, A.: Lingeling and friends entering the SAT challenge 2012. In: Proceed-ings of SAT Challenge 2012; Solver and Benchmark Descriptions. Department of Computer Science Series of Publications B, vol. B-2012-2, pp. 33–34. University of Helsinki (2012)

5. Clarke, E.M., Emerson, E.A.: Design and synthesis of synchronization skeletons using branching time temporal logic. In: Proc. 3rd Workshop on Logic of Programs (LOP 1981). LNCS, vol. 131, pp. 52–71. Springer, Berlin (1982)
6. Daliot, A., Dolev, D., Parnas, H.: Self-stabilizing pulse synchronization inspired by biological pacemaker networks. In: Huang, S.-T., Herman, T. (eds.) SSS 2003. LNCS, vol. 2704, pp. 32–48. Springer, Heidelberg (2003)
7. Dolev, D., Hoch, E.N.: On self-stabilizing synchronous actions despite Byzantine attacks. In: Pelc, A. (ed.) DISC 2007. LNCS, vol. 4731, pp. 193–207. Springer, Heidelberg (2007)
8. Dolev, S.: Self-Stabilization. The MIT Press, Cambridge (2000)
9. Dolev, S., Welch, J.L.: Self-stabilizing clock synchronization in the presence of Byzantine faults. Journal of the ACM 51(5), 780–799 (2004)
10. Fischer, M.J., Lynch, N.A.: A lower bound for the time to assure interactive consistency. Information Processing Letters 14(4), 183–186 (1982)
11. Fuhs, C., Schneider-Kamp, P.: Synthesizing shortest linear straight-line programs over GF(2) using SAT. In: Strichman, O., Szeider, S. (eds.) SAT 2010. LNCS, vol. 6175, pp. 71–84. Springer, Heidelberg (2010)
12. Järvisalo, M., Kaski, P., Koivisto, M., Korhonen, J.H.: Finding efficient circuits for ensemble computation. In: Cimatti, A., Sebastiani, R. (eds.) SAT 2012. LNCS, vol. 7317, pp. 369–382. Springer, Heidelberg (2012)
13. Junttila, T.A., Niemelä, I.: Towards an efficient tableau method for Boolean circuit satisfiability checking. In: Palamidessi, C., et al. (eds.) CL 2000. LNCS (LNAI), vol. 1861, pp. 553–567. Springer, Heidelberg (2000)
14. Kojevnikov, A., Kulikov, A.S., Yaroslavtsev, G.: Finding efficient circuits using SAT-solvers. In: Kullmann, O. (ed.) SAT 2009. LNCS, vol. 5584, pp. 32–44. Springer, Heidelberg (2009)
15. Lynch, N.A.: Distributed Algorithms. Morgan Kaufmann, San Francisco (1996)
16. Manna, Z., Wolper, P.: Synthesis of communicating processes from temporal logic specifications. ACM Transactions on Programming Languages and Systems 6(1), 68–93 (1984)
17. Moscibroda, T., Oshman, R.: Resilience of mutual exclusion algorithms to transient memory faults. In: Proc. 30th Symposium on Principles of Distributed Computing (PODC 2011), pp. 69–78. ACM Press, New York (2011)
18. Pease, M.C., Shostak, R.E., Lamport, L.: Reaching agreement in the presence of faults. Journal of the ACM 27(2), 228–234 (1980)

A   Algorithm Listings

In this appendix, we give two examples of our algorithms—machine-readable versions of all algorithms, verification code, and some illustrations are available online [1].

Table 2 gives a cyclic algorithm for $n = 4$. The rows are labelled with (x_0, x_1), the columns are labelled with (x_2, x_3), and the values indicate $A_0((x_0, x_1, x_2, x_3))$, that is, the new state of the first node in the observed configuration x.

Table 3 shows a non-cyclic algorithm for $n = 6$. Again, the rows are labelled with the first half (x_0, x_1, x_2) of the observed state x and the columns are labelled with the second half (x_3, x_4, x_5) of the observed state x. The values show the new state for each node: $A_0(x), A_1(x), \ldots, A_5(x)$.

Table 2. Cyclic algorithm for $s = 3$, $n = 4$, $f = 1$, and $t = 7$

	00	01	02	10	11	12	20	21	22
00	1	1	1	1	2	1	1	1	1
01	1	1	1	0	2	0	1	1	0
02	1	1	1	1	0	0	1	1	1
10	1	0	0	1	0	0	1	0	0
11	0	0	0	0	0	0	0	0	0
12	0	0	0	0	0	0	0	0	0
20	1	1	1	1	1	1	1	1	1
21	1	1	1	1	0	0	1	1	0
22	1	1	1	0	0	0	1	1	1

Table 3. Algorithm for $s = 2$, $n = 6$, $f = 1$, and $t = 8$

	000	001	010	011	100	101	110	111
000	111111	111111	111111	110101	111011	111111	111111	110101
001	111111	110111	111101	000001	111011	100011	101001	000100
010	111111	111111	111111	110101	001000	001000	001000	000000
011	101111	100011	101001	000000	001000	000000	001000	000000
100	111111	011100	110101	000000	111111	011100	100011	000000
101	110111	000000	000000	000000	100011	000000	000000	000000
110	111111	011100	100011	000000	001000	001000	000000	000000
111	100111	000000	000000	000000	000000	000000	000000	000000

An Asynchronous Self-stabilizing Approximation for the Minimum Connected Dominating Set with Safe Convergence in Unit Disk Graphs*

Sayaka Kamei[1], Tomoko Izumi[2], and Yukiko Yamauchi[3]

[1] Hiroshima University, Japan
s-kamei@se.hiroshima-u.ac.jp
[2] Ritsumeikan University, Japan
izumi-t@fc.ritsumei.ac.jp
[3] Kyushu University, Japan
yamauchi@inf.kyushu-u.ac.jp

Abstract. In wireless ad hoc or sensor networks, a connected dominating set (CDS) is useful as the virtual backbone because there is no fixed infrastructure or centralized management. Safe converging self-stabilization is one extension of self-stabilization, that is, self-stabilization guarantees the system tolerates any kind and any finite number of transient faults and doesn't need any initialization. The safe convergence property guarantees that the system quickly converges to a safe configuration, and then, the system configuration becomes to an optimal configuration without breaking safety. However, the previous works on safe converging algorithm for the minimum CDS assumed a phase clock synchronizer, this is a very strong assumption. In this paper, we propose the first *asynchronous* self-stabilizing $(6 + \epsilon)$-approximation algorithm with safe convergence for the minimum CDS in the networks modeled by unit disk graphs. The first convergence time to a safe configuration in which a dominating set is computed is 1 round, and the second convergence time to an optimal configuration in which an approximation of the minimum CDS is constructed is $O(\max\{d^2, n\})$ rounds, $O(n^6)$ steps.

1 Introduction

Wireless ad hoc or sensor networks have no fixed physical backbone infrastructure and no centralized administration. Therefore, a *connected dominating set* (CDS) formed by processes (*i.e.*, processors) is useful as the virtual backbone for the computation of message routing and other network problems for such networks. Unfortunately, it is known that the minimum CDS problem is NP-hard [1] even in unit disk graphs which are one model of ad hoc or sensor networks. Therefore, for finding a minimum CDS, a lot of approximation algorithms are proposed. A $|D_{alg}|/|D_{opt}|$-approximation algorithm for the minimization problem is an algorithm which guarantees the approximation ratio $|D_{alg}|/|D_{opt}|$, where $|D_{alg}|$ is the size of the solution of the approximation algorithm in the worst case and $|D_{opt}|$ is the size of an optimal (*i.e.*, a minimum) solution.

Self-stabilization [2] is a theoretical framework of fault-tolerant distributed algorithms. A self-stabilizing algorithm can start execution from an arbitrary (illegitimate)

---

* This work is supported in part by KAKENHI No. 22700074, No. 22700017 and No. 23700019.

T. Higashino et al. (Eds.): SSS 2013, LNCS 8255, pp. 251–265, 2013.

system configuration, and eventually leads the system configuration to a legitimate one where the algorithm satisfies its specification. Because of this property, it can tolerate any kind and any finite number of transient faults, such as message loss and memory corruption, as long as no fault occurs while converging to its legitimate configurations.

However, ordinary self-stabilizing algorithms have no safety guarantee while they are converging even if faults and topology changes don't occur. Therefore, while they are converging, any quality of services on networks couldn't be guaranteed. Thus, during the converging period, we would like to guarantee a safety property by extending self-stabilization, called *safe convergence* [3]. When faults occur, a self-stabilizing algorithm with safe convergence (SC-algorithm) converges to a feasible (not optimal) legitimate configuration satisfying a certain safety property as soon as possible. Then, the safety property should be set up to offer minimal quality of services. After that, if no fault occurs for a long enough period of time (*i.e.*, during convergence time), the system configuration automatically converges to an optimal legitimate configuration to provide the best quality of services while it preserves the safety property. As a result, the SC-algorithm needs smaller time complexities to guarantee the safety property than without safe convergence.

Because a CDS can be used for the virtual backbone for routing messages in ad hoc networks, many algorithms for the CDS have been proposed. There are some self-stabilizing algorithms for computing CDSs without safe convergence property, for example [4], [5] and [6]. However, they are not approximation algorithms or without safe convergence property. In [7], the authors modified [6] to add safe convergence property. However, this algorithm assumes the step synchronization using a phase clock synchronizer [8]. That is, every process executes the same step in parallel and in a synchronized manner. This is a very strong assumption. Additionally, they did not show the round and step complexity for converging to an optimal configuration.

Contribution of This Paper: In this paper, we propose a $(6 + \epsilon)$-approximation SC-algorithm for the minimum CDS in unit disk graphs under an unfair distributed daemon (called unfair d-daemon), *i.e.*, we assume an asynchronous system. Note that, our algorithm can compute a CDS in general graphs, but we cannot guarantee the approximation ratio in general graphs. That is, we assume unit disk graphs only for the guarantee of its approximation ratio.

Using our algorithm, a configuration very quickly becomes to a feasible (*i.e.*, not optimal) one, that is, a (non-connected) dominating set is computed in 1 round. Then, as long as no transient fault occurs, a configuration eventually becomes an optimal one in which an approximation of the minimum CDS is computed. In sensor networks, after a dominating set is constructed, until an optimal CDS is constructed, each member of the dominating set temporarily stores sensor data. After that, when an optimal CDS is constructed, each member of the dominating set can start transferring the data on the CDS. To an optimal configuration, in our algorithm, the round complexity is $O(\max\{d^2, n\})$ rounds, and the step complexity is $O(n^6)$ steps, where d and n are the diameter and the number of processes in the network. The round complexity is the number of rounds, in which every processes take at least one steps, in the worst case. That is, some processes may take too many steps in a round. On the other hand, the step complexity is defined as the maximum number of steps taken by any process in the worst case. It is important criterion since it reflects the number of messages exchanged by an algorithm.

Designing such algorithm is not trivial for the following reasons. By means of the safe convergence property, each configuration from a feasible one to an optimal one in the computation maintains the safety property, *i.e.*, the system remains constructing a dominating set in each configuration. To construct an approximation of the minimum CDS, some members of the dominating set in the feasible configuration leave the set. If two neighboring processes leave at the same step because of unfair d-daemon, then there is a possibility that the set will become not a dominating set. Therefore, our algorithm first computes a larger dominating set to guarantee the safety property. After that, it decreases the member of CDS carefully, that is, among each process and its neighbors, any two processes cannot leave the CDS at the same time by voting among neighbors.

Outline of This Paper: This paper is organized as follows. In section 2, we formally describe the system model and the distributed minimum CDS problem. In section 3, we propose a SC-approximation algorithm for the minimum CDS under unfair d-daemon. In section 4, we show the proof of the correctness of the proposed algorithm. In section 5, we give a conclusion and discuss future works.

2 Preliminaries

Let $V = \{P_1, P_2, ..., P_n\}$ be a set of n processes and $E \subseteq V \times V$ be a set of bidirectional communication links in a distributed system. Then, the topology of the distributed system is represented as an undirected graph $G = (V, E)$. We assume that G is connected and simple. In this paper, we use "graphs" and "distributed systems" interchangeably. We assume that each process has a unique process identifier. We also denote the process identifier of P_i by P_i. By N_i, we denote the set of neighboring processes of P_i. By Δ, we denote the maximum degree of the network. Let the *distance* between P_i and P_j be the number of the edges on a shortest path between them. For any set $S \subset V$ and any process $P_i \notin S$, let the distance between P_i and S be the minimum distance between P_i and any $P_j \in S$.

A set of local variables defines the local state of a process. By Q_i, we denote the local state of each process $P_i \in V$. A tuple of the local state of each process $(Q_1, Q_2, ..., Q_n)$ forms a *configuration* of a distributed system. Let Γ be a set of all configurations.

As a communication model, we assume the *state reading model*. In this model, each process can read the local states of neighboring processes without delay. Although a process can read the local state of neighboring processes, it cannot update them; it can only update the local state of itself.

Our algorithm is *semi-uniform*, *i.e.*, there is a specific process P_r and each process except P_r executes the same program. An algorithm of each process P_i is given as an ordered finite set of actions including a priority which is represented by the label of actions. The label of each action is assigned a unique positive integer, and the action with a smaller label has high priority. Each action is constituted as follows: $< label >::< guard >\rightarrow< command >$. Each *guard* is a predicate on P_i's local state and local state of its neighbors. Each *command* updates local state of P_i, the next local state is computed from the current local states of P_i and its neighbors. An action can be executed only if its guard is satisfied. We define that P_i is *privileged* in configuration γ iff at least one guard is satisfied by P_i in γ. When several guards of actions are satisfied simultaneously at P_i, then only one action with highest priority among actions associated to true guards can be executed.

We define a *step* as an atomic execution unit. A step consists of the following three substeps: (1) Reading the local states of all neighbors and evaluating guards, (2) Executing a command associated to a true guard with the highest priority, and (3) Updating its local state. When the three substeps are done, the next step begins.

We assume *unfair distributed daemon* (*i.e.*, scheduler). In each configuration, distributed daemon selects an arbitrary non-empty subset of privileged processes at each step, and selected processes execute their steps in parallel. The unfair daemon can select a set of processes not to stabilize a system, that is, it can forever prevent a process from executing an action except when the number of privileged processes is only one.

For any configuration γ, let γ' be any configuration that follows γ. Then, we denote this transition relation by $\gamma \to \gamma'$. It means that it is possible for the network configuration to change from γ to γ' in one step by executing the algorithm. For any configuration γ_0, a *computation* E of the algorithm starting from γ_0 is a maximal (possibly infinite) sequence of configurations $E = \gamma_0, \gamma_1, \gamma_2, ...$ such that $\gamma_t \to \gamma_{t+1}$ for each $t \geq 0$. Note that, starting from an identical configuration γ_0, there are many executions depending on the scheduler's selections.

Definition 1. (Self-Stabilization) *Let Γ be a set of all configurations. A system S is self-stabilizing with respect to Λ such that $\Lambda \subset \Gamma$ if and only if it satisfies the following two conditions:*
- *Convergence: Starting from an arbitrary configuration, the system eventually reaches a configuration in Λ, and*
- *Closure: For any configuration $\lambda \in \Lambda$, any configuration γ that follows λ is also in Λ as long as no fault occurs.*
Each $\gamma \in \Lambda$ is called a legitimate *configuration.*

Definition 2. (Safe converging self-stabilization) *Let Γ be the set of all configurations, and let $\Lambda_O \subset \Lambda_F \subset \Gamma$. A self-stabilizing system S is safely converging with respect to (Λ_F, Λ_O) if and only if it satisfies the following three conditions:*
- *S is self-stabilizing with respect to Λ_F.*
- *Safe convergence: For any execution starting from a configuration in Λ_F, the configuration eventually becomes one in Λ_O.*
- *S is self-stabilizing with respect to Λ_O.*
Each $\gamma \in \Lambda_F$ is called a feasible legitimate *configuration, and each $\gamma \in \Lambda_O$ is called an* optimal legitimate *configuration.*

We use the definition of *rounds* to compute the time complexity to the feasible legitimate configuration. The first round of a computation E is the minimal prefix E' of E containing the execution of one action of every privileged process of the initial configuration. The second round of E is the first round of E'' where $E = E'E''$. The third and later rounds are defined recursively in the same way.

Definition 3. *Let S be a safely converging self-stabilizing system with respect to (Λ_F, Λ_O). The* first convergence time *(resp.* second convergence time*) is the maximum* *number of rounds (resp. rounds or steps) to become a configuration in Λ_F (resp. Λ_O) from any initial configuration in Γ (resp. Λ_F).*

We give the definition of the dominating set and independent set as follow: A *dominating set* of a graph $G = (V, E)$ is a subset $V' \subseteq V$ such that there are $v \in V'$ and $(u, v) \in E$ for $\forall u \in V \backslash V'$. A dominating set V' of G is *minimal* if no proper subset of V' is a dominating set of G. An *independent set* of G is a subset $V' \subseteq V$ such that $(u, v) \notin E$ for any $u, v \in V'$. An independent set V' of G is *maximal* if no proper superset of V' is an independent set of G. In [9], the following relationship between dominating sets and independent sets is shown.

Theorem 1 ([9]). *Every maximal independent set (MIS) in a graph G is a minimal dominating set of G.*

We give the definition of the minimum connected dominating set (CDS) as follow: A *connected dominating set* of a graph $G = (V, E)$ is a dominating set $V' \subseteq V$ such that the induced subgraph of G by V' is connected. A connected dominating set V' of G is *minimum* if $|V'| \leq |V''|$ for any connected dominating set V'' of G. We call the members of the CDS *dominators*, and others *dominatees*. Each dominatee is *dominated* by at least one dominator.

We consider solving the minimum CDS problem in distributed systems in this paper. We assume that each process P_i doesn't know the global information of the network. We defined the distributed minimum CDS problem as follows.

Definition 4. *Let $G = (V, E)$ be a distributed system, let $cds_i \in \{0, 1\}$ be a local variable of each process $P_i \in V$ that represents whether P_i is in a minimum connected dominating set. The distributed minimum connected dominating set problem is a problem defined as follows.*

- *Each process P_i must decide the value of cds_i as output of P_i, and*
- *The set $\{P_i \in V \mid cds_i = 1\}$ is a minimum connected dominating set of G.*

3 Proposed Algorithm

Our algorithm ASC-CDS is safe converging. We define that the safety property is the condition in which "a dominating set is computed". That is, ASC-CDS computes a dominating set in the first round, and then, it leads the system to a configuration where a $(6 + \epsilon)$-approximation of the minimum CDS is constructed. During the convergence, the system remains constructing a dominating set in each configuration.

ASC-CDS is a conditional composition of CDS in this paper and the Question-Answer algorithm (QA) in [10]. The formal description of the proposed algorithm CDS is shown in Fig. 1 and Fig. 2. Our algorithm CDS is based on the strategy of Wan *et al.*'s algorithm in [11].

First, CDS computes a BFS tree T rooted at P_r for G, *i.e.*, each process P_i computes the distance L_i from P_r. Our algorithm uses an algorithm in [10] as actions 1, 4, 9 and 10 for $P_i \neq P_r$ and actions 1 and 2 for P_r, and uses QA only for the BFS tree construction[1]. Each process P_i executes QA, only when the predicate $Cond_i$ is true, i.e., the tree containing P_i is locally correct (i.e., $GoodTGoodL_i$ is true.), P_i doesn't need to newly join the dominating set in the configuration (i.e., $GoodDS_i$ is true.), and P_i has a consistent local state. If guards of QA and CDS are true at P_i simultaneously, QA is executed before CDS. The algorithm QA manages the request for getting some children on a BFS tree. Each request is sent by action 9 of CDS (i.e., $Req_i = $ ASK). By QA, the request is transmitted to P_r and the process P_i which sent the request with the lowest L_i preferentially gets a permission (i.e., $Req_i = $ REP) from P_r. Then, P_i's neighbors can select P_i as their father in the tree rooted at P_r by action 4. If every neighbor of P_i connects to the tree rooted at P_r, then P_i sets Req_i to OUT to request another permission by action 10. By QA, each process can connect to the tree rooted at P_r in order of increasing of the distance from P_r. For the purpose of illustration below, let k be the height of T on G, and let D_l be the set of processes which have distance $L_i = l$ ($0 \leq l \leq k$).

Next, CDS computes an MIS constructed by *paving* on T (i.e., $\cup_{l=0}^{k} I_l$) by the following way: The root P_r definitely joins a set I_0. Let M_l be a set of processes $P_i \in D_l$ each of which is dominated by (i.e., neighboring to) some processes in I_{l-1}. For each $1 \leq l \leq k$, a set I_l is an MIS of an induced subgraph of G by $D_l \setminus M_l$. That is, the members of the MIS are selected in a greedy manner from P_r to leaves on T.

Property 1. Let T be a BFS tree on G, and L_i be the distance from the root to P_i on T. For any MIS I' *constructed by paving on T for G*, each member P_i of I' which has $L_i = l$ has the following two processes:
- a father $P_j \in N_i$ of P_i on T, and
- a neighbor $P_k(\neq P_i) \in I'$ of P_j has $L_k = l - 1$ or $L_k = l - 2$.

Theorem 2 ([11]). *Let I' be the MIS constructed by paving on a BFS tree. For any P_i in I', the distance between P_i and $I' \setminus \{P_i\}$ is exactly two.*

Last, CDS selects members of a *CDS-tree* defined as follows:

Definition 5. *Let I' be any MIS constructed by paving on a BFS tree T for G. Let $S'(\neq \emptyset)$ be a set of processes each of which is the father of a member in I' on T. A set of processes $I' \cup S'$ is a CDS-tree for G.*

By Theorem 2, the connectivity of the CDS-tree is ensured. In the MIS constructed by paving on T, each member $P_i \in D_l$ of the MIS has a father on T which is neighbor to at least one member of the MIS in D_{l-1} or D_{l-2}. Therefore, the union of the MIS and a set of fathers of members of the MIS is connected. Because the MIS is also a dominating set by Theorem 1, the union is a CDS.

Theorem 3 ([7]). *Let D_{opt} be a minimum CDS. Any CDS-tree is an approximation for a minimum CDS which size is at most $6|D_{opt}| + 5$ in unit disk graphs.*

We assume the output of each process P_i is the variable cds_i, where $cds_i = 1$ (resp. 0) if P_i is a dominator (resp. dominatee). Additionally, the local variable m_i represents

---

[1] The algorithm in [10] is a conditional composition of QA and an algorithm for the BFS tree construction. These actions in CDS are the same as the algorithm for the tree construction.

whether P_i is in the MIS or not, that is, $m_i \neq 0$ (resp. 0) if P_i is (resp. is not) a member of MIS. For each configuration $\gamma \in \Gamma$, we define the following two subsets:

- $MIS(\gamma) \equiv \{P_i \in V \mid m_i \neq 0\}$
- $Doms(\gamma) \equiv \{P_i \in V \mid cds_i = 1\}$

A set of legitimate configurations is defined as follows.

Definition 6. *A configuration γ is in a set of* feasibly legitimate *configurations Λ_F iff $Doms(\gamma)$ is a dominating set. A configuration γ is in a set of* optimally legitimate *configurations Λ_O iff $Doms(\gamma)$ is a CDS-tree.*

To guarantee the safety property, CDS computes a larger dominating set, even if the BFS tree is broken. When the process is not in the tree rooted at P_r, *i.e.* when $T_i = E$, the process joins MIS and $Doms$ by action 1 of CDS. When the process is in tree rooted at P_r, *i.e.* when $T_i = C$, if $P_i(\neq P_r)$ is not dominated by its neighbors P_j with $L_j \leq L_i$, then P_i joins these sets by actions 2. When $T_i = C$, if P_i is in MIS, but not in $Doms$, then P_i joins $Doms$ by action 3. Note that, the composed QA is used only for the construction of T. Therefore, the states of QA don't have influence on the safe convergence.

After that, while CDS constructs a BFS tree, it decreases the members of MIS and $Doms$ carefully to construct a minimum CDS by actions 6, 7 and 8. That is, the process should be careful not to break a condition of dominating set even when it leaves from the dominating set. To guarantee the set remains a dominating set, at most one process can leave the set among the neighbors and itself in each step by the following way: When a process P_i wants to leave the set, P_i sets the value c_i to non 0 value determined by L_i (see Macro *WantLeave*) in action 5. Only if every neighbor P_j allows P_i to leave, that is, P_j sets a_j to P_i by action 5, then P_i can leave MIS by action 7. By the macro *ChangeCand$_i$*, each process P_j selects a neighbor P_i with $c_i \neq 0$ as a_j when L_i is smaller than other P_j's neighbors with $c \neq 0$. Additionally, if there is a process $P_k \in N_i$ with $L_k < L_i$ and $c_k \neq 0$, then P_i selects P_k as a_i, and P_i cannot leave the set. When P_i wants to leave, if there is a neighbor P_j with $m_j = 0 \wedge L_j \geq L_i$ and there is no neighbor P_h of P_j with $m_h \neq 0 \wedge L_h \leq L_j$ other than P_i, then P_i waits for P_j's joining or encourages P_j to join by action 6. After P_j joins, then P_j selects P_i as a_j. By action 8, processes which are neither in MIS nor fathers of MIS leave $Doms$.

4 Proof of Correctness

In this section, we show the proof of correctness of ASC-CDS.

Lemma 1. *Let γ be any configuration in Γ.* **(a)** *A process P_i and all of its neighbors $P_j \in N_i$ cannot leave $MIS(\gamma)$ simultaneously. Additionally,* **(b)** *Any two neighbors $P_j \in N_i$ and $P_k \in N_i$ of P_i cannot leave $MIS(\gamma)$ simultaneously.*

Proof. Assume that P_i and $P_j \in N_i$ leave MIS simultaneously, that is, they execute action 7 in the same step. For P_i's execution of action 7, P_i must hold $a_i =\perp$. For P_j's execution of action 7, $\forall P_l \in N_j[a_l = P_j]$ must hold. Because $P_i \in N_j$, this is a contradiction. Therefore, (a) holds.

Constant

N_i: a set of neighboring processes of P_i.

Shared variable (See [10])

$Req_i \in \{\mathsf{ASK, WAIT, REP, OUT}\}$: a shared variable with QA.

Predicates

$GoodTGoodL_i \equiv \{T_i = C \wedge (P_i = P_r \vee L_i = L_{F_i} + 1) \wedge$
$\qquad\qquad\qquad \forall P_j \in N_i[|L_i - L_j| \leq 1 \vee L_i < L_j \vee T_j = E]\}$

$GoodDS_i \equiv \{m_i \neq 0 \vee \exists P_j \in N_i[m_j \neq 0 \wedge L_j \leq L_i]\} \wedge \{(m_i = 0 \wedge cds_i = 0) \vee cds_i = 1\}$

$Cond_i \equiv GoodTGoodL_i \wedge GoodDS_i \wedge \{a_i = \perp \vee d_i \leq 1 \vee NumDom_i \neq 1 \vee m_i \neq 0\}$

$GPREP_i \equiv \exists P_j \in N_i[T_j = E \vee |L_j - L_i| > 1]$

$Start_i \equiv Req_i = OUT \wedge GPREP_i$

$End_i \equiv Req_i = REP \wedge \neg GPREP_i$

$Allowed_i \equiv (P_i = P_r)$ (See [10])

Local variable for the construction of a BFS tree (See [10])

L_i: the distance from the root process P_r.

$F_i \in N_i$: an id of a father of P_i in the BFS tree.

$T_i \in \{C, E\}$: $T_i = C$ (resp. $T_i = E$) if P_i is (resp. is not) in a tree rooted at P_r.

Local variable for the construction of a CDS-tree

$m_i \in \{0, 1, 2\}$: $m_i \neq 0$ (resp. $m_i = 0$) if P_i is (resp. is not) in the MIS.

$d_i \in [0..\delta]$: the number of neighboring dominator with small or equal distance.

$c_i \in \{0, 1, 2\}$: $c_i \neq 0$ (resp. $c_i = 0$) if P_i wants (resp. does not want) to leave the MIS.

$a_i \in N_i \cup \{\perp\}$: the neighbor to whom P_i allow to leave.

$cds_i \in \{0, 1\}$: $cds_i = 1$ (resp. $cds_i = 0$) if P_i is (resp. is not) in the CDS.

Macro for the construction of a BFS tree (See [10])

$Child_i \equiv \{P_j \in N_i \mid F_j = P_i \wedge L_j = L_i + 1\}$

$ChPar_i \equiv \{P_j \in N_i \setminus Child_i \mid T_j = C\}$

$MinChPar_i \equiv \min\{P_j \in ChPar_i \mid \forall P_t \in ChPar_i[L_j \leq L_t]\}$

Macro for the construction of a CDS-tree

$NumDom_i \equiv |\{P_j \in N_i \mid m_j \neq 0 \wedge L_j \leq L_i\}|$

$WantLeave_i \equiv$ **if** $T_i = C \wedge \forall P_j \in N_i[T_j = C \wedge |L_i - L_j| \leq 1] \wedge m_i \neq 0$ **then**
$\qquad\qquad$ **if** $\exists P_j \in N_i[m_j \neq 0 \wedge L_j < L_i]$ **then** 2
$\qquad\qquad$ **elseif** $\exists P_j \in N_i[m_j \neq 0 \wedge L_j = L_i]$ **then** 1
$\qquad\qquad$ **else** 0
$\qquad\qquad\quad$ **else** 0

$Cand_i \equiv \{P_j \in N_i \mid T_j = C \wedge m_j \neq 0 \wedge c_j \neq 0\}$

$LostCand_i(P_j \in N_i) \equiv$ **if** $L_j < L_i$ **then** 1
$\qquad\qquad\qquad$ **elseif** $L_j = L_i \wedge c_j > c_i$ **then** 1
$\qquad\qquad\qquad$ **elseif** $L_j = L_i \wedge c_j = c_i \wedge m_j > m_i$ **then** 1
$\qquad\qquad\qquad$ **elseif** $L_j = L_i \wedge c_j = c_i \wedge m_j = m_i \wedge P_j < P_i$ **then** 1
$\qquad\qquad\qquad$ **else** 0

$MinCand_i \equiv \{P_j \in Cand_i \mid \forall P_t \in (Cand_i \setminus \{P_j\})[LostCand_j(P_t) = 0]\}$

$ChangeCand_i \equiv$ **if** $T_i = C \wedge a_i = \perp \wedge Cand_i \neq \emptyset \wedge$
$\qquad\qquad$ $\{(m_i = 0 \wedge (NumDom_i > 1 \vee L_{MinCand_i} > L_i)) \vee (m_i \neq 0 \wedge$
$\qquad\qquad$ $(\forall P_j \in N_i[m_j = 0 \vee L_j > L_i] \vee (c_i \neq 0 \wedge LostCand_i(MinCand_i) = 1))\}$
$\qquad\qquad$ **then** $MinCand_i$ **else** $\perp$

Fig. 1. Variables and Macro for each process P_i

Algorithm for process P_r:

Constant: $L_r := 0$; $F_r := P_r$; $T_r := C$; $m_r := 1$; $c_r := 0$; $d_r := 0$; $cds_r := 1$;

Actions

/* Request Start (This is the same as [10]) */

$1::$ $Start_r \rightarrow P_r.Req = \mathsf{ASK}$;

/* Request End (This is the same as [10])*/

$2::$ $End_r \rightarrow P_r.Req = \mathsf{OUT}$;

/* Vote */

$3::$ $a_r \neq ChangeCand_r \rightarrow a_r := ChangeCand_r$;

Algorithm for process $P_i \neq P_r$:

/* Error of tree (This is the same as [10]) */

$1::$ $\{T_{F_i} = E \vee L_{F_i} \geq L_i\} \wedge \{T_i = C \vee m_i = 0 \vee c_i \neq 0 \vee a_i \neq \perp \vee cds_i = 0\}$
       $\rightarrow T_i := E$; $m_i := 1$; $c_i := 0$; $a_i :=\perp$; $cds_i := 1$;

/* Join the MIS */

$2::$ $T_i = C \wedge m_i = 0 \wedge \{\forall P_j \in N_i[m_j = 0 \vee L_j > L_i] \vee (NumDom_i = 1 \wedge$
       $\exists P_j \in N_i[((L_j < L_i \wedge m_j \neq 0) \vee (L_j = L_i \wedge m_j = 2)) \wedge c_j \neq 0])\}$
       $\rightarrow m_i := 1$; $d_i := NumDom_i$; $c_i := 0$; $a_i :=\perp$; $cds_i := 1$;

/* Join the CDS */

$3::$ $T_i = C \wedge cds_i = 0 \wedge (m_i \neq 0 \vee \exists P_j \in N_i[F_j = P_i \wedge m_j \neq 0])$
       $\rightarrow cds_i := 1$;

/* Connect (This is the same as [10]) */

$4::$ $\exists P_j \in N_i[Req.j = \mathsf{REP} \wedge P_j = MinChPar_i \wedge (T_i = E \vee L_i - L_j > 1)]$
       $\rightarrow T_i := C$; $F_i := MinChPar_i$; $L_i := L_{F_i} + 1$; $m_i := 1$;
       $d_i := NumDom_i$; $c_i := 0$; $a_i :=\perp$; $cds_i := 1$; $Req_i := \mathsf{OUT}$;

/* Vote */

$5::$ $T_i = C \wedge (d_i \neq NumDom_i \vee c_i \neq WantLeave_i \vee a_i \neq ChangeCand_i)$
       $\rightarrow d_i := NumDom_i : c_i := WantLeave_i : a_i := ChangeCand_i :$

/* Prepare to leave the MIS */

$6::$ $T_i = C \wedge \forall P_j \in N_i[T_j = C \wedge |L_j - L_i| \leq 1] \wedge m_i = 1 \wedge a_i =\perp \wedge c_i \neq 0 \wedge$
       $\exists P_j \in N_i[m_j \neq 0 \wedge L_j \leq L_i] \wedge \exists P_j \in N_i[m_j = 0 \wedge d_j = 1 \wedge L_j = L_i]$
       $\wedge \forall P_j \in N_i[a_j = P_i \vee (m_j = 0 \wedge d_j = 1 \wedge L_j = L_i)]$
       $\rightarrow m_i := 2 :$

/* Leave the MIS */

$7::$ $T_i = C \wedge \forall P_j \in N_i[T_j = C \wedge |L_j - L_i| \leq 1] \wedge m_i \neq 0 \wedge a_i =\perp \wedge c_i \neq 0 \wedge$
       $\exists P_j \in N_i[m_j \neq 0 \wedge L_j \leq L_i] \wedge \forall P_j \in N_i[a_j = P_i \wedge (m_j \neq 0 \vee d_j > 1 \vee L_j < L_i)]$
       $\rightarrow m_i := 0$; $c_i := 0$; $d_i := NumDom_i :$

/* Leave the CDS */

$8::$ $T_i = C \wedge \forall P_j \in N_i[T_j = C \wedge |L_j - L_i| \leq 1] \wedge cds_i = 1 \wedge$
       $m_i = 0 \wedge \forall P_j \in N_i[F_j \neq P_i \vee m_j = 0]$
       $\rightarrow cds_i := 0$;

/* Request Start (This is the same as [10]) */

$9::$ $Start_i \rightarrow Req_i := \mathsf{ASK}$;

/* Request End (This is the same as [10]) */

$10::$ $End_i \rightarrow Req_i := \mathsf{OUT}$;

Fig. 2. CDS: A safe converging self-stabilizing approximation algorithm for the minimum CDS for each process P_i

Assume that $P_j \in N_i$ and $P_k \in N_i$ leave MIS simultaneously, that is, they execute action 7 in the same step. For P_j's execution of action 7, $\forall P_l \in N_j[a_l = P_j]$ must hold, that is, $a_i = P_j$. However, for P_k's execution of action 7, $a_i = P_k$ must hold. This is a contradiction. Therefore, (b) holds. □

Lemma 2. *Let γ be any configuration in Γ, and γ' be a configuration after any one round execution starting from γ. Then, for each P_i, we have $m_i \neq 0 \vee \exists P_j \in N_i[m_j \neq 0]$ in γ', and $m_i \neq 0 \vee \exists P_j \in N_i[m_j \neq 0]$ is closed after one round.*

Proof. We show that every process holds $m_i \neq 0 \vee \exists P_j \in N_i[m_j \neq 0]$ in γ'. For the contrary, we assume P_i holds $m_i = 0 \wedge \forall P_j \in N_i[m_j = 0]$ in γ'. Note that, because our algorithm is a conditional composition of QA and CDS, some processes may execute only QA in the first round. By the definition of algorithm, P_r holds $m_r = 1$ in γ'. If P_i holds $T_{F_i} = E \vee L_{F_i} \geq L_i \vee T_i = E$ in γ, P_i cannot execute QA by $GoodTGoodL_i$, and the value of m_i becomes 1 by action 1 in the first step. If P_i remains to hold $T_i = E$ in γ', $m_i = 1$ in γ'. If the value of T_i becomes C during one round execution, then P_i firstly executes action 4, and the value of m_i becomes 1. Therefore, we consider only processes with $T_i = C$ in γ' below.

Case 1: Consider the case that P_i holds $m_i = 0 \wedge \forall P_j \in N_i[m_j = 0]$ in γ and keeps this property during one round execution. Then, P_i holds $T_i = C$ in γ, is privileged in action 2 and cannot execute QA by $GoodDS_i$. Therefore, the value of m_i becomes 1 in its first step. This is a contradiction.

Case 2: Assume that every process holds $m_i \neq 0 \vee \exists P_j \in N_i[m_j \neq 0]$ in γ, hence $m_i = 0 \wedge \forall P_j \in N_i[m_j = 0]$ becomes true during the first round. First, we consider only processes with $T_i = C$ in γ.

Case 2-1: Consider the case that P_i holds $a_i \neq \bot \wedge d_i > 1 \wedge NumDom_i = 1 \wedge m_i = 0$ in γ. Let $P_j \in N_i$ be a neighbor with $m_j \neq 0$ pointed by a_i. Then, P_i is privileged in action 5 because $T_i = C \wedge d_i \neq NumDom_i$ in γ. Because $a_i \neq \bot \wedge d_i > 1 \wedge NumDom_i = 1 \wedge m_i = 0$, P_i cannot execute QA by $Cond_i$. Therefore, if P_i executes action 5 as its first step before P_j leaves, then d_i is updated to 1. If $L_j \leq L_i$, then P_j cannot leave by the definition of action 7, this is a contradiction. If $L_j > L_i$, then after P_j leaves, there is a neighbor P_k of P_i with $m_k \neq 0 \wedge L_k \leq L_i$ because $NumDom_i = 1$, this is a contradiction. If the value of m_j becomes 0 by action 7 before P_i executes its first step, then $m_i = 0 \wedge \forall P_j \in N_i[m_j = 0]$ may hold when $L_j \leq L_i$. However, then P_i did not execute its first step, is privileged in action 2, and cannot execute QA by $GoodDS_i$. Therefore, during the first round, P_i executes action 2, then the value of m_i becomes 1. Therefore, in γ', $m_i \neq 0 \vee \exists P_j \in N_i[m_j \neq 0]$ holds. This is a contradiction. Note that, such a process P_i is only in the initial configuration because P_i's neighbors not pointed by a_i cannot leave by action 7 and P_i cannot point to P_j with $L_j \leq L_i$ by a_i when $NumDom_i = 1 \wedge m_i = 0$ by action 5.

Case 2-2: Consider the case that P_i holds $a_i = \bot \vee d_i \leq 1 \vee NumDom_i \neq 1 \vee m_i \neq 0$ in γ. By the definition of algorithm, if $m_i \neq 0 \wedge \forall P_j \in N_i[m_j = 0]$, then the value of m_i cannot become 0. By lemma 1(a), we consider a process P_i with $T_i = C \wedge m_i = 0 \wedge \{a_i = \bot \vee d_i \leq 1 \vee NumDom_i > 1\}$ in γ. For the assumption, all neighbors $P_s \in N_i$ with $m_s \neq 0$ must change the value of m_s to 0 during the first round. By lemma 1(b), the neighbors P_s of P_i leave MIS one by one. Consider when the number of neighbors

P_s of P_i with $m_s \neq 0 \wedge L_s \leq L_i$ becomes only one, then $NumDom_i = 1$. For P_s's execution of action 7, $\forall P_l \in N_s[a_l = P_s]$ must hold. Therefore, P_i must hold $a_i = P_s$ when P_s executes action 7.

- If $NumDom_i > 1$ in γ, then P_i points to other neighbor P_q when P_q leaves. Therefore, P_i updates the value of a_i by action 5 after P_q leaves before P_s leaves. Then, by the action 5, the value of d_i is updated and becomes 1. For P_s's execution of action 7, $\forall P_l \in N_s[a_l = P_s \wedge (m_l \neq 0 \vee d_l > 1 \vee L_l < L_s)]$ must hold. Because $m_i = 0$, $d_i = 1$ and $L_s \leq L_i$, P_s cannot execute action 7. This is a contradiction.
- If $d_i \leq 1$ in γ, then P_s cannot execute action7. This is a contradiction.
- If $NumDom_i = 1 \wedge a_i = \perp$ in γ, then P_i updates the value of a_i by action 5 for P_s's execution of action 7. Then, by the action 5, the value of d_i is updated to 1. For P_s's execution of action 7, $\forall P_l \in N_s[a_l = P_s \wedge (m_l \neq 0 \vee d_l > 1 \vee L_l < L_s)]$ must hold. Because $m_i = 0$, $d_i = 1$ and $L_s \leq L_i$, P_s cannot execute action 7. This is a contradiction.

If $T_i = E$ in γ and $T_i = C$ in γ', then during the first round, P_i executes action 4 and $m_i = 1$ holds. By the above discussion, P_i cannot become $m_i = 0 \wedge \forall P_j \in N_i[m_j = 0]$.

Therefore, in γ', every process holds $m_i \neq 0 \vee \exists P_j \in N_i[m_j \neq 0]$. Additionally, after one round execution, $m_i \neq 0 \vee \exists P_j \in N_i[m_j \neq 0]$ is closed by the proof of **Case 2**.   □

Lemma 3. *(One-round convergence to Λ_F) Let γ be any configuration in Γ, and γ' be a configuration after any one round execution starting from γ. Then, we have $\gamma' \in \Lambda_F$.*

Proof. By the definition of algorithm, P_r holds $m_r = 1 \wedge cds_r = 1$ in γ'. If P_i holds $T_{F_i} = E \vee L_{F_i} \geq L_i \vee T_i = E$ in γ, then by $GoodTGoodL_i$, P_i cannot execute **QA**. Then, P_i executes action 1 in its first step, and is with $m_i = 1$ and $cds_i = 1$ in γ' if P_i remains to hold $T_i = E$ in γ'. If the value of T_i becomes C during one round execution, then P_i firstly executes action 4, and the both value of m_i and cds_i become 1.

To show this lemma, for the contrary, we assume that $Doms(\gamma')$ is not a dominating set, then there is a process P_i with $cds_i = 0 \wedge \forall P_j \in N_i[cds_j = 0]$ in γ'. Then, $T_i = C$ holds. Because $m_i \neq 0 \vee \exists P_j \in N_i[m_j \neq 0]$ in γ' by lemma 2, if $cds_i = 1$ holds for each P_i with $m_i \neq 0$ in γ', then $cds_i = 1 \vee \exists P_j \in N_i[cds_j = 1]$ holds, this is a contradiction. Hence, there is a process P_i with $cds_i = 0 \wedge m_i \neq 0 \wedge T_i = C$ in γ'. However, then P_i cannot execute **QA** by $GoodDS_i$ and is privileged in action 3. Therefore, if P_i did not execute its first step, and is not privileged in actions 1 and 2, then the value of cds_i becomes 1 by action 3 in its first step. If P_i executes action 1 or 2 as its first step, then the value of cds_i becomes 1 in its first step. If P_i executes other actions as its first step, then before the first step, $m_i \neq 0 \wedge cds_i = 0$ holds because there is no action to make P_i to $cds_i = 0 \wedge m_i \neq 0$ by the definition of **CDS**. This is a contradiction because the priority of action 3 is higher than other actions. Therefore, lemma holds.   □

By the proof of lemmas 2 and 3, we can derive the following lemma.

Lemma 4. *(Closure of Λ_F) Let γ be any configuration in Λ_F, and γ' be any configuration after any execution starting from γ. Then, we have $\gamma' \in \Lambda_F$.*

Lemma 5. *If no process is privileged in configuration* γ, *$MIS(\gamma)$ is an MIS constructed by paving on a BFS tree.*

Proof. Let γ be a configuration in which no process is privileged. By the definition of actions 1, 4, 9 and 10 and the constant of P_r, it is clear that the value of L_i, for each P_i, represents the distance from P_r in γ [10]. By other actions, the value of F_i and L_i are not changed. This means that a BFS tree T is computed in γ. By [10], every process has $T_i = C$ in γ.

Assume that $MIS(\gamma)$ is not an MIS constructed by paving on T in γ. Then, $MIS(\gamma)$ is not an independent set (**Case A**), or is an independent set but it is not maximal (**Case B**), or is an MIS but it is not constructed by paving on T (**Case C**).

First, we consider **Case A**, *i.e.*, there are two processes P_i and $P_j \in N_i$ in $MIS(\gamma)$. This means that $m_i \neq 0 \land \exists P_j \in N_i[m_j \neq 0]$ holds at P_i in γ. By the definition of $WantLeave$, if $L_i > L_j$ (resp. $L_j > L_i$, $L_i = L_j$), then we have $c_i = 2$ (resp. $c_j = 2$, $c_i = c_j = 1$) because no process is privileged in action 5. Then, by the definition of $Cand$, $P_i \in Cand_j$ (resp. $P_j \in Cand_i$, $P_i \in Cand_j$ and $P_j \in Cand_i$). By the definition of $LostCand$, either $LostCand_j(P_i) = 1$ or $LostCand_i(P_j) = 1$ can be true, they conflict with each other. Without loss of generality, we consider the case that $P_i \in Cand_j$ and $LostCand_j(P_i) = 1$. Then, because $LostCand_i(P_j) = 0$, $a_i = \perp$ holds by the guard of action 5 in γ. If $\forall P_k \in N_i[a_k = P_i \land (m_k \neq 0 \lor d_k > 1 \lor L_k < L_i)]$, then P_i is privileged in action 7, this is a contradiction. We consider the case that $\exists P_k \in N_i[a_k \neq P_i \lor (m_k = 0 \land d_k \leq 1 \land L_k \geq L_i)]$.

Case A1: Consider the case that $\exists P_k \in N_i[m_k = 0 \land d_k \leq 1 \land L_k \geq L_i]$, let P_k be such a process. Because $L_k \geq L_i$ and $m_i \neq 0$, $NumDom_k \neq 0$ holds. If $d_k = 0$, then P_k is privileged in action 5, this is a contradiction. If $d_k = 1$ and $L_k > L_i$, then P_k is privileged in action 2 because $m_i \neq 0 \land c_i \neq 0$, this is a contradiction. If $d_k = 1$ and $L_k = L_i$, and if all other neighbors of P_i than P_k select P_i as their a, then by action 6, $m_i = 2$. Then, P_k is privileged in action 2, this is a contradiction. If $d_k = 1$ and $L_k = L_i$, and if there is a neighbor P_l of P_i which holds $a_l = \perp$, then P_l is privileged in action 5 because P_i is in their $Cand_l$. If $d_k = 1$ and $L_k = L_i$, and if there is a neighbor P_l of P_i which selects other neighbor than P_i as a_l, we can find a process which is privileged in action 5 or 7 by the following a directed path defined by the value of a pointers, because each process P_a points to a neighbor P_b only when P_a loses to P_b by $LostCand_a(P_b)$.

Case A2: Otherwise, we consider the case that $\forall P_k \in N_i[m_k \neq 0 \lor d_k > 1 \lor L_k < L_i] \land \exists P_k \in N_i[a_k \neq P_i]$, let P_k be a process with $a_k \neq P_i$. If $m_k \neq 0$ (*i.e.*, $P_k = P_j$), by the definition of $ChangeCand_k$, $a_k \neq \perp$ holds because $P_i \in Cand_k$ and $LostCand_k(P_i) = 1$. If $m_k = 0 \land L_k < L_i$, by the definition of $ChangeCand_k$, $a_k \neq \perp$ holds because $P_i \in Cand_k$. If $m_k = 0 \land L_k \geq L_i \land d_k > 1$, then $NumDom_k = d_k > 1$ by action 5, that is, $a_k \neq \perp$ holds. Therefore, in every case, $a_k \neq \perp$. Because $a_k \neq P_i$, there is a neighbor P_q of P_k and $a_k = P_q \land c_q \neq 0 \land m_q \neq 0$ holds by the definition of $ChangeCand_k$. If all neighbors P_l of P_q select P_q as their a_l, then P_q is privileged in action 7, this is a contradiction. If there is a neighbor P_l of P_q which holds $a_l \neq P_q$, then P_l is privileged in action 5 because $P_q \in Cand_l$, or we can find a process which is privileged in action 5 or 7 by the following a directed path defined by the value of a pointers. This is a contradiction.

Next, we assume **Case B**. However, by lemma 2, there is no process such that $m_i = 0 \wedge \forall P_j \in N_i[m_j = 0]$ holds, *i.e.*, $MIS(\gamma)$ is a dominating set. Therefore, $MIS(\gamma)$ is a dominating set and an independent set in γ. According to Theorem 1, this is a contradiction.

Finally, we assume **Case C**. Then, there are two processes $P_i \neq P_r$ and $P_j \in N_i$ such that $m_i \neq 0 \wedge m_j = 0 \wedge L_j = L_i - 1$, and there is no neighbor $P_k \in N_j$ such that $m_k \neq 0 \wedge L_k \leq L_j$ in γ. Then, $\forall P_k \in N_j[m_k = 0 \vee L_k > L_j]$ holds at P_j, and P_j is privileged in action 2. This is a contradiction.

Therefore, $MIS(\gamma)$ is an MIS constructed by paving on T. $\qquad\qquad\qquad$ □

Lemma 6. *If no process is privileged in configuration γ, $\gamma \in \Lambda_O$.*

Proof. We show that $Doms(\gamma)$ is a CDS-tree. By the definition of constant of P_r and the definition of action 4, it is clear that the value of F_i, for each P_i, represents a father of P_i on a BFS tree T in γ. By Lemma 5, the set $\{P_i \mid m_i \neq 0\}$ is an MIS constructed by paving on T in γ. Therefore, by the definition of the CDS-tree, if $Doms(\gamma) = (\{P_i \mid m_i \neq 0\} \cup \{P_j \mid F_i = P_j \wedge m_i \neq 0\})$, $\gamma \in \Lambda_O$. To show the contraposition, we assume $Doms(\gamma) \neq (\{P_i \mid m_i \neq 0\} \cup \{P_j \mid F_i = P_j \wedge m_i \neq 0\})$.

First, assume that $\{P_i \mid m_i \neq 0\} \not\subseteq Doms(\gamma)$, *i.e.*, there is a process P_i such that $m_i \neq 0 \wedge cds_i = 0$. Because of the definition of constant of P_r, P_i is not P_r. Then, P_i is privileged in action 3 in γ. This is a contradiction.

Next, assume that $\{P_j \mid F_i = P_j \wedge m_i \neq 0\} \not\subseteq Doms(\gamma)$, *i.e.*, there are two processes P_i and $P_j \in N_i$ such that $m_i \neq 0 \wedge cds_j = 0 \wedge F_i = P_j$. Because $\{P_i \mid m_i \neq 0\}$ is a MIS, $m_j = 0$ holds at P_j. Then, in P_j, $m_j = 0 \wedge \exists P_i \in N_j[F_i = P_j \wedge m_i \neq 0]$ holds, *i.e.*, P_j is privileged in action 3 in γ. This is a contradiction.

Finally, assume that $Doms(\gamma)$ is a CDS, but not a CDS-tree, *i.e.*, $Doms(\gamma) \supsetneq (\{P_i \mid m_i \neq 0\} \cup \{P_j \mid F_i = P_j \wedge m_i \neq 0\})$. Then, there is a process P_i such that $cds_i = 1$, but neither P_i nor its children are members of MIS. That is, $m_i = 0 \wedge \forall P_j \in N_i[F_j \neq P_i \vee m_j = 0]$ holds at P_i. Then, P_i is privileged in action 8 in γ. This is a contradiction.

Therefore, if no process is privileged in configuration γ, $\gamma \in \Lambda_O$. $\qquad\qquad$ □

Lemma 7. *(Convergence to Λ_O) For any configuration $\gamma_0 \in \Lambda_F$ and any computation starting from γ_0, eventually no process is privileged.*

Proof. For each P_i, the value of variables L_i, F_i, T_i and Req_i are changed only by actions 1, 4, 9 and 10, and these actions are same as [10]. By [10], every process eventually holds $T_i = C \wedge \forall P_j \in N_i[T_j = C \wedge |L_j - L_i| \leq 1] \wedge Req_i = \mathsf{OUT}$, and L_i and F_i eventually represent a BFS tree.

First, we show that, after $T_i = C \wedge \forall P_j \in N_i[T_j = C \wedge |L_j - L_i| \leq 1]$ holds in γ_0, if processes P_j with $L_j < L_i$ don't change the value of any other variables than a_j, then P_i can change the value of m_i at most three times. The value of m_i is changed by actions 2, 6 and 7. Action 2 is joining MIS and action 7 is leaving MIS. The action 6 is a preparation of execution of action 7, *i.e.*, some execution of action 7 need the execution of action 6 before itself. If each process P_i changes the value of m_i forever, then P_i executes action 2 and action 7 (or a pair of actions 6 and 7) repeatedly.

Now, we show that, if P_i executes action 2 in γ_0, then after that, P_i can execute neither action 6 nor 7. For the contrary, we assume P_i executes actions 6 or 7 after action 2 in γ_0. If each process P_l with $L_l < L_i$ holds $c_l \neq 0$, then P_i holds $a_i = P_l$ by action 5 before action 7 because the priority of action 5 is higher than action 7. Therefore, for P_i's execution of action 7 after action 2, each process P_l with $L_l < L_i$ holds $c_l = 0$. Before P_i executes action 2, $m_i = 0 \wedge \exists P_j \in N_i[m_j \neq 0 \wedge L_j \leq L_i]$ in γ_0 by lemma 2. After P_i executes action 2, P_i and $P_j \in N_i$ satisfy the following property: $m_i = 1 \wedge c_i = 0 \wedge a_i = \perp \wedge NumDom_i = 1 \wedge \exists P_j \in N_i[L_j = L_i \wedge m_j = 2 \wedge c_j \neq 0]$ because $P_l \in N_i$ with $L_l < L_i$ holds $c_l = 0$. Let P_j be the neighbor of P_i with $L_j = L_i \wedge m_j = 2 \wedge c_j \neq 0$. For P_i's execution of action 6 or 7 after that, P_i has to hold $a_i = \perp$ and $c_i \neq 0$. Because P_i holds $m_i = 1$, $a_i = \perp$ and $c_i = 0$ after its execution of action 2, before action 6 or 7, P_i has to execute action 5. However, by action 5, $c_i = 1$ holds because $NumDom_i = 1$ and $L_j = L_i$. That is, $LostCand_i(P_j) = 1$ is true because $L_j = L_i \wedge \{c_i < c_j \vee (c_i = c_j \wedge m_i < m_j)\}$. Therefore, P_i updates $a_i = P_j$ by action 5. Then, P_j executes action 7, and then $\forall P_j \in N_i[m_j = 0 \vee L_j > L_i]$ holds. Therefore, P_i cannot execute both of actions 6 and 7. This is a contradiction. Therefore, after action 2 in γ_0, P_i cannot execute actions 6 and 7.

Before the action 2 in γ_0, P_i may execute action 7 or a pair of actions 6 and 7. Therefore, after $T_i = C \wedge \forall P_j \in N_i[T_j = C \wedge |L_j - L_i| \leq 1]$ holds, if processes P_j with $L_j < L_i$ don't change the value of any variables except a_j, then P_i can change the value of m_i at most three times.

By the definition of algorithm CDS, the root process cannot change the value of $m_r = 1$ and $c_r = 0$. Therefore, the processes P_i with $L_i = 1$ cannot change the value of m_i infinitely often. Because the processes P_i with $L_i = h$ cannot change the value of m_i infinitely often, the processes P_j with $L_j = h+1$ cannot change the value of m_k. By the definition of other variables d_i, c_i a_i and cds_i, it is clear that their value cannot be changed infinitely often because the value of m of itself and neighbors cannot be changed infinitely often. Lemma holds.   □

From lemmas 6 and 7, we can derive the following theorem.

Theorem 4. ASC-CDS *is safely converging self-stabilizing with respect to* (Λ_F, Λ_O) *in arbitrary networks. Additionally,* ASC-CDS *is* $(6 + \epsilon)$-*approximation algorithm for the minimum CDS in unit disk graphs.*

For each P_i, the value of variables L_i, F_i, T_i and Req_i are changed only by actions 1, 4, 9 and 10. These actions are same as [10] whose time complexity is $O(n^6)$ steps. Let J be the maximum number of times any process executes action 2 in any computation. We can represent the maximum number of execution of each other action by J. Then, we can derive the following lemma.

Lemma 8. *For any configuration* γ_0 *and any computation from* γ_0, $O(n^6 + J\Delta^2)$ *steps are needed by algorithm* ASC-CDS *until every process is not privileged.*

Each process P_i can execute action 2 in $O(k)$ steps, where k is the height of a BFS tree. Because $k < n$, we can derive the following lemma.

Lemma 9. *For any configuration* γ_0 *and any computation from* γ_0, *the number of execution of action 2 is* $O(n^2)$ *steps until every process is not privileged.*

The round complexity of [10] is $O(d^2)$ rounds. For each leaving MIS, CDS needs $O(1)$ rounds.

Lemma 10. *For any configuration γ_0 and any computation from γ_0, the second convergence time is $O(\max\{d^2, n\})$ rounds.*

From lemmas 3, 8, 9 and 10, we derive the following theorem.

Theorem 5. *The first convergence time is at most 1 round, and the second convergence time is $O(\max\{d^2, n\})$ rounds, $O(n^6)$ steps.*

5 Conclusion

In this paper, we proposed an asynchronous self-stabilizing approximation algorithm for the minimum CDS with safe convergence in unit disk graphs. As an application of the proposed algorithm, a minimum CDS is a virtual backbone in ad hoc or sensor networks. Our algorithm converges to a safe configuration in a round, and to an optimal configuration in $O(\max\{d^2, n\})$ rounds, $O(n^6)$ steps. Our algorithm guarantees that the size of the solution in unit disk graphs is at most $6|D_{opt}| + 5$. Development of a safely converging self-stabilizing approximation algorithm with better approximation ratio or better time complexity is left for future work.

References

1. Clark, B.N., Colbourn, C.J., Johnson, D.S.: Unit disk graphs. Discrete Mathematics 86(1-3), 165–177 (1990)
2. Dijkstra, E.W.: Self-stabilizing systems in spite of distributed control. Communications of the ACM 17(11), 643–644 (1974)
3. Kakuagwa, H., Masuzawa, T.: A self-stabilizing minimal dominating set algorithm with safe convergence. In: Proceedings of the 8th IPDPS Workshop on Advances in Parallel and Distributed Computational Model, p. 263 (2006)
4. Jain, A., Gupta, A.: A distributed self-stabilizing algorithm for finding a connected dominating set in a graph. In: Proceedings of the 6th International Conference on Parallel and Distributed Computing, Applications and Technologies, pp. 615–619 (2005)
5. Drabkin, V., Friedman, R., Gradinariu, M.: Self-stabilizing wireless connected overlays. In: Shvartsman, A. (ed.) OPODIS 2006. LNCS, vol. 4305, pp. 425–439. Springer, Heidelberg (2006)
6. Kamei, S., Kakugawa, H.: A self-stabilizing distributed approximation algorithm for the minimum connected dominating set. In: Proceedings of the 9th IPDPS Workshop on Advances in Parallel and Distributed Computational Models, p. 224 (2007)
7. Kamei, S., Kakugawa, H.: A self-stabilizing 6-approximation for the minimum connected dominating set with safe convergence in unit disk graph. Theoretical Computer Science 428, 80–90 (2012)
8. Herman, T.: Phase clocks for transient fault repair. IEEE Transactions on Parallel and Distributed Systems 11(10), 1048–1057 (2000)
9. Berge, C.: Theory of Graphs and its Applications. Methuen (1962)
10. Cournier, A., Rovedakis, S., Villain, V.: The first fully polynomial stabilizing algorithm for bfs tree construction. In: Fernàndez Anta, A., Lipari, G., Roy, M. (eds.) OPODIS 2011. LNCS, vol. 7109, pp. 159–174. Springer, Heidelberg (2011)
11. Wan, P.J., Alzoubi, K.M., Frieder, O.: Distributed construction of connected dominating set in wireless ad hoc networks. Mobile Networks and Applications 9(2), 141–149 (2004)

Automated Addition of Fault-Tolerance under Synchronous Semantics

Yiyan Lin[1], Borzoo Bonakdarpour[2], and Sandeep Kulkarni[1]

[1] Michigan State University
[2] University of Waterloo

Abstract. We focus on the problem of automated *model repair* for *synchronous* systems. Model repair focuses on revising a model, so that it satisfies a new property while preserving its existing properties. While the problem of model repair has been studied previously in the context of interleaving semantics, we argue that the corresponding solutions are not applicable for several problems encountered in embedded systems. Specifically, in interleaving semantics, only one of the components executes in a given step. On the contrary, in many commonly considered distributed embedded systems, several components can execute synchronously.

We present a polynomial-time sound and complete algorithm for repairing models in *synchronous* semantics (also called *maximum parallelism* semantics). We show that our approach allows us to design *fault-tolerant* systems, where after the occurrence of faults, the system recovers to its normal behavior within a given number of steps. We illustrate our approach by synthesizing a fault-tolerant group membership protocol and a protocol for cache coherence.

1 Introduction

Traditionally, there are two main approaches for providing assurance about correctness of a system: (1) *verifying* that the system meets a desired set of properties (e.g., fault-tolerance), or (2) *synthesizing* the system automatically from scratch in such a way that it meets the desired properties. A disadvantage of the former is that it requires the designer to construct the fault-tolerant model manually. This, in turn, exposes the risk of violating existing properties of the system; i.e., the designer damages the existing sound behavior while adding fault-tolerance to the original model. A disadvantage of the latter is that it may not provide reuse of the existing model. Moreover, depending upon the requirements in the fault-free setting, the latter problem may be undecidable or suffer from high complexity.

An intermediate approach, *model repair*, can alleviate these disadvantages. Specifically, in model repair, one begins with an existing model and subsequently *adds* one or more properties (e.g., safety, fault-tolerance, or timing constraints). More formally, let $\mathcal{M}$ be a model, Σ be a specification (in some logic such as the Linear Temporal Logic), and Π be a (new) property, where $\mathcal{M}$ satisfies Σ but does not satisfy Π. A model repair algorithm takes $\mathcal{M}$, Σ, and Π as input and generates a model $\mathcal{M}'$, so that $\mathcal{M}'$ satisfies Σ and Π simultaneously. Thus, model repair algorithms enhance the robustness of the

T. Higashino et al. (Eds.): SSS 2013, LNCS 8255, pp. 266–280, 2013.

resulting model, while minimizing penalties to performance and overhead [5]; i.e., such algorithms *fix* errors with minimal intervention in the original behavior of the model.

By *interleaving semantics* [18] [12], we mean that in the execution of the program, in every step, one component/process is non-deterministically chosen for execution. The notion of interleaving semantics is inspired by processes that communicate via asynchronous message passing. It has also been extended to shared memory programs where it is used as an abstraction to simplify program design and its proof. In such shared memory programs, it is anticipated that some synchronization would be added during implementation to ensure that action execution is serialized. It has also been extended to component-based programs [7] where the program is viewed from a global state perspective and actions where multiple components collaborate can be viewed as a transition in the global state space that changes the states of multiple processes at once. Likewise, any transition in global state space can be viewed as an interaction among (possibly all) components.

By contrast, *synchronous semantics* (also considered maximum parallelism semantics, e.g. [15]) considered in this paper is motivated by timed execution. Intuitively[1], one step in this system can be viewed as two phases, a read phase and the update phase. In the read phase, each component obtains the states of other components it interacts with. Then, in the update phase, each component utilizes this information to update its state. Synchronous semantics is thus useful in permitting a component to execute independently (and coordinating only on a *clock-tick*). And, it also captures the concurrent execution more precisely. Moreover, since it abstracts modeling of explicit time, it is beneficial in reducing the cost of verification and repair. Also, synchronous semantics is closer to timed execution.

However, in the context of *synchronous semantics*, the opportunities and challenges of the problem has not been addressed. Repairing a model in synchronous semantics creates a new challenge in that if some process transition is removed during repair, then it can introduce new behaviors to the original system. This is due to the fact that if some process, say j, does not execute its transition, then the system execution includes a new global transition, where all processes except j execute. And, such a transition is not part of the original program. This scenario does not occur in interleaving semantics as removal of one process transition only removes the corresponding behavior from the overall system behavior. This scenario also does not occur in systems (e.g., [7], [14] where components utilize explicit coordination.

Contributions

1. We present polynomial-time sound and complete algorithms for repair of models in synchronous semantics to provide three different levels of fault-tolerance, namely, *failsafe*, *nonmasking*, and *masking*. Additionally, the algorithms can be used to ensure that when faults stop occurring the program recovers to its set of legitimate states within a given number of steps.

---

[1] Since the term synchronous semantics has been used with different interpretations in the literature, we note that our definition of synchronous semantics is one given in Definition 3 that captures this intuition.

2. We illustrate our algorithm using a round-based group membership protocol as well as a cache coherence protocol. We also present the results of our experiments on the implementation of the aforementioned algorithms.

2   Modeling Synchronous Programs

2.1   Programs in Synchronous Semantics

Definition 1. A **program** p is a tuple $\langle V_p, R_p \rangle$, where V_p is a set of variables and R_p is a set of processes.

Each variable in V_p is associated with a domain. A state of a program p is obtained by assigning each variable in V_p a value from its respective domain. The set of all possible states of p is called the state space of p (denoted by S_p). Given a variable $x \in V_p$ and a state $s \in S_p$, $x(s)$ denotes the value of x in s.

Definition 2. Let $p = \langle V_p, R_p \rangle$ be a program. A **process** j in R_p is specified as a tuple $\langle W_j, \delta_j \rangle$, where $W_j \subseteq V_p$, and $\delta_j \subseteq S_p \times S_p$.

In the above definition of a process, W_j denotes the variables that process j is allowed to write. In other words, δ_j satisfies the following condition:

$$(s_0, s_1) \in \delta_j \quad \Rightarrow \quad \forall x : x \notin W_j : x(s_0) = x(s_1)$$

Given any two processes j and k, we require that W_j and W_k are disjoint. In addition, for all processes their writable variables are exhaustive; i.e., $\bigcup_{l \in R_p} W_l = V_p$.

Definition 3. Let $p = \langle V_p, R_p \rangle$ be a program, $j = \langle W_j, \delta_j \rangle$ be a process in R_p, and s_0 and s_1 be two states in S_p. Then, (s_0, s_1) is a transition of p in **synchronous semantics** iff the following condition is satisfied:

$$\forall j \in R_p(\,(\exists s_j \in S_p : (s_0, s_j) \in \delta_j \wedge \forall x \in W_j : x(s_1) = x(s_j)) \vee$$
$$(\forall s_j \in S_p : (s_0, s_j) \notin \delta_j \wedge \forall x \in W_j : x(s_0) = x(s_1)))$$

Definition 4. Let $p = \langle V_p, R_p \rangle$ be a program, $j = \langle W_j, \delta_j \rangle$ be a process in R_p, and s_0 and s_1 be two states in S_p. Then, (s_0, s_1) is a transition of p in **interleaving semantics** iff the following condition is satisfied:

$$(\exists j \in R_p : (s_0, s_1) \in \delta_j) \vee ((s_0 = s_1) \wedge \forall j \in R_p : \forall s_j \in S_p : (s_0, s_j) \notin \delta_j)$$

To illustrate the synchronous and interleaving semantics, consider a program, say p_{jk}, where $V_{jk} = \{x, y\}$ with domain $\{0, 1\}$ and $R_{jk} = \{j, k\}$. Thus, the state space of the program is $S_{p_{jk}} = \{00, 01, 10, 11\}$, where the digits denote the values of x and y, respectively. Moreover, process j can write variable x and process k can write variable y. Each process includes transitions that check if the value of x and y are different. If they are different, then the process tries to make them the same by toggling the value of its variable. Thus, the set of transitions of processes j and k are δ_j and δ_k respectively, where $\delta_j = \{(01, 11), (10, 00)\}$ and $\delta_k = \{(01, 00), (10, 11)\}$. Now, transitions of p_{jk} in synchronous semantics are $(01, 10)$, $(10, 01)$, $(00, 00)$, and $(11, 11)$. In inter-leaving semantics, the transitions are $(01, 00)$, $(01, 11)$, $(10, 00)$, $(10, 11)$, $(00, 00)$, and $(11, 11)$.

Notations. We use δ_p to denote the transitions of program p. For the convenience of writing, we use $(s_0, s_1) = \delta_j^1 \cdot \delta_k^1 \cdots$ to denote the transition, where transition δ_j^1 is enabled in process j, transition δ_k^1 is enabled in process k, and so on. If some process, say l, is not specified in this list, then the state of l remains unchanged in transition (s_0, s_1). This is possible only if δ_l does not include any transition that originates in state s_0; i.e., $\forall s_1 \in S_p : (s_0, s_1) \notin \delta_l$. In addition, we introduce the notation $\delta_j \times \delta_k \times \cdots$, where

$$\delta_j \times \delta_k \times \cdots = \{\delta_j^{i_1} \cdot \delta_k^{i_2} \cdots \mid \delta_j^{i_1} \in \delta_j \wedge \delta_k^{i_2} \in \delta_k \wedge \cdots\}$$

to denote a set of program transitions in which each process choose to execute one of its transitions.

Running example. We utilize a protocol to reach agreement on *Processor Group Membership* [11] as a running example throughout the paper. The protocol aims to provide each processor with a consistent membership list of processors in its processor-group. In addition, the protocol tolerates certain faults (e.g., communication delays, processor crashes) in a synchronous distributed system. A processor joins an existing group in three rounds. In the first round, the processor that wants to join broadcasts a *newgroup* message. Due to synchronous nature of the system, in the absence of faults, this message is received by others in the next step. In the second round, upon receiving the *newgroup* message, all processors in the group broadcast a *present* message (to show the willingness of forming a new group with the new processor). Finally, in the last round, all processors in the group recompute their membership list.

We model each processor in the protocol as a process. To compactly represent the set transitions of a process, we utilize *guarded commands* (also called *actions*) of the form:

$$process\ j: \quad guard \quad \longrightarrow \quad statement_1;\ statement_2;\ \ldots;$$

where *guard* is a state predicate over program variables and each *statement*$_i$ is an assignment operations over those variables. This guarded command compactly represents the transitions $\{(s_0, s_1) \mid guard$ is true in s_0 and s_1 is obtained by executing each *statement*$_i$ sequentially from s_0 in one atomic step$\}$.

We describe the protocol based on an instance composed of four processes, namely i, j, k, and l. For brevity of the model, instead of modeling explicit message passing, we use some globally readable variables to denote a broadcast message. Thus, the variables of process j in the program are (1) *joined.j* : $\{true, false\}$, that denotes whether j is joined to a group, (2) *member.j* : set of processors regarded by j as members in its group, (3) *newgroup.j* : $\{true, false\}$, that denotes whether j is interested in joining the group, (4) *present.j* : $\{true, false\}$, that denotes whether j sent a present message in the current round, and (5) *skipped.j* : $\{true, false\}$, used due to the fact that the process that sends the newgroup message should not execute in round 2.

The rounds of the protocol are as shown in Table 1. Specifically, in the first round, any process (if not joined) is allowed to set its *newgroup* to *true* if all the processes'

Table 1. Processor group membership protocol

round 1: $(j$ wants to join the group$) \land \neg joined.j \land_{p \in \{i,j,k,l\}} \neg newgroup.p$
$\longrightarrow \quad newgroup.j := true; \; skipped.j := true;$

round 2: $\begin{cases} \exists p \in \{i,j,k,l\} : newgroup.p \land joined.j \longrightarrow & present.j := true; \\ newgroup.j \land skipped.j & \longrightarrow \quad skipped.j := false; \end{cases}$

round 3: $\begin{cases} \neg joined.j \land newgroup.j \land \neg skipped.j \longrightarrow joined.j & := true; \\ \quad\quad member.j & := \{p \mid present.p = true\} \\ & \quad \cup \{q \mid newgroup.q = true\}; \\ \quad\quad newgroup.j & := false; \\ joined.j \longrightarrow \quad\quad member.j & := \{p \mid present.p = true\} \\ & \quad \cup \{q \mid newgroup.q = true\}; \\ \quad\quad present.j & := false \end{cases}$

newgroup are *false*. The guard of this action includes the constraint "j wants to join the group". This constraint is set to true by the application using the group membership protocol. Note that under synchronous semantics, this action ensures that several processes can request to join the group at the same time. However, until the status of these processes is determined in round 3, another process cannot send a newgroup message. In the second round, all the joined processes show their willingness of forming a group by setting their *present* variable to *true*. The process that sent the newgroup message should not execute in round 2. To model this, the variable *skipped.j* (which is set to *true* in round 1) is reset to *false* in round 2. Finally, in the third round, all the processes enabled in either round 1 or round 2 compute the members as those whose *present* or *newgroup* is true. In addition, the process whose *newgroup* is true mark its *joined* to true and *newgroup* to false simply denoting there is no need to broadcast *newgroup* message forever. Likewise, a process that has already joined the group sets it back to false and waits for other processes to join.

2.2   Specifications

Based on the definition of a program and its different execution semantics, we now define the notion of specification and what it means for a program to satisfy a specification. In the rest of the section, we assume that S_p denotes the state space of program p. And, δ_p denotes the transitions of program p.

Definition 5. *A **state predicate** of p is any subset of S_p.*

Definition 6. *A state predicate S is **closed** in p (respectively, δ_p) iff $\forall(s_0, s_1) \in \delta_p : (s_0 \in S \Rightarrow s_1 \in S)$.*

Definition 7. *A sequence of states, $\sigma = \langle s_0, s_1, \cdots \rangle$ is a **computation** of p iff (1) $\forall j : 0 < j < length(\sigma) : (s_{j-1}, s_j) \in \delta_p$, and (2) if σ is finite and terminates in state s_l, then there does not exist a state s, such that $(s_l, s) \in \delta_p$.*

Following Alpern and Schneider [1], we let the specification of a program consist of *safety properties* and *liveness properties*. Intuitively, a safety property characterizes "bad things" by a set of transitions that the program should not execute.

Definition 8. *A **safety property** is denoted as Sf_p, where $Sf_p \subseteq S_p \times S_p$. A computation $\sigma = \langle s_0, s_1, \cdots \rangle$ **satisfies** the safety property Sf_p iff $\forall j : 0 < j < length(\sigma) : (s_{j-1}, s_j) \notin Sf_p$.*

A liveness property, on the other hand, denotes "good thing" eventually happens during program execution. We, in particular, use *leads-to* properties (denoted $\mathcal{L} \rightsquigarrow \mathcal{T}$) to represent liveness, where both $\mathcal{L}$ and $\mathcal{T}$ are state predicates. Specifically,

Definition 9. *A **liveness property** is of the form $Lv \equiv \bigwedge_i \mathcal{L}_i \rightsquigarrow \mathcal{T}_i$, where $\mathcal{L}_i$ and $\mathcal{T}_i$ are state predicates. A computation $\sigma = \langle s_0, s_1, \cdots \rangle$ satisfies $\mathcal{L}_i \rightsquigarrow \mathcal{T}_i$ iff $\forall j : (s_j \in \mathcal{L}_i \Rightarrow \exists k : j \leq k < length(\sigma) : s_k \in \mathcal{T}_i)$.*

A *specification*, say *spec*, is a tuple $\langle Sf, Lv \rangle$, where Sf is a safety property (as in Definition 8) and Lv is a liveness property (as in Definition 9). We say that a computation σ *satisfies spec* iff σ satisfies Sf and Lv.

Example (cont'd). The safety specification of the group membership protocol requires that any reachable state satisfies the following constraints:

- (Sf_a) Processors in the group agree with each other about group membership.[2]
- (Sf_r) The list of group members is nonempty.
- (Sf_s) After a processor joins a group, it does not leave until a failure is detected or a *newgroup* message is sent.

Definition 10. *Given a program p, a state predicate I, and specification spec, we say that I is a set of **legitimate states** of p iff (1) I is closed in p; (2) Every computation of p that starts in a state in I satisfies spec; (3) $I \neq \emptyset$.*

Example (cont'd). If a process has not joined a group, there is no need to maintain a copy of the members in that group. If a process j joins the group, as required by safety specification Sf_a and Sf_r, $member.j$ should be equal to all other processes in that group and j itself should be in the group. In addition, if some joined process j broadcasts the *present* message (i.e., sets $present.j$ to true), then all other joined processes should perform the same action according to the synchronous semantics. Thus, the legitimates states of the protocol are as follows:

$$I = (\forall j : \neg joined.j \Rightarrow member.j = \emptyset) \vee$$
$$((\forall i, j : i \neq j : (joined.j \wedge joined.i) \Rightarrow (member.i = member.j)) \wedge$$
$$(\forall j : joined.j \Rightarrow j \in member.j) \wedge$$
$$(\exists j : \forall i : i \neq j : (joined.j \wedge joined.i \wedge present.j) \Rightarrow present.i))$$

Definition 11. *We say that a program p **satisfies** spec **from** I iff I is a set of legitimate states of p and every computation in p satisfies spec.*

In the context of the group membership protocol, observe that the protocol satifies its safety specification from the identified legitimate states.

---

[2] Observe that this requirement cannot be satisfied in interleaving semantics since two processes that update group membership cannot update their state in the same step.

3   Problem Statement

In this section, we formally define the repair problem of adding *fault-tolerance* to synchronous programs. Before we describe the problem statement, we first identify how we model faults and their execution in the context of synchronous semantics.

In case of programs with synchronous semantics, faults can be caused due to different reasons. For example, consider the following cases:

– One common type of fault is a process failure. As an illustration, if a program consists of n processes, then in each program transition, all n processes are supposed to execute (unless some have no valid transition in the current state). However, if one of them fails to execute, then the resulting transition is one where $n - 1$ processes change their state. The transition obtained thus can now be viewed as a fault transition. In other words, even though the transition is obtained by execution of a subset of processes, this transition would be modeled as a fault transition.
– Moreover, a fault transition could execute concurrently with original processes. In other words, in one step, all processes execute and concurrently, the fault also updates some program variables. (Conflicting updates by processes and faults needs to be handled in an application-specific method.) In this case, the transition obtained by considering execution of all processes and the fault will be considered as a fault transition.
– Alternatively, execution of faults could be independent of program execution; i.e., the fault occurs *between* two program transitions.

As we can observe from these scenarios, even though the execution of the program itself occurs in synchronous semantics, an interaction between a program and faults can be viewed in terms of interleaving semantics. In other words, faults do not have to synchronize with program actions. Moreover, fault actions can potentially modify all program variables. Furthermore, since the interaction between the program and faults is interleaving in nature, we can utilize existing approaches in the context, where processes in the program execute in interleaving semantics.

Specifically, for the first alternative, suppose that a fault perturbs the state of a program to a state s_0, from which state s_1 is reached by program transition (s_0, s_1). Let the set of variables updated by transition (s_0, s_1) be $write(s_0, s_1)$. This fault, thus, can be modeled in a way, such that only part of variables in $write(s_0, s_1)$ are updated. Likewise, for the second alternative, the fault can be modeled, so that part of the variables in $write(s_0, s_1)$ are updated same as transition (s_0, s_1) while the remaining variables are updated with new values. For the third alternative, the fault can update any variables while the program takes no transitions.

Definition 12. *A set f of **faults** for program p is a subset of $S_p \times S_p$.*

Definition 13. *A sequence of states, $\langle s_0, s_1, \cdots \rangle$ is a **computation of** p **in the presence of** f iff the following three conditions are satisfied:*

– $\forall j : j > 0 : (s_{j-1}, s_j) \in (\delta_p \cup f)$,
– *if $\langle s_0, s_1, \cdots \rangle$ is finite and terminates in state s_l, then there does not exist state s such that $(s_l, s) \in \delta_p$, and*
– $\exists n : n \geq 0 : (\forall j : j > n : (s_{j-1}, s_j) \in \delta_p)$.

Notation. We use $p[]f$ to denote the program transitions in the presence of faults.

Definition 14. *A state predicate T is a* **fault-span** *of program p from I iff (1) $I \subseteq T$, and (2) T is closed in $p[]f$.*

Example (cont'd). In the context of the group membership protocol, we consider the fault, where a process fails to send the *present* message in the second round. Thus, this fault can be modeled as a transition where the faulty process does not set the variable *present* to true while others do:

$$f : \exists p \in \{i, k, l\} : newgroup.p \wedge joined.j \longrightarrow present.j := false;$$
$$\forall q \in \{i, k, l\} :$$
$$\textbf{if } joined.q \textbf{ then } present.q := true;$$

Definition 15. *Let p be a program, I be its set of legitimate states, f be a set of faults, and spec = $\langle Sf, Lv \rangle$ be a specification. We say that p is* **masking** *fault-tolerant to f for spec from I iff*

1. *p satisfies spec from I*
2. *$\exists T : (1) I \subseteq T; (2) p[]f$ satisfies Sf from $T; (3) p[]f$ satisfies $T \rightsquigarrow I$.*

Constraint 2(c) stipulates *fault recovery*; i.e., if a computation of a masking fault-tolerant program leaves its set of legitimate states, it eventually *recovers* back to its legitimate states. A *fail-safe* fault-tolerant program only needs to satisfy constraints 1, 2(a), and 2(b). A *nonmasking* program only needs to meet constraints 1, 2(a), and 2(c).

  Now, we explain the problem of repairing a fault-intolerant program, say p, for adding fault-tolerance and obtaining a repaired fault-tolerant program, say p'. In this paper, we always assume that p satisfies its specification in the absence of faults. Thus, a repair algorithm should not introduce any new behaviors to the program in the absence of faults. Hence, we require that the set I' of legitimate states of the repaired fault-tolerant program is a subset of the set of legitimate states of the original intolerant program. And, in the absence of faults, a computation of p' that starts from a state in I' should exist in the set of computations of p that start from I. Clearly, a repair algorithm should also ensure that the program is masking fault-tolerant.

Definition 16. *Let p be a program and S be a state predicate. The* **projection** *of δ_p on S (denoted $\delta_p|S$) is the set of transitions of δ_p that start in S and end in S; i.e., $\delta_p|S = \{(s_0, s_1) \mid (s_0, s_1) \in \delta_p \wedge (s_0 \in S) \wedge (s_1 \in S)\}$.*

Problem Statement:
Given a program p with the set of legitimate states I,
specification *spec*, and a set f of faults, such that p satisfies *spec* from I;
Does there exist a program p' with legitimate states I',
such that:
C1: $(I' \subseteq I) \wedge (\delta_{p'}|I' \subseteq \delta_p|I')$
C2: p' is masking fault-tolerant to f for *spec* from I'.

4   Repair Algorithms

In this section, we introduce the algorithm that solves the problem stated in Section 3; i.e., the algorithm repairs a fault-intolerant program by adding masking fault-tolerance under synchronous semantics. Before we describe our algorithm, we make certain observations and identify issues that one needs to deal with in repairing a program under synchronous semantics.

A program under synchronous semantics is specified in terms of transitions of its processes. Hence, when we repair the given program to add fault-tolerance, we need to obtain the repaired transitions for each process. However, a repair algorithm itself can require composition of the processes to obtain the corresponding program transitions. One reason for such composition is that the safety specification is often specified in terms of global constraints (e.g., relation of states of different processes). Hence, to evaluate whether the safety specification is satisfied, in our algorithm, we first compute the transitions of the given program by considering the transitions of its processes.

After computing the global transitions of the input program, its computations resemble those of a program in interleaving semantics. Specifically, as Definition 7 states, in a program computation, the program executes one of its transitions (that is obtained by composition of process transitions) in the initial state. Then, in the resulting state, it executes its next transition and so on. Hence, in designing our algorithm, we first utilize ideas from program repair in interleaving semantics.

Applying algorithms for interleaving semantics has the potential that the repaired program cannot be realized under synchronous semantics. To illustrate this, consider a program, say p, with two processes, say j and k. Let s be a state of program p. Furthermore, let j (respectively, k) have two transitions from s, δ_j^1 and δ_j^2 (respectively, δ_k^1 and δ_k^2). This implies that p has four possible transitions from state s, namely, $t_1 = \delta_j^1 \cdot \delta_k^1$, $t_2 = \delta_j^2 \cdot \delta_k^2$, $t_3 = \delta_j^1 \cdot \delta_k^2$ and $t_4 = \delta_j^2 \cdot \delta_k^1$. Suppose that while adding fault-tolerance, some of these transitions may be removed, e.g., to ensure that safety is not violated in the presence of faults. For example, consider the scenario where transition t_4 is removed. While a program involving transitions t_1, t_2, and t_3 is a valid *single-process* program, it cannot be realized as a multi-process program under synchronous semantics. This is because to realize such a program, j (respectively, k) must include transitions δ_j^1 and δ_j^2 (respectively, δ_k^1 and δ_k^2). However, if j and k include such transitions, then the repaired program would also contain transition t_4 which is not acceptable.

A similar problem also arises while synthesizing recovery transitions. Specifically, consider the scenario where transitions t_1, t_2, and t_3 are added as recovery transitions, but t_4 is not added, as it causes the program to loop outside the set of legitimate states. Clearly, in such a case, the repaired program is not realizable under synchronous semantics.

4.1   Adding Masking Fault-Tolerance

Our algorithm for adding masking fault-tolerance (see Algorithm 1), consists of three key steps: *AddSafeRecovery*, *BreakCycles*, and *ConstructSyncProgram* (Lines 1, 2, and 3). Specifically:

Algorithm 1. Adding Masking Fault-tolerance to a Synchronous Program

Input: A program $\langle V_p, R_p \rangle$, where $j \in R_p$ is $\langle W_j, \delta_j \rangle$, legitimate states I, faults f, safety specification Sf.
Output: A masking fault-tolerant program with set of processes transitions $\bigcup_{j \in R_p} \delta'_j$

1: $\delta_{p'}, I', T' := AddSafeRecovery(\delta_p, f, I, Sf)$
2: $\delta_{p'} := BreakCycles(I', T', \delta'_p)$
3: $\bigcup_{j \in R_p} \delta'_j := ConstructSyncProgram(T', \delta_{p'})$

Function: $AddSafeRecovery$ (δ_p, f: transitions, S: state predicate, Sf: safety specification)
4: $ms := smallestfixpoint(X = X \cup \{s_0 \mid \exists s_1 : (s_0, s_1) \in f \land (s_1 \in X \lor (s_0, s_1) \in Sf)\})$
5: $mt := \{(s_0, s_1) \mid (s_1 \in ms) \lor ((s_0, s_1) \text{ violates } spec)\}$
6: $S_1, T_1 := S - ms,\ true - ms$
7: **repeat**
8:    $T_2, S_2 := T_1, S_1$
9:    $\delta_{p_1} := \delta_p | S_1 \cup \{(s_0, s_1) \mid s_0 \in (T_1 - S_1) \land s_1 \in T_1\} - mt$
10:    $T_1 := T_1 - \{s \mid S_1 \text{ is not reachable from } s \text{ in } \delta_{p_1}\}$
11:    $T_1 := largestfixpoint(X = (X \cap T_1) - \{s_0 \mid \exists s_1 : (s_0, s_1) \in f \land s_1 \notin X\})$
12:    $S_1 := S_1 - smallestfixpoint(X = X \cup \{s_0 \mid \forall s_1 \in S_1 \cap T_1 : (s_0, s_1) \notin \delta_{p_1}\})$
13:    **if** $(S_1 = \{\} \lor T_1 = \{\})$ **then**
14:      declare no safe recovery exists and exit
15:    **end if**
16: **until** $(T_1 = T_2 \land S_1 = S_2)$
17: **return** δ_{p_1}, S_1, T_1

Function: $BreakCycles$ (S, T: state predicate, δ_p: transitions)
// Let $rank(s, S, p)$ be the length of the shortest finite computation of transitions p that starts from s and ends in a state in S
18: $\delta_{p'} := \{(s_0, s_1) \in \delta_p \mid (s_0 \in S) \lor ((s_0 \in T) \land (rank(s_0, S, p) > rank(s_1, S, p)))\}$
19: **return** $\delta_{p'}$

Function: $ConstructSyncProgram$ (T: state predicate, δ_p: transitions)
20: **for all** $j \in R_p$ **do**
21:    $\delta'_j = \bigcup_{(s_0, s_1) \in \delta_p} \{(s_0, s_2) \mid \forall x \in W_j : x(s_2) = x(s_1) \land \forall x \notin W_j : x(s_2) = x(s_0))\}$
22: **end for**
23: **for all** $s \in T$ **do**
24:    $trans := \{(s, s_1) \mid (s, s_1) \in \delta_p\}$
25:    **for all** $j \in R_p$ **do**
26:      $\delta^s_j := \bigcup_{(s, s_1) \in trans} \{(s, s_2) \mid \forall x \in W_j : x(s_2) = x(s_1) \land \forall x \notin W_j : x(s_2) = x(s))\}$
27:    **end for**
28:    $A_s := \delta^s_1 \times \delta^s_2 \times \cdots$
29:    **while** $A_s \not\subseteq trans$ **do**
30:      Let $t := (s, r)$ where $t \in (A_s - trans)$
31:      Let k be a process st. $|\delta^s_k|$ is the largest
32:      $\delta^{\{t\}}_k := \{(s, s_1) \mid \forall x \in W_k : x(r) = x(s_1) \land \forall x \notin W_k : x(s_1) = x(s)\}$
33:      $\delta'_k := \delta'_k - \delta^{\{t\}}_k$
34:      recompute δ^s_k and A_s same as Lines 25-28.
35:    **end while**
36: **end for**
37: **return** $\bigcup_{j \in R_p} \delta'_j$

Step 1. The first step adds recovery while ensuring safety properties. The function $AddSafeRecovery$ ignores the structure of the synchronous program and only treats it as a set of transitions. Hence, this function reuses the approach in Add_masking_ft [17] under interleaving semantics. The function first computes the set ms of states from where occurrence of faults only can violate the safety specification (Line 4), and, the set mt of transitions that reach ms (Line 5). Then, in Line 9, it computes the set δ_{p_1} of program transitions including new recovery transitions that does not start in S_1. Using these transitions, the new fault-span T_1 (to ensure closure in Line 11) and the set of legitimate states S_1 (to ensure deadlock freedom in Line 12) are subsequently recomputed. When the repeat-until loop terminates, the function ensures that from any state reached in the presence of faults, it is possible to recover to the legitimate states without violating safety.

Step 2. Although *AddSafeRecovery* ensures that from every state reached in the presence of faults, safe recovery is possible, the resulting program may include cycles outside the set of legitimate states. Hence, we use function *BreakCycles* to break such cycles, so that the program will eventually recover to its legitimate states. To this end, we assign a *rank* to each state in the fault-span, where the rank is the length of the shortest path from that state to a state in the set of legitimate states. After we obtain the ranks, we only include transitions of which the rank of the originating state is greater than the rank of the target state (Line 18),

Step 3. Finally, function *ConstructSyncProgram* ensures that the resulting program can be realized under synchronous semantics. Moreover, during this step, we need to ensure that the resulting program will still guarantee that from any state reached in the presence of faults, the program will (1) recover to a legitimate state, and (2) not violate the safety specification. To ensure the first property, we guarantee that the repaired program does not deadlock in any state reached in the presence of faults. And, to guarantee the second property, we ensure that transitions that were removed in *AddSafeRecovery* or *BreakCycles* are not reintroduced to the repaired program.

To explain this step, we revisit the example, where the program obtained after *BreakCycles* (from state $\mathfrak{s}$) contains transitions t_1, t_2, and t_3, and transition t_4 is removed in previous steps (where $t_1 = \delta_j^1 \cdot \delta_k^1$, $t_2 = \delta_j^2 \cdot \delta_k^2$, $t_3 = \delta_j^1 \cdot \delta_k^2$, and $t_4 = \delta_j^2 \cdot \delta_k^1$). In this case, the resulting program is not realizable under synchronous semantics since realizing it would require process j (respectively k) to execute δ_j^1 and δ_j^2 (respectively, δ_k^1 and δ_k^2). Hence, in this case, we update the program as follows: We change transitions of process j (or k) to ensure that transition t_4 cannot be a transition of the repaired program. This can be achieved by either removing δ_j^2 or δ_k^1. Here, we remove the transition from a process that has the largest (with a tie-break) transitions from state $\mathfrak{s}$. We note that while removing such transitions, there will be at least one transition that remains from state $\mathfrak{s}$. This is due to the fact that if there is only one transition from $\mathfrak{s}$, then it gives only one possible transition for every process. And, this is realizable under synchronous semantics.

Specifically, function *ConstructSyncProgram* first computes the set of transitions of each process (Line 21). Then, from each state $\mathfrak{s}$, it ensures that the set of outgoing transitions is realizable in synchronous semantics. To this end, we compute the set $\delta_j^{\mathfrak{s}}$ of transitions for each process j that originate from state $\mathfrak{s}$ (Line 26). Next, the while-loop (Lines 29-35) considers transitions t that originate in $\mathfrak{s}$ and are removed in the previous steps (Line 30). Let k be the process with largest number of outgoing transitions from state $\mathfrak{s}$ (Line 31). Finally, we remove transitions of k that contribute in t (Lines 32 and 33).

Theorem 1. *Algorithm 1 is sound and complete. And, its time complexity is polynomial in the state space of the input program.*

4.2 Application in Group Membership Protocol

Due to reasons of space, we do not consider line-by-line analysis of Algorithm 1. Instead, we consider the effect of fault f on the fault-intolerant program to explain the changes performed by Algorithm 1 while adding failsafe fault-tolerance. Specifically, consider the scenario, where process i and j are in the group, and process k decides to join while process l decides not to. After the first round where k sets its $newgroup$ to $true$, f perturbs the program. As a result, only process i sets $present.i$ to $true$. The resulting state of the program is not in I. Both processes i and k only have one action to take in the next round which is to compute their $member$ (denoted as δ_i^1 and δ_k^1, respectively). Based on the $present$ and $newgroup$ values of all processes, their $member$ variables are set equal to $\{i, k\}$. For process j, it has two actions it can potentially perform. One is to set $present.j$ to true (denoted as δ_j^1) and the other one is to set $member.j$ to be $\{i, k\}$ (denoted as δ_j^2). Notice that either one of δ_j^1 or δ_j^2 should be performed simultaneously with δ_i^1 and δ_k^1. However, the program transition $\delta_1 = \delta_i^1 \cdot \delta_j^1 \cdot \delta_k^1$ results a state violating Sf_a, since $member.i \neq member.j$. Thus, δ_1 is excluded by Algorithm 1. The program transition $\delta_2 = \delta_i^1 \cdot \delta_j^2 \cdot \delta_k^1$ can remain in the program since the resulting state does not violate the safety specification. Therefore, the failsafe fault-tolerant program is shown below, where round 2 action is repaired:

round 2: $\exists p \in \{i, j, k, l\} :: newgroup.p \wedge joined.j$

$$\bigwedge_{q \in \{i,j,k,l\}} \neg present.q \longrightarrow present.j := true;$$

Observe that the repaired program is failsafe fault-tolerant. Hence, it may not recover to a state in I. There are several possible recovery actions that Algorithm 1 can add to obtain masking fault-tolerance. One action is that when process j finds out that $j \notin member.j$ in round 3, it leaves the group and starts to join again. The same recovery action can be taken when in round 3 two processes p and q have the same members, but one has broadcast $present$ and the other one has not. This recovery action is shown below.

round 3: $\exists q : newgroup.q \wedge joined.j \wedge \neg present.j \wedge$

$\exists p : (present.p \wedge member.p = member.j)$

$\longrightarrow joined.j := false;\ member.j := \emptyset;$

The action shown above is added to the fault-tolerant program because (1) on Line 9 in $AddSafeRecovery$, set of recovery transitions are added (from set of states outside of I to those inside of I, see I in Section 2.2); (2) follow this action, program recovers, the rank decreases along transitions and thus it will not be removed by $BreakCycles$; (3) this action (grouping with others at certain states) is realizable under synchronous semantics, thus it will not be removed by $ConstructSyncProgram$.

5   Experiment and Optimization

In this section, we discuss the implementation of Algorithm 1 and its applications on the case studies. All the experiments in this section are run on a PC with AMD Athlon II X4 2.8 MHz processor with 6GB RAM. Algorithm 1 is implemented symbolically using Glu/CuDD package [21].

To obtain a compact representation, we model the protocols in the case studies using BDDs. The forward/backward reachability calculations in *AddSafeRecovery* (on Line 4,11,12) are implemented as fixpoint calculations. To implement Line 18 in *BreakCycle*, we use the following formula:

$$\delta_{p'} = \delta_p \cap ((S_1 \times S_0) \cup (S_2 \times S_1) \cup \cdots \cup (S_n \times S_{n-1}))$$

Where S_i is a state predicate that includes states whose rank is i, i.e., the shortest path from these states to a state in the invariant is i. Thus S_0 is the invariant. Each S_i is obtained by backward reachability computation from invariant.

For *ConstructSyncProgram*, it is not possible to implement it symbolically since we need to check the outgoing transitions from each state in T. However, we apply other optimizations to improve the performance. For example, given state s, we can compute Δ_i^s and A_s symbolically.

In spite of these optimizations, *ConstructSyncProgram* still remains the bottleneck of Algorithm 1. This is due to the fact that some enumeration of states in T is essential in implementation of *ConstructSyncProgram*. Due to limited space, the experimental results for the three tasks involved in adding fault-tolerance are shown in [22].

6   Related Work

Automated model repair is a relatively new area of research. To the best of our knowledge, this paper is the first work on applying model repair in the context of synchronous systems. Model repair with respect to CTL properties was first considered in [8] and extended in [10] using abstraction techniques. The theory of model repair for memoryless LTL properties was studied in [16] in a game-theoretic fashion; i.e., a repaired model is obtained by synthesizing a winning strategy for a 2-player game. In [5], the authors explore the model repair for a fragment of LTL (the UNITY language [9]). Most results in [5] focus on complexity analysis of model repair for different variations of UNITY properties. Model repair in other contexts includes the work in [3] for probabilistic systems and in [20] for Boolean programs.

Model repair in the context of *addition of fault-tolerance* to fault-intolerant models has been studied from different perspectives. For instance, addition of fault-tolerance using discrete controller synthesis is studied in [13]. This line of research falls short in automatically synthesizing recovery paths and complexity analysis of addition of fault-tolerance as well as issues such as completeness. In particular, unlike our approach, conventional controller synthesis algorithms [19] work within the given behavior of the input model and are unable to find appropriate recovery paths that are not present in the input model. This problem is even more amplified when the input model has complex read/write restrictions, such as in our framework. In [6], the authors propose symbolic heuristics for addition of fault-tolerance to distributed models.

The work in [7] is the closest to the algorithm presented in this paper. The authors show that adding fault recovery to component-based models subject to cyber-physical constraints is NP-complete. The component-based models under investigation are specified in the BIP framework [4][14], where a set of atomic components synchronize by using interaction parametrized by synchronization primitives such as rendezvous and broadcasts. The main difference between the results in this paper and the work in [7] is that the synchronous semantics considered in this paper requires *all* processes to participate in each round of execution, whereas the computation model in [7] is for programs under interleaving semantics.

7   Conclusion

In this paper, we focused on the problem of adding fault-tolerance to programs in the popular synchronous semantics for embedded systems. This work was motivated by the fact that such systems use round based computations and the problem of automatically adding fault-tolerance to them has not been considered previously. Synchronous semantics is also applicable in the execution of physical subsystems in a cyber-physical system. We also argued that algorithms for adding fault-tolerance under interleaving semantics cannot be directly applied in synchronous systems.

One way to model synchronous programs is to utilize formal methods such as timed automata. However, utilizing timed automata can increase the complexity substantially in adding fault-tolerance. Specifically, depending upon the specific formulation, the complexity of adding fault-tolerance in timed automata is polynomial/exponential in terms of the size of the time-abstract bisimulation graph [2]. And, the size of the graph can be substantially larger (normally, exponential in the size of state space). By contrast, the time complexity of our algorithms is polynomial in the state space of the given program. We illustrated our approach with two case studies: A group membership protocol and a cache coherence protocol. For both case studies, we presented experimental results demonstrating the feasibility of adding fault-tolerance in synchronous semantics.

One future work in this area is to develop algorithms for powerset semantics, where in a given step, one or more processes execute their actions. This is more general than synchronous semantics in that in powerset semantics, a process is allowed to execute in every step but is not required to. By contrast, in synchronous semantics, it is required to execute in every step. Another future work is to develop protocols targeted for a specific architecture such as TTA or BIP.

References

1. Alpern, B., Schneider, F.B.: Defining liveness. Information Processing Letters 21, 181–185 (1985)
2. Alur, R., Dill, D.: A theory of timed automata. Theoretical Computer Science 126(2), 183–235 (1994)

3. Bartocci, E., Grosu, R., Katsaros, P., Ramakrishnan, C.R., Smolka, S.A.: Model repair for probabilistic systems. In: Abdulla, P.A., Leino, K.R.M. (eds.) TACAS 2011. LNCS, vol. 6605, pp. 326–340. Springer, Heidelberg (2011)
4. Basu, A., Bozga, M., Sifakis, J.: Modeling heterogeneous real-time components in BIP. In: Software Engineering and Formal Methods (SEFM), pp. 3–12 (2006)
5. Bonakdarpour, B., Ebnenasir, A., Kulkarni, S.S.: Complexity results in revising UNITY programs. ACM Transactions on Autonomous and Adaptive Systems (TAAS) 4(1), 1–28 (2009)
6. Bonakdarpour, B., Kulkarni, S.S., Abujarad, F.: Symbolic synthesis of masking fault-tolerant programs. Springer Journal on Distributed Computing (DC) 25(1), 83–108 (2012)
7. Bonakdarpour, B., Lin, Y., Kulkarni, S.S.: Automated addition of fault recovery to cyber-physical component-based models. In: ACM International Conference on Embedded Software (EMSOFT), pp. 127–136 (2011)
8. Buccafurri, F., Eiter, T., Gottlob, G., Leone, N.: Enhancing model checking in verification by ai techniques. Artificial Intelligence 112, 57–104 (1999)
9. Chandy, K.M., Misra, J.: Parallel program design: a foundation. Addison-Wesley Longman Publishing Co., Inc., Boston (1988)
10. Chatzieleftheriou, G., Bonakdarpour, B., Smolka, S.A., Katsaros, P.: Abstract model repair. In: Goodloe, A.E., Person, S. (eds.) NFM 2012. LNCS, vol. 7226, pp. 341–355. Springer, Heidelberg (2012)
11. Cristian, F.: Reaching agreement on processor group membership in synchronous distributed systems. Distributed Computing 4, 175–187 (1991)
12. Ghosh, S.: Distributed Systems: An Algorithmic Approach. Chapman and Hall/CRC Computer and Information Science Series. Taylor & Francis (2010)
13. Girault, A., Rutten, É.: Automating the addition of fault tolerance with discrete controller synthesis. Formal Methods in System Design (FMSD) 35(2), 190–225 (2009)
14. Gössler, G., Sifakis, J.: Composition for component-based modeling. Science of Computer Programming 55(1-3), 161–183 (2005)
15. Gouda, M.G., Haddix, F.F.: The alternator. Distributed Computing 20(1), 21–28 (2007)
16. Jobstmann, B., Griesmayer, A., Bloem, R.: Program repair as a game. In: Etessami, K., Rajamani, S.K. (eds.) CAV 2005. LNCS, vol. 3576, pp. 226–238. Springer, Heidelberg (2005)
17. Kulkarni, S.S., Arora, A.: Large automating the addition of fault-tolerance. In: Joseph, M. (ed.) FTRTFT 2000. LNCS, vol. 1926, pp. 82–93. Springer, Heidelberg (2000)
18. Lynch, N.A.: Distributed Algorithms. Morgan Kaufmann Publishers Inc., San Francisco (1996)
19. Ramadge, P.J., Wonham, W.M.: The control of discrete event systems. Proceedings of the IEEE 77(1), 81–98 (1989)
20. Samanta, R., Deshmukh, J.V., Emerson, E.A.: Automatic generation of local repairs for boolean programs. In: Formal Methods in Computer-Aided Design (FMCAD), pp. 1–10 (2008)
21. Somenzi, F.: Cudd: Colorado university decision diagram package
22. Lin, Y., Kulkarni, S., Bonakdarpour, B.: Automated addition of fault-tolerance under synchronous semantics. Technical Report MSU-CSE-13-5, Computer Science and Engineering, Michigan State University, East Lansing, Michigan (July 2013)

Naming and Counting in Anonymous Unknown Dynamic Networks[*][**]

Othon Michail[1], Ioannis Chatzigiannakis[1], and Paul G. Spirakis[1,2]

[1] Computer Technology Institute & Press "Diophantus" (CTI), Patras, Greece
[2] Department of Computer Science, University of Liverpool, UK
{michailo,ichatz,spirakis}@cti.gr

Abstract. In this work, we study the fundamental naming and counting problems (and some variations) in networks that are anonymous, unknown, and possibly dynamic. In *counting*, nodes must determine the size of the network n and in *naming* they must end up with unique identities. By *anonymous* we mean that all nodes begin from identical states apart possibly from a unique leader node and by *unknown* that nodes have no a priori knowledge of the network (apart from some minimal knowledge when necessary) including ignorance of n. Network dynamicity is modeled by the 1-interval connectivity model [KLO10], in which communication is synchronous and a (worst-case) adversary chooses the edges of every round subject to the condition that each instance is connected. We first focus on static networks with broadcast where we prove that, without a leader, counting is impossible to solve and that naming is impossible to solve even with a leader and even if nodes know n. These impossibilities carry over to dynamic networks as well. We also show that a unique leader suffices in order to solve counting in linear time. Then we focus on dynamic networks with broadcast. We conjecture that dynamicity renders nontrivial computation impossible. In view of this, we let the nodes know an upper bound on the maximum degree that will ever appear and show that in this case the nodes can obtain an upper bound on n. Finally, we replace broadcast with *one-to-each*, in which a node may send a different message to each of its neighbors. Interestingly, this natural variation is proved to be computationally equivalent to a full-knowledge model, in which unique names exist and the size of the network is known.

1 Introduction

Distributed computing systems are more and more becoming dynamic. The static and relatively stable models of computation can no longer represent the

---

[*] Supported in part by the project "Foundations of Dynamic Distributed Computing Systems" (**FOCUS**) which is implemented under the "ARISTEIA" Action of the Operational Programme "Education and Lifelong Learning" and is co-funded by the European Union (European Social Fund) and Greek National Resources.
[**] A brief announcement of this work has appeared in [MCS12a].

T. Higashino et al. (Eds.): SSS 2013, LNCS 8255, pp. 281–295, 2013.
© Springer International Publishing Switzerland 2013

plethora of recently established and rapidly emerging information and communication technologies. In recent years, we have seen a tremendous increase in the number of new mobile computing devices. Most of these devices are equipped with some sort of communication, sensing, and mobility capabilities. Even the Internet has become mobile. The design is now focused on complex collections of heterogeneous devices that should be robust, adaptive, and self-organizing, possibly moving around and serving requests that vary with time. Delay-tolerant networks are highly-dynamic, infrastructure-less networks whose essential characteristic is a possible absence of end-to-end communication routes at any instant. Mobility can vary from being completely predictable to being completely unpredictable. Gossip-based communication mechanisms, e-mail exchanges, peer-to-peer networks, and many other contemporary communication networks all assume or induce some sort of highly-dynamic communication network.

The formal study of dynamic communication networks is hardly a new area of research. There is a huge amount of work in distributed computing that deals with causes of dynamicity such as failures and changes in the topology that are rather slow and usually eventually stabilize (like, for example, in self-stabilizing systems [Dol00]). However the low rate of topological changes that is usually assumed there is unsuitable for reasoning about truly dynamic networks. Even graph-theoretic techniques need to be revisited: the suitable graph model is now that of a *dynamic graph* (a.k.a. *temporal graph* or *time-varying graph*) (see e.g. [MMCS13, KKK00, CFQS11]), in which each edge has an associated set of time-labels indicating availability times. Even fundamental properties of classical graphs do not carry over to their temporal counterparts. See, for example, [KKK00] for a violation of Menger's theorem, [MMCS13] for a valid reformulation of Menger's theorem and the definition of several cost optimization metrics for temporal networks, and [AKL08] for the unsuitability of the standard network diameter metric.

In this work, we adopt as our dynamic network model the 1-*interval connectivity* model of Kuhn *et al.* [KLO10] building upon previous work of O'Dell and Wattenhofer [OW05]. In this model, nodes proceed in *synchronous rounds* and communicate by *interchanging messages*. Message transmission is *broadcast* in which, in every round, each node issues a single message to be delivered to all its neighbors. In this model, the network may change arbitrarily from round to round subject to the condition that in each round the network is connected. We only consider deterministic algorithms.

We focus on networks in which nodes are initially identical and, unless necessary, do not have any information about the network. In any case, nodes do not know the size n of the network. By *identical* we mean that they do not have unique identities (ids) and execute identical programs. So, this is some sort of minimal reliable distributed system, like, for example, a collection of particularly cheap and bulk-produced wireless sensor nodes. Nodes may execute the same program, because it is too costly to program them individually and their lack of ids may be due to the fact that ids require customization beyond the capabilities of mass production [AFR06]. Our only assumption is the existence of a unique leader that introduces some symmetry breaking. To further break the symmetry introduced by broadcast message transmission and in order to solve naming in dynamic networks, we allow to the nodes to send a different message to each one of their neighbors.

2   Related Work

Distributed systems with worst-case dynamicity were first studied in [OW05]. Their novelty was to assume a communication network that may change arbitrarily from time to time subject to the condition that each instance of the network is connected. They studied asynchronous communication and allowed nodes detect local neighborhood changes. They studied the *flooding* and *routing* problems in this setting and among others provided a uniform protocol for flooding that terminates in $O(Tn^2)$ rounds using $O(\log n)$ bit storage and message overhead, where T is the maximum time it takes to transmit a message.

Computation under worst-case dynamicity was further and extensively studied in a series of works by Kuhn *et al.* in the synchronous case. In [KLO10], among others, *counting* (in which nodes must determine the size of the network) and *all-to-all token dissemination* (in which n different pieces of information, called tokens, are handed out to the n nodes of the network, each node being assigned one token, and all nodes must collect all n tokens) were solved in $O(n^2)$ rounds using $O(\log n)$ bits per message. The requirement for continuous connectivity was first dropped in [MCS12b]. That work proposed a set of metrics for capturing the speed of information spreading in a dynamic network that may be disconnected at every instance and efficient algorithms were developed. Some recent works, e.g. [Hae11], present information spreading algorithms in worst-case dynamic networks based on *network coding*.

The question concerning which problems can be solved by a distributed system when all processors use the same algorithm and start from the same state has a long story with its roots dating back to the seminal work of Angluin [Ang80], who investigated the problem of establishing a "center". Further investigation led to the classification of computable functions [YK96, ASW88]. [BV99] removed the, until then, standard assumption of knowing the network size n and provided characterizations of the relations that can be computed with arbitrary knowledge. Other well-known studies on unknown networks have dealt with the problems of robot-exploration and map-drawing of an unknown graph [DP90, AH00] and on information dissemination [AGVP90]. Fraigniaud *et al.* [FPPP00] assumed a unique leader in order to break symmetry and assign short labels as fast as possible. To circumvent the further symmetry introduced by broadcast message transmission they also studied other natural message transmission models as sending only one message to a single neighbor. Recently, and independently of our work, Chalopin *et al.* [CMM12] have studied the problem of naming anonymous networks in the context of snapshot computation. Finally, Aspnes *et al.* [AFR06] studied the relative powers of reliable anonymous distributed systems with different communication mechanisms: anonymous broadcast, read-write registers, or read-write registers plus additional shared-memory objects.

3   Contribution

We begin, in Section 4, by formally describing our distributed models. In Section 5, we formally define the problems under consideration, that is, naming, counting and some variations of these. Our study begins, in Section 6, from static networks with broadcast. The reason for considering static networks is to arrive at some impossibility results that also carry over to dynamic networks, as a static network is a special case of a dynamic network. In particular, we prove that naming is impossible to solve under these assumptions even if a unique leader exists and even if all nodes know n. Then we prove that without a leader also counting is impossible to solve and naturally, in the sequel, we assume the existence of a unique leader. We provide an algorithm based on the *eccentricity* of the leader (greatest distance of a node from the leader) that solves counting in linear time (inspired by the findings in [FPPP00]). Then, in Section 7, we move on to dynamic networks with broadcast. We begin with a conjecture essentially stating that dynamicity renders nontrivial computations impossible even in the presence of a unique leader. [1] In view of this, we allow the nodes some minimal initial knowledge, which is an upper bound on the maximum degree that any instance will ever have. This could for example be some natural constraint on the capacity of the network. We provide a protocol that exploits this information to compute an upper bound on the size of the network. However, w.r.t. naming, the strong impossibility from Section 6 still persists (after all, knowledge of n does not help in labeling the nodes). To circumvent this, in Section 8, we relax our message transmission model to *one-to-each* that allows each node to send a different message to each one of its neighbors. This is an alternative communication model that has been considered in several important works, like [Hae11], however in different contexts than ours. This further symmetry breaking, though minimal, allows us, by exploiting a leader, to uniquely label the nodes. By this, we establish that this model is equivalent to a full-knowledge model in which unique names exist and the size of the network is known. To arrive at this result, we provide four distinct naming protocols each with its own incremental value. The first presents how to assign ids in a fair context in which the leader will eventually meet every other node. The second improves on the first by allowing all nodes to assign ids in a context where no one is guaranteed to meet everybody else, but where connectivity guarantees progress. Both these are correct stabilizing solutions that do not guarantee termination. Then we provide a third protocol that builds upon the first two and manages to assign unique ids in 1-interval connected

---

[1] By *nontrivial computation* we mean the ability to decide any language L on input assignments s.t. $L \neq \Sigma^*$ and $L \neq \emptyset$, where input symbols are chosen from some alphabet Σ. For example, deciding the existence of any symbol in the input is considered nontrivial.

graphs while terminating in linear time. As its drawback is that messages may be $\Omega(n^2)$ bit long, we refine it to a more involved fourth protocol that reduces the bits per message to $\Theta(\log n)$ by only paying a small increase in termination time.

4 Preliminaries

4.1 The Models

A *dynamic network* is modeled by a *dynamic graph* $G = (V, E)$, where V is a set of n nodes (or processors) and $E : \mathbb{N} \to \mathcal{P}(E')$, where $E' = \{\{u, v\} : u, v \in V\}$, (wherever we use $\mathbb{N}$ we mean $\mathbb{N}_{\geq 1}$) is a function mapping a round number $r \in \mathbb{N}$ to a set $E(r)$ of bidirectional links drawn from E'. Intuitively, a dynamic graph G is an infinite sequence $G(1), G(2), \ldots$ of *instantaneous graphs*, whose edge sets are subsets of E' chosen by a *(worst-case) adversary*. A *static network* is just a special case of a dynamic network in which $E(i + 1) = E(i)$ for all $i \in \mathbb{N}$. The set V is assumed throughout this work to be *static*, that is it remains the same throughout the execution.

A dynamic graph/network $G = (V, E)$ is said to be 1-*interval connected*, if, for all $r \in \mathbb{N}$, the static graph $G(r)$ is connected [KLO10]. Note that this allows the network to change arbitrarily from round to round always subject to the condition that it remains connected. In this work, we focus on 1-interval connected dynamic networks which also implies that we deal with connected networks in the static-network case.

Nodes in V are *anonymous* that is they do not initially have any ids and they do not know the topology or the size of the network, apart from some minimal knowledge when necessary (i.e. we say that *the network is unknown*). However, nodes have unlimited local storage. In several cases, and in order to break symmetry, we may assume a unique *leader node* (or *source*) l. If this is the case, then we assume that l starts from a unique initial state l_0 (e.g. 0) while all other nodes start from the same initial state q_0 (e.g. $\bot$). All nodes but the leader execute identical programs.

Communication is *synchronous message passing* [Lyn96, AW04], meaning that it is executed in discrete rounds controlled by a global clock that is available to the nodes and that nodes communicate by sending and receiving messages. Thus all nodes have access to the current round number via a local variable that we usually denote by r. We consider two different models of message transmission. One is *anonymous broadcast*, in which, in every round r, each node u generates a single message $m_u(r)$ to be delivered to all its current neighbors in $N_u(r) = \{v : \{u, v\} \in E(r)\}$. The other is *one-to-each* in which a different message $m_{(u,i)}(r)$, $1 \leq i \leq d_u(r)$, where $d_u(r) := |N_u(r)|$ is the degree of u in round r, may be generated for each neighbor v_i. In every round, the adversary first chooses the edges for the round; for this choice it can see the internal states of the nodes at the beginning of the round. In the one-to-each message transmission model we additionally assume that the adversary also reveals to each node u a set of locally unique edge-labels $1, 2, \ldots, d_u(r)$, one for each of the edges currently incident to it. Note that these labels can be reselected arbitrarily in each round so that a node cannot infer what the internal state of a neighbor is based solely on the corresponding local edge-name. Then each node transitions to a new state based on its internal state (containing the messages received in the previous round) and generates its messages for the current round: in anonymous broadcast a single message is generated and in one-to-each a different message is generated for each neighbor of a node. Note that, in both models, a node does not have any information about the internal state of its neighbors when generating its messages. Deterministic algorithms are only based on the current internal state to generate messages. This implies that the adversary can infer the messages that will be generated in the current round before choosing the edges. Messages are then delivered to the corresponding neighbors. In one-to-each, we assume that each message m_i received by some node u is accompanied with u's local label i of the corresponding edge, so that a node can associate a message sent through edge i with a message received from edge i. These messages will be processed by the nodes in the subsequent round so we typically begin rounds with a "receive" command referring to the messages received in the previous round. Then the next round begins.

4.2 Causal Influence

Probably the most important notion associated with a dynamic graph is the *causal influence*, which formalizes the notion of one node "influencing" another through a chain of messages originating at the former node and ending at the latter (possibly going through other nodes in between). We use $(u, r) \rightsquigarrow (v, r')$ to denote the fact that node u's state in round r (r-state of u) influences node v's state in round r'. Formally:

Definition 1 ([Lam78]). *Given a dynamic graph $G = (V, E)$ we define an order $\rightarrow \subseteq (V \times \mathbb{N}_{\geq 0})^2$, where $(u, r) \rightarrow (v, r + 1)$ iff $u = v$ or $\{u, v\} \in E(r + 1)$. The causal order $\rightsquigarrow \subseteq (V \times \mathbb{N}_{\geq 0})^2$ is defined to be the reflexive and transitive closure of $\rightarrow$.*

A very important aspect of 1-interval connectivity, that will be invoked in all our proof arguments in dynamic networks, is that it guarantees that the state of a node causally influences the state of another uninfluenced node in every round (if one exists). To get an intuitive feeling of this fact, consider a partitioning of the set of nodes V to a subset V_1 of nodes that know the r-state of some node u and to a subset $V_2 = V \backslash V_1$ of nodes that do not know it. Connectivity asserts that there is always an edge in the cut between V_1 and V_2, consequently, if nodes that know the r-state of u broadcast it in every round, then in every round at least one node moves from V_2 to V_1.

This is formally captured by the following lemma from [KLO10].

Lemma 1 ([KLO10]). *For any node $u \in V$ and $r \geq 0$ we have*

1. $|\{v \in V : (u, 0) \rightsquigarrow (v, r)\}| \geq \min\{r + 1, n\}$,
2. $|\{v \in V : (v, 0) \rightsquigarrow (u, r)\}| \geq \min\{r + 1, n\}$.

5   Problem Definitions

k-labeling. An algorithm is said to solve the k-labeling problem if whenever it is executed on a network comprising n nodes each node u eventually terminates and outputs a *label* (or *name* or *id*) id_u so that $|\{id_u : u \in V\}| \geq k$.

Naming. The naming problem is a special case of the k-labeling problem in which it must additionally hold that $k = n$. This, in turn, implies that $id_u \neq id_v$ for all distinct $u, v \in V$ (so, unique labels are required for the nodes).

Minimal (Consecutive) Naming. It is a special case of naming in which it must additionally hold that the n nodes output the labels $\{0, 1, \ldots, n-1\}$.

Counting Upper Bound. Nodes must determine an upper bound k on the network size n.

Counting. A special case of counting upper bound in which it must hold that $k = n$.

6   Static Networks with Broadcast

We here assume that the network is described by a static graph $G = (V, E)$, where $E \subseteq \{\{u, v\} : u, v \in V\}$. Moreover, the message transmission model is broadcast, that is, in every round, each node u generates a single message to be delivered to all its neighbors. Note that any impossibility result established for static networks is also valid for dynamic networks as a static network is a special case of a dynamic network.

First of all, note that if all nodes start from the same initial state then, if we restrict ourselves to deterministic algorithms, naming is impossible to solve in general static networks, even if nodes know n. The reason is that in the worst-case they may be arranged in a ring (in which each node has precisely 2 neighbors) and it is a well-known fact [Ang80, Lyn96, AW04] that, in this case, in every round r, all nodes are in identical states.

We show now that impossibility persists even if we allow a unique leader and even if nodes have complete knowledge of the network.

Theorem 1. *Naming is impossible to solve by deterministic algorithms in general anonymous (static) networks with broadcast even in the presence of a leader and even if nodes have complete knowledge of the network.*

Proof. Consider a star graph with the leader in the center. ☐

An obvious generalization is that, under the same assumptions as in the statement of the theorem, it is impossible to solve k-labeling for any $k \geq 3$. In the full paper, we also provide some thoughts on a degree-based labeling.

We now turn our attention to the simpler counting problem. First we establish the necessity of assuming a unique leader.

Theorem 2. *Without a leader, counting is impossible to solve by deterministic algorithms in general anonymous networks with broadcast.*

Proof. If some algorithm counts in k rounds the n nodes of a static ring, then it fails on a ring of $k + 1$ nodes.   □

In view of Theorem 2, we assume again a unique leader in order to solve counting. Recall that the *eccentricity* of a node u is defined as the greatest geodesic distance between u and v, over all $v \in V \backslash \{u\}$, where "distance" is equivalent to "shortest path". We first describe a protocol *Leader_Eccentricity* (inspired by the *Wake&Label* set of algorithms of [FPPP00]) that assigns to every node a label equal to its distance from the leader and then we exploit this to solve counting. We assume that all nodes have access to the current round number via a variable r.

Protocol *Leader_Eccentricity.* The leader begins with $label \leftarrow 0$ and $max\_asgned \leftarrow 0$ and all other nodes with $label \leftarrow \bot$. In the first round, the leader broadcasts an $assign$ (1) message. Upon reception of an $assign$ (i) message, a node that has $label = \bot$ sets $label \leftarrow i$ and broadcasts to its neighbors an $assign$ $(i + 1)$ message and an ack (i) message. Upon reception of an ack (i) message, a node with $label \neq \bot$ and $label < i$ broadcasts it. Upon reception of an ack (i) message, the leader sets $max\_asgned \leftarrow i$ and if $r > 2 \cdot (max\_asgned + 1)$ then it broadcasts a $halt$ message, outputs its label, and halts. Upon reception of a $halt$ message, a node broadcasts $halt$, outputs its label, and halts.

Theorem 3. *In Leader_Eccentricity nodes output $\epsilon + 1$ distinct labels where ϵ is the eccentricity of the leader. In particular, every node outputs its distance from the leader.*

Proof. At time 2, nodes at distance 1 from the leader receive $assign$ (1) and set their label to 1. By induction on distance, nodes at distance i get label i at round $i + 1$. In the same round, they send an ack that must arrive at the leader at round $2i + 1$. If not then there is no node at distance i.   □

We now use *Leader_Eccentricity* to solve counting in anonymous unknown static networks with a leader. We additionally assume that at the end of the *Leader_Eccentricity* process each node u knows the number of neighbors $up(u) = |\{\{v, u\} \in E : label(v) = label(u) - 1\}|$ it has to its upper level (it can store this during the *Leader_Eccentricity* process by counting the number of $assign$ messages that arrived at it from its upper level neighbors). Moreover, we assume that all nodes know the leader's eccentricity ϵ (just have the leader include max_asgned in its $halt$ message). Finally, let, for simplicity, the first round just after the completion of the above process be round $r = 1$. For this, we just need all nodes to end concurrently the *Leader_Eccentricity* process. This is done by having node with label i that receives or creates (this is true for the leader) a $halt$ message in round r halt in round $(r + max\_asgned - i)$. Then the nodes just reset their round counters.

Protocol *Anonymous_Counting.* Nodes first execute the modified *Leader_Eccentricity*. When $\epsilon - r + 1 = label(u)$, a non-leader node u receives a possibly empty (in case of no lower-level neighbors) set of $partial\_count_i$ ($rval_i$) messages and broadcasts a $partial\_count$ $((1 + \sum_i rval_i)/up(u))$ message. When $r = \epsilon + 1$, the leader receives a set of $partial\_count_i$ ($rval_i$) messages, sets $count \leftarrow 1 + \sum_i rval_i$, broadcasts a $halt$ ($count$) message, outputs $count$, and halts. When a non-leader u receives a $halt$ ($count$) message, it outputs $count$ and halts.

For a given round r denote by $rval_i(u)$ the ith message received by node u.

Theorem 4. *Anonymous_Counting solves the counting problem in anonymous static networks with broadcast under the assumption of a unique leader. All nodes terminate in $O(n)$ rounds and use messages of size $O(\log n)$.*

Proof. By induction on the round number r, in the beginning of round $r \geq 2$, it holds that $\sum_{u:label(u)=\epsilon-r+1} (1 + \sum_i rval_i(u)) = |\{u : label(u) \geq \epsilon - r + 1\}|$. Clearly, in round $\epsilon + 1$ it holds that $count = 1 + \sum_i rval_i(leader) = |\{u : label(u) \geq 0\}| = n$. □

7 Dynamic Networks with Broadcast

We now turn our attention to the more general case of 1-interval connected dynamic networks with broadcast. We begin with a conjecture stating that dynamicity renders nontrivial computation impossible (see also [OW05] for a similar conjecture in a quite different setting). Then we naturally strengthen the model to allow some computation.

Conjecture 1. It is impossible to compute (even with a leader) the predicate $N_a \geq 1$, that is "exists an a in the input", in general anonymous unknown dynamic networks with broadcast.

In view of Theorem 1, which establishes that we cannot name the nodes of a static, and thus also of a dynamic, network if broadcast communication is assumed, and of the above conjecture, implying that in dynamic networks we cannot count even with a leader [2], we start strengthening our initial model.

Let us assume that there is a unique leader l that knows an upper bound d on maximum degree ever to appear in the dynamic network, that is $d \geq \max_{u \in V, r \in \mathbb{N}}\{d_u(r)\}$. We keep the broadcast message transmission.

Note first that impossibility of naming persists. However, we show that obtaining an upper bound on the size of the network now becomes possible, though exponential in the worst case.

Protocol Degree_Counting. The leader stores in d the maximum degree that will ever appear and begins with $label \leftarrow 0$, $count \leftarrow 1$, $latest\_event \leftarrow 0$, $max\_label \leftarrow 0$, and $r \leftarrow 0$ while all other nodes begin with $label \leftarrow \perp$, $count \leftarrow 0$, and $r \leftarrow 0$. In the beginning of each round each node increments by one its round

---

[2] This is implied because, if we could count, we could have a node wait at most $n - 1$ rounds to hear of an a (provided that all nodes that have heard of an a forward it) and if no, reject.

counter r. The leader in each round r broadcasts *assign* (r). Upon reception of
an *assign* (r_label) message, a node with *label* $=\perp$ sets *label* $\leftarrow r\_label$ and from
now in each round r broadcasts *assign* (r) and *my_label* $(label)$. A node with
label $=\perp$ that did not receive an *assign* message sends an *unassigned* (r) message. All nodes continuously broadcast the maximum *my_label* and *unassigned*
messages that they have received so far. Upon reception of an *unassigned* (i)
message, the leader, if $i > latest\_event$, it sets *count* $\leftarrow 1$ and, for $k = 1, \ldots, i$,
count $\leftarrow$ *count* $+ d \cdot$ *count*, *max_label* $\leftarrow i$, and *latest_event* $\leftarrow r$ and upon
reception of a *my_label* (j) message, if $j > max\_label$, it sets *count* $\leftarrow 1$
and, for $k = 1, \ldots, j$, *count* $\leftarrow$ *count* $+ d \cdot$ *count*, *latest_event* $\leftarrow r$, and
max_label $\leftarrow j$ (if receives both i, j it does it for $\max\{i, j\}$). When it holds
that $r > count + latest\_event - 1$ (eventually occurs) then the leader broadcasts
a *halt* $(count)$ message for *count* rounds and then outputs *count* and halts. Each
node that receives a *halt* (r_count) message, sets *count* $\leftarrow r\_count$, broadcasts
a *halt* $(count)$ message for *count* rounds and then outputs *count* and halts.

Theorem 5. *Degree_Counting solves the counting upper bound problem in
anonymous dynamic networks with broadcast under the assumption of a unique
leader. The obtained upper bound is $O(d^n)$ (in the worst case).*

Proof. In the first round, the leader assigns the label 1 to its neighbors and
obtains an *unassigned* (1) message from each one of them. So, it sets *count* $\leftarrow$
$(d + 1)$ (in fact, note that in the first step it can simply set *count* $\leftarrow d_u(1) + 1$,
but this is minor), *latest_event* $\leftarrow 1$, and *max_label* $\leftarrow 1$. Now, if there are
further nodes, at most by round *count* $+ latest\_event - 1$ it must have received
an *unassigned* (i) message with $i > latest\_event$ or a *my_label* (j) with $j >$
max_label. Note that the reception of an *unassigned* (i) message implies that
at least $i + 1$ distinct labels have been assigned because as long as there are
unlabeled nodes one new label is assigned in each round to at least one node
(this is implied by Lemma 1 and the fact that all nodes with labels constantly
assign new labels). Initially, one node (the leader) assigned to at most d nodes
label 1. Then the $d + 1$ labeled nodes assigned to at most $(d + 1)d$ unlabeled
nodes the label 2, totalling $(d + 1) + (d + 1)d$, and so on.

In the worst-case, each label in $\{0, 1, \ldots, n - 1\}$ is assigned to precisely one
node (e.g., consider a static line with the leader in the one endpoint). In this
case the nodes count $O(d^n)$. □

We point out that if nodes have access to more drastic initial knowledge such as an upper bound e on the *maximum expansion*, defined as
$\max_{u,r,r'}\{|future_{u,r}(r' + 1)| - |future_{u,r}(r')|\}$ (maximum number of concurrent
new influences), where $future_{(u,r)}(r') := \{v \in V : (u, r) \rightsquigarrow (v, r')\}$, for $r \le r'$,
then essentially the same protocol as above provides an $O(n \cdot e)$ upper bound.

8   Dynamic Networks with One-to-Each

The result of Theorem 1, in the light of (a) the conjecture of Section 7, and
(b) the assumption of a broadcast message transmission model, clearly indicates

that nontrivial computations in anonymous unknown dynamic networks are impossible even under the assumption of a unique leader. We now relax these assumptions so that we can state a correct naming protocol. We start by relaxing the assumption of a broadcast message transmission medium by offering to nodes access to a *one-to-each message transmission mechanism*. We also assume a unique leader as without it, even under one-to-each, impossibility persists.

1st Version - Protocol *Fair*

We now present protocol *Fair* in which the unique leader assigns distinct labels to each node of the network. The labels assigned are tuples (r, h, i), where r is the round during which the label was assigned, h is the label of the leader node and i is a unique number assigned by the leader. The labels can be uniquely ordered first by r, then by h and finally by i (in ascending order).

Each node maintains the following local variables: *clock*, for counting the rounds of execution of the protocol (due to synchrony), *label*, for storing the label assigned by the leader, *state*, for storing the local state that can be set to {*anonymous, named, leader*}, and *counter*, for storing the number of labels generated. All nodes are initialized to *clock* $\leftarrow$ 0, *id* $\leftarrow$ $(0, \perp, \perp)$, *state* $\leftarrow$ *anonymous*, and *counter* $\leftarrow$ 0 except from the leader that is initialized to *clock* $\leftarrow$ 0, *id* $\leftarrow$ $(0, 1, 1)$, *state* $\leftarrow$ *leader*, and *counter* $\leftarrow$ 1.

Each turn the leader u consults the one-to-each transmission mechanism and identifies a set of locally unique edge-labels $1, 2, \ldots, d(u)$, one for each of the edges incident to it. [3] The leader iterates the edge-label set and transmits to each neighboring node a different message m_i, $1 \leq i \leq d(u)$ that contains the unique label $(clock, label, counter + i)$. When the transmission is complete, it increases the variable *counter* by $d(u)$. All the other nodes of the network do not transmit any messages (or transmit a null message).

All nodes under *state* = *anonymous*, upon receiving a (non-null) message set the local *label* to the contents of the message and change *state* to *named*. All the other nodes of the network simply ignore all the messages received.

Recall that a naming assignment is correct if *all nodes* are assigned *different* labels. It is clear that *Fair* is a non-terminating correct protocol, given the following *fairness assumption*: the leader node at some point has become directly connected with each other node of the network (i.e., eventually meets all nodes).

Lemma 2. *With one-to-each transmission, under the fairness assumption, and in the presence of a unique leader, protocol Fair eventually computes a unique assignment for all the nodes in any anonymous unknown dynamic network.*

2nd Version - Protocol *Delegate*

We now proceed by presenting a stronger protocol *Delegate* (based on *Fair*) that is correct even without the fairness assumption. To achieve correctness

---

[3] Recall that these edge-labels can be reselected arbitrarily in each round (even if the neighbors remain the same) by the adversary so that a node cannot infer the internal state of a neighbor, based solely on the corresponding local edge-name.

the leader node delegates the role of assignment of labels to all the nodes that it encounters. Thus, without loss of generality, even if the leader does not encounter all other nodes of the network, due to the *connectivity property*, all nodes will eventually hear from the leader. Therefore, all nodes will either receive a unique label from the leader or from another labeled node. The uniqueness among the labels generated is guaranteed since each label can be traced back to the node that issued it using the h parameter.

In *Delegate* the nodes maintain the same variables as in *Fair*. Each turn the leader performs the same actions as in *Fair*. Also similarly to *Fair*, each node that is in $state = anonymous$ does not transmit any message (or transmits a null message if message transmission is compulsory). Each node u that is in $state = named$ performs similar actions as the leader node and transmits to each edge-label i a message containing the unique label $(clock_u, label_u, counter_u + i)$ and then increases the variable $counter_u$ by $d(u)$. All nodes under $state = anonymous$, upon receiving one or more (non-null) messages that contain a label, select the message that contains the lowest label (i.e., the one with the lowest h parameter) and set the local $label$ to the contents of the message and change $state$ to $named$.

Lemma 3. *With one-to-each transmission, and in the presence of a unique leader, protocol Delegate correctly computes a unique assignment for all the nodes in any anonymous unknown dynamic network.*

3rd Version - Protocol *Dynamic_Naming* (terminating)

The protocols *Fair* and *Delegate* compute a correct naming assignment (based on different assumptions) but do not terminate. Essentially the nodes continue to transmit labels forever. We now present protocol *Dynamic_Naming* (based on *Delegate, Fair*) that manages to terminate.

Dynamic_Naming is an $O(n)$-time protocol that assigns unique ids to the nodes and informs them of n. As usual, there is a unique leader l with id 0 while all other nodes have id $\perp$.

The idea here is as follows. Similarly to *Delegate*, all nodes that have obtained an id assign ids and these ids are guaranteed to be unique. Additionally to *Delegate*, we have nodes that have obtained an id to acknowledge their id to the leader. Thus, all nodes send their ids and all nodes continuously forward the received ids so that they eventually arrive at the leader (simple flooding mechanism). So, at some round r, the leader knows a set of assigned ids $K(r)$. We describe now the termination criterion. If $|K(r)| \neq |V|$ then in at most $|K(r)|$ additional rounds the leader must hear (be causally influenced) from a node outside $K(r)$ (to see why, see Lemma 1). Such a node, either has an id that the leader first hears of, or has no id yet. In the first case, the leader updates $K(r)$ and in the second waits until it hears of a new id (which is guaranteed to appear in the future). On the other hand, if $|K(r)| = |V|$ no new info will ever arrive at the leader in the future and the leader may terminate after the $|K(r)|$-round waiting period ellapses.

Protocol *Dynamic_Naming*. Initially, every node has three variables *count* ←
0, *acks* ← ∅, and *latest_unassigned* ← 0 and the leader additionally has
latest_new ← 0, *time_bound* ← 1, and *known_ids* ← {0}. A node with
id ≠⊥ for 1 ≤ *i* ≤ *k* sends *assign* (*id*, *count* + *i*) message to its *i*th neighbor and sets *count* ← *count* + *k*. In the first round, the leader additionally sets
known_ids ← {0, (0, 1), (0, 2), . . . , (0, *k*)}, *latest_new* ← 1, and *time_bound* ←
1 + |*known_ids*|. Upon receipt of *l* *assign* messages (*rid_j*), a node with *id* =⊥
sets *id* ← min_j{*rid_j*} (in number of bits), *acks* ← *acks* ∪ *id*, sends an *ack*
(*acks*) message to all its *k* current neighbors, for 1 ≤ *i* ≤ *k* sends *assign*
(*id*, *count* + *i*) message to its *i*th neighbor, and sets *count* ← *count* + *k*. Upon
receipt of *l* *ack* messages (*acks_j*), a nonleader sets *acks* ← *acks* ∪ (⋃_j *acks_j*)
and sends *ack* (*acks*). A node with *id* =⊥ sends *unassigned* (*current_round*).
Upon receipt of *l* ≥ 0 *unassigned* messages (*val_j*), a node with *id* ∉ {0, ⊥
} sets *latest_unassigned* ← max{*latest_unassigned*, max_j{*val_j*}} and sends
unassigned (*latest_unassigned*). Upon receipt of *l* *ack* messages (*acks_j*), the
leader if (⋃_j *acks_j*)*known_ids* ≠ ∅ sets *known_ids* ← *known_ids* ∪ (⋃_j *acks_j*),
latest_new ← *current_round* and *time_bound* ← *current_round* + |*known_ids*|
and upon receipt of *l* *unassigned* messages (*val_j*), it sets *latest_unassigned* ←
max{*latest_unassigned*, max_j{*val_j*}}. If, at some round *r*, it holds at the leader
that *r* > *time_bound* and *latest_unassigned* < *latest_new*, the leader sends a
halt (|*known_ids*|) message for |*known_ids*| − 1 rounds and then outputs *id* and
halts. Any node that receives a *halt* (*n*) message, sends *halt* (*n*) for *n* − 2 rounds
and then outputs *id* and halts.

Denote by $S(r) = \{v \in V : (l, 0) \rightsquigarrow (v, r)\}$ the set of nodes that have obtained
an id at round *r* and by *K*(*r*) those nodes in *S*(*r*) whose id is known by the leader
at round *r*, that is $K(r) = \{u \in V : \exists r' \text{ s.t. } u \in S(r') \text{ and } (u, r') \rightsquigarrow (l, r)\}$.

Theorem 6. *Dynamic_Naming solves the naming problem in anonymous unknown dynamic networks under the assumptions of one-to-each message transmission and of a unique leader. All nodes terminate in $O(n)$ rounds and use
messages of size $\Theta(n^2)$.*

Proof. Unique names are guaranteed as in *Delegate*. Termination is as follows.
Clearly, if $V \backslash K(r) \neq \emptyset$, either $|K(r + |K(r)|)| \geq |K(r)| + 1$ or $(u, r) \rightsquigarrow (l, r +
|K(r)|)$ for some $u \in V \backslash S(r)$. The former is recognized by the leader by the
arrival of a new id and the latter by the arrival of an *unassigned* (*timestamp*)
message, where *timestamp* ≥ *r*. On the other hand, if $K(r) = V$ then $|K(r +
|K(r)|)| = |K(r)|$ and $\nexists u \in V \backslash S(r)$ s.t. $(u, r) \rightsquigarrow (l, r + |K(r)|)$ as $V \backslash S(r) = \emptyset$.
Finally, note that connectivity implies that $|S(r+1)| \geq \min\{|S(r)|+1, n\}$ which
in turn implies $O(n)$ rounds until unique ids are assigned. Then another $O(n)$
rounds are required until nodes terminate. □

Clearly, by executing a simple $O(n)$-time process after *Dynamic_Naming* we
can easily reassign minimal (consecutive) names to the nodes. The leader just
floods a list of (*old_id*, *new_id*) pairs, one for each node in the network.

Note that the messages sent by *Dynamic_Naming* may be of size $\Omega(n^2)$. We
now refine *Dynamic_Naming* to arrive at a more involved construction that

reduces the message size to $\Theta(\log n)$ by paying a small increase in termination time. We call this 4th version of our naming protocols *Individual_Conversations*. Due to space restrictions, we only give the main idea here.

Protocol *Individual_Conversations* [Main Idea]. To reduce the size of the messages (i) the assigned names are now of the form $k \cdot d + id$, where id is the id of the node, d is the number of *unique consecutive* ids that the leader knows so far, and $k \geq 1$ is a name counter (ii) Any time that the leader wants to communicate to a remote node that has a unique id it sends a message with the id of that node and a timestamp equal to the current round. The timestamp allows all nodes to prefer this message from previous ones so that the gain is twofold: the message is delivered and no node ever issues a message containing more than one id. The remote node then can reply in the same way. For the assignment formula to work, nodes that obtain ids are not allowed to further assign ids until the leader freezes all named nodes and reassigns to them unique consecutive ids. During freezing, the leader is informed of any new assignments by the named nodes and terminates if all report that no further assignments were performed.

Theorem 7. *Individual_Conversations solves the (minimal) naming problem in $O(n^3)$ rounds using messages of size $\Theta(\log n)$.*

References

[AFR06]   Aspnes, J., Fich, F.E., Ruppert, E.: Relationships between broadcast and shared memory in reliable anonymous distributed systems. Distributed Computing 18(3), 209–219 (2006)

[AGVP90] Awerbuch, B., Goldreich, O., Vainish, R., Peleg, D.: A trade-off between information and communication in broadcast protocols. Journal of the ACM (JACM) 37(2), 238–256 (1990)

[AH00]   Albers, S., Henzinger, M.: Exploring unknown environments. SIAM J. Comput. 29(4), 1164–1188 (2000)

[AKL08]   Avin, C., Koucký, M., Lotker, Z.: How to explore a fast-changing world (Cover time of a simple random walk on evolving graphs). In: Aceto, L., Damgård, I., Goldberg, L.A., Halldórsson, M.M., Ingólfsdóttir, A., Walukiewicz, I. (eds.) ICALP 2008, Part I. LNCS, vol. 5125, pp. 121–132. Springer, Heidelberg (2008)

[Ang80]   Angluin, D.: Local and global properties in networks of processors (extended abstract). In: Proceedings of the Twelfth Annual ACM Symposium on Theory of Computing (STOC), pp. 82–93. ACM (1980)

[ASW88]   Attiya, H., Snir, M., Warmuth, M.K.: Computing on an anonymous ring. J. ACM 35(4), 845–875 (1988)

[AW04]   Attiya, H., Welch, J.: Distributed computing: fundamentals, simulations, and advanced topics, vol. 19. Wiley-Interscience (2004)

[BV99]   Boldi, P., Vigna, S.: Computing anonymously with arbitrary knowledge. In: Proceedings of the 18th Annual ACM Symposium on Principles of Distributed Computing (PODC), pp. 181–188. ACM (1999)

[CFQS11] Casteigts, A., Flocchini, P., Quattrociocchi, W., Santoro, N.: Time-varying graphs and dynamic networks. In: Ad-hoc, Mobile, and Wireless Networks, pp. 346–359 (2011)

[CMM12]   Chalopin, J., Métivier, Y., Morsellino, T.: On snapshots and stable properties detection in anonymous fully distributed systems (extended abstract). In: Even, G., Halldórsson, M.M. (eds.) SIROCCO 2012. LNCS, vol. 7355, pp. 207–218. Springer, Heidelberg (2012)

[Dol00]   Dolev, S.: Self-stabilization. MIT Press, Cambridge (2000)

[DP90]   Deng, X., Papadimitriou, C.: Exploring an unknown graph. In: 31st Annual Symposium on Foundations of Computer Science (FOCS), pp. 355–361. IEEE (1990)

[FPPP00]   Fraigniaud, P., Pelc, A., Peleg, D., Pérennes, S.: Assigning labels in unknown anonymous networks (extended abstract). In: Proceedings of the Nineteenth Annual ACM Symposium on Principles of Distributed Computing (PODC), pp. 101–111. ACM (2000)

[Hae11]   Haeupler, B.: Analyzing network coding gossip made easy. In: Proceedings of the 43rd Annual ACM Symposium on Theory of Computing (STOC), pp. 293–302. ACM (2011)

[KKK00]   Kempe, D., Kleinberg, J., Kumar, A.: Connectivity and inference problems for temporal networks. In: Proceedings of the Thirty-Second Annual ACM Symposium on Theory of Computing, STOC 2000, pp. 504–513. ACM (2000)

[KLO10]   Kuhn, F., Lynch, N., Oshman, R.: Distributed computation in dynamic networks. In: Proceedings of the 42nd ACM Symposium on Theory of Computing (STOC), pp. 513–522. ACM (2010)

[Lam78]   Lamport, L.: Time, clocks, and the ordering of events in a distributed system. Commun. ACM 21(7), 558–565 (1978)

[Lyn96]   Lynch, N.A.: Distributed Algorithms, 1st edn. Morgan Kaufmann (1996)

[MCS12a]   Michail, O., Chatzigiannakis, I., Spirakis, P.G.: Brief announcement: naming and counting in anonymous unknown dynamic networks. In: Aguilera, M.K. (ed.) DISC 2012. LNCS, vol. 7611, pp. 437–438. Springer, Heidelberg (2012)

[MCS12b]   Michail, O., Chatzigiannakis, I., Spirakis, P.G.: Causality, influence, and computation in possibly disconnected synchronous dynamic networks. In: Baldoni, R., Flocchini, P., Binoy, R. (eds.) OPODIS 2012. LNCS, vol. 7702, pp. 269–283. Springer, Heidelberg (2012); Journal of Parallel and Distributed Computing (2013), doi:10.1016/j.jpdc.2013.07.007

[MMCS13]   Mertzios, G.B., Michail, O., Chatzigiannakis, I., Spirakis, P.G.: Temporal network optimization subject to connectivity constraints. In: Fomin, F.V., Freivalds, R., Kwiatkowska, M., Peleg, D. (eds.) ICALP 2013, Part II. LNCS, vol. 7966, pp. 657–668. Springer, Heidelberg (2013)

[OW05]   O'Dell, R., Wattenhofer, R.: Information dissemination in highly dynamic graphs. In: Proceedings of the 2005 Joint Workshop on Foundations of Mobile Computing, DIALM-POMC 2005, pp. 104–110. ACM (2005)

[YK96]   Yamashita, M., Kameda, T.: omputing on anonymous networks. i. characterizing the solvable cases. IEEE Transactions on Parallel and Distributed Systems 7(1), 69–89 (1996)

Gathering Asynchronous Oblivious Agents with Restricted Vision in an Infinite Line

Samuel Guilbault and Andrzej Pelc*

Département d'informatique, Université du Québec en Outaouais,
Gatineau, Québec J8X 3X7, Canada
samuel.guilbault@gmail.com,
pelc@uqo.ca

Abstract. We consider the problem of gathering identical, memoryless, mobile agents in one node of an infinite anonymous line of nodes. Agents start from different nodes of the line. They operate in Look-Compute-Move cycles and have to end up at the same node. Our model differs from most of the existing literature on gathering asynchronous oblivious agents in graphs in that the agents have restricted perception capabilities: they can only see at bounded distance d (called the *radius of vision*) from their current location. In one cycle, an agent takes a snapshot of the part of the line at distance at most d from it (Look), makes a decision to stay idle or to move to one of its adjacent nodes (Compute), and in the latter case makes an instantaneous move to this neighbor (Move). Cycles are performed asynchronously for each agent.

An initial configuration of agents is called *gatherable* if there exists a deterministic algorithm that gathers all the agents of the configuration in one node and keeps them idle from then on, regardless of the actions of the asynchronous adversary. (The algorithm can be even tailored to gather this specific configuration.) A deterministic gathering algorithm is *universal* if it gathers all gatherable configurations. We observe that if the vision of agents is unrestricted then a universal gathering algorithm exists. For radius of vision $d = 1$ a universal gathering algorithm is known. By contrast, our main result shows that for any finite radius of vision $d > 1$ there is no universal gathering algorithm. Our result remains valid for rings of size at least $7d + 8$.

Keywords: asynchronous, mobile agent, gathering, line.

1 Introduction

Gathering is one of fundamental tasks in mobile agent coordination. Its aim is to bring mobile entities (agents), initially situated at different locations of some environment, to the same location (not determined in advance) and stop. Agents may operate either in the plane, in which case they usually represent mobile

---

* Supported in part by NSERC discovery grant and by the Research Chair in Distributed Computing of the Université du Québec en Outaouais.

T. Higashino et al. (Eds.): SSS 2013, LNCS 8255, pp. 296–310, 2013.

robots, or in a network, modeled by a simple undirected graph, in which case they may model software agents. Gathering permits, e.g, to exchange information between agents or coordinate their further actions, such as network maintenance.

A lot of effort has been devoted to study gathering in very weak scenarios, where agents represent simple devices that could be cheaply mass-produced. One of these scenarios is the CORDA model, initially formulated for agents operating in the plane [5–7, 14, 20–22] and then adapted to the network environment [9, 17–19]. In this paper we study gathering in a scenario even weaker than the above. Below we describe our model and point out how it differs with respect to that from [9, 17–19].

Consider a simple undirected graph. Neither nodes nor links of the graph have any labels. Initially, some nodes of the graph are occupied by identical agents and there is at most one agent at each node. The goal is to gather all agents at one node of the graph and stop. Agents operate in Look-Compute-Move cycles. Let d be a positive integer, called the *radius of vision* of the agents. In one cycle, an agent takes a snapshot of the part of the graph at distance at most d from its current position (Look), then, based on it, makes a decision to stay idle or to move to one of its adjacent nodes (Compute), and in the latter case makes an instantaneous move to this neighbor (Move). Cycles are performed asynchronously for each agent. This means that the time between Look, Compute, and Move operations is finite but unbounded, and is decided by the adversary for each agent. The only constraint is that moves are instantaneous, and hence any agent performing a Look operation can see other agents at its own or other nodes and not on edges, while performing a move. However an agent A may perform a Look operation at some time t, perceiving agents at some nodes, then Compute a target neighbor at some time $t' > t$, and Move to this neighbor at some later time $t'' > t'$ in which some agents are at different nodes from those previously perceived by A, because in the meantime they performed their Move operations. Hence agents may move based on significantly outdated perceptions, which adds to the difficulty of achieving the goal of gathering. It should be stressed that agents are memoryless (oblivious), i.e., they do not have any memory of past observations. Thus the target node (which is either the current position of the agent or one of its neighbors) is decided by the agent during a Compute operation solely on the basis of the location of other agents perceived in the previous Look operation. Agents are anonymous and execute the same deterministic algorithm. They cannot leave any marks at visited nodes, nor send any messages to other agents.

The only difference between our scenario and that from [9, 17–19] is in what an agent perceives during the Look operation. While in the above papers the agent was assumed to see the entire configuration of all agents in the graph (i.e., it was assumed to have unlimited vision) we assume that it only sees the part of the configuration at distance at most d from its current position, i.e., nodes at distance at most d from the perceiving agent and agents located at these nodes. This model has been used in [10] in the context of ring exploration. We also used a particular instance of this model in [15], for $d = 1$, in the context of gathering in regular bipartite graphs.

An important and well studied capability in the literature on agent gathering is the *multiplicity detection* [14, 17–19, 21]. This is the ability of the agents to perceive, during the Look operation, if there is one or more agents at a given location. It has been shown in [19] that without this capability gathering in networks is usually impossible (even for the ring and even if agents can take global snapshots). Hence in this paper we assume the capability of multiplicity detection. In our model it means that the agent, during the Look operation, can distinguish, for any node at distance at most d from it, if it is empty, if there is a single agent at this node (such an agent is called a *singleton*) or if there is more than one agent at the node (we say that there is a *tower* at this node). It should be stressed that an agent does not see a difference between a node occupied by a or b agents, for distinct $a, b > 1$.

In this paper we study the gathering problem in the infinite network forming a line, i.e., in which all nodes have degree 2. A configuration of agents is called *gatherable* if there exists a deterministic algorithm that gathers all the agents of the configuration at one node and keeps them idle from then on, regardless of the actions of the asynchronous adversary. (The algorithm can be even tailored to gather this specific configuration.) Similarly as in [9, 17–19] we assume that in an initial configuration there is at most one agent per node, i.e., there are no towers. A deterministic gathering algorithm is *universal* if it gathers all gatherable configurations. In this paper we investigate the existence of universal gathering algorithms for the infinite line.

1.1   Our Results

We first observe that if the vision of agents is unrestricted, then a universal gathering algorithm exists for the infinite line. On the other hand, it follows from [15] that for radius of vision $d = 1$ there is a universal algorithm for all regular bipartite graphs. Indeed, applied for the line, our result from [15] implies that the only gatherable configuration for $d = 1$ is a segment of three singletons, and hence the easy algorithm gathering this configuration is universal. Hence it is natural to ask if there are universal gathering algorithms for larger radii of vision. The main result of this paper is a negative answer to this question: we show that a universal gathering algorithm for the infinite line does not exist for any finite radius of vision $d > 1$. Our result remains valid for rings of size at least $7d + 8$.

1.2   Related Work

The problem of gathering mobile agents has been extensively studied in the literature, under many scenarios. Agents move either in a network represented as a graph, cf. e.g. [2, 11–13], or in the plane [1, 3, 5–7, 14, 20–22], they are labeled [11, 12], or anonymous [1, 3, 5–7, 14, 20–22], gathering algorithms are probabilistic (cf. [2] and the literature cited there), or deterministic [1, 3, 5–7, 11, 13, 14, 20–22].

The very weak scenario of anonymous identical agents that cannot send any messages and communicate with the environment only by observing it, was first used to study deterministic gathering in the plane [1, 3, 5–7, 14, 20–22]. The scenario was further precised in various ways. In [5] agents have memory, while in [1, 3, 6, 7, 14, 20–22] they are oblivious, i.e., do not have any memory of past observations. Oblivious agents operate in Look-Compute-Move cycles. The differences are in the amount of synchrony assumed in the execution of the cycles. In [3, 22] cycles are executed synchronously in rounds by all active agents, and the adversary can only decide which agents are active in a given cycle. In [5–7, 14, 20–22] they are executed asynchronously, giving raise to the CORDA model. In this model the adversary is very powerful: it can interleave operations arbitrarily, stop agents during the move, and schedule Look operations of some agents while others are moving. It is proved in [14] that gathering is possible in the CORDA model if agents have the same orientation of the plane, even with limited visibility. Without orientation, the gathering problem was positively solved in [6], assuming that agents have the capability of multiplicity detection. A complementary negative result concerning the CORDA model was proved in [21]: without multiplicity detection, gathering agents that do not have orientation is impossible.

Our scenario is the most similar to the asynchronous model used in [9, 17–19] for rings. It differs from the CORDA model in the execution of Move operations. This has been adapted to the context of networks: moves of the agents are executed instantaneously from a node to its neighbor, and hence agents always see other agents at nodes. All possibilities of the asynchronous adversary concerning interleaving operations performed by various agents are the same as in the CORDA model, and the characteristics of the agents (anonymity, obliviousness, multiplicity detection) are also the same. Unlike in our scenario, [9, 17–19] assume unlimited vision of agents. The restricted vision model used in the present paper has been previously used in [10] for ring exploration. We also used its particular instance in [15] in the context of gathering, for the radius of vision $d = 1$.

A significantly different model of asynchrony for the study of gathering has been used in [4, 8, 11, 16]. In these papers gathering of two agents with no vision is studied, and meeting can occur either at a node or inside an edge. In [8, 11] agents have distinct labels, in [4] each agent knows the coordinates of its position in a global coordinate system, and in [16] agents are identical and anonymous.

2   Terminology and Preliminaries

We consider an infinite line of nodes of degree 2. A node at which there is no agent is called *empty*, otherwise it is called *occupied*. A single agent occupying a node is called a *singleton* and more than one agent occupying a node form a *tower*. An empty node is denoted by 0, a singleton is denoted by 1, and a tower by $*$. The total number of agents is finite but unknown. A configuration is a function on the set of nodes of the line with values in the set $\{0, 1, *\}$. An initial configuration does not contain towers. We say that singletons are adjacent (resp. towers are adjacent, a singleton is adjacent to a tower), if the respective nodes are adjacent. Since the position of a configuration in the line is irrelevant, a configuration can be identified with a finite sequence with terms in $\{0, 1, *\}$, such that the first and the last terms of the sequence are non-zero, using the convention that all nodes outside this sequence are empty. In a configuration $(c_1, \ldots, c_r)$ the terms c_1 and c_r are called *extremities*. A configuration is *symmetric* if the corresponding sequence has an axis of symmetry. There are two types of symmetric configurations: *node-symmetric* if the axis goes through a node, and *edge-symmetric* if the axis goes through an edge. For example, the configuration $(*, 1, 0, 1, 0, 1, *)$ is node-symmetric, the configuration $(*, 1, 0, 1, 1, 0, 1, *)$ is edge-symmetric, and the configuration $(*, 1, 0, 1, 0, 0, 1, *)$ is not symmetric. The *diameter* of a configuration is the maximum distance between any two agents.

A *view* of an agent A with radius of vision d is the set of two sequences

$$\{(a_d, \ldots, a_1, \underline{1}, b_1, \ldots, b_d), (b_d, \ldots, b_1, \underline{1}, a_1, \ldots, a_d)\}$$

if the agent is a singleton, and the set of two sequences

$$\{(a_d, \ldots, a_1, \underline{*}, b_1, \ldots, b_d), (b_d, \ldots, b_1, \underline{*}, a_1, \ldots, a_d)\}$$

if the agent is in a tower. The sequences are of length $2d+1$, the central singleton or tower is underlined for clarity, and a_i and b_i are from the set $\{0, 1, *\}$. We define the view as a pair of sequences one of which is the mirror image of the other, in order to capture the feature of the model that an agent cannot distinguish left from right. A view is symmetric if $a_i = b_i$, for all $i = 1, \ldots, d$. The sequences $(a_1, \ldots, a_d)$ and $(b_1, \ldots, b_d)$ are called the two *sides* of the view of the agent. We use 0^k to denote a sequence of k consecutive empty nodes.

The characteristics of our model imply that a given gathering algorithm may have many executions. This is due to two features of the model. First, since the Look, Compute and Move actions of every agent are asynchronous, different schedules of those actions potentially lead to different executions. Second, any Move action is based on the view of the agent obtained in the preceding Look action. If the view is symmetric and the algorithm prescribes to move when this view is given, the agent cannot distinguish to which of the two neighbors it should move, and each such choice leads to a potentially different execution.

We capture these different possibilities by using the concept of an *adversary* which schedules the Look, Compute and Move actions and chooses to move to one among the two neighbors for symmetric views, each time in a way most detrimental to the algorithm. If we prove that, for some initial configuration and for any hypothetical algorithm, the adversary can make the above choices so as to prevent gathering, it will follow that the given initial configuration is not gatherable, because for any hypothetical algorithm starting from this configuration, some possible execution of it prevents gathering.

We will use the following fact proved similarly as an analogous fact for rings in [19].

Proposition 1. *Edge-symmetric configurations are not gatherable, for any radius of vision and for unrestricted vision.*

The following proposition shows that if the vision of the agents is unrestricted, as in the model from [9, 17–19], then there exists a universal gathering algorithm for the line. The proof of this result is based on ideas from [9, 17–19] and is omitted due to space limitations.

Proposition 2. *There exists a universal gathering algorithm in the infinite line for agents with unrestricted vision.*

3   Nonexistence of Universal Gathering Algorithm for Radius of Vision $d > 1$

In this section we prove our main result: for any finite radius of vision $d > 1$, there is no universal gathering algorithm in the infinite line. (In the sequel we omit the word " finite" qualifying the radius of vision.) We start with the following two lemmas that hold for any radius of vision.

Lemma 1. *A configuration whose both extremities are towers is not gatherable, for any radius of vision.*

Proof. Consider a configuration C whose both extremities are towers, and any hypothetical gathering algorithm for this configuration. Consider an adversary that schedules Look-Compute-Move cycles for agents in rounds in such a way that:

– for every agent an entire cycle is performed in one round,
– all agents in a tower perform corresponding cycles in the same round,
– cycles for agents situated in different nodes are performed in different rounds,

as long as the diameter of the configuration is larger than 1. By induction on the round number it follows that, as long as the diameter is larger than 1, the configuration preserves the invariant that its extremities are towers. Since the hypothetical algorithm should gather the configuration, the diameter must eventually decrease to zero. Indeed, the characteristics of the adversary imply that the diameter can change by at most 1 in a round.

Consider the first round t when the diameter is at most 1. Since the diameter can change by at most 1 in a round, the diameter in round t is exactly 1. Hence the configuration consists of two adjacent towers and the lemma follows from Proposition 1. □

Lemma 2. *Consider any radius of vision and any algorithm that gathers the configuration with two occupied nodes that are adjacent, one of them occupied by a singleton and the other by a tower. Then this algorithm must instruct the tower to stay idle and the singleton to move on the tower.*

Proof. Consider an adversary that schedules Look-Compute-Move cycles for agents in rounds in such a way that:

- for every agent an entire cycle is performed in one round,
- all agents in a tower perform corresponding cycles in the same round,
- cycles for agents situated in different nodes are performed in different rounds,

until the pre-last round of the execution.

Consider the last time in the execution when some agent moves before gathering. The tower and the singleton must be (again) adjacent. Suppose that the instructions of the algorithm are not as stated in the lemma. There are three cases:

Case 1. Both the tower and the singleton are instructed to stay idle.

This contradicts the accomplishment of gathering.

Case 2. The tower is instructed to move on the singleton and the singleton to stay idle.

In this case the adversary schedules the cycles of all the agents of the tower except one simultaneously. They move on the singleton, thus forming a tower, and the remaining agent becomes a singleton. The configuration is as before, which contradicts gathering.

Case 3. The tower is instructed to move on the singleton and the singleton to move on the tower.

In this case the adversary schedules the cycles of all the agents simultaneously. The singleton moves to the node occupied by the tower and the tower to the node occupied by the singleton. The configuration is as before, which contradicts gathering.

The contradiction in all three cases concludes the proof.   □

In order to show that there is no universal gathering algorithm, fix a radius $d > 1$ and consider the following seven configurations, in which every letter $a, b, c, a', b', c', e, f, g$ denotes a singleton. (We use different letters to simplify the arguments).

$C = (a, b, a')$

$C_1 = (a, b, c, 0^{d-1}, c', b', a')$

$C_2 = (a, b, c, 0^{d-2}, e, f, 0, g)$

$C_1' = (a, b, c, 0^{d-1}, e, 0^{d-1}, c', b', a')$

$C_2' = (a, b, c, 0^{d-1}, e, f, 0, g)$

$C_1'' = (a, b, 0, c)$

$C_2'' = (a, b, c, 0, e, f)$

The idea of the nonexistence proof is the following. Depending on the radius of vision $d > 1$ (we will consider cases $d \geq 4$ even, $d \geq 3$ odd and $d = 2$) we will show that some three of these seven configurations are gatherable, but there is no single algorithm gathering all three of them. The proof is split into a series of lemmas. The following four lemmas assert gatherability of some of the above configurations, depending on the radius of vision.

Lemma 3. *Configuration C is gatherable for any radius of vision $d > 1$.*

Proof. The gathering algorithm, regardless of d, is the following: a singleton adjacent to an empty node and to an occupied node moves to the occupied node; a singleton adjacent to two occupied nodes does not move; an agent in a tower does not move. □

Lemma 4. *Configurations C_1, C_2 are gatherable for even radius of vision $d \geq 4$.*

Proof. Consider an even radius of vision $d \geq 4$ and configuration C_1. The gathering algorithm for this configuration is the following. The singleton c (respectively c') goes away from singletons a and b (respectively a' and b') until it gets at distance $d/2$ from b (respectively b'). They can do it because during this trip c and c' are the only singletons that see two adjacent singletons on one side of their view (a and b in case of c and a' and b' in case of c'), and at least another singleton on the other side of their view. All other agents remain idle until they see a tower. At the end of this part singletons c and c' form a tower at the central node. The rest of the algorithm is the following: if an agent sees a tower and no agent between itself and the tower, it goes toward the tower; an agent in a tower does not move. In the second part singletons b and b' join the tower, and then a and a' join the tower, completing gathering.

Consider an even radius of vision d and configuration C_2. Note that each singleton in this configuration has a different view. In particular, no singleton sees a tower and f is the only singleton that sees a unique singleton at distance 2 on one side of its view and more than one singleton on the other side of its view. Initially the singleton f moves on e forming a tower (it is the only singleton that can move initially). The rest of the algorithm is as follows.

1. A singleton that sees a tower on one side of its view and no other agent between itself and the tower and that sees no agent on the other side of its view moves toward the tower.

2. A singleton that sees a tower on one side of its view and no other agent between itself and the tower and that sees the closest agent on the other side of its view at distance less than d moves toward the tower.

3. A singleton that does not see a tower and sees on one side of its view a unique singleton that is at distance d moves toward this singleton.

4. An agent in a tower does not move.

After the tower is formed, singleton g moves toward it independently of singletons a, b and c, finally joining the tower (clause 1 of the algorithm above). These three singletons move as follows. Singleton c moves toward the tower and joins it (clause 2), then b moves to the node adjacent to the tower (clause 2). Then a makes one move toward b (clause 3), then b moves on the tower (clause 2), and finally a moves toward the tower and joins it (clause 1) completing gathering. □

Lemma 5. *Configurations C_1', C_2' are gatherable for odd radius of vision $d \geq 3$.*

Proof. Consider an odd radius of vision $d \geq 3$ and configuration C_1'.
The gathering algorithm for this configuration is the following.

1. A singleton that sees on one side of its view exactly two singletons at distances 1 and 2 and that sees at least one isolated singleton not at distance 2 on the other side of its view moves toward the latter singleton.

2. A singleton that sees on one side of its view exactly one adjacent singleton and that sees a unique singleton at distance $d - 1$ on the other side of its view moves toward the latter singleton.

3. A singleton that sees on each side of its view exactly two singletons at distances 2 and d moves (in one of the two directions, since its view is symmetric).

4. A singleton that sees on one side of its view exactly 2 singletons at distances $d - 2$ and d and that sees on the other side of its view the closest singleton at distance 3 moves toward the latter singleton.

5. A singleton that sees on one side of its view exactly 2 singletons at distances 1 and 3 and that sees on the other side of its view exactly 2 singletons at distances $d - 2$ and d moves toward the singletons at distances 1 and 3. (Note that for $d = 3$ both sides of the view are identical, i.e., the view is symmetric, and in this case the singleton moves on either side).

6. A singleton that sees a tower on one side of its view and no other agent between itself and the tower and that sees no agent on the other side of its view moves toward the tower.

7. A singleton that sees a tower on one side of its view and no other agent between itself and the tower and that sees the closest agent on the other side of its view at distance less than d moves toward the tower.

8. A singleton that does not see a tower and sees on one side of its view a unique singleton that is at distance d moves toward this singleton.

9. An agent in a tower does not move.

First, singleton c (resp. c') moves at distance 2 from e (clause 1). Then, b (resp. b') performs one move toward c (resp. c') resulting in the configuration $(a, 0, b, 0^{d-3}, c, 0, e, 0, c', 0^{d-3}, b', 0, a')$ (clause 2). Then e moves one node in one of the directions, since its view is symmetric (clause 3). Without loss of generality suppose that e moves toward c' resulting in the configuration $(a, 0, b, 0^{d-3}, c, 0, 0, e, c', 0^{d-3}, b', 0, a')$.

At this point the only singleton that can move is c. If $d \neq 3$ then the clause that makes it move is clause 4 and if $d = 3$ then the clauses that make it move are clause 4 and clause 8 but in this case the moves that they imply are identical. In both cases c moves toward e. Now the only singleton that can move is c' (clause 5). For any $d \neq 3$ it moves on e creating a tower, and for $d = 3$ it moves either on e or on b' (as its view is symmetric) also creating a tower.

Once the tower is created, all singletons move toward the tower in a manner similar to that described in the last part of the proof of Lemma 4, they all join the tower one by one on each side of it, thus completing gathering.

Next, consider an odd radius of vision $d \geq 3$ and configuration C_2'. Note that each singleton in this configuration has a different view. In particular, no singleton sees a tower and f is the only singleton that sees a unique singleton at distance 2 on one side of its view and a unique singleton on the other side of its view. Initially the singleton f moves on e forming a tower (it is the only singleton that can move initially). The rest of the algorithm is as follows.

1. A singleton that sees a tower on one side of its view and no other agent between itself and the tower and that sees no agent on the other side of its view moves toward the tower.

2. A singleton that sees a tower on one side of its view and no other agent between itself and the tower and that sees the closest agent on the other side of its view at distance less than d moves toward the tower.

3. A singleton that does not see a tower and sees on one side of its view a unique singleton that is at distance d moves toward this singleton.

4. An agent in a tower does not move.

After the tower is formed, singleton g moves toward it independently of singletons a, b and c, finally joining the tower (clause 1 of the algorithm above). These three singletons move as follows. Singleton c moves to the node adjacent to the tower (clause 2), then b makes one move toward c (clause 3), then c joins the tower (clause 2). Then b moves to the node at distance 2 from the tower (clause 2), then a makes one move toward b (clause 3), then b makes one move toward the tower (clause 2), then a makes one move toward b (clause 3), then b moves on the tower (clause 2) and finally, a moves toward the tower and joins it (clause 1). □

Lemma 6. *Configurations C_1'', C_2'' are gatherable for radius of vision $d = 2$.*

Proof. Consider the radius of vision $d = 2$ and configuration C_1''. The gathering algorithm for this configuration is the following. In the beginning all nodes have different views and c moves toward b, while a and b are idle. Now a segment (a, b, c) is formed and all nodes have different views from those in configuration C_1''. The rest of the algorithm is as for configuration C_1.

Finally, consider the radius of vision $d = 2$ and configuration C_2''. The gathering algorithm for this configuration is the following.

1. A singleton that is an extremity of a segment of length at most 2 and sees an occupied node behind an empty neighbor, moves to this empty neighbor.

2. A singleton that sees 4 other singletons moves to one of the neighbors.

3. A singleton that sees an adjacent tower and sees an empty node behind it moves on the tower.

4. A singleton that sees an adjacent singleton and an adjacent tower moves on the tower.

5. A singleton that sees an adjacent tower and a singleton behind it on one side, and empty nodes on the other side, moves on the tower.

6. An agent that does not satisfy any condition 1 – 5 does not move.

In the beginning only singleton e satisfies one of the conditions 1 – 5, namely condition 1. It moves toward c. Then only singleton f satisfies one of the conditions 1 – 5, namely condition 1. It moves toward e, forming a segment (a, b, c, e, f). Now c is the only agent that satisfies one of the conditions 1 – 5, namely condition 2. W.l.o.g. it moves to e forming a tower. Now the configuration is $(a, b, 0, *, f)$. The singleton f satisfies condition 3 and can move on the tower at any time. The singleton b satisfies condition 1 and can move toward the tower at any time. The adversary can schedule moves of b and f in arbitrary order. After the move of b the singleton a satisfies condition 1 and moves toward b. (The move of f and the moves of a and b are independent and can be scheduled arbitrarily.) After the move of a singleton b satisfies condition 4 and moves on the tower. Then a satisfies condition 1 and can move toward the tower. Singletons a and f move on the tower in arbitrary order either by condition 3 or by condition 5. This completes gathering.   □

The next three lemmas show the nonexistence of a universal gathering algorithm for various classes of radii of vision.

Lemma 7. *There is no universal gathering algorithm for even radius of vision* $d \geq 4$.

Proof. Suppose that there exists a universal gathering algorithm $\mathcal{A}$ for even radius of vision $d \geq 4$. In particular this algorithm must gather configurations C, C_1 and C_2. Consider configuration C. The algorithm must move at least one of the agents or gathering would never occur. There are 3 possible moves in C that agents can do. (Note that a and a' have the same view in C.) Move α is when b moves on one of the adjacent singletons (either a or a'), move β is when a moves on b (resp. a' moves on b) and move γ is when a moves away from b (resp. a' moves away from b).

Now consider configuration C_1. Singletons b and b' in C_1 have the same view as singleton b in C. Singletons a and a' in C_1 have the same view as singletons a and a' in C. Consider the following behavior of the adversary if move α is executed in C_1. The adversary schedules the moves of b on a and b' on a' synchronously, creating a configuration in which towers are at the extremities. By lemma 1, gathering is impossible. Now, consider the following behavior of the adversary if move β is executed in C_1. The adversary schedules the moves of a on b and a' on b' synchronously, creating a configuration in which towers are at the extremities. Again, by Lemma 1, gathering is impossible. Hence we may restrict attention to moves γ for configuration C.

Next consider configuration C_2. Singleton a in C_2 has the same view as singletons a and a' in C. Consider the following behavior of the adversary if move γ is executed in C_2. The adversary schedules singleton a to move away from b before anything else. This results in the edge-symmetric configuration $(a, 0, b, c, 0^{d-2}, e, f, 0, g)$. By Proposition 1, gathering is impossible.

It follows that moves α or β executed in C_1 lead to a non-gatherable configuration and move γ executed in C_2 leads to a non-gatherable configuration, under some behavior of the adversary. This implies that algorithm $\mathcal{A}$ cannot gather configurations C, C_1 and C_2, although these configurations are gatherable (each by a dedicated algorithm), by Lemmas 3 and 4. This contradicts the hypothesis that $\mathcal{A}$ is universal.   □

The proof of the next lemma is similar to that of Lemma 7 and is omitted due to space limitations.

Lemma 8. *There is no universal gathering algorithm for odd radius of vision* $d \geq 3$.

Lemma 9. *There is no universal gathering algorithm for radius of vision $d = 2$.*

Proof. Suppose that there exists a universal gathering algorithm $\mathcal{A}$ for radius of vision $d = 2$. In particular this algorithm must gather configurations C, C_1'' and C_2''.

Consider configuration C_1''. At least one of the agents must move or gathering will never occur. There are 6 possible moves in C_1'': each of the agents can move on one side or the other. Among these 6 moves three lead to a non-gatherable configuration. We analyze these moves below.

1. a moves away from b.

This leads to the configuration $(a, 0, b, 0, c)$ in which a and c have the same view. If b moves in this configuration, this yields (w.l.o.g) the configuration $(a, 0, 0, b, c)$ in which b and c have the same view. If the algorithm instructs them to move on the adjacent singleton, the adversary moves them synchronously causing them to exchange positions and thus yielding the same configuration. If the algorithm instructs them to move away from each other, the adversary schedules the Look-Compute-Move cycle of b first yielding again configuration $(a, 0, b, 0, c)$. This shows that b cannot move in configuration $(a, 0, b, 0, c)$. Hence in this configuration singletons a and c have to move. There are two possibilities: they may either move away from b or toward b. If they move away from b, the adversary moves them simultaneously and thus a, b and c have empty views which prohibits gathering (the adversary may then move a and c farther and farther from b). The other possibility is that a and c move toward b. In this case the adversary schedules the Look-Compute-Move cycle of c first thus yielding again the configuration C_1''. Hence we conclude that neither of the above possibilities can guarantee gathering. It follows that a cannot move away from b in configuration C_1''.

2. b moves on a.

This leads to a configuration containing a tower and the singleton c at distance 3 from it. This is a non-gatherable configuration as the adversary may schedule both the singleton and the tower to move farther and farther from each other.

3. c moves away from b.

This leads to the configuration $(a, b, 0, 0, c)$ and the argument similar to that from case 1 (above) applies.

Hence in configuration C_1'' we can restrict attention to the remaining possible moves. If in configuration C_1'' neither a nor c move toward b, then the only possible move is that of b to the adjacent empty node and such moves would perpetually recreate configurations equivalent to C_1''. Hence we may assume that either a moves on b or c moves toward b. Note that singleton b may move to the adjacent empty node as well, but in this case *both* a moves on b and c moves toward b. Indeed, if only one of these moves could happen, the adversary could schedule moves of b so that a and c always stay idle, in which case configurations equivalent to C_1'' would be perpetually recreated. Denote by λ the move of a on b, by μ the move of c toward b and by ν the move of b to the adjacent empty node in configuration C_1''.

Now consider configuration C. The algorithm must move at least one of the agents or gathering would never occur. There are 3 possible moves in C that agents can do. (Note that a and a' have the same view in C.) Move α is when b moves on one of the adjacent singletons (either a or a'), move β is when a moves on b (resp. a' moves on b) and move γ is when a moves away from b (resp. a' moves away from b). Observe that move γ in configuration C leads to a non-gatherable configuration. Indeed, the adversary schedules a and a' to move simultaneously, thus yielding configuration $(a, 0, b, 0, a')$. From this point on the argument is the same as in Case 1 above. Hence we may restrict attention to moves α and β in configuration C.

Now consider configuration C_2''. Singleton f in C_2'' has the same view as single-ton a in C_1''. Singleton e in C_2'' has the same view as singleton b in C_1''. Singleton a in C_2'' has the same view as singletons a and a' in C. Singleton b in C_2'' has the same view as singleton b in C.

Consider the move λ in configuration C_1'' and moves α and β in configuration C. Since f in C_2'' has the same view as a in C_1'' and a and b in C_2'' have the same view as (respectively) a and b in C, the move λ performed in C_2'' would create a tower at one extremity and the moves α or β performed in C_2'' would create a tower at the other extremity. Hence by Lemma 1 gathering is impossible. This implies that move λ in configuration C_1'' is impossible. Hence also the move ν in this configuration is impossible (recall that ν implies both λ and μ in C_1'') . It follows that the only possible move in configuration C_1'' is the move μ.

In configuration C_2'' either move α or β must occur. The adversary schedules one of these moves first, creating a tower at one extremity. The resulting config-uration is either $D_1 = (*, 0, c, 0, e, f)$ or $D_2 = (*, c, 0, e, f)$. Now neither e nor f can move, as these would be moves λ or ν. Consider the singleton c. There are three cases.

Case 1. c moves toward the tower.

After this move in configuration D_2 the tower does not see any other agent and hence cannot move; after this move in configuration D_1 singleton c is adjacent to the tower, by Lemma 2 it joins the tower, which then does not see any other agent and hence cannot move. In both D_1 and D_2 after the move of c singletons e and f see only each other and hence gathering is impossible.

Case 2. c moves toward e.

The adversary schedules this move first. Since e has the same view as b in configuration C and f has the same view as a in configuration C, move α or β can be scheduled by the adversary to create a tower at the other extremity, which prohibits gathering by Lemma 1.

Case 3. c does not move.

Since no singleton can move in this case, the tower must eventually become adjacent to c. By Lemma 2 the tower cannot move on c and thus gathering is impossible.

This implies that algorithm $\mathcal{A}$ cannot gather configurations C, C_1'' and C_2'', although these configurations are gatherable (each by a dedicated algorithm), by Lemmas 3 and 6. This contradicts the hypothesis that $\mathcal{A}$ is universal. $\square$

The above lemmas imply our main result.

Theorem 1. *There is no universal gathering algorithm in the infinite line for any radius of vision $d > 1$.*

Proof. Lemmas 7 and 8 show that there is no universal algorithm for radius of vision $d > 2$. Lemma 9 shows that there is no universal algorithm for radius of vision $d = 2$. ☐

4 Conclusion

We showed that for any radius of vision $d > 1$ there does not exist a universal gathering algorithm for the infinite line. Our result remains valid for rings of size at least $7d + 8$. Indeed, all configurations used in our proof have at most 7 agents. In a ring of size at least $7d + 8$ the adversary can always guarantee that all agents have the same view as in the infinite line: it may schedule moves of the agents in such a way that they do not see each other on the "other side" of the ring.

References

1. Agmon, N., Peleg, D.: Fault-Tolerant Gathering Algorithms for Autonomous Mobile Robots. SIAM J. Comput. 36(1), 56–82 (2006)
2. Alpern, S., Gal, S.: The Theory of Search Games and Rendezvous. Kluwer Academic Publishers (2002)
3. Ando, H., Oasa, Y., Suzuki, I., Yamashita, M.: Distributed Memoryless Point Convergence Algorithm for Mobile Robots with Limited Visibility. IEEE Trans. on Robotics and Automation 15(5), 818–828 (1999)
4. Bampas, E., Czyzowicz, J., Gąsieniec, L., Ilcinkas, D., Labourel, A.: Almost optimal asynchronous rendezvous in infinite multidimensional grids. In: Lynch, N.A., Shvartsman, A.A. (eds.) DISC 2010. LNCS, vol. 6343, pp. 297–311. Springer, Heidelberg (2010)
5. Cieliebak, M.: Gathering Non-oblivious Mobile Robots. In: Farach-Colton, M. (ed.) LATIN 2004. LNCS, vol. 2976, pp. 577–588. Springer, Heidelberg (2004)
6. Cieliebak, M., Flocchini, P., Prencipe, G., Santoro, N.: Solving the Robots Gathering Problem. In: Baeten, J.C.M., Lenstra, J.K., Parrow, J., Woeginger, G.J. (eds.) ICALP 2003. LNCS, vol. 2719, pp. 1181–1196. Springer, Heidelberg (2003)
7. Cohen, R., Peleg, D.: Robot Convergence via Center-of-Gravity Algorithms. In: Kralovic, R., Sýkora, O. (eds.) SIROCCO 2004. LNCS, vol. 3104, pp. 79–88. Springer, Heidelberg (2004)
8. Czyzowicz, J., Labourel, A., Pelc, A.: How to meet asynchronously (almost) everywhere. ACM Transactions on Algorithms 8, article 37 (2012)
9. D'Angelo, G., Di Stefano, G., Navarra, A.: How to gather asynchronous oblivious robots on anonymous rings. In: Aguilera, M.K. (ed.) DISC 2012. LNCS, vol. 7611, pp. 326–340. Springer, Heidelberg (2012)
10. Datta, A.K., Lamani, A., Larmore, L.L., Petit, F.: Ring exploration with oblivious myopic robots. CoRR abs/1205.5003 (2012)

11. De Marco, G., Gargano, L., Kranakis, E., Krizanc, D., Pelc, A., Vaccaro, U.: Asynchronous deterministic rendezvous in graphs. Theoretical Computer Science 355, 315–326 (2006)
12. Dessmark, A., Fraigniaud, P., Kowalski, D., Pelc, A.: Deterministic rendezvous in graphs. Algorithmica 46, 69–96 (2006)
13. Flocchini, P., Kranakis, E., Krizanc, D., Santoro, N., Sawchuk, C.: Multiple Mobile Agent Rendezvous in a Ring. In: Farach-Colton, M. (ed.) LATIN 2004. LNCS, vol. 2976, pp. 599–608. Springer, Heidelberg (2004)
14. Flocchini, P., Prencipe, G., Santoro, N., Widmayer, P.: Gathering of Asynchronous Robots with Limited Visibility. Theoretical Computer Science 337(1-3), 147–168 (2005)
15. Guilbault, S., Pelc, A.: Gathering asynchronous oblivious agents with local vision in regular bipartite graphs. In: Kosowski, A., Yamashita, M. (eds.) SIROCCO 2011. LNCS, vol. 6796, pp. 162–173. Springer, Heidelberg (2011)
16. Guilbault, S., Pelc, A.: Asynchronous rendezvous of anonymous agents in arbitrary graphs. In: Fernàndez Anta, A., Lipari, G., Roy, M. (eds.) OPODIS 2011. LNCS, vol. 7109, pp. 421–434. Springer, Heidelberg (2011)
17. Izumi, T., Izumi, T., Kamei, S., Ooshita, F.: Mobile robots gathering algorithm with local weak multiplicity in rings. In: Patt-Shamir, B., Ekim, T. (eds.) SIROCCO 2010. LNCS, vol. 6058, pp. 101–113. Springer, Heidelberg (2010)
18. Klasing, R., Kosowski, A., Navarra, A.: Taking advantage of symmetries: Gathering of many asynchronous oblivious robots on a ring. Theoretical Computer Science 411, 3235–3246 (2010)
19. Klasing, R., Markou, E., Pelc, A.: Gathering asynchronous oblivious mobile robots in a ring. Theoretical Computer Science 390, 27–39 (2008)
20. Prencipe, G.: CORDA: Distributed Coordination of a Set of Autonomous Mobile Robots. In: Proc. ERSADS 2001, pp. 185–190 (2001)
21. Prencipe, G.: Impossibility of gathering by a set of autonomous mobile robots. Theoretical Computer Science 384, 222–231 (2007)
22. Suzuki, I., Yamashita, M.: Distributed Anonymous Mobile Robots: Formation of Geometric Patterns. SIAM J. Comput. 28(4), 1347–1363 (1999)

Counting the Number of Homonyms in Dynamic Networks

G.A. Di Luna[1], R. Baldoni[1], S. Bonomi[1], and Ioannis Chatzigiannakis[2]

[1] Dipartimento di Ingegneria Informatica, Automatica e Gestionale Antonio Ruberti
Universitá degli Studi di Roma La Sapienza
Via Ariosto, 25
I-00185 Roma, Italy
{baldoni,bonomi,diluna}@dis.uniroma1.it
[2] Computer Technology Institute & Press "Diophantus" (CTI)
Patras, Greece
ichatz@cti.gr

Abstract. We consider a synchronous distributed system with n processes that communicate through a dynamic network guaranteeing 1-interval connectivity i.e., the network topology graph might change at each interval while keeping the graph connected at any time. The processes belonging to the distributed system are identified through a set of labels $\mathcal{L} = \{\ell_1, \ell_2 \ldots, \ell_k\}$ (with $1 \leq k < n$). In this challenging system model, the paper addresses the following problem: "counting the number of processes with the same label". We provide a distributed algorithm that is able solve the problem based on the notion of energy transfer. Each process owns a fixed energy charge, and tries to discharge itself exchanging, at each round, at most half of its charge with neighbors. The paper also discusses when such counting is possible in the presence of failures. Counting processes with the same label in dynamic networks with homonyms is of great importance because it is as difficult as computing generic aggregating functions.

Keywords: Aggregating Function, Dynamic Networks, Homonyms, Failure, Synchronous System.

1   Introduction

Recently, dynamic distributed systems have attracted a lot of interest from the relevant research community [6,7], due to the fact that static distributed systems do not capture anymore the new kind of software applications that are emerging on the ICT field. Mobile devices, sensors networks and cloud computing definitely changed the way of looking at distributed systems where, for example, the underlying communication graph connecting distributed system's nodes is constantly changing. Mobility of devices, intermittent connectivity due to lossy links and limited power create very challenging system models where what was trivially solvable is a static distributed systems, is now far from being trivial in this new landscape. A critical element in such future distributed systems is the identifier of the devices; the uniqueness of the node IDs is not anymore guaranteed, thus in the more general case, a distributed system of n processes can use a

T. Higashino et al. (Eds.): SSS 2013, LNCS 8255, pp. 311–325, 2013.
ⓒ Springer International Publishing Switzerland 2013

set of labels $\mathcal{L}$ with $1 \leq |\mathcal{L}| \leq n$ [8]. As extreme case, $|\mathcal{L}| = n$ represents a distributed system where all processes have distinct labels. Conversely, $|\mathcal{L}| \geq 1$ represents a system where processes share the same label and we refer to such processes as homonyms and to this setting as *dynamic networks with homonyms*. In the case $|\mathcal{L}| = 1$, we have the classical scheme where all processes are anonymous (i.e., all processes share the same label e.g. [17]). However, very few problems are solvable on dynamic networks with anonymous processes. In [14], the authors conjectured that also basic problems like counting the number of processes in a dynamic network with anonymous processes without additional knowledge is impossible. This paper makes a step in the direction of having a better understanding of which classes of problems are solvable in *dynamic networks with homonyms*.

In this paper we consider the problem of counting the number of homonyms in a dynamic network of n nodes that proceeds by synchronous rounds. This is among the most fundamental problems of distributed computation and is a key function for network management and control. Estimating the size of nodes groups in the same state, for example, is fundamental for topological change detection or automatic network reconfiguration. Thus, counting the size of groups of processes in the same state is equivalent to compute a generic aggregating function.

The vast number of papers appearing in the relevant literature is a clear indication of the importance of the counting problem. A large part of these studies deals with causes of dynamicity such as failures and changes in the topology that eventually stabilize [12]. However the low rate of topological changes that is usually assumed there is unsuitable for reasoning about truly dynamic networks. We envision future networks with highly dynamic changes: neighboring nodes may become immediately unreachable after they have been received a message from them. More specifically we study synchronous computation under worst-case dynamicity as originally introduced by [15] and then refined in [13]. We consider that the communication graph is controlled by an adversary that may introduce or remove any number of edges as long as the graph is connected at any round. Communication along the edges is assumed to be bidirectional and nodes are not aware which edges are made available by the adversary. Each node runs a deterministic algorithm that generates messages on the base of internal state alone. Messages are then delivered to the sender's neighbors, as chosen by the adversary; nodes change their states, and the next round begins.

In a companion paper [11], we introduced a new technique for counting the size of the network that overcomes the lack of unique identities and the constantly dynamic environment by using the concept of *energy-transfer*. Each node is assigned a fixed energy charge, and during each round it discharges itself by disseminating it around to its neighbors. Such technique enforces, at each round, an invariant on the sum of energy among networks' nodes: energy is not created or destroyed. Such invariant is then used to design distributed algorithm solving the counting problem.

In this paper, we design a fully distributed algorithms that is able to apply the *energy-transfer technique* and that output at each process, its number of homonyms.

Counting homonyms is possible under the assumption that each process knows the exact number of nodes n part of the network and it uses as basic building block a distributed algorithm answering to the predicate *"Are there in the network at least* *t processes identified by the same label ℓ_i?"*. Such algorithm exploits the notion of energy-transfer by creating an energy flow for each label ℓ_i, that will flow from every process with a label different from ℓ_i to all the processes identified through ℓ_i, that knowing the size n and looking to their collected energy can compute the lower bound on the number of processes with label ℓ_i and answer to the predicate.

Additionally, we also present a few results showing when counting the number of homonyms of a process is possible in the presence of f failures. We solve this problem with crash stop failures, that are modeled as single remotion event in the dynamic computation: we show that is not possible to detect a failure when $|\mathcal{L}| \leq f$, on the contrary we show that if $|\mathcal{L}| > f + \frac{f^2}{|V|-f}$ then is possible to build a distinguisher $\mathcal{A}_D$ that is able to detect change in the network size, on top of this distinguisher we can build a procedure that is able to count the number of homonyms despite the failures.

The rest of the paper is structured as follows: Section 2 presents relevant previous work, and in Sec. 3 we formally define our dynamic network model with homonyms. In Sec. 4 we show how to answer to predicates $Num_{\ell_i} \geq t$, the correctness of proposed algorithms is formally proved, in the same we discuss why counting homonyms is as difficult as computing generic aggregating functions and finally we show our results on counting homonyms in dynamic networks in the presence of failures (cf. Section 5).

2 Related Work

System model based on homonyms has been introduced in [8]. The authors studied the minimum number of labels needed to solve the byzantine agreement problem [8] in a static distributed system. In the synchronous case considering t byzantine processes, it has been proved that $3t + 1$ labels are necessary and sufficient for agreement while in the partially synchronous case the number of labels must be greater than $(n + 3t)/2$. In [9] byzantine agreement is studied in the presence of an attacker able to forge a limited number of identities. In particular, the authors showed that Byzantine Agreement problem is solvable if and only if $|\mathcal{L}| > 2t + k$ where $t \leq k \leq |\mathcal{L}|$ is the maximum number of identifiers forgeable by a byzantine process.

When we consider fully anonymous static networks $|\mathcal{L}| = 1$, [2] and [17] provided several characterizations for problems that are solvable under certain topological constraints in such a setting. Further investigation led to the classification of computable functions [4,17]. Other well-known studies on unknown networks have dealt with the problems of robot-exploration and map-drawing of an unknown graph [1,10,16] and on information dissemination [5]. Finally, Aspnes *et al.* [3] studied the relative powers of reliable anonymous distributed systems with different communication mechanisms: anonymous broadcast, read-write registers, or read-write registers plus additional shared-memory objects.

Distributed systems with worst-case dynamicity were first studied in [15] by introducing the 1-interval connectivity model. They studied flooding and routing problems in asynchronous communication and allowed nodes detect local neighborhood changes. Under the same model, [13] studied the problem of counting for networks where nodes have unique IDs and provided an algorithm that requires $O(n^2)$ rounds using $O(\log n)$ bits per message. In [14] studied the problem of anonymous counting in this worst-case dynamicity model. They showed that the problem is impossible without a leader process and then examined the case where a leader node is available. They provided an algorithm where given that the nodes know an upper bound on the maximum degree that will ever appear, the nodes obtain an upper bound on the size of the network.

3   System Model

A *dynamic network* is a network whose topology changes along time due to possible failures of nodes or communication links. We consider computations executed in discrete *synchronous* rounds, controlled by a fictional global clock accessible to all the nodes. Thus, all nodes have access to the current round number via a local variable that we usually denote by r. A dynamic network is modeled by a *dynamic graph* $G(r) = (V, E(r))$, where V is a set of n nodes (or processors) and $E : \mathbb{N} \to \mathcal{P}(E')$, where $E' = \{\{u, v\} : u, v \in V\}$, is a function mapping a round number $r \in \mathbb{N}$ to a set $E(r)$ of bidirectional links drawn from E' [13]. Intuitively, a dynamic graph $G(r)$ is an infinite sequence $G(1), G(2), \ldots$ of *instantaneous graphs*, whose edge sets are subsets of E' chosen by a *worst-case adversary*. Initially, we assume that processes do not fail, i.e., the set V is *static* and remains the same throughout the execution. We will relax this assumption later in Section 5 where we will introduce crash failures.

We assume that the dynamic graph/network $G(r) = (V, E(r))$ is 1-*interval connected* as defined in [13]. A network is 1-*interval connected* if for all $r \in \mathbb{N}$, the static graph $G(r)$ is connected. Note that this allows the network to change arbitrarily from round to round always subject to the condition that it remains connected. A very important aspect of 1-interval connectivity is that it guarantees that a message sent by a node and relayed by others at any round will reach all the nodes of the system in at most $|V|$ rounds [13]; a node w influences a node v if v receives a message generated by w. Let us finally remark that a connected network in the static-network case is a particular case of a 1-interval connected dynamic network.

Nodes are homonyms [8], i.e. each process has a label selected form a set $\mathcal{L} = \{\ell_1, \ell_2, \ldots, \ell_k\}$. We assume that $|\mathcal{L}| \leq n$ and that each label is assigned to at least one process. Let us note that when $|\mathcal{L}| = 1$ the system is fully anonymous while $|\mathcal{L}| = n$ the system is fully identified. Moreover, we indicate with $|\ell_j|$ the number of processes with label j. We assume that each process knows the set of labels used in the system and the initial number of processes n. We consider only deterministic algorithms, i.e. algorithms where process actions are determined by the initial state and messages it receives. The state of a node u at a certain round r, identified as $s_u(r)$, is given by the set of all the variable and their current values. To ease of presentation, in the following we sometimes refer to processes using names as v but such names cannot be used by processes themselves in the algorithm.

Nodes communicate by sending and receiving messages via *anonymous broadcast*, in which, in every round r, each node u generates a single message $m_u(r)$ to be delivered to all its current neighbors in $N_u(r) = \{v : \{u, v\} \in E(r)\}$.

4   Answering Predicates $Num_{\ell_j} > t$ with Knowledge of Network Size

In the following, we will focus our attention on fully distributed algorithms able to answer to predicates in the form $Num_{\ell_i} \geq t$, i.e., *"Are there at least t processes with the same label ℓ_i?"*. Let us notice that answering such predicates is an open problem left in [14] and it allows processes to compute more complex functions.

Energy-Transfer Technique. The energy-transfer technique is based on the physical notion of energy preservation. Each process has an initial energy charge and, during the computation, it exchanges its energy with its neighbors without creating or destroying it. This is fundamental to enforce, at each round, an invariant on the sum of energy stored among networks' nodes. Leveraging on the energy stored at each node and knowing the initial size of the network n, it is possible to define algorithms with well defined terminating conditions.

Depending on the function to be computed, processes may act both as as energy collectors (i.e., nodes that do not transfer energy to neighbors) or as energy distributers (i.e. processes that sends a quantity of their energy at each round). Interestingly, this technique is very simple to implement and depends on very limited information about the attributes of a given network.

In the following, we will first show and algorithm, namely *Distributed Answering Predicate greater than* 2 (DAP2), that, given a certain label ℓ_i is able to output the value true iff there exists at least two processes in V identified by the same label ℓ_i, otherwise it output false. In Section 4.2, we will show how it is possible to extend **DAP2** to the generic case where processes are interested to know if the number of processes with a given label ℓ_i are above a certain threshold t.

4.1   An Algorithm to Answer Predicate Like $Num_{\ell_i} \geq 2$

Let us consider a generic process v with a label ℓ_i; at round $r = 0$, v creates an unitary energy charge $< e_{\ell_j}, \ell_j >$ for each label ℓ_j (with $e_{\ell_j} = 1$). At each round, for each label ℓ_j different from its own, v distributes half of the residual energy e_{ℓ_j} to its neighbors while it will collect, acting as a sink, energy marked with its label ℓ_i from all its neighbors. Note that, the transferring method is designed in such a way that there is no creation, neither loss, of energy marked with a particular label ℓ_j. Thus, for each label ℓ_i the sum of energy is equal to $n = |V|$. The presence of another process v_i with label ℓ_j interferes with the sink behavior of v_j that is not able anymore to collect the whole energy in the network. So, v_j can infer, from the quantity of energy that it has collected, the presence of at least another process with label ℓ_j.

Algorithm DAP2 – Evaluating predicate $Num_{\ell_j} \geq 2$ in dynamic networks with Homonyms.

Init: Each process $v_j \in V$ has an energy variable $e_{\ell_j}^j \leftarrow 1$ for each $\ell_i \in \mathcal{L}$ and an integer variable $B \leftarrow |V|$ representing the bound on number of neighbors of node

---

v_j (i.e. $|N_{v_j}(r)| \leq B, \forall r$).

At the beginning of each round r: for each label $\ell_i \neq \ell_j$, v_j sends a quantity of energy $e'_{\ell_i} \leftarrow \frac{e^j_{\ell_i}}{2B}$ to each neighbor, updates its residual energy $e^j_{\ell_i} \leftarrow \frac{e^j_{\ell_i}}{2}$ and then it broadcast a ENERGY(e'_{ℓ_i}, ℓ_i) message to its neighbors. Concerning its label ℓ_j, v_j sends a ENERGY$(0, \ell_j)$ with zero energy. In addition, for each label $\ell_i \neq \ell_j$, v_j disseminates RESIDUAL$(e^j_{\ell_i}, \ell_i, r)$ message containing the residual energy associated with label ℓ_i that v_j is able to transmit at round r, while for label ℓ_j it will send RESIDUAL$(0, \ell_i, r)$, since it will never transmit energy marked with label ℓ_j.

At the end of each round r: v_j receives a set of messages for each label ℓ_i, $S^{\ell_i}_{MSG}$. For each message $m = < e_m, \ell_i > \in S^{\ell_i}_{MSG}$, v_j updates its internal energy charge associated with label ℓ_i as follows: $e^j_{\ell_i} \leftarrow e^j_{\ell_i} + e^{rcv}_{\ell_i} + \overline{e^{sent}_{\ell_i}}$ where $e^{rcv}_{\ell_i} = \sum_{\forall m \in S^{\ell_i}_{MSG}} e_m$ is the energy received from neighbors for the label ℓ_i and $\overline{e^{sent}_{\ell_i}} = (B - |S^{\ell_i}_{MSG}|) \times e'_{\ell_i} = (B - |S^{\ell_i}_{MSG}|) \times \frac{e^j_{\ell_i}}{2B}$ is an adjustment on the energy sent to neighbors at the beginning of the round due to the possible over estimation of the neighborhood size.

Terminating Condition: Exploiting the property of 1-connected graphs about the latest delivery time for a message sent at round r, at each round $r > |V|$, v_j estimates the energy related to its label ℓ_j that still needs to be collected to check if it is the only one with label ℓ_j. To do that, it selects among all the RESIDUAL$(e^j_{\ell_j}, \ell_j, r - |V|)$ messages, the one with maximum residual energy $e^{max}_{\ell_j}$ and it computes an upper bound on the energy associated $\mathcal{E}_{\ell_i}$ to the label ℓ_j stored in the rest of the network and defined as $e^{max}_{\ell_j} \times |V|$. When $e^{max}_{\ell_j} \times |V| < 1$ the algorithm ends and v_j outputs true if $|V| - e^j_{\ell_j} \geq 1$, otherwise it outputs false. Let us notice that v_j needs to disseminate the answer to the predicate; to do that, it broadcasts its result for $|V|$ rounds. Any node $v_k \in V$ delivering a $true/false$ message forward it for $|V|$ rounds then terminates with output $true/false$.

Theorem 1. *Given a dynamic network* $G(r) = (V, E(r))$, *during the execution of* DAP2, *the sum of energy with a particular label* ℓ_i *among all nodes is always preserved.*

Proof. For simplicity we restrict our proof to the energy marked with a single label ℓ_i and we prove that at the end of a round r the sum of energy among all nodes in V is equal to the sum of energy at the beginning of r. Without loss of generality we refer only to the energy $e^j_{\ell_i}$ present in $v_j \in V$. At the beginning of r, v_j sends to to all its current neighbors $N_{v_j}(r) : \{v_1, v_2, ... v_h\}$ a fraction of its energy $\frac{e^j_{\ell_i}}{2|V|}$ and v_j will have a remaining energy of $\frac{e^j_{\ell_i}}{2} + e^j_{\ell_i} \frac{|V| - |N_{v_j}(r)|}{2|V|}$. Let us recall that v_j knows $|N_v(r)|$ only after the reception of messages. The energy initially possessed by v_j was $e^j_{\ell_i}$, at the end of r the sum of energy over nodes in $N_{v_j}(r) \cup \{v_j\}$ is $e^j_{\ell_i}$. Iterating this reasoning over all nodes we have that the conservation of energy is not violated. $\square_{Theorem\ 1}$

Theorem 2. *Given a dynamic network $G(r) = (V, E(r))$, let $\mathcal{E}_{\ell_i}$ be the energy associated to a label ℓ_i kept by nodes identified with a label different from ℓ_i. The algorithm* **DAP2** *ensures that $\mathcal{E}_{\ell_i}$ is monotonically decreasing.*

Proof. The claim simply follows by Theorem 1 and from the assumption of 1-interval connectivity. At any round, in fact, there will exist a node v_i identified by the label ℓ_i that is neighbor of a node v_j with label $\ell_j \neq \ell_i$; thus the node v_j will transfer to v_i a certain amount of energy, that will be permanently stored in v_i (since v_i is a sink for energy related to label ℓ_i). This implies that at each round the energy in $\mathcal{E}_{\ell_i}$ decrease, since the sum of energy is a constant due to Theorem 1.

$\square_{Theorem\ 2}$

We would like to remark that since each node sends just half of its energy, we will have that a node v_i with label ℓ_i will transfer all the energy marked with label $\ell_j \neq \ell_i$ only after an infinite number of rounds. So at any finite round r we will have that a node $v_i \in V$ possesses a not zero amount of energy for each label $\ell_x \in \mathcal{L}$. For this reason the terminating condition of the algorithm is $e^{max}_{\ell_j} \times |V| < 1$, this condition is reached in a finite time, as direct consequence of Theorem 2 because it is implied by $\mathcal{E}_{\ell_i} < 1$. On the contrary a stringent condition $e^{max}_{\ell_j} \times |V| = 0$ would be verified only after an infinite number of rounds.

Theorem 3. *Given a dynamic network $G(r) = (V, E(r))$, if processes know $n = |V|$, then* **DAP2** *correctly evaluates predicate $Num_{\ell_j} \geq 2$.*

Proof. Let Y is the set of processes with label ℓ_j and let us us consider a process $v_j \in Y$. It is sufficient to show that a process v_j broadcasts $true$ if and only if $N_{\ell_j} \geq 2$.

- **v_j broadcasts true $\rightarrow N_{s_j} \geq 2$:** v_j broadcasts true iff $|V| - e^j_{\ell_j} \geq 1$ and $(e^{max}_{\ell_j} \times |V|) < 1$. This happens when we have that all the energy in the network present in nodes with label different from ℓ_i is strictly less then 1 but at the same time v_j has collected strictly less energy that the one it has to collect in a network of size $|V|$. This is only possible if $\exists v_i \in Y$ $v_i \neq v_j$ with the same label ℓ_j, this process acts as a sink for energy in the form $< x, \ell_j >$. Moreover, v_i does not release its initial energy $e^i_{\ell_i}$; this implies that the energy associated to ℓ_i that v_j can receive is less than $|V| - 1$.
- **$N_{\ell_j} \geq 2 \rightarrow v_j$ broadcasts true;** if $N_{\ell_j} \geq 2$ then $\exists v_j \in Y$ $v_i \neq v_j$. This v_i similarly to v_j will act as a sink for energy in the form $< x, \ell_j >$. Moreover it releases the energy marked with ℓ_j that it posses. This means that the energy in the network that v_j could collect is at most $|V| - 1$, from this follows that when $(e^{max}_{\ell_j} \times |V|) < 1$ it must be that $|V| - e^{\ell_j}_{v_j} \geq 1$, so v_j broadcasts $true$.

$\square_{Theorem\ 3}$

4.2 An Algorithm to Answer Predicate Like $Num_{\ell_i} \geq t$

In the following, we will show how it is possible to extend **DAP2** in order to allow each process $v_j \in V$ to evaluate predicates in the form $Num_{\ell_j} \geq t$. The extended algorithm, namely *Distributed Answering Predicate greater than t* (DAPT), takes as input label ℓ_i and outputs the value true iff there exists at least t processes in V identified by the same label ℓ_i, otherwise it output false.

In order to explain the intuition behind the **DAPT** algorithm we restrict to the case when exist exactly two nodes v_i and v_j, identified with the same label ℓ_j during the energy collection phase they can either (i) end up at some round r with a different energy charge (i.e. $e^i_{\ell_j} \neq e^j_{\ell_j}$ at some round r) or (ii) they are symmetric and have exactly the same amount of energy at each round (i.e. $e^i_{\ell_j} = e^j_{\ell_j}$ for any round r).

In the first case, processes can break the symmetry, assume two different logical label $\ell'_j = <\ell_j, e^i_{\ell_j}>$ and $<\ell''_j = \ell_j, e^j_{\ell_j}>$ that will differentiate them for the remaining of the computation and that allow them to be counted according to **DAP2**. Conversely, in the second case the algorithm will define a procedure allowing them to infer, by means of simple equation, the cardinality of the set of processes with the same label ℓ_j and the same quantity of energy. As a consequence, no matter of how the adversary handle the dynamicity of the network, it is always possible to count the number of processes with a particular label ℓ_j.

Algorithm DAPT – Evaluating predicate $Num_{\ell_j} \geq t$ in dynamic networks with Homonyms.

Same as **DAP2** except the terminating condition that is defined as follows.

Terminating Condition: Exploiting the property of 1-connected graphs about the latest delivery time for a message sent at round r, at each round $r > |V|$, v_j estimates the energy related to its label ℓ_j that still needs to be collected as in **DAP2**. Let $e^{max}_{\ell_j}$ be the maximum residual energy for the label ℓ_j. Eventually, v_j will trigger the terminating condition of **DAP2** and thus, $e^{max}_{\ell_j} \times |V| < 1$ and v_j stores an energy charge $e^j_{\ell_j}$.

If $|V| - e^j_{\ell_j} < 1$, then v_j broadcasts COUNT $(\ell_j, 1)$ message, otherwise it broadcasts STATE $(\ell_j, e^j_{\ell_j})$ and this message floods the network.

Then, node v_j waits $2|V|$ rounds. If v_j receives only messages STATE (ℓ_j, e') with $e' = e^j_{\ell_j}$, then v_j broadcasts COUNT $(\ell_j, \lceil \frac{|V|-1}{e^j_{\ell_j}} \rceil)$. Contrarily, if v_j has received at least one message STATE (ℓ_j, e'') with $e'' \neq e^j_{\ell_j}$, v_j sets its label to logical label $\ell'_j \leftarrow <\ell_j, e^j_{\ell_j}>$ and then it broadcasts COUNT(ℓ'_j, nil) and restarts the procedure broadcasting its new label ℓ'_j, collecting the energy associated with ℓ'_j. Each process v_j collects messages in the form COUNT (ℓ_j, Z) until it is able to count the number of processes in state ℓ_j.

Theorem 4. *Given a dynamic network $G(r) = (V, E(r))$, if processes know $n = |V|$, then **DAPT** correctly evaluates predicate $Num_{\ell_j} \geq t$.*

Proof. Without loss of generality, let us assume to have a set Y of processes with label ℓ_j, with $|Y| \geq 1$. Let us consider the first round r_t where process $v_j \in Y$ will satisfy the condition $e_{\ell_j}^{max} \times |V| < 1$. At round r_t, v_j will have a quantity of energy $e_{\ell_j}^j$. Two cases are possible:

case 1: $|V| - e_{\ell_j}^j < 1$: this means that $|Y| = 1$, we boil down into the scenario of Theorem 3 and so v_j correctly broadcasts COUNT$(\ell_j, 1)$.

case 2: $|V| - e_{\ell_j}^j \geq 1$: this condition implies $|Y| > 1$ (cfr. proof of Theorem 3), so v_j knows that there exists a process $v_i \in Y$ such that $v_i \neq v_j$. In this case, since 1-interval connectivity holds, waiting $2 \times |V|$, v_j has necessary to receive at least one message from a process v_i and two cases are may happen:

- v_j receives a message STATE$(\ell_j, e_{\ell_j}^i)$ from v_i with $e_{\ell_j}^j \neq e_{\ell_j}^i$: in this case, v_j can detect that the STATE message is originated by a different $v_i \in Y$. Moreover, v_j sets its label $\ell_j' \leftarrow < \ell_j, e_{\ell_j}^j >$ that is different from the logical label that v_i will set $\ell_i'' \leftarrow < \ell_j, e_{\ell_j}^i >$. Therefore, in the next rounds v_j has to count the processes in the subset $Y_{\ell_j'}$ that is strictly smaller then the original Y since $v_i \in Y \setminus Y_{\ell_j'}$.

- v_j does not receive a message STATE$(\ell_j, e_{\ell_j}^i)$ from v_i with $e_{\ell_j}^j \neq e_{\ell_j}^i$: in this case, for each process $v_i \in Y$, we have $e_{\ell_j}^j = e_{\ell_j}^i$.
  Since the terminating condition $e_{\ell_j}^{max} \times |V| < 1$ is verified we have $\mathcal{E}_{\ell_j} < 1$ this implies the inequality $e_{\ell_j}^j |Y| \geq |V| - 1$. Moreover due to Theorem 1 we have $e_{\ell_j}^j \times |Y| \leq |V|$. From this system of inequalities we derive:

$$\frac{|V| - 1}{e_{\ell_j}^j} \leq |Y| \leq \frac{|V|}{e_{\ell_j}^j}$$

This means that v_j could restrict the size of $|Y|$ at values in the range $[\frac{|V|-1}{e_{\ell_j}^j}, \frac{|V|}{e_{\ell_j}^j}]$. It is easy to show that this range does not include more then one natural number since the inequality $\frac{|V|}{e_{\ell_j}^j} - \frac{|V|-1}{e_{\ell_j}^j} < 1$ it is satisfied for $e_{\ell_j}^j > 1$. So, $|Y| = \lceil \frac{|V|-1}{e_{\ell_j}^j} \rceil$ and $|Y| = |V|$ iff $e_{\ell_j}^j = 1$.

Given the previous analysis, it is easy to show that each node $v_j \in Y$, is able to either: (1) count the processes with the same label, when the energy accumulated is the same $\forall v \in Y$, (2) to be the only process with a label ℓ_j and thus to detect this condition, (3) to detect the presence of a process with the same label but with a different energy charge, this allows it to change its label to a new one and to restart the counting. Let us recall that due to Theorem 2, the terminating condition will always be reached. The count of processes with the original label ℓ_j follows trivially by flooding and collecting all the messages from processes that are in logical labels that derives from ℓ_j. $\square_{Theorem\ 5}$

4.3   From Counting Homonyms to Computing Aggregate Functions

An aggregate function is a particular type of function that, starting from a set of input values, returns an output computed by aggregating each single input provided by each process; example of such type of queries are the sum, max, min, average. In the context of dynamic networks, 1-interval connectivity property could be enough to compute some of them as max and min; however, to compute functions like sum and average, processes need non only to eventually collect all the necessary input, but they also need to know the exact number of duplicate values. The latter point is actually an issue in distributed systems with homonyms.

In the previous Section, we shown how it is possible to count homonyms by means of the algorithms answering to predicates in the form $Num_{\ell_i} \geq t$. This allows processes in the dynamic network to exactly state how many processes are labeled with each label $\ell_i \in \mathcal{L}$ by simply checking, for each label ℓ_i the predicates starting from $Num_{\ell_i} \geq |V|$ and decreasing the threshold until the predicate returns false. To evaluate the predicate sum or average, processes run **DAPT** where the counting is done by considering the composite label obtained by the pair $< value, \ell_j >$ where $value$ is the local value stored by each process and used as input for the aggregation function and ℓ_j is the label of each single process.

5   Counting with Failures

In this section we show how it is possible to extend **DAPT** to work in the presence of failures. In particular, we consider the following failure model: during the execution of a distributed algorithm $\mathcal{A}$ (i.e. **DAPT**), an external adversary is able to remove up to f processes (with $n > f \geq 1$) during a round r_f; this means that the size of the network changes between round r_f and $r_f + 1$. In other words, we assume failures are confined in a single round.

In order to cope with this kind of failures we propose the following approach:

1. Build a distinguisher algorithm, namely $\mathcal{A}_D$, that is able to detect if in the dynamic network $G(r) = (V(r), E(r))$ there is a change of cardinality for the set $|V(r)|$. In the subsection 5.1 we show that is possible to implement a distinguisher algorithm that take an infinite time to detect the network size change, in 5.2 we modify the terminating condition of the algorithm show in section 5.1 in order that it terminates detecting a change of $|V|$ in a finite number of rounds.
2. Detecting the new size of V. In Section 5.3, we show how $\mathcal{A}_D$ can be instrumented to detect at round $r_f > r$ the precise number of failures occurred at round r and to compute the new value of $|V|$.
3. Restarting a new instance of **DAPT** after the round r_f in order to count the homonyms.

5.1   A Distinguisher Algorithm for Networks of Different Size

$\mathcal{A}_D$ is able to distinguish if it is running in a network whose nodes are represented by the set $V : \{v_1, ..., v_n\}$ from a run in a network whose nodes are represented by the set

$V' = \{v_1, ..., v_k\}$, with $n - f \le k \le n$. In particular, $\mathcal{A}_D$ should be able to output true when it is running on V and to output false when it is running on V'. Let us observe that during the execution of **DAPT**, a node $v_i \in |V|$ identified by the label ℓ_i could collect at most $|V| - |\ell_j| + 1$ energy in V and, in the worst-case, $|V| - |\ell_j| - f + 1$ in V' and such difference could be exploited to distinguish $\mathcal{A}_D(V)$ from $\mathcal{A}_D(V')$.

Thus, we modify the terminating condition of **DAPT** with the following one $e_{\ell_j}^{max}|V| = 0$, that is all the energy with label ℓ_j has been transferred to some node with label ℓ_j. When this condition is reached we have (see previous section) a set of nodes Y with the same label ℓ_j and having a symmetric execution history leading them to collect the same energy $e_{\ell_j}^j$. Now if $\mathcal{A}_D$ is running on $|V|$ the following equation has to hold for energy conservation (see Theorem 1):

$$|Y| \times e_{\ell_j}^j = |V| \tag{1}$$

this holds because the sum of energy of nodes belonging to Y has to be equal to $|V|$.

Since, each process v_j knows both $e_{\ell_j}^j$, $|V|$, it can compute, starting from the previous equation, the value of $|Y|$. Let us notice that, to distinguish the two scenarios where we run on V or on V', we need that the value for $|Y_V|$ computed while considering the network with $|V|$ processes and $|Y_{V'}|$, the value of $|Y|$ computed in the network V' (where the size is less then expected), must be not natural numbers at the same time (i.e. at least one of the two must be in the domain of $\mathbb{R} \setminus \mathbb{N}$). In particular, since equation 1 is always holding, when $|Y_V|$ is computed we always obtain a natural number.

When $\mathcal{A}_D$ runs on V' each process in Y has to collect $e_{\ell_j}^j = \frac{|V|-f}{|Y|}$. This is actually due to: (i) the energy in the network is $|V| - f$, (ii) each process in Y has to collect exactly the same energy, (iii) all processes with label different from ℓ_j has 0 energy.

Thus, substituting into equation 1 we obtain as estimate on $|Y|$ the quantity $|Y_{V'}| = \frac{|V||Y|}{|V|-f}$ that could be rewritten as

$$|Y_{V'}| = |Y| + \frac{|Y|f}{|V|-f} \tag{2}$$

When $|Y_{V'}|$ is in $\mathbb{R} \setminus \mathbb{N}$, each v_j can detect that is not in V. Since $|Y|$ is a natural number the only way is to have $\frac{|Y|f}{|V|-f}$ in $\mathbb{R} \setminus \mathbb{N}$. This is true when $\frac{|Y|f}{|V|-f} < 1$ that imposes a condition on the cardinality of Y, i.e.,

$$|Y| < \frac{|V|}{f} - 1 \tag{3}$$

This condition on $|Y|$ means that we can detect there are up to f processes missing when the cardinality of each label is strictly less then $\frac{|V|}{f} - 1$. This condition can be essentially mapped on $\mathcal{L}$ under the hypothesis that processes are equally distributed between labels (i.e. $|\ell_i| = \frac{|V|}{\mathcal{L}}$). So the previous condition could be expressed as $\frac{|V|}{|\mathcal{L}|} < \frac{|V|}{f} - 1$, this is equivalent to:

$$|\mathcal{L}| > f + \frac{f^2}{|V|-f} \tag{4}$$

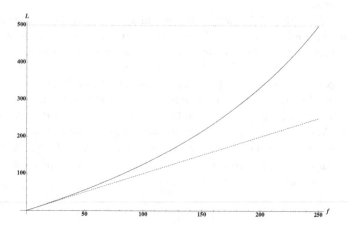

Fig. 1. Number of labels needed by $\mathcal{A}_D$ to tolerate f failure in a network with 500 processes

Figure 1 shows that number of distinct labels (i.e. $|\mathcal{L}|$) needed by $\mathcal{A}_D$ to tolerate f failures in a dynamic distributed network composed by $|V| = 500$ processes. In the same figure the dotted line is the lower bound on the number of labels needed to tolerate f failures by any distributed algorithm. As final remark, let us notice that in order to tolerate $f < \frac{|V|}{2}$ failures in a round, i.e., a minority of failures, we need less label than $|V|$. If the number of failures in a round is greater than or equal to a majority of $|V|$, each process in the systems needs a distinct label.

Interestingly, the threshold $|\mathcal{L}| > f$ is tight as proved by the following Theorem:

Theorem 5. *Given a dynamic network $G(r) = (V, E(r))$, if processes know $|V|$ and $|\mathcal{L}| = f$ there is no algorithm that can distinguish a run on $V = \{v_1, v_2, ..., v_{|V|}\}$ from a run on $V' = \{v_1, ..., v_{|V|-f}\}$*

Proof. Let us consider two static rings, namely R_1 and R_2, made as follows:

$$R_1 = \{v_1^{\ell_1}, v_2^{\ell_2}, ..., v_k^{\ell_k}, v_{k+1}^{\ell_1}, ..., v_{|V|}^{\ell_k}\}$$

and

$$R_2 = \{v_1^{\ell_1}, v_2^{\ell_2}, ..., v_k^{\ell_k}, v_{k+1}^{\ell_1}, ..., v_{|V|-k}^{\ell_k}\}$$

Let us consider a generic Algorithm $\mathcal{A}$ running on a process v with label ℓ_j in R_1, and the same algorithm running on a process w with label ℓ_j in R_2. In order to distinguish R_1 from R_2, $\mathcal{A}$ has to reach two different states on v and w. It is easy to see that process v has the same set of δ-neighbors[1] of w for each value of δ. Thus, they have two neighbors in the same state at distance 1, distance 2,.. up to $\delta = +\infty$. This means that even considering an infinite run v and w will persist in the same state, making impossible to distinguish between a run of $\mathcal{A}$ on R_1 or R_2. $\square_{Theorem\ 5}$

---

[1] The δ-neighborhood of a given node v is the sub-set of processes that are distant from v at most δ.

5.2   A Distinguisher Algorithm Working in a Finite Time

The condition $e_{\ell_j}^{max}|V| = 0$ can be verified only in an infinite run (see Section 4.1). To make the algorithm practical, such terminating condition has to be modified with a condition that can be verified in a finite number of rounds. Let us note that $e_{\ell_j}^{max}|V|$ is monotonically decreasing (see Theorem 2). Thus, it is possible to select a boundary value K and when $e_{\ell_j}^{max}|V| < K$ we get that $\mathcal{E}_{\ell_j} < K$. In the following, we will show how K should be selected to ensure that the terminating condition will be satisfied in a finite time. As in the previous case we consider a set of nodes Y with the same label ℓ_j and having a symmetric execution history; when $e_{\ell_j}^{max}|V| < K$, for any node $v_j \in Y$ we have:

$$e_{\ell_j}^j = \frac{|V| - f - \mathcal{E}_{\ell_j}}{|Y|}$$

Where the terms $-\mathcal{E}_{\ell_j}$ is present because the nodes in Y terminates the collection before to collect all the energy with label ℓ_j. So, computing the value for $|Y_{V'}|$ as in equation 2 we get

$$|Y_{V'}| = |Y| + \frac{|Y|(f + \mathcal{E}_{\ell_j})}{|V| - f - \mathcal{E}_{\ell_j}}$$

Thus, we need to distinguish between the case $f = 0$ and $f \geq 1$. This will in turn allow to distinguish between an execution on V and an execution on V'. Let us define $d_f = \frac{|Y|(f + \mathcal{E}_{\ell_j})}{|V| - f - \mathcal{E}_{\ell_j}}$. When $f = 0$ we have $d_0 = \frac{|Y|\mathcal{E}_{\ell_j}}{|V| - \mathcal{E}_{\ell_j}}$. We can enforce $d_0 < T$ by bounding $\mathcal{E}_{\ell_j} < T\frac{|V|}{|V|+1}$. At the same time we would like that $T < d_x < 1$ when $x \in [1, f]$, this will allow the distinguisher algorithm to recognize when it is running on V'. Since d_f is a monotonically increasing function of f in order to enforce the bound on T we consider d_1. We have $d_1 > T$ if $|Y| > T\frac{|V|-1-\mathcal{E}_{\ell_i}}{1+\mathcal{E}_{\ell_i}}$. This is always verified for $T < \frac{1}{|V|}$, $|Y| \geq 1$ and $\mathcal{E}_{\ell_i} < \frac{1}{|V|+1}$, so we can set $K = \frac{1}{|V|+1}$ and $T = \frac{1}{|V|}$. This essentially means that if we use $e_{\ell_j}^{max}|V| < \frac{1}{|V|+1}$ as terminating condition, we will end up with an $|Y_{V'}|$ that has $|Y_{V'}| - \lfloor|Y_{V'}|\rfloor \in (0, T)$ if $f = 0$ and $|Y_{V'}| - \lfloor|Y_{V'}|\rfloor \in (T, 1)$ if $f > 1$ [2], this allows the distinguisher to discriminate when it is running either in V or in V' in a finite time.

5.3   Using the Distinguisher Algorithm to Count in the Presence of Failures

We assume an instance of $\mathcal{A}_D$ is started at each round by each node v_j with input $|V|$. As a matter of fact, $\mathcal{A}_D$ running on V will always output true until f failures happen at round r_f. For any round $r > r_f$, $\mathcal{A}_D$ outputs false at v_j at round $r + \delta$ where δ is the time needed by $\mathcal{A}_D$ to terminate. When the first instance $\mathcal{A}_D$ terminates with output false at round r', the nodes start sequential runs of $\mathcal{A}_D$, the first run is started at round $r'+1$ with a guess for the network size that is $|V|-1$, if this guess is correct the $\mathcal{A}_D$ will terminate with output true, so the processes know that $f = 1$, otherwise $\mathcal{A}_D$ terminates

---

[2] The condition $|Y_{V'}| - \lfloor|Y_{V'}|\rfloor < 1$ could be simply enforced as in the previous case.

with output false, if this happen the processes start another run of $\mathcal{A}_D$ with network size's guess $|V| - 2$, this procedure is iterated until processes detect the correct number of failures f. Thus, v_j knows the current size of the network, namely $|V'| = |V| - f$, and it can start an instance of **DAPT** that will terminate correctly returning the count of homonyms.

6 Conclusion and Future Work

Counting the number of members in a given group is a fundamental problem for many distributed applications as it is a basic building block to design monitoring, reconfiguration and other management procedures. When considering a dynamic system like sensor networks or cloud systems, counting is far from being trivial and the problem become even more difficult in the presence of homonyms. This paper made a step in the context of dynamic networks with homonyms by designing an algorithm, namely **DAPT**, serving as basic building block to compute generic aggregation functions like counting the number of homonyms or computing the sum/average of the values stored by homonyms. This algorithm exploits the energy-transfer technique to answer the predicate *"There exist in the network at least t processes identified by the same label ℓ_i?"* that is then used to count the exact number of homonyms with the same label ℓ_i. In addition, we also studied how **DAPT** behaves in the presence of at most f crash failures and we found (i) the impossibility to count when the number of failures is the same as the number of labels and (ii) the minimum number of labels needed to count the number of homonyms after that f failures happened. Interestingly enough, we show that our algorithm is still able to count, tolerating the presence of homonyms, until a minority of processes fails (i.e. $f < |V|/2$) while it required a fully identifiable network to count when a majority of processes fails. As a future work, we are going to study if the bound on the number of labels needed to count in the presence of failure is tight. In addition, we plan to extend the analysis in the case of failures happening at any point in time.

Acknowledgement. This work has been partially supported by the Italian Ministry for Education, University, and Research (MIUR) in the framework of the Project of National Research Interest (PRIN) TENACE: Protecting National Critical Infrastructures from Cyber Threats and by the European project PANOPTES.

References

1. Albers, S., Henzinger, M.R.: Exploring unknown environments. SIAM J. Comput. 29(4), 1164–1188 (2000)
2. Angluin, D.: Local and global properties in networks of processors (extended abstract). In: Proceedings of the Twelfth Annual ACM Symposium on Theory of Computing, STOC 1980, pp. 82–93. ACM (1980)
3. Aspnes, J., Fich, F.E., Ruppert, E.: Relationships between broadcast and shared memory in reliable anonymous distributed systems. Distributed Computing 18(3), 209–219 (2006)
4. Attiya, H., Snir, M., Warmuth, M.K.: Computing on an anonymous ring. J. ACM 35(4), 845–875 (1988)

5. Awerbuch, B., Goldreich, O., Vainish, R., Peleg, D.: A trade-off between information and communication in broadcast protocols. Journal of the ACM (JACM) 37(2), 238–256 (1990)
6. Baldoni, R., Bertier, M., Raynal, M., Tucci-Piergiovanni, S.: Looking for a definition of dynamic distributed systems. In: Malyshkin, V.E. (ed.) PaCT 2007. LNCS, vol. 4671, pp. 1–14. Springer, Heidelberg (2007)
7. Casteigts, A., Flocchini, P., Quattrociocchi, W., Santoro, N.: Time-varying graphs and dynamic networks. CoRR, abs/1012.0009 (2010)
8. Delporte-Gallet, C., Fauconnier, H., Guerraoui, R., Kermarrec, A.-M., Ruppert, E., Tran-The, H.: Byzantine agreement with homonyms. In: Proceedings of the 30th Annual ACM SIGACT-SIGOPS Symposium on Principles of Distributed Computing, PODC 2011, pp. 21–30. ACM, New York (2011)
9. Delporte-Gallet, C., Fauconnier, H., Tran-The, H.: Homonyms with forgeable identifiers. In: Even, G., Halldórsson, M.M. (eds.) SIROCCO 2012. LNCS, vol. 7355, pp. 171–182. Springer, Heidelberg (2012)
10. Deng, X., Papadimitriou, C.H.: Exploring an unknown graph. In: Proceedings of 31st Annual Symposium on Foundations of Computer Science, pp. 355–361. IEEE (1990)
11. Di Luna, G., Baldoni, R., Bonomi, S., Chatzigiannakis, I.: Counting on Anonymous Dynamic Networks through Energy Transfer. Technical Report 1, MIDLAB, Sapienza University of Rome (2013)
12. Dolev, S.: Self-stabilization. MIT Press, Cambridge (2000)
13. Kuhn, F., Lynch, N., Oshman, R.: Distributed computation in dynamic networks. In: Proceedings of the 42nd ACM Symposium on Theory of Computing, STOC 2010, pp. 513–522. ACM, New York (2010)
14. Michail, O., Chatzigiannakis, I., Spirakis, P.G.: Brief announcement: Naming and counting in anonymous unknown dynamic networks. In: Aguilera, M.K. (ed.) DISC 2012. LNCS, vol. 7611, pp. 437–438. Springer, Heidelberg (2012)
15. O'Dell, R., Wattenhofer, R.: Information dissemination in highly dynamic graphs. In: Proceedings of the 2005 Joint Workshop on Foundations of Mobile Computing, DIALM-POMC 2005, pp. 104–110. ACM, New York (2005)
16. Panaite, P., Pelc, A.: Exploring unknown undirected graphs. In: Proceedings of the Ninth Annual ACM-SIAM Symposium on Discrete Algorithms, pp. 316–322. Society for Industrial and Applied Mathematics (1998)
17. Yamashita, M., Kameda, T.: Computing on an anonymous network. In: Proceedings of the Seventh Annual ACM Symposium on Principles of Distributed Computing, PODC 1988, pp. 117–130. ACM, New York (1988)

Localizability of Wireless Sensor Networks: Beyond Wheel Extension

Buddhadeb Sau[1] and Krishnendu Mukhopadhyaya[2]

[1] Dept. of Mathematics, Jadavpur University, Kolkata, India
bsau@math.jdvu.ac.in
[2] ACM Unit, Indian Statistical Institute, Kolkata, India
krishnendu@isical.ac.in

Abstract. A network is called *localizable* if the positions of all the nodes of the network can be computed uniquely. If a network is localizable and embedded in plane with *generic configuration*, the positions of the nodes may be computed uniquely in finite time. Therefore, identifying localizable networks is an important function. If the complete information about the network is available at a single place, localizability can be tested in polynomial time. In a distributed environment, networks with *trilateration orderings* (popular in real applications) and *wheel extensions* (a specific class of localizable networks) embedded in plane can be identified by existing techniques. We propose a distributed technique which efficiently identifies a larger class of localizable networks. This class covers both trilateration and wheel extensions. In reality, exact distance is almost impossible or costly. The proposed algorithm based only on connectivity information. It requires no distance information.

Keywords: Wireless sensor networks, graph rigidity, localization, localizable networks, distributed localizability testing.

1 Introduction

A *sensor network* is a network containing some ten to millions of sensors. Wireless sensor networks (WSNs) have wide-ranging applications. To react to an event detected by a sensor, the knowledge about the position of the sensor is necessary. The problem of finding the positions of nodes in a network is known as *network localization*. A wireless ad-hoc network embedded in $\mathbb{R}^m$ may be represented by a *distance graph* $G = (V, E, d)$ whose vertices represent computing devices. A pair of nodes, $\{u, v\} \in E$ if and only if the Euclidean distance between u and v $(d(u, v) = |u - v|)$ is known. Determining the coordinates of vertices in an embedding of G in $\mathbb{R}^m$ may be considered as graph realization problem [9,6,4,1]. A *realization* of a graph $G = (V, E, d)$ in $\mathbb{R}^m$ is an injective mapping $p : V \to \mathbb{R}^m$, which assigns coordinates $(x_1, \ldots, x_m) \in \mathbb{R}^m$ to every vertex in V, such that $|p(u) - p(v)| = d(u, v)$, $\forall \{u, v\} \in E$. The pair (G, p) is called a *framework* of G in $\mathbb{R}^m$. Two frameworks (G, p) and (G, q) are *congruent* if $|p(u) - p(v)| = |q(u) - q(v)|$, $\forall u, v \in V$ (i.e., preserving the distances between all pairs of vertices). A framework (G, p) is *rigid*, if it has no smooth deformation [5] preserving the edge lengths. The distance graph G is *generically globally*

T. Higashino et al. (Eds.): SSS 2013, LNCS 8255, pp. 326–340, 2013.

rigid [5], if all realizations with *generic configurations* (set of points with coordinates not being *algebraically dependent*) are congruent. A set $A = \{\alpha_1, \ldots, \alpha_m\}$ of real numbers is algebraically dependent if there is a non-zero polynomial h with integer coefficients such that $h(\alpha_1, \ldots, \alpha_m) = 0$. The graph G is termed as *globally rigid*, if all realizations of G are congruent.

In real applications, positions of the nodes may either be 1) estimated [10,2,3,8,17] within some tolerable error level or 2) uniquely realized. If all realizations of a network are congruent, the network is called *localizable*. A distance graph is localizable if and only if it is globally rigid. In $\mathbb{R}^2$, all the nodes in a globally rigid graph can be uniquely realized with three *anchors* (nodes with known position). In this paper, we consider the graphs embedded only in plane. Here onwards, all the discussions and results are concerned only in $\mathbb{R}^2$. If the nodes cannot be localized from the given information, location estimation may serve well in several applications. Localization of a network is NP-hard [15] even when it is localizable [7]. A graph is globally rigid, if and only if it is 3-*connected* and *redundantly rigid* [7]. A graph is redundantly rigid, if it remains rigid after removing any edge. Localizability of a graph can be answered in polynomial time [7] while complete network wide information is available in a single machine. To gather complete network information in a single site is infeasible or very costly. On the contrary, finding methods to recognize globally rigid graphs in distributed environments based on local information is still a challenging problem [16].

The rest of the paper is organized as follows. Section 2 describes motivation and contribution of this work. Section 3 introduces some classes of localizable graphs which include trilateration graph and wheel extension as their special cases. Section 4 defines the problem. Section 5 describes the proposed distributed algorithm of localizability testing. Section 6 proves correctness and performance analysis of the algorithm. Finally, we conclude in Section 7.

2   Background and Our Contribution

Trilateration [11,14] technique efficiently localizes a *trilateration graph* starting from three anchors. A trilateration graph is a graph with a *trilateration ordering*, $\pi = (u_1, u_2, \ldots, u_n)$ where u_1, u_2, u_3 form a K_3 and every u_i $(i > 3)$ is adjacent to at least three nodes before u_i in π. However, not all localizable networks admit trilateration ordering. Fig. 1 (a) and 1 (b) respectively show a *wheel graph* and a *wheel extension* graph which have no trilateration ordering. A wheel W_n with

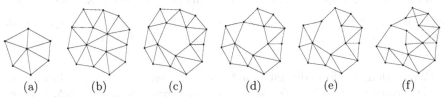

(a)   (b)   (c)   (d)   (e)   (f)

Fig. 1. Examples of some localizable graphs: (a) Wheel graph, (b) Wheel extension, (c) Triangle cycle, (d) Triangle circuit, (e) Triangle bridge, (f) Triangle net

n vertices is a graph consisting of a cycle with $n - 1$ nodes and a vertex which is adjacent to all vertices on the cycle. A *wheel extension* is a graph having an ordering $\pi = (u_1, u_2, \ldots, u_n)$ of nodes where u_1, u_2, u_3 form a K_3 and each u_i, $i > 3$, lies in a wheel subgraph containing at least three nodes before u_i in π. A wheel extension is generically globally rigid and can be identified efficiently and distributedly [16]. However, there are many more localizable graphs which do not have wheel extensions. Fig. 1 (c), 1 (d), 1 (e) and 1 (f) are examples of graphs which are generically globally rigid, but do not have wheel extensions.

Our contributions: In this paper, we introduces some elementary classes of localizable graphs: *triangle cycle, triangle circuit, triangle bridge, triangle notch and triangle net*. Using these classes of graphs, we build up a new family of localizable graphs called *triangle bar*. Trilateration graphs and wheel extensions are special cases of triangle bars. We propose a distributed algorithm that efficiently recognizes triangle bars starting from a K_3 based only on connectivity information. It requires no distance information. In real applications, exact node distance is impossible or costly. However, several localizable graphs still fall outside the class triangle bar. To the best of our knowledge, distributed recognition of an arbitrary localizable network is still an open problem. Some results in this paper stated without proof. Detail proofs are available in [13].

3   Rigidity and Localizability of Triangle Bar

Unique realizability is closely related to graph rigidity [9,6]. The realizability testing of a distance graph $G = (V, E, d)$ is NP-hard [15]. We expect data are consistent to have a realization, if the distance information is collected from an actual deployment of devices. A realization of G may be visualized as a frame constructed by a finite set of hinged rods. The junctions and free ends are considered as vertices of the realization and rods as the edges. With perturbation on the frame, we may have a different realization preserving the edge distances. The realizations obtained by flipping, rotating or shifting the whole structure are congruent. By *flip, rotation* or *shift* on a realization, we mean a part of the realization is flipped, rotated or shifted. If two globally rigid graphs in $\mathbb{R}^2$ share exactly one vertex in common, one of them may be rotated around the common vertex keeping the other fixed. Such a vertex is called a *joint*. If two globally rigid graphs in $\mathbb{R}^2$ share exactly two vertices, rotation about these vertices is no longer possible, but one of the graphs may be flipped, about the line joining the common vertices, keeping the other fixed. This pair of vertices is called a *flip*.

Lemma 1 ([12]). *If two globally rigid subgraphs, B_1 and B_2, of a graph embedded in plane share at least three non-collinear vertices, then $B_1 \cup B_2$ is globally rigid.*

In this section, we formally introduce some elementary classes of localizable graphs: *triangle cycle, triangle circuit, triangle bridge, triangle notch, triangle net*. Using these elementary classes, a larger class of localizable graphs *triangle bar* is formally defined. Results obtained in this section are proved in [13].

3.1   Triangle Cycle, Triangle Circuit and Triangle Bridge

Let $\mathcal{T} = (T_1, T_2, \ldots, T_m)$ be a sequence of distinct triangles such that for every i, $2 \leq i \leq m - 1$, T_i shares two distinct edges with T_{i-1} and T_{i+1}. Such a sequence $\mathcal{T}$ of triangles is called a *triangle stream* (Fig. 2 (a)). $G(\mathcal{T})$ is the graph

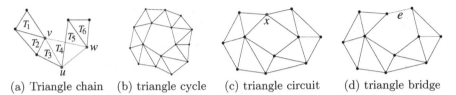

(a) Triangle chain   (b) triangle cycle   (c) triangle circuit   (d) triangle bridge

Fig. 2. Examples of triangle chain, triangle cycle, triangle circuit, triangle bridge

constructed by taking the union of the T_is in $\mathcal{T}$. A node u of a triangle T_i is termed a *pendant* of T_i, if the edge opposite to u in T_i is shared by another triangle in $\mathcal{T}$. This shared edge is called an *inner side* of T_i. Each triangle T_i has at least one edge which is not shared by another triangle in $\mathcal{T}$. Such a non-shared edge is called an *outer side* of T_i. In Fig. 2 (a), $T_4 = \{u, v, w\}$ has two pendants v and w. It has two inner sides uw and uv and one outer side vw. If T_1 and T_m have unique and distinct pendants, then $G(\mathcal{T})$ is called a *triangle chain*. Fig. 2 (a) shows an example of a triangle chain. A triangle chain involves only flips; hence it is rigid. If T_1 and T_m share a common edge other than those shared with T_2 and T_{m-1}, then the union $G(\mathcal{T})$ is called a *triangle cycle*. In a triangle cycle, each triangle has exactly two inner and one outer sides. Fig. 2 (b) shows an example of a triangle cycle. A wheel graph is a triangle cycle.

If $G(\mathcal{T})$ is not a triangle cycle and T_1 and T_m have a unique pendant in common, then $G(\mathcal{T})$ is called a *triangle circuit* (Fig. 2 (c)). The common pendant is called a *circuit knot*. x is the circuit knot of the triangle circuit. Let $\mathcal{T} = (T_1, T_2, \ldots, T_m)$ be a triangle stream corresponding to a triangle chain. T_1 and T_m have unique and distinct pendants. We connect these pendants by an edge e. $G(\mathcal{T}) \cup \{e\}$ is called a *triangle bridge* (Fig. 2 (d)). The edge e is called the *bridging edge*. The *length of a triangle stream* $\mathcal{T}$ is the number of triangles in it and is denoted by $l(\mathcal{T})$.

Lemma 2. *1) Every triangle cycle has a spanning wheel or triangle circuit (a wheel or triangle circuit which is a spanning subgraph of the triangle cycle). 2) Every triangle circuit has a spanning triangle bridge (a triangle bridge which is a spanning subgraph of the triangle circuit).*

We have seen that a rigid realization in $\mathbb{R}^2$ may have *flip ambiguity*, i.e., it may yield another configuration by applying flip operation only. In $\mathbb{R}^2$, if a rigid realization admits no flip ambiguity, then it is globally rigid. Using this, we shall prove the generically global rigidity as follows.

Lemma 3. *Triangle cycle, circuit and bridge are generically globally rigid.*

3.2   Triangle Notch and Triangle Net

Consider a sequence $\mathcal{T} = (T_1, T_2, \ldots, T_m)$ of triangles. Suppose, for $i = 2, 3, \cdots,$ m, each T_i shares exactly one edge with exactly one T_j, $1 \leq j < i$. The node opposite to this sharing edge is called a *pendant* of T_i in $\mathcal{T}$. Fig. 3 shows an example of such a sequence and x is a pendant of T_2. T_1 has no pendant. For

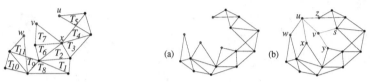

Fig. 3. Triangle tree   **Fig. 4.** (a) Triangle tree (b) u and v are extended nodes

$2 \leq i \leq m$, each T_i has exactly one pendant in $\mathcal{T}$. The graph $G(\mathcal{T})$ corresponding to such a sequence $\mathcal{T}$, is called a *triangle tree*. Fig. 3 is an example of a triangle tree with 11 triangles. $G(\mathcal{T})$ contains no triangle cycle. Otherwise, there always exists a T_j which shares two edges with some triangles before T_j in $\mathcal{T}$. If a triangle T_i shares no edge with T_j, $j > i$, is called a *leaf triangle*. A leaf triangle shares exactly one edge with other triangles in $\mathcal{T}$. It has a unique pendant, called a *leaf knot*. T_5, T_7 and T_{11} are leaf triangles and u, v and w are leaf knots. By construction, any realization of a triangle tree is rigid.

Definition 1. *Let $G(\mathcal{T})$ be a triangle tree. A node v, outside $G(\mathcal{T})$, is called an extended node of $G(\mathcal{T})$, if v is connected by edges (such an edge is called an extending edge) to at least three nodes, each being i) a pendant in $G(\mathcal{T})$; or ii) an extended node of $G(\mathcal{T})$.*

Fig. 4 (a) is a triangle tree, say $G(\mathcal{T})$. Fig. 4 (b) consists of a replica of the graph in Fig. 4 (a) and some more nodes and edges. Fig. 4 (a) does not contain u of Fig. 4 (b). u is adjacent to three pendants w, x and z. So u is an extended node of $G(\mathcal{T})$. The edges uw, ux and uz are the extending edges of u. Similarly, v is adjacent to an extended node u and two pendants s and y. So v is also an extended node of $G(\mathcal{T})$; where vu, vs and vy are the extending edges.

Definition 2. *A graph G is a triangle notch, if it can be generated from a triangle tree $G'(\mathcal{T})$, while G' is proper subgraph of G, by adding only one extended node v if every leaf knot of $G'(\mathcal{T})$ is adjacent to v. v is called the apex of G.*

Fig. 5 (b) shows an example of a triangle notch with the apex v. The triangle tree from which it is generated is separately shown in Fig. 5 (a).

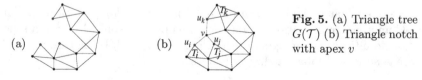

(a)   (b)   **Fig. 5.** (a) Triangle tree $G(\mathcal{T})$ (b) Triangle notch with apex v

Lemma 4. *A triangle notch is generically globally rigid.*

Lemma 5. *Let G be a graph obtained from a triangle tree $G'(\mathcal{T})$ by adding extended nodes. Any extended node along with all pendants and extended nodes adjacent to it lie in a generically globally rigid subgraph.*

Definition 3. *A graph G is called a triangle net, if it may be generated from a triangle tree $G'(\mathcal{T})$ by adding one or more extended nodes and satisfying the following conditions: i) G contains no triangle cycle, triangle circuit or triangle bridge; and ii) there exists an extended node u such that every leaf knot of $G'(\mathcal{T})$ is connected to u by a path (called an extending path) containing only extending edges. The extended node, which is added last, is called an apex of G.*

In Fig. 6 (a), u and v are two extended nodes. The leaf knots t, w and x are connected to u by extending paths. Other leaf knots y and z are connected to v by extending paths. No extending path exists between the y and u, and x and v. So the graph shown in Fig. 6 (a) is not a triangle net. Fig. 6 (b) contains two

(a)   (b)

Fig. 6. (a) Not a triangle net (b) A triangle net

extended nodes u and v. All the leaf knots w, x, y and z are connected to u by extending paths. Fig. 6 (b) is an example of a triangle net. The graph shown in Fig. 6 (b), is generated from a triangle tree by adding extended nodes u and then v. So v is an apex of G. Triangle notch is a special case of triangle net.

Lemma 6. *A triangle net is generically globally rigid.*

3.3 Triangle Bar

A graph G is called a *triangle bar*, if it satisfies one of the followings: i) G can be obtained from a triangle cycle, triangle circuit, triangle bridge or triangle net by adding zero or more edges, but no extra node; ii) $G = B_i \cup B_j$ while B_i and B_j are triangle bars sharing at least three nodes; or iii) $G = B_i \cup \{v\}$ while B_i is a triangle bar, v is a node not in B_i and adjacent to at least three nodes of B_i. Note that triangle cycle, triangle circuit, triangle bridge and triangle net are also triangle bars. These triangle bars will be referred as *elementary bars*.

Fig. 7 shows some examples of triangle bars. The first figure is a triangle cycle.

Fig. 7. Examples of triangle bar

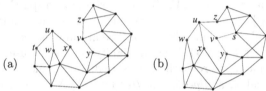

Next two are triangle nets. The fourth figure shows an example of a triangle bar which is obtained by stitching the first three elementary bars through common.

Theorem 1. *Triangle bar is generically globally rigid.*

Theorem 2. *Trilateration graph and wheel extension are triangle bars.*

4   Problem Statement

Let $G(\mathcal{T})$ be a triangle tree where $\mathcal{T} = (T_1, T_2, \ldots, T_n)$. Three nodes in T_1 are chosen as the reference nodes. This triangle is called *seed triangle*. Our goal is to identify a maximal triangle bar containing T_1.

Problem 1. Consider a distance graph $G = (V, E, d)$, generically embedded in plane with a seed triangle T_1. Find a maximal triangle bar containing T_1 in a distributed environment and mark the nodes of the triangle bar as localizable.

We solve the problem using only connectivity information. No distance information is used. Here onwards, we ignore the distance function d and consider the graph $G = (V, E)$. The stated problem is solved by exploiting flips of triangles in G. In order to solve the problem, we introduce the notion of *flip-triangle graph*.

Flip-Triangle Graph: Given a graph $G = (V, E)$, we construct a graph $\mathcal{G} = (\mathcal{V}, \mathcal{E})$ with $\mathcal{V} = \{t_1, t_2, \ldots, t_N\}$ where t_i represents a triangle T_i in G and $\{t_i, t_j\} \in \mathcal{E}$ if and only if T_i and T_j share an edge in G. The graph $\mathcal{G}$ is termed as flip-triangle graph of G, in short $FTG(G)$. If no ambiguity occurs, we use t_i to denote a vertex of $FTG(G)$ and T_i to refer the corresponding triangle in G. A maximal tree in $FTG(G)$ is called a *flip-triangle tree (FTT)*. A connected $FTG(G)$ has unique FTT. Let $\mathcal{T} = (T_1, T_2, \ldots, T_m)$ be a sequence of triangles in G and $\tau = (t_1, t_2, \ldots, t_m)$ be the corresponding sequence of nodes in $\mathcal{G}$. If no ambiguity occurs, $\mathcal{T}$ also means the subgraph obtained from the union of T_is in $\mathcal{T}$. Similarly, τ means corresponding subgraph in $\mathcal{G}$. We describe some properties which are used to develop the proposed algorithm. The detail proofs are available in [13].

Proposition 1. $\mathcal{T}$ *is a triangle cycle of length n in G if and only if τ is an n-cycle in $\mathcal{G}$.*

Proposition 2. $\mathcal{T}$ *is a triangle tree in G if and only if τ is a tree in $\mathcal{G}$.*

Proposition 3. $\mathcal{T}$ *is a maximal triangle tree in G if and only if τ is an FTT in $FTG(G)$.*

Solution Plan: Consider a graph $G = (V, E)$. A triangle bar may be identified in G by three rules as in its definition. First, we find elementary bars in G. If possible, then we stitch them via three common nodes to form a larger triangle bar; or extend a triangle bar $\mathcal{B}$ successively by adding a new node which is adjacent to at least three nodes of $\mathcal{B}$. After computing the $FTG(G)$, the stated problem is solved in a distributed set up as follows:

1. We identify all the components of $\mathcal{G}$. For each component $\mathcal{G}'$ in $\mathcal{G}$, we compute a corresponding spanning tree $FTT(\mathcal{G}')$ which is a maximal subtree in $\mathcal{G}$.
2. Finding triangle cycles is equivalent to finding the cycles in $\mathcal{G} = FTG(G)$ (Proposition 1). We identify a *set of base cycles* (a minimal set of cycles such that any cycle of the graph may be obtained by union of some base cycles and deleting some parts).

3. A triangle chain is also a triangle tree. The generator chains of triangle circuits and bridges and generator trees of triangle nets are uniquely identified by subtrees in $FTG(G)$ (Proposition 2). We identify other elementary bars in G from the FTTs by suitable extensions.
4. We stitch or extend these elementary bars to form a maximal triangle bar in G containing T_1; then we mark the nodes in this triangle bar as localizable.

5 Localizability Testing

This section describes a distributed technique to find the maximal triangle bar with a seed triangle T_1 in three phases. This triangle bar is reported as the localizable subgraph of G.

Representation of Graph and Flip-Triangle Graph: Each node contains data structures suitable for describing and storing necessary information. We assume that each node contains a unique number as its identification (called *node-id*) and a list (**nbrs**) of node-ids of its neighbours. To represent a triangle in computer, we define a data structure, with type name **Trngl**, containing: 1) node-ids of the nodes constituting the triangle; and 2) a list of adjacent nodes in $FTG(G)$ (i.e., triangles sharing its edge in G). The node with minimum node-id among three nodes of a triangle is designated as *leader* of the triangle. The leader contains all the information of the triangle and processes them. Each node v additionally contains a list (**trngls**) of all the triangles containing v as the leader.

Communication Protocols for G and $FTG(G)$: A communication between two adjacent nodes in $FTG(G)$ (i.e., two triangles sharing an edge in G) means communication between their leaders which may involve at most 2-hop communication in G. Intermediate communications via other nodes uses standard communication tools for G (i.e., communication within G). By a communication between a node $s_i \in G$ and a node $t_j \in FTG(G)$ (i.e., triangle T_j), we mean the communication between s_i and the leader of T_j.

5.1 Phase I: Computing the FTG

Phase-I of the algorithm sets up the basic structure of the $FTG(G)$. Before starting Phase I, we assume that every node executes as follows. Each node sends its neighbour list to all its neighbours. On receiving a neighbour list, a node executes the RECVNBRLIST( ) as an atomic operation. Note that each triangle will be identified by three nodes of the triangle. It will be ignored by the nodes other than its leader. However, a leader node identifies all the triangles with this node as the leader. The order of arrival of neighbour list does not affect computing of triangles. Therefore, synchronization is not an issue in this pre-processing. The node lists all these triangles in its list **trngls**. For this pre-processing, each node costs exactly one *unit* (one transmission is treated as one unit of energy) energy. Every node executes RECVNBRLIST( ) exactly one for a neighbour list each neighbour. Each **For** loop runs over neighbour lists

---

1: **procedure** RECVNBRLIST( )   /* s_i = current node */
2:     **Wake** on arrival of neighbours (nbrs$_j$) form s_j
3:     **for** (each common s_k in nbrs$_j$ and nbrs$_i$) **do** /* $\triangle s_i s_j s_k = T$ is identified. */
4:         **if** (s_i is the leader of T) **then**   /* T corresponds new node in $FTG(G)$ */
5:             **for** (each $T' \in s_i$.trngls sharing an edge with T) **do**
6:                 **Push** T' into T.trngls; T into T'.trngls as nbr of each other in $\mathcal{G}$.
                    /* These operations occur in s_i, since s_i is the leader T and T'. */
7:             **end for**
8:             **Store** the new triangle T into s_i.trngls, since s_i is the leader of T.
9:         **end if**
10:    **end for**
11: **end procedure**

1: **procedure** RECVTRIANGLE( )   /* s_i = current node */
2:     **Wake** on arrival of a triangle $T(\triangle s_j s_k s_l)$ such that $j < k < l$
3:     **for** (each $T' \in s_i$.trngls sharing an edge with T) **do** /* an edge TT' for $\mathcal{G}$ */
4:         **Push** T into T'.trngls as a nbr of T' in $FTG(G)$. /* s_i = leader of T' */
5:     **end for**
6:     **if** ($i \in \{j, k, l\}$, say $i = l$)   /* Note that beyond 1-hop, $i \notin \{j, k, l\}$ */
7:         **Send** the triangle T to all nbrs of s_i except s_j and s_k
8: **end procedure**

---

which are finite in size. Since the processes are atomic and loops runs on finite neighbour list, progress is guaranteed. After this pre-processing, Phase I will be triggered. In this phase, each node s_i starts by sending a message for each triangle $T(\triangle s_i s_j s_k) \in s_i$.trngls to s_j and s_k. On arrival of triangle message, a node executes RECVTRIANGLE( ).

Proposition 4. *1. Synchronization creates no problem in Phase I.*
2. The algorithm guarantees the progress and finite termination of Phase I.
3. Phase I of the algorithm computes the $FTG(G)$.
4. The number of triangles transmitted over the whole network is thrice the number of triangles in the network.

Proof. In a node s_i, RECVTRIANGLE( ) checks if a newly arrived T shares an edge with the existing triangles in the list s_i.trngls. Note that a triangle $T' \in s_i$.trngls may share an edge with T. We call such a pair of triangles as *neighbour triangles* of each other. If T' shares an edge with T, then s_i is the leader of T'.

Synchronization: The vertices of $FTG(G)$ are already computed without any synchronization problem. A pair of triangles $\{T, T'\}$ with a common edge in G corresponds an edge for $FTG(G)$. For the synchronization in Phase I, we need to consider two cases: 1) T and T' have the same leader, and 2) T and T' have distinct leaders. In the first case, setting an edge for $FTG(G)$ is already done before Phase I without any synchronization problem. In second case, T will be set as a neighbour of T' when T arrives the leader of T' and vice verse. All the triangles are already computed and listed. RECVTRIANGLE( ) is atomic. Therefore, any order of insertions of triangles into the neighbour triangle list will finally give the same result.

Progress and finite termination: In RECVTRIANGLE( ), **If** block conditions are false beyond 1-hop from s_i and stops resending T. Assumed channels are reliable, every message reaches its destination in finite time. We use Lamport's logical clock. In each node, the value of logical clock does not exceed thrice the number of neighbours; one neighbour list and two triangle messages from each neighbour. It also follows the number of communications from a node.

Computation of FTG(G): Each node receives a neighbour list of a neighbour exactly once. Consider an arbitrary triangle $T(\triangle s_i s_j s_k)$ in G (Fig. 8) while $i < j < k$. Let T is received by s_i, the leader node of T. RECVNBRLIST( ) inserts T into s_i.trngls. No other node incorporates T, though s_j and s_k also identify T. It may be adjacent to the edges in $FTG(G)$ due to sharing its edges with other triangles. The inner **for** loop in RECVNBRLIST( ) sets up the edges which

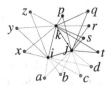

Fig. 8. Examples showing all possible triangle communications

are obtained while T shares an edge with the triangles whose leader is s_i. s_i also sends a triangle message T to s_j and s_k to find and set other edges with T in $FTG(G)$. T shares no edge in G beyond 1-hop. The edges in $FTG(G)$ between T and other triangles with leaders other than s_i are set by RECVTRIANGLE( ). When s_j (or s_k) receives T, it checks whether T shares any triangle in its list trngls sends to sends T to its neighbours other than s_i and s_j. Thus T reaches all the nodes which contains a triangle that may share an edge with T.

Number of triangle transmissions: Each is transmitted exactly thrice. Once from its leader at the starting of Phase I. From each of other two nodes of the triangle, this triangle is resent from RECVTRIANGLE( ).   □

5.2   Phase II: Finding *FTT*s and Elementary Bars

For finding elementary bars, we may assume that G is connected; otherwise, we proceed with the component containing the seed triangle T_1. Phase-II identifies the *FTT* of G containing t_1(i.e., T_1 in G); then elementary bars. This process is triggered by t_1 in G sending a **visit** signal to its adjacent nodes in G.

Representation of *FTT*s of G and Elementary Bars: For this purpose, each node in G (a triangle in G) contains additional five fields:

1. status (assumes **0** or **visited**, initially **0**) is used to indicate the status regarding the processing of the node. After the required processing of a node, status is set to **visited**.
2. eltLst is a list of elementary bars in which this particular node (triangle) is a constituent part; initially it is empty.

3. **parent** contains the immediate ancestor of the triangle in a FTT of G. The seed triangle has no parent; and it is treated as root node.
4. **children** lists direct descendants in $\mathcal{G}$. These are used to set the trees in $\mathcal{G}$.
5. **hearLst** holds the list of received triangles with some extra information that help in identifying elementary bars.

Each node in G also contains similar five fields to store the information regarding pendants, extended knots and elementary bars.

Finding the FTT and Base Cycles in $\mathcal{G}'$: The FTT of $\mathcal{G}$ containing T_1 are identified by distributed BFS on $\mathcal{G}$. If we take any FTT and add to it a new edge from $\mathcal{E}$ a set of base cycles of $\mathcal{G}$ may be obtained. The details of these steps are described in procedure VISITTRIANGLE( ). On arrival of **visit** signal into $t_i \in \mathcal{V}$, VISITTRIANGLE( ) in leader node of T_i sets its status to **visited**. t_i.parent is assigned the value t_j. This helps in backtracking in the tree in $FTG(G)$. After visiting t_i, the process sends **visit** signal to all neighbours in $FTG(G)$. At the same time, t_i sends a **visitNode** signal with T_i to the pendant s_k of T_i with respect to T_j in G for finding elementary bars other than triangle cycles. It sends back a **child** signal to the sender t_j to inform itself as a child. The **child** signal is handled (handler is not described separately) by inserting its sender into the list **children**. If t_i is already visited by some other node t_k, a base cycle in $FTG(G)$ is identified with $t_i t_j$ and sends a **cycle** signal with $t_i t_j$ to t_j and t_k. A cycle in $FTG(G)$ corresponds a triangle cycle in G (Proposition 1). A triangle cycle G, corresponding to a base cycle in $FTG(G)$, contains at least one new triangle which is not a part of any other triangle cycle in G. The outcome may be summarized below as:

Proposition 5. VISITTRIANGLE( ) *identifies the FTT and triangle cycles of G containing T_1.*

Finding Triangle Circuits and Triangle Bridges in $\mathcal{G}'$: Triangle cycles are identified by handling **cycle** signals. In view of the Proposition 3, a FTT generate maximal triangle tree in G. These maximal trees provide maximal triangle bars including appropriate edges and extended knots.

On arrival of a **visitNode** signal with X_j (either a triangle T_j or a node s_j), a node $s_i \in V$ wakes up and VISITNODE( ) stores X_js into a list **hearLst**. If s_i is being visited for the first time as a node in G, s_i set its **status** as **visited** and **parent** to X_j for backtracking. If $X_j = T_j$ and s_i is a pendant of T_j, s_i sends a **visitNode** signal with s_i to all neighbours other those in T_j. Otherwise, if s_i 1) receives a triangle T_j and its parent is a triangle T_k, a triangle circuit is identified; 2) receives a node s_j and its parent is a triangle T_k (either a pendant or extended knot), a triangle bridge or net is identified; and 3) if three **visitNode** signals, it identifies itself as an extended knot and as well as a triangle net. If s_i marks himself as an extended knot it sends **visitNode** signal with s_i to all neighbours except its parent for identifying other extended knots and nets. Note that **visitNode** signal with triangle is sent only to a pendant from the process VISITTRIANGLE( ). The final outcome of this process is described below.

```
 1: procedure VISITTRIANGLE( )  /* t_i =
       current node of G' */
 2:     Wake on a visit signal from t_j
 3:     if (status ≠ visited) then
 4:         Set parent ← t_j
 5:         Set status ← visited
 6:         Send a visit to all neighbours
            in G' other than t_j
 7:         Send a child signal to t_j to
            indicate, s_i is a child of s_j
 8:         Send a visitNode signal to
            s_k ∈ T_i − T_j with T_i qualified
            as triangle
 9:     else  /* a base cycle is found */
10:         Push T_iT_j into eltLst to in-
            dicate, t_i is in the cycle T_iT_j
11:         Send a cycle signal to t_j and
            parent with T_iT_j as elemen-
            tary bar-id
12:     end if
13: end procedure
```

```
 1: procedure ELEMENTARYBARS(x_i) /*
       x_i is the current (t_i ∈ V or s_i ∈ V) */
 2:     Wake on arrival of a cycle signal
        with elementary bar bar-id
 3:     if (bar-id qualifies delete) then
 4:         Del bar-id from eltLst
 5:     else if (bar-id ∉ eltLst) then
 6:         Push bar-id into eltLst
 7:         Send a cycle signal to the
            parent with bar-id
 8:     else/* traced elementary bar */
 9:         Send a cycle with bar-id
            qualified delete to its parent
10:     end if
11: end procedure
```

```
 1: procedure VISITNODE( ) /* s_i =current
       node in G */
 2:     Wake on visitNode with X_j (T_j | s_j)
 3:     Push X_j into hearLst
 4:     if (status ≠ visited) then
 5:         Set parent ← X_j
 6:         Set status ← visited
 7:         if (X_j = T_j)  //T_j = △s_is_ks_m
 8:             Send a visitNode with s_i to
                all s_m ∈ nbrs − {s_k, s_l}
 9:             Send a child signal to parent to
                inform that s_i is a child
10:         else if (X_j = T_j) then
                /* parent = T_k */
11:             Send a cycle signal to t_j and t_k
                with T_js_iT_k as elementary bar-id
12:         else if (X_j = s_j) then
13:             if (parent = T_k) then
                    /* a bridge or net */
14:                 Send a cycle signal to s_j and
                    t_k with s_js_iT_k as bar-id
15:             else if (parent = s_k) then
16:                 if (mark = extended) then
17:                     Send a visitNode with
                        s_i to all s_m ∈ nbrs − {s_k}
18:                     Send a cycle to s_j and
                        s_k with s_js_is_k as bar-id
19:                 else if (|hearLst| = 3) then
20:                     Set mark ← extended
21:                     for all s_j ∈ hearLst do
22:                         Send a cycle to s_k, s_j
                            with bar-id s_js_is_k
23:                     end for
24:                 end if
25:             end if
26:     end if
27: end procedure
```

Proposition 6. *All triangle circuits and triangle bridges in G' are identified by* VISITNODE*( )*.

Identifying Triangle Nets in G': On arrival of a **cycle** signal into x_i (either a node in $FTG(G)$ or pendant or extended knots in G), ELEMENTARYBARS( ) inserts elementary bar-id into the eltLst and in turn sends the same **cycle** signal to its parent until it finds a node in $FTG(G)$ containing same elementary bar-id in respective eltLst. If a matching bar-id is found, it sends **cycle** signal with this bar-id qualified as **delete**. If it finds bar-id qualified as **delete** and bar-id is deleted from eltLst and sends **delete** signal same bar-id qualified as **delete** to its parent until the root node t_1 in $FTG(G)$ is reached.

5.3   Phase III: Identifying the Maximal Triangle Bar Containing T_1

VISITNODE( ) and ELEMENTARYBARS( ) provide a maximal triangle bar for the
FTT. We have obtained a set $\mathcal{M}$ of maximal triangle bars containing T_1. Maximal triangle bars for a FTT do not share any triangle in this FTT. From $\mathcal{M}$,
two maximal triangle bars M_1 and M_2 which have three nodes in common are
replaced by $M_1 \cup M_2$. Repeat these until no replacement. This task may be
achieved by sending a special signal from all nodes of M_1, containing T_1, to their
neighbours. Another M_i sends this special signal if it hears this signal from three
nodes. Finally, a maximal triangle bar in G will be identified.

Proposition 7. *The maximal triangle bar of G containing T_1 is identified in
polynomial time with $O(|E|)$ one-hop communications over the network.*

Mark localizable nodes: At the end of Phase-II when t_1.eltLst is empty, t_1 set
its **status** as **localizable**. The triangle T_1 (i.e., t_1) triggers the Phase-III by
sending the eltLst to all its adjacent nodes (**children**) in $\mathcal{G}$. On arrival of
an elementary bar list into x_i ($t_i \in FTG(G)$ or $s_i \in G$), MARKLOCALIZABLE( )
starts execution. If the current node, x_i, lies in an elementary bar in the received

---

```
1: procedure MARKLOCALIZABLE(x_i)       /* x_i is the current (t_i ∈ V or s_i ∈ V) */
2:     Wake on arrival of an elementary bar list, say barLst
3:     if (barLst ∩ eltLst ≠ ∅ and status ≠ localizable) then
4:         Set status ← localizable
5:         Send a message with eltLst to all nodes in x_i.children
6:     end if
7: end procedure
```

---

list and is not marked as localizable, the process marks x_i as localizable and sends
x_i.eltLst to all nodes in x_i.children.

Theorem 3. *If an elementary bar contains T_1, then all the nodes (in G) of
these bars are marked as localizable through MARKLOCALIZABLE( ) (identifying
the bar through T_1) in the complete run of the algorithm.*

Proof. The result follows from the statements in Proposition 1, 2, 5 6.   □

6   Performance Analysis of the Algorithm

Each of the procedures in the algorithm may contain loops which run only over
a list either **nbrs** or **trngls**. The sizes of these lists do not exceed the number
of neighbours of a node or number of triangles with this node as the leader. The
loops executes without waiting for any signal. Therefore, the finite termination
of each procedure in any individual node is guaranteed. Since the transmission
medium is reliable, every message sometime reaches the destination. Thus, the
whole system terminates in finite time.

Synchronization, Correctness and Progress: Synchronization, progress, finite termination and correctness of Phase I are proved in Proposition 4. Phase II uses BFS tool to find the trees in a connected $FTG(G)$. This ensures that the FTTs are found correctly (Proposition 3). Theorems 1 and 3 establish the correctness of Phase II and III of the algorithm.

Time Complexity: We have used Lamport's logical clock. In the pre-processing before Phase I, the value of this logical clock in a node is equal to the number of its neighbours. The running time complexity of RECVNBRLIST() in each node is $O(n)$ in the worst case. Phase I communicates no message beyond 2-hop. In Phase I, a node can receive three triangles for each triangle in its triangle list. So the value of this clock does not exceed thrice the number of triangles with this node as the leader, i.e. $O(n^2)$ in the worst case. Time complexity for communication in Phase II and III is guided by the BFS of $FTG(G)$ in distributed way. The value of the logical cannot exceeds the number of triangles listed in it, $O(n^2)$ in the worst case. A visit signal from t_1 will reach any other t_i in $FTG(G)$ along its shortest path in between them. In worst case, it may be equal n. This dominates time required to find extended knots. Thus the overall running time complexity of the execution in the whole system is $O(n^2)$.

Energy Complexity: Since message communication dominates the leading consumer of energy, we only count the communications for energy analysis. Every node sends the neighbour list **nbrs** only once. It counts n (number of nodes in the network) transmissions. In view of Proposition 4, the number of message transmissions in Phase I is $O(n^3)$. It is easy to see that, in Phase II and Phase III, each node communicates with its neighbours constant number of times. Hence, the total energy dissipation is $O(n^3)$ in worst.

7   Conclusion

In this paper, we consider the problem of localizability of nodes as well as networks. We do not compute the positions of nodes. So, exact distances are not necessary and error in distance measurements does not affect the localizability testing. We propose an efficient distributed technique to solve this problem for a specific class of networks, triangle bar. The proposed technique distributedly recognizes triangle bar containing a seed triangle while trilateration and wheel extension are special cases of triangle bars. The proposed algorithm runs with $O(|V|^2)$ time complexity and energy complexity of $O(|V|^3)$ in the worst case. In centralized environment Localizability testing can be carried out in polynomial time. Though the proposed algorithm recognizes a class of localizable networks distributedly, several localizable networks remain unrecognized by this technique.

References

1. Aspnes, J., Eren, T., Goldenberg, D., Morse, A., Whiteley, W., Yang, Y., Anderson, B., Belhumeur, P.: A theory of network localization. IEEE Transactions on Mobile Computing 5(12), 1663–1678 (2006)
2. Biswas, P., Toh, K.-C., Ye, Y.: A distributed sdp approach for large-scale noisy anchor-free graph realization with applications to molecular conformation. SIAM J. Sci. Comput. 30(3), 1251–1277 (2008), http://dx.doi.org/10.1137/05062754X
3. Cakiroglu, A., Erten, C.: Fully decentralized and collaborative multilateration primitives for uniquely localizing wsns. EURASIP Journal on Wireless Communications and Networking 2010, Article ID 605658, 7 pages (2010)
4. Čapkun, S., Hamdi, M., Hubaux, J.P.: Gps-free positioning in mobile ad hoc networks. Cluster Computing 5, 157–167 (2002)
5. Connelly, R.: Generic global rigidity. Discrete and Computational Geometry 33(4), 549–563 (2005), http://dx.doi.org/10.1007/s00454-004-1124-4
6. Hendrickson, B.: Conditions for unique graph realizations. SIAM J. Comput. 21, 65–84 (1992)
7. Jackson, B., Jordán, T.: Connected rigidity matroids and unique realizations of graphs. Journal of Combinatorial Theory Series B 94(1), 1–29 (2005)
8. Kwon, O.H., Song, H.J., Park, S.: Anchor-free localization though flip-error-resistant map stitching in wireless sensor network. IEEE Transactions on Parallel and Distributed Systems 21(11) (2010)
9. Laman, G.: On graphs and rigidity of plane skeletal structures. Journal of Engineering Mathematics 4(4) (December 1970)
10. Moore, D., Leonard, J., Rus, D., Teller, S.: Robust distributed network localization with noisy range measurements. In: SenSys 2004: Proceedings of the 2nd International Conference on Embedded Networked Sensor Systems, pp. 50–61. ACM, New York (2004), http://doi.acm.org/10.1145/1031495.1031502
11. Niculescu, D., Nath, B.: Dv based positioning in ad hoc networks. Journal Telecommunication Systems 22, 267–280 (2003)
12. Sau, B., Mukhopadhyaya, K.: Length-based anchor-free localization in a fully covered sensor network. In: Proc. of the First International Conference on COMmunication Systems and NETworks, COMSNETS 2009, pp. 137–146. IEEE Press, Piscataway (2009), http://dl.acm.org/citation.cfm?id=1702135.1702157
13. Sau, B., Mukhopadhyaya, K.: Localizability of wireless sensor networks: Beyond wheel extension. ArXiv e-prints (August 2013), http://arxiv.org/abs/1308.6464
14. Savvides, A., Han, C., Strivastava, M.: Dynamic fine-grained localization in ad-hoc networks of sensors. In: Proc. of the 7th Annual International Conference on Mobile Computing and Networking (MobiCom 2001), pp. 166–179. ACM, Rome (2001)
15. Saxe, J.: Embeddability of weighted graphs in k-space is strongly np-hard. In: Proc. 17th. Allerton Conference in Communications, Control and Computing, pp. 480–489 (1979)
16. Yang, Z., Liu, Y., Li, X.: Beyond trilateration: on the localizability of wireless ad hoc networks. IEEE/ACM Trans. Netw. 18(6), 1806–1814 (2010)
17. Zhu, Z., So, A.C., Ye, Y.: Universal rigidity: Towards accurate and efficient localization of wireless networks. In: IEEE INFOCOM 2010 (2010)

Memory Efficient Self-Stabilizing k-Independent Dominating Set Construction*

Colette Johnen

Univ. Bordeaux, LaBRI, UMR 5800, F-33400 Talence, France

In this paper, we consider the problem of computing a k-independent dominating set in a self-stabilizing manner in case where $k > 1$. A nodes set is a k-independent dominating set (also called maximal k-independent set) if and only if this set is a k-independent set and a k-dominating set. A set of nodes, I is k-independent if the distance between any pair of I's nodes is at least $k + 1$. A set of nodes D is k-dominating if every node is within distance k of a node of D.

In [1], a silent self-stabilizing protocol extracting a minimal k-dominating set from any k-dominating set is proposed. The protocol requires at least $O(k.log(n))$ bits per node. In [2,3] are presented silent self-stabilizing protocol building k-dominating set. These protocols use the hierachical collateral composition of several silent self-stabilizing protocols whose a leader election protocol and a spanning tree construction rooted to the elected leader. So they requires more memory space than the protocol $\mathcal{SID}$.

We propose a memory efficient self-stabilizing protocol building k-independent dominating sets, named $\mathcal{SID}$. The protocol $\mathcal{SID}$ is simple: no used of the hierachical collateral composition, no need of leader election process, neither the building of spanning tree. The protocol $\mathcal{SID}$ is silent; it converges under the unfair distributed scheduler (the weakest scheduling assumption).

The protocol $\mathcal{SID}$ is memory efficient : it requires only $2log((k+1)n+1)$ bits per node. To our knowledge, the protocol $\mathcal{SID}$ requires less memory space than any other protocol solving a similar problem.

Presentation of the Protocol $\mathcal{SID}$

An k-**augmentedID type** value, a, is an tuplet (d, x) such that d is integer with $0 \le d \le k$, and x is a node identifier. Let $a = (d, x)$ be k-augmentedID value. We note $a.dist = d$ and $a.id = x$.

The operation $+1$ on k-augmentedID $\cup \perp$ is defined as follow : $a + 1 = a$ if $a = \perp$ or if $a.dist = k$ otherwise $a + 1 = (a.dist + 1, a.id)$.

The total order relation **dom** on k-augmentedID value is defined as $dom(a, b) = a$ if $b = \perp$, $(a.id < b.id)$, or $(a.id = b.id \wedge a.dist < b.dist)$ otherwise $dom(a, b) = b$.

The total order relation **min** on k-augmentedID value is defined as $min(a, b) = a$ if $b = \perp$, $(a.dist < b.dist)$, or $(a.dist = b.dist \wedge a.id < b.id)$ otherwise $min(a, b) = b$.

---

* This work was partially supported by the ANR project Displexity.

T. Higashino et al. (Eds.): SSS 2013, LNCS 8255, pp. 341–343, 2013.
© Springer International Publishing Switzerland 2013

Algorithm 1. The Protocol $\mathcal{SID}$ on the node v

Shared variables

- $\text{firstHead}(v) \in k\text{-augmentedID}$
- $\text{secondHead}(v) \in k\text{-augmentedID} \cup \perp$

Internal variables

- $\text{firstAugmentedIdSet}(v) = \{a + 1 \in k\text{-augmentedID} \mid$
  $a = \text{firstHead}(u) \vee a = \text{secondHead}(u) \ with \ u \in N_v \wedge a.dist < k \wedge a.id \neq id_v\}$
- $\text{secondAugmentedIdSet}(v) = \{a \in \text{firstAugmentedIdSet} \mid a.id \neq \text{firstHead}(v).id\}$

Macro

- $\text{headUpdate}(v) : \text{firstHead}(v) := (0, id_v); \ \text{secondHead}(v) :=\perp;$
- $\text{ordinaryUpdate}(v) : \text{firstHead}(v) := min(\text{firstAugmentedIdSet}(v));$
  $\text{secondHead}(v) := min(\text{secondAugmentedIdSet}(v) \cup \{\perp\});$

Predicates

- $\text{Head}(v) \equiv \text{firstHead}(v) = (0, id_v)$
- $\text{toResign}(v) \equiv (0, id_v) \neq dom(\text{firstAugmentedIdSet}(v) \cup \{(0, id_v)\})$
- $\text{toElect}(v) \equiv \text{firstAugmentedIdSet}(v) = \emptyset$
- $\text{headToUpdate}(v) \equiv \text{firstHead}(v) \neq (0, id_v) \vee \text{secondHead}(v) \neq\perp$
- $\text{ordinaryToUpdate}(v) \equiv \text{firstHead}(v) \neq min(\text{firstAugmentedIdSet}(v)) \vee$
  $\text{secondHead}(v) \neq min(\text{secondAugmentedIdSet}(v) \cup \{\perp\})$

Rules

$\mathbf{RE}(v) : \neg\text{Head}(v)v \wedge \text{toElect}(v) \longrightarrow \text{headUpdate}(v);$
$\mathbf{RU}(v) : \neg\text{Head}(v) \wedge \neg\text{toElect}(v) \wedge \text{ordinaryToUpdate}(v) \longrightarrow \text{ordinaryUpdate}(v);$
$\mathbf{RR}(v) : \text{Head}(v) \wedge \text{toResign}(v) \longrightarrow \text{ordinaryUpdate}(v);$
$\mathbf{RC}(v) : \text{Head}(v) \wedge \neg\text{toResign}(v) \wedge \text{headToUpdate}(v) \longrightarrow \text{headUpdate}(v);$

A node v is a head if and only if $\text{firstHead}(v) = (0, id_v)$; otherwise the node v is an ordinary node.

Once the system is stabilized, the variable $\text{firstHead}(v)$ contains the identifier of the closest head to v with its distance to v. Similary, the variable $\text{secondHead}(v)$ contains the identifier of the second closest head to v with its distance to v if the second closest head to v exists and its distance to v is lesser than $k + 1$ otherwise the value of $\text{secondHead}(v)$ is $\perp$.

The execution of the rule **RU** or the rule **RU** updates the two shared variables without changing the status of v (i.e. v stays ordinary or head).

The internal variables are used to compute the value of both shared variables. The computation of these values can be done without the use of these internal variables, but the presentation of this procedure is out the scope of this brief announcement. Once the system is stabilized, $(d, id_u) \in \text{firstAugmentedIdSet}(v)$ if and only if (1) $d > 0$; (2) the node u is the closest or the second closest head of a v' neighbor, named w; and (3) the distance between w and u is $d - 1 < k$.

The predicate $\text{firstAugmentedIdSet}(v)$ is empty if v does not have a head at distance lesser than $k + 1$. Notice that in this case, $\text{toElect}(v)$ is verified. So, if v is an ordinary node then the rule **RE** is enabled by v: v will become a head. This rule ensures that any ordinary node is at distance at most k of a head.

The predicate `toResign(`v`)` is verified when `firstAugmentedIdSet(`v`)` contains a node identifier smaller than than v's identifier. In this case, if v is a head, the rule **RR** is enabled : v will become ordinary. This rule ensures that the distance between two heads is at least $k + 1$.

The correctness and the termination of the protocol $\mathcal{SID}$ is proven in [4]. We have established that any terminal configuration of $\mathcal{SID}$ protocol is legitimate: the set of heads is a k-independent dominating set. By *reductio ad absurdam* arguments, we have proven that all maximal computations under any the unfair distributed scheduler are finite.

The computation of the convergence time of the protocol $\mathcal{SID}$ is an open question.

References

1. Datta, A., Devismes, S., Larmore, L.: A self-stabilizing $o(n)$-round k-clustering algorithm. In: 28th IEEE Symposium on Reliable Distributed Systems (SRDS 2009), pp. 147–155 (2009)
2. Datta, A.K., Larmore, L.L., Devismes, S., Heurtefeux, K., Rivierre, Y.: Competitive self-stabilizing k-clustering. In: IEEE 32nd International Conference on Distributed Computing (ICDCS 2012), pp. 476–485 (2012)
3. Datta, A.K., Larmore, L.L., Devismes, S., Heurtefeux, K., Rivierre, Y.: Self-stabilizing small k-dominating sets. International Journal of Networking and Computing 3(1), 116–136 (2013)
4. Johnen, C.: Memory efficient self-stabilizing k-independant dominating set construction. Technical Report RR-1473-13, Univ. Bordeaux, LaBRI, UMR 3800, F-33400 Talence, France (June 2013)

Modeling and Analyzing Timing Faults in Transaction Level SystemC Programs

Reza Hajisheykhi[1], Ali Ebnenasir[2], and Sandeep S. Kulkarni[1]

[1] Michigan State University, MI, USA
{hajishey,sandeep}@cse.msu.edu
[2] Michigan Technological University, MI, USA
aebnenas@mtu.edu

1 Introduction

In order to increase design productivity of SoC (System on Chip) systems, there is a need to move from implementation-driven design at Register Transfer Language (RTL) to higher levels of abstraction. This move introduces a shift in the development of electronic systems, which has been put into practice as Electronic System Level (ESL) design. The importance of ESL has become reality with *Transaction Level Modeling* (TLM) standard TLM-2.0 [1]. The C++-based system modeling language *SystemC* perfectly supports TLM and hence is well-accepted for ESL design in industry. Since the TLM models serve as references for the RTL implementation, it is necessary to study the effect of faults in such models. Also in SoC systems, timing play an important role. Hence, analyzing the system in the presence of timing faults is essential. This paper studies the effect of timing faults on SystemC TLM programs.

Formal verification of finite models created from SystemC programs has been studied extensively in the past decade. Nonetheless, none of the studies addresses the issue of timing faults in the context of SystemC TLM programs. Specifically, [2] focuses on fault-free behaviors and does not support timing faults. Although [2] permits modeling of timing properties (not faults), the generated models are often too large to perform significant analysis. The results in [3] focus on untimed behaviors and does not address timing faults. And, [4] does not address timing faults considered in this paper. The objective of our paper is to develop a methodology to support analysis in the presence of timing faults. Since SystemC TLM programming is typically considered in two forms: loosely-timed (LT) and approximately-timed (AT), we consider both coding styles. In the LT coding style there is a loose dependency between timing and data, while in the AT the dependency between timing and data is stronger. Also the AT coding style captures the global time more precisely.

To model timing faults in SystemC TLM programs, our approach uses three steps: (1) *model extraction,* (2) *timing faults modeling,* and (3) *analyzing the model in the presence of timing faults.* For the first part, we use the ideas in [2] and [3] to extract an UPPAAL timed automata model from the SystemC TLM program. Towards this end, each component in the SystemC TLM program is

T. Higashino et al. (Eds.): SSS 2013, LNCS 8255, pp. 344–347, 2013.

mapped to one or more timed automata. These timed automata interactions capture the communication between SystemC TLM components. This translation is based on a set of rules that identify the semantics of b_transport and nb_transport as well as different primitives in the transaction. For the second part, we consider timing faults and inject them into the extracted timed automata model. Some of the timing faults we consider include transactions (or parts of transactions) that are delayed or finish too quickly. The effect of these faults under LT and AT coding style is different. Specifically, in LT coding style, the effect of a delay would affect all subsequent transactions. However, the order of transactions will not change. By contrast, in AT coding style, such a fault would cause a change in transactions to finish in a different order. Also, the choice of timed automata can cause modeling of these faults more complex. For example, in a timed automaton, a clock can either increase continuously (at the fixed rate for all clock variables) or be reset, but it cannot be set to an arbitrary value. This constraint needs to be satisfied in generating the UPPAAL model. In the third part, we use UPPAAL toolset to verify the extracted model and analyze how the model behaves in the presence of timing faults. Specifically, we evaluate if the UPPAAL model that is subjected to timing faults satisfies 1) deadlock-freedom, 2) timing constraints for the original program, and 3) relaxed timing constraints.

Contributions of the Paper. We present: a) a set of transformation rules to extract the UUPPAAL timed-automata from SystemC TLM program; b) an approach for modeling timing faults in timed automata for SystemC TLM programs; and c) an analysis of the fault-affected model for both loosely-timed and approximately-timed coding styles.

2 Background, Model Extraction, and Fault Analysis

Background. In a TLM model, a *transaction* is an abstraction for an interaction between two or more concurrent processes for either data transfer or synchronization. An *Initiator* is a module that initiates new transactions to exchange data or synchronize with the other module, called the *Target*. In TLM 2.0, the interoperability is introduced as a layer and has a set of main components as follows: *Core interface* which implements blocking and non-blocking interfaces, *Generic payload* which represents transaction objects, *Sockets* that connect initiator and target modules, and *Base protocol* that is a set of rules for using TLM interfaces while sending/receiving generic payload through sockets.

Model Extraction for LT and AT Coding Styles. In a transaction using b_transport interface, we need to consider the timing since one of the sending arguments is *delay*. This argument illustrates the actual starting and ending time of the transaction in future. Hence, we define a synchronization channel in the UPPAAL model to synchronize the Initiator and Target of a transaction. Moreover, in order to guarantee deterministic execution and increase the timing accuracy, a SystemC TLM program that uses loosely-timed coding style benefits from explicit synchronization points by utilizing calls to the *wait()* function. This function is a synchronization-on-demand method that yields the control to the SystemC scheduler. To transform this function into the UPPAAL model, we define a variable *global-clock* that plays the role of the global time in a SystemC TLM program. when the wait function is called, we add the *delay* arguments to the global-clock variable and reset the local clock. Having the AT coding style in a SystemC TLM program, we utilize our rules from [3] along with the ideas from [2] to extract the UPPAAL model.

Fault Modeling and Impact Analysis.   Timing faults could perturb the state of a system to an illegitimate configuration. In other words, the timing faults cause an action/operation to be executed either too early or too late, and, as a result, the operation cannot be performed properly. We introduce a variable $delay_t$ to the fault-free UPPAAL model that can model both early and late timing problems. The maximum value of $delay_t$ (default value is 1) is identified by the designer. The UPPAAL model is further modified to non-deterministically increase the delay argument in b_transport by $delay_t$ in all processes. Regarding executing an action too early, we also introduce a new transition that increases the clock variable by a value less than that of the original transition.

We considered the effect of such timing faults in models that utilize both the LT and AT. Regarding LT model, we present an approach for model extraction that extend the approach in [3] by modeling of timing faults. This approach also utilizes UPPAAL (as opposed to Promela considered in [3]) so that accurate timing properties can be verified. Regarding AT model, we utilize the approach in [2]. We further simplified the resulting UPPAAL model by removing components unaffected by timing faults. This abstraction enabled verification of timing faults in the AT model. We considered the faults when components execute too early or too late. To evaluate our approach, we considered on-chip memory mapped busses in both LT and AT coding styles. In the evaluation, the time for verification in the presence of timing faults was small. However, there was a substantial gap between the verification time of LT and AT examples. For example, the average verification time for the faults where the Initiator executed too late in the LT model was 7.5 ms, whereas in the AT model was 17 s.

3   Future Work

One future work in this area is to automate the analysis of timing faults completely. Currently, our analysis of timing faults is rule-based and identifies the changes that need to be done to the original UPPAAL model. We are currently working on automating these rules to develop a fully automated approach that takes the description of the timing faults from users and automates the analysis.

Acknowledgments. This work is supported by NSF CNS-0914913, NSF CCF-1116546, NSF CNS 1329807 and NSF CNS 1318678.

References

1. Transaction-Level Modeling (TLM) 2.0 Reference Manual,
   http://www.systemc.org/downloads/standards/
2. Herber, P., Pockrandt, M., Glesner, S.: Transforming systemc transaction level models into uppaal timed automata. In: Singh, S., Jobstmann, B., Kishinevsky, M., Brandt, J. (eds.) MEMOCODE, pp. 161–170. IEEE (2011)
3. Ebnenasir, A., Hajisheykhi, R., Kulkarni, S.S.: Facilitating the design of fault tolerance in transaction level systemc programs. Theor. Comput. Sci. 496, 50–68 (2013)
4. Hajisheykhi, R., Ebnenasir, A., Kulkarni, S.: Analysis of permanent, transient, and message faults in transaction level systemc programs, Tech. Rep. MSU-CSE-13-6, Department of Computer Science, Michigan State University, East Lansing, Michigan (July 2013)

Low-Communication Self-stabilizing Leader Election in Large Networks

Thamer Alsulaiman[1], Andrew Berns[2], and Sukumar Ghosh[1]

[1] Department of Computer Science, The University of Iowa
{thamer-alsulaiman,sukumar-ghosh}@uiowa.edu
[2] Department of Computer Science, The University of Wisconsin – La Crosse
aberns@uwlax.edu

Abstract. This paper makes two contributions: (1) On a completely connected network of n anonymous processes, it presents a synchronous randomized algorithm to solve the *weak leader election* problem in expected $O(1)$ time using $O(\sqrt{n}\log n)$ messages with high probability, (2) It presents a self-stabilizing algorithm for the *strong leader election* problem on a completely connected network of processes with unique ids – it stabilizes in expected $O(1)$ number of rounds (or in $O(\log n)$ rounds with high probability) using $O(n)$ messages. In doing so, the algorithm also solves the stabilizing unison problem.

1 Introduction

Given a network of processes, the goal of leader election is to elect a unique process as the leader, and notify every non-leader process about the identity of the leader. This version of the problem is called the *strong* or *explicit* leader election. There is a weaker version of this problem, known as the *weak* or *implicit* leader election that waives the requirement of notification. On a completely connected network of n processes communicating via message passing, Kutten et al. [2] presented a synchronous randomized algorithm that elects a leader in $O(1)$ rounds with a message complexity of $O(\sqrt{n}\log^{\frac{3}{2}} n)$ with high probability. In this paper, we present a variation of [2] that elects a leader in expected $O(1)$ rounds using $O(\sqrt{n}\log n)$ messages with high probability. Subsequently, we present a self-stabilizing algorithm for the strong leader election problem – it stabilizes in expected $O(1)$ number of rounds (or in $O(\log n)$ rounds with high probability) using $O(n)$ messages, which is optimal.

2 Weak Leader Election

We use the synchronous message-passing model $\mathcal{CONGEST}$ on a completely-connected topology. We assume all nodes know an upper bound on n, the number of processes in the system. Algorithm 1 sketches our weak leader election algorithm.

T. Higashino et al. (Eds.): SSS 2013, LNCS 8255, pp. 348–350, 2013.
© Springer International Publishing Switzerland 2013

Algorithm 1. Weak leader election

Variables: $leader(i)$ (initially $\perp$), $voted(i)$ (initially $false$)

Round 1a

Each node becomes an *observer* with probability $\frac{2\log n}{n}$.

Round 1b

Each observer becomes a *candidate* with probability $\frac{1}{\log n}$. Each candidate randomly chooses an *id* from $\{0, 1, \ldots, n^2\}$. Call it *rid*.

Round 2

1. Each candidate sends an election message of (*rid, election*) to a randomly chosen set of $2\sqrt{n}\log n$ neighbors. Call them *voters*. Upon receipt, each voter sets $voted(i)$ to *true*.

2. Each observer sends an *observe* message to a randomly chosen set of $\sqrt{n}$ processes. Call them *agents*.

Round 3

1. Each agent i sends to its observer the value of $voted(i)$.

2. If $leader(i) = \perp$, voter i sends an acknowledgment to the candidate with the largest value of *rid*.

Round 4

1. If a candidate receives $2\sqrt{n}\log n$ acknowledgments, it becomes a leader.

2. If an observer node u does not receive at least one message from an agent i with $voted(i) = true$, then u repeats Algorithm 1 beginning at Round 1b.

In Algorithm 1, a process becomes a *candidate* for election in two steps: first it becomes an *observer* and subsequently zero or more of the observers are chosen as candidates. At least one node becomes an observer with high probability. The observers check if a candidate was elected, and if no candidate is detected, eventually one or more of them choose themselves as candidates for election in a future round.

Theorem 1. *Algorithm 1 solves the implicit leader election problem with high probability. The expected running time of Algorithm 1 is $O(1)$ rounds, while the message complexity is $O(\sqrt{n}\log n)$ in expectation.*

The proof of this theorem can be sketched by noting that, given there is at least one candidate, with high probability, each observer detects its existence, and no observer from Round 1b becomes a leader thereafter. The expected number of candidates after Round 1b is constant. Furthermore, with high probability at least one node has become a candidate in $O(\log^3 n)$ rounds, and with high probability, only one candidate receives all acknowledgements.

3   Self-stabilizing Leader Election

We use a modified version of the weak leader election algorithm to elect a unique *monitor*. The monitor collects the system's state and, if illegal, declares itself as the new leader. These steps will be indefinitely repeated, as in Katz and Perry's paper [1], although a different monitor may be picked in each iteration. Algorithm 2 contains our full program. We assume in this algorithm that all processes have a unique identifier. Note that, since strong leader election has a lower bound of $\Omega(n)$, we use a simpler version of the monitor election algorithm.

Algorithm 2. Self-Stabilizing Leader Election

Execute the following actions continuously based upon variable $round(i)$. Increment $round(i)$ after each round.

Round 0

With probability $\frac{1}{n}$, each process i sends an election message containing $(id_i, election, round(i))$ to every other process. If there is a recipient j such that $round(j) \neq 0$, then upon receipt of the election message, it resets its round number to 0, and clears all incoming channels.

Round 1

Every recipient of an election message returns an *ack* to the election message sender with the largest identifier.

Round 2

The process that receives $(n-1)$ *ack* messages takes up the role of election monitor, and sends out a *query* to every other process, asking them to send the identifier of their leader.

Round 3

A process receiving one or more *query* messages replies with its leader identifier to the query message sender with the largest identifier.

Round 4

A process that receives $(n-1)$ query response messages checks the legality of the configuration. If the configuration is legal then it takes no action. If the configuration is illegal, it sets itself as the new leader and notifies every other process. A process resets its leader only when it receives exactly one such notification.

Theorem 2. *Algorithm 2 is a self-stabilizing leader election algorithm. A legal configuration is reached in expected $O(1)$ rounds, and $O(\log n)$ rounds with high probability. The algorithm exchanges $O(n)$ messages if channels are initially clear, or $O(n^2)$ messages if the channels initially contain arbitrary messages, before reaching a legal configuration.*

The proof of this theorem begins by noting that an election message is sent out in an expected constant number of rounds, at which point the phase clocks are synchronized. The remainder of the proof parallels that of Theorem 1.

References

1. Katz, S., Perry, K.J.: Self-stabilizing extensions for message-passing systems. Distrib. Comput. 7(1), 17–26 (1993), http://dx.doi.org/10.1007/BF02278852
2. Kutten, S., Pandurangan, G., Peleg, D., Robinson, P., Trehan, A.: Sublinear bounds for randomized leader election. In: Frey, D., Raynal, M., Sarkar, S., Shyamasundar, R.K., Sinha, P. (eds.) ICDCN 2013. LNCS, vol. 7730, pp. 348–362. Springer, Heidelberg (2013)

Self-stabilizing Byzantine Resilient Topology Discovery and Message Delivery*

Shlomi Dolev[1,**], Omri Liba[1], and Elad M. Schiller[2,***]

[1] Ben-Gurion University of the Negev, Israel
{dolev,liba}@cs.bgu.ac.il
[2] Chalmers University of Technology, Sweden
elad@chalmers.se

Traditional Byzantine resilient algorithms use $2f + 1$ vertex-disjoint paths to ensure message delivery in the presence of up to f Byzantine nodes. The question of how these paths are identified is related to the fundamental problem of topology discovery. Distributed algorithms for topology discovery cope with a never ending task: dealing with frequent changes in the network topology and unpredictable transient faults. Therefore, algorithms for topology discovery should be self-stabilizing to ensure convergence of the topology information following any such unpredictable sequence of events. We present the first such algorithm that can cope with Byzantine nodes. Starting in an arbitrary global state, and in the presence of f Byzantine nodes, each node is eventually aware of all the other non-Byzantine nodes and their connecting communication links. Using the topology information, nodes can, for example, route messages across the network and deliver messages from one end user to another. We propose the first deterministic, cryptographic-assumptions-free, self-stabilizing, Byzantine-resilient algorithms for network topology discovery and end-to-end message delivery. We also consider the task of r-neighborhood discovery for the case in which r and the degree of nodes are bounded by constants. The use of r-neighborhood discovery facilitates polynomial time, communication and space solutions for the above tasks. The obtained algorithms can be used to authenticate parties, in particular during the establishment of private secrets, thus forming public key schemes that are resistant to man-in-the-middle attacks of the compromised Byzantine nodes. A polynomial and efficient end-to-end algorithm that is based on the established private secrets can be employed in between periodical secret re-establishments.

---

* This is a high level overview of a recent work that appears as an extended abstract [1].
** Partially supported by Deutsche Telekom, Rita Altura Trust Chair in Computer Sciences, Lynne and William Frankel Center for Computer Sciences, Israel Science Foundation (grant number 428/11), Cabarnit Cyber Security MAGNET Consortium, Grant from the Institute for Future Defense Technologies Research named for the Medvedi of the Technion, and Israeli Internet Association.
*** Partially supported by the EC, through project FP7-STREP-288195, KARYON (Kernel-based ARchitecture for bsafetY-critical cONtrol), the European Commission Seventh Framework Programme (FP7/2007-2013) under grant agreement 257007 and through the FP7-SEC-285477-CRISALIS project.

T. Higashino et al. (Eds.): SSS 2013, LNCS 8255, pp. 351–353, 2013.

The Task. The task of *r-neighborhood network discovery* allows each node to know the set of nodes that are at most r hops away from it in the communication network. Moreover, the task provides information about the communication links attached to these nodes. The task *topology discovery* considers knowledge regarding the node's entire connected component. The r-neighborhood network discovery and network topology discovery tasks are identical when r is the communication graph radius. This work presents the first deterministic self-stabilizing algorithms for r-neighborhood discovery in the presence of Byzantine nodes. We assume that every r-neighborhood cannot be partitioned by the Byzantine nodes. In particular, we assume the existence of at least $2f + 1$ vertex-disjoint paths in the r-neighborhood, between any two non-Byzantine nodes, where at most f Byzantine nodes are present in the r-neighborhood, rather than in the entire network. When r is defined to be the communication graph radius, our assumptions are equivalent to the standard assumption for Byzantine agreement in general (rather than only complete) communication graphs. E.g., the standard assumption is that $2f + 1$ vertex disjoint paths exist and *are known* while we present distributed algorithms to find them.

Topology Discovery. The algorithm learns about the neighborhoods that the nodes report. Each report message contains an ordered list of nodes it passed so far, starting in a source node. These lists are used for verifying that the reports are sent over $f + 1$ vertex-disjoint paths.

Each node p_i periodically sends a message to each neighbor. The message sent contains the local topology, the source and an empty path. When a report message, m, arrives to p_i, it inserts m to the queue $informedTopology_i$, and tests the queue consistency until there is enough independent evidence to support the report. The consistency test of p_i iterates over each node p_k such that, p_k appears in at least one of the messages stored in $informedTopology_i$. For each such node p_k, node p_i checks whether there are at least $f + 1$ messages from the same source node that have mutually vertex-disjoint paths and report on the same neighborhood. The neighborhood of each such p_k, that has at least $f + 1$ vertex-disjoint paths with identical neighborhood, is stored in the array $Result_i[k]$ and the total number of paths that relayed this neighborhood is kept in $Count[k]$. We note that there may still be nodes $p_{fake} \in P \setminus N$, for which there is an entry $Result[fake]$. For example, $informedTopology$ may contain f messages, all originated from different Byzantine nodes, and a message m' that appears in the initial configuration and supports the (false) neighborhood the Byzantine messages refer to. These $f + 1$ messages can contain mutually vertex-disjoint paths, and thus during the consistency test, a result will be found for $Result[fake]$. We show that during the next computations, the message m' will be identified and ignored. The $Result$ array should include two reports for each (undirected) edge; the two nodes that are attached to the edge, each send a report. Hence, $Result$ includes a set of directed (report) edges. The term *contradicting edge* is needed when examining the $Result$ set consistency. We say that the edge (p_i, p_j) is *contradicting with the set evidence* $\subseteq$ $edges(N_j)$, if $(p_i, p_j) \notin evidence$, where $p_i, p_j \in P$. Following the consistency test, p_i examines the $Result$ array for contradictions. Node p_i checks the path of each message $m \in informedTopology_i$ with source p_r, neighborhood $neighborhood_r$ and $Path_r$. If every edge (p_s, p_j) on the path appears in $Result[s]$ and $Result[j]$, then we move to the next message. Otherwise, we found a fake supporter, and therefore we reduce $Count[r]$ by one. If the resulting $Count[r]$ is smaller than $f+1$, we nullify the r'th entry of the $Result$ array. Once all messages are processed, the $Result$ array consisting of the (confirmed) local topologies is the output. At the end, p_i forwards the arriving message, m, to each neighbor that does not appear in the path of m. The message sent by p_i includes the node from which m arrived as part of the visited path contained within m.

End-to-End Delivery. We present a self-stabilizing Byzantine resilient algorithm for the transport layer protocol that is based on the discovered topology. We consider a set, $CorrectPaths$, that includes $f + 1$ correct vertex-disjoint paths. For different cases, we guarantee correct message exchange by sending messages over a polynomial number of vertex-disjoint paths:

(1) Constant r and Δ.   It is feasible to consider all paths in r-neighborhoods, when the neighborhood radius, r, and the node degree Δ are constants.

(2) Constant f.   For each possible choice of f system nodes, $\{p_f\}_f$, the sender and the reciter compute a new graph $G(\{p_f\}_f)$ that is the result of removing $\{p_f\}_f$, from G_{out}, which is the graph defined by the discovered topology, $ConfirmedTopology$. Let $\mathcal{P}(\{p_f\}_f)$ be a set of $f + 1$ vertex-disjoint paths in $G(\{p_f\}_f)$ and $Paths = \bigcup_{\{p_f\}_f} \mathcal{P}(\{p_f\}_f)$. The sender and the receiver can exchange messages over $Paths$, because $|Paths|$ is polynomial. Moreover, At least one choice of $\{p_f\}_f$, has a corresponding set $\mathcal{P}(\{p_f\}_f) \supseteq CorrectPaths$.

(3) The case of no Byzantine neighbors   Assume that any Byzantine node has no Byzantine neighbor in the communication graph. Consider the (extended) graph, G_{ext}, that includes all the edges in $confirmedTopology$ and $suspicious$ $edges$. Given three nodes, $p_i, p_j, p_k \in P$, we say that node p_i considers the undirected edge (p_k, p_j) suspicious, if the edge appears as a directed edge in $ConfirmedTopology_i$ for only one direction, e.g., (p_j, p_k). The extended graph, G_{ext}, may contain fake edges that do not exist in the graph, but Byzantine nodes reports on their existence. Nevertheless, G_{ext} includes all the correct paths of G.

Conclusions. The obtained end-to-end capabilities can be used for communicating the public keys of parties and establish private keys, in spite of f corrupted nodes that may try to conduct man-in-the-middle attacks, which classical Public key infrastructure (PKI) does not cope with. Once private keys are established encrypted messages can be forwarded over any specific $f + 1$ node independent paths (one of which must be Byzantine free). The Byzantine free path will forward the encrypted message to the receiver while all corrupted messages will be discarded. Since our system should be self-stabilizing, the common private secret should be re-established periodically.

Reference

1. Dolev, S., Liba, O., Schiller, E.M.: Self-stabilizing byzantine resilient topology discovery and message delivery. In: Gramoli, V., Guerraoui, R. (eds.) NETYS 2013. LNCS, vol. 7853, pp. 42–53. Springer, Heidelberg (2013); CoRR abs/1208.5620, http://arxiv.org/abs/1208.5620

Self-stabilizing TDMA Algorithms for Wireless Ad-Hoc Networks without External Reference*

Thomas Petig, Elad M. Schiller, and Philippas Tsigas

Computer Science and Engineering, Chalmers University of Technology, Sweden
{petig,elad,tsigas}@chalmers.se

Cooperative systems will ultimately carry out risk-related tasks and liberate mankind from mundane labor. The implementation of these systems implies the use of wireless ad hoc networks and their critical component - a medium access control (MAC) layer that satisfies severe timing requirements. Infrastructure-based wireless networks successfully provide high bandwidth utilization and bounded communication delay. They divide the radio into *timeslots* of uniform size, ξ, that are then combined into *frames* of uniform size, τ. Base-stations, or wireless network coordinators can schedule the frame in a way that enables each node to transmit during its own timeslot, and arbitrate between nearby nodes that wish to communicate concurrently. We strive to provide the needed MAC protocol properties, using limited radio and clock settings, i.e., no external reference for collision detection, time or position. For these settings, we demonstrate that there is no solution for the studied problem when $\tau < \max((2-\epsilon)\delta, \chi_2)$, where $\epsilon > 0$, δ is a bound on the number of neighbors with whom each node can directly communicate with, and χ_2 is the chromatic number for distance-2 vertex coloring of the communication graph. The main result is the existence of probabilistic collision-free self-stabilizing TDMA algorithms that have constant communication delay of $\tau > \max(4\delta, X_2) + 1$, where $X_2 \geq \chi_2$ is a number that depends on the coloring algorithm in use. The convergence period is within $\mathcal{O}(\text{diam} \cdot \tau^2 + \tau^3 \delta)$ steps starting from an arbitrary configuration, where diam is the network diameter. We note that in case the system happens to have access to external time references, the convergence time is within $\mathcal{O}(\tau^3)$, and $\mathcal{O}(\tau^3 \delta)$ steps when $\tau > 2\Delta$, and respectively, $\tau > 4\delta$, where $P := \{p_i\}_i$ is the set of communicating nodes, Δ_i is a set of nodes with whom node p_i can communicate using at most one intermediate node for relaying messages and $\Delta \geq |\Delta_i|$. In the context of self-stabilizing systems that have no external reference, we are the first to study this problem (to the best of our knowledge).

The packet *exposure period* refers to the time during which packets may collide. When there is no external reference, the TDMA algorithm has to align its timeslots while allocating them. Existing MAC algorithms circumvent this challenge by assuming that $\tau/(\Delta + 1) \geq 2$. This guarantees zero exposure period with respect to at least one timeslot, s, and *all* transmissions from transmitters that are at most two hops away. However, the $\tau/(\Delta + 1) \geq 2$ assumption implies bandwidth utilization that is up to $\mathcal{O}(\delta)$ times lower than the proposed algorithm. As a basic

---

* The work of this author was partially supported by the EC, through project FP7-STREP-288195, KARYON (Kernel-based ARchitecture for safetY-critical cONtrol). This is a high level overview of a recent work that appears as a technical report in [1].

T. Higashino et al. (Eds.): SSS 2013, LNCS 8255, pp. 354–356, 2013.

result, we show that $\tau/\delta \geq 2$, and as a complement to this lower bound, we focus on considering the case of $\tau/\delta \geq 4$. We present a probabilistic collision-free self-stabilizing TDMA algorithm with communication delay of $\tau\xi$. We show that it is sufficient to guarantee zero exposure period with respect to a single timeslot, s, and a *single* receiver, rather than *all* neighbors. This narrow opportunity window allows control packet exchange, and timeslot alignment. After convergence, there are no collisions of any kind, and each frame includes at most one control packet.

The Task.   We consider the task $\mathcal{T}_{\text{TDMA}}$, that requires all nodes, p_i, to have data packet timeslots that are unique within Δ_i. We note that $\mathcal{T}_{\text{TDMA}}$'s requirements obviously hold when the ratio between the Δ and the frame size, τ, is less than one. Therefore, the studied task also deals with timeslot exhaustion by delivering busy channel indications, $\perp$, to the nodes for which there were no timeslot left.

The Algorithm.   We propose Algorithm 1 as a self-stabilizing algorithm for the $\mathcal{T}_{\text{TDMA}}$ task. The nodes transmit data packets, as well as control packets. Active nodes send data packets during their data packet timeslots. The passive nodes listen to the active ones and do not send data packets. Both active and passive nodes use control packets, which include frame information that includes recently received packets from direct neighbors. Each node aggregates the frame information it receives. It uses this information for avoiding collisions, acknowledging packet transmission and resolving hidden node problems. Passive nodes, p_i, can become active by uniformly, at random, selecting timeslots, $s_i \in [0, \tau - 1]$ that active nodes do not use, sending a control packet in s_i and waiting for confirmation. Once p_i succeeds, it becomes an active node that uses timeslot s_i for transmitting data packets. Node p_i can become passive whenever it learns about conflicts with nearby nodes, e.g., due to a transmission failure.

The hidden node problem refers to cases in which node p_i has two neighbors that use intersecting timeslots. The algorithm uses random back off techniques for resolving this problem in a way that assures at least one successful transmission from all active and passive nodes within $\mathcal{O}(\tau)$, and respectively, $\mathcal{O}(1)$ frames in expectation. The passive nodes count a random number of unused timeslots before transmitting a control packet. We base frame numbers on the clock value, and let active nodes count down only during TDMA frames whose numbers are equal to s_i, where s_i is p_i's data packet timeslot. These back off processes connect all direct neighbors and facilitate clock synchronization, timeslot alignment and timeslot assignment. Once all nodes are active, there are no collisions and each node transmits one control packet once every τ frames.

The code of Algorithm 1 considers on three events. The first event is *timeslot()* (line 1). Actives nodes transmit their data packets upon their timeslot, s_i (line 3). Both, passive and active nodes, transmit control packets when the back off counter, that counts down unused timeslots, $wait_i$, reaches zero (line 6). Active nodes count unused timeslots that belong to frames with $frame() = s_i$ (line 4). The second event is $TransmissionError()$ (line11). Transmission errors indicate failure of the previous attempt to transmit. Active and passive nodes become, and

---

Algorithm 1. Self-stabilizing TDMA Timeslot Allocation, node p_i code

```
1  upon timeslot() do
2    if s() = sᵢ ∧ statusᵢ = active then                    /* send data packet */
3    |  transmit(⟨statusᵢ, Local(FIᵢ), MAC_fetch()⟩); lastTxᵢ ← activeTDMA;
4    else if ¬(statusᵢ = active ∧ frame() ≠ sᵢ) then         /* control packet or back-off */
5    |  if IsUnused(s()) ∧ waitᵢ ≤ 0 then                    /* send control packet */
6    |  |  transmit(⟨statusᵢ, Local(FIᵢ), 0⟩); ⟨waitᵢ, waitAddᵢ⟩ ← BackOff();
7    |  |  if statusᵢ = active then lastTxᵢ ← activeCSMA;
8    |  |  else ⟨sᵢ, statusᵢ, lastTxᵢ⟩ ← ⟨s(), active, passiveCSMA⟩;
9    |  else if waitᵢ > 0 ∧ IsUnused((s() − 1) mod τ) then waitᵢ ← max{0, waitᵢ − 1};
10   |  FIᵢ ← {⟨•, rxTime⟩ ∈ FIᵢ : GetClock() < (timeOut + rxTime) mod c};

11  upon TransmissionError() do
12   |  if lastTxᵢ ≠ activeCSMA then ⟨⟨waitᵢ, waitAddᵢ⟩, statusᵢ⟩ ← ⟨BackOff(), passive⟩;

13  upon ⟨j, tⱼ, tᵢ, ⟨statusⱼ, FIⱼ, m′⟩⟩ ← receive() do
14   |  if ConflictWithNeighbors(FIⱼ) ∧ statusᵢ = active then  /* detect conflicts */
     |  |  ⟨⟨waitᵢ, waitAddᵢ⟩, status⟩ ← ⟨BackOff(), passive⟩;
15   |  if statusⱼ = active then                              /* acknowledge active node */
16   |  |  if m′ ≠ ⊥ then FIᵢ ← {⟨idᵢ, •⟩ ∈ FIᵢ : idᵢ ≠ j} ∪ {⟨j, message, local, tᵢ⟩};
17   |  else if tⱼ = tᵢ ∧ Slot(tⱼ) ∉ Used(FIᵢ) then           /* acknowledge passive node */
18   |  |  FIᵢ ← {⟨idᵢ, •⟩ ∈ FIᵢ : idᵢ ≠ j} ∪ {⟨j, welcome, local, tᵢ⟩};
19   |  if tᵢ < tⱼ then                                       /* converge-to-the-max */
20   |  |  AdvanceClock(tⱼ − tᵢ);
     |  |  FIᵢ ← {⟨•, (rxTime + tⱼ − tᵢ) mod c⟩ : ⟨•, rxTime⟩ ∈ FIᵢ};
21   |  |  if sᵢ ∈ Used(FIᵢ) then ⟨⟨waitᵢ, waitAddᵢ⟩, statusᵢ⟩ ← ⟨BackOff(), passive⟩;
22   |  AddToFI(FIⱼ, tᵢ − tⱼ);                                /* Aggregate information on used timeslots */
23   |  if m′ ≠ ⊥ then MAC_deliver(m′);
```

---

respectively, stay **passive** when they learn whose data packets collide (line 12). The third event is **receive()** (line 13), i.e., the reception of a packet. Node, p_i, becomes **passive** when it identifies a conflict between its data packet timeslot, s_i, and an entry in the received frame information FI_j. (line 14). When the sender is **active**, the receiver records the related frame information using $AddToFI()$ (line 22). A node p_i prepares an acknowledgment for active neighbors in line 16, and for passive neighbors in line 18.

Conclusions. The analysis in [1] considers the timeslot allocation aspects of the studied problem, together with transmission timing aspects. Interestingly, we show that the existence of the problem's solution depends on convergence criteria that include the ratio, τ/δ, between the frame size and the node degree. We establish that $\tau/\delta \geq 2$ as a general convergence criterion, and prove the existence of collision-free TDMA algorithms for which $\tau/\delta \leq 4$. Unfortunately, our result implies that, for our systems settings, there is no distributed mechanism for asserting the convergence criteria within a constant time. For distributed systems that do *not* require constant communication delay, we propose to explore such criteria assertion mechanisms as future work.

Reference

[1] Petig, T., Schiller, E.M., Tsigas, P.: Self-stabilizing TDMA Algorithms for Wireless Ad-hoc Networks withoutExternal Reference. CoRR abs/1308.6475 (2013), http://arxiv.org/abs/1308.6475

Zone-Based Synthesis of Strict 2-Phase Fault Recovery

Fathiyeh Faghih and Borzoo Bonakdarpour

School of Computer Science, University of Waterloo, Canada

Abstract. In this paper, we focus on efficient synthesis of fault-tolerant timed models from their fault-intolerant version. We propose an algorithm that takes a timed automaton, a set of fault actions, and a set of safety and bounded-time response properties as input, and utilizes a space-efficient symbolic representation of the timed automaton (called the *zone graph*) to synthesize a fault-tolerant timed automaton as output. The output automaton satisfies strict phased recovery, where it is guaranteed that the output model behaves similarly to the input model in the absence of faults and in the presence of faults, fault recovery is achieved in two phases, each satisfying certain safety and timing constraints.

1 Introduction

Dependability and time-predictability are two vital properties of most embedded (especially, safety/mission-critical) systems. Consequently, providing *fault-tolerance* and meeting *timing constraints* are two inevitable aspects of dependable real-time embedded systems. However, these two features have conflicting natures; i.e., fault-tolerance deals with unanticipated faults, while meeting timing constraints requires time predictability. This conflict inevitably makes design and analysis of fault-tolerant real-time systems a tedious and error-prone task.

Let Q and P be two predicates that should be reached in phase 1 and 2 of recovery within different time bounds, respectively. In [2], the authors have shown that if Q is not required to be closed in the execution of recovery transitions, then synthesizing a timed automaton [1] with 2-phase recovery is NP-complete in the size of the detailed region graph [1] of the input automaton. On the contrary, if the closure of Q is required and, moreover, $P \subseteq Q$, then the synthesis problem can be solved in polynomial time. The polynomial-time algorithm presented in [2] to solve the latter problem is only an evidence for proving the complexity of the problem and is not an efficient practical solution with potential for implementation. This is simply because the size of a detailed region graph grows incredibly huge even for small models.

With this motivation, in this paper, we propose a time- and space-efficient algorithm for synthesizing timed automata that provide 2-phase recovery, where Q is required to be closed and $P \subseteq Q$, while no new behaviors are added in the absence of faults.

T. Higashino et al. (Eds.): SSS 2013, LNCS 8255, pp. 357–359, 2013.

2 Problem Statement

Given are a fault-intolerant timed automaton TAD with semantic model $\mathcal{SM} = (S, s_0, T)$ and legitimates states LS, a set F of faults, and specification $SPEC$, such that TAD satisfies $SPEC$ by starting from any legitimate state LS (denoted $TAD \models_{LS} SPEC$). Our goal is to develop an algorithm for synthesizing an automaton TAD' with legitimate states LS' from TAD, such that TAD' is F-tolerant to $SPEC$ from LS' [2]. By F-tolerant, we mean that [2] when the state of a system is perturbed by faults, the system is required to either directly return to its legitimate states LS within $\theta \in \mathbb{Z}_{\geq 0}$ time units, or, if direct recovery is not feasible, then it should first reach an *intermediate* recovery predicate Q within $\theta \in \mathbb{Z}_{\geq 0}$ (i.e., phase 1), from where the system reaches LS within $\delta \in \mathbb{Z}_{\geq 0}$ time units (i.e., phase 2). We require that the algorithm for adding fault tolerance does not introduce new behaviors to TAD in the absence of faults. These constraints are formally stated below, where $T \mid LS$ denotes the set of transitions T that start and end in LS.

Problem statement. Given a fault-intolerant timed automaton TAD with semantic model $\mathcal{SM} = (S, s_0, T)$, a set F of faults, intermediate predicate Q, where $LS \subseteq Q$, and specification $SPEC$, such that $TAD \models_{LS} SPEC$, our goal is to propose an algorithm for synthesizing an automaton TAD' with $\mathcal{SM}' = (S', s_0', T')$, and legitimate states LS' from TAD, such that:

1. $LS' \subseteq LS$,
2. Q is closed in T',
3. $(T' \mid LS') \subseteq (T \mid LS')$, and
4. TAD' is F-tolerant to $SPEC$ from LS'.

---

3 The Synthesis Algorithm

Our zone-based algorithm consists of the following steps:

1. *(Automaton enhancement)* The input model is enhanced, so that the corresponding zone graph is more efficient and is augmented with delay transitions that can be utilized for adding 2-phase recovery.
2. *(Zone graph generation)* Next, the zone graph (a space-efficient representation of a timed automata) of the enhanced input automaton is generated. We utilize an existing algorithm from the literature of verification for this step.
3. *(Adding recovery behavior)* To enable 2-phase recovery, we add possible transitions among the zones of the zone graph. In this step, new zones may be added to the zone graph.
4. *(Backward zone generation)* For the newly added zones in the last step, we identify the backward reachable zones to ensure that the new zones do not introduce terminating computations.

5. *(Cycle removal)* Since adding recovery transitions may create cycles, the algorithm removes the possible cycles to ensure correct recovery.
6. *(Zone graph repair)* The zone graph is modified, so that it satisfies the safety properties in the presence of faults, and also does not introduce any deadlock states.

4   Implementation

We have implemented our algorithm to evaluate the efficiency of our proposed synthesis method. We model a timed automaton with faults and automatically add switches to the the input model (Step 1). Then we generated the zone graph of the enhanced automaton with zones being marked with LS, $Q - LS$, and $\neg Q$. The rest of the algorithm (Steps 2 – 6) is then performed on the generated zone graph. The result is a synthesized zone graph, which can be used to generate the fault-tolerant timed automaton. We tested our algorithm on two case studies and compared the synthesis time to the zone graph generation time for the intolerant input automaton with fault (before enhancement). This comparison enables us to analyze synthesis versus corresponding verification time.

In our first case study, by increasing the model size, the zone graph generation time increases considerably, which turns out to be the bottleneck of our algorithm. However, this step outperforms the zone graph generation time for the original automaton with faults. This is because the fault leads to bad states, and a significant number of reachable zones are cut by our pruning switches added in the first step of the algorithm. In the second case study, the bottleneck is mostly on the step for adding transitions among zones. The reason is due to the fact that in this model, the fault does not lead the computation to reach bad states and, hence, our pruning strategy does not help in this regard.

5   Conclusion

In this paper, we focused on synthesizing fault-tolerant timed models from their fault-intolerant version. The type of fault-tolerance under investigation is *strict 2-phase recovery*, where upon occurrence of faults, the system is expected to recover in two phases, each satisfying certain constraints. Our contribution is a synthesis algorithm that adds 2-phase strict fault recovery to a given timed model, while not adding new behaviors in the absence of faults. The algorithm works on a space-efficient representation of timed models, know as the *zone graph*. To our knowledge, this is the first instance of such an algorithm.

References

1. Alur, R., Dill, D.: A theory of timed automata. Theoretical Computer Science 126(2), 183–235 (1994)
2. Bonakdarpour, B., Kulkarni, S.S.: Synthesizing bounded-time 2-phase recovery. Springer Journal of Formal Aspects of Computing (FAOC) (to appear)

Analyzing Convergence and Reachability of Asynchronous Iterations

Yoshisato Sakai

Corporate Software Engineering Center, Toshiba Corporation, Kawasaki, Japan
yoshisato.sakai@toshiba.co.jp

Abstract. Asynchronous iterations are computation schemes suitable for distributed systems with unpredictable delays and occasional loss of data in their communication links. This paper provides novel methods based on fixpoint computations to analyze convergence and reachability of them. They reduce memory usage to avoid the problem of state explosion by exploiting some assumptions on communication delays to eliminate message buffers and to decompose state space into elements.

Let n be the number of nodes of a distributed system, S_i be the set of all states of the i-th node, and $S = S_1 \times \cdots \times S_n$ which is assumed to be a finite set. The i-th element of a vector $u \in S$ is denoted by $u_i \in S_i$. We use three operators defined as $\text{proj}_i Z = \{x_i \mid (x_1, \ldots, x_n) \in Z\}$, $\text{box } Z = (\text{proj}_1 Z) \times \cdots \times (\text{proj}_n Z)$, and $\text{img}_f Z = \{f(r) \mid r \in Z\}$ for any $Z \subseteq S$ and $f : S \to S$. We denote the greatest and least fixpoints of $\tau : 2^S \to 2^S$ by $\nu Z. \tau(Z)$ and $\mu Z. \tau(Z)$, respectively.

An *asynchronous iteration* [3] with respect to $f : S \to S$ is a sequence $\{x(k)\}_k$ such that

$$
x_i(k) = \begin{cases} x_i(k-1) & (i \notin \alpha(k)) \\ f_i(x_1(\beta_1(k-1)), \ldots, x_n(\beta_n(k-1))) & (i \in \alpha(k)) \end{cases} \tag{1}
$$

where $x(0) \in S$ is a given initial value, $\{\alpha(k) \subseteq \{1, \ldots, n\}\}_k$ represents the set of nodes which make (non-deterministic) state transitions at time k, and $\{\beta(k) \in \{0, 1, \ldots\}^n\}_k$ represents effects of unpredictable delays in communication links. We denote this $\{x(k)\}_k$ by $\text{async}(f, \alpha, \beta, x(0))$. Similarly to [3], we assume that, for any $i \in \{1, \ldots, n\}$, [A1] $0 \leq \beta_i(k) \leq k$ for any $k \in \{0, 1, \ldots\}$, [A2] $\{k \mid i \in \alpha(k)\}$ is an infinite set, and [A3] $\{k \mid \beta_i(k) = l\}$ is a finite (possibly empty) set for any $l \in \{0, 1, \ldots\}$.

Our proposal is to serve the following theorems for analysis, although their proofs are omitted for lack of space.

Theorem 1 (convergence). *For any* $\text{async}(f, \alpha, \beta, x(0)) = \{x(k)\}_k$, *there exists* p *such that* $\{x(k) \mid k \geq p\} \subseteq \nu Z. \text{box img}_f Z$.

Theorem 2 (reachability). *For any* $\text{async}(f, \alpha, \beta, x(0)) = \{x(k)\}_k$, *it holds that* $\{x(k) \mid k \geq 0\} \subseteq \mu Z. \text{box}(\{x(0)\} \cup \text{img}_f Z)$. *Reversely, for any* $x(0) \in S$ *and* $y \in \mu Z. \text{box}(\{x(0)\} \cup \text{img}_f Z)$, *there exist* α, β, *and* p *such that* $y = x(p)$ *where* $\{x(k)\}_k = \text{async}(f, \alpha, \beta, x(0))$.

T. Higashino et al. (Eds.): SSS 2013, LNCS 8255, pp. 360–362, 2013.

Because the operator 'box' is a monotonic predicate transformer (see [2, Chap. 6] for its definition and related properties on fixpoint), we can calculate $\nu Z.\,\text{box}\,\text{img}_f\,Z$ and $\mu Z.\,\text{box}(\{x(0)\} \cup \text{img}_f\,Z)$ with

$$X(0) = S, \quad X(k+1) = \text{box}\,\text{img}_f\,X(k)\,, \tag{2}$$

$$Y(0) = \emptyset, \quad Y(k+1) = \text{box}(\{x(0)\} \cup \text{img}_f\,Y(k))\,. \tag{3}$$

They yield $\{X(k)\}_k$ and $\{Y(k)\}_k$ for which there exist p and q such that

$$X(0) \supsetneq \cdots \supsetneq X(p) = X(p+1) = \cdots = \nu Z.\,\text{box}\,\text{img}_f\,Z\,, \tag{4}$$

$$Y(0) \subsetneq \cdots \subsetneq Y(q) = Y(q+1) = \cdots = \mu Z.\,\text{box}(\{x(0)\} \cup \text{img}_f\,Z)\,. \tag{5}$$

We can rewrite (2) and (3) into computationally less expensive formulas such as

$$X_i(0) = S_i, \quad X_i(k+1) = \{f_i(x) \mid x \in X_1(k) \times \cdots \times X_n(k)\}\,, \tag{6}$$

$$Y_i(0) = \emptyset, \quad Y_i(k+1) = \{x_i(0)\} \cup \{f_i(x) \mid x \in Y_1(k) \times \cdots \times Y_n(k)\} \tag{7}$$

where $X(k) = X_1(k) \times \cdots \times X_n(k)$ and $Y(k) = Y_1(k) \times \cdots \times Y_n(k)$.

To discuss the performance of our proposal, we assume that the system under analysis has m links and, for simplicity, $s = |S_1| = \cdots = |S_n|$. Whereas $|S| = s^n$, the total size of state sets explored by the proposed methods is at most ns because $|X_i(k)|, |Y_i(k)| \le |S_i| = s$. In contrast, conventional tools for model checking require models of links which keep past messages to emulate delays. Under the assumption that these messages are senders' states themselves, each of link models needs an s-bit buffer to store subsets of S_i (as in Fig. 2 shown later). Therefore, the size of the state set of the entire system is $s^n \cdot 2^{ms}$, which is the product of those of all nodes and links. This is extremely larger than the case of our proposal. Moreover, fairness constraints due to [A2] and [A3] impose extra costs on model checking, while our proposal does not suffer from such costs.

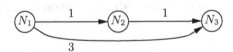

Fig. 1. Example system for convergence analysis

These observations seem to be supported by the following example. Figure 1 shows a distributed system with 3 nodes and 3 uni-directional communication links ($n = 3$, $m = 3$). The shortest distances from N_1 to other nodes can be computed by an asynchronous iteration w.r.t. $f_1(x) = 0$, $f_2(x) = (x_1+1) \bmod s$, and $f_3(x) = \min\{(x_1 + 3) \bmod s, (x_2 + 1) \bmod s\}$ where, e.g., $s = 2^3$.

The author tried convergence analysis for this example with two programs; let N stand for NuSMV [1] (version 2.5.4 without zChaff) invoked with the -dynamic option in addition to the input script shown in Fig. 2, and P for an experimental program which implements our proposal using binary decision diagrams to compute (6). Both of them were successful in analysis; N reported

```
MODULE   node(id, x, c, y, d)        DEFINE    w := 3;
VAR      out: unsigned word[w];      IVAR      run: boolean;
ASSIGN   next(out) := case !run: out;  id = 1: uwconst(0,w);
              id = 2: x+c;  x+c < y+d: x+c;    TRUE: y+d;   esac;
JUSTICE  run;


MODULE   link(inp)                    DEFINE  w := 3; s := 8; -- s = 1<<w
VAR      buf: unsigned word[s];
IVAR     dur: unsigned word[s]; out: unsigned word[w];
ASSIGN   next(buf) := buf & dur | (uwconst(1,s) << inp);
TRANS    bool((next(buf) >> out)[0:0]);
JUSTICE  !bool(dur[0:0]); JUSTICE !bool(dur[1:1]); JUSTICE !bool(dur[2:2]);
JUSTICE  !bool(dur[3:3]); JUSTICE !bool(dur[4:4]); JUSTICE !bool(dur[5:5]);
JUSTICE  !bool(dur[6:6]); JUSTICE !bool(dur[7:7]);


MODULE   main      DEFINE  w := 3; c0 := uwconst(0,w); c1 := uwconst(1,w);
                           c2 := uwconst(2,w); c3 := uwconst(3,w);
VAR      n1: node(1, c0, c0, c0, c0); n2: node(2, 112.out, c1, c0, c0);
         n3: node(3, 123.out, c1, 113.out, c3);
         112: link(n1.out); 113: link(n1.out); 123: link(n2.out);
CTLSPEC  AF AG (n1.out = c0 & n2.out = c1 & n3.out = c2);
```

Fig. 2. NuSMV script for checking convergence

$AF\,AG(x = (0,1,2))$ is true, and P yielded $\nu Z.\,\mathrm{box\,img}_f\, Z = \{(0,1,2)\}$. Each of them implies that, starting from any initial state, the system executing the asynchronous iteration eventually converges to the correct state and stays there forever. However, P was significantly faster than N; P consumed only 0.02 seconds while N required 89 seconds.

In the case of another example where $n = 512$, $m = 1294$, and $s = 2^{20}$, the program P based on our proposal completed convergence analysis successfully within 18 minutes. The author thinks this example is too large for NuSMV. We hope to explain more details in future opportunities.

References

1. Cimatti, A., Clarke, E., Giunchiglia, E., Giunchiglia, F., Pistore, M., Roveri, M., Sebastiani, R., Tacchella, A.: NuSMV 2: An openSource tool for symbolic model checking. In: Brinksma, E., Larsen, K.G. (eds.) CAV 2002. LNCS, vol. 2404, pp. 359–364. Springer, Heidelberg (2002)
2. Clarke Jr., E.M., Grumberg, O., Peled, D.A.: Model checking. MIT Press, Cambridge (1999)
3. Üresin, A., Dubois, M.: Parallel asynchronous algorithms for discrete data. J. ACM 37(3), 588–606 (1990)

Ring Exploration by Oblivious Robots with Vision Limited to 2 or 3

Ajoy K. Datta[1], Anissa Lamani[2], Lawrence L. Larmore[1], and Franck Petit[3]

[1] School of Computer Science, University of Nevada Las Vegas, USA
[2] MIS, Université de Picardie Jules Verne Amiens, France
[3] LIP6, INRIA, CNRS, UPMC Sorbonne Universities, France

1 Introduction

The problem of exploring a finite discrete space by autonomous mobile robots is a basic building block for many applications. Space to explore is partitioned into a finite number of locations represented by a graph, where nodes represent indivisible locations that can be sensed by the robots, and where edges represent the possibility for a robot to move from one location to the other. We address the *terminating exploration* problem which requires that starting from a configuration where no two robots occupy the same node, every node needs to be visited by at least one robot, with the additional constraint that all robots eventually stop moving.

We assume weak settings: The robots are *oblivious*, *i.e.*, no memory of any past behavior of themselves or any other robot. They all follow the same algorithm and no robot can distinguish any two other robots. There is no mean to distinguish any node or edge labeling. Furthermore, the robots have no (direct) means of communicating with each other. However, robots are endowed with visibility sensors enabling to see robots located on nodes.

Consider the terminating exploration on *ring networks*. This problem with such weak robots has been widely investigated [2–4], however assuming *unlimited visibility*, *i.e.*, each robot can sense the n nodes of the ring. Let us consider stronger settings by adding another constraint: *myopia*. A *myopic* robot has limited visibility, *i.e.*, it cannot see the nodes located beyond a certain fixed distance ϕ. If $\phi = 1$, then a robot can sense robots located on its own node and at its immediate neighboring nodes. If $\phi = 2$, then a robot can sense robots corresponding to $\phi = 1$ and the neighbors of its neighboring nodes. And so on. Studying the impact of myopia strength (*i.e.*, the size of the visibility radius) is clearly motivated by limiting the vision capacities that each agent is required to have. In [1], it is shown that, if $\phi = 1$, then no deterministic terminating exploration is possible in the semi-synchronous model. The result is valid for any $k < n$—k is the number of robots, n is the number of nodes in the ring.

In this brief announcement, we present two general algorithms for each case, $\phi = 2$ and $\phi = 3$. We first need to define the terms $\phi.group$ and $d.block$. The former refers to any maximal elementary path in which there is one robot every node at distance at most ϕ of each other. A $d.block$ is any maximal elementary

T. Higashino et al. (Eds.): SSS 2013, LNCS 8255, pp. 363–366, 2013.

Fig. 1. *Middle*   **Fig. 2.** *Terminal*   **Fig. 3.** *Intermediate*

path in which robots are at distance d. The *size* of a d.block is the number of robots in the d.block. Both algorithms assume the following result[1]:

Theorem 1. *For any $2 \leq k < n$, $n > 10$ and $\phi \in \{2, 3\}$, no deterministic exploration protocol $\mathcal{P}$ exists in the semi-synchronous model if in the initial configuration γ_0, the k robots do not form a ϕ.group, i.e., they are not located on a maximal elementary path in which there is one robot every node at distance at most ϕ of each other.*

In other words, the robots must be close enough to form a unique visibility block—ϕ.group—in γ_0. Intuitively, Theorem 1 is proven by showing that if the robots are not in a single ϕ.group in γ_0, then for any Protocol $\mathcal{P}$, there exists some executions of $\mathcal{P}$ that bring the system into configurations that are undistinguishable from γ_0.

2   Visibility $\phi = 2$

We provide a general deterministic exploration protocol for any ring of size greater than 19 ($n \geq k\phi + 1$), that uses 9 robots. It works starting from any configuration satisfying Theorem 1.

The number of robots located on a node u_i is called *multiplicity* of u_i and is denoted by M_i. A configuration is said to be *Middle* (refer to Figure 1) if there exists a sequence of consecutive nodes $u_i, u_{i+1}, \ldots, u_{i+5}, u_{i+6}$ such that: (i) $M_j = 2$ for $j \in \{i, i+1, i+5, i+6\}$, (ii) $M_{i+2} = 1$, and (iii) $M_j = 0$ for $j \in \{i+3, i+4\}$. Similarly, a configuration is said to be *Terminal* (Fig. 2) if there exists a sequence of nodes $u_i, u_{i+1}, \ldots, u_{i+4}$ such that: (i) $M_j = 2$ for $j \in \{i, i+3\}$, (ii) $M_{i+1} = 0$, (iii) $M_{i+2} = 4$, and (iv) $M_{i+4} = 1$. Finally, a configuration is *Intermediate* (Fig. 3) if there exists a sequence of nodes $u_i, u_{i+1}, \ldots, u_{i+6}$ such that: (i) $M_j = 2$ for $j \in \{i, i+1, i+5, i+6\}$, (ii) $M_j = 0$ for $j \in \{i+2, i+4\}$, and (iii) $M_{i+3} = 1$. The algorithm works in two phases.

1. *Organization Phase.* The aim of this phase is to build the *Middle* configuration. Robots at the border of the ϕ.group move towards their neighboring node inside the ϕ.group they belong to, until they create a tower. The role of the tower is to give a temporary orientation to the neighboring robots which move in the opposite direction of such a tower. In order to prevent

---

[1] In the long version, we provide two extra algorithms for both cases $\phi = 2$ and $\phi = 3$. The former ($\phi = 2$) works with 7 robots only. The latter ($\phi = 3$) uses 5 robots and is show to be optimal in terms of number of robots. However, both of them start from the particular ϕ.group where all the robots form a single 1.block.

the creation of another tower, robots move in a given order such that, at the end, each tower becomes neighbor of a 1.block of size 3. Two other towers are then created to build the *Middle* configuration. Observe that since we consider an asynchronous setting, one side of the ϕ.block can be faster then the other side. However, there is exactly one robot that is not allowed to move unless *Intermediate* configuration is reached.

2. *Exploration Phase*. The starting configuration of this phase is the *Middle* configuration. A set of robots is elected ($T1, T2, R1$ in Fig. 1) to perform the exploration task while the other robots stay still as a landmark ($T'1, T'2$) in Fig.1). *Terminal* configuration is created at this end of this phase to indicate the end of exploration task.

3   Visibility $\phi = 3$

We provide a general deterministic exploration protocol for any ring of size greater than 22 ($n \geq k\phi + 1$), that uses 7 robots. It works starting from any configuration satisfying Theorem 1. Using the same definition of multiplicity as in Section 2, a configuration is said to be *Set* (Fig. 4) if there exists a sequence of 5 nodes $u_i, u_{i+1}, \ldots, u_{i+4}$ such that: (*i*) $M_j = 2$ for $j \in \{i, i+4\}$, (*ii*) $M_{i+1} = 3$, and (*iii*) $M_j = 0$ for $j \in \{i+2, i+3\}$. Similarly, a configuration is *Final* (Fig. 5) if there exists a sequence of 4 nodes $u_i, u_{i+1}, \ldots, u_{i+3}$ such that: (*i*) $M_j = 2$ for $j \in \{i, i+1\}$, (*ii*) $M_{i+2} = 0$, and (*iii*) $M_{i+3} = 3$.

Fig. 4. *Set*   **Fig. 5.** *Final*

1. *Set-Up Phase*. The goal of this phase is to create Configuration *Set*. To do so, one tower is created at each border of the ϕ.*group*. The aim is to give an orientation to the robots allowing them to create a 1.block of size 3 with a tower as a neighbor at each of its borders. The robot that has a symmetric view moves to one of its adjacent nodes (chosen by the adversary) to create a new tower. The remaining single robot moves to its adjacent empty node to create the desired configuration.

2. *Exploration Phase*. Starting from Configuration *Set*, the isolated tower (with 2 robots) remains idle while the other robots explore the ring asynchronously in the opposite direction. The phase ends by reaching Configuration *Final*.

References

1. Datta, A.K., Lamani, A., Larmore, L.L., Petit, F.: Ring exploration by oblivious agents with local vision. In: 33rd International Conference on Distributed Computing (ICDCS), pp. 347–356 (2013)
2. Devismes, S., Petit, F., Tixeuil, S.: Optimal probabilistic ring exploration by semisynchronous oblivious robots. Theoretical Computer Science (TCS) 498, 10–27 (2013)
3. Flocchini, P., Ilcinkas, D., Pelc, A., Santoro, N.: Computing without communicating: Ring exploration by asynchronous oblivious robots. Algorithmica 65(3), 562–583 (2013)
4. Lamani, A., Potop-Butucaru, M.G., Tixeuil, S.: Optimal deterministic ring exploration with oblivious asynchronous robots. In: Patt-Shamir, B., Ekim, T. (eds.) SIROCCO 2010. LNCS, vol. 6058, pp. 183–196. Springer, Heidelberg (2010)

Scalable Estimation of Network Average Degree

Taisuke Izumi and Hironobu Kanzaki

Graduate School of Engineering, Nagoya Institute of Technology
{t-izumi,h.kanzaki.359}@nitech.ac.jp

Abstract. In massive networked systems, it is an important problem to obtain a certain kind of network statistic such as average degree or clustering coefficient. In this paper, we propose a one-shot scalable average degree estimation algorithm, which allows a monitoring node outside of the target network obtains the average degree with $o(n)$ message complexity. The proposed algorithm is based on the method by Goldreich and Ron (GR), which is well-known in the context of property testing. In this sense our algorithm is a "network version" of it. While the original GR algorithm can be regarded as a pull-based scheme in the sense that the monitoring node can get information only from randomly chosen nodes, our algorithm utilizes push-based schemes, that is, each node in the target network can actively send information to the monitoring server. The primary contribution of this paper is that such push-based schemes actually yield better message complexity.

1 Introduction

Knowing statistical information of massive networked system is useful in both scientific and engineering aspects: While it is one of recent trends to understand the behavior and structure of dynamic large-scale networks, such a structural property is often measured by a statistical information such as the clustering coefficient. From engineering viewpoints, getting such information seems to be useful for the self-organization of networks with a certain kind of efficiency, such as low-diameter, much bandwidth, and so on. While full-information centralized approaches, where a single monitoring server aggregates all topological information of the target network, is a trivial solution, it is far from practice in massive networks. Thus, inherently we needs a scalable solution for estimating the information. In this context efficiency is measured by the amount of communication aggregated by the server, and scalability means that the server only needs a number of messages *sublinear* for the network size n.

In this paper, we consider the problem of average degree estimation. Since computing the exact value of average degree using only $o(n)$ messages is obviously impossible, we rather focus on its approximation. The background idea of our result is the concept of *property testing*, which is a new algorithmic paradigm that only allows algorithms to takes $o(n)$ time for computing solutions. For the

T. Higashino et al. (Eds.): SSS 2013, LNCS 8255, pp. 367–369, 2013.
© Springer International Publishing Switzerland 2013

problem of average degree estimation, the sublinear-time algorithm by Goldreich and Ron is well-known (say GR)[3]. It obtains $(1 \pm \varepsilon)$-approximation of the average degree of input graphs with $O\left(\frac{\sqrt{n}\log^2 n}{\varepsilon^{3.5}}\right)$ time complexity (which is equivalent to query complexity) for any constant $\varepsilon < 1/2$. We show a new degree estimation algorithm based on GR in the setting of distributed computing. The main difference between property testing and distributed computing is that the input instance (the target graph) is also computing entities: While the original GR algorithm is regarded as a pull-based scheme in the sense that only the monitoring server can actively get information, the distributed setting allows the push-based schemes, which imply that the nodes organizing the input instance (i.e., the network) can actively send some information to the server. Importantly, in push-based schemes, the node in the network can decide whether it should send a message to the server or not according to its local information. The primary contribution of this paper is that such push-based schemes actually have a merit. More precisely, for any $\varepsilon < 1/2$, our algorithm achieves $O\left(\frac{\min(\bar{d}/\sqrt{\varepsilon}, \sqrt{n})\log n}{\varepsilon^{3.5}}\right)$ message complexity and approximation factor $(1 \pm \varepsilon)$, where $\bar{d}$ is the actual average degree of the target network. For sub-dense instances with average degree $o(\sqrt{n})$, our algorithm yields better message complexity.

2   Related Work

To the best of our knowledge, this paper is the first one studying about the interconnection between distributed computing and property testing. However, a number of results considering some related topics appear at different contexts. We briefly introduce them.

Monitoring information with sublinear message complexity is also considered in data-stream models. Cormode et.al. study the problem of distributed functional monitoring[1], which shows a way of scalably computing a function over distributed multiple streams. It shows that the message complexity of several fundamental functions such as frequency moments and entropy.

For sampling-based computation of average value, Motowani et.al. show a weighted sampling scheme[4]. It shows that the average of n values can be approximated from sublinear number of samples by using the weighted sampling that chooses each value with the probability proportional to its weight.

There is much literature about the property testing. For average degree estimation, the first result is one by Feige[2]. It proposes a 2-approximation algorithm by using only uniform sampling of nodes, and shows that approximation factor two is tight if we can utilize only uniform sampling. The algorithm by Goldreich and Ron, stated above, breaks that bound by allowing the sampling from neighbors in addition to uniform sampling over all nodes[3].

3   The Model, Problem, and Result

The distributed system considered in this paper consists of n processes connected by links, and one special process A, called *monitoring server*. The processes organize a network, which is represented by an undirected graph $G = (V, E)$. where V corresponds to the n processes and denoted by $V = \{v_0, v_1, \cdots, v_{n-1}\}$. Note that monitoring sever A is regarded as a process outside of network G. Each process in V can communicate with each other if they are connected by a link in E. The monitoring server A is connected with any node in V. The system proceeds its execution following the discrete synchronous time $t = 0, 1, 2, \cdots$. At each time, all processes including A can send a message to their neighbors. We assume that the size of each message is restricted to $O(\log n)$ bits. We also assume that every communication is reliable and thus no loss or corruption occurs.

The problem of average degree estimation requires monitoring sever A to obtain the information about the average degree (denoted by $\hat{d}$) of G with using as few messages as possible. In this paper we consider an approximate version of degree estimation, which is defined as the problem of obtaining a value $\tilde{d}$ such that $(1 - \varepsilon)\bar{d} \le \tilde{d} \le (1 + \varepsilon)\bar{d}$ holds.

To achieve sublinear message complexity in push-based schemes, it seems to need some assumption about the knowledge of number n of nodes in G. Thus we assume that each node knows the exact value of n. Note that this assumption can be relaxed a little bit: Our algorithm can be easily modified to work under the assumption that each node commonly knows some two values n_l and n_u such that $n_l \le n \le n_u$, $n_l = O(n)$ and $n_u = O(n)$.

For the model and problem stated above, we show the following theorem:

Theorem 1. *For any $\varepsilon < 1/2$ and $\beta \le \varepsilon/4$, there exists an algorithm that outputs a value $\tilde{d}$ satisfying $(1 - \varepsilon)\bar{d} \le \tilde{d} \le (1 + \varepsilon)\bar{d}$ with probability at least $2/3$ and uses $O\left(\frac{\min(\bar{d}/\sqrt{\varepsilon}, \sqrt{n}) \log n}{\varepsilon^{3.5}}\right)$ messages.*

References

1. Cormode, G., Muthukrishnan, S., Yi, K.: Algorithms for distributed functional monitoring. In: Proceedings of the Nineteenth Annual ACM-SIAM Symposium on Discrete Algorithms, SODA 2008, pp. 1076–1085. Society for Industrial and Applied Mathematics, Philadelphia (2008)
2. Feige, U.: On sums of independent random variables with unbounded variance and estimating the average degree in a graph. SIAM Journal on Computing 35(4), 964–984 (2006)
3. Goldreich, O., Ron, D.: On estimating the average degree of a graph. Electronic Colloquim on Computational Complexity, ECCC (2004)
4. Motwani, R., Panigrahy, R., Xu, Y.: Estimating sum by weighted sampling. In: Arge, L., Cachin, C., Jurdziński, T., Tarlecki, A. (eds.) ICALP 2007. LNCS, vol. 4596, pp. 53–64. Springer, Heidelberg (2007)

Synthesizing Round Based Fault-Tolerant Programs Using Genetic Programming

Ling Zhu and Sandeep Kulkarni

Department of Computer Science and Engineering, Michigan State University,
East Lansing, MI 48824, USA
{zhuling,sandeep}@cse.msu.edu

Abstract. In this paper, we present an approach to synthesize round based distributed fault-tolerant programs using stack based genetic programming. Our approach evolves a fault-tolerant program based on a round based structure and the program specification. To permit such evolution, we use a multi-objective fitness function that characterizes the correctness of the program in the absence of faults, in the presence of a single fault and in the presence of multiple faults. This multi-objective fitness function attempts to synthesize a program that works equally well in all these scenarios. We demonstrate the effectiveness of our approach using two case studies: a byzantine agreement problem and a token ring problem.

1 Introduction

We focus on the model synthesis and model repair using genetic programming. Genetic programming (GP), as an evolutionary algorithm-based methodology, automatically constructs a program targeted towards a user-defined task. GP starts with an initial population of individual programs and evolves them into an optimized solution based on the objective functions. In each generation, GP selects candidate individuals, i.e., programs that have high fitness value, and applies computational analogs of biological mutation and crossover to reproduce new programs (called offsprings). By iterating this process the best solution close to the objective is evolved. tion. Moreover, the computation of the fitness function needs to be efficient.

Our specific focus is on using genetic programming to develop round-based distributed programs. Intuitively, in a round based program, each process executes in rounds. In each round, a process receives messages from all its neighbors (or all processes in a fully connected network). Subsequently, this process utilizes these messages and its local state to send messages in that round. These messages would, in turn, be received in the next round and so on. Round based algorithms offer several advantages. For one, if the individual processes are deterministic then the round based program is also deterministic. Hence, evaluating the fitness function based on *how good the program is* becomes easier. Second,

T. Higashino et al. (Eds.): SSS 2013, LNCS 8255, pp. 370–372, 2013.

round based algorithms can be implemented even if the processes in a distributed program execute without tight synchronization. Towards this end, we need to include a round number in every message and require processes to wait for messages from the desired round and buffer messages from future rounds. Third, traditional distributed algorithms can be viewed as round-based algorithms under synchronous semantics where in each step, each process executes one its transitions. And, these programs can be revised to obtain programs in interleaving semantics using refinement techniques.

Contributions of the Paper. The main contributions of the paper are as follows. (i) We evaluate the feasibility of synthesizing round-based fault-tolerant programs using genetic programming. (ii) We identify multiple objectives for different conditions that the program needs to satisfy. (iii) We illustrate our approach using two case studies: byzantine agreement and token ring. The byzantine agreement case study illustrates the feasibility of our approach in the context of byzantine faults that are traditionally considered to be the most challenging. The token ring program illustrates a mechanism to utilize our approach for programs that are not inherently round based.

2 Genetic Programming for Synthesizing Fault Tolerant Program

The overall framework is as follows: the user defines the program variables (with their domain), a skeleton of program actions, faults and desired fault-tolerance requirements. GP (genetic programming) utilizes these inputs to generate corresponding programs and evaluates them in several distinct scenarios by simulating the given program in a round-based manner to identify if it violates given properties. In each scenario the fitness functions is computed according to the information learnt from the specific simulation. These fitness functions from different scenarios constitute multiple objectives and the final goal of GP is to find programs that obtain best fitness value in all objectives.

Program Representation. In this work, we consider round-based distributed programs that each consists of a finite number of processes. A process is associated with a set of variables, each with a finite domain. These processes execute in a round-based manner. A distributed program is comprised of one or more actions and each action conditionally executed in every round. The conditions used in actions are evolved by GP. In this work, statements themselves are not evolved by GP. Instead, they are specified by the designer.

Description of Genes. The program generated during evolution is encoded into integer vectors which represent conditions and Boolean operators in the corresponding program. Then during the program evaluation these integer vectors are decoded into a pair of stacks, an *operator stack* and a *values stack*. These two stacks constitute the conditions used in the evolved program.

Fitness and Genetic Operator. We evaluate the evolved program by partial execution (up to a predetermined number of steps) to identify if it satisfies specification. A typical fault-tolerant program has several objectives that identify the desired behavior in the absence of faults, in the presence of a single fault, in the presence of multiple faults, etc. Each objective is partitioned into one or more properties. To evaluate the correctness of program the fitness value of each objective is calculated by checking if the execution (or multiple execution sequences) satisfy all properties in that objective. We apply non-dominated sorting(NSGAII [1]) to preserve all the elites and emphasize the good solutions. For genetic operator single point crossover and one bit flip mutation are applied to GP.

3   Experiments

In the experiment we considered two programs: byzantine agreement and token ring program. To synthesize byzantine agreement we consider three cases: (1) when no process is byzantine, (2) when some non-general is byzantine, and (3) when the general is byzantine. The goal of GP is to evolve programs that work equally well in all these cases. For token ring program we consider three cases for the token ring circulation: (1) in the absence of faults and (2) in the presence of one fault, and (3) in the presence of multiple faults. In both cases GP successfully find the best solutions that are identical that in [2] and [3] respectively. We are able to synthesize the program in a reasonable amount of time. Also, the evolved program can be found even if the structure provided is not ideal. Detailed results could be found in technical report [4].

4   Conclusion

In this work, we focus on the use of genetic programming to synthesize round based fault-tolerant programs. We begin with a population of initial (random) programs. Subsequently, we evaluate their fitness based on the level to which it satisfies its specification. We utilize multi-objective fitness function to evaluate these individual. Subsequently, these programs are evolved based on fitness functions, mutations and crossover. This approach was successfully used to synthesize byzantine agreement and token ring program.

Acknowledgments. This work is supported by NSF CNS-0914913, NSF CNS 1329807 and NSF CNS 1318678.

References

1. Deb, K., Pratap, A., Agarwal, S., Meyarivan, T.: A fast and elitist multiobjective genetic algorithm: Nsga-ii. IEEE Transactions on Evolutionary Computation 6(2), 182–197 (2002)
2. Lamport, L., Shostak, R., Pease, M.: The byzantine generals problem. ACM Transactions on Programming Languages and Systems 4(3), 382–401 (1982)
3. Kulkarni, S.S., Ebnenasir, A.: Adding fault-tolerance using pre-synthesized components. In: Dal Cin, M., Kaâniche, M., Pataricza, A. (eds.) EDCC 2005. LNCS, vol. 3463, pp. 72–90. Springer, Heidelberg (2005)
4. Zhu, L., Kulkarni, S.S.: Synthesizing round based fault-tolerant programs using genetic programming (MSU-CSE-13-9), 15 (August 2013)

Self-stabilizing DAG-Constructing Protocols with Application to Geocast in MANET

Koichi Ito[1,2], Yoshiaki Katayama[1], Koichi Wada[3], and Naohisa Takahashi[1]

[1] Nagoya Institute of Technology, Gokiso-cho, Showa-ku, Nagoya, Aichi, Japan
[2] ANDEN, Co., LTD., Japan
[3] Hosei University, 3-7-2 Kajino-cho, Koganei, Tokyo, Japan

Abstract. We propose a self-stabilizing protocol for DAG construction on MANET and show that the geocast protocol using the proposed protocol is better than known geocast protocol by computer simulations.

Keywords: Self-stabilizing, DAG, Geocast, MANET.

1 Introduction

A *directed acyclic graph* (DAG) is a directed graph with no directed cycle. GeoTORA[1], which is one of the protocols for geocasting in MANET, uses a DAG-based approach. In the use of a DAG for geocasting in MANET, it is important to construct a DAG that has high robustness or high accuracy of geocast message delivery. To maintain a DAG adapting to change of the network topology, we propose a self-stabilizing DAG constructing protocol.

A DAG constructing self-stabilizing protocol has been proposed in [2]. This protocol $\mathcal{DAG}_{NO}$ uses a distance from the nearest sink. To enhance the accuracy of the geocast delivery, we propose a new self-stabilizing DAG constructing protocol $\mathcal{DAG}_{AO}$, which uses distances from all sinks. We perform some computer simulations to evaluate the performance of the geocast protocols that use $\mathcal{DAG}_{NO}$ and $\mathcal{DAG}_{AO}$ for constructing a DAG, and GeoTORA. The simulation results show that our geocast protocol can deliver a message to geocast group members with high accuracy although the communication overhead slightly increases.

2 Protocol $\mathcal{DAG}_{AO}$ (Fig.1)

Important assumptions for $\mathcal{DAG}_{AO}$ are the followings. A graph $G = (V, E)$ and a set of sink nodes $T(\subseteq V)$ are given. Each node has a totally ordered identifier and knows an upper bound of $|V|$, and communicates with neighbors by using shared variables. The scheduler is strongly fair distributed daemon.

In $\mathcal{DAG}_{NO}$, to determine the direction of an edge, a distance from the nearest sink and ID are used. On the other hand, $\mathcal{DAG}_{AO}$ uses distances from all sinks and ID. Since the number of the reachable sinks is exptected to be increased by using $\mathcal{DAG}_{AO}$, the accuracy of a geocast message delivery can be enhanced.

T. Higashino et al. (Eds.): SSS 2013, LNCS 8255, pp. 373–375, 2013.

$L_{tmp} := \phi$
for all $P_j \in N_i$ //N_i:a set of neighbors' ID
  for all $(P_k, l_k) \in L_j$ // L_j: $L_j = \{(P_k, l_k)|P_k \in \mathcal{P}, l_k = dist(P_j, P_k)\}$
    if $(P_k \neq P_i) \wedge (l_k < N - 1)$ **then**
      if $L_{tmp}[P_k] = \infty$ **then** $L_{tmp} := L_{tmp} \cup \{(P_k, l_k + 1)\}$
      else if $l_k + 1 < L_{tmp}[P_k]$ **then** $L_{tmp}[P_k] := l_k + 1$
$L_i := L_{tmp}$
if t_i **then** $L_i := L_i \cup \{(P_i, 0)\}$:$Out_i := \phi$
else $Out_i := \{P_j | \forall P_j \in N_i, (L_j <_d L_i) \vee ((L_j =_d L_i) \wedge (P_j < P_i))\}$
// $<_d$: lexicographical order of two sets after sorting members of each set

Fig. 1. Protocol $\mathcal{DAG}_{AO}$ on node P_i

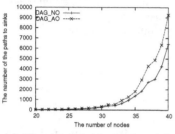

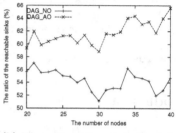

(a) The number of paths to sinks   (b) The ratio of the reachable sinks

Fig. 2. Comparison of property of DAGs

3   Comparison $\mathcal{DAG}_{AO}$ and $\mathcal{DAG}_{NO}$

Protocols $\mathcal{DAG}_{AO}$ and $\mathcal{DAG}_{NO}$ can correctly construct a DAG on MANET. We evaluate the each protocol's property of paths from any node to any sink on a DAG because we intend to use the proposed protocol for a geocast protocol. Hence, we use the following performance metrics: *the number of paths to sinks* is defined as the total number of paths to all sinks from a non-sink node, and *the ratio of reachable sinks* is defined as the ratio of the number of reachable sinks from each node and the number of all sinks. In the experiments, a random unit disc graph is used. That is, nodes are randomly allocated with in 1000×1000 field and edges are defined between two nodes whose distance is less than 250.

    Fig.2 shows that, on both metrics, $\mathcal{DAG}_{AO}$ constructs a better DAG than $\mathcal{DAG}_{NO}$. When a DAG is used as a path to sinks, it may be better that there are many paths and reachable sinks.

4   Performance Evaluations on Geocast

We perform some computer simulations to evaluate the accuracy of the geocast protocols AOGP(using $\mathcal{DAG}_{AO}$), NOGP(using $\mathcal{DAG}_{NO}$) and GeoTORA. If a source process sends a geocast packet and at least one of the processes in the geocast region receives the geocast packet, we call the entire scenario *one success*.

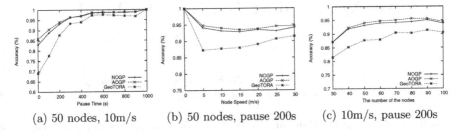

(a) 50 nodes, 10m/s   (b) 50 nodes, pause 200s   (c) 10m/s, pause 200s

Fig. 3. The Accuracy comparisons

The *accuracy* is defined as the ratio of the number of one successes for the number of geocastings. The simulations are done by using ns-3, with IEEE802.11b range loss model on a 1000×1000 rectangle field. The geocast region is a circle of radius 150 meters around the coordinate (250,250). The nodes move according to the random way point model.

Fig.3 shows that AOGP achieves better accuracy than the others. We also evaluate total size of packets for a geocasting and show that $\mathcal{DAG}_{AO}$ needs more message size than the others. This is a trade-off between the accuracy and the total size of messages.

5 Conclusion

We show that the proposed protocol $\mathcal{DAG}_{AO}$ provides better DAG than $\mathcal{DAG}_{NO}$ and can construct a better geocast protocol than known one (GeoTORA). But the proposed protocol needs more overhead than the others because $\mathcal{DAG}_{AO}$ uses distances from all sinks while $\mathcal{DAG}_{NO}$ uses only a distance from the nearest sink. And the average length of paths to sinks of a DAG constructed by $\mathcal{DAG}_{AO}$ is little bit longer than that is constructed by $\mathcal{DAG}_{NO}$.

If we try to adopt $\mathcal{DAG}_{AO}$ to practical MANET, it will be needed to reduce overhead as much as possible for energy efficiency.

The full paper of this work will be found at:
http://repo.lib.nitech.ac.jp/?lang=en

References

1. Ko, Y.B., Vaidya, N.: Geotora: a protocol for geocasting in mobile ad hoc networks. In: Proceedings of International Conference on Network Protocols, pp. 240–250 (2000)
2. Miura, T., Katayama, Y., Wada, K., Takahashi, N.: A fault-containing self-stabilizing protocol for constructing a directed acyclic graph. IPSJ SIG Technical Report. AL 2011 (20), 1–8 (2011) (in Japanese)

An Agile and Stable Neighborhood Protocol for WSNs

Gerry Siegemund[1], Volker Turau[1], Christoph Weyer[1],
Stefan Lohs[2], and Jörg Nolte[2]

[1] Institute of Telematics, Hamburg University of Technology, Hamburg, Germany
{gerry.siegemund,turau,c.weyer}@tu-harburg.de
[2] Distributed Systems Group, Brandenburg University of Technology, Cottbus
{slohs,jon}@informatik.tu-cottbus.de

Abstract. Self-stabilizing algorithms (SSA) are defined on the assumption that either the system's topology is fixed over time or topology changes are isolated events occurring at a very low rate. These assumptions are not valid in wireless sensor networks (WSNs) where link qualities change rapidly. The contribution of this paper is a neighborhood management protocol (NMP) providing a neighborhood relation sufficiently stable to apply existing SSAs in WSNs.

1 Motivation

Real world usage of SSAs is different to the theoretical approach where link changes are mostly handled as seldom temporary events. Message loss and varying path propagation lead to concurrent link changes, therefore, changing the local view of each node. Alterations of the neighborhood relation may force nodes to invoke rules leading to updates of their states possibly triggering more rule executions in the entire network. Ultimately, an algorithm running on top of a vigorously changing topology will not converge to a stable state. To illustrate this problem consider the execution of a self-stabilizing spanning tree algorithm (see Fig. 1 left). The consequences of such instabilities (edge e) for the spanning tree algorithm may be even more severe than in the figure, they might result in loops, interfering tremendously if the tree is used for routing purposes. Fig. 1 (right) illustrates this phenomenon for a standard maximal independent set (MIS) algorithm. The unstable edge e causes all nodes to change their state, resulting in an oscillating behavior.

To solve the underlying problem the need for an NMP, providing a sufficiently stable neighborhood relation to execute SSAs, arises. The goal of an NMP is to maintain a neighborhood relation such that the resulting topology is stable, and fulfills certain criteria such as connectedness of the induced graph. Essential abilities of NMPs are: Agility – ensures that the protocol adjusts quickly to new or failing nodes or links – and fault tolerance – ignoring transient faults, like burst errors, to make the topology more stable.

T. Higashino et al. (Eds.): SSS 2013, LNCS 8255, pp. 376–378, 2013.

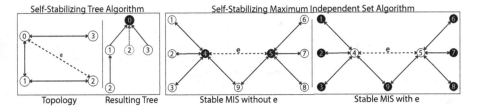

Fig. 1. Influence of unstable link e. Left: Execution of a self-stabilizing spanning tree algorithm: The parent of node 2 oscillates between nodes 0 and 1. Right: Execution of a self-stabilizing MIS algorithm: The disappearing link e has global influence. In both cases the outcome would remain stable if the edge e would not be considered.

2 Neighborhood Management Algorithm

The proposed NMP Mahalle$^+$ forms a stable network topology on top of a physical network despite transient faults. In contrast to other NMPs, Mahalle$^+$ does not only use a neighbor list L but also a preparation list P. Potential neighbors, i.e, nodes from which messages where received, are stored in the P until theses entries are found to be sufficiently promising to be promoted to L.

Mahalle$^+$ maintenance data, containing all members of the neighbor list L, a sequence number, and the id of the connected component the node belongs to, is regularly broadcasted by every node. If the sender id of a received message is a member of P or L then its stored neighborhood data and the link quality measure Q are updated. Q is evaluated by a link quality estimator (LQE), which uses sequence numbers to detect lost messages and calculates Q (Mahalle$^+$ works with any LQE, e.g., EWMA, WMEWMA).

L and P do not only contain the ids of neighbors and Q but also information deducted from the neighbors of a neighboring node. These are, the symmetry of a connection – found by appearance of the own id in the neighbor list received from a neighbor – and the number of overlapping neighbors between the current node and a particular neighbor – calculated by comparing all neighborhood table entries among each other. Furthermore, the number of unknown neighbors to the current and a neighboring node is determined.

In case the sender id is unknown and P is not full, the id is added to P. Otherwise, the message is discarded. From P a node is either evicted or the entry is moved to L (see Figure 2). The decision is based first on the current quality value Q of the link and on the available space of L. If L is not full and $Q > Q_{min}$, where Q_{min} is a minimum value depending on LQE, channel, and environment, the neighbor is moved to L. A node remains only for a limited time in P to qualify to become a member of L. If L is full, but there is a promising new entry (with $Q > Q_{min}$) in P which could be added, the eviction policy of Mahalle$^+$, stated in Fig. 3, comes into place. These rules act as filters and are applied incrementally in a top down manner.

Since symmetric links are favorable, asymmetrical links are replaced first (R1). An additional SSA is in place to conduct which nodes are already in a

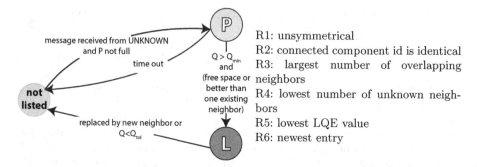

Fig. 2. Neighborhood transitions   Fig. 3. Mahalle⁺'s eviction rules

connected component. Nodes of neighboring components are prioritized to form one globally connected topology (R2). The next rule filters out nodes that have the largest number of overlapping neighbors (R3). The rationality of this rule is that these nodes are connected through one of the other common neighbors with high probability. Thus, removing this node has the lowest likelihood of compromising connectivity. After that, nodes with the lowest number of unknown neighbors are considered (R4). These nodes increase the connections of the direct neighborhood raising the local connectivity (i.e., closeness centrality) but are less helpful to build a connected topology. Rule R5 utilizes Q, the node with the worst link quality will be discarded. If all fails, the node with the youngest timestamp is discarded. Finally, nodes are removed from L if Q drops below the tolerable value Q_{tol}.

3   Conclusion

Mahalle⁺ is an NMP that can be used with any LQE while being suitable for a variety of applications. It is fast converging, stable, and finds well connected topologies even in high density networks. It provides a high degree of neighborhood stability and therefore increases the applicability of SSAs in WSNs.

In a series of simulations using OMNeT++ with the MiXiM framework we were able to show that in all scenarios Mahalle⁺ outperforms a well known NMP: TinyOS's Link Estimation Exchange Protocol (LEEP). This is, first of all, due to the preparation list, which monitors and screens appropriate neighbors before considering them as such. Therefore, hardly any bad neighbors will interfere with other SSAs running on top of Mahalle⁺, enabling the usage of SSAs in WSNs. This was confirmed by evaluating the execution of two different SSAs running on top of an overlay topology produced by the NMP: spanning tree and MIS. Both algorithms showed a much more stable behavior when executed on top of Mahalle⁺ compared to LEEP.

Acknowledgment. This research was funded by the Deutsche Forschungsgemeinschaft (DFG), contract number TU 221/6-1.

Author Index